UNDERSTANDING TOSCANINI

UNDERSTANDING TOSCANINI

A Social History of
American Concert Life

JOSEPH HOROWITZ

UNIVERSITY OF CALIFORNIA PRESS
Berkeley • Los Angeles

University of California Press
Berkeley and Los Angeles, California

First California Paperback Printing 1994

Library of Congress Cataloging-in-Publication Data

Horowitz, Joseph, 1948–
    Understanding Toscanini : a social history of American concert
life / Joseph Horowitz.
        p.   cm.
    Originally published: New York : A.A. Knopf, 1987.
    Includes bibliographical references and index.
    ISBN 0-520-08542-6 (pbk.)
    1. Toscanini, Arturo, 1867–1957.   2. Conductors (Music)—
Biography.   3. Music—United States—History and criticism.
I. Title.
ML422.T67H65   1994
784.2'092—dc20
[B]   93-38873
                                                                                            CIP
                                                                                            MN

Manufactured in the United States of America
        1   2   3   4   5   6   7   8   9

For my parents and my sister

It is therefore not true to assert that men living in democratic times are naturally indifferent to science, literature, and the arts; only it must be acknowledged that they cultivate them after their own fashion and bring to the task their own peculiar qualifications and deficiencies.

—TOCQUEVILLE, *Democracy in America* (1835)

Contents

IV. After Toscanini

Appendices

Notes

Index

Illustrations follow page 244

Acknowledgments

For a period of years, while I was working to understand Toscanini, the Performing Arts branch of the New York Public Library became something like my office. For my purposes, the Music Division's resources were wonderfully complete, its staff members always friendly, knowledgeable, alert. Manhattan's public library system makes me feel lucky to live in New York. Of the other archival resources I used, the most important were those of the New York Philharmonic, where Frank Milburn and Barbara Haws could not have been more helpful. I also benefited from the scholarly expertise of Howard Shanet of Columbia University, the central historian of the New York Philharmonic; Ezra Schabas of the University of Toronto, who knows all about Theodore Thomas; and John Mowitt of the University of Minnesota, who helped me to explain certain writings of Theodor Adorno. David Hamilton, Terri Jory, Linda Sanders, Greg Sandow, and Jeffrey Spielberg read the manuscript and contributed valuable advice. Kathleen Hulser critiqued the manuscript in addition to stimulating me, again and again, to scutinize and update my attitudes toward culture and its dissemination. Two others who helped in various ways were Agnes Bruneau and my agent, Robert Cornfield. Notwithstanding its idiosyncrasies, Robert Gottlieb believed in *Understanding Toscanini* from the first, and his cohorts at Knopf—in particular, Eva Resnikova and Mary Maguire—oversaw its editing and production with the most painstaking attention.

Introduction: Toscanini and the Ways of Culture

*R*eaders of this book who reached record-buying age by 1950 will have no trouble remembering Arturo Toscanini (1867–1957). High priest of the music appreciation movement of the thirties and forties, he commanded an imprimatur more influential than that of any classical musician before or since. During his years with the Metropolitan Opera (1908–15) and the New York Philharmonic (1926–36), he was regularly proclaimed the "greatest conductor of his time," even "of all time." With the NBC Symphony (1937–54), formed in his behalf by David Sarnoff's Radio Corporation of America, he became the beneficiary of a voracious, multimedia promotional apparatus the likes of which Paganini and Liszt could not have imagined. Toscanini partisanship in America was more than effusive; it was peculiarly intense. Even tabloid newspapers and mass-circulation magazines jealously guarded his First Musician eminence. According to *Life*, to which he seemed "the greatest living master of music," Toscanini was as well-known as Joe DiMaggio. *Time*, for which he "brought the music of Beethoven, Schubert, Wagner, and Verdi to life as no other man has," twice put him on its cover. When Toscanini died, the New York *Times*'s page-one obituary documented the majesty of the Toscanini reputation and diversity of the Toscanini constituency. "Both as an operatic and symphonic conductor," the *Times* recklessly reported, "he achieved a stature no other conductor before him had attained." A sidebar headlined TOSCANINI FOUGHT AGAINST FASCISM began: "A fine musician, Toscanini was also a human being of profound sensibilities who did not hesitate to take a stand on the side of what he considered the right." A full column of condolence messages began with statements by President Eisenhower and New York City Mayor Robert Wagner.[1]

Though the New York *Herald Tribune*'s Lawrence Gilman once attributed Toscanini's unique fame to "simple recognition of his unique greatness," mere "greatness"—and Toscanini can legitimately be called a "great conductor"—does not account for the onslaught of proprietary reverence and pride propelling his United States career. In fact, the cult was revealingly short-lived: Toscanini's death made him mortal. How did Toscanini become an object of unmitigated veneration in America?

To study how Americans perceived Toscanini is to study how they perceived themselves. As a personality, even as a musician, Toscanini embodied "self-made" virtues distinguishing the New World from the parent culture of Europe. In political terms, he symbolized the good fight against Hitler and Mussolini. As the dominant figurehead for Great Music, he furnished proof of New World high-cultural achievement and traced Great Music's dissemination within the United States. Directed and embroidered by Sarnoff, Gilman, and other music appreciation apostles, the Toscanini cult charted a course linking Great Music to a great public—a new, democratized arts constituency, transcending Toscanini and his times. My topic, broadly put, is the growth of this constituency, its pressing need for a Toscanini, and the consequences for both.

The Toscanini movement's infectious cultural populism capped long-term evolutionary tendencies toward today's concert and operatic forms. As music changed, it cultivated different numbers and types of listeners. The listeners, a countervailing force, influenced what sort of music was written and played, where it was presented, and the ambience of the musical event.

The chaste, declamatory operas of Caccini and Peri correlate with the cultivated Florentine intelligentsia of 1600; later operas, obsessed with drama, spectacle, or vocal display, formed and were formed by other audiences. In the eighteenth-century courts of Germany and Austria, music bowed to the taste of a Frederick the Great, an enthusiastic dilettante who rejected the new *Empfindsamkeit;* or an Anton Esterházy, who disbanded the Haydn-led court orchestra and opera cherished by his father. In London, a relatively broad public was influential. Reared on Elizabethan and Restoration theater, it rejected grandiose Continental opera in favor of semioperas like Purcell's *Fairy Queen* and ballad operas like John Gay's *Beggar's Opera;* when Handel became England's foremost composer, he found himself moving from operas in Italian to rousing biblical oratorios in English.

Modern audiences have proven incalculably bigger and broader than those of Renaissance, baroque, and early Classical times. Their sheer weight of numbers has mandated a new production scale: larger halls and orchestras, and symphonies and operas louder, more colorful, more emotionally intense than any written before. This transformation of scale has signaled a profound transformation in scope and tone of symphonic and operatic culture generally.

The loss or reduction of court and church patronage was a crucial early factor in the modern scheme. The Napoleonic Wars and the Congress of Vienna diminished the fortunes of European princes, and secularized or dissolved many ecclesiastical states and prince-bishoprics. With less aristocratic largesse to go around, aristocratic operatic establishments shaded into state establishments subsidized by taxes and box office revenues. In 1768, the Imperial Opera in Vienna was put in charge of commercial management on behalf of the court—a system already working effectively in Italy. In 1831, a similar arrangement was implemented in Paris, where commercialized opera under the July Monarchy coincided with the shrewd ostentation of the Meyerbeer style. An expanding audience base accompanied the rise of public concerts, including those of Vienna's Gesellschaft der Musikfreunde and London's Philharmonic Society, both formed in 1813, and of Paris's Société des Concerts du Conservatoire, formed in 1828. Composers, meanwhile, cut adrift from court moorings, became free-lancers with no fixed role. Berlioz supported himself as a journalist. Paganini and Liszt made their livings as itinerant virtuosos; their magnificent showmanship catered to popular followings more massive and varied than any enjoyed by the composer-performers Mozart and Beethoven. In opposition to the cult of the virtuoso, a composer's cult arose, worshiping a pantheon of dead masters, of whom the "Romantic" Beethoven stood highest. Around the same time, sudden growth in the music publishing industry underlined trends toward music's commodification. Formerly, music dilettantes and professionals had blurred together, as had intimate concerts with daily life; now audiences became more diverse and impersonal, prey to shrewd merchandisers of music and musical events. A more recent transformational stage, following World War I, was powered by new technologies. Radio, recordings, and television made music ubiquitous. Its organization during the same period became ever more commercial. The audience for concerts and opera, ever more democratic, now revered a *performers'* pantheon serving the revered dead masters. Contemporary composers grew increasingly specialized, estranged from the mainstream.[2]

Viewed in the fullest context, the initial phase of modern musical culture paralleled political and industrial revolution, vital social and intellectual change. The English-language idea of "culture" as the body of the arts, or general state of intellectual development, is itself a turn-of-the-nineteenth-century coinage. The catalyst was a sudden increase in literacy and readership, driving up book sales in the final decades of the eighteenth century. In particular, a floodtide of novels created and saturated a middle-class market for popular fiction. "Culture," in its new definition, noted and censured this development; Coleridge endorsed culture when he said of novel reading: "It produces no improvement of the intellect, but fills the mind with a mawkish and morbid sensibility." Concomitantly, "art" changed from meaning "skill" to connoting the imaginative arts generally; and many a Romantic "artist," at odds with society and industrial civilization, seemed a bohemian "genius" (another new meaning) prone to florid or contentious individuality. Of the popular authors, Byron represented this new cult of personality, while Henry Mackenzie, Ann Radcliffe, and Sir Walter Scott were representative mass-producers spewing stereotyped, sentimentalized plots and characters en route to the more enduring mass productions of Dickens.[3] In music, the Romantic geniuses included Berlioz, Paganini, Liszt, and Wagner, while Auber and Donizetti epitomized the mass-producers. These developments variously impugned and vindicated democratized taste.

A subsequent nomenclature, familiar today, calls "high culture" what Coleridge and other early critics of the novel called "culture" merely. Its sprawling, majority antithesis, oblivious of class pedigrees, is "mass culture" —an imprecise term roughly interchangeable with "popular culture," and not necessarily pejorative. Theoretically, high culture is acquired selectively and actively, mass culture passively, even unconsciously. Superseding regionalized "folk cultures" of earlier times, mass culture may be said to have begun with the late eighteenth century's burgeoning public of readers and listeners. It reached ingenious fruition as fortified and expanded by twentieth-century communications technology. The full panoply of contemporary mass culture includes break dancing, the Super Bowl, Muzak, *Star Wars*, "Dallas," and subway graffiti.

When not rejecting or ignoring high culture, mass culture mounts it on a pedestal and worships on bended knee. It is here, within mass culture's upper precincts, that the elitist critique remains irresistible. *Ulysses* is made into a movie, Picasso into a coffee-table book. *Moses and Aron* is marketed for nudity and violence, existentialism for cocktail conversation. "Theater" is epitomized by *Death of a Salesman* on Broadway with Dustin Hoffman, "opera" by *La Bohème* on television with Luciano Pavarotti. This post–World War I hybridization of mass and high culture has been named "midcult" by the late Dwight Macdonald. In a landmark 1960 essay, "Masscult and Midcult,"[4] Macdonald, stigmatizing both, wrote of midcult that it has "the essential qualities of masscult [but] decently covers them with a cultural figleaf," and that it "pretends to respect the standards of high culture while in fact it waters them down and vulgarizes them." Macdonald's midcult examples included eminently profitable, palatable artists and artifacts—John Steinbeck, Rodgers and Hammerstein, *The Old Man and the Sea, Our Town*—as well as such distribution apparatus as the Book-of-the-Month Club and the Great Books series of Mortimer Adler and Robert Hutchins. Midcult's ambiguity, Macdonald argued, makes it the most insidious cultural stratum: ostensibly raising mass culture, it corrupts —packages and petrifies—high culture. It "threatens to absorb both its parents." It may become "stabilized as the norm of our culture."

One need not endorse Macdonald's wholesale depreciation of midcult to find the concept useful. Midcult's own argument that it paves the way to high culture is not always specious. But midcult is complexly problematic, not simply positive. And Macdonald was correct to stress its American genesis. More than Europeans, Americans abhor elitism and apply democratic values with broad strokes. In the realm of music, the nineteenth-century rise of the public concert and commercialization of opera here proceeded without court or state subsidies—a circumstance favoring both personal enterprise and marketplace exigencies. The absence of kings and princes seems also to have fostered a craving for surrogate royalty; in any event, the cult of personality, dragging high culture downward, has for over a century more dramatically articulated the musical scene here than abroad. The technological machinery of twentieth-century midcult, finally, is first and foremost American machinery impacting on marketing, scale, emotional pitch, and personal style. To ponder the health of contemporary operatic and symphonic culture is to ponder the diverse ramifications of a vast, democratized audience headquartered in the United States.

Macdonald defined midcult as high culture diluted for mass sales and consumption. This was one effect—the most controversial—of Toscanini worship and music appreciation. Rapid, widespread dissemination of symphonies and operas after World War I did not foster singing and chamber music in the home, as the more modest nineteenth-century popularity of Beethoven, Schubert, Mendelssohn, Schumann, and Brahms had done. Rather, playing their radios, phonographs, and televisions, many new listeners appropriated at arm's length a canon of fossilized "masterpieces" more homogeneous (and, incidentally, more marketable) than the full gamut of genres and styles cultivated by musicians themselves. No book-of-the-month club had a salesman to rival Toscanini. No midcult writer possessed Toscanini's aura of centrality, of actually mythic stature. Steinbeck was never called the "world's greatest novelist." *Our Town* was not known to be the "world's greatest play." Propagated by RCA and NBC, by *Time* and the New York *Times,* Toscanini's cult was the definitive midcult phenomenon for music in this century.

In undertaking to "understand Toscanini," I have written a different kind of book. Unlike most writings on mass culture—a proliferating body of scholarly articles and books—it is not theoretical, but a detailed case study. Unlike most treatments of music in performance, it attempts to apply a broad sociocultural context. (Two valuable precedents, both pertinent to understanding Toscanini, are Arthur Loesser's *Men, Women and Pianos: A Social History* and Howard Shanet's *Philharmonic: A History of New York's Orchestra.*) Finally, *Understanding Toscanini* has little in common with other writings on Toscanini. While copious, the Toscanini literature mainly documents the cult unwittingly. Even Harvey Sachs's *Toscanini*— the best and most recent Toscanini biography, and an essential aid to my own research—fails to acknowledge the Toscanini madness swelling Toscanini's American career.

Like Sachs, I never heard Toscanini "live": born in 1948, I encountered him first on records just before his Beethoven and Brahms ceased to seem "definitive." *Understanding Toscanini* therefore contains no personal impressions of Toscanini or his concerts such as those found in Filippo Sacchi's *The Magic Baton,* Howard Taubman's *The Maestro,* B. H. Haggin's *Conversations with Toscanini,* Samuel Antek's *This Was Toscanini,* and George Marek's *Toscanini,* among other books. I have dispensed, as well, with interviewing Toscanini's colleagues and friends. A patient perusal of Toscanini-related magazine articles and newspaper reviews has served my purposes best. This is because my topic is less Toscanini than the manner in which he was perceived, procured, appreciated, marketed, and used. My sources unconsciously document the midcult dynamic better than any conscious testimony could.

I present my findings in four parts. Part I, "Setting the Stage," begins with the nascent musical institutions of Gilded Age America. In addition to musicians, my dramatis personae include Mark Twain, who maps the American psyche of the period, and P. T. Barnum, whose mass culture expertise was unrivaled by any contemporary. Part II, "Toscanini in America," is by far the longest of my four. Chronicling peak periods of the Metropolitan Opera and the New York Philharmonic, and the seventeen-year history of the NBC Symphony, I construct a detailed narrative of Toscanini's American career stressing the extramusical appeal of his personal and political attributes, and how these attributes were publicized and mythologized. My purview includes the advent of radio, television, and the long-playing record, as well as the power brokers Arthur Judson and David Sarnoff, and the Toscanini rivals Gustav Mahler, Willem Mengelberg, Leopold Stokowski, and Wilhelm Furtwängler (of whom Furtwängler figures prominently throughout *Understanding Toscanini* as a Toscanini antipode). My core analysis of this Part II material—the core, in fact, of the entire book—will be found in the two sections treating "The National Context" of the NBC Symphony experience. Here, dwelling on the meaning of audience expansion, my range of references includes Walter Damrosch's "Music Appreciation Hour," Sinclair Lewis's *Babbitt,* and the mass culture analyses of Theodor Adorno. Both to simplify my narrative and to stress Toscanini's extramusical appeal, I have practically excluded from "Toscanini in America" the sound of Toscanini's music. This becomes the subject matter of Part III, "Toscanini on Records," in which—abandoning the context of the image-makers' "Toscanini"—I consider the musical influence of the actual Toscanini and evaluate his "greatest conductor" reputation. My concluding Part IV, "After Toscanini," begins with "The Collapse of the Cult," which carries the Toscanini story into the 1960s and 1970s. I hope readers will be quick to perceive the pertinence of understanding Toscanini to understanding the current cultural scene, and make their own observations. Some observations of my own constitute the balance of Part IV, pondering the Toscanini cult's "Long-Term Legacies." These I have collected as the "Great Performances" syndrome, under a rubric borrowed from the Public Broadcasting System, and connoting a midcult reduction of high culture circumscribed by the old Old World.

While aspects of the "Great Performances" syndrome obviously afflict Europe, *Understanding Toscanini* studies America as midcult's heartland. Similarly, Toscanini and the Toscanini cult both flourished abroad, but readers interested in Toscanini's European career, and also in many details of his real-life personal history, will find them in Harvey Sachs's book, not here. In some ways, not in others, the Toscanini cults of Britain, Italy, Germany, Austria, and Israel paralleled the course and causes of his American celebrity. But my interest is in cult headquarters: the United States, where the fame and influence of the Toscanini icon peaked.

A final note on sources.

I am often surprised at the indiscriminate use of newspaper reviews in books about musicians—as if critics were interchangeable. Rather, a writer on Toscanini in America must know, for example, that of the music critics in New York's daily press just before World War I, two were better than the rest: W. J. Henderson and Henry E. Krehbiel. Each, moreover, had his strengths and weaknesses: Henderson's specialties were opera and the voice; Krehbiel was a Beethoven scholar and disliked modernism. Also, like all critics, Henderson and Krehbiel conveyed implicit information about themselves in passing explicit judgment on others. Krehbiel's prickly reaction to Mahler, as we shall see, reveals a prickly pride in New World culture.

This secondary information—the inadvertent content of a review—may reflect a substantial body of opinion. In this regard, I would distinguish between "maverick" critics, whose views are personal merely, and "mainstream" critics, who speak for multitudes. Of the interwar Toscanini critics, any who did not endorse his "world's greatest" status were mavericks by definition—the most prominent being Virgil Thomson of the New York *Herald Tribune,* who often relied on friction with conventional wisdom to ignite the energy of his own opinions. Of the Toscanini adulators, the contentious B. H. Haggin, who called other true believers false, was a maverick. Olin Downes of the New York *Times* was the model mainstream critic in the Toscanini camp. No less than Thomson relished being in the minority, Downes cherished the majority, whose viewpoint boosted the resonance and security of his own. Downes's ideal critic was one who so identified with an audience as to disappear into it.[5] His reviews are packed, as Thomson's are not, with information about a huge constituency of shared feeling and experience.

In many instances, the identity of a publication clarifies a critic's identity. The *Herald Tribune* was a "gentleman's paper" of modest circulation, a place a maverick could feel at home. The *Times* was, and is, the central "newspaper of record," whose monolithic bulk lends dangerous weight to its critics' views. Thomson could denigrate Toscanini in disregard of popular opinion. Downes was obligated at least to acknowledge what most others thought when he disagreed with them. More to the point, he was personally predisposed to orthodoxy. Thomson believed that the Metropolitan Opera, and the New York Philharmonic under John Barbirolli, were not part of New York City's "intellectual life," and enjoyed ignoring both institutions. As the *Times*'s chief music critic, Downes could not feel as estranged, and did not.*

In writing of the "genius act" in "Masscult and Midcult," Dwight Macdonald observed: "There is a strange ambivalence. The masses put an absurdly high value on the personal genius, the charisma, of the performer, but they also demand a secret rebate: he must play the game—*their* game —must distort his personality to suit their taste." Read with due regard for between-the-lines messages, reviews and other writings on Toscanini assemble a rounded portrait of a diligently sought and manufactured "Toscanini." The real Toscanini acted as a mirror whose reflected light illuminated American energies and insecurities, innocence and experience.

---

*The short tenures of Stanley Kauffmann and Richard Eder as chief *Times* drama critic were object lessons in the paper's cultural orthodoxy; neither was predisposed to boost conventional Broadway fare. Today, this may be changing: rather than propounding from on high, *Times* critics increasingly write in the once-proscribed first person.

I · Setting the Stage

"*T*his Venice, which was a haughty, invincible, magnificent republic, . . . is fallen a prey to poverty, neglect, and melancholy decay," wrote Mark Twain.

Her glory is departed, and with her crumbling grandeur of wharves and palaces about her, she sits among her stagnant lagoons forlorn and beggared, forgotten of the world. . . .

We reached Venice at eight in the evening and entered a hearse belonging to the Grand Hotel d'Europe. At any rate, it was more like a hearse than anything else, though to speak by the card, it was a gondola. And this was the storied gondola of Venice!—the fairy boat in which the princely cavaliers of the olden time were wont to cleave the waters of the moonlit canals and look the eloquence of love into the soft eyes of patrician beauties, while the gay gondolier in silken doublet touched his guitar and sang as only gondoliers can sing! This the famed gondola and this the gorgeous gondolier!—the one an inky rusty old canoe with a sable hearse body clapped onto the middle of it, and the other a mangy, barefooted guttersnipe with a portion of his raiment on exhibition which should have been sacred from public scrutiny. . . .

I began to feel that the old Venice of song and story had departed forever. But I was too hasty. In a few minutes we swept gracefully out into the Grand Canal, and under the mellow moonlight the Venice of poetry and romance stood revealed. Right from the water's edge rose long lines of stately palaces of marble; gondolas were gliding swiftly hither and thither and disappearing suddenly through unsuspected gates and alleys; ponderous stone bridges threw their shadows athwart the glittering waves. . . .

The Venetian gondola is as free and graceful in its gliding movement as a serpent. . . . The gondolier *is* a picturesque rascal for all he wears

no satin harness, no plumed bonnet, no silken tights. His attitude is
stately; he is lithe and supple; all his movements are full of grace. . . . This
is the gentlest, pleasantest locomotion we have ever known.

Mark Twain's contradictory impressions of Venice, received during a
five-month tour of Europe and the Holy Land in 1867 and published two
years later as *The Innocents Abroad,* document the vicissitudes of a bar-
barian/aesthete. He ridiculed the spectacle of Old World culture gone to
seed, debunked the sentimental imagery of moonlit trysts—and was himself
seduced.

Meticulously, greedily, he worked at exorcising his susceptibility. "We
have seen pictures of martyrs enough and saints enough to regenerate the
world. I ought not to confess it, but . . . to me it seemed that when I had
seen one of these martyrs I had seen them all." As for the Cathedral of St.
Mark: "I could not go into ecstasies over its coarse mosaics, its unlovely
Byzantine architecture, or its five hundred curious interior columns from
as many distant quarries. Everything was worn out. . . . Under the altar
repose the ashes of St. Mark—and Matthew, Luke, and John, too, for all
I know. Venice reveres these relics above all things earthly." Like Venetian
religion, Venetian government was venal and tyrannical, as reconstrued by
Mark Twain: "The patricians alone governed Venice—the common herd
had no vote and no voice. . . . Men spoke in whispers in Venice, and no
man trusted his neighbor; not always his own brother." Mark Twain found
the residents of nineteenth-century Venice slothful, slow, and mainly poor.
The titled descendants of Renaissance dukes and doges he found "effeminate," "airing their nobility in fashionable French attire," "eating ices and
drinking cheap wines."

Mark Twain's "show me" tone betrayed him. He used his heresies to
subvert the awe he felt but did not want to show. His insistence on a
modern, democratic *New* World as the measure of all things registered
some innocence, but also willful naiveté: more than affronted, he was
discomfited by privilege and pretension borne of history. His perceptions
of the "forlorn and beggared" were oddly voyeuristic; he took too keen a
pleasure in seeing "princely cavaliers" and "patrician beauties" stripped of
bygone glamour.

Ralph Waldo Emerson, in his famous 1837 address "The American
Scholar," urged America's artists and intellectuals to cease listening to the
courtly muses of Europe. Mark Twain tried: in his ambivalence abroad, his
scowling innocence, he embodied the proud-to-be-transplanted offspring of
a rooted parent culture. A rambunctious manchild rejecting and succumb-
ing to the father image of courtly Europe, he eyed the parental keyhole
anxiously, contemptuously, hungry for knowledge. *The Innocents Abroad*

was the first of numerous Mark Twain books and stories with trans-Atlantic locales. Samuel Langhorne Clemens, part of whose layered, contradictory identity was called Mark Twain, spent nearly one-sixth of his life in Europe. At one time, he resolved to settle in England. With Henry James, he was, in Leslie Fiedler's words, one of "the two writers of their generation by whom Europe was most obsessively felt as an enigma to be endlessly attacked, precisely because it could never be entirely solved."[1]

In *The American*, published eight years after *The Innocents Abroad* but set less than a year after Mark Twain's 1867 visit to France and Italy, James situated an innocent Californian in an enticing, confounding Old World setting. For the purposes of understanding Toscanini, however, Mark Twain's identity quest is the more pertinent. James wrote for a learned elite. Clemens, who once proclaimed he would "rather be damned to John Bunyan's heaven" than read James's *The Bostonians*, was—as Mark Twain—called the "people's author." He could, as his most recent biographer has stressed, gratify his readers' need for "literature" and reassure them he was no *littérateur*, that "fancy talk and three-dollar words [were] just as alien to him as to any storekeeper or clerk."[2] This new, unrefined constituency included an evolving middle class prefiguring more numerous, confident, and consolidated middle-class audiences to come, and already democratizing the books, newspapers, magazines, and lectures of the Gilded Age.

Facing inland to the west, the nouveaux riches were less cosmopolitan than previous generations of mercantilist businessmen. Unconnected to overseas trade or to coastal aristocracies, they turned to confront Old World values by exercising a prerogative unknown to their parents: the European excursion. Mark Twain's own 1867 tour of Europe and the Holy Land, abroad a chartered steamer named *Quaker City*, was representative. It was initiated by Henry Ward Beecher, the charismatic Brooklyn preacher, and organized by one of Beecher's Sunday-school superintendents. The passengers, of certifiable character and credit if not impeccably bred, were prominent Brooklynites enticed by Beecher's name and those of other celebrities. In his Preface to *The Innocents Abroad*, Mark Twain declared his intention to embody the experiences of these first-time pilgrims without regard for the delicate sensibilities of those who knew foreign lands already.

Shedding generations of insularity, the *Quaker City* pilgrims explored the Old World with sudden, raw curiosity. Hugging their Baedekers, dogging their English-speaking guides, they fastened on every accredited landmark. Mark Twain, who called his male companions "boys," submitted to this streamlined agenda as willingly as if Europe were a candy shop being cased. His verdicts, as in Venice, were decisive, zealous, and contradictory. He compared Lake Como unfavorably with Lake Tahoe; it was narrower, he complained, than the Mississippi River. The Arno he called a "creek." The exterior of St. Peter's seemed to him "not a twentieth part as beautiful" as the United States Capitol. The Milan Cathedral, however, he found a "vision," a "miracle," "the princeliest creation that ever brain of man conceived." Like the other *Quaker City* tourists, he aspired to a gentility he understood as "cultured" yet would not relinquish the prerogatives of a cranky frontiersman. He surveyed Old World wares with a combination of docile obedience and unvarnished chauvinism.

To treat Mark Twain as the spokesman for an evolving Middle America oversimplifies his case. Notwithstanding the Preface to *The Innocents Abroad*, his perspective on the pilgrims' ambivalence was itself ambivalent. He was at times embarrassed by their vulgar patriotism, or titillated by their aping of patrician decorum. Still, the pilgrims' ambivalence abroad did not contradict the artist's ambivalence so much as parody it. Samuel Clemens's public touristic countenance, bristling with pride, mired in uncertainty, personified Gilded Age America as highlighted by the rubbing action of Europe. Grappling with his cultural ancestry, he seemed, as an authorized biographical sketch put it, "characteristically American in every fiber."[3]

In nothing was this characteristic American more typical, finally, than in the beliefs sustaining his resilience in the face of history's daunting traditions. In Rome he pointed toward his credo, exclaiming: "What is it that confers the noblest delight? . . . Discovery!" To which he added, rhetorically: "What is there . . . for me to see that others have not seen before me?" Mark Twain's faith resided not merely in the present, but in his own experience. In Europe, he was the absolute empiricist who must see for himself. The quintessential American, he embodied the quintessential self-made man. He characterized his kind as "hurrying" and "restless." He proclaimed himself an unabashed materialist for whom first-rate railways and turnpikes, among other modern accessories to egalitarian advancement, meant more than a "hundred galleries of priceless art treasures" and their scholarly adherents. He pointedly buttressed his enthusiasm for the Milan Cathedral and the Venetian gondola with appreciative references to purely mechanical feats. Admiring the roof of the former, he likened its curved beams to the fore-and-aft braces of an American steamboat. Admiring the latter, he fixed on the gondolier's "marvelous skill":

> He cuts a corner so closely, now and then, or misses another gondola by such an imperceptible hairbreadth that I feel myself "scrooching," as the children say, just as one does when a buggy wheel grazes his elbow. But he makes all his calculations with the nicest precision, and goes darting in and out among a Broadway confusion of busy craft

with the easy confidence of the educated hackman. He never makes a mistake.

Like his ambivalence abroad, the keynotes of Mark Twain's self-reliance —his empiricism, his restless haste, his zest for mechanical efficiency— provide clues to understanding Toscanini.

The conflicts with which Mark Twain faced his Old World inheritance necessarily figured in all the American arts. Musicians of the Gilded Age registered the symptoms of dependency: envy and gratitude, challenge and docility vis-à-vis the European fount. Given America's cultural inferiority complex, even Mark Twain was more universally admired in England and Germany than in the United States. To this inverse chauvinism, pitting American composers against such Continental luminaries as Wagner and Brahms, were added disadvantages specific to music. Britain's creative legacy, a crucial influence in American drama, literature, and art, omitted great symphonies and operas. And the American frontier, a wellspring of imagery in American novels, plays, and paintings, seemed less transportable into its concert halls and opera houses.

If, as of its one hundredth birthday, America had no composers to set beside Mark Twain and Henry James, or Melville and Whitman, or John Copley, Gilbert Stuart, and Benjamin West, its musical life, then as now, mainly highlighted performers. Here the ambivalence syndrome dictated a spectrum of charged relationships to Old World art. In Paris, Americans were snubbed at the Conservatoire and the Opéra because, as the Opéra director once put it, theirs was "an industrial country—excellent for electric telegraphs, but not for art." Some Americans agreed. The most intangible, least "useful" of the arts, music seemed to them the most dispensable. An 1853 editorial in the Pittsburgh *Evening Chronicle* expostulated: "From the language of the musical critiques of the Eastern press, one would suppose that there was nothing else worth living for in this life but music. . . . The Americans are a musical people, but we want to be educated up to the science and so long as nine-tenths of our people do not know even the A.B.C. of music, it is folly for them to listen to the most finished and eloquent combinations of it." At another extreme, there were Americans who would transplant Old World music verbatim. The stronghold of this constituency was the German immigrant community. Its preferred musical medium was the orchestra, its venue the concert hall, its core agenda the Beethoven symphonies. In between those who would ignore Old World music and those who would import it whole came a stratum evoking Mark Twain and all he stood for. Its temper seized on the American passion for pageantry and display, circuses and parades—so pronounced in Mark Twain's Hartford that he moved the kitchen of his house closer to Farmington Avenue "so the servant can see the circus go by without running into the street." Its trappings crackled with the type of ballyhoo—press puffery, posters and advertisements, banners and medallions—relished by Mark Twain the sometime publisher and promoter. Its medium was the celebrity tour, its venues included tents and equestrian rings, and its agenda ranged from Rossini to "Yankee Doodle." Its effect was to adulterate Old World art with a leveling Yankee veneer. As Mark Twain in *The Innocents Abroad* made a pantheon of "Milton, Shakespeare, and Washington," New World entrepreneurs hawked Old World singers and instrumentalists in a manner common to sideshow freaks, blackface minstrels, and other native attractions.[4]

As of 1869, when lavish first editions of *The Innocents Abroad* were marketed door to door by subscription agents, the most successful American concert impresario was the redoubtable ballyhooer Phineas Taylor Barnum. The most successful American practitioner of symphonic imports was Theodore Thomas, conductor of his own itinerant orchestra. It was characteristic of Barnum that he offered to manage Thomas. It was characteristic of Thomas that he refused to sign with Barnum. But Barnum did succeed in signing, at enormous cost, the "Swedish Nightingale," Jenny Lind. In his autobiography, he called her American tour of 1850–51 "an enterprise never before or since equaled in managerial annals"—and this was no ballyhoo.[5]

Barnum was already the acknowledged master of every trick of the huckster's trade. His first, triumphant humbug, in 1835, had been "the most astonishing and interesting curiosity of the world": Joice Heth, whom he claimed was 161 years old and had, as George Washington's nurse, been the first person "to put clothes on" the first President. Seven years later he christened a five-year-old midget "General Tom Thumb" and created one of the entertainment prodigies of the century. Barnum housed Tom Thumb's carriage and royal presents in his American Museum, an establishment also containing giants and a thin man, monkeys and crocodiles, and a diorama of Napoleon's funeral. Gradually, Barnum's empire came to encompass more pedigreed attractions. For the museum, he acquired animal rarities of bona fide scientific interest, carefully catalogued and numbered. For his tours, he acquired Jenny Lind. It did not matter that he had never heard her sing—"her reputation was sufficient for me." More than a supreme artist, "the divine Jenny" had been acclaimed a personage of extraordinary generosity. Her eminence, moreover, was the hard-won redemption of a harsh childhood. In this combination of attributes Barnum sensed a bonanza: not just fistfuls of cash, but armloads of prestige. As his *Autobiography* attested:

Taking all things into the account, I arrived at the following conclusions:

1st. The chances were greatly in favor of immense pecuniary success; and 2d. Inasmuch as my name has long been associated with "humbug," and the American public suspect that my capacities do not extend beyond the power to exhibit a stuffed monkey-skin or a dead mermaid, I can afford to lose fifty thousand dollars in such an enterprise as bringing to this country, in the zenith of her life and celebrity, the greatest musical wonder in the world. . . .

The manner in which Jenny Lind was presented to the public, Barnum knew, would tell all. In this regard, his ambition was to achieve the greatest possible humbug compatible with a modicum of dignity. He engaged as his European emissary John Hall Wilton, an Englishman who may have proposed the Barnum-Lind alliance in the first place. Wilton was instructed to offer as much as $1,000 per concert. The resulting contract forced Barnum to borrow and cajole in order to raise $187,500. This accomplished, he began bellowing his publicity. Barely modulating his first promotional premise—that the singer was an actual angel come down from on high—he prepared biographies bypassing her more esoteric qualifications in favor of evidence of piety, philanthropy, and eagerness to visit the United States. According to one Barnum announcement: "A visit from such a woman, who regards her high artistic powers as a gift from Heaven, for the amelioration of affliction and distress, and whose every thought and deed is philanthropy, I feel persuaded, will prove a blessing to America." Topping the din of notices, anecdotes, and testimonials came Barnum's bogus disclosure that Jenny had asked to be received with a song written for the occasion. In one week, over seven hundred texts reached Barnum's committee of judges. When the winning entry, "Greeting to America," was lampooned as "The Manager and the Nightingale," Barnum had his agents help disseminate it, too. Finally, he had Jenny give two concerts in Liverpool within a day of departing for New York, the first to be reviewed by a specially procured London critic.

Jenny's ship arrived on September 1, 1850. The welcoming crowd overflowed onto the spars and rigging of adjacent vessels, and blackened nearby roofs. Many were trampled and hurt when the gates to the pier gave way; at least one man was swept into the sea (and rescued). Riding beside Barnum in a decorated carriage, Jenny passed under two triumphal arches of evergreens, one reading "Welcome, Jenny Lind," the other, surmounted by an American eagle, "Welcome to America." A throng of ten thousand greeted her at the Irving Hotel; by 11 p.m., twice as many had gathered. Two hundred musicians, escorted by twenty brigades of firemen, arrived by torchlight to serenade the visitor with "Yankee Doodle" and "Hail, Columbia." In the days that followed, newspapers ran special columns tracking the movements of "the most popular woman in the world at this moment—perhaps the most popular that ever was in it." According to the New York *Herald,* Jenny's advent was "as significant an event as the appearance of Dante, Tasso, Raphael, Shakespeare, Goethe, Thorvaldsen, or Michael Angelo." She had "changed all men's ideas of music as much as Bacon's inductive system revolutionized philosophy." And still the nightingale had yet to warble.

For Jenny's debut Barnum chose Castle Garden, New York's largest place of amusement, once a fort. Rather than sell tickets, he staged an auction before a paying audience of thousands; the highest bidder, a Barnum acquaintance, spent $225 for his choice location. In four colors, the tickets corresponded to colored seat numbers, lamps, rosettes, and wands —a gimmick, but favoring decorum. All five thousand customers were in place when Jenny appeared to sing opera excerpts by Bellini, Meyerbeer, and Rossini, some Scandinavian songs, and the "Greeting to America" as set by her German-born music director, Julius Benedict. The orchestra played the overtures to Weber's *Oberon* and Benedict's *The Crusaders.* A baritone offered Rossini's "Largo al factotum." The hall rang with approbation. At the evening's close, vociferous calls for "Barnum!" united the artist and her impresario onstage. This was the first of ninety-three such events, during which the Jenny Lind mania never flagged. In Boston, Jenny was feted with fireworks and a torchlight parade. Both of her Washington concerts were attended by President Fillmore, his family, and every member of his cabinet; she was also received at the White House. In Madison, Wisconsin, she found herself singing in a pork butcher's shed decorated in her behalf. In Philadelphia, the hall was a horse ring. According to Barnum's relentless publicists, she donated part of her proceeds to charity in most of the nineteen cities she visited. Also charitable was her willingness to review Barnum's Great Asiatic Caravan, including ostriches, monkeys, and ten elephants drawing a chariot.

With receipts totaling $712,000 and ticket prices of up to $650, Jenny's tour was more profitable than any Barnum had undertaken with Tom Thumb—in fact, more profitable than any other of his enterprises. For Jenny, it marked the greatest triumph of her career. But to what degree was Jenny's triumph Barnum's? She was an accredited singing sensation, idolized in Berlin and London. Mendelssohn called her "as great an artist as ever lived." Clara Schumann thought her "the warmest, noblest being" she had encountered among artists. But though Barnum called her "the greatest musical wonder in the world," she did not surpass other musical wonders, as had Paganini and Liszt. Even among sopranos, she did not necessarily eclipse Henriette Sontag. Henry Chorley, the important British music journalist, recorded that the two halves of her range were of different quality (the lower weak and often out of tune, the upper rich and brilliant), that her breath control was consummate, that her ornaments were original, that her acting was eloquent so long as the required sentiments were snow white. Her charismatic saintliness, which she maintained with a will, belied offstage lapses into smugness, irritability, and shrewd self-aggrandizement. Barnum, by comparison, was all he seemed. World paragon of hokum, he ensured that, as one admirer put it, the nightingale "always kept her angel face to the public." Tenaciously, unconsciously, he tailored her portrait to America's prevailing feminization of culture, embodied by homemakers and ladies of charity who, as revered angels of art and compassion, cultivated the parlor spinet, sentimental fiction, and other "uplifting" diversions.[6] Transcending greed, Barnum's ambition was actually aesthetic. The public understood and applauded. "The bigger the humbug," he affirmed, "the better the people like it."

Jenny herself furnished proof of Barnum's genius, if proof were needed, when she decided to dispense with his services and seize the benefits of her celebrity. In the course of forty post-Barnum American concerts, her audiences dwindled, her profits plummeted, and her private persona began to show. Her gala departure, on May 29, 1852, was witnessed by a fraction of the multitudes that had greeted her arrival. Her legacy to the New World was dwarfed by Barnum's legacy: a case study in maximizing mass appeal by trading on supreme puffery and personal imagery rather than supreme talent, even where supreme talent existed. Max Maretzek, a rival impresario, lamented:

[Jenny Lind's] visit to this country might have exercised the most salutary influence upon the taste and development of Art. . . . Blind by nature to every consideration of this character, [Barnum] came to the conclusion that, as an artist, the fair Swede would be at the best a very uncertain speculation. In consequence of this, he determined upon working her as a curiosity, as he had done with the Feejee Mermaid, and other of his pseudo-irregularities of nature. It was purely a matter of the most perfect indifference to him, whether she produced any enthusiasm as a songstress, provided she excited curiosity, as angel, woman, or demon. . . .

Reputation was manufactured for her, by wholesale. It was not merely made by the inch, but was prepared by the cart-load. . . . Everywhere, the curiosity to see her was stronger than the enthusiasm after hearing her, and great as her merit most unquestionably was, the "humbug" of her manager was by far the most powerful attraction to her concerts.

Fondly recalling Jenny's flawless veneer, Barnum himself pronounced: "It is a mistake to say that the fame of Jenny Lind rested solely upon her ability to sing. She was a woman who would have been adored if she had had the voice of a crow."[7]

The cult of the Swedish Nightingale epitomized the ballyhoo tradition in American music, but did not initiate it. As of the preceding decade, a series of imported singers and instrumentalists had been flamboyantly courting New World wealth. Their essential qualifications were two: a certified European reputation and an appreciable aura of celebrity. Among the first to mesmerize was Ole Bull, the Norwegian violinist. Beginning in 1843—the year after Barnum acquired Tom Thumb—he made five American visits. He could bow all four violin strings at once. The outstanding imported singing sensation, apart from Jenny Lind, was Henriette Sontag, in 1852. A "public serenade" outside her hotel, modeled on the Barnum-Lind precedent, degenerated into pandemonium: parading musicians were blocked by a cheering, screaming mob unwilling to relinquish space under Sontag's balcony. Blows were exchanged, instruments were mangled, music was shredded, and the singer retired in anger and bewilderment. Leopold de Meyer, known as the "Lion Pianist," was the first celebrity pianist to tour America, arriving in 1845. Like Ole Bull's, his programs featured his own sleight-of-hand concoctions, larded with such Americana as "Yankee Doodle." Meyer was soon eclipsed by the Parisian keyboard virtuoso Henri Herz. Herz's Barnum was Bernard Ullmann, whose brainstorms included "A Thousand Candles"—an accessory so prodigiously advertised that it packed the hall. Ullmann also managed the American debut of the debonair Sigismond Thalberg, capitalizing on his snob appeal with "matinees musicales" for "ladies belonging to the first families of the city." The only American of such gaudy eminence was Louis Moreau Gottschalk, a pianist so exotic—his father was a cultivated Englishman educated in Germany; his mother was of upper-class French descent; he studied in Paris from the age of thirteen—as to seem European. Gottschalk was a matinee idol: his dreamy eyes and *beau idéal* profile made women storm the stage and clutch for his white gloves. So successful was his American return of 1853 that Barnum himself felt inspired to bid $20,000 a year for his services, and Gottschalk felt able to decline.

Eleven years later, Gottschalk had occasion to observe:

I am daily astonished at the rapidity with which the taste for music is developed and is developing in the United States. At the time of my first return from Europe I was constantly deploring the want of public interest for pieces purely sentimental [i.e., possessing inherent "feeling"]; the public listened with indifference; in order to interest it, it became necessary to astound it; grand movements, tours de force, and noise had alone the privilege in piano music, not of pleasing, but of making it patient with it. I was the *first* American pianist, not by my artistic worth, but in chronological order. Before me, there were no piano concerts except in peculiar cases—that is to say, when a very great name arriving from Europe placed itself by its celebrity before the public, which, willing or unwilling, through curiosity and fashion rather than from taste, made it a duty to go and see the lion. Now piano concerts are chronic. . . . From whatever cause the American taste is becoming purer, and with that remarkable rapidity we cite through our whole progress.[8]

This very "purification" worked to Gottschalk's disadvantage. A vibrant artist, admired by Berlioz and Victor Hugo, he was increasingly taken to task for ignoring Beethoven, Weber, Mendelssohn, Chopin, and Schumann in favor of his own Creole-derived miniatures and operatic pastiches of the Liszt/Thalberg variety. A strong antidote, in 1872–73, was a 215-concert American tour undertaken by the formidable Anton Rubinstein. Rubinstein, too, played his own music, including a new set of "Yankee Doodle" variations. More significant, however, were the mighty doses of Bach, Beethoven, Chopin, and Schumann he meted out. Even by European standards, Rubinstein's American programs were rarefied. Still, he did not escape the ballyhoo tradition. His manager, Maurice Grau, agitated for bonbons and encores; when he lost, he translated so much Bach-and-Beethoven playing into a feat of "vast knowledge, herculean power, and unmatched skill" none but Rubinstein would attempt. Rubinstein himself resented the trappings of his American celebrity—the photographs in shop windows and on wallboards, the onslaught of autograph seekers and social invitations—but was powerless to stem the tide. As the hero of George W. Bagby's "Jud Brownin Hears Ruby Play," a favorite recitation for thirty years, he actually passed into American folklore:

By jinks, it was a mixtery! He fetched up his right wing, he fetched up his left wing, he fetched up his center, he fetched up his reserves. . . . He opened his cannon—round shot, shells, shrapnels, grape, canister, mines, and magazines—every living battery and bomb a-going at the same time. The house trembled, the lights danced, the walls shuck, the sky split, the ground rocked—heavens and earth, creation, sweet

potatoes, Moses, ninepences, glory, tenpenny nails, Sampson in a 'sim-
mon tree—Bang!!! . . .

    With that bang! he lifted himself bodily into the air, and he come
down with his knees, fingers, toes, elbows and his nose, striking every
single solitary key on the pianner at the same time.

    . . . I knowed no more that evening.[9]

Like Lind, Gottschalk, and other American favorites, Rubinstein was also
lavishly feted in the Old World, where Paganini and Liszt were recent
Promethean exemplars of the performing musician as Romantic hero.
Europe, too, knew musical pageantry and gimmickry (Paganini's repertoire
included farmyard imitations). But Europe, while it gave birth to musical
Romanticism, spawned no P. T. Barnum or Jud Brownin to amplify and
popularize it. Americans were found to possess a distinct aptitude for celebrating feats of heroic individualism; as Lewis Mumford has written, "pioneering may in part be described as the Romantic movement in action."
Moreover, even for the United States, the decade beginning in 1840, when
the first influx of celebrity musicians coincided with the onset of Barnum's
peak phase of humbuggery, was a period of swelling dimensions and coursing vitality—Texas, California, and Oregon were wrested or annexed; the
gold rush began; the electric telegraph went into service; the railroads proliferated. For every European raised to be a good citizen who knew his place,
there was an American possessed of what Gottschalk termed "the insatiable
avidity of our people for novelty and change," what Tocqueville termed
"extreme fluctuations" and "impatient desires." In music, public concerts
were swiftly supplanting soirees and church services as prime venues. As in
Europe, larger, more varied audiences abetted the cult of the virtuoso; as not
in Europe, the absence of native royalty and paucity of native conductors,
singers, and instrumentalists abetted celebrity cults all the more. What the
New World lacked in indigenous resources it was prepared to entice with
dollars and applause. Casting an eye on America's eager, impressionable
listeners, Robert Schumann commented:

    The [European] public has lately begun to weary of virtuosos, and . . . we
    have too. The virtuosos themselves seem to feel this, if we may judge from
    a recently awakened fancy among them for emigrating to America; and
    many of their enemies secretly hope they will remain over there; for, taken
    all in all, modern virtuosity has benefited art very little.

To which Eduard Hanslick, the dean of Viennese music critics, later added:
"America was truly the promised land, if not of music, at least of the
musician."[10] One further factor shaped the New World's musical suscep-

tibilities: insofar as charismatic looks and acrobatic passagework craved a popular following, the cult of the virtuoso resonated with the democratic ethos. Barnum, again, is the locus classicus. When mobs of New York "fashionables" congregated outside the hotel of the recently arrived Jenny Lind, he worried that so much *beau monde* attention would ruin his prospects. His three-ring circuses had no bad seats. Not only his pocketbook but his principles dictated that he woo an enlarged, heterogeneous audience. Like Mark Twain (with whom he carried on a friendly correspondence), he was self-made and respected self-made men; his lectures and autobiography preached that experience was the best teacher.

In fact, as a hybridization of American know-how with European talent, concert giving in the ballyhoo tradition betrayed the ambivalence of innocents abroad. Such a ballyhoo specimen as "Jud Brownin Hears Ruby Play" is a near cousin of Mark Twain in Venice. Jud's willfully naive metaphors—he likens Rubinstein's huge piano to "a distracted billiard table on three legs," his whirring hands to "a sugar squirrel turning the wheel of a candy cage," his jangling sonorities to "a circus, and a brass band, and a big ball, all going at the same time"—appoint the New World the measure of all things. A rambunctious manchild, he tells his neighbor, "That's fine music, that is," then jumps on his seat to yell, "Go it, my Rube!" In part, George Bagby's satirization of Europe's premier active pianist registers appropriative American energies, dynamically absorbing Old World culture in a protean New World milieu; in part, it is an act of accommodation, easing the tensions of perceived inferiority.

If the ballyhoo tradition mellowed over time, it never quit. Decades after Rubinstein's barnstorming, a lesser artist, Ignace Jan Paderewski, won the most thorough American adulation of any pianist. Like Jenny Lind, he inspired far-flung merchandising ploys: Paderewski wigs, shampoos based on "the Paderewski formula," candy, soap, and mechanical toys shaped in his image. Like Gottschalk, he hypnotized the ladies: they fainted, they shrieked, they hung by their chins on the lip of the stage. Like Rubinstein, he melted into folklore, familiar, as "Paddy," to legions of schoolboys and farmers. His appeal began with his chrysanthemum of pale red hair, his dreamy countenance, his lordly bearing, all affirmed by trappings—he traveled in his own railroad carriage, attended by a valet, a tuner, a manager, a chef, and two porters—befitting foreign royalty. His Barnum, Hugo Görlitz, would distribute free tickets to students pledged to stampede "as though overcome with a mad desire to get a nearer view of Paderewski performing his magic." His first American tour, in 1891–92, netted $95,000 —unheard of for a pianist. In later years, his American earnings were estimated to exceed $1,000 per selection, including encores.[11]

Paderewski's first visit to the United States coincided with the first appearance of a second famous European pianist. Ferruccio Busoni, too, was handsome and charismatic, but his artistry was less external. Busoni's periodic American residences were dictated by pressing financial needs. He inspired no toys or shampoos, provoked no fainting spells, engendered no folk humor or press puffery. He loathed slogging through the hinterlands after the fashion of Gottschalk, Rubinstein, and Paderewski. Once, in a Western town, he found himself alongside a screen on which were flashed the various sections of the sonata he was playing: "Introduction," "First Subject," "Bridge," "Second Subject." On another occasion, in Texas, he glanced up from the keyboard to find a sign reading: "Don't shoot the pianist; he's doing the best he can." American conviviality and irreverence left him melancholy and estranged; even the metropolises he found depressingly raw. Of a Boston appearance, he wrote to his wife in 1904: "Yesterday's concert was very nice, great success, two laurel-wreaths; I played my best. But they don't understand it, and it is almost useless playing to them." In Chicago, the conductor Felix Mottl warned him not to attend the opera —"and he was right." He wrote his wife from Des Moines in 1910: "I need not practice any more, just keep the playing going. The latter has changed a little. One involuntarily responds to the demands for a brilliant technique which are made by the Americans." A month later, from Chicago, he wrote: "Good God, the method they have here of turning people into celebrities makes one's heart sink into one's boots. Is it possible such a small, ordinary person like X can really be a great artist? Even from an 'opera singer's standpoint'? I cannot believe it, and I have never heard of her being extraordinarily good in any of her roles. But every nigger knows her name." Of Los Angeles he observed in 1911: "The town is an American provincial town (at least at first sight) with skyscrapers, and the usual street sights. It is a fresh wonder to me every day how *such* a town, so tasteless and bare, could be built in *such* a country. Why must this marvelous gift of Nature be besmeared in such a way? . . . What is this pride they have of being 'practical'?"[12]

Busoni was a trenchant observer of the American scene, but unsympathetic. Other touring musicians found more to admire. Gottschalk, though mainly a confirmed expatriate (he was better appreciated in France and Latin America), found occasion to praise the "practical and utilitarian spirit" of Americans, the education offered American women, and the ingenuity of American hokum ("The American lure is a science and an art"). Paderewski found Americans devoted listeners and generous, personable companions. Even the harried Rubinstein was quoted calling the United States "the land for those who love liberty," and declaring he would like his children to be American citizens.[13]

Its enterprise, affability, and egalitarianism were lively virtues of the ballyhoo tradition—yet conducive to questionable taste and reckless enthusiasm.

While a virulent presence on the musical scene, ballyhoo was never ubiquitous. Alongside, industrious and well-dispersed, a countertradition took hold. Even on Jenny Lind's tours the accompanying orchestra was known to perform proper German overtures. One occasional member of the Jenny Lind violins was the young Theodore Thomas. In American musical annals, he would become P. T. Barnum's inspired antithesis: a tireless itinerant purveyor of overtures, symphonies, and concertos. Like Mark Twain, he would go to Europe to peruse Old World culture, but not as an ambivalent innocent. Born in Germany in 1835, he revisited his homeland with a single purpose: artistic replenishment at the source. Mark Twain was beached in the Old World; Thomas established an Old World beachhead in the New.

He arrived in the United States in 1845, part of a massive German immigration begun about a decade earlier, and peaking in the 1880s. In conjunction with arriving Scandinavians, Italians, and Eastern Europeans, the Germans modified prevailing Anglo-American cultural norms. Their ranks swarmed with musicians. Gottschalk, something of a Germanophobe, met one in St. Louis in 1862: "I was introduced to an old German musician with uncombed hair, bushy beard, in constitution like a bear, in disposition the amenity of a boar at bay to a pack of hounds. I know this type; it is found everywhere." A year later he remarked: "All the musicians in the United States are German."[14] Paralleling a burgeoning musical idealism abroad, the immigrant Germans pledged allegiance to German "masterworks" and foreswore the ballyhooed "virtuosos"; more than an esteemed profession, music was for them a holy cause. Barnum and the ballyhooers aspired to reach all who could be amazed; the Germans aspired to teach all who could be converted. Early converts included legions of New Englanders even purer than their masters. Lowell Mason (1792–1872), as influential as any American-born musician of his time, was president of Boston's Handel and Haydn Society, co-founder of the Boston Academy of Music, and the author of twelve hundred original hymn tunes; as educator, conductor, organist, and composer, he embodied German models. His son William (1829–1908), whose four years in Germany included studies with Liszt, introduced many Beethoven piano sonatas to America. John Sullivan Dwight (1813–93), the leading American music critic of his time, was a Transcendentalist who looked to music to cure materialism by "familiarising men with the beautiful and the infinite." As editor of *Dwight's Journal of Music*, he revered "scientific" German masters, and so was Gottschalk's chief nemesis. Other *Dwight's* contributors included Alexander Wheelock Thayer (1817–97), author of a landmark biography of Beethoven, and the Alsatian-born Frederic Louis Ritter (1834–91), whose *Music in America* (1883) declared: "The people's song . . . is not to be found among the American people."

With its expanding German core, America's "serious music" establishment was a mid-nineteenth-century outpost, but no backwater. Manning the theater and opera pits, accompanying the ballyhooed imports, launching chamber music and choral ventures, teaching and espousing Beethoven, newly resident Germans implanted Central European traditions in city after city. As of 1841–42, New York, already the nation's musical hub, offered two to four concerts per week for the September-to-May season. The repertoire was much the same as in Europe. Concurrently, in 1842, the Germans founded the first great symbol of their New World aspirations and achievements: the New York Philharmonic Society. The prime makers of the New York orchestra were William Scharfenberg and Henry Christian Timm, both German born, and Ureli Corelli Hill, who had studied in Germany with Ludwig Spohr. The first principal conductor, Theodor Eisfeld, and his successor as of 1862, Carl Bergmann, were natives of Wolfenbüttel and Ebersbach. Initially 42 percent German, the Philharmonic musicians were 70 percent German by 1855. Programming leaned heavily on the Beethoven symphonies; symphonies by Mozart, Mendelssohn, and Schumann were also frequently given. As of 1875, German music constituted 80 percent of the repertoire.[15]

The New York Philharmonic's early birth—the Vienna Philharmonic was founded the same year; Berlin would not have a permanent concert orchestra for another four decades—signaled a New World propensity for orchestra breeding. The American symphonic tradition was not immune to ballyhoo: among the prime Castle Garden attractions in the decade of Jenny Lind were the "monster concerts" of Louis Antoine Jullien, who conducted his orchestra of one hundred from a tapestried throne, and whose pièce de résistance was a *Fireman's Quadrille,* in which three companies of firemen rushed in to extinguish actual flames. But the essential symphonic tone was devotional. This feature, and the heartiness of the American symphonic species generally, were largely Theodore Thomas's doing. His orchestral experience began with broad exposure as a teen-age violinist: in Jullien's orchestra; in orchestras touring with Lind, Sontag, and other celebrities (he considered Sontag's music director, Carl Eckert, "the only really fully equipped and satisfactory conductor who visited this country during that period"); and, from 1854, in the New York Philharmonic (whose lax rehearsal discipline he deplored).[16] From 1855, he was a member of William Mason's chamber music organization (Mason later recalled his twenty-year-old violinist as "the dominating influence, felt and acknowledged by us all"). He first conducted an orchestra of his own in 1862. Beginning in 1864, the Theodore Thomas concerts were a regular—often nightly—feature of New York's music life. Thomas's orchestra began touring in 1869; in Chicago, as in New York, it would give up to fifty concerts per visit. And, like the touring virtuosos of the ballyhoo tradition, Thomas and his men followed the railroad tracks north to Buffalo, Detroit, and Minneapolis, south to Mobile, New Orleans, and Atlanta, west to California. Their core itinerary of twenty-eight cities in twelve states became known as the "Thomas Highway." They visited points on the map where railroad stations and churches were the only places to perform. Once, in Utah, Thomas was gravely advised to program as many wedding marches as possible. The program for one Iowa concert began with the *Tannhäuser* Overture, the Andante from Beethoven's Fifth, and Weber's *Invitation to the Dance* as "adapted for orchestra by Hector Berlioz." A local critic reported:

> The first piece was that fine trilogy which Hector Berlioz, with exquisite art, made from Wagner, Beethoven, and Weber. The thought of Hector Berlioz evidently . . . was to put after the passionate action of the one the ocean-like, star-like, measureless calm and harmony of the symphony. After you have bathed in that luxury and languor long enough, there comes Von Weber's *Invitation to the Dance*. Oh! There has been nothing heard in Keokuk like that trilogy as Thomas's Orchestra gives it.

More eloquent testimony of Thomas's hinterlands impact was this 1927 third-person reminiscence by Charles Edward Russell in *The American Orchestra and Theodore Thomas:*

> In 1877, Theodore Thomas came to the town where the boy lived. . . . The playing of [Schumann's] "Träumerei" seemed something unbelievable. Theodore Thomas had orchestrated the piano score and united with it as a trio the Schumann "Romanza." Only the strings were used without the basses. At the end, the beautiful melody grew softer and softer, slowly fading until it seemed to be drifting in the air, first into Shelley's shadow of all sounds, then the daintiest gossamer and filament of elusive and fairy music. . . . Then it grew fainter, and still slowly fainter . . . With all intension, rapt, leaning forward, the listeners were following it. Of a sudden they awoke to the fact that Mr. Thomas had laid down his baton and there was no sound. For the last minute there had been none. The violinists had continued to move their bows without

touching the strings, but so strong was the spell, these thralls had believed they still heard that marvelous elfin melody. A strange gasping noise arose as two thousand people suddenly recovered their breath and consciousness, and then looked at one another to see if all this were real.

Evidence still exists that to all impressionable persons hearing that concert, life was never the same afterward. It was not alone that they had heard something beautiful; there had been shown to them things and potentialities they had never suspected. . . .

This striking level of symphonic achievement was sustained without patrician favors that had supported earlier European endeavors, and were to be vital to future American orchestras; in fact, Thomas could not keep his orchestra intact without constant concerts generating constant revenues. Fortuitously, he was self-made in the American mode. In Germany, he had been taught the violin by his father. In New York, he had helped support his family by playing for dances and weddings, and in theaters. Touring the South at the age of eleven, he had acted as his own manager, publicist, and ticket taker. As a self-reliant, iron-willed adult (his enemies called him brutal), he hardened his constitution with icy baths and gymnastics every morning; according to the critic Richard Aldrich, "He could take up almost any of his subordinates and lay him upon the table without apparent effort." William Mason called him "born to command."

Like many another German musician, Thomas disdained popular music as a sensual indulgence having "more or less the devil in it." He spoke of "master works" as a "character-building force" and "uplifting influence." He called concerts "sermons in tones." Characteristically, his was a practical weaning strategy, interspersing classical overtures, movements from symphonies, and excerpts from the latest "music of the future" with lighter fare by Lanner, Johann Strauss, Jr., Offenbach, and the like. But he would reprogram the "better" pieces with table-pounding insistence. When audiences complained they did not like Wagner, he declared he would play Wagner until they did. He felt duty-bound to keep abreast of important new music and to let the public hear it at least once. Eventually he was able to perform entire symphonies and concerts wholly devoted to Wagner, Brahms, or Richard Strauss. The list of music he was the first to play in the United States comprises repertoire staples old and new: Bach's First, Second, and Third orchestral suites; Beethoven's Second and Third piano concertos and *Grosse Fuge;* Berlioz's *Harold in Italy* and *Romeo and Juliet,* Part II; Brahms's "Haydn" Variations and Second and Third symphonies; Bruckner's Fourth and Seventh symphonies; Dvořák's Sixth and Seventh symphonies and Symphonic Variations; Elgar's *Cockaigne Overture* and "Enigma" Variations; Grieg's First *Peer Gynt* Suite; Handel's *Royal Fire-*

works Music; Haydn's "Oxford" and "Surprise" symphonies; Liszt's First Piano Concerto and *Mazeppa;* Mozart's Sinfonia Concertante for violin and viola and symphonies Nos. 39 and 40; Schubert's "Unfinished" and "Great" C major symphonies; Schumann's *Genoveva* Overture; Sibelius's Second Symphony; Strauss's *Also sprach Zarathustra, Don Quixote, Ein Heldenleben,* and *Till Eulenspiegel;* Wagner's Ride of the Valkyries, Wotan's Farewell, *Siegfried Idyll,* and overtures and preludes to *Die Meistersinger, The Flying Dutchman,* and *Parsifal.*

The performances themselves were of a sort not to distract attention from the music, but superbly disciplined all the same. Americans had heard nothing as good before. Commenting on its 1869 concerts in Boston, *Dwight's Journal* called the Thomas orchestra comparable with the best in Europe. Two years later, Anton Rubinstein told his American hosts: "I have found in America something that I least expected to find. . . . Never in my life, although I have given concerts in St. Petersburg, Vienna, Berlin, Paris, London, and other great centers, have I found an orchestra that was as perfect as the organization Theodore Thomas has created and built up." In 1873 the New York *Post* editorialized:

> Mr. Thomas found, as soon as his work and intention became clearly understood, and rose above the strata of spasmodic adventures and dis- honest enterprises with which the people had long been deceived, that he was welcome. Now, then, these two great things appear to have been achieved: First, there has been produced in New York an orchestra inferior to none of its size in the great world. . . . Second, a comprehen- sion of the works of the great composers has been animated all over the country. Where in former days an orchestra would, in stirring abroad, pass into a chilling atmosphere, it now encounters applause and warmth. The change has been great, it might almost be said marvellous.

Theodore Thomas himself was not given to such grandiloquent pro- nouncements. Alert to rival enticements, he remained a stern, un-Romantic messiah, wrestling the demons of ballyhoo for America's musical soul.

"What a paradise this land is," wrote Samuel Clemens to William Dean Howells from Frankfurt in 1878. "What clean clothes, what good faces, what tranquil contentment, what prosperity, what genuine freedom, what superb government!"[17] German streets and parks were better kept than America's. German trains were prompter. In American universities, Ger- many stood for academic freedom, and for advanced scholarship in science, medicine, philosophy, and jurisprudence. In music, the German hegemony actually increased during the last quarter of the nineteenth century. When someone was needed to play the oboe or clarinet, the French horn or double bass, native-born Germans or their offspring filled the breach. More than ever, German extracurricular pursuits bred local choruses and string quartets. As these ventures grew in scale and number, their devoutly wished-for consummation, disseminating fortresses of high German culture, was a New World network of permanent symphony orchestras.

One signal event, in 1877, was the New York Philharmonic's decision to appoint as its first eminent conductor its chief rival: Theodore Thomas. During Thomas's thirteen-season regime, Beethoven was by far the most-performed composer, followed by Wagner, Schumann, Schubert, and Mozart. As of 1892, all but three Philharmonic musicians were Germans. America's second permanent orchestra was the New York Symphony, established in 1878 by another influential German, Leopold Damrosch (whom the jealous Thomas allegedly vowed to "crush"), and conducted after 1885 by his son, Walter, also German born. It was Walter Damrosch and the New York Symphony who in 1891 inaugurated Carnegie Hall with a five-day festival at which Tchaikovsky, the guest of honor, was moved to exclaim: "Amazing people these Americans! Compared with Paris . . . the frankness, sincerity and generosity in this city . . . and its eagerness to please and win approval, are simply astonishing." But the period's prime orchestral benchmark was the founding of the Boston Symphony in 1881. This was the brainchild of Henry L. Higginson, a Boston financier who had studied music in Vienna. Emulating the personal patronage of Old World kings and princes, yet dedicated to democratic public service, Higginson resolved to hire a world-class orchestra for Boston. The musicians would be full-time employees. The conductor would enjoy artistic freedom. As owner and administrator, Higginson would pay all salaries and make up all deficits. The orchestra's first six conductors—George Henschel (1881–84), Wilhelm Gericke (1884–89, 1898–1906), Arthur Nikisch (1889–93), Emil Paur (1893–98), Karl Muck (1906–08, 1912–18), and Max Fiedler (1908–12)—were Central European. Nikisch and Muck were among the musical luminaries of Europe. A quarter-century before World War I, the Boston Symphony was America's premier orchestra, having surpassed both New York orchestras in stature, stability, and frequency of performance. Credible witnesses compared it favorably to the best European ensembles; in Europe, it was grudgingly acknowledged a light in the wilderness.

Higginson's philanthropy had no greater admirer than Theodore Thomas, whose Philharmonic schedule of six subscription concerts per season was one-eighth the Boston Symphony's twenty-four subscription pairs, and whose forced annual migrations were finally exacting a physical toll. Thomas's yearning for a full-time, fully endowed orchestra found expression in his resolve to "go to Hell if they gave me a permanent orchestra." He wound up going to Chicago, where local businessmen pledged to underwrite a new orchestra for him. Under Thomas's baton, the Chicago Orchestra, founded in 1891, quickly matured; Richard Strauss and Eugène Ysaÿe were among the European visitors who marveled at its discipline and refinement. Thomas died in 1905, to be succeeded by his German assistant conductor, Frederick Stock. Among Thomas's many eulogists, Richard Strauss observed: "What we Germans owe him shall be held in everlasting remembrance."

Other American orchestras with early starts included the Cincinnati Symphony, whose first conductor, in 1895, was the American-born, Belgian-and-German-trained Frank Van der Stucken; the Pittsburgh Symphony, which enjoyed an early heyday from 1898 to 1904 under the Irish-born, German-trained Victor Herbert; the Philadelphia Orchestra, whose first conductor, in 1900, was the German Fritz Scheel; the Minneapolis Symphony, whose first conductor, in 1903, was the German Emil Ober-hoffer; and the St. Louis Symphony, which, after tentative beginnings in 1880, was newly organized in 1907 under Max Zach, an Austrian. This remarkable proliferation was unparalleled abroad. In Germany itself, as in Austria, Italy, and France, opera was paramount; the Leipzig Gewandhaus orchestra, the Berlin Philharmonic, the Meiningen Orchestra under Hans von Bülow were conspicuous exceptions to a rule relegating professional orchestras to theatrical service, concert performances being left to ad hoc groups including amateurs. The United States, by comparison, was neces-sarily less a home to stage performances sung in Italian, German, and French. As for opera in English, it was Theodore Thomas who, as artistic director of the short-lived American Opera Company, discovered that American music lovers also resisted the sung vernacular. To a degree, Thomas's endorsements of symphonic masterworks had the effect of mak-ing a virtue of necessity. Strengthening a bias inculcated by Schumann and other Romantic worshipers of the dead Beethoven, he specifically preached that "a symphony orchestra shows the culture of a community, not opera." He disdained gaudy singers and instrumental virtuosos. His arguments for music as an elevating antidote to business "fatigue" identified "instrumental music" as "especially restful" because it appealed to the unfettered intellect and imagination "whereas in vocal music the interpretation is bound by the text." In Chicago, he declared that the city's endemic "excitement and nervous strain" recommended symphonic relaxation.

"A symphony orchestra shows the culture of a community" proved an immensely popular dictum, stimulating continued orchestral growth along the onetime Thomas Highway. However incongruously, turn-of-the-century America could—and did—consider itself the world's best home for concert orchestras and their Germanic canon. When the Boston Symphony was launched, its supporters proclaimed: "A symphony orchestra pure and simple does not exist in all of Europe. That is to say, that in no city in Germany, Italy, France or Russia is there an orchestra which is made up of players whose *only* business it is to perform such music as is to be found on programmes of symphony concerts." When Chicago started its orchestra ten years later, local enthusiasts noted that Boston and Leipzig were the only cities whose orchestras offered more paired subscription concerts than Chicago's twenty. Theodore Thomas's derogation of opera was widely adopted; instrumental music was found nobler and purer. The term "symphony orchestra" was itself an expensive American coinage, first used in 1878 by Leopold Damrosch.[18] At the same time, the American-style symphony orchestra remained essentially emulative of the European original. Its repertoire was German, its players were of Central European extraction, its conductors went home to Germany every summer.

Two other areas of pronounced Germanic impact on American music bear mentioning: composition and criticism. In composition, German models crowded out America's own musical past. After the Civil War, especially, more nearly vernacular American styles—Gottschalk's, for one—were superseded by an approved German style based in New England and fathered by America's first professor of music, Harvard's John Knowles Paine (1839–1906). Paine's spiritual progeny included Amy (Mrs. H.H.A.) Beach, George Chadwick, Arthur Foote, Edward MacDowell, and Horatio Parker, all felicitous Germanic practitioners. In music criticism, the father figure was John Sullivan Dwight. His chief successors were, in Boston, Philip Hale and in New York, Richard Aldrich, Henry T. Finck, W. J. Henderson, James Gibbons Huneker, and Henry E. Krehbiel—a pantheon prevailing well into Toscanini times. The insatiably inquisitive Huneker—he was an accomplished pianist; a dazzling essayist published in New York, London, Paris, Berlin, and Vienna; an author of books on art, literature, and music (including a classic study of Chopin), as well as of a novel—cut the broadest swath; H. L. Mencken called him "a divine mongrel [who] knew no nationalities and no schools." Also notably eclectic was Hale; having studied in Berlin, Munich, and Paris, he revered Debussy and d'Indy as well as Beethoven. The caustic, scholarly Krehbiel qualified as the probable "dean" of New York music critics; of German extraction, he produced an English-language edition of Alexander Thayer's great work on Beethoven, was an early and ardent Wagnerian, and honored the classical symphonists with a purist's fierce integrity. Henderson, also an authoritative Wagnerian, was a gentler writer with special expertise in opera. In such company, Aldrich and Finck, both of whom studied in Germany and with Paine at Harvard, were lightweights. The former, once Krehbiel's assistant, was as temperate as Henderson without possessing Henderson's incisiveness. The latter, whose studies included stints in Berlin and Vienna, was yet another Wagnerian, with enthusiasms more passionate, less reliable than Aldrich's. His outspoken belief in music's moral efficacy ("the best way to eradicate savage impulses") reflected entrenched Germanic loyalties that, if diluted in some of his colleagues' writings, dominated the music pages of the New York press.

Mediating the oil-and-water separation of the ballyhoo and Germanic traditions was a third New World musical current in which both traditions intermingled: opera. To schematize these relations further: Italian opera gravitated toward ballyhoo, German opera toward symphonic sobriety.

Most Americans did not understand Italian or German. Echoing a famous prediction by the English essayist Joseph Addison—that a time would come when his countrymen would be curious to know "why their forefathers had to sit together like an audience of foreigners in their own country and . . . hear whole plays acted before them in a tongue they did not understand"—Philip Hone, an important New York City diarist, thus reported the opening of a new Italian opera house in 1833: "The performance occupied four hours—much too long, according to my notion, to listen to a language which one does not understand. . . . Will this splendid and refined amusement be supported in New York? I am doubtful."[19]

And yet the operatic language barrier was not insuperable. For one thing, many late-nineteenth-century Americans, including most New Yorkers, had been born abroad. For another, a certain class of patrons actually preferred the exoticism of an unfamiliar tongue. In *The Innocents Abroad,* Mark Twain claimed to have discovered in the register of an Italian hotel such signatures as "John P. Whitcomb, Etats Unis"; "Wm. L. Ainsworth, travailleur"; "George P. Morton et fils, d'Amérique." His comment: "I love this sort of people. A lady passenger of ours tells of a fellow citizen of hers who spent eight weeks in Paris and then returned home and addressed his dearest old bosom friend Herbert as Mr. 'Er-bare!' . . . This entertaining idiot, whose name was Gordon, allowed himself to be hailed three times in the street before he paid any attention, and then begged a thousand pardons and said he had grown . . . accustomed to hearing himself addressed as 'M'sieu Gor-r-*dong.*'" To affluent or upwardly mobile Whitcombs, Ainsworths, Mortons, and Gordons, the snob appeal of Old World culture was least resistible when garnished with Italian, German, or French verse. A box at the opera, moreover, furnished a suitable after-dinner destination for well-attired rich folk. To these attractions were added others less elitist: venerable amateur choral societies had cultivated a taste for the singer's art; the ballyhooed visits of Lind, Sontag, and other charismatic warblers had spread operatic culture beyond the ranks of debutantes and dilettantes.

For most of the nineteenth century, the result of opera's assorted New World assets and debits was mixed: an absence of institutions as enduring as the state operas of the Old World or the New York Philharmonic of the New, partly offset by mighty waves of transitory exposure. The cash rewards that lured Lind, Sontag, and Rubinstein also lured whole operatic troupes assembled abroad. If Americans heard Lind only in concert, they heard Sontag in opera, and also Marietta Alboni, Giulia Grisi, Maria Malibran, Mario, Adelina Patti.

A crucial catalyst, setting the pattern for what was to come, was the 1825 New York visit of a company headed by Manuel García, the famous Spanish singer, impresario, and teacher. Its repertoire favored Rossini but also included one Mozart opera, *Don Giovanni* (with García, a tenor, in the title role). Krehbiel, in his indispensable *Chapters of Opera* (1908), inferred that García's troupe had been "a poor affair, the orchestra not much better than that employed at the ordinary theater . . . and the chorus composed of mechanics drilled to sing words they did not understand." But New York had not before heard Italian opera of comparable authenticity, and its impact was great. The García company toured, and so did many others, implanting Italian and French opera in San Francisco, New Orleans, Chicago. A landmark in this dissemination was the opening in 1854 of New York's Academy of Music: following three failures, the city's first auditorium found capable of sustaining a commitment to opera. It was here that German opera first achieved a fashionable New World berth. Among the rival impresarios vying for management was the same Bernard Ullmann who had packaged Henri Herz with "A Thousand Candles" and sold Sigismond Thalberg to "ladies belonging to the first families of the city." Ullmann's operatic merchandising, according to Krehbiel, proved "utterly unconscionable"; among his prize possessions was an insignificant soubrette advertised as a lineal descendant of Charlemagne. The Academy of Music's most enduring, most successful impresario was London's James Henry Mapleson, who took charge in 1878—the same year the New York Symphony became the second permanent American orchestra. His artistic stable included the likes of Italo Campanini, Patti, Francesco Tamagno. Ablaze with vocal incandescence, the Academy under Mapleson shone more brightly than any previous American operatic undertaking. The stagings, the conducting, the chorus and orchestra contributed but dimly, however, and the commercial wrappings exuded ballyhoo. Krehbiel recalled Mapleson's attempt to stage a "spontaneous" torchlight serenade for Patti as "the most pitiful affair that I have ever witnessed . . . a humiliation of the great artist." James Huneker's 1918 autobiography contains these further recollections:

> In opera the cheap spectacular ruled. Singers were advertised like freaks, and managers always a half a step from ruin. That manager is become an extinct type. Only the pen of Charles Dickens could have character- ized the late Henry Mapleson, the Colonel, as he was affectionately named. . . . The particular artistic ointment used by the Colonel as a cure-all for irritated "artistic" vanity was antique flattery. If promises were rejected he applied, and with astonishing results, the unguent of fat praise; he literally smeared his singers. Then, conscious that another night had been saved . . . the Colonel would exclaim in that prodigious voice of his: "My boy! I say! What about a cold bottle!"[20]

Not the Academy but the 3,615-seat Metropolitan Opera House, opened in 1883, became an operatic showcase commensurate in prestige with the orchestral showcases of New York and Boston. Its rationale was not artistic but social. The Gilded Age had produced a new stratum of fashionable New York wealth whose ambitions, like those of the older Knickerbocker stock, included a Park Avenue apartment, a Newport villa, and—copying Old World prerogatives—a box at the opera. (Henry James called opera "the only approach to the implication of the tiara known in American law" and "the great vessel of social salvation.") The private boxes at the Academy being already full, a larger and more opulent opera house was commis- sioned and built. One inevitable result was a war between Mapleson's company and the Metropolitan. The Metropolitan won, but at a surprising cost: from 1884 to 1891, it catered to Wagner, whose operas the box-holders loathed. The entire repertoire was sung in German, and Germans, then making up one-sixth New York City's population, made up the majority of the audience. The singers included Marianne Brandt, Amalie Materna, and Albert Niemann, all Bayreuth principals, and the indefatigable Lilli Lehmann. The chief conductor, following Leopold Damrosch's death mid- way through the first German season, was Anton Seidl, a member of Wagner's household for six years and later a conductor in Leipzig and Bremen; in New York, where operatic performances had never before been commandingly integrated, he was instantly revered.

Especially in the eyes of such Germanophiles as Krehbiel, the Metropoli- tan's German regime rescued opera from the celebrity ballyhoo of Ull- mann, Mapleson, and other commercialists. In fact, given the newness of *Der Ring des Nibelungen* (completed in 1874), *Tristan und Isolde* (1859), and *Die Meistersinger* (1867), and the stature of the performers, it was a historic undertaking, capitalizing on American anything-is-possible enterprise. A less favorable opinion, however, dominated the Metropolitan's private boxes, the bustle and gabble from which drew frequent rebukes downstairs and up. In 1890–91, the chairman of the directors' "amusement committee" requested that the last act of *Die Meistersinger* be sung first, as it was "the only act with music in it"; another director maintained that stockholders reserved the right to disturb listeners in the stalls. As of 1891–92, the directorship terminated all German offerings in favor of opera in Italian and French. After several more seasons of squabbling, a trilingual status quo emerged with Maurice Grau, the former Anton Rubinstein impresario, in charge. He proved adept as both peacemaker and administrator, and the house enjoyed fabled years of bad scenery, bad ballet, erratic conducting, and prodigious individual vocal attainments by the likes of Emma Calvé, Emma Eames, Nellie Melba, Lillian Nordica, Pol Plançon, Jean and Edouard de Reszke, and Marcella Sembrich.

The Metropolitan's Golden Nineties were tarnished, in 1898, by the sudden death of Anton Seidl at age forty-seven. His distinguished successor at the head of the Metropolitan's German wing, Franz Schalk, stayed only a year, to be followed by lesser lights. A second misfortune, in 1903, was the retirement of Maurice Grau and the appointment of Heinrich Conried in his place. Born in Austria, Conried had arrived in New York as an actor, later becoming the manager of a small German theater and of operetta companies. To the management of opera he brought unbridled boldness, shrewd business instincts, and clownish ignorance; as one critic put it, he "knew no more about opera than an ordinary chauffeur knows about airplanes." When Felix Mottl, a conductor of Seidl's stature, complained that a mezzo-soprano was singing a soprano role in *Das Rheingold*, Conried is said to have replied: "You know that, my dear Mottl. I know that and so did the composer. But does the public know that?"[21] On other occasions, Conried was found not to know what the composer knew. Mottl put up with Conried for a year, then quit the house.

While the new regime was not without its artistic triumphs, most bore the stamp of quick-buck artistry. One such, highlighting Conried's first season, was the phenomenally profitable first non-Bayreuth run of Wagner's *Parsifal*, a work the composer and his widow had forbidden outside the Wagner shrine. It took Conried to flaunt these wishes, and to squelch ensuing petitions and litigation, in the interest of a certain commercial killing. But Conried's crowning feat was his exploitation of a new vocal prodigy, Enrico Caruso. Contrary to contemporary reports, Conried did not bring Caruso to the Metropolitan; he had already been signed for 1903–04 by Grau. According to Conried's biographer: "Those who knew Mr. Conried declared that he never thoroughly enjoyed opera unless Caruso sang." Part of the reason was that Conried's contract entitled him to a share of the company's profits; Caruso became his prime investment. Intent on extracting his money's worth, Conried presented the resilient young tenor more than fifty times per season; in 1905–06, Caruso's sixty-one dates amounted to more than one-third of all performances. As W. J. Henderson commented in the *Sun:* "The fact now to be recorded is that the public has gone to the opera in the season just ended, almost solely for the purpose of hearing Enrico Caruso. The public has not cared a rap what opera was sung." Caruso's friend Victor Herbert commended "the warm glow of his democratic modesty and personal charm," and so did legions of Caruso cultists. Like Jenny Lind's, his New York residence was regularly besieged, and passers-by would stop to gape. Quipped Huneker: "Why, there are men in this land of ours who would rather be Caruso than the President of the United States of Europe."[22]

Conried came to pay the price of ignoring his artillery in favor of one big gun. On November 16, 1906, Caruso was arrested in the monkey house of the Central Park Zoo for allegedly pinching the buttocks of a Mrs. Hannah K. Graham. He had to force his way through an enormous crowd in order to appear in court two weeks later. There, in a trial lasting two days, he was accused of two earlier fondling offenses. Denounced as a pervert, he was found guilty and fined ten dollars. At every stage, the "Monkey House Scandal" made headlines. Confronted by demands that he be deported and by daily shipments of abusive mail, Caruso fell prey to blinding headaches. These ended following a performance of *La Bohème* during which his admirers silenced a nest of hissers with frantic cheers and applause. But the Monkey House Scandal hurt Conried—it is believed to have precipitated an illness leading to his death less than three years later. A second blow was the opening, a few blocks from the Metropolitan, of the Manhattan Opera House on December 3, 1906. This was the brainchild of Oscar Hammerstein, whose opera credentials were barely more auspicious than Conried's own. After amassing a fortune as the inventor of revolutionary cigar-making machinery, Hammerstein (who was invariably seen smoking one of his long black cigars) had become a trailblazing theatrical entrepreneur possessed of a Barnum-scaled flair for self-promotion. Unlike Conried, however, Hammerstein knew music; he once won a five-hundred-dollar wager by writing an opera ("the worst on record," in the opinion of Carl Van Vechten) in twenty-four hours.[23] In fact, his stewardship of the Manhattan Opera revealed a capacity for astute musical judgment. He went shopping in Europe and returned with Amadeo Bassi, Alessandro Bonci, Mary Garden, John McCormack, Maurice Renaud, and Mario Sammarco. His principal conductor was the formidable Cleofonte Campanini. He introduced New York to *Elektra, Louise, Pelléas et Mélisande,* and *Thaïs.* Salting the rivalry between the two New York houses was Hammerstein's publicity expert, Billy Guard, who advertised Bonci as "the new and better Caruso" and spread rumors that Caruso had lost his voice. In fact, the timing of the Monkey House Scandal, and certain revelations concerning the complainant—that she had given the police a false address; that she did not appear at the trial; that she was a close friend of the arresting officer —suggested to some a Billy Guard coup.

Conried fought back by packing Caruso onstage even more frequently than before and by presenting the American premiere of Richard Strauss's scandalous *Salome,* which he hoped would prove a second *Parsifal.* Assessing the former tactic, Henry Krehbiel observed that it was "getting difficult to keep the Caruso cult on its old hysterical plane." The latter tactic backfired when after the premiere the directors declared *Salome* "objectionable and detrimental to the best interests of the Metropolitan Opera House" and forbade further performances. In Conried's defense it might be pointed out that the opportunistic, unmusical opera director was a species not unknown in Europe; and that with no state subsidy, he was forced to try pleasing the public taste in general and the taste of the celebrity-conscious boxholders in particular. Even so, the Metropolitan had never so contradicted the decorum of the Germanic tradition, or so evoked the mentality of Colonel Mapleson's "cheap spectaculars."

And there were further counts against the foundering Conried management: that the French artists and new French operas anchoring Hammerstein's success had been offered first to Conried; that Luisa Tetrazzini, a Hammerstein sensation, had been under contract to the Metropolitan and allowed to escape. Even the directors were made to realize that the house needed a stronger artistic profile. Meanwhile, the New York Philharmonic faced similar problems arising from a similar cause. Following Theodore Thomas's departure for Chicago in 1891, Anton Seidl had taken his place. His work again proved ear-opening. Moreover, as at the Metropolitan, his presence was linked to new prosperity. And, as at the Metropolitan, his demise proved unmooring: following five unsuccessful seasons under Emil Paur and Walter Damrosch, the orchestra chiefly opted for a galaxy of guests, including Edouard Colonne, Willem Mengelberg, Fritz Steinbach, Richard Strauss, Felix Weingartner, and Henry Wood. Any one of these eminent musicians might have made a feasible Seidl replacement; as stopgap visitors, they contributed to the orchestra's general decline in competence, stability, and prestige.

The twofold loss of Seidl was compounded by exciting developments abroad: supplanting the traditional supremacy of celebrity vocalists, pianists, and violinists, the day of the celebrity conductor was swiftly dawning.

Its chief prophets had been Richard Wagner and his onetime disciple Hans von Bülow; its chief contemporary apostle was Arthur Nikisch. Its central document, Wagner's *On Conducting* (1869), espoused the overthrow of self-effacing time beating in favor of more personal, improvisatory methods; specifically, Wagner prescribed interpolated tempo changes as "a positive life principle of all our music." In practice, Wagner's theory added to the traditional canons of discipline and technical proficiency Lisztian license and charisma. "When he conducts he is almost beside himself with excitement," one observer reported; "Wagner controlled the orchestra as if it were a single instrument and he was playing it."[24] More than dictatorial authority, Wagner's conductor of the future would exude intense personal magnetism. The pale, morbidly sensuous Nikisch, the Leipzig Theater's first conductor from 1882, more than fulfilled this prophecy. He was idolized. He mesmerized his orchestra. His readings were fabulously pliant, incandescently exciting.

By Wagnerian standards, Theodore Thomas seemed a dour Kapellmeister. He was appreciated for his integrity, his force, his repose, his clarity. By the turn of the century, however, this was not enough. Thomas's obituary in the New York *Times* called him an ideal exemplar of "the older generation of music lovers," versus "the 'modern' conductor that has evolved from Wagner's influence." Six years later, in 1911, the *Musical Courier,* making comparisons with "the big virtuoso conductors of the present period," declared him "a human metronome, a drill master who never yielded for a moment to a flexible or emotional indiscretion, as he would have called it." In New York, Thomas was jealous of Seidl, and had reason to be: in the eyes of Krehbiel, Huneker, and other sophisticates, Seidl represented what Thomas was not. Wagner's own protégé, Seidl had also served beside Nikisch in Leipzig. He was rumored to be an atheist and Liszt's illegitimate son. He could, in Henry Finck's opinion, make an orchestra "sing and sigh and whisper, exult, plead and threaten, storm, rage and overwhelm, as no other conductor could." His friend Huneker later recalled: "His profile was sculptural. So was his manner. But a volcano beneath. . . . His expression was eminently ecclesiastical. . . . His Gothic head I've seen in medieval triptychs, as a donator at Bruges or Ghent or else among the portraits of Holbein. . . ." A taciturn man, Seidl may have been too private to embody all the glamour of the Wagner-Bülow-Nikisch species. But he came closer than anyone in his wake. Walter Damrosch, the dean of New York conductors in concert and opera both, was a plodder with unsurpassed social connections. Frederick Stock, Thomas's successor in Chicago, was more capable, but not the celebrity type. Boston had already had Nikisch from 1889 to 1893, but had not been ready for him; Philip Hale, evoking the genteel ghost of John Sullivan

Dwight, had complained: "It is seldom . . . under Mr. Nikisch, that you have any theme given in frank simplicity; that a *piano* is observed strictly for more than two or three consecutive measures. Thus in a symphony of Mozart or Haydn, there is almost constant overstress. . . ." Karl Muck, supreme among Nikisch's pre–World War I Boston successors, was modern yet scholarly; as a candidate for American veneration, however, he was insufficiently exotic (after the manner of the princely Paderewski) or democratic (the amiable Caruso).[25]

What the American musical establishment needed, post-Seidl, post-Conried, was a pair of celebrity conductors, one to save the Metropolitan, the other to save the New York Philharmonic. Or, better, a single celebrity to rescue both and consolidate competing operatic and symphonic, ballyhoo and Germanic strains. In the glamour milieu of opera, with its continued susceptibility to virtuosic display and promotional hyperbole, he might attain the mass appeal of a Lind or Caruso. In the devotional symphonic milieu, with its "master works" and "sermons in tones," he might attain the lordly elevation of a Thomas or Seidl. Unlike Thomas, Henry Higginson, Colonel Mapleson, and other pioneers, he would inherit rooted, prestigious institutions. His diverse, aspirant audience could comprise every past or present New World cultural constituency: the circus mobs P. T. Barnum diverted toward aesthetic pleasure; the emerging nouveaux riches Mark Twain ridiculed and yet partly personified; the fledgling patrons of the Thomas Highway, trained to judge symphonic prowess the bellwether of community culture; the mild-mannered ladies of breeding who were the schoolteachers, librarians, parlor pianists, and music club organizers of the Gilded Age; the new and old wealth that coveted opera boxes as signatures of status; the genteel intellectual patriarchs who held the musical arts ethically indispensable; the stalwart Germans, eagerly desirous of more and better Beethoven and Wagner.

Within the larger scheme of New World/Old World ambivalence, a multipurpose podium celebrity could assuage longterm fears of inadequacy and satisfy the American hunger for novelty and achievement. Plausibly promoted as the "best" and "greatest," appropriated as thoroughly as Thomas had been and Caruso would be, he might become a national treasure: a cultural token Americans could flaunt as the symbol of their coming of age and guardian of their self-esteem. Bestriding the New World's uncluttered musical landscape, with its post-adolescent cravings and enthusiasms, he could achieve such fortune, adulation, and influence as could never be his on the crowded, aging ramparts of musical Europe.

II · Toscanini in America

The Metropolitan Opera, 1908–15

Around the turn of the twentieth century, Europe's leading Austro-German and Italian opera houses were transformed by individuals of Napoleonic force and fortitude. These were the Vienna Opera under Gustav Mahler, who became artistic director in 1897 at the age of thirty-seven, and La Scala of Milan under Arturo Toscanini, who became principal conductor in 1898 at the age of thirty-one.

In terms of culture, Mahler and Toscanini were natural rivals. In terms of policy, they were embattled allies. Both were small, excitable men whose ruthless idealism stirred achievement, turmoil, and intrigue. Dismissing tradition as a barrier to cultural renewal, pursuing a vision of integrated musical theater, they mounted new and neglected operas and refashioned the warhorses. They discarded unruly singers and ruled those they brought or kept. They intimidated audiences into arriving on time and keeping quiet. They made enemies and answered them with scorn. They were celebrities symbolizing a new order.

Romain Rolland described Mahler: "A long, clean-shaven face, hair tousled over a pointed skull and receding from a high forehead, eyes constantly blinking behind his glasses, a strong nose, a large mouth with narrow lips, sunken cheeks, and an ascetic, ironic and desolate air. He is extraordinarily highly strung, and caricatured silhouettes have popularized his resemblance to an epileptic cat on the conductor's podium." Born in a Bohemian village to German-speaking Jewish parents, he became a Catholic in 1897. "I am thrice homeless," he would say. "As a Bohemian in Austria, as an Austrian among Germans, as a Jew throughout the world, everywhere an intruder." His early conducting posts included one in Leipzig, where he led more than two hundred performances in a season. In Vienna, he removed the claque, closed the doors to latecomers, and eliminated all customary cuts in *Tristan* and other huge operas. He thought nothing of refusing leave to singers and was perennially enraged at the orchestra, which he believed conspired against him. He stressed the German repertoire, which he considered supreme, yet introduced works by Charpentier, Giordano, Leoncavallo, Offenbach, Puccini, Saint-Saëns, and Smetana. Aligning himself with the Secessionists, he collaborated with Alfred Roller on stagings that overthrew naturalism with symbolic lighting and simplified scenery. As a conductor his trademarks included textural clarity and mercurial emotionalism. According to Bruno Walter: "His every appearance in the orchestra pit was preceded by the tenseness with which one looks forward to a sensation. . . . Before the opening of the [last] act, he was invariably received with a hurricane of applause." A critic remarked in 1910: "Only [such] a man, completely blind to the world, led only by his holy vision, could have succeeded for years on end in conducting the Imperial Royal Opera in Vienna as if we were in Athens at the time of the great tragedies."[1]

Toscanini, among the handsomest men to wield a baton, had the face of a sculpted deity: the mask aristocratically molded, the skin lustrous and uncannily smooth, the eyes dramatically submerged in pools of shadow. At once ascetic and dreamy, his countenance elaborated the enigma of his obsessive, near-sighted gaze, variously described as "fiery," "brilliant," "blazing with excitement and spiritual light," yet—like the gaze of the blind—vacant, unfocused, wistful. Born and raised in Parma, home of Italy's most notoriously demonstrative opera audiences, the son of a tailor and sometime Garibaldi redshirt, he boasted of remaining a *contadino*—a peasant—all his life; he despised titles, privileges, and airs. After graduating, as a cellist, from the Parma Conservatory, he made an impromptu podium debut in Rio de Janeiro in 1886, conducting *Aida* when no one else could do the job. Following a period as an itinerant conductor of rising reputation, he became music director of Turin's Teatro Regio in 1895, an appointment he began with the first *Götterdämmerung* by an Italian company. Six weeks later he led the world premiere of *La Bohème*. At La Scala he made the women take off their hats, darkened the house, and outlawed encores. He led the Italian premieres of *Euryanthe, Eugene Onegin,* and *Pelléas et Mélisande.* He presented the first Italian production of *Siegfried* and the closest thing to an uncut Italian *Meistersinger.* His temper was already legendary. When the tenor mistimed an entrance during an ill-fated revival of *La forza del destino,* Toscanini stopped and made him beg   again. When he grew dissatisfied with the soprano in *Norma,* he canceled the production following Act I of the dress rehearsal. Feodor Chaliapin, Toscanini's Mefistofele in Boito's opera in 1901, left this account:

> The conductor looked quite ferocious to me. A man of few words, unsmiling, he corrected the singers harshly, and spared nobody. Here

was a man who really knew his job, and one who would brook no contradiction. I remember his turning to me in the middle of rehearsal, and asking in rasping tones if I intended to sing the opera as I was singing it then [in half-voice].

"No. Certainly not," I said, embarrassed. "Well," he replied, "I have not had the honor of going to Russia and hearing you there. Thus I don't know your voice. Please be good enough to sing as you intend to do at the performance."

I saw that he was right, and I sang in full voice. Often he would interrupt the other singers, offering advice, but he never said a word to me. I didn't know how to take this, and it left me with a feeling of uncertainty. . . .

The [next day's] rehearsal began with the Prologue. I gave it full voice, and when I had finished Toscanini paused for a moment, his hands lying on the piano keys, inclined his head a little, and uttered one single word in a very hoarse voice.

"Bravo."

It was quite unexpected . . . Elated by this success, I sang with tremendous enthusiasm, but Toscanini never uttered another word. . . .

At the rehearsals that followed . . . Toscanini, who produced, would come and watch me, order me to stand this way, that way, the other, sit like this, like that, walk that way, not this way. He would wind one of my legs round the other corkscrew-fashion, or make me fold my arms à la Napoleon. In fact what I was being instructed in was the technique of provincial tragedians, something with which I was already too well acquainted. If I asked him why he found this or that pose necessary, he replied with the utmost confidence: "Perchè questa è una vera posa diabolica" (because it is a truly diabolic pose). . . . [Later, Toscanini relented, and let Chaliapin reveal his own famous characterization.][2]

Another eminent foreign witness, Siegfried Wagner, was astonished by the quality of Toscanini's Scala *Tristan* in 1901.

Mahler, the pariah, was manic, morbid, insecure. His heights and depths of turmoil, relieved by droll jokes and pious reveries, are written in his music. His wife, Alma, nineteen years his junior, was touched by his "childish helplessness" and wounded by his selfishness. When her own composing interfered with her attentions to him, he ordered her to give composing up. Toscanini was rooted, iron willed, indestructible. A notorious, irresistible philanderer, he kept his shoes highly polished, and wore Eau de Cologne d'Orsy even on his mustache. Whereas Mahler, in the pit, would glare at latecomers and whisperers with an outsider's disdain, Toscanini, the *contadino,* would turn on his tormenters with the fury of a brother betrayed. These vilifications of the public were as famous as his behind-the-scenes ragings against singers and orchestras. When at the Milan premiere of *Euryanthe* in 1902 the audience demanded a repeat of the overture, Toscanini instead twice began the first scene. When the shouts of "Bis!" grew more insistent, he angrily dropped his baton and vanished; though he returned to repeat the overture, it was the only encore that evening. The following season, during a performance of *Un ballo in maschera,* Toscanini ignored thunderous pleas that Giovanni Zenatello be permitted to repeat "È' scherzo od è follia." He left the theater after the first act and did not return for three years. Equally revealing, however, was his way of sealing the acclaim for *Pelléas et Mélisande* in 1908: he applauded the audience. He was a tyrannical democrat.

The intransigence with which Mahler and Toscanini set high artistic goals ensured their long-term disgruntlement. And Mahler wanted more time to compose. In May 1907—ten years after he had begun work in Vienna—Mahler's resignation was made known. Toscanini's resignation was announced in February 1908—ten years following his arrival at La Scala, of which three had been spent elsewhere. Both announcements were greeted with dismay, satisfaction, and a torrent of rumors. Mahler might have also been speaking for Toscanini, in advance, when he explained to a newspaper: "No [operatic] theater in the world can be kept at a level where one performance is equal to another. But this is exactly what repels me in the theater. For of course I wanted to see all my performances on the same high level—that is, to attain an ideal which is simply unattainable."[3] One additional factor was common to both departures: Mahler and Toscanini were wooed, in turn, by New York's Metropolitan Opera. And with wads of dollars to invest in famous European talent, the Metropolitan succeeded both times. Quite suddenly, Mahler and Toscanini, twin deities in Vienna and Milan, became rival conductors in the same house. In America, their dual eminence ended; more than eclipsed, Mahler would be routed.

It was Heinrich Conried, the opera director who thoroughly enjoyed opera only when Caruso was singing, who made Mahler an offer he could not refuse: three months' work for 75,000 kronen ($15,000), with all travel and hotel expenses paid. In Vienna, Mahler's salary had been 24,000 kronen plus gratuities and pension. Never wealthy, he was determined to set aside more time for his symphonies and more money for his family.

Mahler believed in omens. Two omens preceding his first journey to America were devastating. On July 5, 1907—only days after the contract with Conried was finalized—his elder daughter, Maria Anna, died at the age of five. A few days later Mahler was found to have a diseased heart and was forbidden to climb, bicycle, or swim.

With the Mahlers' arrival in New York in December 1907, the distractions of new tasks in a new setting were palliative for a time. The Manhattan harbor itself, its two rivers crowded with tugboats and freighters, ribbed by heroic bridges, shadowed by ranks of vertical buildings, was in breathtaking contrast to Vienna. And Conried, who had the Mahlers to lunch at his apartment, proved equally diverting. "This first, fantastic luncheon-party, the flat itself and our host's utter innocence of culture, kept us in concealed mirth until we were in the street again and could burst out laughing," Alma later recalled.

> In Conried's smoking-room, for example, there was a suit of armor which could be illuminated from within by red lights. There was a divan in the middle of the room with a baldachino and convoluted pillars, and on it the godlike Conried reclined when he gave audience to the members of the company. All was enveloped in somber, flounced stuffs, lighted up by the glare of colored electric lights. And then, Conried himself, who . . . was now going to "make" Mahler.[4]

In his suite at the Hotel Majestic, Mahler spent most of the day in bed and forbade mention of his dead child's name. Alma suffered hallucinations. But at the opera house, the orchestra passed muster and the singers surpassed Vienna's. Meanwhile, Mahler's arrival was being favorably noted in the New York press. He had already been advertised, upon signing with Conried, as Europe's "most famous" conductor and a composer of stature. Now the soprano Olive Fremstad, rehearsing *Tristan* under Mahler's baton, told the New York *Times:* "Gustav Mahler's greatness cannot be over-estimated. I heard a performance of *Fidelio* at his theater in Vienna, and it made me cry to watch him. He is a small man, but his force is tremendous and he absolutely hypnotizes his men and his singers. . . . I am sure that . . . the New York public will make the acquaintance of a great man." Also, flattering storm warnings were being sent out: Mahler was a reorganizer, a stickler for detail, a martinet. According to the New York *Sun,* "musicians aware of his peculiarities" were predicting that "he would have a profound influence at the Metropolitan or leave at the end of a week."[5]

In fact, Mahler had mellowed. Well before leaving Vienna, he had quieted his frenetic baton technique. Now he relinquished his mania for total control. According to Alma Mahler:

> Mahler was very different in New York. He not only introduced all the usual cuts, but invented new ones in order to abbreviate the operas. He was merely amused, too, by lapses in the settings which in Vienna would have roused him to fury. It was not because his mind was distracted by the anxiety his illness caused him, or that he did not take the New York public seriously—on the contrary, he found the public there entirely of his own way of thinking. The reason was that his whole attitude to the world and life in general had changed. The death of our child and his own personal sorrow had set another scale to the importance of things.[6]

After Roller, the settings for *Tristan* seemed farcical. Musically, however, Mahler's American debut, on January 1, 1908, was a complete success. *Musical America* reported:

> There could be no doubt of the spirit in which the audience had come prepared to receive the noted German whom New York has gained at the expense of Vienna, for when he came forward to take his place at the conductor's desk he was greeted with a storm of applause such as is generally reserved for tried and proven favorites. That no disappointment was felt in his work was demonstrated subsequently between the acts when the same effusive cordiality insisted upon his appearing before the curtain to share the honors with the singers.

In the *Tribune,* Krehbiel wrote: "It was easy to recognize in Mr. Mahler's work last night that he is a master of his art whom New Yorkers will take particular delight to honor. It was a strikingly vital reading which he gave to Wagner's familiar score . . . eloquent in phrasing, rich in color, elastic in movement and always sympathetic with the singers." In the *Sun,* Henderson wrote: "Mr. Mahler knows well how to hunt Wagner's melody, from the top of the ruled page to the bottom, and let the auditors hear it. What he did last night was admirable, an honor to himself and charged with respect for the regenerator of the drama in music." In the *Times,* Richard Aldrich wrote: "Mr. Mahler's conducting resulted in a reading of the score that is comparable with the best that New York has known—the readings of Anton Seidl and of Felix Mottl. It was, on the whole, a finer reading than Mottl's, conceived in a larger mould, with all its finesse and subtlety, and with a greater power in the dramatic climaxes. . . . He gives the unmistakable impression of à man of commanding authority and of keen insight." A member of the orchestra told the influential *Musical Courier* that "Mahler

is the supreme Wagner conductor in the world," and the *Courier* agreed
with him. Alma, a superb musician, felt she had for the first time heard the
second act "sung as pure music" by Fremstad and Heinrich Knote. Mahler
himself "swam in bliss."[7]

Not three weeks later, Mahler wrote to Roller, urging him to seek a
position at the Metropolitan:

> The audiences here, and all the factors affecting the artist—not least
> the board themselves (most of whom are multi-millionaires)—though
> corrupt and misguided are—in contrast with "our people" in Vienna
> . . .—unsophisticated, hungry for novelty, and in the highest degree
> eager to learn. . . .
>
> For your information, you would have a season of approximately five
> months here. . . . *Last not least*—I think you can demand a salary of 15,000
> dollars. . . .
>
> Seize the opportunity, my dear fellow, if you receive an offer and if
> there is nothing to detain you in Vienna.—The people here are tremen-
> dously unspoilt—all the crudeness and ignorance are—*teething troubles.*
> *Spite* and hypocrisy are to be found only among our dear immigrant
> compatriots. Here the dollar *does not reign supreme*—it's merely easy to
> earn. Only one thing is respected here: *ability* and *drive!*

Then Mahler wrote to Willem Mengelberg, urging him to take over the
Boston Symphony Orchestra:

> The position in Boston is the finest any musician could wish for.—
> It is the *first* and *highest* in this whole continent.—*A first-class* orchestra.
> A position of absolute authority. A social position that no musician can
> ever attain in Europe.—A public more eager to learn and more grateful
> than any European can imagine. Your New York experiences are no
> criterion. Here in New York the theatre is the center of attraction, and
> concert-going is confined to a small minority.
>
> And now to what must also help to tip the scales for you: the salary.
> If you are approached, ask for 20,000 dollars. . . . You can live very
> comfortably indeed on 6,000 to 8,000 dollars, putting the rest aside. If
> I were you I should not hesitate to accept the offer. . . .
>
> It would be wonderful for me to have you nearby again. I shall
> probably also be spending the next few years here in America. I am quite
> entranced with this country, even though the artistic satisfaction to be
> got out of the Metropolitan is very far from what it might be.
>
> I write in great haste, wanting you to have this letter as soon as
> possible. Please answer immediately, even if quite briefly.[8]

Musical America truthfully reported "Mahler Amazed at Love of Art Here," and quoted him as follows:

> Before I set out for New York I had heard all sorts of stories about "the land of dollars." You know the nonsense that is said of it. Well, I have been amazed to see how ridiculously untrue those stories were. I have been impressed at every turn by the interest you show in art; and the more I have seen of America the more I have become convinced that those who speak ill of it have only themselves to blame for what they grumble at. My experience at the Metropolitan has been pleasant in the extreme. The singers and musicians have done their utmost to cooperate with me. And what artists they are![9]

Unknown to Mahler, he was standing in the path of an Italian juggernaut.

The Italians' first victim was Heinrich Conried. Spurred by Oscar Hammerstein's example, and by unignorable evidence of Conried's clownishness and declining health, the Metropolitan's executive committee had resolved to revamp the house's artistic image. According to Mahler's letters and Alma's recollections, Mahler was asked to take over Conried's job. Five years earlier, Mahler confided to a friend, he would have "been unable to resist such an alluring offer."[10] Considering his current needs, he resisted it firmly. Toscanini, who had been sounded out by the Metropolitan as early as 1903, was contacted next. He stipulated that he would be available only in tandem with La Scala's director, Giulio Gatti-Casazza. On February 4, 1908, a cable from Milan announced that Toscanini had been engaged to conduct at the Metropolitan. Eight days later, the Metropolitan board announced the hiring of Gatti-Casazza. To allay fears of receding German influence on repertoire and casting, Andreas Dippel, a veteran multipurpose tenor, was retained in a vague administrative capacity. Toscanini and Mahler were to be "joint musical directors." Two months later, Toscanini's salary for the three seasons beginning in 1908–09 was fixed at 25,000 lire per month plus expenses—about the same as what Mahler was earning. But whereas Mahler had made himself available for three months annually, Toscanini was to be at the company's disposal throughout each five-month season.

The New York press identified Toscanini as Italy's foremost conductor and a difficult man to please. From the start, two pieces of biographical data were seized upon: that he conducted everything from memory, and that he had made his conducting debut, in a Rio de Janeiro *Aida,* as an instrumentalist substituting in an emergency. Introducing a story destined to be as lovingly embroidered as that of Washington and the cherry tree, *Musical America* got the city and the opera wrong:

> He began his musical career as a cellist, and was playing in that capacity in the orchestra during the regular opera season at Buenos Aires when the regular conductor was suddenly taken ill. He immediately volunteered to take his place, and since there was no one else, his offer was accepted. The opera was *Lohengrin,* and after opening the score the new conductor did not turn a page, directing the entire performance from memory, and so remarkably that there was no further question as to his future profession.

Toscanini's New York debut, in *Aida* on November 16, 1908, was splendidly received. Krehbiel wrote: "Of the new conductor it must be said that he is a boon to Italian opera as great and as welcome as anything that has come out of Italy since Verdi laid down his pen. In the best sense he is an artist, an interpreter, a re-creator. . . . Signor Toscanini brought to the understanding and the emotions of the audience all of Verdi's score, body and soul, as it lives in him, mixing with it an abundance of sympathetic affection." From the first, Krehbiel put Toscanini's mnemonic feats in perspective: "He used no book; but that is matter of small importance except as it influenced the performance. It is, of course, as a brilliant German musician [Bülow] once said, much better that a conductor should have the score in his head than his head in the score; but unless he can convey his knowledge to the musicians under him it will avail him nothing. Evidently Signor Toscanini's head and heart are full of Verdi's music, and his transmission of what he knows and what he feels is magnetic." Henderson wrote: "As to the artistic success of Arturo Toscanini there was not the slightest question. No one who was at all acquainted with the recent annals of opera in Europe expected anything else." Aldrich called Toscanini "a dominating power, a man of potent authority, a musician of infinite resource."

Toscanini's first concert performance at the Metropolitan, of Verdi's Requiem on February 21, 1909, was so heavily attended that "the crush of standees was discomforting"; three extra performances were scheduled, plus two for 1910. His first *Falstaff,* the following month, acquainted New Yorkers with one of his specialties; the *Musical Courier* called it "an artistic achievement unparalleled."[11] By the end of the season he had led forty-five performances of ten operas, four concerts, parts of three benefit programs, and eighteen tour performances. In subsequent years Toscanini's pace, if anything, accelerated. His eventual seven-season total, including tours, was 446 performances of 31 operas.[12]

The churning wheels of the Italian juggernaut threw sparks in all directions. When Mahler arrived, there had been expressions of surprise at his mildness. Toscanini's behavior occasioned no such surprises. According to a much-rehearsed story, Geraldine Farrar interrupted one of his outbursts to remind him she was a star. "Only the sky has stars," he is said to have replied. Farrar was one of five celebrity singers—the others were Caruso, Emma Eames, Marcella Sembrich, and Antonio Scotti—who in November 1908 signed a worried letter to the directors on behalf of Andreas Dippel, who perceived himself being bypassed by the Italians. Caruso was reported to have gone so far as to threaten resigning when Toscanini's appointment was announced. Eames and Sembrich did retire early in 1909, although both decisions had long been brewing. With Farrar, Caruso, Scotti, and the rest of the company's pampered soloists, Toscanini prevailed. Throughout the house he inspired admiration, respect, and fear. When during a performance of *Euryanthe* he stopped conducting to silence talkers in the audience, the result was "a sudden and complete hush."

Three further obstacles to the hegemony of the new regime were duly removed. Declaring that "the operatic war is suicide," Oscar Hammerstein agreed to give up producing opera in Boston, Chicago, New York, and Philadelphia for ten years in exchange for more than $1,000,000 paid by the Metropolitan. Dippel left the Metropolitan administration to take charge of the new Chicago Grand Opera, comprising remnants of Hammerstein's organization. And Gustav Mahler made his last appearance in the Metropolitan's pit on March 21, 1910—around the same time as Hammerstein's withdrawal and Dippel's departure.

Mahler's strong start, on January 1, 1908, had been sustained for a time. During the remainder of the 1907–08 season, he triumphed in *Die Walküre*, *Don Giovanni*, *Fidelio*, and *Siegfried*. *Don Giovanni*, with a cast including Bonci, Chaliapin, Eames, Gadski, Scotti, and Sembrich, gave New York a taste of the winged ensemble style that had set a new Mozart standard in Vienna. For *Fidelio*, Mahler transplanted Roller's famous settings and introduced his interpolation of the *Leonore* Overture No. 3 before the final scene. Commented the *Musical Courier* critic: "I can say that so finished, so complete in every detail, so expressive, so tempered and yet so dramatically powerful a performance as that overture has never been given in this city. It was the acme of perfection in orchestral conducting. . . . After hearing that, can anyone blame the *Musical Courier* for paying no attention to the orchestral concerts given in this city by men like [Vassily] Safonoff and Damrosch?"[13]

The *Courier*'s commentary was prescient—with one eye cocked in the direction of the approaching Italians, Mahler was already contemplating leaving the Metropolitan for a New York orchestral post. At first, the converging opera autocrats had paid one another long-distance compliments. "I hold Mahler in great esteem," Toscanini had told Gatti, "and would infinitely prefer such a colleague to any mediocrity." And Mahler had written to Roller from New York: "The management plan [is] to appoint *Toscanini*, a *very well-thought-of* conductor, to take charge of Italian opera, and hand, as it were, German opera over to me." Then, inevitably, a collision course was charted. In late February 1908, Mahler perceived "a noticeable cooling off of the powers that be" in New York; in early March, he sensed " 'things' are moving towards the formation of a Mahler orchestra entirely at my disposal." By fall 1908, Mahler better appreciated the scope of Toscanini's intentions and wrote to Dippel in New York:

. . . In the discussion of my contract—of this you are a witness—I explicitly stated that I wished to retain for the new season the works which I have already rehearsed and conducted in New York. This was promised me, and I dispensed with a written assurance to this effect in the contract only at your request. And, while I have recently—in deference to the wishes of my colleague—left everything to the discretion of the new director, I have nevertheless expressly retained *Tristan* for myself. I lavished a great deal of effort on the *Tristan* last season, and may reasonably assert that the form in which the work now appears in New York is my intellectual property. If Toscanini, for whom I have the greatest respect, without knowing him, and whom I count it an honor to be able to greet as a colleague, were to take over *Tristan* before my arrival, then obviously the work would be given a completely new stamp and I should be completely unable to take on the work in the course of the season. I must therefore request you most earnestly to reserve the conducting of this work to me and therefore not to put it into the repertoire before December 17.[14]

Mahler got his way: the next Metropolitan *Tristan* took place on December 23, 1908, and he conducted it. The same season, Mahler led *The Bartered Bride*, *Fidelio*, *Le nozze di Figaro*, and *Pique Dame*. By February 1909, however, the real outcome of the *Tristan* collision had been determined: Mahler, careening to the side, would leave the Metropolitan to take charge of the New York Philharmonic. Toscanini, his forward impetus barely deflected, annexed *Tristan* on November 27, 1909. According to Bruno

Walter, Mahler commented: "Toscanini conducts it in a manner entirely different from ours but magnificently in his way." According to Alma, Mahler and she "always felt that [Toscanini's] Wagner suffered from an excess of Italian accent." In Alma's view, Mahler relinquished *Tristan* unwillingly.

> Toscanini immediately took it in hand and rehearsed it all over again in a manner entirely different. Mahler bitterly resented this and took no further pleasure in opera in New York. . . . Instead of thanking him, Toscanini from the first moment contemptuously ignored him. He even went so far as to hold him up to scorn during rehearsals. He was always telling the orchestra that Mahler "could not do that" and that he had no understanding of *Tristan*. We went to the first night of this production of Toscanini's. The nuances in his Wagner were distressing.

Many years later Toscanini told Howard Taubman that Mahler's *Tristan* had "no passion in it; but the poor man was tired and sick." He told B. H. Haggin that Mahler was a "crazy man."[15]

The question of whether Toscanini's Wagner was compromised by an Italian accent is as illuminating as any raised during his Metropolitan Opera tenure. In 1908, the year of Toscanini's first New York *Götterdämmerung*, Italian Wagner conductors were practically an unknown species. The following season, in addition to the *Tristan* performances that unnerved Mahler's wife, Toscanini led *Die Meistersinger*. The press was agog at the power and security of these three readings. But there was not the same chorus of unqualified acclaim that greeted Toscanini's Verdi and Puccini. Two critical camps emerged: those who found Toscanini's Wagner superb and yet Italianate, and those who found Toscanini's Wagner supreme. Toscanini's first New York Wagner reviews already defined the combat zone. Max Smith, who was to become Toscanini's most fervent journalistic partisan as well as a personal friend, wrote in the New York *Press:*

> Think of the peculiar situation: An Italian conducting a German work, and not only challenging comparison with the best German leaders who have appeared here, not excluding Seidl, but proving himself superior to most of them in their own territory! . . . Toscanini was the real "star" of last night's *Götterdämmerung*.
> . . . It was significant of everything Toscanini did that he accomplished results without blurring the music by haste or losing rhythmical strength by slowness. Rhythm tense and incisive thrilled and throbbed

in his reading; there was not a moment of relaxation, of dullness. Everything had musical intention and meaning; everything was based on sound artistic principles and inspired by burning temperament. From beginning to end Wagner's score, made clear and transparent by Toscanini's masterly analytical powers, revealed its most hidden treasures.

And did Toscanini once over-sentimentalize, a thing one might easily excuse in an Italian? Not a bit of it. Under his sweeping baton he brought out the heaving melodies of Wagner's music with wonderful plasticity and emotional energy. But there was no admixture of sugar; in fact, Toscanini often showed a distinct desire to avoid sentimentality, as in the Gutrune theme, which he took faster than usual. His reading was rugged, rather than sentimental.

The whole performance, orchestrally considered, represented a gradual crescendo of power and intensity. The last act never was performed here with such an overpowering accumulation of concentrated feeling. The funeral march, in itself one of the greatest compositions of all times, was stupendous.

The enemy position was well articulated by Henderson in the *Sun:*

At the outset it may be said that taking into account the temperament and acquired tastes of an Italian musician the interpretation of the score by Mr. Toscanini was thoroughly commendable. It would be injustice to others and flattery to this conductor to say that it was a great reading. It would be equally unjust to deny that, granting its emotional outlook (which is by no means indefensible), it was a good reading.

Mr. Toscanini naturally feels above all the sensuous quality of Wagner's melody, and it is this in all its ebb and flow that he seeks and exposes. Whenever the sensuous beauty of the melody is such as to tempt a conductor to dwell unduly on the phrase, to exaggerate the rhetorical pause, to smooth out all the rugged edges of the instrumental declamation Mr. Toscanini yields to it with avidity and spreads the syrup on the bread as thin as possible.

The results of such treatment are easily noted. In most of the first act they took shape in elongations of tempi till the scenes at times lost their innate strength. Hercules was transformed into Apollo with an accentuation of the effeminacy always noted in statues of the latter god. But there was another side to the picture. Whenever the sensuous beauty of the pure melody was to be exposed only by deepening its lines by adhering to the firmly dramatic nature of its contours, Mr. Toscanini rose to the occasion. This was, for example, notably the case in the splendid choral passage of the second act, which went with admirable verve.

. . . It remains to say . . . that the orchestra had been well drilled in the conductor's ideas and that certain failures in cohesion and in solidity of tone were due to the nature of the reading rather than to technical deficiencies in the playing.

And so it went. Of Toscanini's *Tristan,* Algernon St. John-Brenon of the New York *Telegraph* wrote: "There may be a Teutonic way of interpreting *Tristan und Isolde.* There may even be a delicatessen way. But Mr. Toscanini's way is the Wagnerian way." Huneker issued this more qualified encomium:

[Toscanini] belongs to the Brahmin conductors; to the company of Richter, Levi, Seidl, Mottl, Mahler. A more poetically intense *Tristan* than his reading with the lovely Fremstad as the impassioned Isolde, I have seldom heard. Toscanini is a superman. In that frail frame of his there is enough dynamic energy with which to capture Gehenna. He is all spirit. He does not always achieve the ultimate heights as did Seidl, as does Arthur Nikisch. While his interpretation of *Tristan* is a wonderfully worked-out musical picture, yet the elemental ground-swell, which Anton Seidl summoned from the vasty deep, is missing. But what ravishing tone-colors Toscanini mixed on his orchestral palette!

Aldrich of the *Times* thought Toscanini's first Metropolitan *Meistersinger,* on March 26, 1910, his highest local achievement. But *Musical America* thought the *Meistersinger* performance, while "superb" over all, inferior to Toscanini's *Tristan* to the degree that *Meistersinger* seemed more inherently "Teutonic": "At moments now and then one felt that a trifle more of the stolidly and ponderously muscular might have been more to the purpose." The detailed reportage of the *Musical America* review is full of interest:

. . . The score constantly exhaled exquisite poetry; and without ever sacrificing any of the multicolored glories of Wagner's orchestration the Italian conductor succeeded in maintaining so continent a dynamic scale that every word uttered by the singers carried its full value. His tempi were in many cases different from those of his predecessors, many of them inclining toward greater rapidity. His reading of the overture was superb, and it was most noteworthy how he emphasized its wonderful polyphony by accentuation of certain melodic inner voices which are often suffered to pass unheard in the contrapuntal melee. Perhaps he hurried a trifle over the wonderful love theme heard in the first act, as

Walther gazes after Eva when she leaves the church, but he made ample amends for this in the accompaniment to Walther's trial song. Wondrously beautiful was his work in the second act during the scene between Sachs and Eva, in the ethereal summernight music at the appearance of the watchman, and again in the indescribably lovely episode after the riot.[16]

The ultimate test of Toscanini's catholicity took place in the Germans' own symphonic citadel: on April 13, 1913, he led the Metropolitan Opera Orchestra in Beethoven's Ninth Symphony. The magnitude of the event was acknowledged. The first day tickets went on sale, the demand was so great that over a thousand people were turned away. The audience was crammed with musicians; Caruso was among the standees. Max Smith wrote a twenty-five-inch review in which the keynote ran: "This was not playing in the ordinary sense. It was the burning utterance through multitudinous voices, all responding to one galvanic influence, of emotional ideas conceivable only in music." Even Karl Muck and the Boston Symphony, Smith continued, could not match the "impassioned vehemence" of the Toscanini–Metropolitan Opera account. "No unprejudiced person competent to pass judgment can well deny that last night's production of Beethoven's masterpiece surpassed any previous performance of the work, including the comparatively recent ones under Gustav Mahler and Felix Weingartner." Other reviewers reached a surprisingly united consensus: Toscanini had led a thrilling performance of Beethoven's Ninth, remarkable for its textural clarity, crisp rhythms, singing *melos,* and unaffected fervor. The fourth movement was the best. The second and third were too brisk. Krehbiel was in the majority when he wrote:

> Signor Toscanini put a little too much strain not only upon his performers but also upon himself. His tempi . . . seemed to indicate that he was laboring under a somewhat abnormal nervous strain. . . . He did wonderful things [in the] finale. There he inspired his singers to a feat which was without parallel, we make bold to say, in the history of the work in America. From beginning to end that all but impossible composition was sung. It was sung with a precision, a volume, an attention to nuance, a distinctness of utterance (the original German text was used), an unfaltering justness of intonation, which held veteran concert goers spellbound. Everybody was letter perfect.
> . . . The scherzo last night was taken at a quicker speed than Beethoven prescribed, and the effectiveness of the trio, in particular, was marred and some passages were blurred. Nor was the flight to the empyrean in the

variations quite so transfiguring as it might have been. But the music held
the listeners in an irresistible grip, nevertheless.

Krehbiel would have been surprised to learn that such lavish praise of
Toscanini's Beethoven would seem damnably faint a mere generation
later. Nor would Henderson's and Huneker's reservations about Toscanini's Wagner, however qualified, have been peaceably received by
New York critics and audiences of the next generation. What are we to
make of these reviews seven decades after the fact? To Max Smith, Toscanini's mildest detractors seemed sullied by German loyalties. And, as-
suredly, ingrained Teutonism was part of the context in which
Toscanini's first New York symphonic performance was heard. But there
is another part of this context that bears scrutiny. The most distinguished
Italian operatic conductor on the New York scene preceding Toscanini's
arrival was the Manhattan Opera's Cleofonte Campanini, who barely appeared at the Metropolitan. The Central European conductors who had
led Wagner and Beethoven in New York and Boston, on the other hand,
composed a daunting pantheon. In addition to Mahler, both Mottl and
Seidl—with Hermann Levi and Hans Richter, Wagner's chief protégés at
Bayreuth—had led *Tristan* at the Metropolitan, as had Franz Schalk en
route to taking charge of the Vienna Opera. Seidl had also conducted the
New York Philharmonic in Beethoven, as had Fritz Steinbach and Felix
Weingartner. Nikisch, who led the Boston Symphony from 1889 to 1893,
was widely regarded as the leading symphonic conductor of his time.
Muck, who succeeded Nikisch in Boston as of 1906, possessed Wagnerian
credentials fully as impressive as Seidl's or Mottl's. By the end of World
War I, all these master exponents of the German repertoire had passed
from the American scene.

Surveying New York operatic affairs between 1908 and 1918, Krehbiel
observed:

> During the period of which I am writing, even in journals of dignity
> and scholarly repute the gossip of the foyer and the dressing rooms of
> the chorus and ballet stood in higher esteem with the news editors than
> the comments of conscientious critics. . . . If in this [the newspapers]
> reflect the taste of their readers, it is a taste which they have instilled and
> cultivated, for it did not exist before the days of photo-engraving, illus-
> trated supplements and press agents. . . . The phenomenon, inasmuch as
> it marked the operatic history of the decade of which I am writing more
> emphatically than any period within a generation, is deserving of study.

Leo Slezak, a Metropolitan artist from 1909 to 1913, intensely admired the energy, authority, and "passion for accuracy" Toscanini brought to the house, yet also had cause to reflect:

> Press work! Publicity! This is the basis which governs everything in the U.S.A. Whether a thing is good or bad, no matter so long as it is talked about. . . . This even applies to those [artists] who are at the top of their profession and want to continue earning top-scale fees! Life moves quickly in the U.S.A. and the greatest sensation of the day is forgotten by the evening. Everything is on such a vast scale, that one must shout louder than one's neighbors if one is to attract any notice at all.
>
> It becomes a question of constantly keeping one's name before the public and of not being too particular about the methods used for the purpose. In order to achieve this, one employs a press agent. . . . His principal duty is to produce some new "stunt" every week—however fatuous it may be—to drag round the U.S. press. If the press agent has a sufficiently vivid imagination, one may read things about oneself in the papers which should make one blush for shame, but after a year in the U.S. one gets hardened to things of that kind.[17]

In his memoirs, Slezak, whose sense of humor was once described as "undisciplined," claims to have posed for American reporters with a goat and tortoise as mascots ("I cannot sing unless this goat is in the concert hall and the tortoise loves me and wags its tail when I speak to it"). Toscanini tolerated no stunts or press agents, yet was inevitably a prime beneficiary of the growing public relations mentality. From the start, his phenomenal memory furnished a trove of trivia. One typical item, appearing in both *Musical America* and the Boston *Transcript*, attested:

> [Toscanini] was about to graduate from the conservatory, and, as a candidate, had to play a composition at sight. The composition on this occasion was written by one of the professors of the conservatory, and was long and bristled with all sorts of technical difficulties. Toscanini overcame these with ease, and, as he was a quick sight reader, had no trouble in passing the test. Some years afterward he happened to meet this professor at the house of a friend, and during the course of the evening, which was devoted to music, Toscanini asked him if he would give an opinion on a composition which he would play. The professor acquiesced and Toscanini sat down and played from memory the piece composed for the sight-reading test. "A very poor composition," exclaimed the professor almost before Toscanini had finished playing.

"You composed it," retorted Toscanini, laughing. "I never did," replied the other. "I could not write so badly." And then Toscanini explained what it was, but the professor, still skeptical, hunted out the manuscript and found to his surprise that Toscanini was right and had played the piece note for note, though he had only seen it once, and that for the occasion of his examination in sight reading.

More pungent were Toscanini's fits of temper:

> It is well understood here . . . that Mr. Slezak's failure to appear was the culmination of certain difficulties in existence for some time between Mr. Slezak and Mr. Toscanini, and that, preceding last evening's performance Mr. Toscanini stated, simply but emphatically, that he would not conduct if Mr. Slezak sang.
>
> It was also said to be the case that Mr. Toscanini refused to conduct when Miss Farrar sang on Tuesday evening.
>
> Gossip has it that the real reason for the *Tristan und Isolde* postponement last week was Arturo Toscanini's anger at two of the principals who failed to appear at the rehearsal he had called.
>
> Reports were circulated on Monday along Broadway and Fifth Avenue to the effect that the orchestra at the Metropolitan had struck and would not play any more under Toscanini, owing to his having insulted two members of their body.[18]

And yet Toscanini was said to be afflicted with "a sphinx-like reticence of speech" and to be so shy that applause caused him physical pain. His foibles were endearingly plebeian:

> Arturo Toscanini, the Metropolitan Opera conductor, is superstitious about the number "thirteen." He conducted a recent performance of *Cavalleria rusticana* at the Metropolitan although there were others to conduct it, simply to remove a possible thirteen "hoodoo" from the premiere of *Ariane et Barbe-bleue.* He had discovered that he had previously this season conducted twelve first performances, including novelties and revivals, and he did not want *Ariane* to be the thirteenth.[19]

Max Smith was Toscanini's chief publicist in the press during his Metropolitan Opera years. In contrast to the lordly Krehbiel, and to such temperate types as Henderson and Aldrich, Smith was ready to take up the cudgels when his man was crossed, or even in anticipation of such contradiction:

No doubt the musical philistine was well represented in last night's audience, which included a large number of professional men and women. From him we shall surely hear in due time that Toscanini was quite out of his element. Great men always arouse antagonism among the small fry.

> Whenever *Die Meistersinger* has its annual revival in the Metropolitan Opera House under the direction of Arturo Toscanini certain persistent critics solemnly inform the public that an Italian conductor, be he ever so enlightened, cannot possibly do justice to a score so essentially Teutonic.
> . . . Truth to tell, a study of Wagner's writings . . . bears out the opinion that Toscanini's performance of the score would have more than satisfied the famous composer's demands. Far from underrating the merits of foreign musicians, indeed, Wagner criticized severely those of his country.

Smith was as carping toward Toscanini's colleagues as toward his own:

> In Toscanini's first season in New York, when he had to spend more time on an orchestra unaccustomed to his ways than he does now, accusations, nursed by malice, were brought against him of following such questionable methods, the intimation being that he compelled the opera company to spend large sums of money for orchestral rehearsals which he needed only as an aid to his memory. Yet all the time Gustav Mahler, who conducted from score habitually, held rehearsals even more frequently.

Smith also complained that Nikisch was "pretentious, pompous, theatrical," and that Weingartner made "mincing gestures . . . calculated, no doubt, to show how he can bend great forces to his will by the turn of his little finger."

In a critical community dominated by armchair aesthetes, Smith was messianic, always on his feet. Thirsty for converts, he pled his case in national magazines, rehearsing with fearless redundancy the particulars of Toscanini's unscheduled debut, absolute diligence, and fabled memory. In *Century Magazine* he wrote:

> In New York, Toscanini has conducted twenty-two operas. The number of pages in the full scores of those works, as, thanks to Lionel Mapleson, librarian of the Metropolitan Opera Company, I have ascertained, is approximately ten thousand. Yet that does not nearly represent

the prodigious amount of material that he has filed away in his mind, ready for immediate use. In countries outside of the United States he has conducted by heart not only seventy other operas, thus bringing the number of operatic scores he has committed to memory to the stupendous figure of ninety-two, but has also produced various oratorios, symphonies, and tone-poems.

Of greater interest, in the same article, is Smith's delineation of the Toscanini virtues in juxtaposition with certain stereotypical defects.

"When Toscanini leaves his house, he knows exactly where he is going," one of his admirers remarked in discussing the conductor's ways, "and he proceeds in that direction as eagerly as a hound on a trail. That is something you rarely find among musicians, most of whom wander about with their heads in the clouds."

Toscanini does not conform to the traditional type of absent-minded musician. Neatness, order, punctiliousness, nicety, are characteristic of the man as well as of the artist.

Unlike certain other conductors—Nikisch, Strauss, Mahler, and Mottl —the Italian master is never satisfied with giving vague indications.

Toscanini approaches his task objectively rather than subjectively and that explains why he succeeds so well with music of various schools and epochs. . . . He has no sympathy with the trend of modern conducting, as exemplified by Nikisch, who not only shapes his readings to suit his individual taste, but actually presumes to change the orchestration set down by the composer. His all-absorbing ambition is to reproduce music in a way absolutely true not only to the letter, but to the spirit of the creating mind.

And in a *Vanity Fair* article, Smith wrote: "Eminently sane in his ways of thinking, a man of common sense, despite his artistic temperament, [Toscanini] would not admit for a moment that the ability which his admirers call genius, came from any but perfectly simple and normal sources."[20]

These tributes to practicality, efficiency, and objectivity, all of which designated Toscanini "one of us," were widely, if less militantly, echoed. This is how the *Musical Courier* praised Toscanini's *Falstaff:*

The *Falstaff* score is as well fixed in Toscanini's mind as it was in the mind of the composer, if not more rigidly and firmly. Few composers can ever do this with their own works. The consequence is that there is a smooth performance and more than that—an elegant, well interpreted, genuinely artistic production. . . . There is no question of doubt. The operation is performed not only artistically but scientifically.

More than signifying musical acuity, Toscanini's powers of memory appealed specifically to children of the Gilded Age. Mark Twain had admired the Venetian gondoliers' precise calculation and confident execution; in the years of the first Model T (1909) and the first Ford assembly line (1913), Toscanini was found as flawless and economical as a machine. Smith praised his "photographic vision." The New York *Sun* said: "Toscanini's mind has been compared to an American phonograph." Putting the case more baldly still, a Chicago paper wrote:

> . . . To his orchestra, he represents simply the brain of the organization. Why this is so, concerns them little. It is tradition, it is custom, and he is Toscanini—the commander in chief.
>
> But the last man you ask may hint at the true reason. "He knows his business," one of them said the other day, and in that remark is the kernel of truth that explains it all. . . .
>
> For he possesses that trait of the born conductor, not to be acquired, except at the expenditure of generous energy—a self-reliance born of exhaustive knowledge. He has studied, he has planned, he has rehearsed as according to that plan and there is nothing further to be done. Therefore he stands quietly before the severest, most unkind critics in the world, the orchestral musicians, and they respect him as they respect no one else related to the organization.
>
> He is the man who knows his business.

That the criterion of good business is good money was not lost on Max Smith: "A man like Toscanini is worth more than any one 'star' even in financial terms. That is why the Italian conductor's services are now in demand in every musical center of the world, enabling him to earn in a year almost twice as much as the President of the United States."[21]

As Max Smith's Toscanini campaign scaled new heights of embattled advocacy, the rumors swarming in Toscanini's wake reached peak intensity in response to a single burning question: Would he stay or would he leave? During the 1913–14 season, various scribes at their listening posts reported hearing that Toscanini had threatened to resign. Ever more obstreperous threats were heard about in 1914–15. Gatti-Casazza, too, was said to be contemplating departure. A New York critic observed: "Opera gossip until recent years had its inspiration in the whimsies of prima donnas. Up-to-date chroniclers find a more fruitful field in speculation as to the intentions of a general manager, or of a conductor."[22]

In point of fact, Toscanini's contract was to expire in April 1915, and he was indecisive about renewing it. The New York job was wearing him down physically. As at La Scala, he found that no amount of vigilance and cajoling could sustain Olympian standards on a day-to-day basis. As he eventually told Max Smith in a letter:

> . . . Please, dear friend, make this explicit declaration on my behalf concerning my spontaneous withdrawal from the Metropolitan, and even make it public if necessary: "I have given up my position at that theatre because my aspirations and artistic ideals were unable to find the fulfillment I had dreamt of reaching when I entered it in 1908. Routine is the ideal and the basis of that theatre. This can suffice for the artisan, not for the artist."
>
> "Renew yourself or die." *Voilà tout.* This is the *only* reason which made me leave the Metropolitan. All the others that have circulated in the papers are false and unfounded. . . .[23]

But there were other reasons to leave New York. Toscanini was increasingly eager to conduct symphonic concerts. A nationalist, he wished to be home in Italy in wartime. Geraldine Farrar, with whom he was having an affair, was demanding that he abandon his family for her.

The end came following a pair of flawed *Carmen* performances on March 18 and April 13, 1915. Long enraged over economies imposed by the management, Toscanini blamed missed entrances and other lapses on insufficient rehearsal time. He told Gatti that he would conduct Mascagni's *Iris* on April 14 and nothing more—his remaining seven dates, including an enormous symphonic program, were void. He returned to Italy saying he was finished with the Metropolitan.

Or was he? No one knew for sure. Otto H. Kahn, the chairman of the Metropolitan executive committee, refused to give up; through European emissaries, he assured Toscanini that he could dictate the terms of his return. Gatti-Casazza did what he could to help; on July 16, 1915, he wrote to Kahn from Milan:

> [Toscanini] rehashes all the old accusations against the Metropolitan to justify his conduct. To these accusations I responded thus: Excuse me, Maestro, what can you complain about, considering that everyone at the Metropolitan, from Mr. Kahn down to the lowest staff member, is ready to do whatever you wish? Is it a question of financial conditions? We can

always reach an understanding on that. Is it a question of a title? In that case, why have you refused that of General Music Director? Is it a question of repertoire, artists, rehearsals, performances, etc.? But I wish for nothing more than to go along with you whom I consider an associate, not an employee, and whom I try to satisfy in everything possible. If I cannot always comply with your ideas, it is because you often do not state them. . . .

I ask you, Mr. Kahn, how can one argue and make decisions under these conditions, while trying not to vex such an opponent? Not even Job in the Bible was put to such a test of patience.[24]

All summer long, the New York press buzzed with speculation: Toscanini had suffered a "complete physical breakdown" and was "almost certain" to stay put in Italy; Toscanini was reconsidering and a happy verdict was now "assured." The guessing continued into the fall. On September 4, 1915, *Musical America* reported that Toscanini's firm resolve to leave the Metropolitan "became definitely known this week." Ten days later, Henderson wrote in the *Sun:*

The annual expression of doubt as to the return of Arturo Toscanini to the conductor's desk at the Metropolitan Opera House has been emphasized this year by the war in Europe, in which the Italian conductor has taken a great interest. . . . So far there has come no definite word to anybody in authority at the Metropolitan from either Toscanini or Gatti-Casazza that the conductor [is] not coming. The season here does not begin until Nov. 15, so there is ample time for Signor Toscanini to change his mind, just as he has been doing for so many years.

By the end of September, all observers had seemingly concluded that, at the very least, the new season would have to begin Toscanini-less. For those who, like Max Smith, considered him the "greatest living conductor," Toscanini's absence could only be calamitous. The admiration other critics felt for Toscanini the artist was diminished by irritation with Toscanini the man. Surveying the qualifications of two Toscanini replacements, the *Musical Courier* went so far as to predict:

From the standpoint of art the season will suffer in no way. The splendid work done by Giorgio Polacco is already very well known to the patrons and, judging from the theatres in which Mr. Bavagnoli has directed, it is reasonable to assume that he, too, is a thoroughly competent conductor. But the public seems to like "stars" at the conductor's desk as on the stage. Evidently Mr. Gatti-Casazza has planned to avoid the rising of any new conductorial stars this season that might obscure the light which will still feebly illuminate us, shining from distant Italy. It may be that the orbit of this particular star will swing once more in the direction of America before the beginning of another season.

Musical America summed up:

. . . Toscanini's failure to return to this country next season is being viewed from two different standpoints by some of the artists who have been under his direction. Some say, frankly, that while they admire his genius and consider him perhaps the greatest conductor of opera there is in the world today, they would not particularly miss him, for the reason that his great talent and mastery of stage effect were offset by his frightful irritability and his habit of perpetually abusing the artists, the chorus, and the orchestra during rehearsals, and never losing an opportunity of hurling invective at poor Gatti-Casazza, whenever he saw him, whether on the stage or in the wings.

The result, they said, was, that by the end of the season half the company was in a state of nervous collapse.

On the other hand, there are several artists, notably among the younger ones, who seem to appreciate Toscanini's interest in their work, and who are much inclined to view his irritability and tendency to vituperation as simply characteristic of "the artistic temperament."

As one said recently:

"I believe dat some arteest no like Toscanini call them 'peeg.' Dat meana nodding wida da Maestro. Wen 'e call people 'peeg,' 'e ees only mean to tell dem that they don't seeng or do da worrk good, an' 'e want dem to do da worrk good, so to please da publeek. 'E no mean wen 'e call you 'peeg,' dat you is a *porco* to be cook an' eat. Dat is what is call in French, *façon de parler*. Eet ees da way 'e talk.

"I 'ave learn much from da Maestro. I 'ave learn so much dat I am please eef ee call me 'peeg' many time, so I make big success."

H. T. Parker of the Boston *Transcript* sealed Toscanini's Metropolitan tenure with this balanced assessment:

. . . The nervous force within him he infused into music and play, singers, band and audience, until, when he was at his highest and fullest and in music that stirred him, it made the atmosphere of the opera house electric. It was his glory to outpour this unique power of personality; it is his misfortune that he will brook not the smallest limitation to it.[25]

Reading such panegyrics today, one can only envy Metropolitan Opera audiences of the Toscanini-Gatti period. The roster of singers comprised an international elite—and this in a period amply endowed with superb exponents of the standard repertoire. The orchestra and chorus were honed to peak potential. The stagings, if less progressive than those Mahler had thought to introduce, could scarcely have risked non-committal efficiency. In the view of the Viennese Mahler biographer Egon Gartenberg, the Metropolitan repertoire "deteriorated" once the Italians took over in 1908.[26] Granted, a seven-season New York schedule including fresh stagings of Catalani's *La Wally*, Franchetti's *Germania*, Giordano's *Madame Sans-Gêne*, Leoni's *L'oracolo*, Puccini's *Le Villi*, and, by Wolf-Ferrari, *Il segreto di Susanna*, *L'amore medico*, and *Le donne curiose*, reflects chauvinism as well as enterprise.* But in light of such undertakings as the world premiere of *La fanciulla del West* and the American premieres of *Boris Godunov* and *Der Rosenkavalier*, Gartenberg's judgment is harsh.

In the long view, Toscanini helped consolidate a repertoire trend originating under Maurice Grau: notwithstanding his flair for Beethoven and Wagner, the operas he and Gatti mounted were overwhelmingly Italian. In other respects, however, he represented a staying of the tide: the pressures that kept his Metropolitan tenure short eventually truncated his legacy. In the absence of incandescent leadership, the celebrity singers regained the upper hand, rupturing the *Gesamtkunstwerk* ideal. The orchestra and chorus deteriorated. In fact, the enduring significance of Toscanini's first New York appointment was less institutional than personal: his seven Metropolitan seasons launched his New World celebrity.

The story of Mahler's postoperatic New York career constitutes a dark postscript to the first stage of Toscanini's American success. In two years, his detour from the Metropolitan Opera House to Carnegie Hall proved a dead end.

As at the Metropolitan in 1907, the Mahler regime at Carnegie Hall began

---

*Mahler's track record was better: of the eight operas he conducted in New York, four (*Fidelio, Die Walküre, Siegfried, Tristan und Isolde*) were staples, the novelties being the first New York staging of *Pique Dame*, with Slezak and Destinn; the New York premiere of *The Bartered Bride*, for which dancers were imported from Bohemia; *Don Giovanni*, which was not seen again at the Metropolitan until 1929; and *Le nozze di Figaro*, which received five Metropolitan Opera performances during the subsequent twenty years.

auspiciously. As at the Metropolitan, a group of millionaires resolved to arrest financial and artistic decline. In 1909—the year after Toscanini arrived in New York—the New York Philharmonic was reorganized. From having been a shaky musicians' cooperative, it became the subsidized luxury of a group of philanthropic socialites. Desirous of laying the groundwork for a more permanent orchestra worthy of comparison with the Boston Symphony, these "guarantors," headed by Mrs. George R. Sheldon, pledged to make good any deficits for three years, expanded the season from eighteen to forty-six concerts, arranged for the orchestra's first tour, and passed the baton to Mahler, who received it as a scepter. Mahler hired a new concertmaster, Theodore Spiering, as well as new principal brasses and woodwinds. He rebalanced the strings, which had been bass heavy. He insisted that the Philharmonic not reduce its size on tour. And he told the press he would strive to make his orchestra the best in the United States and the equal of any in the world.

> "It will be my aim to educate the public," said Mr. Mahler, as he sat in his rooms in the Savoy Hotel, shortly after his arrival from Europe, "and that education will be made gradually and in a manner which will enable those who may not now have a taste for the best later to appreciate it. The basis of the season's programs will be classic music. There will be special cycles, such as the Beethoven, for those who love this lofty symphonic music and for the education of my orchestra, and the historical, in which we shall play the music from the time of Bach down to the modern composer."[27]

Mahler conveyed his private opinion of the New York Philharmonic in a letter to Bruno Walter: "My orchestra here is a real American orchestra. Untalented and phlegmatic. It's uphill work." Spiering later recalled that, despite some recalcitrance, the Philharmonic under Mahler was "swept along to undreamed-of heights of achievement." A Viennese observer who heard Mahler in New York remembered:

> For someone who had had the privilege of hearing a Philharmonic Concert under Mahler in Vienna, the outward aspect of a concert in New York was heart-rending: the audience, the greater part of which came too late and ran off before the end of the concert, the clinical and graceless Carnegie Hall, the cool discipline and austere impersonality of the orchestra (I can with warmth register two exceptions: the outstanding leader Spiering and the excellent horn-player Reiter, who both really understood Mahler). And yet, for those with ears and hearts, performances which are unforgettable![28]

As for the New York critics, they greeted the reconstituted Philharmonic with growing optimism. Of Mahler's reading of the *Leonore* Overture No. 3 on November 19 the *Musical Courier* reported: "The great conductor gave a marvellously inspired and inspiring performance of this most uplifting of all overtures. The audience applauded the feat to the echo and displayed more enthusiasm than ever before has been noted in a New York concertroom after a Beethoven performance." The Funeral March from *Götterdämmerung,* given at a subsequent concert covered in the same review, "rose to heights of new grandeur. . . . Not even Seidl, in his palmiest days, ever gave us such a concert performance of Wagner. It was nothing short of sublime."[29]

As Mahler's symphonic interpretations became better known, however, reviewers found more to criticize than they had in the opera house. Like Wagner, Mahler believed that differences between modern instruments and those Bach and Beethoven knew dictated doublings and rescorings to clarify and rebalance clotted textures. Upon repeated exposure, some New York critics found that this policy promoted Mahler's imprint more than the composer's. In particular, Mahler offended Henry Krehbiel, whose feuding post-Metropolitan Mahler reviews evoke Eduard Hanslick's broadsides against Wagner or Philip Hale's against Nikisch. Of Mahler's version of Beethoven's Fifth he wrote:

> . . . The first evidence of erraticism occurred in the famous cadenza, in the first movement.
>
> This Mr. Mahler phlebotomized by giving it to two oboes and beating time for each note—not in the expressive adagio called for by Beethoven, but in a rigid andante. Thus the rhapsodic utterance contemplated by the composer was turned into a mere connecting link between two parts of the movement. Into the cadence of the second subject of the third movement, Mr. Mahler injected a bit of un-Beethovenian color by changing the horn part so that listeners familiar with their Wagner were startled by hearing something very like Hagen's call from *Götterdämmerung* from the instruments which in the score simply sustain a harmony voice in octaves. In the finale Mr. Mahler several times doubled voices (bassoons with cellos) and transposed the piccolo part an octave higher. Here he secured sonority which aided him in building up a thrilling climax, but did not materially disturb Beethoven's color scheme. The question of the artistic righteousness of his act may be left to the decision of musicians.[30]

Krehbiel also disliked Mahler's own music; assessing the First Symphony, he dubbed the composer "a prophet of the ugly." Mahler retaliated by forbidding Krehbiel, for years the Philharmonic's program annotator, from writing program notes for any of his compositions.

And Krehbiel was the least of Mahler's troubles. Notwithstanding positive predictions in the press, the lengthened season resulted in swaths of empty seats; "probably the smallest that ever attended a Philharmonic concert in fifty years" and "perhaps the smallest in number that ever gathered at a Philharmonic concert" are typical descriptions of the houses Mahler attracted.[31] Meanwhile, the strong-willed matrons of the guarantors committee began to have second thoughts about Mahler's appointment. In retrospect, their disaffection was inevitable. Mahler asked no advice and cultivated no graces. One pivotal confrontation, in January 1910, arose during a rehearsal of the Schubert-Liszt *Wanderer* Fantasy. Mahler stopped the orchestra to discuss a point with Busoni, who was the soloist. According to one version of the incident,[32] a guarantor in attendance interpreted the interruption as a work stoppage. In any event, a dispute followed in which the ladies of the committee informed Mahler that his behavior would never do.

In the summer of 1910, Mahler and the guarantors committee were at odds over his salary. The following season, the guarantors established a program committee (four ladies to two musicians) to supervise what music Mahler would conduct. Mahler did his share to fan the flames, encouraging one of his second violinists to inform on enemies of the conductor. Others in the orchestra found out and demanded the man's dismissal. When the guarantors acceded, Mahler took it as a personal affront. In her memoirs, Alma Mahler described the climactic blowout:

> . . . One day in the middle of February, [Mahler] was required to attend at Mrs. Sheldon's house. . . . He found several of the male members of the committee there and was severely taken to task. The ladies had many instances to allege of conduct which in their eyes was mistaken. He rebutted these charges, but now at a word from Mrs. Sheldon a curtain was drawn aside and a lawyer, who (as came out later) had been taking notes all the time, entered the room. A document was then drawn up in legal form, strictly defining Mahler's powers. He was so taken aback and so furious that he came back to me trembling in every limb; and it was only by degrees that he was able to take any pleasure in his work. He decided to ignore all these ladies in the future.[33]

Days later, Mahler's health took a turn for the worse. On February 21, he conducted for the last time. Alma was grateful for the many expressions of solicitude she encountered on the street: "Never in my whole life have I met so much genuine warmth of heart and delicacy of feeling as in

America." But her gratitude did not extend to the guarantors. In May, by which time the Mahlers had returned to Vienna, she told an American interviewer that she held the Philharmonic responsible for her husband's decline: "You cannot imagine what Mr. Mahler has suffered. In Vienna my husband was all powerful. Even the Emperor did not dictate to him, but in New York, to his amazement, he had ten ladies ordering him about like a puppet."* The guarantors, the article continued, denied these accusations, "insisting that [their relations with Mahler] were always agreeable, and that the illness of the conductor came about through his extreme nervousness."[35]

May 18, Mahler was dead. Vienna gave him a hero's funeral. The Philharmonic guarantors chose Josef Stransky, a Bohemian of no international standing, to take Mahler's place. In New York, word-of-mouth duly acclaimed Stransky the "greatest conductor in the world."[36]

Krehbiel's objections to Mahler's score tampering were not unprecedented abroad. But, as an American, he had a sharper ax to grind. Even his favorable review of Mahler's New York debut in *Tristan* began on a pugnacious note: "Herr Mahler . . . is a newcomer whose appearance here, while full of significance, is not likely to excite one-half the interest in New York that his departure from Europe did on the other side of the water." When Mahler implemented his "historical cycles" to "educate" the Philharmonic audience, Krehbiel was more than dubious: he was affronted. Additional

---

*In the context of America's genteel tradition, with its culture-bearing ladies of charity, the Philharmonic's powerful female guarantors were not the anomaly they seemed to Mrs. Mahler. All of America's music clubs, and most choruses, were women's organizations. According to Theodore Thomas, Midwestern advances in musical understanding were due "almost wholly to women. They have more time to study and perfect themselves in all the arts. They come together in their great clubs and gain ideas. Then they travel abroad." In Cincinnati, where Thomas directed the May Festival (1873–1905), women founded the Cincinnati Symphony (1895). Thomas's second wife, Rose Fay Thomas, was helpful in the founding of the Chicago Orchestra (1891), of which Thomas was the first music director. The Chicago Orchestra's third manager was Anna Millar (1895–99). In New York, Jeanette Meyers Thurber sponsored Thomas's young people's concerts (1883), formed the short-lived American Opera Company (1886), and coaxed Dvořák to America to direct her National Conservatory of Music (1892–95).[34] It seems reasonable to infer that with the gradual professionalization of music administration and expansion of the symphonic audience base, the direct influence of leisured women on musical affairs waned in favor of salaried men. This was certainly the case at the New York Philharmonic, where Arthur Judson's managerial omnipotence obliterated the memory that female amateurs had once been in charge.

performances of well-known Beethoven symphonies, he commented, could scarcely be deemed "essential to . . . artistic salvation by any process of reasoning, or stretch of the imagination." In fact, everything about Mahler must have struck Krehbiel as objectionably didactic: not merely his programming of symphonic staples but his rescorings and interpretive machinations suggested an attitude of "I know better" or "I am closer to the source." If any part of Europe's musical heritage seemed well appropriated in the United States, it was the symphonic masterworks Mahler was re-teaching. Anyway, for Krehbiel authority resided less in received teachings than in the text. This attitude, flattering to Americans, was vulgarized by Max Smith when he wrote: "Toscanini approaches his task objectively rather than subjectively and that explains why he succeeds so well with music of various schools and epochs."*37

Normally, Krehbiel was a prudent critic. It was Mahler's acidic chauvinism that unmasked his own. Much as Krehbiel charged in the *Tribune*, Mahler neither knew nor cared about America's musical accomplishments. In aspiring "to raise popular musical standards and make the New York Philharmonic Orchestra the best in this country and the equal of any in the world," he had this to say to *Musical America* about whose standards were highest: "The best orchestra in the world today . . . is, to my mind, that of Vienna. Munich, Dresden, Berlin and Paris have splendid organizations, but that of Vienna attained under Hans Richter a perfection that I know of nowhere else."38 Characteristically, Mahler did not think to mention Boston. While Toscanini was also driven to upgrade New York's musical resources according to his own ideals, his "sphinx-like silence" served him better than Mahler's exhortations, and what comments he did confide to the press were favorable to existing American standards.

A conclusive baring of the wounds Mahler had unwittingly inflicted while in New York was prompted by his death. Krehbiel seized this opportunity to deliver a withering fifty-inch postmortem that began:

> Gustav Mahler is dead, and his death was made to appear in some newspaper accounts as the tragic conclusion of unhappy experiences in New York. As a matter of fact . . . [he] was a sick man when he came to New York three years ago. His troubles with the administration of the Philharmonic were of his own creation, for he might have had the absolute power which he enjoyed for a space in Vienna had he desired it. He was paid a sum of money which ought to have seemed to him fabulous from the day on which he came till the day when his labors

*See page 64.

ended, and the money was given to him ungrudgingly, though the
investment was a poor one for the opera company which brought him
to America and the concert organization which kept him here. He was
looked upon as a great artist, and possibly he was one, but he failed to
convince the people of New York of the fact, and therefore his American
career was not a success. His influence was not helpful but prejudicial
to good taste. It is unpleasant to say such things, but a sense of duty
demands that they be said.[39]

In what followed, Krehbiel characterized Mahler as a spendthrift, a possible
liar, and a musical vulgarian. As in all Krehbiel's writing, his intellectual
credentials are imposing; even his dismissal of Mahler's symphonies is
incisively argued. But the undercurrent of personal resentment exacerbat-
ing his Mahler allergy was never so naked as here. Knowing too well that
Mahler's *Tristan* and *Fidelio* had been found path-breaking in Vienna,
Krehbiel wrote of the former that it was "in no sense revolutionary, and
there was even disappointment in the circumstance that there was nothing
except things with which the cognoscenti were only too familiar in the
stage management—a department which needed reformation." Of *Fidelio*
at the Metropolitan Krehbiel now wrote that while "much ado was made"
over Roller's sets and Mahler's musical alterations, "they were not accepted
here as inspired revelations." Discussing Mahler's Eighth Symphony,
Krehbiel took a swipe at "German criticism" for never having questioned
the propriety of joining a church hymn to Goethe's *Faust*, Part II. Finally,
and leaving no doubt that it was not Beethoven but America that Mahler
had besmirched, Krehbiel concluded:

It is a fatuous notion of foreigners that Americans know nothing about
music in its highest forms. Only of late years have the European newspapers begun to inform their readers that the opera in New York has some
significance. Had their writers on music been students they would have
known that for nearly a century New Yorkers have listened to singers
of the highest class—singers that the people of the musical centers of the
European continent were never permitted to hear. Mr. Mahler early
learned a valuable lesson at the opera, but he never learned it in the
concert room. He never discovered that there were Philharmonic subscribers who had inherited not only their seats from their parents and
grandparents, but also their appreciation of good music. He never knew,
or if he knew he was never willing to acknowledge, that the Philharmonic audience would be as quick to resent an outrage on the musical
classics as a corruption of the Bible or Shakespeare. He did not know that
he was doing it, or if he did he was willing wantonly to insult their

intelligence and taste by such things as multiplying the voices in a Beethoven symphony . . . by cutting down the strings and doubling the flutes in Mozart's G minor, by fortifying the brass in Schubert's C major until the sweet Vienna singer of nearly a century ago seemed a modern Malay running amuck, and—most monstrous of all his doings—starting the most poetical and introspective of all Schumann's overtures—that to *Manfred*—with a cymbal clash like that which sets Mazeppa's horse on his wild gallop in Liszt's symphonic poem. . . . But the man is dead and the catalogue might as well be closed. Of the unhappy relations which existed between him and the Philharmonic Society's promoters it would seem to be a duty to speak; but the subject is unpleasant; those most interested know the facts; the injury that has been done cannot be undone, and when it becomes necessary the history may be unfolded in its entirety. It were best if it could be forgotten.

So savage was Krehbiel's attack on the dead man that the pianist Ossip Gabrilovich, supported by others of prominence, felt called upon to issue a pamphlet in reply. Some New York critics were also indignant. The *Musical Courier,* in an unsigned June 7 commentary entitled "The Detractors of Mahler," mounted a barbed rebuttal worthy of Krehbiel himself and reading, in part:

> It was a silly thing to bring a supreme judge like Mahler from Europe and place him under the direction of a petticoat jury. We are told that Mahler wanted his own way. He was an autocrat, and it is un-American to be an autocrat. We hear a great deal of talk about this un-Americanism. . . .
>
> And likewise we say that it is un-American to allow a very great conductor to have his way with an orchestra, forgetting that his way is the only way that will make that orchestra great and worthy of its venerable name. Still, our vanity is flattered. We demonstrated to Gustav Mahler that it would not do to try European despotism in our advanced civilization. . . .

The story of Mahler's New York Philharmonic debacle is packed with meaning for the cultural arena Toscanini would come to dominate. In conjunction with the passing of the Boston Symphony's Esterházy-like Henry Higginson in 1919, the Philharmonic's 1909 reorganization marked the end of one-man patronage or cooperative self-remuneration as models of symphonic financing in America. Instead of state subsidies, as in Europe, the American norm would be subsidization by committees of millionaires responsible for donating or raising money. In return, the millionaires would expect, if not an artistic voice, acknowledgments and courtesies, or at least borrowed glamour. Delicate relations between an orchestra's music director and its benefactors became a trademark of American symphonic affairs. Certain conductors, of which the sociable Walter Damrosch, the flamboyant Leopold Stokowski, and the intimidating Toscanini would furnish contrasting examples, charmed or transfixed their paymasters. Others, following Mahler's example, tended to aggravate a deep-seated ambivalence toward offered transfusions of Old World culture. Krehbiel's role, too, anticipated future troubles—in particular, those of Wilhelm Furtwängler, whose violation of New World personality and artistic canons would antagonize influential millionaires and critics, and whose triumphant adversary would be Toscanini.

For its recitals, symphonies, and operas, its pianists, conductors, and singers, the United States at the time of Mahler's death remained basically dependent on Europe. It naturally revered the nurturing parent culture, yet ever more resentfully resisted continued dependency. The relationship was infinitely volatile.

Interlude, 1917–25

During Toscanini's last season at the Metropolitan Opera, one argument proposed against his threatened departure was that America was a haven from an Old World gone berserk. The Great War had no comprehensible cause and was an ocean away. But in subsequent months the war drew closer. America's entry, in April 1917, signaled a selective transformation of its feelings toward Europe. And this transformation transformed feelings toward the European high culture America had absorbed.

No temperate chronicler of the war fever that gripped America escaped noticing what Ludwig Lewisohn termed its "peculiarly unmotivated ferocity." Families who resisted "flying squads" promoting bond purchases found their homes painted yellow. Red Cross leaders warned that German-Americans had sneaked ground glass into bandages. Supposed draft dodgers were forced to kneel and kiss the flag. More than fifteen hundred alleged spies and traitors were arrested; others were shot or hanged.

Prosecution of the enemy within was inflamed by the United States Government's first large-scale attempt to manufacture propaganda, capitalizing on expanded literacy and improved communications technology. The Committee on Public Information, chaired by the newspaperman George Creel, was a planned instigator of mass opinion generally, and of Germanophobia specifically—making its activities doubly pertinent to understanding Toscanini.

The problem facing Creel was that most Americans were unsure why Germans were enemies. In particular, there was the problem of American emulation of German music, scholarship, pedagogy, and science. To stamp out the image of the civilizing German, a different stereotype was needed. To this end, the word *Kultur* was appropriated and poisoned. German politics were condensed to "Prussian militarism" and made the war's sole cause. German diplomacy was reduced to "boasting, double-dealing, and deceit," German combat to "wanton murder" of Belgian babies. The new mentality was doled out in CPI books, films, lectures, expositions, and advertisements. The CPI's *Conquest and Kultur* summarized the German war effort as follows:

> The pied pipers of Prussianism . . . have led the German people to conquest and to ignominy and to infamy. . . . Before them is the war god to whom they have offered up their reason and their humanity, behind them the misshapen image they have made of the German people, leering with bloodstained visage over the ruins of civilization.

A CPI advertisement in the *Saturday Evening Post*, entitled "Spies and Lies" and bearing a drawing of a black-hatted eavesdropper, read in part:

> German agents are everywhere, eager to gather scraps of news about our men, our ships, our munitions. It is still possible to get such information through to Germany, where thousands of these fragments—often individually harmless—are patiently pieced together into a whole which spells death to American soldiers and danger to American homes. . . . Do not become a tool of the Hun. . . .

A CPI advertisement in New York University's *Alumni News* showed white buildings in flames over the text:

> In the vicious guttural language of Kultur, the degree A.B. means Bachelor of Atrocities. Are you going to let the Prussian Python strike at your Alma Mater, as it struck at the University of Louvain? The Hohenzollern fang strikes at every element of decency and culture and taste that your college stands for.[1]

Given the centrality of German music and musicians on the American concert stage, and the formidable popularity of German opera, the impact of such denunciations was traumatic. Before the war, America's musical community had prided itself on its neutrality: as if in compensation for the absence of an indigenous heritage, leading orchestras and opera houses had picked and paid for the ranking musical celebrities of Europe. Now, the posture of neutrality was dropped. During the closing months of the war, and for some years afterward, American orchestras lost enthusiasm for the German repertoire. Some smaller orchestras, cued by violent protests, banned German music altogether. In New York, the Philharmonic decided not to program any living German composers, and so returned certain Richard Strauss warhorses to the stable. The Metropolitan Opera banned German opera in any language—a policy more severe than in France, where no wartime repertoire restrictions were imposed, or England, where Wagner was temporarily done in English. Mrs. William Jay, instrumental in persuading the Metropolitan to abandon Beethoven, Mozart, and Wagner, contended: "Given in the German language and depicting scenes of violence, German opera cannot but draw our minds back to the spirit of greed and barbarism that has led to so much suffering."[2]

Whereas musical institutions could adapt and survive, some individual musicians could not. Those who were foreign born—which is to say, nearly all those who mattered—were automatically under suspicion. Caruso, though a certain military reject for reasons of age and health, was criticized for not enlisting in the Italian army. He atoned by singing at Liberty Bond rallies at the rate of three per month, and by purchasing quantities of Italian war notes. For artists born in Germany and Austria, the burden of the prescribed hysteria could be insupportable. At the Metropolitan, Gatti-Casazza decided to do without certain tainted singers. Fritz Kreisler, criticized for his pacifist views, withdrew from the concert stage. Frederick Stock of the Chicago Symphony also voluntarily retired for a time, as did several of his players.

Some German- and Austrian-born musicians, while sympathetic to the Central Powers, were dissuaded by American benefactors from leaving American posts. This was the case with Ernst Kunwald, conductor of the Cincinnati Symphony, and Karl Muck, conductor of the Boston Symphony; to their benefactors' surprise, both were deported to Fort Oglethorpe, Georgia, as enemy aliens. Of all the victimized musicians, Muck fell furthest. In Boston, as in Germany, he was judged one of the leading musical personalities of his generation. Hawk-nosed, erect, supercilious, he was also the outward embodiment of a Creel-style "spy." And so it was alleged that Muck had been overheard plotting to blow up the birthplace of Henry Wadsworth Longfellow, and that he was sending messages to German submarines from his cottage in Seal Harbor, Maine. On October 30, 1917, the Providence, Rhode Island *Journal* declared: "It is as good a time as any to put Professor Muck to the test. The Boston Symphony Orchestra should play 'The Star Spangled Banner' in Providence tonight." Though it was not Muck's decision but that of the orchestra's founder, Henry Higginson, and its manager, Charles A. Ellis, Muck's "refusal" to play the national anthem was widely reported. At this, Theodore Roosevelt issued a statement inviting Muck to go back to where he came from, and an agent of the Department of Justice recommended that the Boston Symphony be prohibited from giving concerts without proper patriotic trappings. Thereafter, Muck did conduct "The Star-Spangled Banner"—and was criticized for his "torpid rendition." He also offered to resign, but Higginson would not hear of it. When the orchestra was to play in Baltimore, where "The Star-Spangled Banner" was born, the furor was such that the concert was banned. When the orchestra played in New York, hundreds of policemen were needed to control the crowd outside Carnegie Hall. On March 18, 1918, Muck was arrested and taken to Fort Oglethorpe, where Kunwald had been living since the previous December. Upon leaving for Europe—permanently—following the Armistice, Muck told the press that the United States was a country "controlled by sentiment which closely borders on mob rule."

In the aftermath of the Muck debacle, no American orchestra could go shopping for a new music director in the usual places. That is why the Boston Symphony, whose previous leaders had been Georg Henschel, Wilhelm Gericke, Arthur Nikisch, Emil Paur, Max Fiedler, and Muck, was next led by two Frenchmen: Henri Rabaud (1918–19) and Pierre Monteux (1919–24). Meanwhile, the Philadelphia Orchestra, conducted since 1912 by the flamboyant, London-born Leopold Stokowski, became the first orchestra to challenge Boston's American supremacy. Rather than stick with the low-key Monteux, the Boston trustees elected to counter Stokowski with a Russian: Serge Koussevitzky. By provoking the Red Scare of 1919–20, the Bolsheviks had ensured continued political paranoia in the United States. Soviet turmoil also ensured the westward departure of scores of eminent musicians, including, in addition to Koussevitzky, Jascha Heifetz, Vladimir Horowitz, Gregor Piatigorsky, Nathan Milstein, and Sergei Rachmaninoff. With their impeccable political credentials, these charismatic émigrés were destined to further dilute the German musical presence in America.

During these times of exaggerated hostility to political outsiders, Toscanini's loyalties were never in doubt. Militarism and monarchism incensed him. From Plato's *Republic* he copied out the words: "Freedom in a democracy is the glory of the state, and, therefore, in a democracy only will the freeman of nature deign to dwell."[3]

Toscanini was no erudite student of politics. His republican schooling, such as it was, was partly rooted in his father's glory days in the Risorgimento: as a member of Garibaldi's redshirts, Claudio Toscanini had campaigned against the Spanish Bourbons in the south of Italy and against the Austrian emperor in the north. A second political base was the egalitarian culture of Parma, where Toscanini was born and raised. In all Italy, Parma was celebrated for the irreverence of its opera clientele. Singing that would elsewhere elicit cheers, boos, or indifferent applause incited in Parma's Teatro Regio a running commentary. Wrong notes were corrected en masse. An awkward costume or gesture risked a volley of wisecracks. (Toscanini was fond of an anecdote about two warriors in *Norma* who happened to have enormous noses. Trumpeted a voice from the dread *loggione:* "I can't hear you—turn your noses up a bit!") The Regio was embedded in a larger democracy of which it was the hub. Many of the tradesmen who manned the "lion's den" were amateur musicians. Claudio Toscanini occasionally sang in the Regio chorus; two apprentices in his tailor's shop helped dress the singers. Parma was a republican stronghold.

All this forms the background to Toscanini's wartime patriotism. When in 1914 his sometime friend Puccini declared that German occupation would cure administrative chaos in Italy, Toscanini, in the words of his daughter Wally, "turned into a wild beast."[4] When Italy at first remained neutral in the widening European conflict, Toscanini advocated intervention and territorial acquisition; the Trentino, northeast of Milan, still belonged to the same Emperor Francis Joseph from whom his father had tried to help wrest it under Garibaldi. When in 1915 Italy declared war on the Central Powers, Toscanini set about organizing and conducting benefit performances in Milan and Rome. He followed military events with such intense interest that he kept track of troop movements with flagged pins on a map.

Finally, when the urge to see for himself grew irrepressible, Toscanini formed a military band and took it to the front. In August 1917, while Italian troops assaulted the contested Monte Santo, Toscanini and his band gave a program of marches and anthems. After each selection, Toscanini shouted "Viva l'Italia!" He was later decorated for bravery under fire. In October, leading his band during an Italian retreat, he refused to move without orders to fall back. Only when Austrian shells began landing nearby were the players dismissed.

These feats of courage were widely noted in the American press. One account of the Monte Santo concert, in the Kansas City *Times,* added these details:

> Tranquil and calm, his baton seemed to be directing a concert, showing repeated contempt for danger.
> The Italian soldiery stormed enemy positions, a thunder of guns filled the air, gray green uniforms blending with the landscape and helmets plumed with glittering cock's feathers advanced steadily and by rushes upon the Austrian trenches, and the band played on. . . .
> . . . Did it play well or poorly? Be certain the maestro knew. No burst of shrapnel deafened him to the trombone's false entry. Above "the drums and tramplings of three conquests" taking place simultaneously

a quarter mile away, he heard the performance of his snare drummer and observed the clarinet player's careless habit of keeping time with his foot. . . .

An account in the *Brooklyn Daily Eagle* expressed hope for "an ending of the war that may send [Toscanini] back to us safe and sound," and predicted: "As a patriot who has helped to carry one of our allies to one of its most stirring victories there is no place big enough to hold the welcome which New York will give to Toscanini if he comes." The *Musical Courier,* however, distanced itself from these celebrations. Citing aspects of the New York *Times* version of the Monte Santo concert, the *Courier* observed:

> . . . With the "Austrian barrage fire at its height," the Italian soldiers would have needed super-human ears to have "taken the trenches—to the music of his [Toscanini's] band" even if it were "sheltered only by a huge rock." . . . How convenient that the story should come over just in time to slip into a Monday holiday paper, when a good story is as scarce as roses in December. Arturo Toscanini is too good a musician and too good a patriot to need that kind of a press boost.[5]

The Toscanini fatigue shown by the *Musical Courier* was cumulative. Two years before, when Toscanini left the Metropolitan, the same publication had already wearied of the glare of his spotlit accomplishments. Then, during the war, it had unavoidably taken part in an ongoing Toscanini watch, chronicling the conductor's various benefit concerts as well as the usual stormclouds trailing his activities.

One of Toscanini's most publicized tirades erupted in 1919 during a rehearsal of Beethoven's Ninth in Turin. Enraged by the seeming nonchalance of a member of the second violins, he struck the man's bow with his baton—whereupon the bow, according to most accounts, rebounded into the player's eye. In a lawsuit, Toscanini was absolved through the intervention of the "theoretical philosophy" professor Annibale Pastore, who explained that Toscanini was prey to fits of "sublime frenzy" pre-empting his "normal personality." Pastore's testimony, savored in the American press, continued:

> [Toscanini] becomes transfigured by genius . . . so that the inhibitory nerves are completely paralyzed. In a paroxysm of inspiration he falls a tragic prey to the tyranny of art, and the faculty of distinguishing good

from evil is subordinated to the extreme ebbs and flows of sensibility.
. . . So impossible is anything like a quiet return to normal equilibrium
that throughout the night after a performance he continues in a state of
pitiful nervous exhaustion, exaltation. He cannot sleep, his teeth chatter
incessantly, the muscles of his arms and legs become painfully rigid, and
the whole organism vibrates like the subsoil after a terrible earthquake.[6]

At the heart of the Toscanini watch was the same worried question that
had shadowed his final season at the Metropolitan: Would he return? Inevitably, he was a leading candidate to succeed Karl Muck in Boston (others
approached about the post, for which no Germans needed apply, were
Rachmaninoff and Sir Henry Wood). For a time, in 1919, Toscanini was
said to have accepted a Boston offer. The same year, he was reported to have
agreed to succeed the late Cleofonte Campanini at the Chicago Opera.
Meanwhile, the Metropolitan continued sending emissaries to woo him
back to New York.

As it happened, Toscanini was not in the mood to conduct anywhere
in 1919. With Italy a shambles, the Armistice found him taciturn. In later
life, his vocation in music proved visibly rejuvenating. Now, his sudden
paucity of musical activity since 1915 had caused his motor to run down.
The issue was not resolved until July 1920—twenty months after the war
ended. Submitting to pleas for Italian cultural renewal, Toscanini agreed
to return to La Scala as "plenipotentiary director." At least initially,
America would also be accommodated. The new, hand-picked Scala orchestra would tour the United States, beginning in December 1920. On
the committee of guarantors for the tour was Otto Kahn, still chairman of
the Metropolitan Opera's executive committee, still pressing for Toscanini's services.

Along the Toscanini watch, the Milan orchestra's impending visit dominated the Atlantic horizon. Ugo Ara, who had negotiated with Toscanini
on behalf of Kahn and the other guarantors, told New York reporters that
Toscanini had become "the idol of the Italian people," "worshipped" as
"their national hero." Souvenir programs for the tour promoted Toscanini's war-enhanced prestige. "The return to America of Arturo Toscanini, after five years of absence, during which the longing for his
powerful and fascinating art has never ceased, constitutes in itself a musical
event of supreme importance," the programs stated, adding that the Toscanini orchestra was "the greatest ever formed in Italy," and that its American visit was the outcome of "six months of secret negotiations and two
special trips." Illustrations for the programs included a photograph of
Toscanini and his military band posing at Monte Santo after having performed under a "storm of shot and shell," and a sketch of Toscanini by

Caruso captioned "the time of kings has not passed, despite all revolutions." A third illustration, showing Toscanini's residence, carried this description:

> In spite of its humble appearance, the balcony has been declared a national monument. From here, almost four centuries ago, Saint Charles Borromeo preached to the people of Milan one of those memorable sermons which seemed to have the power of transforming the human soul into a thing of gladness. Today, another missionary lives here, one whose sermons in music have such a compelling influence upon his countrymen as to have gained for him the title "Animator of Souls."

The Toscanini orchestra's American tour was part of an eight-month training mission beginning and ending in Italy. Theodore Thomas's grueling whistle-stop tours had been leisurely by comparison. In sixteen weeks the orchestra gave sixty-eight concerts in dozens of North American cities, including some as small as Columbus, Davenport, Hutchinson, Topeka, and Tulsa. Two concerts at New York's Hippodrome alone attracted sixteen thousand customers. Of the tumult engulfing the orchestra's first New York appearance, on December 28, 1920, at the Metropolitan Opera House, *Musical America* reported:

> The audience that filled the house to bursting . . . was a sight to behold. It contained all the vast disparate elements of the city's musical population. In its heterogeneous ranks were represented the class of Italians whose musical horizon is bounded by Italian opera and Italian singers, American opera-goers of more liberal artistic disposition, the concert-going public in its several phases and musicians proper . . . big and little, from near and far—in short, the musical Who's Who this side of Chicago. They sat—or stood—tense, expectant, as in anticipation of some heaven-wrought miracle. They hung breathless on the music, as in a kind of a sacred terror. . . . The applause that greeted Mr. Toscanini when he first came upon the stage was heated and prolonged and many rose deferentially. It was not a circumstance however, to the torrential outbreaks that followed the performance of the various numbers on the program, particularly the first half. Here pandemonium was unloosed and the house rioted, stamped, cheered and screamed frantically in mad, orgiastic jubilation.[7]

Everywhere, in fact, Toscanini's American tour was tumultuously received. In some cities the musicians were showered with gifts, including silver forks, hand-stitched pillows, and a live goose. In Camden, New Jersey, the orchestra made a series of Victor Talking Machine recordings

—Toscanini's first—whose advertised future availability, "in keeping with the Victor Policy of presenting the recordings of the greatest artists," meant even more recognition and publicity.

Poetic justice demanded critical validation of the Toscanini groundswell. But in New York the critics failed to reach a verdict. About the orchestra itself there was substantial agreement: it was excellent, if less good than the best American groups. Its discipline and responsiveness were universally praised. Toscanini, it was found, extracted performances that were polished, precise, and finely nuanced. Attacks and cutoffs in the Toscanini orchestra were remarkably crisp. Textures were crystalline and singingly sustained. What the critics disagreed about was what they had always disagreed about: Toscanini's feeling for German music. Richard Aldrich's middle-of-the-road response to Toscanini's Brahms and Richard Strauss summarized the opposing points of view.

> It was a curiously and at times strangely alluring Italianate performance of [Brahms's Second Symphony]. . . .
>
> Besides a somewhat deliberate opening tempo, there were to be noted all through the symphony that translucent clarity in the exposition of all the voices, that perfect finish of the ensemble and in the turning and the molding of each phrase, that flexibility of tempo that were to be noted in the previous concerts [of the Toscanini orchestra]. Whatever the reading of the symphony may have been, it was quite evident that it was an exact reproduction of Mr. Toscanini's idea of it; that it was played just as he wanted it. Certain portions seemed unsubstantial, lacking in weight, as in the adagio. The feeling of the whole was essentially lyric, and of course, in a way, that is the true character of the symphony. There were certain phrases that you will perhaps never hear played with such a golden concentration of musical beauty. There were others that needed a more rugged statement. On the whole, for all its beauties, the reading of the symphony seemed rather small, short-breathed and over-detailed. But it called forth bravos from Mr. Toscanini's trusty supporters, and applause from the more soberly musical. . . .
>
> Mr. Toscanini repeated what Mr. Mengelberg had played in the afternoon, Strauss's tone poem, *Don Juan.* There were here, again, great finish and clarity in the orchestral playing, rhythmic tension, concentrated and burning passion; and something lacking in the mere weight and power of the thing. It had beauty and power, however, which were recognized.[8]

Aldrich's reservations repeated those Krehbiel, Huneker, and Henderson had expressed about Toscanini's prewar performances of *Meistersinger,*

Götterdämmerung, Tristan, and Beethoven's Ninth. But the postwar Toscanini groundswell added a new element to the reviews of other, less temperate reservationists: an explicit disavowal of popular opinion. This estrangement had been growing. When Toscanini led the Ninth at the Metropolitan in 1913, the performance was marred, in Henderson's phrase, "by untimely thunderclaps of applause" from "enthusiasts who knew not Beethoven." To some writers, the Toscanini enthusiasts thereafter seemed ever more a breed apart. When the enthusiasts held their breaths while Toscanini changed his mind about leaving the Metropolitan, or trumpeted news of his bravery under fire on the Italian front, *Musical Courier* and *Musical America* grew fatigued. When the Toscanini orchestra excited new heights of Toscanini enthusiasm, the fatigue of some holdouts turned into something like disgust. *Musical America* assessed the Toscanini orchestra's first New York concert as follows:

> The extensively prevalent tendency to consider Mr. Toscanini in the light of a semi-divine being and as immune from the frailties and failings of conductors more earthly in mold does that admired artist no service or benefit. Properly acclaimed for his tremendously energetic, vital and impassioned treatment of operatic works, he has yet to prove himself as a symphonic conductor. His [1913 New York performance of Beethoven's] Ninth Symphony, for all the heated commentaries it generated, failed to decide that point past question.
>
> Last night . . . once more his exposition of Beethoven was fraught with disappointment for those not irrevocably committed to his adoration. He read the [Fifth] symphony not with straightforwardness and forthright power . . . but with incredible preciosities, hyper-refinements and a scheme of nuance so studied in its exaggeration as to rob the work of all spontaneity, all true dramatic suggestiveness and heat, all honesty and rugged, combative spirit. . . . He evinced in the first movement a fondness for novel effects of tempo, for languorous elongations and sentimentalities. . . . The opening of the finale was aggressively blatant.

Another critic stemming the Toscanini tide with a finger in the dike was Sylvester Rawling of the New York *World,* whose review of the same concert misquoted Sir W. S. Gilbert as follows:

> "Bow, bow, bow, before the Lord High Executioner!," the familiar lines from *The Mikado,* haunted me at the first of a series of concerts in an invasion of America by Arturo Toscanini and his Italian La Scala Orchestra, which took place at the Metropolitan Opera House last night. Mr. Toscanini for some seasons was the leading conductor of the Metro-

politan Opera Company. He established himself as a master among maestros. He was an autocrat. The other conductors had little opportunity for rehearsals. Everything was à la Toscanini. He achieved big things. Then he went away.

The war intervened. Mr. Toscanini suffered and served in Italy with all self-abnegation and sacrifice. Now that peace is restored he comes back. The lure of America is great. Stories have been told of tempting offers that he has refused to take charge of American symphony orchestras. They are of no consequence now. Here he is in America at the head of an orchestra of his own selection, challenging recognition as a symphonic rather than an operatic conductor. How does he stand the test? Only negatively well. Mr. Toscanini's gift of controlling an orchestra, of making it reflect his wishes, his desires, his inspiration, remains supreme. In this he has no rival; but he is essentially dramatic in interpretation; his vogue is of the stage. He removed Beethoven's immortal Fifth Symphony—by his pianissimos that couldn't be heard, by his variety of dynamic expression—from the realm of absolute music to the domain of the theater. What Italian composer wrote that Latinized Fifth Symphony, I kept asking myself. Save in the climax of the last movement, a really great achievement on Mr. Toscanini's part, I found no trace of the sturdy Teutonism of Beethoven. . . .[9]

Meanwhile, critics in the Toscanini camp kept pace with the Toscanini tidal wave—this was the very gist of the *Musical Courier*'s assessment of the same concert that *Musical America* and the New York *World* complained about: "It is no exaggeration to say that [Toscanini] fulfilled in every particular the wonderful things his auditors expected of him." When Toscanini and the orchestra boarded a liner to return to Italy, more than two thousand people crammed the pier. Aboard a big tugboat steaming alongside, a band played the Italian national anthem while "Italian-American girls cavorted in native costume." Toscanini responded by calling his hundred men on deck and conducting "The Star-Spangled Banner."[10]

By the time the Toscanini orchestra completed the second leg of its itinerary in June 1921, it had logged 133 concerts in just under eight months —in the opinion of the Toscanini biographer Harvey Sachs, "the longest and roughest tour ever undertaken by a major orchestra." Then came the main event: the reopening of La Scala. This time Giulio Gatti-Casazza, who had stayed on at the Metropolitan, was not to be the lightning rod for Toscanini's thunderbolts. Angelo Scandiani, the new general director, served at Toscanini's pleasure. It was Toscanini who oversaw the theater's modernization, who was final arbiter of costumes and props, and who ruled the stage, shouting and singing, during rehearsals. According to Filippo Sacchi, who knew Toscanini: "Even Toscanini was possibly never quite so single-mindedly creative in his work as he was at this time in the Scala. Music was always an absolute religion with him: but never did he seem more utterly, almost mystically dedicated. For the very first time in his life, at fifty-four years old, he was the master of a great theater . . . without any possibility of interference."[11]

At the heart of the undertaking were Toscanini's piano rehearsals with individual singers. He had always been a tireless coach, but had never produced singers so molded to his ideals of musical-dramatic veracity. Toti dal Monte, one of his favorite sopranos, has recalled how he taught her to treat the nonlegato articulation in "Caro nome" as the panting breaths of a woman in love—and also his fury upon hearing that she had sung Gilda for another conductor with various traditional high notes and cadenzas back in place. Aureliano Pertile, Toscanini's favorite tenor, was a model of intelligence and malleability; "If one is capable of doing well and of overcoming the awe one feels before such a person," Pertile said of Toscanini, "one obtains everything—stimulus, sureness, self-confidence, in addition to an artistic formation." Toscanini taught the thirty-three-year-old Mariano Stabile to sing Falstaff word by word, note by note. "At precisely ten o'clock we began to go over the monologue from the third act, 'Mondo ladro, mondo rubaldo,'" Stabile later recalled. "And until one or one-thirty I repeated those words, because he wanted me to bring forth a sort of regurgitation, that *oahhh* of the fat man, the drunkard, the glutton."[12]

It was *Falstaff*, with Stabile, with which Toscanini reopened La Scala on December 26, 1921. Twenty-three years before, he had begun his first Scala term with *Die Meistersinger*. Now, with a Wagnerian housewarming out of the question, Verdi would be paramount, and the new regime concentrated on the Verdi canon. Outside the Italian repertoire, Toscanini led his first productions of *The Magic Flute, Fidelio,* and *Parsifal. Tristan* was given in a drastically simplified staging by Adolphe Appia, the prophetic Swiss scenic artist. A major novelty of these years was Boito's monumental *Nerone,* his life's work, left unfinished when he died in 1918. Toscanini and Vincenzo Tommasini completed the orchestration. The elaborately mounted 1924 premiere (one crowd scene included a chariot drawn by four white horses) was a triumph, but the opera's success was short-lived.

Other important Scala premieres of the twenties were of Pizzetti's *Dèbora e Jaéle,* Puccini's *Turandot,* and Stravinsky's *Le Rossignol.* Compared to his previous policies in Turin, Milan, and New York, however, Toscanini now showed more limited interest in new work. Elsewhere in

Europe, the decade's important first performances included Berg's *Woz-zeck*, Hindemith's *Cardillac* and *Neues vom Tage*, Janáček's *The Cunning Little Vixen* and *The Makropoulos Affair*, Krenek's *Jonny spielt auf*, Schoenberg's *Die glückliche Hand*, Strauss's *Intermezzo*, and Stravinsky's *Mavra* and *Oedipus Rex*. In 1925, Toscanini, an early champion of Debussy, Mussorgsky, Richard Strauss, and Wagner, attended a festival given by the International Society for Contemporary Music in Venice, and exclaimed at the close: "Now they should disinfect the theater."[13]

Not only did Toscanini's age and past service beg forgiveness for such relative intolerance; at no other time was his artistic mission so enlarged by social responsibilities. Italy was beset by transportation breakdowns, inadequate food distribution, chronic poverty and inflation. The political situation, aggravated by frustrated war claims in Istria and Dalmatia, was as chaotic. Striking and rioting peaked in 1920, when many factories were occupied by workers. From its battered and disused cultural institutions Italy did not seek imports or iconoclasm; the pressing need was for stability and self-esteem. Verdi was a natural remedy. The conductor Gianandrea Gavazzeni later attested: "The public with Toscanini, during that era, was educated to consider the theater not as something for amusement, but as something with a moral and aesthetic function, which enters into the life of a society, in the life of a culture."[14]

But its very centrality, and the political leitmotiv of the times, meant that La Scala's new era could not endure—and that Toscanini's political identity would crystallize in fuller and more provocative form. He had already inserted himself into a postwar diplomatic imbroglio: when the city of Fiume, among the most disputed properties on the eastern Adriatic coast, was seized by troops under Gabriele D'Annunzio in September 1919, Toscanini elected to perform there with his orchestra and lend support to the adventure. The reorganization of La Scala was itself a political act. In close consultation with Emilio Caldara, the Socialist mayor of Milan, Toscanini devised a democratized financing scheme under which the boxes, formerly the property of hereditary holders, were liberated for occupation by the public at large.

The chief catalyst for Toscanini's emergence on the world political stage, however, was Benito Mussolini. So aroused was Toscanini's patriotism in 1919 that he agreed to place his name on Mussolini's slate of candidates for parliament. Toscanini was not the only distinguished Italian who found himself impressed by Mussolini's forcefulness two years before the Fascist movement became the Fascist party. And there were aspects of early Fascist policy he could not help agreeing with. Unlike some of the Socialists whose ranks he had abandoned in 1914, Mussolini strenuously supported the war, the army, and the flag. At the same time, he advocated an Italian republic in which titles of nobility would be abolished and ecclesiastic properties confiscated. Though all the Fascist candidates lost in 1919, Mussolini was appointed prime minister by King Victor Emmanuel III three years later. He had come to stand for brute authority and did not disavow the royal imprimatur. Toscanini was now heard to declare: "If I were capable of killing a man, I would kill Mussolini." When, at La Scala, noisy Fascists demanded that the party hymn, "Giovinezza," be played, Toscanini smashed his baton and left the pit. Only after one of the company's directors announced that the hymn would be heard at the evening's close could the opera continue. Toscanini returned, finished the performance, and told his singers and orchestra to go home. The hymn was played on the piano.

This was the first in a series of confrontations in the course of which Toscanini, more than at Monte Santo, rendered heroic extramusical service. He detested the slogan-shouting crowds, the megalomaniacal speeches, the censorship and secret police. His political instincts were as unshakable as any ideology. Mussolini, based in Rome, was made to feel unholy at La Scala. He must have pondered shutting it down or purging its administration. But under Toscanini La Scala was prestigious for Italy. And Toscanini's moral authority was intimidating.

For several years, a peculiar truce prevailed. Mussolini was photographed with Toscanini and his principal singers. At La Scala's invitation, he conducted a tour of inspection, during which he took Toscanini's arm. Plans were laid to bring the company to Rome and to make Toscanini a senator. But Toscanini never became a senator, and he fell ill when the promised visit to Rome came due. In 1925 all theaters were instructed to display pictures of Mussolini and of the king. No such pictures were displayed at La Scala.

Animosities underlying this strained courtship flared into the open in December 1923, when Toscanini's friend Giuseppe Gallignani, director of the Milan Conservatory since 1897, was dismissed by the Fascists. Overwhelmed, Gallignani threw himself out a window. The same day, Toscanini sent a telegram to the Ministry of Public Education in Rome: "Maestro Gallignani, who did what no Minister or Director-General knew how to do for our Conservatory, has committed suicide. Gentlemen of the Ministry of Public Education, Ministers and Directors-General: I tell you that this suicide will weigh upon your consciences forever." This was one reason Toscanini was summoned to see Mussolini when Mussolini visited Milan two years later. Toscanini's friends, thinking it safer that he comply, bundled him into a car and practically carried him to the prefecture. There

Toscanini, who was kept standing, stared at a spot on the wall above Mussolini's head while being harangued for intransigence and warned of reprisals against La Scala. Later that day—December 28, 1925—he left Italy for New York, where he had been engaged to conduct fifteen concerts with the New York Philharmonic.

No implication of this unprecedented development, requiring a seven-week leave of absence, escaped Toscanini's enemies in Rome or his friends in Milan and America. Even in the best of times, his resilience in operatic affairs was limited. No less than at La Scala from 1898 to 1908, or at the Metropolitan, the ordeal of instilling dedication amid the hurlyburly of rotating casts and operas had led to frustration and anger. With Mussolini threatening to encroach on La Scala's extraterritoriality, Toscanini's resilience was tested the more. Meanwhile, the trans-Atlantic Toscanini hunt continued. However indifferent he might have seemed, Toscanini appreciated the bait. An American orchestral post was a plausible haven for an embattled fifty-eight-year-old operatic conductor; the musicians were excellent and well behaved, the audiences were more than loyal, and the resident philanthropists seemed limitlessly wealthy.

Mussolini's suspension of democratic guarantees on January 3, 1925—a turning point in Fascism—may have been decisive. Three months later, Max Smith, conferring with Toscanini in Milan, was able to wire the Philharmonic that the quarry had been bagged.[15]

The New York Philharmonic, 1926–29

*T*he appointment of Josef Stransky to succeed Gustav Mahler in 1911 gave the New York Philharmonic its most obscure conductor since the pioneer days of Theodor Eisfeld and Carl Bergmann. Whatever the artistic merit of Stransky's regime, he presided over a period of continued expansion. Anton Seidl, during what many remembered as the Philharmonic's glory years (1891–98), had led a mere dozen concerts a season. The combined schedules of Mahler's two seasons (1909–11), reflecting the ambitions of Mrs. George Sheldon's upstart guarantors, totaled 101 concerts. A year later, Stransky led 84 concerts in a single season. In 1920–21, a coast-to-coast tour swelled the traveling schedule alone to 94 concerts. At the same time, the orchestra was able to announce that its concerts enjoyed "the largest subscription since their inauguration."[1]

Under Stransky, Philharmonic audiences grew not only bigger, but broader. To the habitués—a group variously music minded, civic spirited, and status conscious—were added many novices. Stransky's repertoire, sweetened with desserts, reflected as much. It was Stransky, too, who led the Philharmonic in its first recordings—in preradio times, a substantial stride for audience building. In 1911, Joseph Pulitzer's will established a permanent New York Philharmonic endowment fund contingent on a more democratic support base, reinforcing current trends. The Philharmonic was made a membership corporation, "with a membership of not less than one thousand paying dues." The first Young People's Concerts were given. Special performances were held at Madison Square Garden and at army camps. Members of the Philharmonic Society were offered lectures and Evenings of Light Music.

With the Philharmonic finally operating on a scale commensurate with the Boston Symphony, it was bound to acquire a more eminent music director. Between 1921 and 1923, Stransky was eased out, and Willem Mengelberg was eased in. Two additional newcomers made the Philharmonic management more potent than before. In 1921, the telegraph magnate Clarence Mackay was named chairman of the board. Husband of the singer Anna Case, father-in-law of Irving Berlin, and a longtime director of the Metropolitan Opera Association, Mackay was so influential in New York musical circles that when Oscar Hammerstein antagonized Mackay's wife in 1909, New York society withdrew patronage from Hammerstein's Manhattan Opera, hastening its end. A year after Mackay's appointment, Arthur Judson became manager of the New York Philharmonic and executive secretary of its board. Already manager of Stokowski's Philadelphia Orchestra and of booking offices in Philadelphia and New York, Judson was a power broker. He tellingly called himself a "salesman of fine music."

Mengelberg, a diligent rehearser, did his part to upgrade performance standards. According to Winthrop Sargeant, a Philharmonic violinist under Mengelberg and Toscanini before becoming a well-known music critic, Mengelberg transformed the Philharmonic into "if not the most inspired, at least the most spectacularly well-trained orchestra in America."[2] The celebrated Mengelberg–New York Philharmonic recording of *Ein Heldenleben* (1928) is both inspired and spectacularly well played. But Mengelberg's main commitment lay elsewhere. Whereas Koussevitzky lived in Boston, Stokowski in Philadelphia, and Stock in Chicago, Mengelberg made his home in Amsterdam, where he had led the Concertgebouw Orchestra since 1895. He conducted only half the Philharmonic's concerts. New York's primary concert orchestra continued to lack an artistic profile as distinctive as Boston's, Philadelphia's, or Chicago's.

This, as of January 1925, formed the backdrop for the most important New York podium debut since Mahler and Toscanini arrived at the Metropolitan Opera. The debutant was Wilhelm Furtwängler, Nikisch's successor as principal conductor of the Berlin Philharmonic since 1922. Furtwängler's ten New York concerts were a distinct success. The last one, a nonsubscription event on January 30, attracted an audience crammed with musicians. Furtwängler was given a fifteen-minute standing ovation. The orchestra, which joined in the applause, presented him with a silver loving cup. Furtwängler was impressed by the orchestra and by the hospitality, wealth, and vitality of New York City. His secretary, Berta Geissmar, later wrote:

> Many of the great international artists were in the United States at that time, and we saw them frequently. At the house of Frederick Steinway, the venerated chief of the famous music firm, such a galaxy of musical genius and brilliance used to assemble as I have never seen elsewhere. I remember a dinner where Casals, Furtwängler, Gabrilowitsch, Landowska, Kreisler, Rachmaninoff, Stokowski and other famous people were

present. Mr. Steinway's hock was memorable too! Our stay in New York was exciting and strenuous but rushed past us like a dream.

When Furtwängler returned in 1925–26 and 1926–27, the ovations diminished. Throughout his three-season association with the Philharmonic, however, rumors circulated that he would shortly replace Mengelberg as principal conductor: according to Geissmar, he was offered the directorship for 1925–26 but turned it down because of European commitments.[3]

In the musical press, as in Carnegie Hall, the years since Mahler's Philharmonic ordeal had marked a passing of the old guard—of the chief chroniclers of what proved to be Furtwängler's only three visits to the United States, the *Sun*'s W. J. Henderson alone remained from prewar days. Huneker had died in 1921, Krehbiel in 1923; Finck had retired in 1924. At the *Times*, which had emerged as New York's prestige newspaper, Olin Downes had succeeded Richard Aldrich in 1924. At the *Herald Tribune*, product of a 1924 merger and second in distinction to the *Times*, Lawrence Gilman had been music critic since 1923. Winthrop Sargeant, who knew all three men as colleagues, once offered these thumbnail portraits:

> The greatest man of the New York music criticism . . . was W. J. Henderson. . . . Henderson's great prestige arose partly from his honest informality and clear thinking. But it was also due to his great age. He had belonged to the generation of James Gibbons Huneker and Henry Edward Krehbiel, a generation of legendary dignity in the eyes of most younger critics. . . .
>
> Lawrence Gilman of the *Herald Tribune* was a . . . suave, sensitive and rather morose gentleman of extremely aesthetic appearance who wore a fur-collared overcoat, worked for hours over each carefully turned paragraph, and produced a type of elegantly tortured prose that many New York concertgoers regarded as literature. Gilman shut out the coarse sounds of the nonmusical world by wearing plugs of cotton in his ears, except when he was on the job. At concerts, he would remove his overcoat, sit, remove his earplugs, and listen with polite concentration. When he left the concert hall the earplugs would be back securely in place. The other great man was Olin Downes. . . . A man of great enthusiasms, Downes lacked entirely the appearance of judicial calm that characterized his confreres. He was rather heavily built and a hearty good-natured extrovert. He would flail his arms and air his opinions with unconcealed excitement. He was a champion of causes—whether they were the music of Sibelius or the betterment of the economic lot of his colleagues. His reactions were always passionate. What he liked, he liked very much, and what he disliked he hated.[4]

Of Furtwängler's first Philharmonic concert, on January 3, Henderson wrote: "a success of unquestionable character. . . . The lofty grandeur of [Brahms's First Symphony] stood forth in all its majesty." Downes called the Brahms performance "perhaps the most thrilling in the writer's experience." Gilman found that Furtwängler possessed "the stride, the gesture, the address of a major prophet." Henderson, never an effulgent critic, continued to admire Furtwängler through the next two seasons. Gilman, over the same period, amplified certain complaints—that Furtwängler succumbed to "ritarditis"; that by intensifying details he sacrificed continuity—which he had suggested in his first review, yet he retained enthusiasm for the "fervid absorption" and "kindling mastery" of Furtwängler at his best. Downes's Furtwängler reviews, however, grew so peevish they became a point of contention in the pages of the *Times* itself.

In retrospect, even Downes's favorable appraisal of Furtwängler's American debut foreshadowed disaffection. He wrote: "Mr. Furtwängler did not indulge in 'readings' or 'interpretations' of the works that he placed before the audience. He was content to perform the music. . . . The audience found last night that nothing was more stirring than simply Brahms' C minor Symphony." Yet Furtwängler was a meddlesome Brahms interpreter. As he performed the First Symphony, the introduction to the first movement was made slower, more massive, more portentous than Brahms's "un poco maestoso." This was the gist of Gilman's description of the passage in question:

> The opening pages of the symphony . . . were unforgettably read. . . . The momentous, fateful . . . beat of those inexorable eighth notes in the bass, with the superb ascent in the strings up to the high B flat, acquired a spaciousness and an authentic grandeur that were new in our fairly long experience of this symphony. The passage had the essential note of somberly heroic beauty, of melancholy splendor; and it was all extraordinarily enhanced and amplified. Possibly it was too slow, according to the strict canon, but we are rather disposed to believe that the canon is wrong.

As he got to know Furtwängler better, Downes's partiality to textual fidelity could only dictate disillusion. Reviewing Furtwängler's second Philharmonic concert, he complained: "There were occasions when the conductor was paramount, when he was disposed to individual tempi, dynamics and phrasings, with results not invariably indicated in the compositions." In the same review, Downes offered this provisional overview: "It seems probable . . . that [Furtwängler] is fundamentally a classic rather than a modern in his feeling, and this we say in spite of the divagations from the law above mentioned. The modern intensities of Wagner's *Tristan* seemed in part to escape him." But "modern" music—by which Downes meant late Romantic—was Furtwängler's forte. Gilman, in his first Furtwängler review, was on the mark when he surmised:

> He has that largeness of style, that sweep of vision, that intensifying and vitalizing power which are necessary to the community of music that is conceived in the passionate and heroic vein, the great Romantics. . . . He seems . . . like the kind of conductor for whom the music of Brahms, of Strauss, of the more urgent Beethoven, of Wagner in certain of his phases, cries aloud. For he has warmth and fire . . . a broad and encompassing vision, an enlarging imagination.[5]

Downes's disappointment may have accounted for his decision to skip Furtwängler's final appearance of the season—the January 30 concert at which the musicians bestowed their present, and which other critics hailed as momentous. After that, in 1925–26 and 1926–27, his Furtwängler criticism grew increasingly harsh. Of a 1926 concert he wrote: "Last night [Furtwängler] exulted in noise, a tendency to which he has become prone this season." On another occasion, Downes found Furtwängler's renditions "of an unusually rough and obstreperous nature. There were exaggerations of pace, sonority and phrasing. There was unnecessary and too frequently unsuccessful striving after effect."[6]

In certain respects, Downes's disdain suggested an exaggerated echo of Henry Krehbiel's anti-Mahler fulminations. Krehbiel could be prickly about Old World condescension toward New World culture. Downes was more partisan by nature. With regard to New World partisanship, his instincts were doubtless sharpened by World War I. His first book, *The Lure of Music,* was a 1918 layman's guide omitting all German and Austrian composers (resulting in a chronological survey of great music beginning with Rossini). Reviewing Furtwängler, he had occasion to complain about programs "made in Germany." He once took "certain European critics" to task for rejecting Koussevitzky's moderate tempo for the finale of Beethoven's Fifth when in fact it proved the same as Furtwängler's: "Would these critics have altered their opinion if Mr. Koussevitzky had been a German?" He characterized Furtwängler's performance of Weber's *Freischütz* Overture as sentimental and tending to drag—and hence "in a vein that many of Mr. Furtwängler's countrymen, in particular, might endorse." Krehbiel had objected to Mahler's score tampering; Downes found Furtwängler's readings willful with regard to tempo, dynamics, phrasing, and rubato. He found Furtwängler's

rendition of Schumann's Fourth engrossing "in spite of" its straying "far
from the directions of the score."[7]

Downes's implicit belief in a single, definitive reading arising from adherence to the composer's text was more extreme than fidelity in in-
strumentation as espoused by Krehbiel. Rather, it evoked Max Smith's
criterion of "objectivity." For that matter, Downes's threefold aversion to
imprecision, subjectivity, and Germanic "sentimentality" placed him
squarely in the Toscanini camp of which Max Smith had been the leading
prewar publicist. This, as much as anything, accounted for Furtwängler's
post-1925 deterioration as documented by Downes: as of January 1926—one
year after Furtwängler's New York debut—Toscanini had joined the ranks
of the Philharmonic's guest conductors; he and Furtwängler were rival
contenders for Willem Mengelberg's job.

With the appointment of Clarence Mackay in 1921, the Philharmonic's
board of directors was vitalized by a millionaire chairman as single-mindedly determined to import Toscanini as Otto Kahn had been—and, in fact,
remained—at the Metropolitan Opera. It was Mackay to whom Max Smith
reported from Milan in 1925. He had been courting Toscanini there, on
Mackay's behalf, since 1923. Pursuing what had become his "main ambition"
in life, Smith first failed to win over Toscanini, then succeeded, then failed
again when Toscanini changed his mind, then finally succeeded by caution-
ing Toscanini that "it would make a very bad impression on America if he
postponed his engagement with the Philharmonic Society for another
year, the more so as a great many people, their minds poisoned against
him, had been prophesying that he would not live up to his promises."[8]
The final agreement called for fifteen concerts between January 14 and
February 7, 1926, for which Toscanini would receive $24,000; the orchestra
would also pay his travel expenses and—a novel provision—his American
income tax. He would be given six preparatory rehearsals at the outset of
his engagement.

If, as Smith reported to Mackay, Toscanini seemed "much interested in
his coming work with the Philharmonic," his American partisans were
giddy with excitement. Four days before Toscanini's New York Philharmonic debut, Olin Downes produced a panegyric, "The Return of Arturo
Toscanini," declaring in part:

> In listening to operatic and orchestral interpretations of Toscanini it has
> often seemed that after all the statement holds true of the quality of the
> Italian mind, the racial mind that has the finest facture of any in the
> world; the genius which, at its height, combines marvelously the qualities

of analysis and perception, the objectivity of form, and the consuming fire of creative passion. . . .

If ever there was a man who justified the theory of aristocracy built upon the fundamental conception that men are not born free and equal, that some are immeasurably superior to others, and that their superiority is justification for their control of others' acts and destinies, that man is Arturo Toscanini. . . . It is with something more than the curiosity that awaits the appearance of a famous guest conductor that the Philharmonic audiences will gather to meet Mr. Toscanini.[9]

And something more than curiosity was satisfied by Toscanini's first Philharmonic concerts, for which Carnegie Hall's boxes were decked with American and Italian flags, and its rear areas choked with standees. According to Henderson, a professional New York concert-goer since 1887, Toscanini at Carnegie Hall "evoked an enthusiasm . . . eclipsing any such acclaim probably ever before experienced within the walls of the honorable and timeworn edifice." Equally unprecedented was the Toscanini adulation unleashed in the press. Having issued a stentorian preliminary endorsement, Downes now spoke in a hush:

Arturo Toscanini made his first appearance at the head of the Philharmonic Society of New York last night in Carnegie Hall. The . . . audience was one of the most distinguished of the season. This audience listened, tense with excitement, to all and each of the performances, and its applause was tumultuous on every possible occasion.

Mr. Toscanini was conducting a famous American symphony orchestra for the first time. . . . With it he worked his sovereign will and those who were present will not forget the occasion.

Lawrence Gilman's review of the same concert began:

At 8:37 last night a slender, gray-haired man with extraordinary deep-set eyes walked briskly and rather nervously across the stage of Carnegie Hall, as if he were trying to reach the conductor's stand without being seen. He did not quite make it, for as he stepped on to the podium he was greeted by an outburst of clapping and cheering from an audience that rose as one music lover to its feet, just as if the slight and embarrassed figure who stood bowing in evident discomfort had been a premier or a pianist, instead of merely the greatest conductor in the world.

. . . For this was the great event of the musical year: the return to New York of the incomparable Toscanini.[10]

Three weeks later, in an essay entitled "What Toscanini Achieved," Gilman pondered an "ideal" performance of Schubert's "Unfinished" Symphony given on January 24 by Toscanini and the Philharmonic:

Three centuries ago it occurred to some amazing master of words to say of a horse that God had "clothed his neck with thunder." For us, the horse was invented when the phrase was born.

One day, much later, a Toscanini brooded upon a score of Schubert's . . . and a new work came into being. Some will remind us that there was an "Unfinished" Symphony before Toscanini's day, just as others will say that there were horses before the Council of Forty-seven gave us the King James Version. There are times when we are inclined to doubt it.

Music has a way of disclosing itself in these unprecedented revelations. Some veil is drawn, and a moment of sudden light floods and transfigures the divine face.[11]

Not every critic helped lead the cheers. Much as Downes and Gilman took up where Max Smith had left off in the prewar New York press, it fell to the seventy-year-old Henderson to resume and amplify the strains of Toscanini fatigue. We have already observed Henderson regretting the "untimely thunderclaps of applause" emitted by "enthusiasts who knew not Beethoven" when Toscanini led the Ninth in 1913, and two years later yawning over "the annual expression of doubt as to the return of Arturo Toscanini to the conductor's desk at the Metropolitan Opera House." Now, reviewing Toscanini's Philharmonic debut, Henderson wrote:

The concert of the Philharmonic Society last night in Carnegie Hall was one of those musical events which might well be turned over to the star descriptive reporter. It was not a concert at all; it was the return of the hero, a Roman triumph staged in New York and in modern dress. The hero was Arturo Toscanini, one time conductor at the Metropolitan and now lord high admiral of La Scala in Milan. That the directors of the Philharmonic had made no mistake in engaging him was proved by the selling out of the house far ahead.

For these are days when the plain workaday utterance of music will not suffice for a populace incessantly demanding new ways of saying old truths and ready to sink into apathy unless mental stimulants are liberally administered. In such conditions the true merits of such a temperamental conductor as this famous Italian are likely to be obscured behind a red screen of what those who hear with their eyes believe to be inspiration of the moment and sorcery of the baton.

As his review made clear, Henderson continued to hold Toscanini in high regard—he called him, in passing, "one of the world's great conductors." But what Henderson principally perceived, overshadowing music by Haydn, Respighi, Sibelius, Wagner, and Weber, were rites of worship no previous conductor had enjoyed. Gilman had already pronounced Toscanini "the priest of beauty, the consecrated celebrant, abstracted, absorbed, awaiting gravely the trembling of the Temple's veil." Buoyed by new acolytes in high places, the still rising tide of Toscanini enthusiasm had produced a personality cult of messianic intensity.[12]

Like Toscanini and Mahler, New York rivals fifteen years before, Toscanini and Furtwängler were a study in contrasts. The Italian was short, compact, decisive. The German was tall, gangly, visionary. Toscanini's parents were poor. Furtwängler's father was an eminent archeologist, his mother a painter; as a child, he was educated by tutors, and taken to tour ruins and museums in Italy and Greece. While not worldly, Toscanini was of this world; as Max Smith had put it, Toscanini "was said to know exactly where he is going . . . he proceeds in that direction as eagerly as a hound on a trail." Furtwängler wandered in a fog. The cellist Enrico Mainardi once accompanied Furtwängler through Rome while he led an invisible orchestra: "Around us amazed respectful pedestrians looked at this unusual figure who walked along singing and making gestures. . . . The only one who did not notice anything, of course, was Furtwängler himself. . . ." When Toscanini made up his mind, there was no changing it. Furtwängler vacillated; Friedelind Wagner, who was not his enemy, once wrote: "He never managed to make a decision in his life and go through with it." Toscanini was glamorous, fastidious. Furtwängler was awkward; even his table manners were poor. In New York, at postconcert receptions, he unwittingly offended influential members of the Philharmonic Society. According to Berta Geissmar, "Sometimes it seemed that he was only completely at ease with his enormous dog." Toscanini was combative when crossed. Furtwängler was self-doubting. Olin Downes's reviews wounded him so much that he reportedly had a friend ask the *Times* to send another critic to his concerts—a possible reason Downes, when he saw Furtwängler's portrait on a friend's piano in 1931, exclaimed: "Take that swine's picture away from there!"[13]

These differences were, if anything, accentuated on the podium. Toscanini manipulated his baton with fluent strokes. Furtwängler quivered, even spat and stamped. Watching Toscanini in action, Stefan Zweig marveled at his "mysteriously mournful" countenance: "He never attains what Nietzsche calls the 'brown happiness' of relaxation, of self-content."[14] Con-

ducting the great slow movements of Beethoven and Bruckner, Furtwängler, his blue eyes veiled and half-shut, his lips slightly parted, radiated uplift.
Toscanini demanded maximum polish and efficiency. Furtwängler's beat
was famously vague; rather than wielding a razor on command, his orchestra attacked with an energy welling up from within. Toscanini favored a
firm pulse and forthright musical shapes. Furtwängler blurred the edges,
admitting a void.

Addressing questions of musical interpretation, Toscanini and Furtwängler clinched their disaffinities. "Tradition," even "interpretation," were for
Toscanini odious terms; when challenged on a musical point, he would
pound the score because it, not he, was the arbiter. Furtwängler wrote:
"They talk about 'strict adherence to the score.' . . . The *spiritual* problems
with which the great classical masterpieces are in fact concerned have long
since been relegated to oblivion." Toscanini took his tempo from the composer's markings at the head of a movement. Furtwängler said: "The question of tempo is one which cannot be separated from the interpretation of
the piece as a whole, its spiritual image." Toscanini reportedly said of the
first movement of the *Eroica:* "To some it is Napoleon, to some it is
Alexander the Great, to some it is philosophical struggle; to me it is Allegro
con brio." Furtwängler wrote: "Beethoven's subjects develop in mutual
interaction like the characters in a play. In every single subject of every
Beethoven work a destiny is unfolded." Because he experienced music as
an otherworldly calling, Furtwängler insisted that music and politics were
distinct. For him to have led a military band on a battlefield or to have
conducted a waterfront rendition of "The Star-Spangled Banner" would
have seemed a profanation.[15]

Toscanini and Furtwängler first met in 1924 at La Scala, where Furtwäng-
ler led a pair of concerts; during a rehearsal, Toscanini impulsively rushed
onstage to shake Furtwängler's hand. A year later, Furtwängler visited
Milan to attend some of Toscanini's operatic performances. But in New
York in early 1926, around the time of Toscanini's Philharmonic debut,
Furtwängler was overheard flaying Toscanini in conversation with Edgard
Varèse. As Toscanini, too, was a jealous colleague, this antipathy may have
been returned. The following season—Furtwängler's third with the Philharmonic—the rivalry came to a head. Toscanini, with a one-month Philharmonic contract, was unable to conduct any of his scheduled January
performances owing to illness and nervous depression. On the verge of
leaving New York without having appeared onstage, he decided to lead two
February programs of Beethoven symphonies: the First, Third, Fifth, and
Ninth. But Furtwängler, scheduled to begin a three-month Philharmonic
stint upon Toscanini's departure, had been under the impression that *he*
was to conduct the Ninth Symphony at his final concert. He wound up

conducting Brahms's Requiem instead. Privately, it was alleged that Toscanini had feigned his illness and threatened not to appear in New York unless he, and not Furtwängler, conducted the Ninth.[16]

Whether these suspicions were correct or not, they opened a formidable rift—not merely between Furtwängler and Toscanini, but between Furtwängler and the Philharmonic. In fact, Arthur Judson and Clarence Mackay were fervently courting Toscanini, as was Maurice Van Praag, the Philharmonic's personnel manager. Van Praag considered Toscanini "the only great conductor living today." Mackay, who in cables to Max Smith in Italy promised to "do his utmost" to accommodate Toscanini's wishes, was said to have underwritten half the cost of Toscanini's 1926 and 1927 engagements. He also arranged for NBC to broadcast one of Toscanini's 1927 performances of Beethoven's Ninth (probably Toscanini's first radio transmission), explaining: "I believe that these concerts are of such importance that they should be made available to as great a public as possible, and in presenting them to the great 'invisible' audience we are following out the rapidly expanding educational policy of the Society."

Toscanini's Beethoven concerts were received as ecstatically as his first Philharmonic concerts had been in 1926. Gilman wrote: "Mr. Toscanini bade farewell to us . . . amid such a blaze and roar of frenzied enthusiasm and affection as must have persuaded him (if he needed persuasion) that New York cannot easily be reconciled to the possibility that he may not be here again—if such a calamity really is in store for us." Of the major critics, only Henderson did not treat Furtwängler's return on February 10 as a denouement. The day before, Toscanini had signed a contract to lead "approximately forty-two" Philharmonic concerts the following season as a "regular" conductor. On March 3 the Philharmonic announced that Furtwängler would not appear with the orchestra in 1927–28, even as a guest, because his open dates could not "be coordinated with the time which the Philharmonic has available."*[17]

This turn of events stunned the city's Furtwängler admirers. Several wrote angry letters to the *Times*, one of which read in part:

Mr. Furtwängler's lack of popularity may be traced in great measure to the absence of those qualities which New York characteristically demands. He is not a handsome figure. He is rather graceless in his gestures. He becomes absorbed in the music in front of him and forgets all about the audience behind. He accepts applause with a certain indifference. He does not bow graciously. He gets the musicians to play for him

---

*A false claim, according to Daniel Gillis's *Furtwängler in America*, p. 19.

from within and does not impose those military requirements from
without which are so easily and obviously effective in the eye of that
large percentage who come primarily to gape and marvel at the fact that
more than a hundred men can be made to play as if one. . . .[18]

Some letter writers cast unnamed "critics" in villainous roles. So controversial was Downes's partisanship—more extreme than Gilman's, because
Downes's crusader mentality admitted but one god—that he felt the need
to defend himself in a self-revealing thirty-six-column-inch rebuttal entitled
"Furtwängler's Conductorship":

> The *Times* publishes today letters from supporters of Wilhelm Furt-
> wängler, who protest against the conclusion of his engagement as con-
> ductor of the Philharmonic Orchestra. The grounds taken for these
> protests are substantially those raised in other letters published in these
> columns of late weeks, since the announcement of Mr. Furtwängler's
> departure. The assertion is made, and apparently believed by certain
> correspondents, that the termination of Mr. Furtwängler's engagement
> is due to a lack of appreciation of his work and even hostility toward him
> on the part of the critics. It is deduced from these premises that the critics
> have influenced an unthinking public to stay away from Mr. Furtwäng-
> ler's concerts and have prejudiced the management of the Philharmonic
> so that it has failed to re-engage him. To these general observations is
> added the insinuation, to be noted in another column, that the men or
> the man principally responsible for the politics of the Philharmonic are
> not sufficiently informed on matters pertaining to the musical art to
> know what conductor it is best for them to engage, or whose advice to
> take in determining so important a question.
>
> The facts are otherwise than the letters of Mr. Furtwängler's adher-
> ents would indicate. A consensus of critical opinion, coming from differ-
> ent quarters, without the slightest prejudice or collusion, has rated Mr.
> Furtwängler's performances less highly than those of either of his col-
> leagues, Messrs. Mengelberg and Toscanini of the Philharmonic, this
> season. It has not been the design or the pleasure of the reviewers
> concerned to give expressions to these estimates. With one of them, at
> least, it has been a matter of private regret and disappointment that a
> conductor who promised as greatly as Mr. Furtwängler when first he
> arrived in New York should fall so far below his early standards. . . . Mr.
> Furtwängler has not maintained during the season anything like the
> technical and artistic level of his opening and historic performance of
> Brahms's First Symphony with the Philharmonic Orchestra. This is not
> opinion, but fact. . . .

But there is another element in this situation more important, more determinate by far, and far less subject to influences of written criticism than many believe. We refer to the verdict of the public. It is a fact that may be ascertained by the curious that the public, which originally greeted Mr. Furtwängler with warm and spontaneous acclaim, has given its silent verdict upon his performances by patronizing them in lesser degree than it patronized the performances of his fellow-conductors. This is a matter which must and should count with a great orchestral organization.

Patronage has not only to be considered from the point of view of those who must finance an orchestra, it has to do with the effect of orchestral concerts upon the public. A symphony orchestra is making propaganda [for] music. If one conductor attracts a smaller audience than another, the public will benefit the less by the orchestra's ministrations. This [is] the vital principle involved in the engagement of any orchestral conductor, and the fact is that in the last analysis it has been the public and not the reviewers or the management of the orchestra which has given a lukewarm verdict on Mr. Furtwängler's incumbency.

Another matter which touches directly upon the public interest is the apparent limitation of Mr. Furtwängler's repertory. Like many other German conductors lacking wide experience outside their own country, his repertory has been limited, particularly in his first two seasons, and when he ventured outside the stock German repertory it was not always with happy results. German conductors as a class, when they come to America, have to outgrow certain nationalistic musical leanings. It is often astonishing and sometimes unwelcome to them to discover that American audiences are accustomed to a broad and catholic repertory; that American standards of performance are considerably higher—not lower, but higher than those which obtain today in Europe; and, finally, that by virtue of sheer wealth, if nothing else, there come to American cities such as New York many great conductors of various nationalities whom the public estimates regardless of their foreign reputation and entirely upon the merits of their performances.

It is hardly to be gainsaid by unprejudiced individuals that in point of variety of programs and also sympathetic insight into music of different periods, nationalities and schools, Mr. Furtwängler's nearest competitors have surpassed him. It is also a fact that the technical standards of the Philharmonic under Messrs. Mengelberg and Toscanini have been for virtuoso finish and beauty of tone superior to those of Mr. Furtwängler. These are hard things to say, but it seems that the time has come when a few plain words are desirable in reply to unfounded charges and extreme opinions.

One more observation is due to the wise and admirable actions of Mr.
Mackay and his associates in their development to its present high level
of artistic accomplishment of the Philharmonic Orchestra, an orchestra
which is now one of the very best in the country. For years they had
made efforts to bring Mr. Toscanini to this city as head of the Philharmonic. At last they succeeded. Their efforts were completely justified by
the results. Mr. Toscanini was recognized as one of the greatest if not
the greatest conductor who has led either the Philharmonic or any other
American orchestra in recent years. Mr. Toscanini has gained by virtue
of his genius and nothing else, the admiration and support of reviewers
and audiences wherever and whenever he appeared. He has put a fine
edge on the technical accomplishment of an orchestra heavily indebted
for its technical standards to the faithful labors of Willem Mengelberg.
Mr. Mengelberg, in turn, during his half of the Philharmonic season
which has just ended, gave more interesting programs and more brilliant
performances than he had achieved in his two preceding engagements.
If, as many have claimed, the sensational successes of Toscanini affected
both Mengelberg and Furtwängler in their spirits and accomplishments,
the response of Mr. Mengelberg was extremely impressive and gave
further evidence of his great inherent qualities as a musician and conductor. Under these circumstances it does not appear to the present commentator, and it is not the majority opinion, that the direction of the
Philharmonic has shown anything less than sound sense and high artistic
policy in re-engaging Messrs. Mengelberg and Toscanini for next year
—it having been stated that Mr. Furtwängler could not come to America
at that time—and in having prevailed upon Mr. Toscanini to stay, if his
health permits, from the time Mr. Mengelberg leaves to the end of the
1927–28 Philharmonic season.[19]

In thus answering his critics, Downes multiplied their grounds for complaint. Far from "lacking wide experience" outside Germany and Austria,
Furtwängler had conducted in Denmark, England, Hungary, Italy, and
Sweden. Toscanini's symphonic experience, by comparison, was limited—
and so, judging from his New York concerts, was his repertoire. In a little
over four weeks with the Philharmonic in 1926 and 1927, he had mainly
selected the works with which he would be associated for the next twenty-
five years, including Beethoven's Third, Fifth, and Ninth symphonies,
Schubert's "Unfinished," the Nocturne and Scherzo from Mendelssohn's
A Midsummer Night's Dream, Brahms's "Haydn" Variations, the Prelude
and *Liebestod* from *Tristan,* the Funeral March from *Götterdämmerung,* and
La Mer. As novelties, he had presented Respighi's *Pines of Rome,* two
excerpts from Stravinsky's *Petrouchka,* and miniatures by Victor de Sabata,

Giuseppe Martucci, Jean-Jules Roger-Ducasse, and Vincenzo Tommasini. Furtwängler, whose repertoire Downes found parochial, had in four months led the Philharmonic in *Don Juan* by Walter Braunfels, Bruch's *Kol Nidrei*, Dvořák's *Hussite* Overture and Rondo for cello and orchestra (Opus 94), Hindemith's Concerto for Orchestra, Miaskovsky's Seventh Symphony, Prokofiev's First Violin Concerto, Respighi's second set of *Ancient Airs and Dances*, Schoenberg's *Verklärte Nacht*, Sibelius's *Tempest* Overture, the *Sinfonia Domestica* and an interlude from *Intermezzo* by Richard Strauss, and Stravinsky's *Firebird* Suite and *Rite of Spring*. Downes's distinction between "opinion" and "fact," and uncomplicated faith in the latter, testified to an empiricism as oddly unencumbered as Toscanini's own when, in principle, he reduced music to the notes and nothing more. Downes's populist-utilitarian theory of culture, reckoning value in terms of the greatest good for the greatest number, again documented a problematic reductionism.

The Philharmonic's March 4 announcement of Furtwängler's impending absence throughout 1927–28 left him scheduled to lead the final month of 1926–27 programs as a lame duck. At Carnegie Hall, his partisans showered him with applause and assailed Olin Downes with frigid stares. Joseph Szigeti, a soloist at two of Furtwängler's last New York concerts, has described "the uneasy, strained atmosphere backstage, the demonstrative ovations out front that seemed to protest against a 'fait accompli'. . . and the resigned, forgiving smile of the obviously hurt artist, a smile that seemed to answer the acclaim with a philosophical 'too late!' " Szigeti also wrote: "Granted that the emergence of the Nazi regime became an insurmountable obstacle to [Furtwängler's] return . . . how do we explain away his absence between 1927 and, say, 1932?"[20] The Philharmonic's guest conductors during this period included Thomas Beecham, Walter Damrosch, Ossip Gabrilovich, Vladimir Golschmann, Arthur Honegger, Erich Kleiber, Clemens Krauss, Willem Mengelberg, Bernardino Molinari, Fritz Reiner, Ottorino Respighi, Leopold Stokowski, and Bruno Walter. Furtwängler never again appeared on an American stage.

The Toscanini forces made easy work of disposing of Mengelberg. For the 1927–28 season, Mengelberg and Toscanini were both listed as principal conductors, but under the circumstances this parity could not endure. A stickler for idiosyncratic interpretive detail, Mengelberg had drilled the orchestra with finicky precision. Toscanini struck like a tornado, scattering Mengelberg's details like so many pieces of paper. Winthrop Sargeant, a member of the Philharmonic violins at the time, has recalled:

Toscanini was not interested in principles. He was inspirational, not logical. His aim was not to teach a tradition, but to bend the bowing, fingering, breathing, and the very emotions of the last second fiddler or bass clarinettist to every mercurial shading of his implacable will. He had no use for a well-oiled machine. He started methodically converting the Philharmonic into a dependent organism, every member of which seemed to become a mere extension of his own agile brain, body and emotions. For Toscanini, the orchestra player had no will of his own. He became a hypnotized creature reflecting one single will—the will of the maestro.[21]

Mengelberg mounted a rear-guard action, exaggerating his methods, criticizing Toscanini's. But the players' heads were turned; Mengelberg's careful instructions were not just ignored, but ridiculed. His departure is quickly summarized. In 1927–28, Mengelberg's name had come first in the listing of the Philharmonic's two principal conductors. In 1928–29, the order was reversed. As early as February 1929, the Philharmonic sent an emissary to Europe "in an effort to pin [Toscanini] down about whether Mr. Mengelberg should be engaged or not." The report back was that Toscanini "saw no reason why Mengelberg should not be engaged again."[22] Mengelberg conducted the orchestra in 1929–30, but not in 1930–31. Simultaneously, a reorganization took place that enhanced the Philharmonic's personnel and elevated its status: the New York Symphony, the city's second orchestra, was absorbed by the Philharmonic as of 1928–29. Toscanini was given chief responsibility for selecting which New York Symphony members would retain jobs, and which Philharmonic members would not.* Walter Damrosch, the New York Symphony's conductor since 1885, expected to become a regular guest, but was permitted less than three weeks with the amalgamated orchestra.**

---

*Officially, the orchestra was thereafter known as the New York Philharmonic-Symphony. Most people, however, continued calling it the New York Philharmonic.

**In the period between Theodore Thomas and Toscanini's arrival at the Philharmonic, Damrosch was perhaps the most conspicuous figure on the American symphonic scene. In addition to giving up to forty subscription concerts a season, his New York Symphony toured extensively, engaged important guests, and played interesting repertoire. He led his own opera company from 1894 to 1900, attracting major singers. He was a frequent and persuasive lecturer. Widely admired for his generous impulses, broad outlook, optimism, energy, and ease of manner, he also furnished an object lesson in mobilizing great wealth in behalf of high culture. His marriage in 1896 to Margaret Blaine, daughter of a leading national politician, was attended by Supreme Court justices, cabinet members, and the President of the United States. Damrosch

New York was now a one-orchestra city. All that remained was to make Toscanini a one-city conductor. As Mackay and Judson watched attentively, Mussolini's shadow darkened La Scala. As early as May 7, 1926—not four months following Toscanini's Philharmonic debut, and immediately following renewed reports of Toscanini's problems with the Fascists—Judson wrote to Mackay: "This puts us in the position of being compelled to make an immediate decision for the season 1927–28. . . . I have reason to suspect that Mr. Kahn may seize this opportunity to get [Toscanini] for the Metropolitan, which would, of course, be disastrous for the Philharmonic." Maurice Van Praag visited Toscanini in Milan in the company of Max Smith and his wife. Van Praag reported back to Mackay: "[Toscanini] told me how kind you were to him last winter, and how happy he was with the Philharmonic; but when he came back to La Scala he could not stand to hear their terrible playing. I then asked him why it was he bothered with them at all, when you Mr. Mackay were willing to give him the best orchestra in the world to conduct without any friction or discontent." Artistically, La Scala was not yet in eclipse. In 1925–26, Toscanini led two important premieres there: the first Italian performance of Debussy's *Le Martyre de Saint-Sébastien*, to a text by D'Annunzio, and the first performance anywhere of *Turandot*. In 1926–27, he conducted his only *Don Carlo*, his first *Fidelio*, and, in celebration of the Beethoven centenary, the nine symphonies. In 1927–28, he conducted the premiere of a new Pizzetti opera, *Fra Gherardo*. But the personal costs of running an opera house while

---

and his wife entertained constantly, inviting artists, journalists, and the very rich. His handsome features and "dreamy" German accent early endeared him to well-connected young women, who flocked to his musical lectures. He was equally successful winning the affection and respect of Andrew Carnegie, who built Carnegie Hall for him and eventually arranged that he receive a $5,000 birthday gift every year. Another diehard Damrosch supporter was the oil magnate Harry Harkness Flagler, who underwrote the New York Symphony's 1920 European tour and much else. Damrosch's musical facility and lavish backing made him amazingly resilient: unable to gain a foothold at the Metropolitan, he formed his own opera company; unsuccessful with the New York Philharmonic in 1902–03, he reconstituted his own orchestra. He was savagely ridiculed by critics who resented his access to wealth and caste prerogatives. George Martin, in *The Damrosch Dynasty* (1983), portrays his opponents as an obnoxious cabal and undertakes a modest rehabilitation of his reputation as a conductor. But, given its frequency and its sources, the press's anti-Damrosch testimony remains all too credible. And his one substantial recording, of Brahms's Second with the New York Symphony, is the most incriminating document of all—a spastic interpretation, rushing forward and holding back to no coherent purpose. One understands why Toscanini, Judson, and Mackay cashiered Damrosch. Again, he bounced back, becoming radio's foremost musical pedagogue (see page 202). On balance, Damrosch was a positive yet frustrating presence; he could never have made an important career in Germany.

staving off the Fascists were grave. By 1928, Toscanini was suffering from shoulder and back pains, and chronic insomnia. In August he wired Judson: "After next season I take leave definitely from the theater." A performance of *Aida* on May 14, 1929, proved the last time he conducted an entire opera in Italy. A day later, he left with his company to take Vienna and Berlin by storm. Upon his return to Italy, what was ever more widely rumored became fact: Toscanini would leave La Scala.[23]

In America, Clarence Mackay, Arthur Judson, Olin Downes, Lawrence Gilman, and the Toscanini legions stood poised to greet the dawn.

The New York Philharmonic, 1929–36

At sixty, Toscanini did not wish to shoulder an entire season's workload. Even after Mengelberg's departure, he never conducted more than fifteen weeks per season with the New York Philharmonic at Carnegie Hall. But he conducted the Philharmonic more than anyone else did (in those days, the New York orchestral year lasted only from October to April), and imprinted himself so forcefully that when he presided, the Philharmonic was his alone. Under Toscanini, the orchestra attained heights of virtuosity unmatched in its previous or subsequent history. Moreover, to judge from testimony and recordings, this was the most precise embodiment ever of the Toscanini sound—luminous, transparent, electric.

It was a phenomenon widely analyzed. From his seat in the second violins, Winthrop Sargeant decided the crucial ingredient was a "continuous psychology of crisis"—that, like people trapped in a sinking ship or a burning building, the members of Toscanini's Philharmonic found themselves capable of prodigious feats, pursuing a necessary course of action out of desperation. Others attributed the Philharmonic's diligence to new pride. Alfred Wallenstein, the orchestra's first cellist throughout the Toscanini years, regularly rehearsed the cellos separately: "That would be hard to do today; but it was possible then; and we wanted to do our best." A combination of fear and pride also induced the players to study their parts at home —a practice, if Sargeant is to be believed, previously thought heretical.

A further, florid dimension of Toscanini's reign was his continued susceptibility to astonishing fits of temper. According to Fred Zimmerman, a double bassist in Toscanini's Philharmonic:

> Not only the musical phrase that came out different from what he expected upset him: *anything* that wasn't as he expected it to be upset him. Once, in a temper, he dug his hands into the pockets of his jacket

so violently that he tore them away. He made a tremendous effort to control himself, turning his back to us and saying: "No, Toscanini, no! *Calmo—calmo—calmo!*" Then he began to conduct again; but the passage went no better; and in renewed anger he started to dig his hands into his pockets again, but found they weren't there, since he had torn them away. This new frustration made him so furious that he began to tear the jacket itself to pieces. Another time he attempted to break his stick; but this one only bent and wouldn't break; and this made him so angry that he began to bite it.

Though at one point the musicians' union discouraged rehearsal visitors so the players wouldn't be seen being insulted by Toscanini, the Philharmonic tolerated his tantrums. And yet, in Wallenstein's opinion, Toscanini's fuse was shorter in America than in Italy:

> I really think that if he had spoken English as well as he did French or his own language he wouldn't have had occasion to blow up as much as he did. I think it was the impediment in communication that caused many explosions here that wouldn't have happened in Europe. They happened there too, but not to the extent that they happened here. . . . Once after the war he was conducting a Wagner program in Milan; and at the rehearsal he was so sweet to the orchestra that afterwards I asked him about it. "Everybody was playing out of tune, and you didn't say anything. If it were New York you would be on top of them—as a matter of fact you would walk out." And he said: "Because in New York I know they can do it, but here I know they cannot."[1]

That "in New York they can do it" was knowledge cherished by Americans. Equally cherished was the hope that Europe would notice. Wresting Toscanini from La Scala had taken a mighty effort, motivated by a mighty desire. One selling point had been the Philharmonic's superb training and personnel—of which Toscanini, as much as anyone, was aware. But Europeans continued to rank German and Austrian orchestras highest. In fact, the only American orchestra ever to have been heard in Europe was Walter Damrosch's unremarkable New York Symphony. Lawrence Gilman vented his impatience in a *Herald Tribune* column of October 20, 1929:

> Talking recently with a distinguished London colleague—one of the most eminent and magistral of living music critics—we asked him what he thought of a certain interpretation of Toscanini's.

"I have never heard Toscanini conduct," he replied briefly.

Doubtless our question was a tactless one. We had forgotten for the moment that Mr. Toscanini has never conducted in England, and that most English music critics are not in the habit of traveling abroad to hear music. They wait, as a rule, for the mountain to come to Mahomet. Which is about what the music critics and music lovers of Berlin and Paris and Leipzig and Vienna do. . . .

We doubt if our British colleague would have believed us if we had told him that . . . America had been listening for twenty years, off and on, to performances of operatic and symphonic music under Arturo Toscanini the like of which most European capitals had never heard.

Toscanini himself appreciated that Berlin and Paris and Leipzig and Vienna had yet to hear him conduct a symphonic program. When in the Philharmonic negotiations Judson and Mackay had dangled the prospect of a European tour, Toscanini had shown great interest. Now the tour was to take place. The itinerary included Berlin, Paris, Leipzig, and Vienna, and eleven other cities in Belgium, Czechoslovakia, England, Germany, Hungary, Italy, and Switzerland. Gilman observed: America was sending "the best that it has to offer. . . . The mountain was going to Mahomet."

That the Philharmonic's excitement over winning Toscanini should have inspired a tour is easy to understand. Only a little less obvious are the reasons the Philharmonic was not inspired to tour the United States. Its desire for European approval may be gauged against the larger social backdrop. The orchestra left New York for Le Havre on April 27, 1930—six months after the United States had been plunged into its worst period of bankruptcies, unemployment, and hunger. Toscanini was not among the victims of the Great Depression: his Philharmonic salary ranged as high as $110,000 for fifteen weeks of work, plus payment of his federal and state income taxes and of steamship passage to and from New York—per service, about eighty times what was paid the average orchestra member, and more than double the rate paid such guest conductors as Bruno Walter and Otto Klemperer.[2] Yet the Philharmonic Society's governing millionaires were no longer guarantors of solvency, as they had been in Mahler's time: financially, the Toscanini years were a period of mounting deficits, of cost cutting and fund raising. Did straitened circumstances call into question an unprecedented month-long trans-Atlantic tour? Not really: far from inviting criticism for ignoring America's hour of need, the tour was understood as a patriotic service. Under Toscanini, the Philharmonic was ideally equipped to validate American achievement in the citadels of musical culture.

In this regard, and every other, the tour was a sensation. The acclaim

for the opening concerts, in Paris, set the tone. Emile Vuillermoz wrote in
Excelsior: "Toscanini has crossed Paris like a meteor, a shooting star. Here,
truly, is a master, not only a conductor, but a master of all conductors." In
Berlin, among those listeners left with unforgettable memories were Walter, Klemperer, Erich Kleiber, and George Szell. Szell, who also heard the
orchestra in Prague, later described his reaction as "Toscanini shock." At
a farewell party following the final concert, in London, Toscanini paid
tribute to the orchestra with a rare speech:

> My heart is sad. The thought that this evening we have given the last
> concert of our tour and that tomorrow we shall be separated after seven
> weeks of cordial and affectionate association moves me deeply. What I
> am particularly moved to tell you is of the great joy I have experienced
> in discovering every day more and more that enthusiasm and love which
> you have expended in trying to make every concert better than the
> previous one and how you accomplished it without the least signs of
> weariness. You have been wonderful, wonderful.

But even while saluting his players, Toscanini himself was the inevitable
center of attention. On two continents, he was the most glamorous conductor of the day.[3]

Toscanini's moderate New York schedule permitted a multitude of
European engagements. In between taking the Philharmonic abroad and
resigning from it six years later, he led concerts and operas in Bayreuth,
Bologna, Brussels, Copenhagen, London, Monaco, Paris, Salzburg, Stock-
holm, and Vienna. His first appearances at the Wagner festival in Bayreuth,
within weeks of the close of the Philharmonic tour, were momentous. Even
more than Verdi, Wagner was the musical god of Toscanini's youth. His
first visit to Bayreuth, in 1899, was undertaken in the spirit of an acolyte.
Now, invited by Siegfried Wagner over the objections of Karl Muck and
other keepers of the flame, he returned as the first non-German to conduct
in Wagner's own theater.

Toscanini reportedly refused payment for his Bayreuth performances.
From the start, however, the Bayreuth ideal of art as religion was sullied
by secular drama and intrigue. Following his initial rehearsal in the Festspielhaus pit, Toscanini decided the orchestra was impossible and prepared
to leave. Though Siegfried made peace, Toscanini's continued displeasure
caused the players to call him "Toscanono." Among much else, he began
correcting long-standing mistakes in the parts. Meanwhile, Muck, perceiving himself displaced, adopted an attitude of unconcealed hostility. With

members of the family and other initiates taking sides, the Toscanini affair was upstaged by the unexpected death of Siegfried Wagner, aged sixty-one. Toscanini, Muck, and Karl Elmendorff participated in a memorial concert in which Toscanini was assigned the *Siegfried Idyll*. Musically, the unquestioned high point of this singular Bayreuth Festival was the Toscanini *Tristan*, featuring Rudolf Bockelmann, Alexander Kipnis, Nanny Larsén-Todsen, and Lauritz Melchior. Kipnis was not alone in finding Toscanini's *cantabile* Wagner revelatory. And Toscanini's presence proved revelatory at the faltering Bayreuth box office. On September 4, fifteen days following Toscanini's final Bayreuth appearance that season, the New York *Times* announced that he would make Bayreuth his permanent home and take over musical direction of the festival.

Toscanini did return to Bayreuth in the summer of 1931—and, significantly, Muck did not. But there was no question of his settling there and assuming an administrative post. With the benign Siegfried no longer on the premises, the house of Wagner was mired in controversy. To the dismay of her sisters-in-law, the directorship had passed to Siegfried's English-born widow, Winifred. Heinz Tietjen, a conductor famed for his impenetrable diplomacy, was angling to become Winifred's sergeant-at-arms and outrank an eminent newcomer, Wilhelm Furtwängler. While Toscanini was not directly involved in these affairs, Furtwängler, his recent victim in New York, remained his chief European rival. Their relationship was never calm. On this occasion, misunderstanding arose over another memorial program for Siegfried, to be conducted by Toscanini, Furtwängler, and Elmendorff. Toscanini's rehearsal proved traumatic: he walked out in a rage, then sat facing the wall in Siegfried's study while Winifred and Tietjen pleaded with him to return to the Festspielhaus. Furtwängler completed the rehearsal. Toscanini refused even to attend the concert. His disappearance was widely attributed to what one German correspondent called "a sense of rivalry forcefully repressed."[4]

As in 1930, Toscanini's performances—especially of *Parsifal,* which he had taken over from Muck following a reported deathbed petition to Siegfried—managed to transcend the rumors and jealousies in which he figured. But before leaving he informed Winifred that he would not return for the next festival, to be held in 1933. Two months later, the New York *Times* learned of his decision and reported it in a story whose barely concealed subtext contrasted New World wholesomeness with Old World fatigue.

Arturo Toscanini will not conduct opera again at Bayreuth, it has been learned from an authoritative source. And the reason: Simply that Toscanini was not satisfied with the conditions in which he worked. . . .

When Toscanini complained of the quality of the orchestra and of its constantly shifting personnel, Mme. Wagner explained that those conditions were not easy to remedy, but all that was possible would be done. . . .

It is said that the wrath of Toscanini gathered as the 1931 season progressed at the Festspielhaus and he saw his own activities subjected to expediency and commercialism. He found himself hampered and hindered in his aim. It seems evident that Mme. Wagner was dabbling in politics. . . .

Friends here received letters from visitors at Bayreuth telling of Toscanini's irritation when on certain occasions Mme. Wagner took him to the throngs who drank beer and ate Schinkenbrot in the restaurant of the Festspielhaus between the acts. Certainly he is not the man to relish this sort of thing. . . .

Toscanini is a man of extraordinary energy and endurance, but the time has come to treat his arm considerately and husband his strengths. In future there will be longer periods of rest between Philharmonic-Symphony engagements, an arrangement certain to be advantageous to conductor and orchestra.[5]

Like so many Toscanini "decisions," this one proved subject to change. The politics in which Bayreuth's directress now "dabbled" were those of her longtime friend, the Wagner admirer and National Socialist leader Adolf Hitler. Toscanini liked Winifred Wagner but loathed the Nazis. In June 1932, Winifred met him in Paris and changed his mind about the 1933 festival. In January 1933, Hitler's appointment to the chancellorship prompted third thoughts. In March 1933—the month Hitler was voted dictatorial powers—Toscanini let it be known that persecution of Jewish musicians had worsened the prospects of restoring his Bayreuth ties. Toscanini's own worsening relationship with the Nazis was by then common currency in the press.

But it was in Fascist Italy, not Fascist Germany, that Toscanini was bruised by the political storm winds preceding World War II. The 1930 Philharmonic tour, passing through Italy, had renewed the "Giovinezza" skirmishes that had complicated Toscanini's final, doomed years at La Scala. Then, on May 14, 1931, having again refused to perform the Fascist anthem, Toscanini was pummeled by thugs outside Bologna's Teatro Comunale upon arriving to conduct a memorial concert for Giuseppe Martucci. His chauffeur, acting quickly, managed to return him to his hotel. There, nursing superficial head wounds, Toscanini roared with indignation while a mob shouted obscenities from the street below. Informed that his safety could not be guaranteed past 6:00 a.m., he left at

1:20 a.m. for Milan, where his passport was confiscated and his house put under surveillance. News of the attack ignited international indignation. Koussevitzky, whose relationship to Toscanini was never close, canceled his upcoming concerts at La Scala and wrote to the theater's administrator: "Maestro Toscanini does not belong only to Italy, but to the whole world." Though Toscanini's passport was returned within weeks, he was not permitted to conduct in Milan that August, nor in Turin the following year.

This buildup of hostilities on two European fronts could only drive Toscanini into deeper alliance with the United States. In June 1931—the month after the Bologna assault—Olin Downes wrote an article for the *New York Times Magazine,* "Again Toscanini Battles for His Art," in which Toscanini's incorruptible love of freedom was equated with his incorruptibility in music, and his raging against the Fascists analogized to his rehearsal tantrums. Downes even made light of the lawsuit-provoking injury Toscanini's angry baton had inflicted in Turin in 1919.

> Unreasonable? Perhaps. Difficult, because of his exorbitant artistic demands? Certainly. Which do you prefer: a reasonable mediocrity who will conform, adapt himself to the world as it is and let the ideals of his art suffer, or a man of really transcendent genius, a lonely and incomparable figure in his art, whose life and whose one thought is the service of that art and the approach, as nearly as it may be achieved by human beings, to perfection. With Toscanini this is a daily battle, one that must be fought anew at every rehearsal and performance.
> . . . And so . . . Toscanini, in his own proud field, holds glorious and despotic sway. . . .

Throughout Toscanini's New York Philharmonic tenure, in fact, a tightening weave of political and artistic strands strengthened his image.

The keystone of the Philharmonic's 1932–33 season was a Beethoven cycle occupying its final five Sunday afternoons. The cycle began on March 26 with the *Egmont* Overture, invoking Goethe's paean to heroism in the cause of freedom. Seven days later, the Sunday-morning newspapers carried front-page accounts of Nazi boycotts of Jewish stores. Also front-page news was a cable sent from New York to Hitler by eleven musicians protesting persecution of their German colleagues for political or religious reasons. Noting that Toscanini's signature led the list "at his own request," the *Times*'s coverage was headlined "Toscanini Heads Protest to Hitler." Toscanini mounted the podium at Carnegie Hall the same afternoon as *Egmont* incarnate, receiving a stamping ovation unusual even for him. The

program also included the *Eroica* Symphony—whose dedication to Napoleon, according to a well-worn anecdote, was shredded by Beethoven,
repudiating the hubris of power. Two days later, the Berlin radio banned
all Toscanini broadcasts and recordings. These events activated new speculation about Toscanini's possible withdrawal from Bayreuth. According to
the *Times*, it was "believed in musical circles" that his endorsement of the
protest cable "meant that he would not go to Bayreuth this year." Ossip
Gabrilovich issued a statement urging Toscanini to renounce Bayreuth.
Fritz Kreisler issued a statement deploring the "moral pressure" being
applied by Gabrilovich and others; in Kreisler's opinion, Toscanini could
better serve as an "ambassador of peace and harbinger of good will" by
fulfilling his Bayreuth commitments and upholding the inviolability of art
by politics. Winifred Wagner issued a statement insisting there was "not
one word of truth" to reports Toscanini would abandon Bayreuth. Toscanini himself declined to issue any statements. According to the *Times*
analysis: "This was believed to indicate that as yet nothing had occurred
to cause Mr. Toscanini to alter his original intention to go to Bayreuth."
All this took place the week prior to April 9, when Toscanini led the
Philharmonic in the ne plus ultra of curled-lip defiance: Beethoven's Fifth.
The Sunday after that, he conducted the Overture to *Coriolan*, with its
theme of autocracy undone by arrogance. The final Beethoven program,
on April 23, ended the season. The final work: the *Leonore* Overture No.
3, whose allusions to *Fidelio* make it Beethoven's most explicit symphonic
version of "Sic semper tyrannis."[6]

To call to mind the ferocious idealism of any of these Beethoven symphonies and overtures is to know the potency of the New York performances Toscanini flung in the teeth of the fascists. He himself was aroused
to repudiate private entreaties from Hitler. In Italy that May, he showed
Fritz Busch a letter in which Hitler declared how happy it would make him
"to greet Toscanini in Bayreuth." Busch wrote in his memoirs:

> What was depressing Toscanini, from his youth closely attached to
> the art of Richard Wagner, and its greatest interpreter, was anxiety for
> the future of the Bayreuth Festival. Feeling thus he asked me, "What will
> Bayreuth do if I refuse?" "Then they will invite me, Maestro," I said.
> Toscanini was speechless. "That is to say, they *have* invited me. Tietjen,
> who expects your refusal, has already taken steps."
>
> I was delighted at his astonishment and added with a laugh, "Of
> course, I will refuse, like you." Toscanini shut his mouth, which had
> remained open from astonishment, and purred, in his warm, melancholy
> voice, *"Eh, caro amico!"* We were both silent, and a feeling of great
> sorrow came over us.[7]

On May 28, Toscanini wrote to Winifred Wagner:

> The sorrowful events which have wounded my feelings as a man and as an artist have not undergone any change, contrary to my every hope. It is therefore my duty today to break the silence which I had imposed upon myself for two months and to inform you that for my tranquillity, for yours, and for everyone's, it is better not to think any longer about my coming to Bayreuth.
>
> With unchangeable friendship for the House of Wagner,
>
> Arturo Toscanini.

On June 6, the New York *Times* reported Toscanini's decision on page one; as in other accounts in the American press, his "unchangeable friendship" for the Wagners was omitted from transcripts of the letter to Winifred. Bruno Zirato wired Toscanini on behalf of the Philharmonic: "We all are tremendously pleased [by] your decision."[8]

The following Philharmonic season brought a second, expanded Beethoven cycle, comprising fourteen all-Beethoven concerts. The political message was now indelible. Toscanini was given a standing ovation when he appeared onstage to begin the cycle on January 11. The same month, a delegation of Jewish leaders presented him with a certificate inscribed "in recognition of his magnificent act in refusing to direct the 1933 Wagner festival at Bayreuth." Two months later, his sixty-seventh birthday brought congratulatory messages from Mayor Fiorello La Guardia, Governor Herbert Lehman, and President Roosevelt, as well as a cover story in *Time* beginning:

> Conversation hushed in thousands of U.S. homes last Sunday afternoon. In New York's Carnegie Hall a great audience rose to its feet as a slender little man with a stick under his arm made his way as swiftly and inconspicuously as possible to the conductor's stand. For him the business of the afternoon was Beethoven's Sixth Symphony, the Franck D minor. But for once he had to pause until the audience had shown its reverence for Arturo Toscanini.[9]

Meanwhile, repudiated by Italy, and having repudiated Germany, Toscanini concentrated his European activities in Vienna and Salzburg, where the growing fascist presence could only precipitate another confrontation with tyranny. His third series of concerts with the Vienna Philharmonic, in the fall of 1934, included a performance of the Verdi Requiem in memory of Engelbert Dollfuss, the Austrian chancellor murdered the preceding summer. Dollfuss's successor, Kurt von Schuschnigg, presented Toscanini with a copy of the first-edition piano-vocal score of *Fidelio* with corrections in Beethoven's hand. *Fidelio* was one of two operas Toscanini conducted in Hitler's backyard at the Salzburg Festival that summer. The other was *Falstaff*, with a cast including Mariano Stabile and other Scala stalwarts. Hugo Burghauser, president of the Vienna Philharmonic, later commented:

> [Performances] with an Italian ensemble [were] never done in Salzburg even with Mozart, whose operas were mostly written originally in Italian; and it was unheard of that in a German town like Salzburg, three miles from the border of the Third Reich, an Italian should come, an anti-Fascist . . . and should establish there the first Italian performance of *Falstaff*. There were a lot of objections and difficulties; but it was done. . . .

Artistically, the Salzburg *Falstaff* was recognized as one of Toscanini's landmark accomplishments. Herbert Peyser of the New York *Times* was not alone in calling it "astounding . . . from start to finish utterly phenomenal." Peyser's account continued:

> Such virtuosity of teamwork as the Festspielhaus witnessed tonight is something even the most experienced operagoer is likely to encounter a half dozen times in his musical life. And only the drastic idealism of a Toscanini could summon an ensemble of this evening's perfection into being.
>
> The conductor's treatment of Verdi's score is, of course, no secret to New York operagoers. But it seems since Toscanini's Metropolitan days to have gained in vitality, in magical color, in flexibility and indescribable subtleness of beauty. Moreover, it appeared to be suffused tonight with a quality akin to transfiguration.

If in the context of embattled humanism, 1935, *Fidelio* seemed a flung gauntlet, Verdi's Indian-summer satire on human vanity was the more exquisitely poignant offering.[10]

Having already meted out the most extreme encomiums, Olin Downes and Lawrence Gilman yet managed to document Toscanini's enhanced prestige during the years in which he perfected the New York Philharmonic and took it on tour, conquered Bayreuth and Salzburg, endured Mussolini's thugs, and repudiated Hitler via letter and petition, *Fidelio* and

Falstaff. Even when not freshly illuminating Toscanini's art, their accounts continued to shed light on the basis and scope of his appeal.

Downes, as ever, eschewed the detailed musical reportage that had distinguished Toscanini and Mahler reviews from before the Great War. Rather, he laid renewed stress on Toscanini's inspired subservience to the composer's blueprint:

> Mr. Toscanini restudies his Beethoven whenever he plays him. He does not make sudden alterations in his readings, or seek by new detail to make fresh sensations for his audiences. He only tries, each season, to come nearer to the wishes of the composer, to be more faithful, if that is possible, to the spirit that is behind the notes on the music paper.

What chiefly lent variety and flavor to Downes's Toscanini reviews were his appraisals of communal rituals uniting the conductor and his adherents. But these were no irrelevance: in chronicling the sheer ceremony of Toscanini's concerts—their grand rites of secular religiosity, unknown a century before—Downes suggested the psychological underpinnings of dead-master and Toscanini reverence in urban-industrial times. This is how Downes opened and sealed the year of the second Beethoven cycle:

> The first Toscanini concert of the season by the Philharmonic-Symphony Orchestra took place yesterday evening in Carnegie Hall. This meant an auditorium again crowded to capacity with the most impressive audience of the season—an occasion when music lovers in all walks of life assembled to hear Mr. Toscanini's interpretations and do homage with him to the genius of Beethoven. For this concert was the first of the Beethoven series that Mr. Toscanini will give here. . . .
>
> The entire audience rose when Mr. Toscanini entered. He was obviously in the best of physical health, and his energy and concentration on his task were evident in his quick advance to the podium, his bow, brief and courteous, and the rap of the baton on the stand of the nearest player. These are the Toscanini rites. They betoken the quality of the man and the musician and the things the public has come to expect of him.
>
> The public was not disappointed. . . .

> No one who was present yesterday afternoon in Carnegie Hall will forget the occasion, or his own part in it: the final concert of the season by the Philharmonic-Symphony Orchestra with Arturo Toscanini conducting the third and last of his Sunday Wagner programs. . . .
>
> The audience cheered Mr. Toscanini after the overture. Its homage

at the end, when also there was much cheering, came from a deeper
source and a more overwhelming emotion. It was a consecrating
occasion. . . .

The audience was moved in many cases past applause or any other
visible manifestation. With the conductor invisible, the performance
would have delivered its own message. In addition, there was the sight
of the man himself, and that in his face and bearing which betokened in
advance of the rap of the baton the great things that were to be done.
The man and the musician were recognized as one by the gathering, so
fervent in its gratitude and so unwilling to leave the presence of a
supreme artist.[11]

Downes was the very bellwether of popular adulation. His accounts of
Beethoven, Wagner, and Toscanini rites, in which he personified the lay
listener infatuated with revered art, were a populist variation on the Germanic tradition earlier served by Thomas and Seidl, John Sullivan Dwight
and Henry Krehbiel. As we have seen, their tone derived in turn from
Old World worshipers of dead masters. The young Richard Wagner, for
one, had written of believing in "God, Mozart, and Beethoven, likewise in
their disciples and apostles." This was the language now embroidered by
Lawrence Gilman. Like Downes, Gilman endorsed and respected vox
populi. Unlike Downes, he documented Toscanini's triumphs from a
height, matching Toscanini's escalating stature with escalating religious
metaphor.

Mr. Toscanini has increased this season our already incalculable debt to
him. His influence here, the greatness of his example as a prophet and
a priest of art, are immeasurable. By endless demonstrations, of unswerv-
ing rectitude and astonishing completeness, he has proved to us that the
great artist need depend for his spiritual sustenance upon no elements
less rare than simplicity and selflessness and faith. And he has shown us,
as St. Francis did, the startling and terrible beauty of that which is forever
kindling and alight: that pure flame of the imagination, "burning in the
void."

Gilman tirelessly wrought new variations on the sacerdotal theme: Toscanini was the "custodian of holy things," the "priest of beauty," the
"guardian of spiritual themes." Inevitably, he elevated Toscanini to as high
a plane as the composers he served:

Almost without exception the few supreme creative artists, at least in
music, have been religious—not in the narrower sense of that word, but

in its free and ultimate and sublimating sense. Today, is it not rather the supreme interpreters who are religious in that ultimate and dedicatory sense: is it not to them that the custody of the Grail has passed? Is it not they, the few who are truly consecrated and elect, the priests and guardians of immortal beauty, who are filled with that mystical power of creative faith which can turn an act of service into a miracle of resurrection?[12]

In the hierarchy of Toscanini worship, Downes and Gilman, succeeding Max Smith, headed an inner circle of scribe-disciples. During the Philharmonic years this inner circle expanded, the most notable newcomers being Howard Taubman, who joined Downes's staff in 1930; Samuel Chotzinoff (formerly an accompanist for Efrem Zimbalist and Jascha Heifetz), who was music critic for the New York *World* from 1925 to 1930 and for the New York *Post* from 1934; and B. H. Haggin, who wrote for the *Brooklyn Daily Eagle* from 1934 and for *The Nation* from 1936. An early Taubman review shows how closely his Toscanini appraisals mirrored the style and substance of Downes's:

> Arturo Toscanini directed a performance of the *Eroica* at the second concert of the Philharmonic-Symphony Orchestra's Beethoven cycle at Carnegie Hall yesterday afternoon that Beethoven would have known best how to value. For, from what we know of the limitations of individual and ensemble of his day, the composer could not have heard a realization of his creation that was the peer of this one except in his imagination. Mr. Toscanini, at the height of his powers as a sovereign musician and a perceptive human being, has made himself the great Ludwig's most eloquent vicar among us.
>
> Perfection and magnificence are two much-abused words, but if their pristine meaning could be recaptured they would be applied only to interpretations like these. This was a miracle of recreation. . . .
>
> It is as impossible as it is unnecessary to recount the innumerable felicities of performance. All that can and need be told is what the interpretation meant to the auditor. The reaction of yesterday's capacity audience was unmistakable in its meaning. At the end of the *Eroica*, there was a deafening outburst of cheering and applause. This was continued for many minutes while Mr. Toscanini came out for repeated bows. New York's concert halls have seldom been the scene of such a spontaneous and unanimous demonstration of approval.

This was Chotzinoff's account of Toscanini's first 1928–29 Philharmonic concert:

Though it takes more than one swallow to make a summer, Mr. Toscanini is sufficient for a musical season. That maestro, after nearly giving
this department heart failure by refusing to embark for these shores on
schedule time, finally arrived. But even his presence in the vicinity of
Carnegie Hall has never been a guarantee that he would lead his orchestra at the appointed time. . . . Therefore Mr. Toscanini's arrival a few
days before his scheduled concert only opened up fresh anxiety. Even
reports that he had begun rehearsals failed to allay our fears. The country
is loaded down with professional guest-conductors, and it might easily
happen that at the last moment, as we sat in Carnegie Hall, Mr. Judson,
the Philharmonic-Symphony's manager, or one of his aides, would appear on the stage to inform us that Mr. Toscanini being indisposed, Mr.
So-and-so, the eminent conductor of the Sioux City Symphony Orchestra, had kindly consented to take his place. But nothing so grotesque
occurred, and Mr. Toscanini duly emerged from the wings of Carnegie
Hall last Thursday evening looking well and eager, and the season,
which had hitherto seemed a dull one for even the town's kindliest
reviewer, became on the moment vibrant.

Of the new disciples, Haggin was the odd man out, a maverick who, in
Nicolas Slonimsky's characterization, "held unalterable opinions" and
"adopted a polemical manner of personal journalism, disregarding all conventional amenities." From the first, he was a proprietary Toscanini specialist, disdaining not only lesser musicians, but Toscanini disciples lesser than
himself. His judgments were terse, acidic, and sure, as these early specimens
show:

> The years have not caused Mr. Toscanini to feel differently about his
> tempos in the second movement [of Beethoven's Seventh] and the Trio
> of the third: they are faster than most; and he is right.

> [Toscanini's] performance of [Beethoven's] Eighth was a succession of
> the usual miracles of phrasing and tone.

> In the first movement [of Beethoven's Ninth, Toscanini] still imparts his
> own driving intensity—for the notion that Mr. Toscanini does not im-
> press anything of himself on the music he plays is, of course, absurd.

Like his maverick tone, Haggin's forum in *The Nation*, where his notices
appeared beside James Agee's on film, Clement Greenberg's on art, and
Joseph Wood Krutch's on theater, conferred credibility among intellectuals
who disdained the daily press.[13]

. . .

It speaks volumes for the virulence of the Toscanini cult that, even in the face of Downes's pious accountings of the "Toscanini rites" and Gilman's religious imagery, it incurred no sustained disinterested commentary in mainstream newspapers and periodicals. W. J. Henderson, while no Toscanini foe, seemed to be the only major New York critic sufficiently removed from the altar to suffer the old Toscanini fatigue. Complaining of "prima donna conductors" in 1934, he wrote: "Critical comment . . . is almost entirely directed to the 'readings' of mighty magicians of the conductor's wand. . . . Can [the public] ever again be trained to love music for its own sake and not because of the marvels wrought upon it by supermen?"[14]

But Henderson was an old guardsman on his last legs (he died in 1937 at age eighty-one); his gentlemanly rebukes could be ignored. The period's most combative cult opponents, meanwhile, were not credentialed observers of the musical scene but marginal provocateurs. One outstanding polemic appeared in the November 1930 issue of *American Mercury:* "Toscanini's Big Stick" by Edward Robinson:

> Ever since that hysterical evening at Carnegie Hall four years ago, when with extraordinary festivity he triumphantly returned to America as conductor of the New York Philharmonic Orchestra, Arturo Toscanini has steadily progressed along a path of unprecedented adulation and acclaim. With each succeeding concert the chorus of enthusiasm has mounted higher and higher, until by now he has become an object of intense, almost fetishistic adoration. The worshippers—recruited, since the recent European tour, from two continents—include critics and audiences alike. The former, with monotonous unanimity, publicly prostrate themselves, and the ticket buyers flock jubilantly along. Those who may remain unbelievers are silent in their dissent, reluctant, perhaps, to interpose a sceptic's smirk into a picnic that is being so hugely and so generally enjoyed.

Robinson objected not only to the cult but to its object. Toscanini's interpretive signature, in his view, was a "phenomenal capacity for maintaining a persistent tempo with the mechanical rigidity of a metronome." And he charged Toscanini with so manhandling the Philharmonic that players who had excelled under Mengelberg now sounded dull or anxious.

Such writings, seldom seen in any event, were lost on Downes and Gilman. There was, however, one area of Toscanini criticism which elicited, if not actual concern, a concerted substantive response in the pages of the *Times* and the *Herald Tribune,* and this was repertoire. Here, the Toscanini critics included the cultists themselves, who regularly complained that Toscanini allotted too much rehearsal and concert time to music of little worth—in particular, to Italian miniatures by the likes of Martucci, Tommasini, and Leone Sinigaglia. A second, more sweeping criticism of the Toscanini repertoire, not endorsed by the cultists, was that too much time was allotted to warhorses by Beethoven, Brahms, and Wagner, crowding out new and/or American music. Unusually blunt versions of the latter were delivered by the composers Daniel Gregory Mason, Marc Blitzstein, and Douglas Moore. Mason, in *Tune In, America* (1931), called Toscanini's concerts "museums of the masterpieces of musical art in the past," servicing "fashion-enslaved, prestige-hypnotized minds." Blitzstein wrote in the January 1932 issue of *Modern Music* that "this otherwise wonderful conductor has either the most execrable taste in contemporary music, or else a wanton and cynical attitude on the subject which makes one wonder if his artistic conscience is limited to music before 1900." Moore, in a 1934 exchange with Lawrence Gilman in the *Herald Tribune,* charged the Philharmonic with standing "at the bottom of the list of major American orchestras in its encouragement of the creative spirit of today."[15]

Both Downes and Gilman conceded that Toscanini programmed too much negligible Italian music. Taking up the repertoire question in his Sunday column of November 22, 1931, Downes further called Toscanini's neglect of American composers "his greatest weakness as a program maker" but added: "Of course, the day of the American orchestral composer waits partly upon the day of the brilliant and authoritative American conductor." With regard to recent letters voicing further complaints, Downes had appealed to Arthur Judson for "first hand information on a number of . . . points." He proceeded to quote at length from a "long and interesting letter" he had received from Judson in reply, beginning:

> Mr. Judson submits . . . that certain classic compositions specified in the *Times* of October 25 by William M. Strong "not to be played for from two to five years" should, on the contrary, be heard "not only once a season but some of them several times a season. The objection to the performance of these works lies in our attitude toward music. In place of listening to works as one does to the plays of Shakespeare, for example, as really great works, we listen to the interpretation of this or that prima donna conductor. That being the case, it is no wonder we get tired of them. We Americans are too anxious for the sensational and too little concerned with the content of the work. I am beginning to sense a

change in the right direction, and I believe within the next few years the Beethoven Fifth, no matter how badly played, will be welcomed because of the message it conveys. . . ."

Judson also wrote to Downes: "There are certain composers like Bruckner and Mahler who have not yet been accepted heartily by the American public. Certain of their works are played from time to time and it may be that they will gradually attain their permanent place in the repertory. . . . We can only go as far as the public will go with us." This pronouncement by the Philharmonic's manager and prepotent "salesman of fine music," reproduced without demur, summarized policies few major conductors of any period would have sanctioned: for familiar music, Judson prescribed frequent performances; for unfamiliar music, a wait-and-see policy. His rebuke of prima donna conductors was self-interested. Toscanini, whose authority he resented, hurt ticket sales for other Philharmonic conductors; to Otto Klemperer, Judson once remarked: "This Toscanini is going to ruin our business."*[16]

Compared to Downes, Gilman volunteered a more systematic and informative response to the repertoire question. His core arguments appeared

---

*Born in 1881 in Dayton, Ohio, Judson was America's supreme musical power broker in the 1930s and -40s. He was a violinist as a young man and headed the music department at Denison University from 1900 to 1907. In addition to the New York Philharmonic, which he managed from 1922 to 1956, his bases were the Philadelphia Orchestra, which he managed from 1915 to 1935, and his own concert bureau, out of which he created the nation's largest bureau, Columbia Concerts (later Columbia Artists), in 1930. He also presided over Community Concerts, a key Columbia subsidiary. He was a founder of the Columbia Broadcasting System, of which he remained the second largest individual stockholder. At Columbia Concerts, he managed practically all major conductors active in the United States excepting Toscanini, as well as important instrumentalists. Orchestras across the country sought and took his advice on which conductors and soloists to engage. Though he denied it, he also influenced repertoire. Leopold Stokowski, with whom he battled over programming in Philadelphia, called him "a natural enemy of new music."[17] Of the principal conductors with whom Judson dealt as manager of the New York Philharmonic, Toscanini was a law unto himself. Judson tolerated the adventurous programming of Dimitri Mitropoulos (1950–58). As we shall see, he crossed swords with Artur Rodzinski (1943–47). His influence over Toscanini's youthful successor, John Barbirolli (1936–43), is suggested by an exchange of letters (March 5 to September 17, 1936) in which he can be observed shaping repertoire for Barbirolli's first stint with the orchestra (see Appendix A). Judson was ousted as head of Columbia Artists in 1948 but remained with the firm until 1963. He founded a rival management company at the age of 82, then died in 1975. (For more evidence of Judson's antipathy toward American music, see Claire Reis's *Composers, Conductors and Critics* [1955]. For a more positive view of Judson, see Philip Hart's *Orpheus in the New World* [1973] and Cecil Smith's *Worlds of Music* [1952].)

in a series of Sunday columns written in response to letters similar to those Downes received. Replying on May 25, 1930, to a disgruntled Toscanini admirer, he analyzed Toscanini's 1929–30 Philharmonic programs and wrote:

> Mr. Toscanini gave in the Borough of Manhattan 230 performances of individual works, and of these 230 performances more than two-thirds (160, to be precise) were of compositions which are either acknowledged masterpieces, or works of such salience and distinction—as Ravel's *Bolero* and Borodin's *Polovetzian Dances,* for instance—that there could be no question of their acceptability on a symphonic program. In view of this showing, is it quite fair to charge Mr. Toscanini with giving us a paucity of good music? We think not.

At the same time, Gilman observed:

> We think it may fairly be said that [Toscanini] is, for an exceptionally fine-grained artist, often strangely insensitive to the presence of inferior qualities in a musical composition. . . . Going through his repertoire for the last four years in New York one could weep over the memory of the paltry works upon which this superlative artist has squandered golden hours and Heaven knows what reserves of energy and devotion.
>
> But there is nothing to be done about it. Realists accept the fact that Mr. Toscanini is a law unto himself. . . . One takes him or leaves him. Most concert-goers prefer to take him. Speaking for ourselves, we confess that we would rather hear Mr. Toscanini conduct a performance of the C major scale than hear Mr. Batonovich or Mr. Fortepiano conduct a performance of the First Symphony of Brahms.

On February 8, 1931, Gilman examined Toscanini's 1930–31 repertoire to date and reached similar conclusions:

> We have no intention of claiming that Mr. Toscanini is an ideal program-maker; but "right is right," as Mr. Bingle used to insist; and we suspect that those who have charged Mr. Toscanini with neglecting good composers in favor of composers less good have not examined the records in the case. . . .
>
> What the record shows . . . is that performances of music by old and modern masters on Mr. Toscanini's programs so far this season have greatly outnumbered his performances of music by inferior composers. The proportion, it will be noted, is 4 to 1 (seventy-six representations of music by the masters, nineteen of music by the others).

Gilman's most revealing defense of Toscanini's programs appeared on June 15, 1930, answering these letters from B. H. Haggin and from a retired music critic, Charles L. Buchanan:

Dear Mr. Gilman:

Reading and re-reading your [column of May 25], I am impelled to ask whether a concert is given in order that a conductor may conduct the C major scale superlatively well, or in order that music may be heard, even if played less than superlatively well. Implied in the law which Mr. Toscanini is unto himself is the assumption that a concert is given in order that a conductor may conduct, and in practice that is why it *is* given. You accept Mr. Toscanini's law because you accept the assumption, as most people do. But in theory, concerts are given in order that all music may be heard which should be heard.

I feel that you accept Mr. Toscanini's law too easily. It is by no means true that he must behave as outrageously as he does if he is to produce his performances; I have no doubt that when he began to conduct he did not behave in that way. But discovering that he could indulge his temper and not suffer the usual consequences, he indulged it. And not only temper, but everything connoted by what you call "law unto himself.". . .

B. H. Haggin

Dear Sir:

. . . As regards Mr. Toscanini's programs a nice question arises: What good purpose is served by importing Mr. Toscanini to play for us for the thousandth time the *Liebestod* or the Brahms D major Symphony to the neglect of Carpenter's *Skyscrapers*, Grainger's *Spoon River*, Gershwin's *Rhapsody in Blue*? Is it ignorance or just plain snobbishness (the latter always a concomitant of an uncultured person or people) which keeps these works off a Philharmonic program? Furthermore, has Mr. Toscanini or any conductor, for that matter, a right to indulge his individual likes and dislikes before an audience in which there are no doubt many persons that would enjoy hearing an occasional bit of Grieg, Chabrier, Tchaikovsky? . . .

Charles L. Buchanan

On preferring Toscanini's C major scale to another conductor's Brahms First, Gilman now wrote:

We hasten to assure [Mr. Haggin] that we still hold to that preference. . . . Some of us would rather hear Wanda Landowska play a single bar

of Mozartean ornamentation than hear Mr. Poundergood play the whole
of the D minor Concerto. We would rather hear Friedrich Schorr sing
"Das Ende! Das Ende!" in the second act of *Die Walküre* than hear the
ordinary German baritone sing the entire role of Wotan. . . .

Finally, addressing a crucial issue, Gilman argued:

> There is implicit in the letters of both our correspondents the assump-
> tion that music is independent of the great interpreter: that the inter-
> preter (the conductor, in this case) is needed only for the purpose of
> directing the music's course and keeping it in order, like a kind of
> symphonic traffic policeman; and that any competent policeman is good
> enough for the purpose.
>
> But that, alas, is a fallacy. The secrets of great music do not lie open
> to the mastery of any honest, God-fearing mediocrity . . . who chooses
> to peer into its baffling eyes. The blunt truth is that only a great conduc-
> tor is good enough to conduct great music. Only a great conductor, in
> fact, can bring it to life. We are not hearing the C minor Symphony of
> Brahms at all when we hear it at the hands of a mediocre conductor. We
> are being fooled by a dummy and a ventriloquist. . . .
>
> All music that is worth the mystical and agonizing process of re-
> creation can be fully released from its casing of lifeless symbols only by
> those choice and singular artists who bring to it the paradoxical blend
> of imperious will and profound humility which the great interpreter
> exhibits. It is unfortunately true that the great interpreter, like other
> artists of genius, is likely, as our correspondents complain, to be "outra-
> geous," "dictatorial," "inconsiderate," imperfectly domesticated. He is
> likely, in brief, to be impossible. . . . But catch him as he studies or
> prepares the *Eroica,* or that *Liebestod* which Mr. Buchanan thinks must
> now be squeezed quite dry after a thousand handlings—catch him then,
> and it is possible that you may think of him for the moment not as an
> arrogant, intractable egoist, but as brother to the knight "who has knelt
> through his long office, and who has the piety of his office."

No less than Downes when he likened Toscanini's "glorious and des-
potic sway" to his intransigent antifascism, Gilman defended behavior that
had embarrassed members of the Philharmonic itself. Both writers thrilled
to the spectacle of cowering players and smashed batons.

As aired in the mainstream press, the debate over Toscanini's repertoire
fitfully elucidated basic questions concerning the Philharmonic's place in

New York's cultural life. But it crucially elucidated the posture of the Toscanini adherents. Downes and Gilman were actually not bothered by the paucity of American music on Toscanini's programs. They seemed indifferent to the paucity of contemporary European music. And they liked hearing the warhorses over and over again.

This regressive bias was not the outcome of dogmatic narrowness. As any perusal of their writings on new music will show, neither critic was closed-minded. Gilman tried to be judiciously appreciative when confronting the unknown. Downes was eagerly curious—quick to praise or vilify, and just as quick to change his mind. But in a period of compositional quest and experimentation, both clung to the old-fashioned notion that music succeeded according to the veracity, strength, and virtuousness of personalized feelings it—and its interpreters—embodied. Post-*Sacre* Stravinsky spoke a language they did not know. To the extent that the Second Viennese School used the language of Beethoven, Brahms, and Wagner, they did not hear it.[18] As for the newer Toscanini disciples, Chotzinoff, Taubman, and Haggin were no better versed in the latest European and American music, and Chotzinoff and Haggin seemed distinctly less interested in it.

Increasing critical indifference or hostility toward what music Toscanini ignored focused renewed scrutiny on what music he performed. In addition to the always unpopular samplings of minor twentieth-century Italians, a growing body of nineteenth-century works was pronounced unworthy of Toscanini. Downes, more than Gilman, introduced this element of highbrow discrimination—as when, reviewing the Philharmonic concert of October 10, 1929, he devoted four long paragraphs to Brahms's Third Symphony, which Toscanini had never before conducted in New York, and three long paragraphs to Dawn and Siegfried's Rhine Journey from *Götterdämmerung,* which Toscanini had extracted and arranged somewhat differently than others had. Regarding the remainder of the program, he wrote: "Why the revival of trivial music by Rossini, and of what worth the claptrap score of Tommasini?" The latter, his Variations on "Carnival of Venice," was a premiere found to be based on "certain of the showy and meretricious 20 variations which Paganini invented for a cheap theme." The former, the Overture to *L'Italiana in Algeri,* was "perfectly conventional operatic fustian, written for the days and the public which never listened to the overture to an opera, anyhow." When in January 1936 Toscanini gave important first American performances of Cherubini's Symphony in D and the Verdi String Quartet (as arranged for string orchestra), Downes wrote: "The Cherubini symphony has beautiful measures but is repetitious and in sum tedious. . . . Nor can very much more be said for Verdi's string quartet symphony . . . though it is richer music."[19]

Downes was even capable of loftily dismissing the "Pastoral" Symphony as "a work which for all its charm has never ranked among the great creations of Beethoven." Chotzinoff, writing in a similar vein, reached a different conclusion when he renumbered the Beethoven symphonies "in accordance with the true position of each in the spiritual scale. They would follow then, perhaps, in this order: No. 1, 2, 4, 5, 3, 7, 8, 6, 9." But it was the taciturn Haggin who carried the hair-splitting to its apex as Toscanini's Philharmonic period drew to a close. Writing in the *Brooklyn Daily Eagle*, he thought nothing of protesting the inclusion in a Beethoven program of "such a comparatively feeble work" as the Violin Concerto, or—in the face of two Martucci pieces, Dukas's *Sorcerer's Apprentice*, and Richard Strauss's *Death and Transfiguration*—recording his "resentment" that Toscanini should devote himself "to anything less than the finest, the greatest music."[20]

Gilman had already wept "over the memory of the paltry works" upon which Toscanini had "squandered golden hours" in the context of arguing that "only a great conductor is good enough to conduct great music." The argument now emerging was that only great music was good enough for a great conductor. The Toscanini disciples would become guardians of a canon of masterpieces—in Haggin's phrase, "the finest, the greatest music" —of which Toscanini was the one great purveyor. This holy of holies— even Beethoven's Violin Concerto and "Pastoral" Symphony could not gain admittance—would comprise the best of Haydn, Mozart, Beethoven, Schubert, Brahms, and Wagner, with gilding by Mendelssohn, Berlioz, Debussy, and Richard Strauss. No premiere, no enterprising revival could give greater pleasure than a certified major work. As Downes put it upon hearing Toscanini conduct *Ein Heldenleben* following seventeen Philharmonic performances under three conductors the preceding eight seasons: "Mr. Toscanini interpreted this score for the first time in New York, and a first time by Toscanini can well be more important than a novel composition."[21]

To give Toscanini his due, notwithstanding his admitted weakness for Italian cameos, he stuck as close to the canon of acknowledged masterpieces as any disciple could have reasonably desired. Of his eleven Philharmonic seasons, during four of which he led fewer than thirty New York concerts, seven included performances of the *Tristan* Prelude, seven included performances of the *Eroica* Symphony, eight included performances of the Brahms "Haydn" Variations, and nine included performances of the *Meistersinger* Prelude. All told, works by Beethoven, Brahms, and Wagner made up 40 percent of his programs—about one-third more than the American orchestral norm. Beethoven alone constituted nearly 20 percent of Toscanini's New York repertoire—about twice the national average.[22]

Moreover, Toscanini's infrequent deviations from the "finest and greatest" were so mild as to be inconsequential. He caused some annoyance with Honegger's *Pacific 231*, dismissed by Chotzinoff as "a piece of modernist hardtack." Following Koussevitzky's lead, Toscanini presented Roussel's Fourth Symphony when it was new; Downes found it "pretty effeminate," and Chotzinoff wrote that "like most modern music it is a cadaver, without sense or soul." Not once, however, did Toscanini offer a composition by Bartók, Hindemith, or Mahler. The only Prokofiev he conducted was the "Classical" Symphony. The only Ravel was *Boléro* and the second *Daphnis et Chloé* Suite; the only Stravinsky, *Fireworks* and excerpts from *Petrouchka*. The only American works he conducted—none of which he took on tour to Europe—were Abram Chasins's *Flirtation in a Chinese Garden* and *Parade*, Howard Hanson's Symphony No. 2, Ernest Schelling's *Impressions from an Artist's Life*, Bernard Wagenaar's Symphony No. 2, and Hans Wetzler's *The Basque Venus* (though both Wagenaar and Wetzler were foreign born, Wagenaar took American citizenship, and Wetzler's parents were American). As for his controversial Italian loyalties, the only one of twenty-two Italian composers to challenge the predominance of Beethoven and Wagner on Toscanini's Philharmonic programs was his friend Respighi, whose music turned up in nine of Toscanini's eleven seasons, including five seasons' worth of *Pines of Rome*. Stravinsky, who observed Toscanini in rehearsal at La Scala in 1926, remarked in his autobiography: "What a pity it is that his inexhaustible energy and his marvellous talents should almost always be wasted on such eternally repeated works that no general idea can be discerned in the composition of his programs, and that he should be so unexacting in the selection of his modern repertory!" In Toscanini's own view, cited repeatedly in the American press, he was dedicating himself to "coming nearer to the truth" of the Classical and Romantic masters; younger conductors could seek out new music, as he himself once had done. His disinclination to tangle with thorny contemporary works was partly the result of a technical problem: as a number of musicians have testified, he had difficulty beating complex rhythms. According to Winthrop Sargeant: "There were passages even in Strauss's *Till Eulenspiegel* that taxed his sense of rhythmic orientation. He never attempted Stravinsky's *Sacre du printemps*, and I am sure that if he had it would have proved an almost impossible ordeal for him." The crux of Toscanini's aversion to new music, however, was sheer distaste. The works he heard at contemporary music concerts in 1925 and 1926 enraged him. Of Bartók's tonal, traditionally structured *Music for Strings, Percussion, and*

Celesta, he told Artur Rodzinski: "If *that* is music, I leave it to you, the younger generation. It says nothing to me."[23]

In lieu of innovation, the most exotic features of Toscanini's Philharmonic programs were idiosyncratic groupings from among his favorite works. In particular, his preference for upbeat endings forced odd shifts of style and mood. He would finish a concert with the Good Friday Spell from *Parsifal* followed by *Till Eulenspiegel;* or the *Parsifal* Prelude plus excerpts from Franck's *Psyché* and Smetana's *The Moldau;* or the Prelude and *Liebestod* from *Tristan* plus Tchaikovsky's *Romeo and Juliet.* Toscanini treated Siegfried's Funeral March as a bloody filet mignon, with, say, the Nocturne and Scherzo from *A Midsummer Night's Dream* as hors d'oeuvres and the *Euryanthe* Overture or *Pines of Rome* for dessert.

To listeners like Charles Buchanan, Toscanini's high hand in these matters seemed self-serving. In retrospect, Toscanini's programs served the cult in even more ways than Buchanan and other gadflies perceived. However unwittingly, his propagation of acknowledged masterpieces meant propagating the repertoire of maximum mass appeal. It meant drawing attention to Toscanini interpretations of masterpieces frequently heard under other batons. For that matter, since the masterpiece canon excluded both the baroque and impersonal modern modes, it inherently glorified the conductor, whose job it was to absorb and radiate the noble or tender personal sentiments with which its overtures, suites, and symphonies (Toscanini infrequently conducted concertos) were imbued. Finally, the canon was indifferently served by Toscanini's American rivals. With the passing of Nikisch and Muck from the Boston scene, and of Seidl and Mahler from New York, Beethoven, Brahms, and Wagner were nearly orphaned save for Toscanini's sponsorship. Such luminaries as Sir Thomas Beecham, Furtwängler, Erich Kleiber, Otto Klemperer, Clemens Krauss, and Bruno Walter were all heard with the New York Symphony and/or the New York Philharmonic, but only as guests. Koussevitzky in Boston and Stokowski in Philadelphia were major figures, but not for their readings of the German warhorses. Walter Damrosch, conductor of the New York Symphony prior to its absorption by the Philharmonic in 1928, was a good program maker but a routinier. And the German repertoire at the Metropolitan, once the province of Seidl, Mahler, and Toscanini himself, had been relegated to Artur Bodanzky. In Europe, meanwhile, Furtwängler was more than ever hailed as Nikisch's successor. Muck remained active in Hamburg until 1933, when he moved on to Stuttgart. Beecham was London's reigning conductor through 1941. Kleiber remained director of the Berlin Opera until 1934, after which South America became his base. Klemperer was a leading Berlin conductor until 1933; his term with the fledgling Los Angeles Philharmonic (1933–39) did not end his relative

American obscurity. Krauss directed the Vienna State Opera until 1934, then undertook major posts in Berlin and Munich. Walter led the Leipzig Gewandhaus Orchestra until 1930 and thereafter conducted in Vienna; in 1938, he moved to France.

For all their popularity, the acknowledged masterpieces lacked inspired exponents in the United States during Toscanini's New York Philharmonic tenure.

Only against a hundred-year backdrop of orchestral culture can one appreciate the full irrelevance of Toscanini's stiffening allegiance to the canonic symphonies.

The first important conductors, it must be recalled, conducted quantities of new music. Most were themselves important composers: Weber, Mendelssohn, Berlioz, Liszt, Wagner. Not until around 1870 did orchestras consolidate a museum identity as showcases for dead masters.* Concurrently, with Bülow and then Nikisch, a species of virtuoso performance-specialists took up the baton. Even so, a number of prominent conductors continued to dabble in composition; others—Mahler and Strauss, above all —continued the lineage of august composer-conductors. As before, every conductor of consequence sponsored contemporary music. Wagner, Brahms, Bruckner, Mahler, and Strauss all enjoyed prominent podium advocates. Even such modernists as Stravinsky, Schoenberg, Berg, and Hindemith did not altogether lack major sponsorship during the early decades of the twentieth century. Meanwhile, in America, exposure to contemporary symphonic music followed the same pattern, insofar as the outstanding symphonic conductors—Nikisch, Muck, Seidl, Mahler—were the same on two continents. Theodore Thomas, the one important exception, did more than his share to keep the United States abreast of European developments. When the American symphonic milieu grew more distinct after World War I, Koussevitzky and Stokowski were leaders, as were Klemperer (like Furtwängler, himself a productive composer) and others abroad, in maintaining allegiance to the contemporary scene.

---

*The repertoire of the Leipzig Gewandhaus Orchestra, with a continuous history from the late eighteenth century, shows these percentages of works by dead composers: 13 percent in 1781–85, 23 percent in 1820–25, 39 percent in 1828–34, 48 percent in 1837–47, 61 percent in 1850–55, 76 percent in 1865–70. The repertoires of Vienna's Gesellschaft der Musikfreunde, London's Philharmonic Society, and Paris's Société des Concerts shifted comparably after 1850. And yet as late as 1840 most Viennese and Parisian concertgoers denigrated the notion that the greatest music might be music of the past.[24]

In one respect, however, American orchestras could not import or emulate Old World practices. American composers had no fixed place in a musical community modeled after German norms. As early as 1854, William Henry Fry and George Bristow, New York's two best-known mid-century orchestral composers, stirred a furor over the Philharmonic's "systematized effort to extinguish American music": in its twelve years of existence, Bristow fumed in the press, the Philharmonic Society had seen fit to program "either by mistake or accident, one single American composition, an overture of mine."* Yet the German stranglehold on repertoire actually strengthened after the Civil War.** More than before, missionary efforts were made in behalf of the literature of earnestness and moral uplift, with Beethoven as its apex. When in 1874 Theodore Thomas wrote that "my aim has been to make good music popular," he was vouching not for a cross section of periods and styles, but for the German symphonic classics. Eight years later, as conductor of the New York Philharmonic, he enunciated a "Philharmonic Creed": "To endeavor always to form a refined musical taste among the people by the intelligent selection of music; to give, in order to accomplish the desired result, only standard works, both of the new and old masters, and to be thus conservative and not given to experimenting with the new musical sensations of the hour." And in his autobiography Thomas wrote: "The man who does not understand Beethoven and has not been under his spell has not half lived his life. The master works of instrumental music are the language of the soul and express more than those of any other art."[25]

World War I, as Muck and Kunwald suffered to find out, weakened German symphonic hegemony in America. Simultaneously—and not so coincidentally—the American composer came of age. Aaron Copland has written: "Contemporary music as an organized movement in the USA was born at the end of the First World War." In addition to Copland, those who severed the umbilical cord to Germany included George Antheil, Henry Cowell, George Gershwin, Howard Hanson, Roy Harris, Walter Piston, Wallingford Riegger, and Roger Sessions. Hanson took charge of the Eastman School of Music declaring: "The time is come for American creative art with its freshness, wholesomeness and freedom from the decaying thought of Europe, to take its place as a world leader"; he organized his American Composers Concerts in 1925. Of the major American orchestras, the Boston Symphony was the most patriotic: during his twenty-five-

---

*Actually, the Philharmonic had also performed the Americans Dodworth and Mason.

**See page 28.

year tenure (1924–49), Koussevitzky (who would tell his players, "The next Beethoven vill from Colorado come!") gave premieres of sixty-six American works, many of which he programmed more than once. Walter Damrosch, at the head of the New York Symphony, commissioned Gershwin to compose his piano concerto; Damrosch also performed new works by Copland, Hanson, and Deems Taylor, among other Americans.[26] The New York Philharmonic, too, ended its neglect of native-born talent: whatever his stature as an interpreter, Mahler's successor, Josef Stransky, programmed more performances of American compositions than all his predecessors combined. Even Willem Mengelberg, a celebrity conductor based in Holland, led the Philharmonic in music by Rubin Goldmark, Henry Hadley, Hanson, Ernest Schelling, and Taylor. Hadley himself, as the Philharmonic's associate conductor from 1920, presided over the so-called "Greater Americanization of the Philharmonic": in the three seasons beginning in 1922–23, he conducted twenty concerts featuring twenty-three performances of American works.

The demise of the Americanization of the Philharmonic coincided with the advent of Arturo Toscanini. Overnight, the Philharmonic was transformed from a modern international dealership to a showcase for German antiquities. As in the days of Thomas and Seidl, "new music" meant Brahms, Wagner, and Strauss. Timely eight decades later were Bristow's and Fry's denunciations of "systematized efforts to extinguish American music," of concerts "devoted to the distant and the dead." Thomas's Philharmonic Creed of 1882, which he himself was too progressive to live up to, was first actualized by Toscanini, who more truly stressed "only standard works" and was not "given to experimenting with the new musical sensations of the hour."

Howard Shanet, the best and most recent historian of the Philharmonic, has summarized the Toscanini anomaly:

> The Philharmonic allowed itself to be distracted by considerations of glamor and prestige. Toscanini had shaped the Philharmonic into the most glorious musical instrument in America, but as far as its relevance to the musical needs of New York at that moment was concerned, it might just as well have been in Berlin or Vienna or Milan. Its superb performances were being used on the one hand to reinforce the already overbalancing weight of the German-Austrian music of the past in the background of the New York public, and on the other hand to parade before the jealous ears of American composers the works of Respighi, de Sabata, Tommasini, Martucci, Sinigaglia, Pizzetti, Busoni, Castelnuovo-Tedesco, Wolf-Ferrari, Bossi, and Sonzogno.[27]

The anomaly transcended the New York context. That great music required great performers, and great performers required great music, were new dictates. No major conductor previous to Toscanini had been so divorced from the important music of his time.

How did Toscanini feel about leaving new music "to the younger generation"? If this bothered him, he kept it to himself. The question nags because Toscanini's career to date had embodied an expansive, idealistic calling. As an operatic conductor, he had wrestled to make La Scala and the Metropolitan palaces of art, and to rescue opera from expedience, routine, and false glamour. He had proselytized for Wagner, *Pelléas*, and *Boris* when they were new to Italy. Later, when he concentrated on Verdi, his larger purpose was postwar Italian renewal.

But if Verdi in Milan had been conducive to national pride, Beethoven in New York was conducive to cultural self-neglect. It is true that Toscanini made the Philharmonic a greater orchestra than it had been. But it was already a great orchestra when he arrived, and thriving. It is true that Beethoven seemed a timely antidote to Fascist belligerence abroad. But Toscanini would have programmed Beethoven in New York anyway. After decades of grueling operatic work, he wanted to conduct the symphonic classics. With the Philharmonic, the opportunity was ready-made. Never before had Toscanini's mission been so preponderantly personal. He continued to live in Milan, Mussolini notwithstanding. His friends were Italians.

It was not Toscanini but the cultists who determined that America would host his culminating mission in life. As the messiah of music, Toscanini was observed spreading the gospel for Beethoven, Brahms, and Wagner throughout the New World—not as an interpreter, sullying the texts, but as a fundamentalist preacher extolling his canon of acknowledged masterpieces.

No less than the Germanic warhorses cramming Toscanini's Philharmonic repertoire, his appointed Philharmonic mission signified a regression to the nineteenth century: the unpredicted reappearance of Theodore Thomas–style "sermons in tones." As formulated by the cult, the rationale of Toscanini's music education campaign was communal moral uplift. In such a mouthpiece as Lawrence Gilman, the very stiffness of Thomas's own moralizing pronouncements was evoked. If Toscanini himself made no pronouncements, it was just as well: to Thomas's evident incorruptibility he was perceived to add the lofty countenance of a Paderewski, the charisma of a Caruso, the personal divinity of a Jenny Lind. His silence itself became a celebrity attribute, enhancing his reputation for probity.

One further, crucial attribute of the Toscanini mission ensured it would overshadow Theodore Thomas's educational legacy. Following Thomas's death in 1905, a pair of communications breakthroughs helped transform America's concert community from a leisured elite to a variegated mass public. The first regular radio broadcasting station, established in Pittsburgh in 1920, proved so successful that two years later 564 broadcasting stations were licensed in the United States alone. Electrical recording, implemented in 1925, transformed the phonograph's ability to reproduce the sound of a full orchestra. Conducting at the Metropolitan Opera House through 1915, Toscanini was primarily a local phenomenon. Conducting the New York Philharmonic, Toscanini was heard everywhere. Beginning in 1930, the Philharmonic's Sunday-afternoon concerts were carried by the Columbia Broadcasting System to an audience estimated in 1934 at nine million. The intermission commentators for these broadcasts included Olin Downes and Lawrence Gilman. In 1926 and 1929, Toscanini made his first electrical recordings—of Haydn's Symphony No. 101 (the "Clock") and Mozart's Symphony No. 35 (the "Haffner"), plus miniatures by Dukas, Gluck, Mendelssohn, Rossini, and Verdi—with the New York Philharmonic. In 1936, Toscanini and the Philharmonic recorded Beethoven's Seventh, the Brahms "Haydn" Variations, four Wagner excerpts, and two Rossini overtures.* As early radio and recordings characteristically thickened orchestral speech, the incisive, relatively lean Toscanini sound proved particularly adaptable. The impact of his 1936 recordings on the Depression-wracked, Toscanini-starved recordings market had trade magazines proclaiming "the return of the record."[28]

Unlike Leopold Stokowski, Toscanini himself was no eager adherent of the new technology. He disliked making recordings. Even more than refusing to articulate the messianic role his disciples had assigned him, he invariably spurned speaking requests. He would not have dreamed of speaking

---

*The New York Philharmonic archives show the following salaries for conductors recording with the Philharmonic between 1928 and 1936:

1928–29
Mengelberg: 7 sessions, 24 sides. Salary: $7,000
Toscanini: 7 sessions, 18 sides. Salary: $13,833.13
1929–30
Mengelberg: 6 sessions, 28 sides. Salary: $6,000
Toscanini: 1 session, 3 sides (including one remake). Salary: $1,833.34
1931–32
Beecham: 1 session, 10 sides. Salary: $750
1936
Toscanini: $1,833.33 per session

from the stage, as Stokowski and Walter Damrosch—both incorrigible "music for everyone" advocates—did when they wished to urge a friendly reception for unfamiliar works. Even when the Depression held the Philharmonic in its grip, Toscanini turned down appeals to speak over the radio in support of urgent fund-raising efforts.* Yet salesmanship was germane to the new mass media. If Toscanini would not promote himself and his product, others would do it for him.

As an opera autocrat, Toscanini had superintended every detail of production. In Milan, he was said to live at La Scala. But Toscanini's New York Philharmonic led a life of its own. He was not even music director in the accepted sense of the term. Arthur Judson was the orchestra's full-time administrator. Judson and Clarence Mackay were the long-range policy makers. When Toscanini was in New York, his word was law. When he was in Europe, others held sway. Never before had he relinquished so much responsibility. In fact, without realizing it—there was no way he could have known—the imperious Toscanini was relinquishing control of his American destiny.

Toscanini's departure from the New York Philharmonic followed a familiar pattern. The first round of rumors circulated in the fall of 1935. "The possibility that Arturo Toscanini may retire as conductor and general musical director of the New York Philharmonic-Symphony Orchestra at the end of this season became known yesterday," the *Times* reported on November 19, and other papers followed suit. Toscanini's age (sixty-eight) and health problems (recurrent shoulder and arm pains) were the stated reasons for his possible departure. The Philharmonic Society now revealed that Toscanini's retirement had been "regarded as imminent for two or three years," and broached the possibility of shortening the season should the Philharmonic become Toscanini-less. Samuel Chotzinoff, in the *Post*, pondered a more severe contingency plan: "Would it not . . . be the better part of wisdom to abandon our symphony concerts for a season, or until Mr. Toscanini's influence over us has vanished? It may take one year or five. . . . When that moment arrives we can start all over again with a clean slate."[29]

Within a day of the first alarms, Toscanini was reported denying,

---

*But he did sanction a 1934 fund initiated in his name. Contributors received a card "from Toscanini" with a Toscanini photograph and signature facsimile. It read: "Your reply to the appeal on my birthday for contributions for the Philharmonic-Symphony Society campaign fund has deeply touched me and I wish you to accept my heart-felt thanks."

through a spokesman, that he had any intention of leaving the Philharmonic. The issue resurfaced upon his arrival, January 17, 1936, on the French liner *Lafayette*—an event described in the New York *American* as igniting a "near riot." When reporters clambered aboard the docked ship to pursue their retirement inquiries, Toscanini bolted down two flights of stairs and locked himself in his stateroom, from within which he could be heard conversing in rapid, high-pitched tones. His eventual disembarkation was shielded by a shoving, impromptu bodyguard including his wife, who, as portrayed in a *Herald Tribune* report, "spread her arms with the protective belligerence of a hen which has sighted a hawk." Glowering behind raised coat lapels, Toscanini refused to parley. Mrs. Toscanini, described as "slightly less taciturn," denied the retirement rumors on her husband's behalf.

Behind the scenes, Toscanini was in fact slipping away from Mackay and Judson. Hoping to reduce Depression deficits, the Philharmonic had first, in 1934, considered merging with the Metropolitan Opera, then, a year later, thought of shrinking the orchestra. Though Toscanini's vetoes proved decisive in both instances, the proposals perturbed him. Then the society inflicted further injury by failing to consult Toscanini before engaging Sir Thomas Beecham, whom Toscanini considered a dilettante, to conduct for three weeks in 1935–36. By early 1935, the Philharmonic was volunteering incentives and concessions to no avail. The board's formal announcement, on February 13, stated: "After a half century of continuous conducting, the Maestro feels the necessity for a release from the great responsibility of presiding as music director of a permanent orchestra." The possibility of a shortened 1936–37 season was again aired, as was the Chotzinoff plan: if the musicians' union was not amenable to less work for less pay, the board warned, the orchestra might be disbanded.

Toscanini's final 1935–36 appearances with the Philharmonic were believed by many to be his final appearances in the United States. Everything he meant to Americans—his seven years with the Metropolitan Opera, his 1920–21 tour with the Scala orchestra, his eleven years of service to the Philharmonic, his symbolism as a champion of democracy in Europe and divine culture bearer for the New World—would be consummated in two great events: the season's closing subscription concert on the Sunday afternoon of April 26, 1936, and a special farewell concert three days later.

The rites of farewell befitted the occasion. Manifestations of reverence, friendship, and hysteria commingled in one mighty paean. At the April 26 concert, the program for which consisted of Mozart's G minor Symphony, K. 550, Beethoven's *Leonore* Overture No. 3, and Schubert's "Great" C major Symphony, the culminating ovation was judged by Olin Downes

"the greatest demonstration this writer has ever seen in a concert auditorium" and by Lawrence Gilman "unparalleled in recent musical history."
The audience remained on its feet for fifteen minutes; not half a dozen
persons were seen leaving the hall. Even after dismissing the orchestra,
Toscanini was recalled repeatedly to the stage. Finally, he shut himself in
his dressing room and wept. Gilman, embroidering remarks from his Sunday column of April 5, read an intermission tribute beamed to millions of
radio listeners, concluding:

> Toscanini is leaving us; and we who have listened to him discerningly,
> season after season, are well aware of what we are about to lose. But we
> must face the fact with all possible fortitude and philosophy. We are
> confronted, as an American statesman once observed, with a condition
> and not a theory. Mr. Toscanini, vicar of the Immortals, is bound by
> mortal laws. He has served the Immortals long and gloriously, and with
> incomparable devotion; and now he would lighten his burden. He is
> sixty-nine years old. He would conduct when he chooses—not when
> conducting becomes burdensome and exhausting. And so we must do
> without him.
>
> To minimize his loss would be an act of treachery toward our assumed
> allegiance to that ideal of lofty and self-effacing service which this great
> artist has exemplified. It would be an act of gross ingratitude to an
> interpreter who has re-created the music of the masters with unforgetta-
> ble beauty and fidelity.[30]

Since the April 29 farewell, with music by Beethoven and Wagner, was
a nonsubscription event, the competition for seats added new drama to
Toscanini's already tumultuous leave-taking. Tickets, specially inscribed
with a facsimile of Toscanini's signature, were sold out the day the concert
was announced. Speculators drove ticket prices up to one hundred dollars
and more. Thirty minutes before concert time, 140 standing room places
went on sale. The line to the box office stretched eastward along the
sidewalk from Seventh Avenue to Sixth, where it buckled and sprawled
onto the street. When, at 8:16, standing room sales were announced closed,
a throng estimated at five thousand bore down on Carnegie Hall. A police
detachment of over sixty men, including five on horses, struggled to liberate
the main entrance. Two mounted policemen were swept against a wall.
Over one hundred ticket seekers managed to pour through a fire escape and
into a balcony before police plugged the leak and arrested four men. Some
in the crowd claimed to have purchased standing room on the fire escape
itself. Postconcert, however, the anticipated clamor inside the hall was cut
short: the applause had barely begun when a photographer, later identified

as Frank Muto of Hearst's International News Photos, rushed to the edge of the stage and set off a flashbulb directly in Toscanini's face. While Muto fled from a contingent of policemen, Toscanini, whose extreme myopia rendered him susceptible to disorienting afterimages, staggered to the wings. Maurice Van Praag, the Philharmonic's personnel manager, appeared and told the dazed assemblage: "This is the saddest thing I have had to do in my twenty-odd years with the orchestra. Mr. Toscanini was almost blinded by that flash. He is too upset to take any bows. He is sorry. He asks me to say that he loves you all." The audience now hissed and booed at photographers taking pictures from the stage, then dispersed. Responding to hostile glares, Frank Muto, his camera confiscated, was heard to comment: "It might have been a good picture." Meanwhile, over the radio—CBS had broadcast the final forty-five minutes of the concert, the Beethoven selections having failed to dislodge "Gang Busters"—Van Praag's description of the "almost blinded" Toscanini was taken literally, so that radio stations coast-to-coast were besieged with telephone inquiries.

The next day's newspapers bubbled with accounts of the unruly ticket line, the mounted policemen, and the obnoxious flashbulb. The *Times* alone devoted three stories, totaling nearly one hundred column inches, to the event. The Toscanini disciples reacted variously. Chotzinoff signed off as follows: "So ended Mr. Toscanini's eleven years of service to the musical public of New York and, through radio, to the nation at large. The writer of this bare report is at the moment too much moved to extol this service or to contemplate a future without the presence of this peerless musician and great gentleman." Haggin, in the *Brooklyn Daily Eagle,* pronounced:

> In the course of its long musical life New York has seen notable careers end in memorable farewell performances, but none of these, I venture to say, has had the significance of Arturo Toscanini's farewell concert with the Philharmonic-Symphony Orchestra at Carnegie Hall last night. In these other instances one great artist passed, but others remained; when Mahler passed there was Muck, when Muck passed there was Toscanini, but the significance of last night's concert is that Toscanini passes and there is nobody with the same combination of gifts as conductor, musician and artist. . . . Last night the splendid Philharmonic-Symphony Orchestra of Arturo Toscanini, and Beethoven's music as they played it, passed out of existence together, and we shall hear nothing like them next year and many years thereafter.

Downes began: "The atrocious act of vandalism which followed Arturo Toscanini's concluding concert with the Philharmonic-Symphony Orchestra last night in Carnegie Hall put an abrupt and a shocking end to a demonstration which in the normal course of events would have been greater than the one of last Sunday afternoon when Mr. Toscanini conducted in the same place." Gilman alone managed to say something new about Toscanini on the occasion of his exodus. Passing over the likes of Liszt, Rubinstein, Bülow, Richter, Joachim, Busoni, Mahler, and Nikisch, he now proclaimed Toscanini "the greatest musical interpreter who ever lived." Gilman further wrote that "Toscanini's fame is probably without a parallel in the records of music," which fact he found "one of the major validations of our period and our race." He closed his review of Toscanini's last concert with this crowning epiphany:

> There are those who say that late last night, in Carnegie Hall, long after Toscanini and his orchestra and his listeners had gone to their refreshment or their rest, and the doors had been shut and bolted, and the lights put out, a group of Immortals gathered in the darkness and the quiet of the auditorium. It seemed as though infirmity had dropped from them. One, no longer deaf, listened quietly to one whose pain had gone; and this one, more easily articulate than the rest, was heard to say—it seemed with incredulity—"I am he that liveth, and was dead."

On May 2, the day Toscanini left for Europe aboard the French liner *Champlain,* three pertinent statements were issued to the press: a letter to Toscanini from President Roosevelt, expressing his appreciation "for all you have done for music during your stay among us"; a letter to the President from Toscanini, in which he seemed already overcome with nostalgia for the place he was leaving; and a rare public statement from Toscanini, which read in part:

> I depart from New York today after eleven years of happy association with its great orchestra. I should like this message to be taken as a personal good-bye and expression of heartfelt gratitude to the thousands of persons who have come to my concerts, to the men of my orchestra who have worked so faithfully and magnificently with me for all these many seasons, to the innumerable unknown friends throughout the country who have sent me messages and letters, and to the board of directors and the management of the Philharmonic-Symphony Society.
>
> The time has come for me to go, but I leave with deep regret. I shall never forget, as man or as conductor, any smallest detail of my life and work in America. . . .

To foil reporters, Toscanini boarded the *Champlain* hours early and locked himself in his cabin. A private detective stood guard at the door until the ship sailed.

The response to Toscanini's apparent retirement from United States concert life in 1936 seems hyperbolic half a century later. In fact, the confessions of despair, even the prescriptions of fortitude in the face of catastrophic loss, accurately reflected the extent of the Toscanini dependency. More than "the greatest musical interpreter who ever lived," Toscanini was the personification of great music, its appointed guardian and purveyor. Abroad, as America's supreme cultural emissary, he seemed to signify the New World come of age. He was actually irreplaceable.

For the venerable Philharmonic Society, Toscanini's services had incurred a further, financial dependency. He was, as the press put it, the Philharmonic's "only drawing card" during the Depression years. The higher his star ascended, the more lowly his rivals seemed. Guest conductors, even Otto Klemperer and Bruno Walter, sold fewer tickets. Hard times made empty seats unaffordable: during the Toscanini years, the Philharmonic's earned income generally fell, and its deficit generally increased.[31] The board's proposal to shorten the 1936–37 season arose from certain knowledge that the Toscanini cult had engendered a constituency whose first loyalty was neither to concert music nor to the Philharmonic.

While the cult would continue to flourish, for the Philharmonic per se Toscanini's legacy was surprisingly ephemeral. His sheer absence overshadowed his inheritable accomplishments. Rather than stability, his peculiarities had fostered a perpetual cycle of rescue and abandonment. As none could predict from one season to the next whether Toscanini would return, planning and programming had been piecemeal, not consolidating as in Boston and Philadelphia. It is true that, like Koussevitzky and Stokowski, Toscanini had molded a distinctive sound. But compared with theirs, this was a fragile achievement, based less on rooted habits than on a psychology of crisis that only Toscanini's presence could activate.

Normally, world-class orchestras retain distinguishing musical attributes even under unexceptional guest leaders. During the Toscanini years, the members of the Philharmonic behaved like truants even under exceptional guests. The perils faced by Toscanini's successor would be twice as great. The crucial question faced by the board was not whether to shorten the season or shrink the orchestra but who would take Toscanini's place. According to conventional wisdom, the question answered itself: there was only one Toscanini. As Chotzinoff had reasoned the preceding November, when the resignation rumors began (and when Klemperer was in the midst of a twelve-week stint with the Philharmonic, to be followed by twenty-four days of Beecham):

> It is by this time quite obvious that Toscanini is one of those curious manifestations of genius that occurs perhaps once in a century. He is incomparable in the very literal sense of the word, and it is not only unjust but cruel to apply his standards to his colleagues.
>
> It may be wise to admit that for the moment Toscanini has ruined the taste of Philharmonic-Symphony subscribers for any performances that fall short of the perfection he has accustomed them to. I think that if we are willing to admit that premise the problem of what to do about our orchestra will not appear so baffling as it now seems. Perhaps Mr. Stokowski or Dr. Koussevitzky, as head of the Philharmonic-Symphony, could solve the problem, but it is doubtful that these men would abandon their secure positions with their own orchestras to undertake so hazardous a venture. Short of these two possibilities there is literally no one either here or abroad who could carry on when Mr. Toscanini departs.[32]

Following the announcement of Toscanini's resignation on February 13, much attention focused on Stokowski, who was in fact disengaging himself from Philadelphia. Beecham and Klemperer were also considered front runners. Toscanini himself, however, nominated his most authentic rival: Wilhelm Furtwängler. To many in Europe, Furtwängler, if not "the greatest musical interpreter who ever lived," seemed Toscanini's superior in the German repertoire. As both Toscanini and Furtwängler were jealous colleagues who struck sparks when their paths crossed, Toscanini's recommendation came as a surprise. The New York Philharmonic itself had hosted the most extended Toscanini-Furtwängler confrontation, culminating in Furtwängler's exodus. Harvey Sachs speculates that Toscanini nominated Furtwängler "partly because he wished to give him a clear alternative to remaining in [Hitler's] Germany."[33] At the same time, one gathers from stray remarks that Toscanini respected the musician in Furtwängler.

While Furtwängler's reputation was more than ever concealed from Americans by the Toscanini cult, his activities occasionally gained notice in the American press. The perceived tensions between Furtwängler and Toscanini at the 1931 Bayreuth Festival did not go unreported. In May 1932, in a minor cause célèbre, Furtwängler was discovered likening American orchestras to "pet dogs" (*Luxushunden*) in a speech honoring the fiftieth anniversary of the Berlin Philharmonic. To Furtwängler, whose rapport with the New York Philharmonic's "dog owners" had not been smooth, the absence of government subsidies in the United States implied that orchestras were deemed less essential there than in Europe. When the "pet dogs" analogy stirred American resentment, he took pains to explain to the New York *Times* that he "intended to convey the idea that orchestras had grown to be more of a necessity to German communities than elsewhere on account of the greater age of German musical culture and national traditions, as compared with which American musical development is young."[34] This argument seemed merely to reinforce an underlying bias claiming German music as German spiritual property.

What mainly earned Furtwängler a place in United States newspapers in the years following his Philharmonic appearances, however, was the appointment of Adolf Hitler to the German chancellorship in January 1933. Soon enough, the Nazis were manhandling orchestras and opera companies. Furtwängler's response was more concealed, less concise than Toscanini's. Today, we can appreciate that, while he may have been a naive, unreconstructed nationalist, Furtwängler was no Nazi. At the time, the information received by Americans was incomplete and confused. In Furtwängler's favor, it was established that he had written an open letter to Joseph Goebbels protesting the persecution of Jewish musicians, refused to "Aryanize" his orchestra, invited Jewish soloists, written a second open letter defending Paul Hindemith against Nazi vilification, and finally, in November 1934, resigned from the Berlin Philharmonic and Berlin State Opera. Against Furtwängler, it was learned that he was a member of the Reich Music Chamber and a Prussian councillor of state, and that he had decided to return to Germany's tainted musical life as a "guest conductor" in April 1935. According to *Time,* it was also alleged that, as a "slave to Nazidom," he had been "slow to protest" when Jewish musicians were exiled from Germany, and that "the complaint he finally did register was either softened or withdrawn."[35]

All this preceded Toscanini's departure from the New York Philharmonic and his proposal that Furtwängler succeed him. Furtwängler was amenable, so long as he could continue conducting in Europe. The Philharmonic was amenable, so long as Furtwängler did not accept other permanent conducting posts. On February 28, 1936—fifteen days after disclosing Toscanini's resignation—the Philharmonic board named Furtwängler principal conductor for 1936–37. The Nazis then intervened, announcing Furtwängler's reinstatement as director of the Berlin State Opera—a reinstatement Furtwängler, in Cairo, was apparently not told about. Hitler's occupation of the Rhineland occurred on March 7. Two days later, Ira Hirschmann, a vice-president of Saks Fifth Avenue and a former Philharmonic board member, announced the formation of an anti-Furtwängler committee. Boycotts and mass cancellations of subscriptions were threatened. On March 15, Furtwängler withdrew by cable: "Political controversy disagreeable to me. Am not politician but exponent of German music which belongs to all humanity regardless of politics." *Time* reported his decision under the heading NAZI STAYS HOME.

In retrospect, this outcome seems inescapable. As of 1930, New York City's population of 6,930,446 was estimated to include 1.75 to 2 million Jews —and Jews were estimated to make up more than half the Philharmonic's audience. With Hitler's rabid anti-Semitism already embedded in German national policy, and Furtwängler serving Germany at Hitler's pleasure, Jews were bound to resist Furtwängler. Did Furtwängler's swift capitulation to Hirschmann's campaign reflect sudden sensitivity to American Jewish feelings? As likely, he considered his own sensitivity to Olin Downes and the Toscanini cult. And Goebbels reportedly warned Furtwängler he could not return to Germany if he left for New York. The German conductor Heinz Unger has written:

> It was obvious to me that political interference in matters of art, as everything else that happened in the Nazi era, must have been abhorrent to [Furtwängler], and the numerous cases of his intervention for victims of the system proved where he stood. But why, why had this man to whom the whole world would have been open, not left the Germany of Hitler, as so many other artists and scientists of pure "Aryan" origin had done? This was the question which so many of his friends in other countries asked themselves.
>
> Shortly after the war I received an indirect answer. It was in Barcelona where I happened to meet a conductor from Germany whom I had not seen since my own emigration, Franz von Hoesslin, a former Bayreuth conductor, later living in voluntary exile in Switzerland. I had known von Hoesslin in the old Berlin days, and we had a long and intimate conversation on that day in Barcelona. Our thoughts turned to Furtwängler. Why had he not left Germany? Hoesslin told me of his own conversations with Furtwängler on this subject. Yes, Furtwängler knew that he was likely to be welcomed everywhere in the world, if he should decide to turn his back on Germany, that he would probably be successful and celebrated wherever he went. But—would he be understood? Understood in the way he *wanted* to be understood? All his roots were in German music; leaving Germany would set him adrift. Not that he would not continue to serve that art to which he was most closely and most naturally bound; but would *his* way of playing music go to the hearts of his listeners in the same way as it did in Germany? Who outside Central Europe would realize or appreciate the difference between the message of Beethoven's Ninth Symphony as he felt it and—let us say— Toscanini's Beethoven? No, he needed his German audiences and orchestral players as much as they needed him, more than ever, in fact, in

those dark years; and so he stayed within the community into which he had been born.[36]

Some months after Furtwängler decided against taking over the Philharmonic, Toscanini saw him in Paris and criticized him for not having fought harder against Hirschmann. Yet Toscanini never saw fit to speak up for Furtwängler's candidacy; the announcements of Furtwängler's New York appointment did not even acknowledge Toscanini's recommendation. Yehudi Menuhin has pertinently remarked:

> [Toscanini] was totally intolerant of other conductors. . . . Following a concert I gave for the "restoration appeal" of La Scala in Milan [after World War II] which Toscanini attended, we sat at dinner together and he left no conductor unscathed and was encouraged in this by his followers and flatterers. I found myself feeling ever more isolated. I tried to recall a name which had not yet been mentioned, which had not yet been dismissed. I suggested that perhaps Bruno Walter was a conductor of quality.
> "A sentimental fool," was Toscanini's reply.

In his autobiography, Menuhin writes: "Toscanini, I believe, was partly responsible for New York's resistance to Furtwängler."[37]

The conductor the Philharmonic eventually chose to succeed Toscanini was the thirty-six-year-old John Barbirolli. The appointment was inauspicious: Barbirolli's prior posts were in Glasgow and Leeds; as recently as 1932, he had yet to conduct a Beethoven symphony. The kiss of death, however, was the one eventuality sure to confound the Philharmonic more than Toscanini's absence: his competing presence.

The NBC Symphony, 1937–45

*D*avid Sarnoff rose from rags to riches to command the first great electronic communications empire. His prominent keepsakes included portraits of Abraham Lincoln, born in a log cabin, and Guglielmo Marconi, self-taught in telegraphy. Of Sarnoff's career, Karl Compton, the president of the Massachusetts Institute of Technology, remarked: "[It] illustrates what can be accomplished when native ability, ambition, and character find scope in private enterprise in a land of opportunity." A *Life* film documentary called Sarnoff "the incarnation of the American Dream."[1]

Sarnoff was born in 1891 in a village of wooden huts in Russia. Nine years later, he entered the teeming melting-pot culture of New York City's Lower East Side. His first job was as a butcher's errand boy. By the age of thirteen he had left school and purchased a newsstand. Eight years later, as an American Marconi telegrapher with a craving for self-improvement, he won national attention when, singlehandedly, he transmitted news of the sinking *Titanic* for seventy-two hours without sleep. While others continued to see the "wireless" or "radio" mainly as a message service, he foresaw, in 1915, an inexpensive "radio music box" capable of disseminating concerts, lectures, athletic contests, and "events of national importance" to millions of homes, including many "far removed from cities." His prescience was rewarded in May 1921, when he became the boy-wonder general manager of the Radio Corporation of America, which had recently expropriated American Marconi. Not two months later, he engineered a landmark public relations coup, arranging blow-by-blow radio coverage of a championship boxing match between Jack Dempsey and France's Georges Carpentier. The event's patriotic appeal was buttressed by an appeal to humanitarianism: the American Committee for Devastated France received a share of the radio proceeds. As many as three hundred thousand were estimated to have heard the bout in theaters, lodge halls, ballrooms, and barns. Sarnoff was RCA's enthroned corporate mastermind by the time it spawned the National Broadcasting Company in 1926. In 1930, he was named RCA president. Meanwhile, the radio music box idea was mushrooming. The Depression actually helped: theater and film audiences diminished; home audiences grew. As of 1938, NBC owned over 142 broadcasting stations, furnishing access to virtually all of the 88 percent of American homes possessing one of 25 million radios. According to social workers, destitute families valued their radios over their refrigerators, furniture, or bedding. Broadcasting's potential for transforming public opinion was unprecedented, and Sarnoff knew it. In a 1924 message, he foresaw radio spreading "the supreme music, education and entertainment of the country," and contended that commercial stations should not only broadcast but pay for programs "contributed by public and educational interests." In 1927 he pronounced: "Through what other medium of communications could a musical, cultural, and entertainment service have been rendered to many millions of homes throughout the world? What other instrumentality developed by man bears a greater unifying force? By what means of communication could we have hoped to reach, simultaneously and effectively, unnumbered thousands of isolated homes throughout the country with the same message of education, information, or service as that now rendered by radio broadcasting?"[2]

And yet the phenomenal growth of radio was not matched by a concomitant "message of education, information, or service." In retrospect, the issue of government versus private control was crucial. Early on, it became apparent that various public radio proposals—for regulation of broadcasting as a public utility, for reserving a fixed percentage of wavelengths for a federal broadcasting chain, for government control at the municipal or state level—lacked sufficient backing to stave off commercial hegemony. Sarnoff, a key public radio opponent, at one point favored the creation of perhaps six "super power broadcast stations" to blanket the country, maintained and supported by the industry itself through a common fund of radio manufacturers and dealers. But the emerging reality, supported by the Department of Commerce, was less idealistic: toll broadcasting—the hiring of commercial radio facilities by advertisers. NBC and the rival Columbia Broadcasting System, founded in 1928, came to own or control nearly every high-power station. Simultaneously, advertising agencies became the producers of nearly all sponsored network shows, usually out of autonomous radio departments; as one radio advertising pioneer put it in 1928, the agencies were "planning the programs, engaging the artists, and writing the announcements, just as they prepare plans, copy, and art for printed advertisements."[3] The earliest radio programming had been an openminded potpourri of news, phonograph records, and local talent, of live music, storytelling, and lectures on every imaginable topic; after 1930, notwithstanding numerous quality offerings—including a plethora of live concert and opera broadcasts unequalled after World War II on AM, FM, or TV —standardized colloquial fare ruled the dial. The rambunctious "Amos 'n Andy," begun in 1928, was radio's first national hit, followed by a spate of vaudeville-format variety shows featuring Rudy Vallee, Eddie Cantor, and other celebrity hosts. Radio news was circumscribed by political censorship; pacifism, critiques of public utilities or banks, and the rise of organized labor were all typically deemed "too controversial." Commercials, minimal at first, grew longer, more numerous, more aggressive.

This swift deterioration of early ideals was noted and deplored. In Congress, the Wagner-Hatfield amendment, to set aside 25 percent of all radio frequencies for nonprofit broadcasting, won strong support. Though the amendment lost in 1934, the threat of government intervention in behalf of "educational radio" helped inspire NBC to make room for such pedagogic offerings as the "University of Chicago Round Table" and "America's Town Meeting of the Air." A comparable initiative was undertaken by CBS. Under William S. Paley, its president from 1928, the second network began a news service and banned commercials for laxatives. As of 1930, CBS broadcast the New York Philharmonic every Sunday afternoon. In 1937 a gripping radio play, Archibald MacLeish's "The Fall of the City," opened a CBS berth to ranking poets and dramatists. The CBS upsurge rankled Sarnoff, engendering a period of tit-for-tat competition. When in 1937 CBS inaugurated a Shakespeare series with Walter Huston, Burgess Meredith, and Edward G. Robinson, NBC retaliated with a Shakespeare series featuring the faded, fabled John Barrymore. To counter CBS's "American School of the Air," NBC began a "University of the Air" under James Rowland Angell, the retiring president of Yale University. To counter CBS's "Norman Corwin's Words Without Music," NBC devised its poetry series "Fables in Verse." But Sarnoff's trump, and the keystone of NBC's revitalized cultural bill, was its answer to CBS's New York Philharmonic broadcasts: Arturo Toscanini, the world's greatest conductor, presiding over NBC's own house orchestra from NBC's own Radio City studios.

Though credited to Sarnoff by NBC publicists, the Toscanini project originated with the vice-president in charge of programming, John Royal. In the venerable tradition of P. T. Barnum, James Henry Mapleson, and Oscar Hammerstein, Royal was an entrepreneur of bold instinct and broad experience. He had made his name in vaudeville and had also been press agent for Houdini. A magazine piece once described him as a "big, nervous, clever and didactic showman," "cheerful, confident, breezy," sweeping through NBC's corridors "like a white haired tornado." It was Royal who thought to hire Barrymore—because Barrymore's seemed the American theater's most legendary name. There was no question whose name was most legendary in music.[4]

Sarnoff needed no convincing that Toscanini would be NBC's most sensational acquisition. He resolved to engineer a second coming, and hired Samuel Chotzinoff to help. This was the right move: in the course of Toscanini's Philharmonic affiliation, Chotzinoff and his wife, Pauline— who was Jascha Heifetz's sister—had come to command a social clique encircling Toscanini. The Toscaninis were frequent dinner guests at the Chotzinoffs' West Eighty-fifth Street apartment. "At those dinners," the Chotzinoffs' friends Russell and Marcia Davenport once reported, "Pauline had served special Toscanini dishes prepared with her own hands in a panic of anticipation. Afterward Toscanini would sit on the couch with the ladies grouped closely around him, and talk in his low, husky voice, and make jokes; and the atmosphere of the room would glow with warm and apparently casual friendship. But under the surface nobody was really casual. On the contrary everyone was tense with awe and adoration. It is scarcely an exaggeration to say that these people lived to hear Toscanini's music. And it is only a slight exaggeration to suppose that several of them would have died for him, had he asked it."[5]

Initially, Sarnoff tried coaxing Toscanini back to America with offers of NBC-sponsored tours with the Philharmonic or the Philadelphia Orchestra. From Milan, Toscanini said no. Sarnoff then proposed a special NBC Toscanini orchestra and sent Chotzinoff to Italy to plead in person. Chotzinoff, described by the Davenports as a "gentle, timid, sensitive soul," undertook this mission fearfully. In Toscanini's presence, he at first said nothing of Sarnoff's offer. Once he summoned the courage to make his appeal, he stressed the huge audience NBC commanded and the hand-picked orchestra it promised to assemble. To Chotzinoff's surprise, Toscanini agreed, choosing Sarnoff's minimum offer: a ten-week contract. Contacted by Chotzinoff, Sarnoff at once telegraphed a contract from New York. Toscanini would conduct ten concerts from NBC's studios over a ten-week period beginning in December 1937, plus—at his own request—two benefit concerts from Carnegie Hall that NBC could broadcast at its prerogative. NBC would furnish a "first class" orchestra for all twelve concerts. Toscanini would appear "only under NBC auspices" for the duration of the ten weeks. His salary would be $40,000 plus the pertinent income tax.[*]

---

*Toscanini's after-taxes salary of $3,334 per concert was phenomenal in its day. In 1931–32, for example, the New York Philharmonic paid Toscanini $110,000, plus taxes, for 60 concerts. John Barbirolli was paid *$10,000* for his first Philharmonic season, 32 concerts

Toscanini signed the contract on February 4, 1937. The same evening, Chotzinoff and Sarnoff conferred via telephone. A transcript of their conversation crackles with barely controlled excitement. Sarnoff suggests that NBC immediately prepare a press release. Twice Chotzinoff advises that the release be "very dignified." Twice Sarnoff assures Chotzinoff of a "dignified statement." Chotzinoff comments: "I think this is the greatest scoop of the century."[7]

To some at RCA, their president's willingness to spend $40,000 on a part-time orchestra leader, plus additional money on the orchestra itself, seemed irresponsible. But as *Fortune* pointed out in January 1938, "Mr. Sarnoff, in working out the details of his gesture, was not in any music lover's trance." The Toscanini acquisition was a coup that would "make NBC the biggest corporate name in music and bring to a climax the long evolution of 'good' music on the air."

Fortune's analysis amassed a list of reasons the Toscanini-NBC venture made business sense. Congress was agitating for better radio programming. NBC was locked in competition with CBS for prestige presentations, and CBS's top music showcase was Toscanini's old orchestra. The Toscanini presence would consecrate any orchestra bearing NBC's name, enhancing the name itself. RCA could expect to sell more radios. If Toscanini could be induced to make recordings with the NBC Symphony for RCA Victor, the Victor line would profit. NBC's new highbrow glamour was bound to impress prospective advertisers. As for the expense of manning a symphony orchestra—as Sarnoff well knew, the American Federation of Musicians had recently negotiated a contract requiring NBC to increase its staff orchestra to 115. Though some of the specially recruited NBC Symphony personnel commanded formidable salaries, in allotting Toscanini 92 musicians NBC was allotting fewer musicians than it would have to employ anyway. What is more, as the Toscanini concerts would only require fifteen hours a week, the musicians would be available for other NBC work.

To substantiate its argument, *Fortune* conducted a poll. The results, tabulated prior to Toscanini's first NBC concert, showed that 62.5 percent of all Americans liked to listen to classical music on the radio, and that 42.7 percent wanted to hear more radio music. But "the really startling fact that *Fortune*'s survey unearthed," according to the article, was that

---

in 1936–37. In the early 1940s, Eugene Ormandy was said to be making about $50,000 a season (about 100 concerts) in Philadelphia, Serge Koussevitzky about $75,000 a season (about 75 concerts) in Boston.[6]

of all the people in the U.S.—Negroes, poor whites, farmers, clerks, and millionaires—39.9 percent have heard of the name of Arturo Toscanini; and of those who have heard of him, no less than 71 percent can identify him *as an orchestral conductor.* In other words, more than one-fourth of the U.S. knows this short dynamic Italian who has always scorned publicity and builds his music to please only himself and incidentally the recondite connoisseurs. More than a fourth of the U.S. knows who he is and what he does. The Southwest and the Mountain States had the greatest trouble in identifying him; and only 25.5 percent of the poor and 12.8 percent of the Negroes had ever heard of him. But his name was known to 63.8 percent of the prosperous, and of these 80 percent identified him correctly. In New York City, where he conducted the Philharmonic for ten years, 90.8 percent have heard of him, and 95.7 percent of these know who he is. In other cities the figures are: Chicago, 57 and 56.5 percent; St. Louis, 48.1 and 84.6 percent; and Philadelphia, 33.6 and 78.4 percent.

The Toscanini audience, *Fortune* concluded, is "certainly a mass audience."

Toscanini had reasons of his own to welcome the NBC venture. When Chotzinoff got around to writing about his mission to Milan many years later, he made it into a lion-taming act: Toscanini was in a "somber mood," conversation was "strained," lacking in "the old warmth." For two weeks, twice a day, the Chotzinoffs visited the Toscaninis "dutifully but hopefully." Only then was Sarnoff's plan tentatively broached.[8] But the *Fortune* article, written not long after the fact, describes a less arduous courtship, with Chotzinoff telling Toscanini why he had come a day after arriving. In retrospect, it seems implausible that Toscanini could have abandoned the United States upon leaving the Philharmonic; by 1936, he was too embedded in the American scene to disengage himself so readily.

Certainly there was no place for him in Italy, and not merely because he could not conduct there. The government transcript of a monitored phone conversation with an Italian lady friend, identified as "Signora Ada," reveals Toscanini's suffocation as of October 1935—shortly after Mussolini outlawed all foreign newspapers.

> Toscanini: . . . You have to read and know only what they want—there must be only one head! This is no longer living!
> Ada: It's frightful! Worse than Russia! . . .
> Toscanini: I can't wait to leave, because I can't stand it any longer! These things shock me . . . To see people enslaved in this way! Talk about black slavery . . . We are white slaves. . . . It's a suffering that annihilates me.[9]

Far from Hitler and Mussolini was Palestine, where, beginning in December 1936, Toscanini conducted the inaugural concerts of the Jewish immigrants' orchestra later to become the Israel Philharmonic. Though this initial visit to the Middle East made a stunning impression worldwide, Palestine could hardly become Toscanini's base of activities. In Europe, meanwhile, he returned repeatedly to Vienna and to the Salzburg Festival.

By the time Sarnoff hired Chotzinoff, Salzburg had emerged as Toscanini's main artistic venue after New York. In 1936, his Salzburg schedule carried over *Fidelio* and *Falstaff* from 1935 and added *Die Meistersinger*—a significant choice, as this was Bayreuth repertoire. Attending the stage rehearsals was Olin Downes, whose *Times* accounts poked fun at Old World culture bearers:

> And he caught them. He caught them, again and again. He caught them on their own ground, he obliged them to observe their own traditions. Has or has not the delightful remark that he made at a stage rehearsal of *Meistersinger* been cabled? When he objected that the Meistersingers in the first act were on the wrong side of the stage, and was assured that this time it was he who was wrong, he invoked the score.
>
> "Do you want to look at it?" And the score supported him. "But," it was objected, "Signor Toscanini, we do it here in the exact tradition as it is done under the supervision of Frau Winifred Wagner at Bayreuth." "This all may be," was the effect of Toscanini's reply; "we will nevertheless follow Wagner's directions and not those of any one else." "But what about Frau Winifred Wagner?" "Ah," says Toscanini, *"Papa ist mehr klug als Mama"* ["Papa is wiser than Mama"]. And again he had them.[10]

A great event of the 1937 Salzburg season was the final confrontation of Toscanini and Furtwängler, who was making his first appearance at the festival: Toscanini opposed Furtwängler's decision to conduct at Bayreuth that summer and told him so. By the time Hitler occupied Austria the following March, Toscanini had resolved not to return. Furtwängler took over Toscanini's Salzburg *Meistersinger* at the 1938 festival. Toscanini had now barred himself, or was barred, from conducting in Germany, Austria, and Italy.

Even during Toscanini's "final" performances with the New York Philharmonic in April 1936, plans were being laid for a postfarewell visit: without committing himself, Toscanini had sanctioned the possibility of touring the United States with the Philharmonic the following April. This turned into one of the NBC-sponsored tour plans Toscanini rejected prior to Chotzinoff's Milan mission. Toscanini's "no," conveyed to Judson and Mackay on December 14, 1936, came within days of Barbirolli's New York appointment—a choice Toscanini opposed in favor of Artur Rodzinski, scheduled to begin a seven-week guest stint with the Philharmonic in February 1937. Like other observers, Toscanini may have felt that Judson mainly wanted a conductor he could control. Rodzinski, something of a Toscanini protégé, was known to be a superb orchestra trainer—and an erratic, irascible man. Mrs. Toscanini informed the Philharmonic by letter: "Maestro did not think it was right to announce the engagement of Barbirolli after only a brief period with the orchestra and before the other [contending guest] conductors started their terms. . . . Secondly, Mr. Toscanini himself would have liked an official communication of the engagement of Mr. Barbirolli just as a matter of courtesy. . . . He was quite offended by this lack of respect and courtesy."[11]

In other words, as of January 1937, when Chotzinoff was dispatched to Milan, Toscanini was done conducting in Italy, Germany, and Austria, and had just broken with Judson and Mackay over Barbirolli. There can be no doubt that his disinclination to return to the New York Philharmonic was no disinclination to return to America. Stranded in Italy, where he retained six huge scrapbooks of letters from listeners to the Philharmonic broadcasts, he itched to work. Samuel Barber, who visited him at his Isolino San Giovanni island retreat, later told Charles O'Connell, RCA's classical music director from 1930 to 1944, that by the time Chotzinoff arrived, "the old Maestro had had enough of leisure." O'Connell's account continues:

> If the telephone rang or a cable arrived, [Toscanini] would complain pitifully to Barber that now that he had retired, the cruel world wouldn't leave him alone. But on such days as the little boat brought no mail, the telephone was silent, the cables uncommunicative, Toscanini would complain with equal bitterness that the world had quickly forgotten him. From this it might be deduced that the Maestro was a little impatient for activity, energy being the touchstone of his whole nature.

The NBC offer furnished a way to resume work in New York without "capitulating" to the Philharmonic. According to Erich Leinsdorf, who encountered Toscanini in Rome early in 1937, "he was as pleased and excited by [the NBC Symphony] prospect as anyone could be. It was obvious that he wanted to return to New York, less than a year after having given up his post with the Philharmonic there." And Sarnoff's offer was sweetened by the prospect of revenge. Around this time, Rodzinski's wife received a letter from Cia, Toscanini's daughter-in-law:

We have been thinking so much about you both these past days because everybody in the Toscanini house took very much to heart this unkind thing that was done to dear Maestro [Rodzinski] by those people of the Philharmonic. And I have to tell you that if Toscanini agreed to return to America it was because he wants to give a lesson to the Philharmonic. He likes your husband very much.[12]

Chotzinoff, who purportedly told Sarnoff late in 1936 that Toscanini would "never come back," may have felt like a mouse wooing a lion. In fact, the lion wanted to be wooed. In Charles O'Connell's view: "When Chotzinoff arrived . . . he had a remarkably simple and easy task before him, although he didn't know it." To which Leinsdorf adds: "When I met in New York the complete cast of characters around Toscanini, I noted that Samuel Chotzinoff . . . took full credit for bringing the prodigal conductor back to the States. I had been present in Rome when Maestro spoke of the plan and at that time the doorman of the Astor Hotel could have collected his signature of agreement."[13]

Notwithstanding Chotzinoff's repeated appeals for dignity, and a directive from Sarnoff ordering unusual caution, NBC's announcement of its "scoop of the century" signaled the most intense symphonic promotion since the *Fireman's Quadrille* enflamed Louis Antoine Jullien's "monster concerts." Network publicists labored to concoct every feasible "first," "most," "best," and "biggest." Toscanini was billed "the greatest living conductor," "the world's greatest conductor," and—tellingly—"NBC's great conductor." Sarnoff was quoted as finding "more gratification" in the Toscanini contract "than any other single agreement to which I have been a party." The coming NBC Symphony was called "the first full-size, full-time major orchestra to be maintained by an American broadcasting organization"—even though the musicians, as NBC employees, would regularly disband to do other studio work.[14]

NBC's press releases produced the desired sensation, but also unexpected alarms. "The signing of Mr. Toscanini was construed by some as a competitive thrust against the New York Philharmonic-Symphony Orchestra," the *Herald Tribune* commented, adding that "surprise was felt in some circles that Mr. Toscanini should choose to return to American audiences exclusively by way of the radio." The *Times* flatly stated: "The organization led by John Barbirolli now encounters serious competition." In fact, the Philharmonic was thrown into an uproar. Not only had Sarnoff and Toscanini countered its national broadcasts—in which Judson, whose Columbia Concerts Group was a CBS subsidiary, had a double stake; Barbirolli, on the job only three months, might now never establish a local following. Bruno Zirato cabled Mrs. Toscanini on February 8: "Very surprised Maestro's acceptance radio proposal. Would like to know if Maestro has considered ill effects that this contract would have on our season. . . . I am the recipient of hundreds of phone calls from press, public and subscribers seeking information whether Philharmonic will suffer financially or would lose its prestige. . . ." Toscanini himself cabled back: "Was surprised at your surprise. I will ask nothing of Sarnoff, who will arrange things to suit his own interest just as the Philharmonic has done and will always do."[15]

Toscanini could afford to ignore questions of rivalry between NBC and the Philharmonic. But these questions required answers from Olin Downes and other populist disciples for whom Toscanini's highest significance was moral-educational, as well as from Sarnoff, himself a cultural populist whose declared purposes in resurrecting Toscanini included "enriching musical appreciation in our country" and "encouraging the support of local symphony orchestras everywhere." Downes tried silencing the Philharmonic's worries in a Sunday essay whose illogic held up a mirror to NBC's tangled motives. David Sarnoff, Downes began, did not intend to "institute competition or rivalry in the concert field." Toscanini's concerts would "not be given in a concert hall, but in the studios of NBC." Granted, there would be competition with the Philharmonic "on the air." But this, unlike competition "on the ground," was "healthy and productive" and would "redound to the benefit not only of radio audiences but of the great American orchestra institutions, through the interest in symphonic music which good radio performances tend to stimulate." As a "further element in the situation," Downes continued, a radio performance "never equals the effect of the one at which the hearer is personally present." Rather, "the radio performance makes people eager to hear and see the real thing. . . . Thus radio is a 'feeder' for performances such as those of the Philharmonic-Symphony. . . ." Downes concluded by adding that "if, as a sort of by-product, these arrangements serve to remind the directorate of the Philharmonic-Symphony that it may not be the wisest course to engage for three seasons a young and relatively untried conductor and entrust the fortunes of the orchestra wholly to his guidance for that period, nothing will be lost by that."[16]

Defenders of the Philharmonic must have thought: If a radio concert could "never equal" the real thing, was radio the place for Toscanini? Their more immediate concern, however, was: When would the Toscanini broadcasts take place? From the first, Sarnoff had pledged to avoid Sunday afternoons, when the Philharmonic was aired. But his original proposal, Thursday night, proved just as controversial, as this was each week's "first night" for Philharmonic subscribers. NBC therefore slated its concerts for

Saturday night. Downes concurred; this new time period, he wrote, was "calculated to increase the number of Mr. Toscanini's listeners and further extend the influence his concerts are certain to have upon the whole future of symphonic broadcasting and therefore upon the dissemination and the standards of orchestra performance in this country."[17]

But the Saturday slot was more indignantly received than the Thursday slot had been. For one thing, as America's "night out," Saturday was a dead night for radio; NBC would not have to bump a single regular client to make room for Toscanini. Furthermore, with the Philharmonic, the Metropolitan Opera, the Boston Symphony, and the General Motors and Ford concerts all broadcast on Saturday or Sunday, fine music already surfeited the airwaves on weekends, versus a weekday drought. Finally, as the managers of the St. Louis and Cincinnati Symphonies pointed out in letters to the *Times,* the vast majority of America's orchestras performed on Saturday nights. "If NBC really wishes to give radio audiences the Toscanini concerts," wrote Theodore Gannon of the Cincinnati Symphony, "they should not pick the worst radio night of the week. A few cancelled commercials would go a long way toward indicating the sincerity of the broadcasters to sacrifice in behalf of good music." Downes now changed his mind:

> If Toscanini performs on Saturday nights . . . thousands will not hear him who otherwise would do so. . . . Orchestras would lose patrons and Toscanini would lose a part of his audience. . . . If [this] should occur a large percentage of the service and the good-will developed by this new artistic enterprise would be lost. There would be found in various quarters grounds for the charge, already preferred by parties disturbed by the Toscanini engagement, that its actual purpose was that of a great corporation using its resources to discourage competition, stifle initiative, and dominate in the musical field.[18]

This time NBC would not budge. Its final schedule called for ten Saturday-night Toscanini concerts beginning on Christmas Eve, to be preceded by Saturday-night concerts led by Pierre Monteux ("brilliant French conductor, considered the best in his native land," according to NBC) and Rodzinski ("among the most brilliant of the younger school of conductors").

Rodzinski, at Toscanini's request, now commandeered the selection and training of the NBC Symphony. If Rodzinski's wife, in her memoirs, is to be believed, he soon discovered NBC intending to overrely on its existing radio ensemble. Sarnoff, in one early public statement, mentioned retaining "at least forty" NBC musicians in a Toscanini orchestra comprising "more than eighty." According to Halina Rodzinski, only after "detailed conversations" with Sarnoff, in which Rodzinski insisted Toscanini would never accept the pending arrangements, did the network decide to retain only thirty-one members of its seventy-four-man 1937 staff orchestra, to be augmented to ninety-two for Toscanini.[19] Having decided to follow Rodzinski's advice, however, Sarnoff did not stint, hiring members of the Chicago, Cincinnati, Cleveland, Detroit, and Minneapolis orchestras, among others. The NBC Symphony concertmaster would be Mischa Mischakoff, formerly concertmaster of the Chicago Symphony; Sarnoff would reportedly pay him $450 a week. The violas would be led by Carlton Cooley, formerly first viola of Rodzinski's Cleveland Orchestra, and William Primrose of the London String Quartet—among seven quartets contributing personnel to the NBC strings. Victimized orchestras, less lavishly endowed than Sarnoff's network, decried his "raids." A more alarming denunciation came from Toscanini in Milan. Alerted that NBC was discharging musicians to make way for the new Toscanini men—a logical consequence of retaining less than half the existing staff group—he cabled his withdrawal. Chotzinoff swiftly cabled back that, far from subtracting musicians from its payroll, NBC was creating new orchestral jobs. This little lie, which put Toscanini at ease, began a pattern of appeasement cum deception that would characterize the network's dealings with its most prestigious employee.

Rodzinski, an unflinching taskmaster, drilled the reconstituted orchestra into shape as planned. Meanwhile, the publicity machine cooed:

> The National Broadcasting Company has for several months spared no time, effort or expense to bring together a symphonic organization worthy to take the same high place among the orchestras of the world that Toscanini long has occupied among conductors. . . . The NBC Symphony orchestra has been assembled from the finest available musicians in order to make it one of the world's best orchestras. . . . Selection of the personnel . . . was carried out in accordance with a criterion never before used in assembling a major symphonic aggregation. Most of the players in each section of the orchestra are instrumentalists with ability and experience qualifying them to fill the first chair of the section or to play solos. . . . In choosing the players, the National Broadcasting Company kept in mind the need to fulfill the unusually exacting conditions of radio which transmits faithfully the most delicate nuances of orchestral music. Standards for a major radio orchestra, it was assumed, were higher than those for an ordinary orchestra.

The first concerts, under Monteux, took place on November 13 and 27. Rodzinski conducted performances on December 4, 11, and 18. Swiftly purchased, anxiously prepped, the weeks-old NBC Symphony was a racehorse straining at the bit. The Master would now take the reins.

. . .

Everyone knew Toscanini's New World restitution was a gamble. He had already resigned his new job once. At the same time, his admirers did not seek too peaceful a homecoming. Was Toscanini, now seventy, a scourging angel still?

These fears were quickly put to rest. Toscanini arrived in New York on December 13 aboard the *Conte di Savoia.* While the liner was in quarantine, Toscanini and his wife were surprised in the lounge by two flashbulb-popping photographers. Turning purple and then white, Toscanini began popping one of the photographers with his fists. According to a translation in the next morning's *Herald Tribune,* he was also screaming, in Italian: "You pigs! You murderers! Ha! I have a better, a brilliant idea. Ah, no. I shall not slap their faces. I will buy a gun and shoot both of them. That's it. I'll shoot both of them. I, Toscanini, shall rid the world of such pests!" A nun now grabbed Toscanini to restrain him. Mrs. Toscanini pleaded: "No, no. No, no, no. Don't get a gun. You can't do that." Toscanini broke loose, chasing one of the photographers forty yards down the deck while passengers gasped. He then retired to his suite, where he kept two visitors —David Sarnoff and John Royal—waiting outside for nearly an hour. "Oh, we're just a couple of bodyguards, apparently," Sarnoff commented to the press.

Toscanini's initial NBC rehearsal several days later excited morbid curiosity. In The Hague the previous March, he had refused to proceed until the Residentie Orkest had replaced two brass players. Displeased with an oboist in London the following October, he had left a radio studio vowing never again to lead the BBC Symphony. Samuel Antek, an NBC Symphony violinist, left this account of the first NBC tryout:

> . . . Suddenly, from a door on the right side of the stage, a small, solidly built man emerged. . . . In his hand he carried a baton. In awed stillness we watched covertly as he walked up the few steps leading to the stage.
>
> As he stepped up to the podium, by prearranged signal we all rose, like puppets suddenly propelled to life by the pent-up tension. . . .
>
> He looked around, apparently bewildered by our unexpected action, and gestured a faint greeting with both arms, a mechanical smile lighting his pale face for an instant. Somewhat embarrassed, we sat down again. Then, in a rough, hoarse voice, he called out "Brahms!" He looked at us piercingly for the briefest moment, then raised his arms. In one smashing stroke, the baton came down. A vibrant sound suddenly gushed forth from the tense players like blood from a severed artery. . . .
>
> With each heart-pounding timpani stroke in the opening bars of the

Brahms First Symphony his baton beat became more powerfully insistent, his shoulders strained and hunched as though buffeting a giant wind. His outstretched left arm spasmodically flailed the air, the cupped fingers pleading like a beseeching beggar. His face reddened, muscles tightened, eyes and eyebrows constantly moving.

As we in the violin section tore with our bows against our strings, I felt I was being sucked into a roaring maelstrom of sound—every bit of strength and skill called upon and strained into being. Bits of breath, muscle, and blood, never before used, were being drained from me. I sensed, more than I heard, with near disbelief, the new sounds around me. Was this the same music we had been practicing so assiduously for days? Like ships torn from their mooring in a stormy ocean, we bobbed and tossed, responding to these earnest, importuning gestures. With what a new fierce joy we played![20]

The program for Toscanini's NBC Symphony debut consisted of a Vivaldi concerto grosso, Mozart's G minor Symphony, K. 550, and Brahms's First. As at all subsequent performances in NBC's Studio 8H, no tickets were sold (except on the black market); having a guests-only audience avoided the tax on public entertainments where admission is charged. On this occasion, more than fifty thousand requests for tickets had to be turned down.[21] Sarnoff opened the concert by briefly welcoming the "beloved Maestro." The music was received with tense adoration. Uncertain of broadcast etiquette, the audience barely breathed following the Vivaldi work. After the Brahms, it roared. Toscanini was recalled to the stage seven times.

The press was amazed. In an article for *Radio Guide,* Leonard Liebling, editor-in-chief of the *Musical Courier,* called the concert the biggest radio event since King Edward's abdication. The New York *Post,* in an editorial, said it "outweighed our last note to Japan in conversation." *Time* commented: "Even those US lowbrows who were listening in to this highbrow stuff could feel the hypnotic power that was welding 92 separate instrumental voices into one voice." *Time* termed Toscanini the "no. 1 interpreter of Beethoven's and Mozart's symphonies" and observed that his salary, which NBC publicized, probably made him the highest paid conductor in history.

Praise for the specially imported "radio maestro" was a vacillating blend of circus hyperbole and hushed euphoria, the encomiums of P. T. Barnum in behalf of Jenny Lind, of Billy Guard in behalf of Caruso, of Theodore Thomas in behalf of great music rolled into one. On January 4, NBC's popular Dorothy Thompson devoted her entire "People in the News" broadcast to "the perfect, the complete artist of music," source of "the greatest artistic performance that one can see and hear anywhere in the world today." As touted by NBC's own publicists, the crux of Thompson's portrait was an "eyewitness account of a top secret rehearsal," beginning:

The first thing that overwhelmingly impressed me was that he conducts his rehearsals without a score, without a note in front of him. I knew, of course, that he so conducts public concerts. But to conduct a *rehearsal* from memory—a rehearsal, where the orchestra is suddenly stopped, and forced to play a passage over from a single note, or where a few bars by woodwinds or by horns must be repeated, means that Toscanini must have one of the most extraordinary brains on earth. He knows by heart, bar by bar, note by note, passage by passage, backward and forward, every scrap of the great symphonic and operatic literature of the world.

Thompson also reported that "nothing short of perfection" satisfied Toscanini, that he rehearsed "in four languages," that his rage when he was displeased seemed like "a combination of indignation, contempt, and heartbreak." Invoking New World tenets of youth, vigor, and efficiency, she concluded: "He has the grace and agility of a boy, the temperament of a man of thirty, and the working power of a perfect machine." (The text of Thompson's Toscanini broadcast was reprinted in the *Herald Tribune* thirteen days later "in response to a great many requests.")

Toscanini was also presented to a national mass audience as *Cosmopolitan*'s "Cosmopolite of the Month" for March. The magazine's Toscanini profile was written by Samuel Chotzinoff, still music critic of the *Post*. Chotzinoff retold Toscanini's emergency debut in Rio, his rebuke to Geraldine Farrar, and other parables. "To gain the homage of the entire musical world as Toscanini has done," Chotzinoff wrote, "an interpretive artist must embody the musical ideals of every nation. For Italians, Toscanini is the supreme interpreter of Rossini, Verdi, and Puccini. For Germans, he is the supreme interpreter of Beethoven and Wagner; for Austrians, of Haydn, Mozart, and Schubert. For the French, he is the very mouthpiece of Debussy and for the English the finest exponent of Elgar." (Toscanini's Elgar repertoire consisted of the "Enigma" Variations and the Introduction and Allegro for strings.)

The same week that it promoted Chotzinoff's *Cosmopolitan* article, NBC's publicity department contributed an inimitable story of its own: "World's Largest Drum Rushed to New York for Toscanini Concert." As Toscanini could find no bass drum resonant enough for the Verdi Requiem, the network had conducted a search leading from Manhattan to the University of Chicago, whose band was found to possess a drum measuring eight by four feet—"reputedly the largest in the world." The university would not loan it until NBC had agreed to insure it. At first, the Twentieth

Century Limited was to carry it, but no car on that train had doors big enough. Now it was en route to New York aboard a Pennsylvania Railroad train including "the one express car in existence"—discovered, fortuitously, on a Chicago railroad siding—"whose doors are capacious enough to admit it." (A second, quieter press release some days later, titled "Drum Selected for Toscanini Concert," disclosed that the Chicago drum was "being returned"; Toscanini had preferred one belonging to an American Legion post in Greenwich, Connecticut.)

The ballyhoo continued, even mounted, throughout Toscanini's first NBC season. The culminating event was his "farewell concert" of March 5, 1938, which was made the staging ground for a dramatic disclosure. The announcer's introduction for that broadcast—not extemporized, but scripted to sound extemporaneous—began:

> Ladies and gentlemen, we are speaking from the NBC studios in Radio City. . . . In the studio there is an air of tenseness during these few minutes before the concert begins, a feeling that this is a particularly momentous program—and we feel sure that the members of the radio audience have a similar feeling. Mr. Toscanini has chosen a program which in itself makes the evening a gala occasion. Once in a while Mr. Toscanini consents to conduct an all-Wagner concert, and when he does so it is eagerly looked forward to by all music lovers. Tonight we are to have the rare treat of hearing such a program. . . .
>
> When the series of NBC Symphony concerts was originally planned, it was with a twofold hope: first, of providing an opportunity for people everywhere . . . to hear great music under the best possible circumstances; and also, of focusing increased attention on symphonic music, and in this way stimulating interest in the many fine orchestras maintained and supported in cities throughout the country. The extent to which these hopes have been achieved in the last few months has been due in large measure, we feel, to the amazing genius and tireless enthusiasm of Mr. Toscanini as conductor of the NBC Symphony Orchestra. We sincerely believe that the concerts performed under his direction have marked the climax of a great epoch in the National Broadcasting Company's history and in the development of music in America. . . .

An intermission feature was an address by Chotzinoff, who this time termed Toscanini "the greatest musical interpreter of our time—perhaps of all time." It was "generally agreed," Chotzinoff told his audience of millions, that under Toscanini's baton "the great masterpieces of music of all ages achieve their loftiest, their most perfect expression." Reinforcing increasingly intimate behind-the-scenes observations by Dorothy Thompson and others, he called Toscanini humble, assiduous, and passionate, and praised his "simplicity with friends." There was nothing old-fashioned, nothing Old Worldly about Toscanini: "The tempo of the modern world suits him perfectly, for it flatters his nervous energy and inexhaustible vitality. He finds the locomotive unbearably slow. He begins to enjoy motoring when the speedometer registers eighty miles per hour. He is waiting impatiently for the inauguration of trans-Atlantic air service. . . ."

Now David Sarnoff stepped to the microphone:

> Ladies and gentlemen: Tonight's performance is the last in the present series of radio concerts by the NBC Symphony Orchestra under the baton of Arturo Toscanini. That would be a sad statement to make were it not for the more cheerful news I am privileged to give you at this time.
>
> The good news is that Maestro Toscanini has agreed to come back to us in October of this year, and to conduct another series of radio concerts with the NBC Symphony Orchestra, beginning in November. . . . There is still another piece of good news. It is that Maestro Toscanini has signed an agreement with the National Broadcasting Company for a period of three years. . . .*
>
> The National Broadcasting Company is an American business organization. It has employees and it has stockholders. It serves their interests best when it serves the public best. We believe in this principle and maintain it as our guiding policy. This is why we organized the new NBC Orchestra and invited the world's greatest conductor to direct it.
>
> Much as all of us in NBC admired Maestro Toscanini before he joined us last fall, our admiration for him has grown with each succeeding week. And to that statement I would like simply to add that we have also come to love him.

Sarnoff concluded by reading a letter from Toscanini himself, expressing gratification that his concerts had "carried joy and serenity to remote regions and to the humblest abodes."[22]

"It was nearly midnight when that musician whom Mr. Sarnoff had conservatively called 'the world's greatest conductor' completed what the director of the NBC might also have called, without extravagance, the most exciting and memorable series of orchestral concerts given in our time," wrote Gilman in the next morning's *Herald Tribune.* "Before a distin-

---

*The contract stated that, in the United States, Toscanini could conduct *only* under NBC auspices during the three-year period.[23]

guished studio audience that included no less noteworthy a visitor than Mr. Thomas Mann, Mr. Toscanini led his astonishing orchestra—as yet scarcely four months old—through a program of transcendent music, marvelously played, that must often have been a startling revelation of beauty and splendor to many of those millions who listened at their radio." Downes wrote in the *Times:* "All rejoiced in the presence of this preeminent musician, and the certainty that he is not to depart for any long interval from us. His position today, thanks to the vision and the broad policies which have brought him here, is more international and more predominant in his art than ever before." Chotzinoff wrote in the *Post:* "Mr. Toscanini may bring ecstasy to his listeners, but to those who would retell their experiences in words he brings despair. Humanity is so made that it gets quickly used to wonders and miracles, and we may become complacent about his labors among us. It would be a pity if we did. For Mr. Toscanini happens to be the sole prophet of an art that does not speak to us directly."

Both the *Tribune* and the *Times* ran editorials. The *Tribune*'s read in part:

> The truth that was evidently discerned by the NBC when it engaged the most fanatically uncompromising of musical idealists to direct the undertaking which it has just brought to a peak of unexampled popular success was no less surprising a one than this: That the vast increase in the popular appetite for the greatest things that music has to offer is neither a delusion nor a hope nor a dream. It is an actuality, already obvious to the more penetrating among the hard-boiled and the realistic; increasingly obvious to others. . . .
>
> Toscanini, a miracle of youthful elasticity and strength and endurance, an even more vital and compelling artist than before, will return to us next season, and for two seasons after that. Perhaps he may decide to spend most or all of his time among us. He belongs in America. Nowhere else can he command the scope and the facilities for realizing to the full that vision of a democratic musical culture which is taking shape and substance in this country. Nowhere else is he so widely loved and reverenced. Nowhere else, perhaps, is he so needed—"to give news," as Thoreau said, "of traveling gods, and to assure the purpose of the free."

The *Times* editorial began: "Mr. David Sarnoff, who began his life in America as a messenger boy, has again glorified his office."

A month after finishing his first NBC season, Toscanini traveled to Palestine a second time and spent most of April there, conducting the

Palestine orchestra seven times. The visit was more dangerous than in 1937; both Bronislaw Huberman, who helped organize the orchestra, and the Zionist leader Chaim Weizmann had advised him not to come. According to John Royal, who accompanied Toscanini part of the time, the Toscanini party was transported in an armored car guarded by British soldiers; in Jerusalem, an Arab bomb nearly hit the vehicle. The New York *Times* quoted Toscanini as saying: "I like to go into Jewish homes, eat Jewish food and feel the pulse of Jewish life." Meanwhile, Nazi propagandists, also quoted in the *Times,* vilified "Toscanini and his Jewish boosters," terming him "the champion of Jewish art in German countries." In New York, it was rumored that Toscanini might be part Jewish—speculation furthered both by the Nazis and by Toscanini himself.[24]

The months that followed found Toscanini also conducting in London and in Lucerne, where a new international summer festival was begun outside the Nazi orbit. He spent most of the summer, however, in Italy. As in 1931, his passport was confiscated by Mussolini, provoking detailed news accounts and indignant commentaries leading to its return. That October, at Toscanini's first NBC rehearsal for 1938–39, the orchestra acknowledged his continued antifascist profile with a prolonged ovation. Back in Europe in the summer of 1939, he conducted in London and Lucerne. Hitler invaded Poland that fall. Upon returning to America, Toscanini finally left his apartment in downtown Manhattan's Hotel Astor in favor of the five-acre "Villa Pauline" in Riverdale, overlooking the Hudson River. His son, Walter, later moved his family there as well. Toscanini's daughter Wanda had married Vladimir Horowitz in 1933 and already resided in New York. Only Wally, the elder Toscanini daughter, remained in Italy.

Toscanini now lived in exile in the United States. There were no more trips to London, Lucerne, or Palestine. During his first three NBC seasons, he did take the orchestra to Baltimore, Boston, Chicago, Newark, Pittsburgh, Providence, and Washington, D.C. Then, in the summer of 1940, Sarnoff engineered something grander. With Europe enveloped in combat —Italy entered the war June 10; France surrendered twelve days later— Toscanini and his radio symphony undertook a South American tour, performing sixteen concerts (six of which were broadcast home) in Buenos Aires, Rio de Janeiro, São Paolo, and Montevideo between June 13 and July 10. Chotzinoff, as NBC's "director of serious music," told the New York *Herald Tribune* from Uruguay that a Montevideo audience had "threatened to tear down the house unless the Maestro came out again." As the New York *Post*'s music critic, he reported from Buenos Aires that "the adulation for [Toscanini] is so genuine and intense that [the crowd] bangs on the windows of [his] car demanding that the light be switched on so it might see his face." The emotional peak of the visit was reached in Montevideo, where on July Fourth Toscanini called a surprise rehearsal. "Gentlemen, this is your Independence Day," he announced. "We will play 'The Star-Spangled Banner.'" The orchestra excitedly complied, standing, after which Toscanini rushed to his dressing room. There he was found in tears by Edwin Wilson, an American diplomat who had been invited to the "rehearsal" by John Royal. Afterward, Royal told the press that he had never heard a more inspiring rendition of the national anthem. Speaking of the tour as a whole, he said: "All the American diplomats and businessmen in Buenos Aires, Rio de Janeiro, Montevideo, and São Paulo declared this was the biggest event that ever occurred for strengthening the ties between the United States and the nations to the south of us." According to Royal, America's ambassador to Argentina, Norman Armour, had called NBC's forces "the American Fifth Column."[25]

The rationale for Toscanini's visit was in fact partly diplomatic. Germany and Italy had already sent orchestras and opera troupes to South America. This cultural propaganda had caught the United States State Department empty-handed. Yet the idea of an American symphonic friendship mission originated neither in Washington nor at Radio City. As early as 1937, Leopold Stokowski, having begun to sever his ties to Philadelphia, envisioned touring South America with an American orchestra of his own. Stokowski regretted that the Philadelphia Orchestra board had never seen fit to sponsor a foreign tour. He understood the timeliness of a goodwill gesture to the south. In consultation with the State Department and the Pan American Union, he laid plans for an All-American Youth Orchestra with which he could appear in several South American cities. Since Stokowski was an RCA recording artist, Sarnoff was approached as the prospective underwriter. He nibbled, then changed his mind: Why not send NBC's orchestra and conductor instead? This plan suited Toscanini: his return to South America had long been sought there, and Stokowski was, with Koussevitzky, his chief American rival. Sarnoff's withdrawal, in recent years described by one Stokowski loyalist as a "vicious" act,[26] might have dealt the All-American Youth Orchestra a fatal blow but for another rivalry: CBS's William Paley picked up the tab, and Stokowski became a Columbia recording artist. The All-American Youth Orchestra left for Buenos Aires, Rio, São Paolo, and Montevideo in July—the same month Toscanini and the NBC Symphony returned to New York.

Toscanini's South American triumph capped phase one of the Toscanini-NBC partnership. The press remained awestruck. The promotional machinery hummed and clicked. Toscanini declared himself more satisfied than ever with the orchestra. Occasional baton splinters and overturned music stands were smilingly tolerated. But these smiles proved premature.

In an early, widely quoted announcement of the NBC Symphony, Chotzinoff had spoken of "an entirely new and different orchestral organization," distinct from existing studio groups. Only later did it become apparent that NBC Symphony personnel would also play for other network shows. Toscanini, immersed in his music, seemed either not to know or not to care until December 27, 1940. That evening, during a rehearsal of Beethoven's *Missa Solemnis* in Carnegie Hall, members of the NBC Symphony one by one stopped playing, crouched low to the floor, and sneaked offstage. One player, Carlton Cooley, crept away on his hands and knees. The reason was that Toscanini's rehearsal was running late, and they were overdue for a broadcast under Frank Black in Studio 8H. Apparently instructed by Chotzinoff, H. Leopold Spitalny, the orchestra's personnel manager, had positioned himself at the rim of the stage behind Toscanini and was silently supervising the exodus. Toscanini did not notice at first. When he did, he wheeled and roared: "CHOTZINOFF!" Chotzinoff fled the hall. Toscanini shredded his collar and made for his dressing room. Though he led the *Missa Solemnis* as scheduled, there were repercussions. Fearing Toscanini would resign, the orchestra drew up a petition pleading that he stay. When signatures were solicited after a rehearsal, Spitalny objected, blurting out: "How do you know we *want* him back?" To one player, Toscanini confided: "I cannot understand something. When my son-in-law give concert in a city, if they don't want him back the next year, they don't ask him to write letter of resignation." "Why do you mention that, Maestro?" "Because NBC want me to write letter of resignation." "You mean they don't want you back?" "That is right." Around the same time, Toscanini heard that Hugo Burghauser, a bassoonist he had known abroad as president of the Vienna Philharmonic, had been refused employment at NBC, countermanding Toscanini's own recommendation. Burghauser had been told by Chotzinoff that while Toscanini could veto new players, Chotzinoff and Spitalny did the hiring. This contradicted numerous NBC statements. Toscanini began not to answer phone calls and letters from NBC. At one point, he met with William Paley. In April 1941, he sent Sarnoff an ambivalent and conciliatory letter of resignation, reading in part:

> My old age tells me to be high time to withdraw from the militant scene of Art. I am tired and a little exhausted—the dreadful tragedy which tears to pieces unhappy humanity saddens me and makes me crazy and restless:—how can I find peace, heart, wish and strength in order to meet with new responsibility and new work? As for me, it is impossible . . . so that my dear David don't be hesitating any longer and make up

at once your plan for the next season. . . . Later on if my state of mind, health and rest will be improved and you will judge my cooperation advantageous enough for the NBC call me and I shall be glad to resume once more my work. Believe me dear Sarnoff I am sad at heart to renounce the joy to conduct that very fine orchestra you formed for me and gave me so great satisfaction![27]

Sarnoff now hired Leopold Stokowski to head the NBC Symphony. Whether temporary or permanent, it was the most enterprising, most logical move. With his snow-white nimbus, ice-blue eyes, and sculpted nose; his obscure lineage, exotic accent, and untraceable musical education; his film roles, two marriages and divorces, and liaison with Greta Garbo, Stokowski was the one American musical celebrity who possessed something like Toscanini's mystique. On the podium, he was a disarming showman, partial to batonless finger-ballets and feline lunges. Early in his career, he had dramatized his musical memory by dropping scores to the floor and pushing aside his music stand. In a famous experiment with the Philadelphia Orchestra in 1926, he had the house lights extinguished and a huge spotlight played on his hands from below, crowning his head with a silver aureole while projecting massive shadows of his sweeping arms and hands. Beginning in 1934, when he was ostensibly forty-seven—actually fifty-two—years old, he had gradually disengaged himself from Philadelphia in favor of Hollywood. Three movies—*The Big Broadcast of 1937*, *One Hundred Men and a Girl* (1937), and *Fantasia* (1940)—had increased his fame. His last appearances with the Philadelphia Orchestra, in March 1941, happened to coincide with Sarnoff's need for a Toscanini replacement. And hiring Stokowski meant returning him to RCA Victor, where he was missed.

An overt Stokowski-Toscanini rivalry dated back to 1930, when Arthur Judson, sensing a rare opportunity to sell good music, had engineered a conducting contest. For two weeks, Stokowski led Toscanini's New York Philharmonic while Toscanini led Stokowski's Philadelphia Orchestra (Judson managed both orchestras, plus his stellar roster of soloists, at the time). The New York players' truculent resistance to Stokowski fueled accusations he was a dilettante. He did not have Toscanini's ear, memory, or moralistic intensity. He was frankly uninterested in textual fidelity. He less resembled a "high priest" than a high pagan, learned in extemporaneous sound magic and sensuality. These differences and others were borne out during Stokowski's first NBC Symphony season.

Stokowski was as outspoken an advocate of cultural populism as Toscanini, the populist figurehead, was mute. Stokowski's book *Music for All of Us* (1943) begins:

> Music is a universal language—it speaks to everyone—is the birthright
> of all of us. Formerly music was chiefly confined to privileged classes in
> cultural centers, but today, through radio and records, music has come
> directly into our homes no matter how far we may live from cultural
> centers. This is as it should be, because music speaks to every man,
> woman, and child—high or low, rich or poor, happy or despairing—
> who is sensitive to its deep and powerful message.

Like Sarnoff and also Walt Disney, with whom he collaborated on *Fantasia*,
Stokowski (underneath his autobiographical smoke screen) was of unassuming parentage and patchily educated. Like Sarnoff and Disney, he was
emboldened by self-made success to consider democratizing technological
initiatives that might have repelled more patrician personalities. Among the
visions unfolded in *Music for All of Us* is that of a "recreational center" with
a tower beaming music to thousands of outdoor listeners: "gay, popular
music for dancing—stirring marches—music from operas and operettas—
and the finest symphony concerts." At night, "colored light will be pro-
jected—which in time will create new phases of an art of color in motion
and form." If Stokowski's music-and-light tower has so far proved a pipe
dream, he had by 1941 buttressed with achievements the mountain of plati-
tudes his speeches and writings had amassed. No conductor showed more
enthusiasm for the phonograph's future as a music disseminator. With the
Philadelphia Orchestra, he had conducted the first electric orchestral recording; the first, experimental stereophonic recording; and the first, experimental long-playing recording. In 1936, he had taken the Philadelphia
Orchestra on the first transcontinental orchestral tour. *Fantasia*, released
four years later, eventually helped bear out Stokowski's pronouncement
that motion pictures were "an ideal medium" to realize his "ultimate aim
. . . to bring the beauty of music to the greatest number of men, women
and children *all over the world.*" To his intense frustration, he had never
enjoyed a radio berth comparable to the New York Philharmonic's or the
NBC Symphony's. Sarnoff's offer represented a form of national exposure
Stokowski had long coveted.[28]

Part of Stokowski's vision of a democratic musical culture was an educated audience. This, to him, meant a progressive audience, versed in the
acknowledged masterpieces yet open to the latest heresies. In Philadelphia,
he had presented world or American premieres of such important additions
to the literature as Berg's *Wozzeck*; Copland's *Dance Symphony*; Falla's *El
amor brujo*; Griffes's *White Peacock*; Mahler's Eighth Symphony and *Das
Lied von der Erde*; Rachmaninoff's *Rhapsody on a Theme of Paganini*; Schoenberg's *Gurre-Lieder*, First Chamber Symphony, *Die glückliche Hand*,
Variations for Orchestra, and Violin Concerto; Shostakovich's First Sym-

phony; Sibelius's Fifth, Sixth, and Seventh symphonies; Stravinsky's *Song of the Nightingale* and *Symphonies of Wind Instruments;* Varèse's *Amériques* and *Arcana;* and Webern's Passacaglia. When Arthur Judson, members of the board, and many subscribers griped and balked, Stokowski implemented Youth Concerts restricted to listeners of high school and college age: "Most adults," he asserted, "have difficulty in absorbing ideas and impressions . . . they are hopeless." In *Music for All of Us* he called for state-subsidized broadcasts and recordings of "the most outstanding new compositions of younger composers, so that all music lovers over the whole country can hear them and have an opportunity to follow these latest developments of their national art."[29]

At NBC, as in Philadelphia, Stokowski was as good as his word—his ponderous homilies again sprang to life. He eagerly tutored his radio audience; in one on-the-air interview, he used recorded rehearsal excerpts to help introduce Prokofiev's sixteen-year-old *Love for Three Oranges* Suite. Though NBC did not broadcast it, he conducted a children's concert; the program included works by child composers, orchestrated by other hands for the occasion. The eight broadcast concerts he led in 1941–42 included works by six American composers.

Stokowski's NBC debut season did not idle Toscanini. He led the NBC Symphony in five war bond benefits and two recording sessions. Also in 1941–42, he conducted the Philadelphia Orchestra three times, and, after some shouting and soul-searching, consented to remount the podium of the New York Philharmonic in order to cap the orchestra's centenary with a Beethoven cycle.* His attention was distracted, however, by the spotlight

---

*Part of the coaxing process was described in an October 15, 1941 letter from Walter Price to Marshall Field, both eminent members of the Philharmonic's board. Having responded evasively to overtures from the Philharmonic conveyed by Field, Toscanini had visited Price at his home. Price now wrote to Field:

> I told [Toscanini] with the utmost frankness that I thought he had treated our Society in a way that contrasted most unfavorably with the liberal, fine and courteous way in which we had treated him.
> I told him that, no matter what his decision was, his failure to acknowledge your letter except through a communication made to Zirato and his indifference to your second letter, showed neither a spirit of fair play nor an evidence of the courtesy which was due to us from him.
> . . . It seemed to me that, while he wanted to come to the Philharmonic for the Centennial season, in a way, his pride at being grouped with ten conductors prevented him from so doing.
> Every man has the defects of his qualities; and while Toscanini is conscious of the fact that he is regarded as the premier conductor of all time, he, I think, holds to the idea that he can do anything he wants to and get away with it.

now bathing Stokowski at Radio City. Soon Toscanini's "state of mind, health, and rest," all factors figuring in his resignation letter to Sarnoff, improved sufficiently to permit resumption of his former duties. In 1942–43 and 1943–44, Toscanini and Stokowski co-conducted the NBC Symphony, leading about two dozen concerts each.

The orchestra now acquired a split personality. Stokowski, seeking a smoother, plusher sound, toyed with acoustics, reseated the musicians, and abolished uniform bowings. His broadcast repertoire included, in addition to much traditional fare, a nonstop barrage of American and/or new works, including Schoenberg's Piano Concerto (a premiere, with Eduard Steuermann) and Copland's *Short Symphony* (an American premiere)—probably the two most difficult contemporary compositions the NBC Symphony ever tackled, as well as two of the most important.*

It was merely fitting that the incongruous dual regime should have begun with a head-on collision. In December 1941, Stokowski had persuaded NBC to buy the rights to the first American performance of Shostakovich's Seventh Symphony, finished that year and said to reflect Soviet resistance to the German siege of Leningrad. A copy of the score was flown to New York, where Toscanini perused it and decided that he, not Stokowski, would play it first. In June 1942, Stokowski wrote to Toscanini:

> At our meeting a few weeks ago, you asked me not to broadcast any of the music of Brahms, but said that I should broadcast the modern music. I agreed to do this, although I must confess I was reluctant to give

---

He told me with apparent satisfaction of the abrupt way in which he had left the Scala and the Metropolitan. . . .

His inferences were that, every time he had been identified with an organization and left it, definitely degenerating tendencies rapidly developed.

It is not necessary for me to go into the details of the argument which he made to me. I told him that he would often lay his hand upon his heart and talk about his responsibilities to music and the obligation which he had to bring out the truth of what the composer had written.

I told him he had an equal obligation to play a similar role in his relationship with people who for many years have bowed reverentially to any suggestion which he might make. . . .

At times the conversation grew very heated. As I tell you, he was here for three hours and I was pretty well played out when he left. . . .

. . . I am of the opinion that the sooner he is eliminated as a factor, the better it will be for the [Philharmonic], because his conditions, his whims and his attitude almost offset his great ability and capacity. . . .[30]

*In all, Stokowski's thirty-two NBC Symphony broadcast concerts included twenty-five American works by twenty-four composers.

up the music of Brahms, because that is part of our repertoire that I particularly love. I feel strongly that this understanding between us should be kept.

About 10 years ago, when I was in Russia and Shostakovich was comparatively unknown, it was I who perceived his great gifts, believed in him, and against much opposition was the first to play his music in the United States. At that time I became friends with Shostakovich, and since then we have been in correspondence. I have a most tremendous love and enthusiasm for his music. . . .

That is why last December I requested NBC to obtain broadcasting rights for Shostakovich's Seventh Symphony. . . .

Now that you know all these facts, I feel confident you will wish me to broadcast this symphony, and that it will be with your approval and in harmony with the agreement we made together. . . .

Toscanini replied:

I admire Shostakovich music but I don't feel such a frenzied love for it like you. I had promised a time ago to receive the new score as it arrives from Russia. In effect, two men of the Am-Russ Music Corporation brought to me the film and some days later the first copy of the score. . . .

As you can imagine, I eagerly looked into it for a few days. . . . At once I was deeply taken by its beauty and its anti-Fascist meanings, and I have to confess to you, by the greatest desire to perform it.

Don't you think, my dear Stokowski, it would be very interesting for everybody, and yourself, too, to hear the old Italian conductor (one of the first artists who strenuously fought against Fascism) to play this work of a young Russian anti-Nazi composer. . . .

Further dialogue proved fruitless; Toscanini performed Shostakovich's Seventh with the NBC Symphony on July 19; Stokowski, unmollified, performed it with the NBC Symphony five months later.[31]

If the music editor Felix Greissle is to be believed, Toscanini also tried to prevent Stokowski's premiere of the Schoenberg Piano Concerto in February 1944. Toscanini regarded the NBC Symphony as his property and would not have it scarred by Schoenberg's "wrong" notes. Proprietary feeling also moved him to police the orchestra's guest conductors, as Oscar Levant once remarked, "like a house dick." Levant and others have described Toscanini's outrage when George Szell rehearsed Beethoven's Second Symphony measure by measure "until finally Toscanini couldn't stand it any longer and harangued at Szell, 'It's my orchestra! My orchestra and my intellectual capacity for the interpretation of Beethoven! It's an insult to me!' " When Bruno Walter rehearsed the NBC orchestra in Mozart's G minor Symphony, K. 550, shortening Toscanini's *molto arco* bow strokes, Toscanini began yelling and banging his fists against a wall. Yet, compared with Stokowski, Szell and Walter were musically kindred to Toscanini. In December 1942, writing to a friend who worked for NBC, he called Stokowski "that *orrible* man and *dishonest* artist," and added: "I cannot look at his *stupid* face without shuddering!"[32]

Toscanini could not have kept this antipathy a secret from Sarnoff and company. On June 12, 1944, NBC announced that Stokowski's contract would not be renewed. According to network sources, Toscanini had decided that having two such disparate conductors hurt the orchestra. As was widely noted, this explanation left much unexplained. From the beginning, NBC had arranged for NBC Symphony musicians to perform regularly under several batons; of the staff conductors, Frank Black alone led dozens of sessions a year. Virgil Thomson, whom Stokowski consulted for advice during his final innings at NBC, has left no doubt that as far as Stokowski was concerned, "too much" contemporary music was a key factor in his ouster. According to RCA Victor's Charles O'Connell, General Motors, which had begun sponsoring the previously unsponsored NBC Symphony broadcasts, "intimated" to Stokowski some displeasure with his programming. But in O'Connell's view Stokowski was mainly undone by Toscanini, Chotzinoff, and Walter Toscanini. Stokowski himself had this to say:

> If I am an acceptable American conductor who enjoys bringing music of American composers to the American public, it would seem fair that I should have the same consideration as a conductor who has not made himself an American citizen [Stokowski took American citizenship in 1915] and who very seldom plays American music and who ignores the inventions and new methods of broadcasting which have mainly developed in the United States. . . . The people of the United States have the right to hear the music being composed by young talented Americans as well as all the great music of all countries composed by great masters. The radio stations are permitted by the Government to use certain wavelengths. This gives the radio stations *privileges* and also demands of them to fulfill their *responsibilities* to the American people. . . .[33]

Stokowski's departure erased his nascent legacy—the radio talks, the children's concert, the important premieres. As for repertoire, during the three NBC seasons he shared with Stokowski, Toscanini led works by eleven Americans; during his thirteen other NBC seasons, he led works by only seven.

In retrospect, the four-year saga of Toscanini's resignation, co-conductorship, and full reinstatement help to define the authority of "NBC's great conductor." Toscanini, to whom alternative philosophies were rival philosophies, would brook no rivals at NBC. At the same time, Toscanini's power was itself distinctly circumscribed. No normal orchestra could have accepted his resignation as painlessly as Sarnoff's diversified network had. If necessary, the network could jettison Toscanini and the orchestra altogether. Even at the Philharmonic, where he exercised no such omnipotence as at La Scala, Toscanini was conceivably "irreplaceable." At NBC, his employers were prepared to make special efforts to tolerate, placate, and delight him; they were also prepared to restrict his rehearsal and hiring prerogatives if necessary. Some NBC executives considered Toscanini an extravagance. In terms of dollar value, Jack Benny, Bob Hope, and Rudy Vallee carried more weight.

The Toscanini-Stokowski jousts at Radio City were shadowed throughout by combat abroad. Two months after Toscanini's resignation letter, Hitler invaded Russia. Pearl Harbor came six months later. George Marek, an RCA Victor manager as of 1950, has plausibly conjectured that America's declaration of war was a factor in Toscanini's decision to return to NBC. The war was unquestionably a factor in his war against Stokowski.

Stokowski led benefit concerts and army bands from coast to coast. But, like the man himself, his politics could seem bizarre or enigmatic. Once, in Philadelphia, he had conducted his Youth League in "The Internationale" —not, as outraged right-wingers proclaimed, because he espoused Marx, but because he liked the piece; as a Stokowskian ploy to stave off criticism, he had the Communist anthem sung in French. Toscanini, by comparison, was fervent and forthright. Not only his dream of a republican Italy, but his proud, dominating temperament—his reckless refusal to be pushed around—underscored his repugnance for Hitler and Mussolini.

In a September 26, 1943 *New York Times Magazine* article entitled "His Music Speaks for Freedom," Howard Taubman wrote: "It is an article of faith for [Toscanini] to seek out and perform works that have the power to stir and heighten democratic aspirations." In addition to the Shostakovich Seventh, Toscanini led three Soviet works after Hitler made war on Stalin: Kabalevsky's Second Symphony and *Colas Breugnon* Overture, and the Shostakovich First. Earlier, when Russia forcibly annexed the Karelian Isthmus and other border territories, he had led an all-Sibelius concert. In addition to his New York Philharmonic Beethoven cycle of 1942, with its freedom-fighting overtones, he led the NBC Symphony in ten all-Beethoven concerts between Pearl Harbor and VJ Day. Of the American works he now programmed, one became a Toscanini specialty: "The Star-Spangled Banner" in his own orchestration. This he would conduct facing a singing audience, eyes blazing, and singing along in his hoarse baritone. The manuscript of his arrangement was auctioned for one million dollars in war bonds in 1943.*

Other wartime Toscanini beneficiaries included the War Orphan Committee, the Child Welfare League, and the Infantile Paralysis Fund. At one benefit concert with the New York Philharmonic, Toscanini signed a blank check in case the evening's fund-raising goal was not met. Seats for an NBC Symphony war bond benefit with Vladimir Horowitz were available only through war bond purchases; over ten million dollars in bonds was sold. One Infantile Paralysis Fund benefit over NBC elicited a letter from the President to Toscanini reading in part: "The magnificent contributions you have made to the world of music have always been highlighted by your humanitarian and unyielding devotion to the cause of liberty." Toscanini replied: "I assure you, my dear Mr. President, that I shall continue unabated in the same path that I have trod all my life for the cause of liberty."[35]

A singular moment in Toscanini's war crusade was the announcement of Mussolini's downfall midway through an all-Verdi NBC concert on July 25, 1943; Toscanini clasped his hands and gazed aloft. The day after Italy's surrender five weeks later, he conducted a special half-hour broadcast he called "Victory Symphony, Act I." The program consisted of the first movement of Beethoven's Fifth, the *William Tell* Overture, the Garibaldi Hymn, and "The Star-Spangled Banner." In a rare statement to the press, he exclaimed: "I am overwhelmed with joy. . . . I can only say blessed Italy, at last you are free to join the Allies who are struggling to keep alive the flame of liberty in the world." The same month, writing painstakingly in English, he composed a 350-word plea for *Life:* "To the People of America —by Arturo Toscanini." The editors noted: "Never before has Maestro Toscanini written for publication—not even on his own subject of music. . . . He is generally recognized, of course, as the greatest living master of music. Here, however, he speaks as a wise, though impassioned patriot, and as a man whose faith in the ideal of human freedom has never wavered." Toscanini's article called on Americans to seek an Italian solution rejecting Italy's king, Victor Emmanuel III, and prime minister, Pietro Badoglio. It began: "I am an old artist who had been among the first to denounce

---

*George Marek recalls a story told by Toscanini's friend Marcia Davenport. Toscanini was watching the 1953 Eisenhower inauguration on television. "The military band struck up 'The Star-Spangled Banner,' playing it in the wrong tempo and with bad intonation. Toscanini, scandalized, jumped up, clapped his hands to indicate the right tempo, and shouted, '*Madonna*, why didn't they call me?' "[34]

Fascism to the world. I feel and believe that I can act as interpreter of the soul of the Italian people—these people whose voice has been choked for twenty years, but, thanks to God, just now is shouting for peace and liberty. . . ."[36]

For years Hollywood had tried coaxing Toscanini onto the screen with offers of up to $250,000. With Italy's future undecided, he now agreed to participate without fee in a progapanda movie for the Office of War Information, to be shown in Italy and other liberated European countries. In December 1943, he was filmed conducting the NBC Symphony in the Overture to *La forza del destino* and in an obscure 1862 Verdi opus of which he had given the American premiere the preceding January: *The Hymn of the Nations.* The latter was written on commission to a peace-and-brotherhood text by Arrigo Boito. Verdi's choral setting includes strains from the Garibaldi Hymn, the "Marseillaise," and "God Save the King." Toscanini added "The Star-Spangled Banner" and altered the words of the Garibaldi Hymn so that Jan Peerce, rather than singing "Italy, my country," sang "Italy, my betrayed country" where Boito asked for heaven's protection until his fatherland was wholly freed. For the Office of War Information film, Toscanini also inserted "The Internationale." He was shown editing *The Hymn of the Nations* at the keyboard "to honor the great free Allies of today." A second brief sequence showed him operating his home phonograph with nervous, impatient gestures, then pacing his living room to the Garibaldi Hymn while a narrator commented: "Americans know that this son of a soldier of Garibaldi refused to allow his music to become the servant of tyrants. . . . When the Führer rose to power in Germany, Toscanini withdrew from Bayreuth. When Austria was forced into the Reich, Toscanini was heard no more at Salzburg." A review by Louis Biancolli, music critic of the New York *World-Telegram,* called the film "a gripping work of art." Of Toscanini's participation, Biancolli wrote: "The show is the Maestro's all through [in his] double role of world's top batonist and unwavering foe of tyranny. Every crescendo seems a punch at Fascism." Biancolli proposed that Toscanini be given an Academy Award.[37]

Another momentous event in Toscanini's antifascist crusade was an immense Red Cross benefit at Madison Square Garden on May 25, 1944. The performing forces included the NBC Symphony, the New York Philharmonic, the All-City High School Chorus, and five vocal soloists. The program consisted of four Wagner excerpts, the final act of *Rigoletto, Hymn of the Nations,* and "Stars and Stripes Forever." With the arena crammed to capacity, the concert netted over $120,000—which, according to the New York *Times,* was believed to represent "the largest amount ever realized from the sale of tickets for any performance of serious music," and included $11,000 for a Toscanini baton auctioned by Mayor La Guardia during the intermission, and $10,000 from the sale of one hundred copies of a souvenir program autographed by Toscanini.[38]

Toscanini was now wrapped in the flag. The patriotic spectacles he headlined may seem naive nearly half a century after the fact; in 1944, mindful of Toscanini's actual heroism, Americans did not think to marvel that no patriotic native musician symbolized the American cause as Toscanini did, or that Toscanini's innate pugnacity and theatricality were pertinent beyond his politics. The long view back cannot recapture the trauma of fanatic enemies and Americans killed in combat; yet it can prove clarifying. In this regard, the 1944 Madison Square Garden souvenir program is a telling memento of Toscanini's most lucrative benefit performance. The first and most prominent photograph is a full-page Toscanini profile posed and shadowed to conceal a possible Christ-like growth of beard. A double-page picture spread, two pages further in, shows the conductor's birthplace, two childhood portraits, and a 1917 photograph documenting Toscanini's combat-zone band concerts. The most prominent of the full-page advertisements reads: "Arturo Toscanini Records Exclusively on Victor Red Seal Records" ("You may choose from the works of Beethoven, Brahms, Haydn, Mozart and other masters—played in thrilling, flawless performances . . ."). The booklet also includes an appreciation of Toscanini by Winthrop Sargeant and a reproduction of Toscanini's score of *Hymn of the Nations* showing where he changed Boito's words to read "Italia, patria mia tradita." Finally, each musical selection except "Stars and Stripes" is illustrated. Rather than war goddesses on airborne steeds, the Ride of the Valkyries is made to show Allied bombers in formation. If this unique interpretation appropriates Wagner to make war on Germany, the booklet as a whole has less the effect of appropriating Toscanini for the war effort than of appropriating the war effort on behalf of Toscanini.[39]

For VE Day, a year following the Madison Square Garden benefit, Toscanini broadcast "Victory Symphony, Act II," in which he "finished" the Beethoven's Fifth performance he had begun in 1943 as "Victory Symphony, Act I." "Victory Symphony, Act III," for VJ Day the following fall, was a broadcast of the *Eroica;* Toscanini was introduced as "music's symbol of democracy militant." Even more than during his Philharmonic years, when his dealings with Bayreuth had made front-page headlines, Toscanini's soldierly aplomb heightened his charisma. Three further parallels to the Philharmonic period consolidated the imagery of greatest conductor, temperamental genius, and indispensable culture bearer. These were Toscanini's tantrums, his accredited repertoire, and his diminishing competition.

Samuel Antek's blow-by-blow account of the first of half-a-dozen "great [Toscanini] flare-ups" at NBC both illustrates the magnetic drama of Toscanini's rehearsal tirades and illuminates their cause and effect. The music was the Scherzo of Beethoven's Ninth:

> We were all very intent. Toscanini was driving on, covered with perspiration, when suddenly he stopped everything. "The celli!" he screamed. "The celli! Not dah-de-dah-h-h, but duy-de dah!" Were they stupid? So-o-o-o, they were taking it easy. They were sitting back in their chairs. There was no bite, no life, in the sound! They had no respect for the great music! They were asleep! They were insulting Beethoven! They were insulting *him!* No! Not with Toscanini would they play that horrible way! . . . The raging tempest was unleashed. With a torrent of insults he broke his baton, picked up the score, began to pound it, tore it up, kicked at the stand, and then pushed it off the stage. Then, bellowing at the top of his lungs, he began to claw at his collar until his hand caught in the chain of the watch he carried in his breast pocket. With a furious wrench he pulled it away, glared at it with unseeing eyes, and, in a vicious lunge, smashed it to the ground where the watch spilled in all directions. *No-o-o! No-o-o!* He was through! Finished! He would never conduct this orchestra of jackasses again! He stomped off and walked around the outer rim of the stage, shouting his disgust and smashing his clenched fist violently down on the seats as he passed. We still heard him when he left the hall, his oaths reverberating down the corridor as he headed toward his dressing room.

At the next day's rehearsal, Antek continues, Toscanini entered smiling and fresh. He had brought along a cheap Ingersoll watch inscribed "for rehearsals only." The orchestra was now "tremendously alert."

> Toscanini's rage, somehow, always achieved a musical purpose. Childish, petulant, unreasoning as it was, we somehow respected and admired his capacity to be so moved and aroused by his feeling for his work. It was as though Toscanini, through his temper, through the fear, sympathy and resentment he inspired in the men, had made us all feel how important the music was to him and to us. . . . His tantrums did not have the premeditated, sadistic, sarcastic quality of lesser men. To him, the enormity of the crime of an infraction of good taste was an insult to the Muse herself—not to him personally.

To Antek, who in another description likened Toscanini's cries to "the horrible shrieking of stuck bulls in a slaughterhouse I once visited in Chicago," Toscanini seemed a victim of involuntary, visceral susceptibilities; in revering Toscanini, Antek pitied him. To Chotzinoff and other sideline adulators, Toscanini's rages were a ceaseless divertissement. According to Howard Taubman, a system of coded telephone bulletins was devised to keep NBC executives posted on rehearsal conditions at Studio 8H: "Clear, calm," "Breeze coming up," "Rough wind," "Gale blowing," "Tornado." "S.O.S." meant Toscanini had barricaded himself in his dressing room. Taubman himself wrote: "He is used to having his way. Whether you call it temperament or not, it does not diminish the delightful quality of the things that occur when Toscanini is annoyed."[40]

Advancing age made Toscanini's NBC rehearsal traumas seem the more awesome; the episode Antek describes occurred when Toscanini was seventy-two. His NBC repertoire also at times belied his age. Mainly, however, Toscanini perpetuated the repertoire of mass appeal. As previously noted, of his eleven seasons with the New York Philharmonic, during four of which he led fewer than thirty New York concerts, nine included performances of the *Meistersinger* Prelude, eight included performances of the Brahms "Haydn" Variations, seven included performances of the *Eroica,* and seven included performances of the *Tristan* Prelude. Of Toscanini's seventeen NBC Symphony seasons, usually comprising thirteen to twenty concerts, nine included the *Meistersinger* Prelude, eight included the *Eroica,* eight included the *Tristan* Prelude, and seven included the "Haydn" Variations. *La Mer,* presented by Toscanini during five New York Philharmonic seasons, was given during nine seasons over NBC. As with the Philharmonic, Toscanini at NBC never programmed anything by Bartók, Berg, Hindemith, Mahler, or Schoenberg. The only Stravinsky he led was a single performance of excerpts from *Petrouchka.* The only Prokofiev was the "Classical" Symphony. The only works by Ravel were *Boléro,* the *Daphnis and Chloé* Suite No. 2, and *La Valse.* With the Philharmonic, Toscanini had given two Bruckner symphonies, the Fourth and the Seventh; at NBC, he gave none.

As we have seen, both Toscanini's war on Stokowski and America's war on Hitler spurred broadcasts of American and Soviet music. Here, Toscanini's choices were mild, but they included works of enduring interest: Barber's Adagio for Strings; Copland's *El Salón México;* Gershwin's *An American in Paris,* Concerto in F, and *Rhapsody in Blue;* Griffes's *The White Peacock;* Grofé's *Grand Canyon Suite;* Harris's Third Symphony; Shostakovich's First and Seventh. NBC broadcasts of Martucci's Piano Concerto and First and Second symphonies, plus many miniatures, reflected Toscanini's continued allegiance to twentieth-century Italians. Also qualifying as Toscanini novelties were Kurt Atterberg's Sixth Symphony; Berlioz's *Romeo and Juliet;* Cherubini's C minor Requiem and Symphony in D; Falla's *El amor brujo;* Kalinnikov's First Symphony; Kodály's *Dances of Marósszek* and *Háry János* Suite; Liszt's *From the Cradle to the Grave* and *Orpheus;* Joachim's orchestration of Schubert's "Gastein" Symphony; Sibelius's Fourth; and Vaughan Williams's *Fantasia on a Theme by Thomas Tallis.* Many of these nonstandard items were newly acquired by Toscanini when he was in his seventies. Still, the heterodox list is a short one; in a period when other American orchestras were more than doubling their quota of contemporary compositions, especially by Americans and Russians, Toscanini's NBC Symphony repertoire essentially replicated his Philharmonic repertoire.

As for Toscanini's diminishing competition—his Philharmonic period had benefited from a relative paucity of plausible rivals: Artur Bodanzky of the Metropolitan Opera and Walter Damrosch were not major international figures; Koussevitzky in Boston and Stokowski in Philadelphia were, but not as exponents of the canonized German repertoire once served in New York and Boston by Furtwängler, Mahler, Mengelberg, Mottl, Muck, Nikisch, Schalk, Seidl, Strauss, and Weingartner. Now, at NBC, Toscanini saw his competition dwindle further—and this despite a startling influx of musical talent. Of the conductors who left Europe during or just before World War II, five were luminaries of the first rank: Thomas Beecham, who was London's leading conductor of concerts and operas; Fritz Busch, who in Dresden had created one of Europe's vanguard operatic ensembles; Erich Kleiber, who had led historic performances of *Jenůfa* and *Wozzeck* as head of the Berlin State Opera; Otto Klemperer, under whose leadership Berlin's Kroll Opera had been Europe's most forward-looking; and Bruno Walter, who had left cherished legacies in Berlin, Munich, and Vienna. Yet none of these master conductors secured a permanent position in Toscanini's vicinity. Positions were not lacking. Stokowski had announced his resignation from the Philadelphia Orchestra in 1934. But the Philadelphia board, which, according to Stokowski, had earlier ignored his recommendations that it engage Furtwängler and Walter as guests, in 1938 named Eugene Ormandy music director in Stokowski's place. Equally unexciting was the New York Philharmonic board's appointment of the young John Barbirolli—like Ormandy in Philadelphia, an Arthur Judson selection—following Toscanini's resignation and the breakdown of the plan to hire Furtwängler. Beecham overtly sought Toscanini's New York post. Klemperer coveted both the New York and Philadelphia podiums but was opposed by Judson—partly, Klemperer later claimed, for his having insisted on programming an unpopular Mahler symphony with the Philharmonic in 1935. Toscanini and Rodzinski, who spread vicious rumors, and Downes, who wrote unfavorable reviews, helped make Barbirolli's seven-year Philharmonic tenure a tormented one. Walter was offered Barbirolli's job but

considered himself too old, becoming instead a frequent guest and sometime "musical advisor" with the Philharmonic. Barbirolli's successor as
chief conductor, in 1943, was the nerve-wracked, nerve-wracking Rodzinski, who had broken with Toscanini in 1939. Even Rodzinski's admirers did
not call him a major interpreter. He reinstilled orchestral discipline only to
resign in 1947 during a power struggle with Judson, who was allegedly bent
on usurping artistic control in order to promote the roster of soloists and
conductors he also managed. In Rodzinski's view, Judson was the reason
a dozen major conductors had "marched in ghostly parade" before Philharmonic audiences, with only Toscanini taking hold. Winthrop Sargeant,
among others, traced the Philharmonic's vicissitudes to a second source:
"For too many years [the Philharmonic's] initiative, its volition, its only
coordinating and unifying principle, had issued from . . . the hypnotic will
of Toscanini."[41]

Less surprising, but equally unexciting, was the Metropolitan Opera's
response to the conductors' exodus: with the death of Bodanzky in 1939, the
German repertoire—made paramount by Kirsten Flagstad and Lauritz
Melchior—was mainly inherited by the twenty-seven-year-old Erich
Leinsdorf, a onetime Toscanini assistant at Salzburg. Klemperer was not
invited to conduct at the Metropolitan until very late in his career (he
accepted but had to cancel); disappointed in New York and Philadelphia,
he found work in California, where as conductor of the Los Angeles
Philharmonic (1933–39) he was once asked to perform the *Pathétique* Symphony without its depressing finale. Kleiber did receive offers from the
Metropolitan, but found them insufficiently tempting; he is said to have
disliked the "industrial quality" of American musical life. Beecham conducted at the Metropolitan for three seasons (1941–44), during one of which
he led only six performances; having failed to secure the New York Philharmonic, he wound up conducting the Seattle Symphony (1941–43). Busch,
who had been considered for the Philharmonic in 1937 (Toscanini had
recommended him after Furtwängler's appointment fell through),* con-

---

*The Philharmonic board's decision not to press for Busch's appointment was based not
only (as has been reported) on his pending European commitments, but also on his
country of origin. Walter Price wrote to Toscanini on March 31, 1935:

> The Committee are deeply indebted . . . for your kind recommendation. . . . Mr.
> Busch advises that . . . he has European obligations continuing for the whole season
> and is fixed for several years to come, so that he could only come by cancelling or
> rearranging these matters.
> The reaction of the Committee [is that] it would not be fair to him to ask him
> to cancel or rearrange [his plans]. They take into consideration this fact, that we have
> just been through this very unpleasant German business [with Furtwängler] and we

ducted many Mozart and Wagner performances at the Metropolitan for four seasons (1945–49); ill at ease in New York (where one concert promoter complained he was "not a showman"), he returned to Europe, where at Glyndebourne he had begun instilling priorities—conducting, ensemble, staging—supplanting the star system entrenched in New York.[43] Walter alone established something like an enduring relationship with the Metropolitan, mainly conducting Mozart and Beethoven there from 1940 to 1945, then making scattered appearances in later years. An American resident from 1939, he might have played a fuller role. But the Metropolitan after World War I was no conductor's house. Meanwhile, at NBC, Toscanini's Beethoven and Brahms, Verdi and Wagner brandished a dynamism and instrumental finesse unknown at the Judsonized Philharmonic since his departure in 1937, unknown at the star-struck Metropolitan since his departure in 1915.

As carryover traits from his Philharmonic days, Toscanini's patriotic appeal, rehearsal tirades, canonized repertoire, and meager competition perpetuated vital aspects of his cult. At the same time, the NBC concerts spawned a new symphonic species bound to instill the cult in new ways. This was not merely due to the network's merchandising mindset—to plugging "NBC's great conductor," "the finest available musicians," and "the world's biggest drum" after the fashion of radios, vacuum tubes, Edgar Bergen and Charlie McCarthy. The by-invitation-only audiences, the one-concert-per-program schedules, the regular dismemberment of the orchestra into smaller ensembles for "Harvest of Stars," "The Eternal Light," and other commercial shows under any of a dozen conductors—these were anomalies tending to isolate the world's first major commercial-radio orchestra from the normal symphonic milieu. Its listeners, too, could be isolated and controlled.

Symbolic of this isolation was the NBC Symphony's special home. Studio 8H, part of the resplendent Radio City complex Sarnoff had opened

---

have got to be very careful; that we should not ask somebody to change his plans and then find a hostility here that would be disadvantageous to him. We are much influenced by your feeling that he is a most desirable man, but at the same time, in the light of his cable, in which he clearly states that all his time is now filled up, we feel, until the resentment of the Jewish people subsides against anything apparently German, it is unfair to Mr. Busch to allow him to cancel or change his plans. . . .

You see the overhead of [the] orchestra is colossal and with you, our main bower, going, we have got to be very careful, because somebody has got to bear the deficit if there is any, and the Jewish people represent the largest part of our audiences. . . .[42]

Among musicians, Busch was a prominent antifascist; he had left Germany in 1933.

in 1933, was, in theory, NBC's most "scientific" radio auditorium, "the largest broadcasting studio in the world," engineered to meet unique broadcasting criteria. It differed in crucial respects from Carnegie Hall, ten blocks uptown. With a seating capacity of 1,200 and more, 8H was smaller by three-fifths. Its decor was starkly streamlined. And its acoustics, to which the functional-looking decor contributed, were antiseptic: hard, cold, and dull—from the seats, on recordings, and over the airwaves. Onstage, the musicians had trouble hearing one another. Charles O'Connell called Studio 8H "one of the most unsatisfactory musical rooms, from an acoustic point of view, I have ever known."[44] But Sarnoff, overruling O'Connell, would not abandon it.

The synthetic audience, the unnatural sound, the impersonal hall with its glass-faced control booth overlooking the stage all reflected a stranding of the musical event. In Studio 8H, NBC embellished Toscanini's concerts with a show of reverence and ballyhoo paralleling its skewed promotional language. Extraordinary precautions were taken to ensure silent listening: the programs were printed on rattleproof materials; ticket holders with coughs were asked to leave. Over the radio especially, the network could command what was heard and "seen." Sign-off announcements included: "Mr. Toscanini returns to the stage to accept the audience's applause in his customary unassuming way," and "The enthusiasm of the audience in the studio, I feel sure, is only an echo of what all of us are feeling after hearing this final concert under Mr. Toscanini's direction." John Barbirolli, a Toscanini admirer even when his admiration was unreturned, wrote home after attending his first NBC Symphony concert in 1938: "I came away musically exalted and otherwise terribly depressed and disgusted at the way they run things at NBC. . . . Admission is free and by ticket and it is the strangest sensation-mongering audience with all sorts of theatrical stunts and altogether upsetting." Virgil Thomson commented in 1946:

The NBC hall is not a pleasant place to hear music in. Not only are the acoustics, as is well known, deplorable; but the manners of the staff are in no way encouraging to personal expansiveness. At every turn one is disciplined, guided, scolded, administered. It is almost impossible to get into the place or out of it without being pushed around mentally or physically by somebody in a uniform. The "watchdogs of capital," as one of my composer friends [Roy Harris] calls all this uniformed personnel, do not, with their police-like severity, create an atmosphere of welcome or of ease. They make it difficult, in fact, to listen to music with a free mind.[45]

Sarnoff had inaugurated the NBC Symphony on egalitarian premises: ignoring the fact that Toscanini's Philharmonic concerts had been nationally broadcast for years, he spoke of fostering an unprecedented radio audience for great music. But the use of Studio 8H meant that Toscanini's live audience would shrink to a fraction of what it had been. And NBC's ticket system meant that what audience was left was an elite. Such arm's-length democracy, implemented in behalf of the musical democrat who had abolished hereditary boxholders at La Scala, could not pass unnoticed. NBC's Dorothy Thompson noticed it, and strategized as follows in her "People in the News" broadcast of January 4, 1938:

> . . . Actually, you who listen to Toscanini's orchestra on Saturday nights in your own home *hear* the music better than those who manage to get the priceless seats to see as well as hear. For the broadcasting studio is acoustically designed for the radio audience, not for the studio audience, who miss something of the brilliance of the sound, particularly of the strings, in an auditorium where everything is somewhat dampened in order to heighten the effects for the really chosen hearers, who are you.

Yet the bulk of Thompson's report rejoiced in her own powers of sight. "Watch the left hand," she excitedly told the blind chosen hearers. "It is one of the most beautiful and eloquent hands in the world." Elsewhere she confessed: "It is a shame that we do not yet have television so perfected that the home audience can see Toscanini, as well as hear the music which he seems, with his baton, to evoke not only out of the orchestra, but out of the air, out of the elements."

Toscanini's new invisibility made him the more inaccessible—not merely never heard to speak, but never seen to conduct. Concomitantly, he became the more legendary. With NBC in command, both the legend and the man became more malleable. Chotzinoff, Walter Toscanini, and others dedicated to fulfilling Toscanini's every need now formed a newly protective, insulating coterie. His professional itinerary atrophied. The early NBC tour dates—in Baltimore, Boston, Chicago, Newark, Providence, Pittsburgh, Washington, D.C., South America—were not followed up. As for other orchestras, they practically ceased to exist for Toscanini. He did not conduct a complete, staged opera after *Die Meistersinger, Falstaff, Fidelio,* and *The Magic Flute* in Salzburg the summer of 1937. He was contractually bound to record only for RCA.

The musical costs of the NBC hothouse may be imagined. Many members of the orchestra felt its best concerts took place on tour, liberated from

parched acoustics, from hand-picked audiences, from the strains of undertaking a single, do-or-die performance per program. Toscanini himself, it
has been suggested, was made to suffer more than a decade of symphonic
inbreeding. He might have maintained contact with leading American and
European orchestras, with their audiences, historic halls, and nourishing
musical traditions. Tantalizingly, he might again have conducted opera:
according to the opera producer Herbert Graf, plans were laid for staged
presentations of *Falstaff* and *La Traviata* under Toscanini in New York,
but financial guarantees did not materialize. Toscanini wound up doing
both operas by halves in radio installments.[46]

Like NBC's refusal to abandon Studio 8H, Toscanini's shrunken field
of operations showed the importance attached to displaying him on NBC
property. Sarnoff was a sincere believer in disseminating high culture, as
validated by the world's greatest conductor—but under an NBC marquee.
NBC sponsorship guaranteed more than enhanced network prestige;
it made the swollen American Toscanini arena yet bigger and more volatile, manipulable by practiced experts in telling hearers what to see and
think. Toscanini himself was sequestered, facilitating exploitation of the
Toscanini totem in the interest of unrestricted, undiscerning mass consumption.

The NBC Symphony, 1937–45:
The National Context I

*P*ondering the relative classlessness of American society of the 1830s, Tocqueville had written:

> . . . The servant never considers himself as an entire stranger to the pleasures and toils of his master, nor the poor man to those of the rich; the farmer tries to resemble the townsman, and the provinces to take after the metropolis. No one easily allows himself to be reduced to the mere material cares of life; and the humblest artisan casts at times an eager and a furtive glance into the higher regions of the intellect. People do not read with the same notions or in the same manner as they do in aristocratic communities, but the circle of readers is increasingly expanded, till it includes all the people.

A century later, the farmer, the provinces, and the metropolis were integrated as never before, and America's "circle of readers" had expanded immeasurably. A "second industrial revolution" had powered "new prosperity." Radio and movies, the automobile and the telephone had penetrated the island communities of smalltown America, spreading and standardizing city mores. Frederick Lewis Allen, the first historian of the twenties, documented "waves of contagious excitement" seizing on mass-produced names, news, and commodities: Rudolph Valentino, Charles Lindbergh's flight, Henry Ford's Model A. Mass culture and consumption were spurred by specialists in mass behavior. The mayhem at Valentino's funeral—tens of thousands rioted; hundreds were trampled; the chapel was gutted by souvenir seekers—began with one Harry Klemfuss, who as the undertaker's press agent had provided early photographs of the funeral cortege mimed by stand-ins. Unlike Barnum, Bernard Ullmann, and other nineteenth-century ballyhoo experts, men like Klemfuss practiced ballyhoo and nothing but. Ivy Lee, a former reporter, and Edward Bernays, a graduate of George Creel's Committee on Public Information, made "public relations" respectable white-collar work. Ascending in tandem with the publicist was the advertising specialist. In *Crystallizing Public Opinion* (1923), Bernays argued that the public relations counsel "is not merely the purveyor of news; he is more logically the *creator* of news"; and advertisers created new needs. To buy, observed John Dewey in 1930, had become as much an American duty as saving had once seemed. The United States had become a "consumer society."[1]

Reverence for wealth and commercial success made Ford a god, and business a religion. And yet, following Tocqueville, the twenties and thirties also saw a democratization of "higher regions of the intellect." With more money to spend and more time to spend it (the five-day work week became commonplace in offices and factories), Americans patronized movies and baseball games as never before—and also museums and concerts. They bought vacuum cleaners and refrigerators—and recordings of Beethoven and Chopin. This web of material and cultural strivings was documented in a landmark treatment of America's consumer-age Everyman: *Middletown* (1929) by Helen and Robert Lynd.

Middletown (actually Muncie, Indiana), in the Lynds' sociological study, is a community characterized by "a monetary approach to the satisfactions of life," a "diffusion of new urgent occasions for spending money" as created by advertisements, magazines, and movies. The local newspaper baldly maintains: "The American citizen's first duty to his country is no longer that of citizen but that of consumer. Consumption is a new necessity." In Middletown, the fine arts are—like cars, kitchen appliances, and dressy clothes—articles of prescribed consumption. Phonographs, a curiosity as late as 1900, had come to be considered such a necessity that the father in a family of three, laid off in 1923, testified: "We strapped a trunk on the running board of the Ford, put the Victrola in the back seat with the little girl, and went off job hunting. Wherever we lived all summer we had our music with us." Of working class and "business class" families surveyed by the Lynds, one-third of the former, and more than three-fifths of the latter, had one child or more taking music lessons, reflecting more "time spent on music" than their parents had invested as children. And yet, in keeping with the Middletown pattern of increasingly passive, mechanized, and commercialized leisure time, nonvicarious musical activity had diminished in the home: in proportion to an upsurge of radio and phonograph listening, there was less playing and singing. The community's once popular singing societies had also atrophied. Instead, its organized musical life, mainly in the hands of business-class women, centered on music club meetings and club-sponsored concerts. "Music for adults has almost ceased to be a matter of spontaneous, active participation," the Lynds observed, and added: "The mothers of the present generation of children were brought up in a culture without Victrola and radio when the girl in the crowd who could play while the others sang or danced was in demand."[2] (In a sequel, *Middletown in Transition* [1937], the Lynds documented a post-Depression return to twenties cultural values, stressing competitive spending and possessing, and reflecting the resumed impact of industrialization and urbanization.)

While no precise demographics exist for the new culture consumers who swelled audiences for the visual arts, music, and literature during the twenties and thirties, the "new middle classes" of the same period are unquestionably pertinent. These aspirant, upwardly mobile white collar types had weekends and evenings free. Their acquisitive habits, cravings for respectability, and intellectual naiveté made them easy targets for ridicule. Much as Mark Twain's *Innocents Abroad* caricatured the rising cultural ambitions of emergent middle classes during the Gilded Age, the cultural strivings of the new middle classes were parodied by Sinclair Lewis in *Babbitt* (1922). The real estate salesman George F. Babbitt is a joiner, a social climber whose self-esteem hinges on the esteem of the crowd. His living room is a still-life study in vicarious refinement:

> Against the wall was a piano . . . but no one used it save [the Babbitts' ten-year-old daughter] Rinka. The hard briskness of the phonograph contented [the Babbitts]; their store of jazz records made them feel wealthy and cultured, and all they knew of creating music was the nice adjustment of a bamboo needle. The books on the table were unspotted and laid in rigid parallels. . . .

Though he does not realize it, high culture perplexes Babbitt, intimating satisfactions his world of things can never incorporate. When the well-traveled wife of the local construction magnate visits, Babbitt is wide-eyed:

> "I suppose you'll be going to Europe pretty soon again, won't you?" he invited.
> "I'd like awfully to run over to Rome for a few weeks."
> "I suppose you see a lot of pictures and music and curios and everything there."

And he is in awe of the blue blood of Sir Gerard Doak, who passes through town on a coal-buying mission. Yet this same George Babbitt is disinclined to tour Europe "as long as there's our own mighty cities and mountains to be seen." In scenes reminiscent of the *Quaker City* pilgrimage of *The Innocents Abroad,* his insecurities produce diatribes against "snobs," "highbrows," and "the decayed nations of Europe." Babbitt's definitive high-culture credo comes in an address before the Zenith Real Estate Board:

"Our Ideal Citizen—I picture him first and foremost as being busier than a bird-dog, not wasting a lot of good time in day-dreaming or going to sassiety teas or kicking about things that are none of his business. . . .

"In politics and religion this Sane Citizen is the canniest man on earth; and in the arts he invariably has a natural taste which makes him pick out the best, every time. In no country in the world will you find so many reproductions of the Old Masters and of well-known paintings on parlor walls as in these United States. No country has anything like our number of phonographs, with not only dance records and comic but also the best operas, such as Verdi, rendered by the world's highest-paid singers.

"In other countries, art and literature are left to a lot of shabby bums living in attics and feeding on booze and spaghetti, but in America the successful writer or picture-painter is indistinguishable from any other decent businessman. . . ."[3]

One hears echoes of Lewis's caustic voice in the Lynds' comment that music in Middletown "seems to serve in part as a symbol that one belongs," and in Frederick Lewis Allen's explanation of Lindbergh reverence in terms of "spiritual starvation": "There was the god of business to worship —but a suspicion lingered that he was made of brass." A later, influential version of shallow culture-consumption among the new middle classes is C. Wright Mills's *White Collar* (1951), in which "mass leisure" is explained in terms of mass alienation. Staffing ever larger, more bureaucratized offices, the new middle classes were less rooted, socially and psychologically, than self-sufficient entrepreneurs they displaced. Similarly, new blue-collar types, manning larger, more impersonal factories, were less secure than displaced artisans. The result, according to Mills, was a psychology of conformism, of eager material and cultural aspiration. Writing less condescendingly of the psychological costs of post–World War I economic and social transformations, and of Depression-era fear and shame, a prominent recent cultural historian, the late Warren Susman, fashions a view of the thirties as "*the* decade for participating and belonging," for "conforming" and "fitting in" to a larger whole, for finding new, stabilizing symbols and myths in movies and other new mass-participation formats while striving for a more respectable, more ingratiating mien.[4]

At the same time, the culture-consumption movement evoked Tocqueville's benign characterization of eager glances cast toward higher realms of cultivation and knowledge. As surely as some converts to popularized high culture were lazy, craven Babbitt types, or disoriented, displaced entrepreneurs and artisans as described by Mills, others felt a healthy hunger for broader horizons. High school and college enrollment had shot up after World War I. The war itself had offered firsthand glimpses of Old World arts and learning to soldiers and nurses, most of whom had never visited Europe before. In John Dos Passos's *U.S.A.*, J. Ward Morehouse, modeled after Ivy Lee, comments while in Paris: "Maybe it's taken the war to teach us how to live. We've been too much interested in money and material things. . . ."[5] A popular song inquired: "How Ya Gonna Keep 'em Down on the Farm? (After They've Seen Paree)."

Sometimes stirred by envy and dislocation, sometimes by innocent curiosity and egalitarian instinct, a leveling impulse swept through the preserves of high culture after World War I. Differently motivated, fledgling initiates shared a common need: for intellectual grounding and self-confidence, for lessons in the rudiments of creativity and learned discourse. The consumer society answered with a new type of cultural product—neither patrician nor plebeian, intimidating nor patronizingly plain.

The Book-of-the-Month Club, begun in 1926, and proliferating "great books" courses for adults were symptoms of a culture-dissemination mentality that also produced its own great books: H. G. Wells's *Outline of History* (1921) and *Short History of the World* (1922), Hendrik van Loon's *The Story of Mankind* (1921), James Harvey Robinson's *The Mind in the Making* (1921), John Arthur Thomson's *Outline of Science* (1922), John Drinkwater's *Outline of Literature* (1923–24), George A. Dorsey's *Why We Behave Like Human Beings* (1925), Will Durant's *The Story of Philosophy* (1926), Charles and Mary Beard's *The Rise of American Civilization* (1927), John Cowper Powys's *The Meaning of Culture* (1929), and John Langdon-Davies's *Man and His Universe* (1930). The historian James Steel Smith, surveying this "spectacular eruption of popular effort to popularize knowledge," has labeled the 1920s the "day of the popularizers," an "unparalleled cultural happening" reflecting expanding literacy, education, and leisure in the context of mass media and mass marketing. According to Smith:

> The principal popularizers of the 1920s happily and frankly [acknowledged] that their chief intention was to reach the hoi polloi. Frequently and openly all expressed their wish not so much to reach an educated, critical audience but to get the attention of an uninformed, unsophisticated audience eager to learn from them. They were unashamed about their eagerness to teach the *general* intelligent public, which they felt the scholars and critics were neglecting.

In an introduction to the 1931 edition of *Outline of History,* Wells half-teasingly noted the unavailability of prior histories "sufficiently superficial" for the "ordinary citizen" to absorb. Thomson, in his introduction to *Outline of Science* (subtitled "A Plain Story Simply Told"), wrote:

> What then is the aim of this book? It is to give the intelligent student-citizen, otherwise called "the man in the street," a bunch of intellectual keys by which to open doors which have been hitherto shut to him, partly because he got no glimpse of the treasures behind the doors, and partly because the portals were made forbidding by an unnecessary display of technicalities.

The tone of the popularizers, summarized by Smith, was one of "chirpy ebullience, happy energy." Without sacrificing dignity, they endeavored to simplify and entertain, as by connecting facts with people and stories. Durant said his purpose was "to humanize knowledge by centering the story of speculative thought around certain dominant personalities."[6]

Cranked down a notch, such pedagogic goals found a natural venue in radio—a medium itself connotative of the "hoi polloi" and "man in the street." Hostile to abstraction, friendly to anecdote and personality, the airwaves seemed a logical dispenser of unforbidding knowledge. The voice of chirpy ebullience and happy energy seemed a radio voice. With radio's coming of age in the 1930s, its upbeat main attraction was the standardized variety bill built around such national celebrities as Eddie Cantor, Bing Crosby, and Rudy Vallee. Second in popularity were the serials; "The Lone Ranger," new in 1933, was playing three times a week to twenty million people six years later. The single most listened-to show in 1937–38 was "Major Bowes," an amateur hour with audience balloting in which hog callers vied with fledgling opera singers. Concurrently, as we have seen, government and public interest groups, aroused by the profanation of early broadcast ideals articulated by David Sarnoff and others, helped generate more learned fare, including the "University of Chicago Round Table" on NBC and CBS's "American School of the Air." On closer scrutiny, the evolution of these high-culture showcases discloses an ongoing debate over popularization.

Two competing philosophies vied to shape radio's version of the "day of the popularizers." One, advocated by the National Committee on Education by Radio (NACER), wanted to reserve certain frequencies for independent, non-commercial stations. The other, advocated by the National Advisory Council on Radio Education (NACRE), wanted "Cooperation" between educators and commercial broadcasters—the former as guests, the latter as hosts.[7] Naturally, NBC and CBS preached Cooperation; NBC, in fact, played more than a passing role in NACRE's founding and functioning. As NACRE rhetoric made clear, questions of tone were as germane to the debate as questions of content: radio education, in the commercial view, was "radio" first, "education" second. In contrast to the university classroom milieu more nearly endorsed by NACER, NACRE conceived radio education as a higher species of showmanship. A lesson's success depended on the "radio personality" of its teacher, and the class's sheer size. In an address to the NACRE faithful in 1931, Henry Adams Bellows, a CBS vice president, warned that segregating educators on special noncommercial wavelengths would "condemn them to remain unheard and disregarded." Commercial broadcasters, he continued, would gladly offer educators a berth "provided they do not bore their hearers into open desertion." NBC's "Aspects of the Depression," a series of thirty-two weekly talks, was developed with NACRE input to attain "the most popular sort of presentation consistent with scientific scholarship."

Adherents of Cooperation comprised an alliance of university and radio leaders. Opponents included members of the university community partial to NACER and members of the radio community hostile to prescribed high culture. Prominent among the latter was the swashbuckling John Royal, whom another NBC executive once characterized as having "no respect for educational features" and "lacking in appreciation of anything cultural." In 1933, NBC, with Royal in charge of programming, dropped eighteen local productions of the University of Chicago. Chicago president Robert Hutchins, a key NACRE loyalist, now accused commercial broadcasters of having acquired from their advertisers "the delusion that a mass audience is the only audience." The controversy climaxed in 1934 when the newly created Federal Communications Commission held hearings on a proposal (modeled after the defeated Wagner-Hatfield amendment) to set aside a fixed number of radio frequencies for nonprofit use. Fearing an American version of the British Broadcasting Corporation, NBC and CBS denounced the specter of "controlled radio" as a threat to democracy. CBS's William Paley produced statistics showing that his network already was devoting 70 percent of its airtime to public-interest programming. NBC's Merlin Aylesworth introduced Freeman Gosden (Amos) and Charles J. Correll (Andy) as "philosophers to the American people"; the pair testified that their skits incorporated tips on taxes and tooth care. A landmark FCC report to Congress, dated January 1935, rejected the case for reserving nonprofit frequencies. In putting to rest industry fears of an "American BBC," the commissioners removed a key incentive to Cooperate. The long-term result was a genre of radio instruction mediating between the philosophies of "Amos 'n Andy" and of such NACRE flagships as the "University of Chicago

Round Table," discontinued in 1938. NACRE itself, having pronounced "systematic education by national network broadcasting" a "useless attempt," was a shell by late 1937.

More than before, American radio now endorsed a popularizing "middle tradition" calculated to serve the maximum number of high-culture consumers. Versus Durant, Thomson, and Wells, the new gurus included William Lyon Phelps, Alexander Woollcott, and Clifton Fadiman—each a pleasing, approachable personality in his own right. As the nation's premier popularizer of literature, the chatty, cheerful Phelps was known as "Billy."[8] He frequently contributed to newspapers and popular magazines before quitting his Yale professorship and taking to the air in 1933. As a headline performer on "The Swift's Hour" in 1934 and 1935, he delivered weekly five-minute talks on literature and the theater. One Phelps mini-lecture praised Thornton Wilder's *Heaven's My Destiny* and thanked Wilder for writing short books, dubbed James Hilton a worthy replacement of Conrad and Hardy, identified the "greatest biography" of the season, and pronounced "the best picture I ever saw" a film based on "the best novel in the English language": *David Copperfield.* Such advice seemed as easy to follow as instructions showing how to fix a leaky faucet or cook a cheese soufflé. "The entire intellectual wealth of mankind is within the reach of every humble person," Phelps explained. "You've got a mind. Why not cultivate it? Not every person can become a personage, but every person can be a personality." "Personality" conferred popularity among neighbors, status among customers.

Beyond simplifying knowledge to facilitate quick consumption, Phelps stroked the egos of unlettered consumers: he condoned business-class mores more conspicuously than did the popularizing authors of the 1920s. The resulting ambivalence, recycling the familiar syndrome of New World respect and trepidation toward Old World learning, found expression in such typical "Swift's Hour" encomiums as "the genial, informative Billy Phelps of Yale" and "the friendly and engaging Billy Phelps of Yale." As the Yale professor, Phelps (whose circle of friends included George Santayana) represented accredited high culture. As the genial Billy, addicted to golf and short books, he refuted lingering Gilded Age stereotypes associating learning with angelic ladies and sissy clergymen. Phelps's upper-class accent was mitigated by his brisk, informal delivery. His avowal of relative esoterica was mitigated by Middletown sympathies: he assured his audience that the best books were the best sellers; he frankly disliked modernism and deliberately ignored the movement for "proletarian literature"; he was not above putting in a good word for Swift's "foods distinguished by their excellence." He conveyed love for literature and endorsed premium ham.

.   .   .

Given its variety format and pedagogic bent, "The Swift's Hour" touted music in addition to books and food. The co-host, with Phelps, was Sigmund Romberg, composer of *The Student Prince* and some seventy other operettas. Romberg, whose Hungarian name and accent enhanced his pedigree, conducted compositions of his own plus classical hors d'oeuvres processed for easy ingestion. Schubert's "Ave Maria" was reworded to fit a narrative based on Schubert's life. Phelps would frequently comment on Romberg's part of the proceedings—as in describing Paris's Latin Quarter by way of introducing an excerpt from *La Bohème.* He once quoted a "workman" as confiding that "he didn't know music, or know how to read one note from another, yet . . . Professor Phelps, through a radio program, had brought him an understanding of music, such as he had never had before."

As we have seen, many an assertive mediator preceded Phelps's efforts to harmonize music and the masses. Barnum and other ballyhoo experts used musical celebrities to entice audiences as curious and variegated as circus throngs. Such latter-day ballyhooers as Colonel Mapleson and Heinrich Conried cultivated opera throngs indifferent to which opera Tamagno or Caruso happened to be singing. Meanwhile, in the Germanic tradition, Theodore Thomas weaned fledgling symphonic audiences with "sermons in tones." Following the turn of the century, Arturo Toscanini, whose Latin charisma matched Tamagno's or Caruso's, and whose symphonic credentials ultimately looked as good as any German's, gained an American following bigger, broader, and more fervent with each passing decade. His performance of Beethoven's Ninth in 1913 riveted listeners who "knew not Beethoven." His 1920–21 whistle-stop tour with the Scala orchestra was said to trigger "pandemonium," "orgiastic jubilation." His New York Philharmonic debut in 1926 was called "a Roman triumph staged in modern dress." His popularity upon becoming NBC's "radio maestro" in 1937—nearly 40 percent of all Americans knew his name—reflected in music the same popularizing impulse pushing "great books," NACRE, and "The Swift's Hour."

As Toscanini's celebrity attested, culture's new audience, tutored by Will Durant, H. G. Wells, the "University of Chicago Round Table," and Billy Phelps of Yale, feasted on great music. Radio offered the Metropolitan Opera and the NBC Symphony on Saturdays, the New York Philharmonic and "The Ford Hour" on Sundays: as of 1939, these four well-known longhair broadcasts were said to reach more than 10 million families a week. Additional live broadcast concerts and operas, and portions of "serious" music emanating from network studios, had diminished since the early thirties. Still, an average Sunday afternoon gave New York City radio listeners perhaps three "light classical" studio concerts and as many studio recitals in addition to the Philharmonic broadcast; an average Sunday evening added three or four more live concerts and recitals in addition to "The Ford Hour"; and the weekday schedule might include more than a dozen live broadcasts of hinterlands orchestras (Rochester, Indianapolis, Cleveland, Cincinnati), studio orchestras, and studio recitals.* Moreover, when the radio was off, the phonograph was on. As of 1920, it was standard equipment in the living room of George Babbitt. Seven years later, it seemed essential in Middletown. The record industry slumped badly in the early years of the Depression but more than rebounded in the mid-1930s. Far from undermining the phonograph, radio music spurred record sales; so did technological advances, making "high fidelity" a household term by 1934. RCA Victor's sales rose 600 percent between 1933 and 1938, with symphonic, not popular, releases leading the way. Toscanini's eagerly awaited 1936 recordings were an important stimulus, as were budget-priced "music appreciation" albums with standard repertoire and unidentified RCA artists. In 1940, Columbia Records signed the New York Philharmonic and began competing with RCA's Boston Symphony, NBC Symphony, and Philadelphia Orchestra. A price war and skyrocketing sales

---

*Radio studies by Paul Lazarsfeld, a leading figure in American empirical social research beginning in the late thirties, reinforce the impression of a significantly broad high-culture audience. A study of radio listening habits by Lazarsfeld's Princeton Radio Research Project, reported in the April 1939 *Harper's*, estimated that 21.5 percent of the American public preferred listening to "classical" music, and 52.8 percent preferred listening to both "classical" and "popular" music. Of the first group, 31.3 percent were categorized as "prosperous," 24.7 percent as "upper middle class," 20 percent as "lower middle class with regular jobs," 14.8 percent as "poor or unemployed," and 17.2 percent as "Negro." The percentages for the second group were 32.7, 34.8, 20, 26.9 and 32.7. Lazarsfeld's *The People Look at Radio* (1946) included this chart:

PROPORTION LIKING TO LISTEN TO CLASSICAL MUSIC IN
THE EVENING BY SIZE OF TOWN AND EDUCATION

	COLLEGE	HIGH SCHOOL	GRAMMAR SCHOOL
Cities 100,000 and over	62	35	29
Towns 2,500 to 100,000	50	35	22
Under 2,500 and farms	49	24	12

Fortune had published roughly comparable findings in 1938 (see page 154). But audience *ratings*, showing the number of listeners to various classical music radio broadcasts, were much lower—illuminating the risks of asking people what they "liked to hear" rather than what they actually listened to. Even more questionable were Lazarsfeld-type studies of listener motivation (see page 240).

resulted. Babbitt's 1920 collection was of "jazz records" that made him "feel wealthy and cultured"; by 1940, he would have been certain to own albums of Beethoven and Brahms. Other record collectors, including intellectuals who had never been able to take an orchestra home with them, seized the phonograph's bona fide teaching potential, playing and replaying their albums until they could recognize and place all the standard symphonies, and many others besides.[9]

If radio and phonograph habits indicated rising music consumption in the home, proliferating orchestras indicated rising music consumption in the community. "A symphony orchestra shows the culture of a community," Theodore Thomas had preached, and the "symphony orchestra" became an American specialty. But even Thomas could not have envisioned his dictum's extraordinary appeal. As late as 1927, Charles Edward Russell could write, in *The American Symphony Orchestra and Theodore Thomas:* "Without sounding the ever-ready pipe of vainglory, we may justly affirm that in one division of representative art the American achievement has gone beyond debate. The grand orchestra is now more than our foremost cultural asset; it has become our sign of honor among the nations." Of the good effects of orchestral proliferation, Russell, whose many other books included *Why I Am a Socialist,* predicted: "It might change the whole American character; it might in the end scourge us of materialism." To other Americans, the orchestra furnished proof of civic achievement, or an accessory to vast personal wealth, or a way of attracting tourism and investment. When Thomas was criticized for the severity of his programs, his stock retort was: "Do you wish them to be inferior in standard to those of the Boston orchestra?" When Chicago dedicated its Orchestra Hall in 1904, one orator declared: "Chicago has been the most public spirited city in the world. We are proud of our rapid growth in wealth and population, but we are not satisfied with the merely industrial growth of our city. . . . We look through the dust and smoke [to see] a school for the nation, as Pericles declared Athens was the school for Greece." When Rudolf Ganz was conductor of the St. Louis Symphony (1921–27), he is said to have called his orchestra a force in "helping to sell shoes" for the nation's footwear capital.[10] Such attitudes were parodied by Sinclair Lewis, who had Chum Frink, resident poet of Babbitt's business circle, address the Boosters' Club as follows:

> "Some of you may feel that it's out of place here to talk on a strictly highbrow and artistic subject, but I want to come out flatfooted and ask you boys to O.K. the proposition of a Symphony Orchestra for Zenith. Now, where a lot of you make your mistake is in assuming that if you don't like classical music and all that junk, you ought to oppose it.

. . . [But] culture has become as necessary an adornment and advertisement for a city today as pavements or bank-clearances. It's Culture, in
theaters and art-galleries and so on, that brings thousands of visitors to
New York every year. . . .

"Pictures and books are fine for those that have the time to study 'em,
but they don't shoot out on the road and holler 'this is what little old
Zenith can put up in the way of Culture.' That's precisely what a
Symphony Orchestra does do. Look at the credit Minneapolis and Cincinnati get. An orchestra with first-class musickers and a swell conductor
—and I believe we ought to do the thing up brown and get one of the
highest-paid conductors on the market, providing he ain't a Hun—it
goes right into Beantown and New York and Washington; it plays at
the best theaters to the most cultured and moneyed people; it gives such
class-advertising as a town can get in no other way. . . ."

It is inconceivable that Zenith did not possess a symphony orchestra by
1940. Everyplace else did. According to a 1939 survey, the number of American orchestras had increased from 17 before World War I to *270;*[11] other
surveys arrived at even higher totals. Meanwhile, a strategy called "organized audiences" was routing recitalists to the hinterlands in ever increasing
numbers. The Community Concerts Corporation, a 1928 subsidiary of the
Arthur Judson management, sent its salesmen to Zenith, Middletown, and
other budding music markets to secure subscriptions *before* touring singers
and instrumentalists were selected and signed; with the money booked in
advance, concert series could be guaranteed with no risk to the local spon-
sors or to Judson and his musicians. A further infusion of concert music
was provided by the Federal Music Project of the Works Progress Administration, created in 1935 "to give such cultural values to communities that a
new interest in music would be engendered and the audience base expanded." The WPA maintained numerous orchestras, opera units, and
chamber ensembles in addition to concert bands, dance bands, and choral
groups. Through 1939, when it was reorganized and placed under state
control, the Music Project gave 225,000 free or popularly-priced performances, attended by 150 million people, many of whom had been strangers
to live concert music.

Some strangers to music were so uplifted that, as for Charles Edward
Russell, their "life was never the same afterward." For others, uplift was
chiefly cosmetic. The former group hungered for knowledge; the latter,
having helped field a "first-class orchestra," needed coaxing to pay for and
listen to the prescribed symphonies and concertos. As it happened, remedies for both groups were in the wind—and not merely because the day of
the popularizers had dawned. Prior to World War I, the era of grand

philanthropic gestures, when a handful of millionaires could guarantee the solvency of an orchestra, was already ending; millionaires remained indispensable, but could no longer finance symphonic deficits without small-fry help. As early as 1911, as we have observed, the New York Philharmonic discarded its committee of millionaire guarantors in favor of a membership corporation of more than a thousand dues payers. Concurrently, its first Young People's Concerts were given, as well as special lectures, Evenings of Light Music, and performances at Madison Square Garden and at army camps. Beginning in 1922—the year Judson became the Philharmonic's manager and Clarence Mackay its energetic chairman of the board—these tendencies increased. Given his orchestral responsibilities in Philadelphia, plus his seven-year-old booking agency, Judson had begun amassing a national domain partial to economies of scale: the bigger the potential audience, the more concerts he could schedule; more concerts meant higher returns per artist. The year of Judson and Mackay's arrival, the Philharmonic embarked on a plan to secure "a wider popular audience" via "the education of a new public." Young People's Concerts, expressly endorsed as an audience-building tool, were stepped up to a substantial annual series. The Philharmonic was named the regular orchestra for the summertime concerts at Lewisohn Stadium, where the seating capacity topped twenty thousand and tickets could be had for as little as twenty-five cents. With the introduction of Sunday-afternoon Philharmonic broadcasts in 1930, dues-paying listeners became "radio program members" of the Philharmonic-Symphony Society and were mailed program notes for all radio concerts.[12]

While not every orchestra had a Judson or a Mackay, curricular expansion was mandatory for the interwar period. What Joseph Pulitzer had endorsed as a matter of principle in bequeathing a democratic New York Philharmonic endowment fund became a matter of survival. Orchestras everywhere established classes and lectures, "pops" and children's concerts, and women's auxiliary committees with responsibilities for fund raising and promotion. In another place, at another time, these efforts might have proved deluded; in America in the thirties and forties, they rhymed with "The Swift's Hour," the Metropolitan Opera and New York Philharmonic broadcasts, and the sudden boom in recordings. To the degree that the objective was to accommodate Charles Edward Russells, opportunities for deeper engagement were created. But this was partly a by-product: over all, then as now, symphonic curricular expansion was as much an undertaking in marketing as in education. Music salesmen capitalized on the new prosperity, the new leisure time, the new communications technologies, the new propensity for "waves of contagious excitement," the "spiritual starvation" of the new white-collar masses. Their frequent strategy was quicker than teaching the practice of music; piano lessons, unappealing to reluctant husbands and fathers, would have been irrelevant, even counterproductive. It was more dignified than bald advertising and public relations. It was "music appreciation."

The techniques of NACRE and Billy Phelps proved precisely applicable to music. Symphonic masterpieces could be preached with "happy energy." The man on the street could learn to listen without enduring "unnecessary displays of technicalities." A "popular sort of presentation" of musical fundamentals could be reconciled with "scientific scholarship." How-to instructions, applied to lists and rankings of the "best" and "greatest," could help confer personality, popularity, and status. To this end, newspaper and magazine readers, radio and phonograph owners, were bombarded with articles, broadcasts, recordings, and guidebooks identifying the components of sonata form, the essential piano concertos, the members of the woodwind family, the stories of the Strauss tone poems. Music appreciation was applauded by schools and foundations impressed by its egalitarianism. Corporations, impressed by its scope, invested in it. Famous musicians endorsed it—and were famously remunerated.

Half a century before and more, ballyhooers and earnest Germans had spurred popular access to "serious" music in the United States. Between the world wars, the American musical public grew more popular still. It would be misleading to suggest that great music's aura of exclusivity was negated, for this would have canceled half its appeal. Rather, to partake in great music's exclusivity was made a democratic privilege.

Music appreciation had a father figure in its heyday: the venerable Walter Damrosch. When his New York Symphony was appropriated by Toscanini's New York Philharmonic in 1928, Damrosch did not fade away, but campaigned anew as radio's first prominent studio conductor. Already, on November 15, 1926, he had taken part in the first chain broadcast over the new NBC network. In 1927, he became NBC's music advisor. In 1928, he inaugurated the "NBC Music Appreciation Hour," a weekly daytime series aimed primarily at students.

Music appreciation, or something like it, had first appeared in a small number of American public schools around the turn of the twentieth century. For students who neither read music nor performed it, courses in listening were begun, stressing musical structure and the lives and works of the great composers. By 1910, the phonograph, replacing the player piano, notably supplemented such instruction. Later, the radio, too, became a valued classroom aid.* In 1926, schools in Cleveland instituted a course of study built around the Cleveland Orchestra's broadcast youth concerts. Damrosch's programs, two years later, were the first children's concerts to be broadcast nationally. By the time Damrosch turned seventy-five in 1937, his "Music Appreciation Hour" was said to reach seven million students in seventy thousand schools, as well as three to four million adults. David Sarnoff, hosting a "Seventy-Fifth Birthday Anniversary" banquet at the Hotel Pierre, called Damrosch "America's leading ambassador of music understanding and music appreciation" and added: "Schoolchildren probably know the voice of Walter Damrosch better than the voice of any other living person in America today. . . . He occupies a position in music that is unique, and justly places him in the ranks of those who have elevated civilization."[13] Of these three mighty claims, the third warrants close attention.

Damrosch's radio curriculum was divided into four categories of musical knowledge: the instruments of the orchestra, "the ways in which music becomes expressive," musical forms, and the lives and works of the great composers. Damrosch interspersed his talks with musical examples performed by studio musicians under his baton. Classroom listeners (the broadcasts took place weekday mornings and afternoons) were provided with workbooks. Compared with many later music appreciators, Damrosch was a sophisticated practitioner. He had conducted concerts and operas for more than forty years, and was also long established as a friendly, unpedantic lecturer. A composer himself, he took a keen interest in much American and new music. The catholic repertoire that had distinguished his New York Symphony concerts remained in evidence on the "Music Appreciation Hour": to illustrate the oboe, he performed the Scotch Idyll from Saint-Saëns's *Henry VIII;* to illustrate "motion in music," he chose Percy Grainger's *Mock Morris,* Liadov's *The Mosquito,* and part of Honegger's *Pacific 231* (whose American premiere he had led). And yet as a popular embodiment of "serious music," Damrosch was in some respects all too plausible. His paternal manner (he began each lesson by intoning "Good morning, my dear children!") made him seem even older than he was. His German pedigree (born in Breslau, trained in Dresden) made him seem the more distant. Winthrop Sargeant, who played in the New York Symphony just before the music appreciation broadcasts began, remembered its white-

---

*Simultaneously, instrumental music, previously taught privately or in music schools, was a growing presence in the public school curriculum; it was in the period immediately after World War I that school bands proliferated.

haired, "absolutely imperturbable" conductor beating time "like the mechanical pendulum of a grandfather clock. . . . In spite of his kindly . . . always infinitely well-mannered presence, one felt that one was somehow seeing and talking to a great musical symbol rather than a man."[14]

For his young listeners, Damrosch's distant yet soothing aura pervaded the music he appreciated. He taught music listening, not music making.* Moreover, he prescribed a pantheon of dead Germans and Austrians: Bach, Handel, Haydn, Mozart, Beethoven, Schubert, Wagner, and Brahms were the only composers invariably allotted a lesson apiece. That his pedagogy, however well informed, did not preclude misleading banalities is suggested by this workbook quiz on Beethoven, from February 2, 1940:

1. Beethoven achieved fame (only after his death.) (during his lifetime.) (in early childhood.)
2. Throughout his career he experienced (much sorrow and affliction.) (constant happiness.)
3. The development of his personality (had no effect on his music.) (influenced the development of his art.)
4. Beethoven's music differs from Mozart's in its greater (perfection of form.) (cheerfulness.) (dramatic effectiveness.)
5. The Larghetto from the Second Symphony is notable for its (devotional serenity.) (exquisite grace.) (deep melancholy.)

1. If Bach was the founder of modern music structure, what characteristic of modern music started with Beethoven?
2. How did Beethoven's changes in the orchestra enable him to carry out this new type of musical expression?

Presenting Beethoven's Fifth, Damrosch likened the second movement to "a walk in a lovely garden, in which one finds a statue erected to the memory of some national hero." He set its second theme to the words:

> For the Hero has come,
> Sound the trumpet and drum!
> He has fought
> The good fight
> He has won!

---

*Damrosch did encourage music-making skills as co-editor of the Universal School Music Series, whose songbooks made famous symphonic tunes "speak" after the fashion of the Beethoven Fifth theme on this page.

While these were poisonous associations, the surest shortcomings of the "Music Appreciation Hour" were its omissions. Notwithstanding Damrosch's catholicity, nearly all the music he played and discussed was orchestral (occasional baroque and keyboard extracts were dressed in anachronistic symphonic garb). And, notwithstanding his inclusion of such "modern American composers" as Barber, Griffes, Randall Thompson, and Gershwin (whose Concerto in F and *An American in Paris* he had premiered), and such "modern European composers" as Debussy, Hindemith, Ravel, Sibelius, and Stravinsky, nearly all the music he played and discussed was comfortably traditional. *The Rite of Spring*, which might have excited his impressionable charges, was blacklisted. So were Schoenberg, atonalism, and serialism. When in 1932 Leopold Stokowski proposed broadcasting "modernistic" music to schoolchildren so they could "develop a liking for it," Damrosch issued a press release "deeply deploring" Stokowski's plan. "Children should not be confused by experiments," he wrote.[15] For Damrosch's schoolchildren, music as a contemporary art form ceased to exist except as a dilute residue of the nineteenth century.

In the years following the debut of the "Music Appreciation Hour," music appreciation became a radio mainstay. Its prevalence throughout the thirties paralleled that of broadcast concerts and operas—not least because appreciators helped build audiences, boost ratings, and enhance the commercial value of "The Ford Hour," "The Voice of Firestone," and "The General Motors Concert." (When concert and opera broadcasts diminished in the forties, so did the music appreciation shows: Damrosch's went off the air in 1942; by 1950, there were practically no concerts left on commercial network stations.)

Musical facts and anecdotes, in addition to stocking Damrosch-style lectures, infiltrated "Information, Please," "Professor Quiz," and other general-interest programs. NBC's "Fun in Music" offered voice and instrumental lessons. And radio concerts came equipped with "commentators" who, as talking program notes, appraised the works performed. Like other interwar popularizers, radio's music appreciators spanned a gamut of styles. At one extreme were such populists as Billy Phelps and Sigmund Spaeth, who as the "tune detective" traced "I'm Always Chasing Rainbows" to Chopin's Fantaisie-Impromptu and—his most celebrated dissection—"Yes, We Have No Bananas" to the "Hallelujah" chorus, "Bring Back My Bonnie to Me," "Aunt Dinah's Quilting Party," and *The Bohemian Girl.* At the opposite extreme, signaling pockets of network idealism unimaginable a generation later, was the pianist-composer Abram Chasins, whose "Piano Pointers" on CBS and "Chasins' Music Series" on NBC were workshops for musically literate pianists. Among the commentators, J. Andrew ("Major") White, early of CBS, was a sometime sports announcer; another CBS man, Norman Brokenshire, once explained that the "Italian" Symphony was written by Mendelssohn and orchestrated by Bartholdy. The first radio commentators for the New York Philharmonic included Olin Downes and Lawrence Gilman. Of an-other order was the urbane yet unpretentious Deems Taylor, who took over the Philharmonic broadcasts in 1936–37. As a notable composer, Taylor valued contemporary music. As a musical insider, he viewed celebrity performers with as little mystified reverence as the music itself. His introduction to the first of three printed collections of his radio talks included this cautionary note: "Many a potential music lover is frightened away by the solemnity of music's devotees. They would make more converts if they would rise from their knees."[16]

Concert managers, orchestras, and radio networks were not the only music providers with an incentive to preach audience expansion between the wars; recordings furnished a fourth inevitable music appreciation outlet —or, rather, a supplement to the third, for the Radio Corporation of America, ruler of the largest radio network, had taken over the largest American record manufacturer, the Victor Talking Machine Company, in 1929. Victor, now the "RCA Victor" division of RCA, commanded an unsurpassed international roster of singers, instrumentalists, conductors, and orchestras. RCA also stood behind the National Concert and Artist Corporation, sole rival to Arthur Judson's managerial empire. In addition to facilitating broad radio, phonographic, and concert exposure for RCA/NBC artists, these symbioses fostered a trove of varied "educational" materials in which music appreciation's commercial strategies, reflecting the emergence of a vast, manipulable music public, were starkly revealed.

Victor had entered the music appreciation business before World War I. Its director of education as of 1910, Frances Elliott Clark, was in fact a leading music-appreciation pedagogue, having been supervisor of music for Milwaukee. Victor's popular *Victor Book of the Opera*, first published in 1912, gave the stories of over seventy operas and translated the major arias. It also listed and endorsed all pertinent Victor recordings, even where the Victor catalogue listed competing versions of a given aria. In 1913, Victor brought out the first of many editions of *What We Hear in Music*, a music appreciation text "for use in the home, high schools, normal schools, colleges and universities. Also for special courses in conservatories and music clubs." Its thirty-six lessons were keyed to more than 350 Victor recordings. Over one-fourth of its pages were given over to "analyses of records"—a de facto Victor sales catalogue. In addition to the vital recordings, *The Victor Book of the Opera* was held "indispensable in presenting operatic numbers." A sample *What We Hear in Music* lesson, on Beethoven, included a list of his thirty-one "greatest works." The text began:

> Ludwig van Beethoven (1770–1827) is the greatest personality in the history of music. His works marked the culmination of the Classical School of music and opened the doors to the Romantic School. It is difficult to study Beethoven, for his genius is colossal, his sublimity so overwhelming that it compels one's awe and reverence as well as one's admiration. . . .
>
> Beethoven's works are still rightly regarded as the greatest models of instrumental form. New orchestral effects, new methods of portraying dramatic ideas, some changes in form, it is true, have come into music since his time, but nothing which has not been suggested in Beethoven's music. . . .

Another RCA music consumption volume was *Music Appreciation for Children,* first published, as *Music Appreciation for Little Children,* in 1920. It stressed boyhood experiences of the great composers. "The Boyhood of Beethoven," illustrated with a "Bust of Beethoven as a Child" already somber and wild-haired, fantasized:

> Ludwig's father was a tenor singer. . . . I'm sorry to say that Mr. Beethoven wasn't a kind father at all and that was one of the reasons why Ludwig grew to have a strange, unhappy disposition. . . .
>
> . . . Unthinking people, who couldn't understand this strange, scowling lad, often laughed at him for his queer, wild ways. They couldn't see that in his heart Ludwig was really a strongly affectionate boy who loved his friends dearly. Even his playmates—for Ludwig did of course play sometimes, though rarely—never could understand why at times he refused to play when they asked him to join in a merry game, but would steal away and moodily sit alone and apart. . . .
>
> At this time Ludwig loved to improvise, that is, to compose music at the piano or violin. . . .

The Victor Book of the Opera, What We Hear in Music, and *Music Appreciation for Children* were all continued by RCA Victor after 1929. Subsequent additions to the company's music appreciation canon included the junior-high-school text *Music and Romance* (1930), *Form in Music* (1945), and, on a less earnest note, *The Victor Book of Musical Fun* (1945), a collection of quiz games, anecdotes, and cartoons. RCA's core publications, however, were offshoots of *The Victor Book of the Opera: The Victor Book of the Symphony* (1934, 1948), *The Victor Book of Concertos* (1948), *The Vic-*

tor Book of Overtures, Tone Poems and Other Orchestral Works (1950), and
The Victor Book of Ballets and Ballet Music (1950). Coordinated with
RCA's necessary production of album notes, these were layman-oriented
program-note compilations. As author of *The Victor Book of the Symphony*
and *The Victor Book of Overtures, Tone Poems and Other Orchestral Works,*
RCA's Charles O'Connell, an experienced conductor, produced audience-
expansion aids less naive than *What We Hear in Music,* less arthritic than
Walter Damrosch's radio lessons. Of *The Rite of Spring,* proscribed by
Damrosch, O'Connell wrote:

> Few will quarrel with the dictum that *Le Sacre* is the most significant,
> the most original, though not necessarily the most ingratiating of Stra-
> vinsky's works. There are musicians of rank who do not hesitate to assert
> that it is *the* most significant work in modern music. No "modern"
> composition has provoked so much discussion; none—at the time of the
> premiere of *Le Sacre*—had departed so daringly, so radically, and so
> finally from the accepted canons of harmony and structure; none since
> has been received with such a commingled uproar of praise and condem-
> nation.

At the same time, *The Victor Book of the Symphony* did not escape the taint
of music appreciation parochialism. Spanning more than a hundred works,
from Bach's Second "Brandenburg" to the Polka and Fugue from Wein-
berger's *Schwanda,* it represented the music most performed by "four major
American symphony orchestras during the past three years"—a criterion
penalizing recent and American music. Nor was O'Connell immune to
hortatory distinctions between masterworks, invariably Promethean, and
minor works impugned by their concision, humor, or objectivity. Of Beethoven's Eighth Symphony he wrote:

> The Eighth Symphony, charming as it is, no more represents the mature
> and full-statured Beethoven than does the First. The heroic proportions
> and valorous spirit that distinguished the Third, the fierce and god-like
> rages of the Fifth, the vigor and bacchanalian abandon of the Seventh—
> there is little if any of these qualities to be discovered in the Eighth, nor
> is there much that could be regarded as evidence of the forthcoming
> Ninth and last of the symphonies.

At the back of *The Victor Book of the Symphony* came "A List of Modern
Victor Recordings of Symphonic Music" and an essay, "The Modern
Phonograph: Radio," asserting:

The importance to music of modern methods of reproducing sound is parallel to that of the printing press to literature, philosophy, and the whole sum of the world's knowledge. There is this vital difference: Books preserve in cold type the great thoughts of the ages, priceless even though disembodied, but electrical reproduction actually re-creates the living organism of music, giving it voice and movement and compelling vitality.

At the back of *Form in Music* came a "Minimum List of RCA Victor Records"—forty-six selections, ranging in length from the *Don Giovanni* minuet to Sibelius's Second Symphony, "recommended by the author as a minimum list for the successful use of *Form in Music.*" At the back of *The Victor Book of Musical Fun* came a "Coda" reading in part:

> May we . . . respectfully direct your attention to our companion books, *The Victor Book of the Symphony, The Victor Book of the Opera* and the Victor catalogue "The Music America Loves Best." Your enjoyment of our quizzes and your appreciation of our anecdotes will be raised an octave when supplemented with recorded music. The three B's never had a better friend than Thomas Edison, whose electric light made it possible for us to see in the dark and whose phonogram (voice-written) shed a lot of light on the great masters.

RCA advertisements called *The Victor Book of Opera, The Victor Book of the Symphony, What We Hear in Music, Music and Romance,* and *Music Appreciation for Children* "*musts* for the music-lover's library." A sixth volume, the Victor catalogue, was touted as the "Key to the World's Greatest Storehouse of Music":

> If you are a student or lover of music—even though you do not own a modern phonograph with its inevitable complement of Victor Records —you will find Victor's Record Catalog of inestimable worth in guiding you toward greater musical enjoyment.
>
> Primarily, of course, the Catalog is an index to Victor's imposing array of records. But since nearly all the world's great music is Victor-recorded, the Catalog is also a volume of panoramic scope . . . a 388-page encyclopedia of musical facts gathered over a period of 30 years, indexed and cross-indexed to form one of the most valuable of all musical references.
>
> Let us suppose that you know the aria "Vesti la giubba," but cannot remember the opera or composer. The Victor Catalog will give it to you

in an instant. Let us suppose that you are familiar with the opera *Carmen* by name, but would like to recall its leading arias. The Catalog will give you that too. . . .

The company's most elaborate advertisement was the *Victor Record Review,* a monthly "magazine of musical fact and comment" begun in 1938. This guide "in the discovery of whole tonal continents" contained reviews (all favorable) of new releases (all RCA Victor), plus pertinent articles about RCA artists and repertoire. A sample item, from Volume 1, Number 1:

> At press time comes the sad news of the death of Feodor Chaliapin, the great Russian basso. Stricken with anemia, the 65-year-old singer mumbled in his final moments, "What theatre am I in?" Then, grasping his throat, he faltered, "I can't sing here." After that he made no sound. Chaliapin's voice, however, is not stilled. He made a number of magnificent records for Victor. . . .

Also included in *The Victor Record Review* was program information for "The Music You Want When You Want It"—Victor's radio showcase, broadcast up to six days a week over some sixty stations from Hartford to Hollywood.

Beyond Victor's library of educational materials, music appreciation spawned shelves of self-help books and articles. Of the various symphonic Baedekers, *Philip Hale's Boston Symphony Program Notes* (1935) and *The Standard Concert Guide* (1908, 1917, 1930, 1949), containing Chicago Symphony program notes by George Upton and Felix Borowski, were insufficiently hortatory to qualify as music appreciation. But Olin Downes's *Symphonic Masterpieces* (1935) was a bona fide appreciation product, aimed at music's "many new listeners." So was David Ewen's *Music for the Millions* (1944, 1946, 1949), a huge program-note compendium whose title bespoke its intent. B. H. Haggin's *A Book of the Symphony* (1937) contained simple structural analyses of masterworks by Haydn, Mozart, Beethoven, Schubert, Brahms, Tchaikovsky, and Franck. For those who could not read his musical examples, Haggin furnished a stark symbol of lay competence: a ruler with which to measure distances from the outer groove of a phonograph record; thus, the development section of the first movement of Beethoven's Fifth was documented as commencing at $2\frac{7}{16}$ inches as recorded by Koussevitzky and the London Philharmonic, at $2\frac{1}{16}$ inches as recorded by Weingartner and the London Philharmonic, at $1\frac{6}{16}$ inches as recorded by Richard Strauss and the Berlin State Opera Orchestra. If *The Victor Book of the Symphony, Symphonic Masterpieces,* and *A Book of the Symphony* helped laymen ascertain which symphonies to listen to, other publications advised which records to buy. RCA's *Victor Record Review* was an early example of the monthly record magazine, a category also including *The New Records* and *The American Music Lover*. Haggin, in his *Music on Records* (1938, 1942, etc.), undertook the dual purpose of advising (1) readers who "want to know which . . . works are the greatest . . . ; which are enjoyable though of lesser stature; which are of little consequence though by great composers; which to acquire first, which later, which not at all; and (2) readers who want to know which recording of a work offers the best performance, the best-sounding reproduction, which recording to avoid, and in some instances what is offered by different recordings." Haggin's simple, certain, and copious instructions attracted a devoted readership; among his disciples was the poet John Berryman, who assiduously acquired the albums Haggin prescribed and played them up to forty times until he "knew" the contents.[17] Newspapers and magazines, meanwhile, recommended which radio programs to tune in. George Marek, thirteen years away from becoming an RCA executive, even wrote a pamphlet, *How to Listen to Music Over the Radio* (1937), carrying endorsements of radio listening by Kirsten Flagstad, Lotte Lehmann, Ezio Pinza, Eugene Ormandy, Leopold Stokowski, and Deems Taylor. Davidson Taylor, chief of concert music for CBS, added these pointers:

> The radio should be turned up until the volume fills the room pleasantly, but not until it starts annoying neighbors. . . . If your loud-speaker shakes or rattles, naturally you turn it down. . . .
> It's possible that your set is not located in the best spot of the room. Have a look at it. Does it face the listeners? It should, in general. . . .
> It's worth while to tune carefully. . . . Careless tuning will destroy the brilliance of the broadcast; it will eliminate some overtones. . . .

Supplementing pedagogical books, articles, recordings, and concerts, finally, was the music classroom for adults. Not only did orchestras take to sponsoring lectures intended to broaden their audiences, but free instruction was offered in some two hundred fifty music-teaching centers maintained by the WPA's Federal Music Project. And a celebrated network of "layman's music courses" was established by Stokowski's first wife, Olga Samaroff, an accomplished concert pianist. The layman's courses and WPA centers notably transcended the consumerism, antiquarianism, and religiosity of so many other music appreciation endeavors. More than the lives of the great composers and the canon of acknowledged masterpieces, the WPA curriculum included instrumental instruction and lessons in singing, theory, and composition. Samaroff, while reliant on the phonograph as a homework accessory, and scornful of the clumsy dilettante still honored by champions of *Hausmusik,* invoked ear training and score reading as aids to "active listening." The WPA's Index of American Composers and Composers' Forum Laboratories were landmark efforts to catalogue and perform American scores up to and including the latest "experimental" heresies. In *The Layman's Music Book* (1935), Samaroff listed these "points to be remembered" about "modern tendencies": "There has been *modern music* in every age"; "The history of our musical art makes it seem impossible to assume that any concept of consonance and dissonance is final and unalterable"; "A rich musical life should include the greatest things of the past and a vital interest in modern creative music."

Aaron Copland, in a 1936–37 music appreciation lecture course at New York's New School, took Samaroff's points a step further by refusing to segregate "modern music"; he took for granted its place in a historical continuum beginning centuries before the baroque and also including jazz. Copland's lectures were published in 1939 as *What to Listen for in Music;* reprinted in eleven languages and revised in 1957, it is the most enduring of all music appreciation handbooks. "No composer worthy of the name would be content to prepare you to listen only to music of the past," Copland explained in a preface.

> I have often observed that the mark of a real music lover was an imperious desire to become familiar with every manifestation of the art, ancient and modern. Real lovers of music are unwilling to have their musical enjoyment confined to the overworked period of the three B's. The reader, on the other hand, may think that he has accomplished enough if he has been led to a richer understanding of the accepted classics. But it is my belief that the "problem" of listening to a fugue by Handel is essentially no different from that of listening to a similar work by Hindemith.

Discussing melody, Copland moved directly from Schubert to Carlos Chávez. His discussion of rhythm included appreciative references to Gershwin, African drummers, and Cuban rhumba bands, as well as mild derogation of "nineteenth century composers" for indulging in "an overdose of regularly recurring downbeats." His refusal to talk down to the laity led him toward abstract inquiries he himself had puzzled over: "The question remains, How close should the intelligent music lover wish to come to pinning a definite meaning to any particular work? No closer than a general concept, I should say. . . ." Other music appreciators bent their knees or held the masterpieces aloft. Copland looked music in the face.

Most people want to know how things are made. They frankly admit, however, that they feel completely at sea when it comes to understanding how a piece of music is made. Where a composer begins, how he manages to keep going—in fact, how and where he learns his trade—all are shrouded in impenetrable darkness. . . .

One of the first things most people want to hear discussed in relation to composing is the question of inspiration. They find it difficult to believe that composers are not as preoccupied with that question as they had supposed. The layman . . . forgets that composing to a composer . . . is like eating or sleeping. It is something that the composer happens to have been born to do; and, because of that, it loses the character of a special virtue in the composer's eyes.

George Marek's *How to Listen to Music over the Radio* reassured: "You can enjoy a Beethoven symphony without being able to read notes, without knowing who Beethoven was, when he lived, or what he tried to express." Olin Downes once wrote: "The listener does not have to be a tutored man or a person technically versed in the intricacies of the art of composition to understand perfectly well what the orchestra [is] saying to him."[18] Copland stressed:

No composer believes that there are any short cuts to the better appreciation of music. . . . It is very important for all of us to become more alive to music on its sheerly musical plane. . . . The intelligent listener must be prepared to increase his awareness of the musical material and what happens to it. . . . Above all he must, in order to follow the composer's thought, know something of the principles of musical form.

Except for a handful of crackling asides ("as for the popularizers, who first began by attaching flowery stories and descriptive titles to make music easier and ended by adding doggerel to themes from famous composers . . ."; "This popular idea of music's [always having concrete] meaning —stimulated and abetted by the usual run of musical commentator . . ."), Copland was too much the gentleman to dispute "popularizers" and "commentators" explicitly. Implicitly, *What to Listen for in Music* critiqued in substance the appreciation genre it exemplified in purpose.

As the pretelevision decades were motion picture decades, no discussion of music's popularizing venues would be complete without visiting the movies.

Even the silent screen was musical: smaller theaters had pianos or organs, while the big movie palaces had sizable resident orchestras used both to accompany films with reprocessed Wagner and Tchaikovsky and to furnish between-films entertainment. Deems Taylor's gloomy survey of "Music" in Harold Stearns's influential *Civilization in the United States* (1922), preceding the heyday of music appreciation and orchestral proliferation, included this ray of hope:

> The greatest present-day force for good, musically, in this country, is the large motion-picture house. . . . The larger houses today can boast a musical equipment that is amazingly good. . . . The picture house allows [the listener] to pretend that he is going solely to see the films, and needn't listen unless he wants to. He finds that "classical" music is not nearly so boresome as many of its admirers. Freed from the highbrow's condescension, unconscious of uplift, he listens and responds to music like the prelude to *Tristan*, the *Walkürenritt*, the "New World" Symphony, Tchaikovsky's Fourth, and the *Eroica*.

At New York's Capitol Theater, the orchestra numbered up to eighty-five pieces. Its soloists included Jan Peerce. Its conductors included Erno Rapee, who might give a Sunday-morning Mahler symphony at a dollar a ticket, and Eugene Ormandy, once the orchestra's concertmaster.*

With the advent of "talkies" in the late twenties, the movie-palace orchestra was doomed, yet sound accompaniments to films grew more glamorously symphonic: every theater, no matter how small, now enjoyed the services of an unseen orchestra. Two American composers wrote important film scores: Virgil Thomson for *The Plow That Broke the Plains* (1936), *The River* (1942), and *Louisiana Story* (1948); Aaron Copland for *Of Mice and Men* (1939), *Our Town* (1940), and *The Red Pony* (1948). But Thomson's and Copland's styles were too spare, too unsentimental for movie audiences of the thirties and forties. Hollywood glamour dictated another type of "serious music": as in the concert hall, European imports. Among the first were Erich Wolfgang Korngold and Max Steiner, both Vienna trained, both irredeemably Romantic. Korngold, whose opera *Die tote Stadt* (1920) was a sensation in its day, began by adopting Mendelssohn for Warner Bros.'

---

*Given their adaptability and acute sense of timing, Rapee and Ormandy became leading radio studio conductors. Ormandy later graduated from the Judson Radio Corporation to become conductor of the Minneapolis Symphony (a Judson "farm club"), then of Judson's Philadelphia Orchestra. Commenting in later years on his Philadelphia debut, Ormandy recalled conducting *Till Eulenspiegel* on short notice: "Of course, I knew *Till Eulenspiegel* very well. We played it at the Capitol."[19]

A Midsummer Night's Dream (1935). In the years that followed, he composed his own succulent accompaniments to *Anthony Adverse* (1936), *The Prince and the Pauper* (1937), *The Adventures of Robin Hood* (1938), and other screen epics, each lushly orchestrated and embroidered with operatic leitmotivs. Steiner's pièce de résistance was his opera-long score for *Gone With the Wind* (1939), whose swooning theme song may be traced, à la Sigmund Spaeth, to Beethoven's Fifth Cello Sonata (second movement, measure 49).

Meanwhile, with music appreciation at its height, suave or tempestuous embodiments of charismatic longhairs became favorite American and British screen icons. Composers were glorified in *The Constant Nymph* (1943), conductors in *Unfaithfully Yours* (1948), divas in *Metropolitan* (1935), violinists in *Intermezzo* (1939) and *Humoresque* (1946), pianists in *When Tomorrow Comes* (1939), *The Great Lie* (1940), *Dangerous Moonlight* (1949), *Hangover Square* (1945), *The Seventh Veil* (1945), and *Deception* (1946). *Both* romantic leads were pianists in *I've Always Loved You* (1946)—the epitome of a film genre in which extracts from the warhorse piano concertos furnished a running musical commentary. Meanwhile, Hollywood's own composers— of whom Korngold and Bernard Herrmann were practiced hands at operatic, symphonic, and chamber music—invented fresh vehicles for the instrumentalists and singers of Hollywood's invention. Korngold composed a virtuosic cello concerto for *Deception*. For *The Constant Nymph*, he wrote *Tomorrow*, a tone poem for orchestra, contralto, and chorus. Steiner's score for *Four Wives* (1939) included a *Symphonie moderne*. Richard Addinsell's phenomenally popular *Warsaw Concerto* punctuated *Dangerous Moonlight* (known in America as *Suicide Squadron*). *Hangover Square* climaxed with Herrmann's *Concerto macabre*, performed by a deranged pianist in a burning room. Most memorable of all was Herrmann's gripping, parodistic recitative and aria from *Salammbô*, the bogus grand opera twice sampled in *Citizen Kane* (1941).

While the symphonic resonance of Hollywood soundtracks and plots reinforced music appreciation lessons, some films skirted music appreciation itself. In the Disney-Stokowski *Fantasia* (1940), Beethoven's "Pastoral" Symphony, Schubert's "Ave Maria," and other masterworks acquired plots and cartoon actors, even Mickey Mouse. Music education of a sort was also dispensed by the streamlined biographies *The Melody Master* (with Alan Curtis as Schubert, 1941), *A Song to Remember* (with Cornel Wilde as Chopin, 1944), *Rhapsody in Blue* (with Robert Alda as Gershwin, 1945), *Song of Love* (with Paul Henreid as Schumann, Katharine Hepburn as Clara, and Robert Walker as Brahms, 1947), *Song of Scheherazade* (with Jean-Pierre Aumont as Rimsky-Korsakov, 1947), and *The Great Caruso* (with Mario Lanza as Caruso, 1951). Whereas Stokowski was merely glimpsed in silhouette in *Fantasia,* and José Iturbi dubbed Wilde's pianism in *Song to Remember,** Hollywood's conscious intent to disseminate great music did not preclude on-screen performances by actual performers. With the coming of sound, Beniamino Gigli, Giovanni Martinelli, and Tito Schipa delivered arias in one-reelers proving that movies could sing. Complete operas and concerts were ruled out, however, in favor of highbrow cameos in friendly lowbrow settings. As bit players with show-stopping musical acts, the kings and queens of Carnegie Hall and the Metropolitan Opera were made to seem unintimidating party guests. In *One Hundred Men and a Girl* (1937), Stokowski rescued unemployed musicians. In *They Shall Have Music* (1939), Jascha Heifetz helped save a settlement music school. The personable Iturbi was MGM's representative concert pianist; *Music for Millions* (1944) and *Holiday in Mexico* (1946) were among the seven movies in which he appeared. And then there were the opera stars: Lanza, Lauritz Melchior, Grace Moore, Ezio Pinza, Lily Pons, Gladys Swarthout, and Lawrence Tibbett, among others, made multiple screen appearances.

The closest Hollywood came to filming unadulterated "serious music" in feature-length performance was *Carnegie Hall* (1947), with arias and symphonic excerpts sung and played from Carnegie Hall's stage and studios by Heifetz, Peerce, Gregor Piatigorsky, Pinza, Pons, Fritz Reiner, Artur Rodzinski, Arthur Rubinstein, Risë Stevens, Stokowski, and Bruno Walter. The picture also served to demonstrate Hollywood's pagan resistance to full-fledged music appreciation rites. The performance cameos were linked by the story of a cleaning woman whose son becomes a famous pianist. And, while not tampering with its music, the film's producer, Boris Morros, could not resist visual embellishments. As Piatigorsky later recalled:

> [Morros] engaged me for the picture *Carnegie Hall.* I did not see the script, but I was told that it would be an authentic history of the famous hall. The list of performers in the picture was formidable. . . . My query as to what I should perform was answered, "Anything you wish." The contract signed, I asked again, but the identical answer had a slight modification: "Anything you wish, providing it's not over two minutes long."
>
> I played [Saint-Saëns's] "The Swan." Well, it's not something unusual for a cellist to live in the company of this bird. There is nothing wrong with it: the music is fine, the bird is noble, as is the legend of its death; but there is hardly anything worthwhile that cannot with some

---

*Iturbi's contemporary recording of a Chopin polonaise sold over a million copies.

effort be transformed into a travesty. In Carnegie Hall I recorded the piece with a harp. Finding the sound satisfactory, the next day I came for the shooting of the picture. To my bewilderment, instead of being photographed with the one harpist with whom I made the recording, I found myself surrounded by half a dozen or so ladies with harps. They all were alike, wearing identical flowers, gowns, and expressions.

"Can they play the harp?" I asked Mr. Morros.

He said, "No."

"What are they doing here?"

"I need them for the background." The busy producer had no time for further conversation. He was arranging the positions of the group, giving orders to cameramen, and hurrying me to the make-up room. Unaccustomed to theatrical beautification, I disbelievingly watched my face undergo drastic changes. With "voluptuous" lines around my eyes and with my face coated with something like a pink stucco, I returned to Mr. Morros. "You look gorgeous," he said.

"Just gorgeous," he repeated after my sequence of *Carnegie Hall* had been completed.

I attended the "premiere" of the picture and stormed out of the theater after "The Swan." The sight of the cellist wrapped in a bouquet of harpists was devastating, but my postmortem cries did not last, and this experience became a souvenir not unlike one of the comical or sad snapshots one finds in an old family album.[20]

Popularizing philosophy in 1926, Will Durant endeavored to "humanize" knowledge and expand its audience by "centering the story of speculative thought around certain personalities." Music-appreciation middlemen like Damrosch, Downes, Haggin, and Marek were indispensable, but could not themselves personify great music. Beethoven could, but a living symbol would be fresher, more dramatic. As no contemporary composer embodied Beethoven's fanatic dedication and universal appeal, the obvious alternative was a contemporary performer who could embody Beethoven. The obvious performer was Toscanini.

His disciples had already anointed him music's messiah. His new NBC home was bigger, wealthier, higher powered than his homes at the Metropolitan Opera and New York Philharmonic had been. David Sarnoff's brand of cultural populism was more grandiose than any envisioned by concert managers or orchestral boards, and buttressed by merchandising expertise untouched by the usual high-culture proprieties. All this ensured new scope and virulence for the Toscanini cult. Simultaneously, the disciples, too, entered their most vibrant phase. More than had the Philharmonic, or CBS on its behalf, NBC stressed maximizing the Toscanini constituency. The disciples responded with music appreciation texts indoctrinating the layman in the significance of great music and Toscanini both.

The flagship in this enterprise was a glorified listener's companion to the NBC Symphony broadcasts: *Toscanini and Great Music* (1938) by Lawrence Gilman. In an Author's Note, Gilman avowed "unpayable debts of gratitude" to Sarnoff, "for having conceived and effected the restoration of Toscanini to the musical life of America,"* and to Samuel Chotzinoff, "whose cooperation, tact, wisdom, and devotion equipped him as ambassador extraordinary in the successful accomplishment of a difficult task." Gilman's threefold purpose was to elucidate "Toscanini the priest of music, and . . . certain masterworks that he reveals, and the significance of their interaction for the democratic culture of our time." Concerning "democratic culture," Gilman wrote: "Within the last decade or so the average man has discovered, chiefly through the agency of phonograph recordings and radio broadcasts, that the art of music is not the province of a few incomprehensible specialists, but a vast and boundless continent of the mind, inexhaustible in its riches for the spirit." Toscanini's "unexampled weekly concerts" over NBC signified "a new extension and significance to our ideas concerning the democratization of musical culture."

The body of *Toscanini and Great Music* recycled various of the author's essays and program notes. Toscanini—"the most illustrious conductor who ever lived," a "vehicle of revelation" whose "fame is probably without parallel in the annals of music"—was visualized preaching to grateful New Worlders—"we who have heard him oftenest, and have known him, as an artist, longest and best."

How often, especially in these later years of Toscanini's association with symphonic music in America, his return has been looked upon as the cardinal event of the musical season in New York! How long, and how affectionately, New Yorkers have known that familiar and characteristic ritual of inauguration . . .

Now, three decades after he first came to the United States, Toscanini, a prodigy of youthful resilience and strength and endurance, an even more vital and compelling artist than before, has returned to us again, and one may hear the First Musician of the world conduct sym-

---

*In fact, in a letter to Sarnoff (September 27, 1938), Gilman gratefully noted that Sarnoff "encouraged" him to write *Toscanini and Great Music*. He added: "The book will be published two days before the Maestro's opening concert [of the second NBC Symphony season]."[21]

phonic music broadcast by an orchestra established and supported for no other purpose than that he should make of it a perfected vehicle for the widest possible diffusion of great music; and these concerts enter the receiving sets of who shall say how many million homes?

The new NBC audience required education in great music; great music required a great interpreter. The bulk of Gilman's opening essay, "The Music Behind the Notes," elaborated the second proposition, familiar from his newspaper columns:

> The secrets of music do not lie open to the mastery of any conductor who chooses to peer into its baffling eyes. The blunt truth is that only a great conductor can read or impart them.
>
> There are few musical fallacies more respectable and hoary than . . . the fallacy that a conductor, aside from discharging a few obvious and elementary functions, need merely, in the sanctified phrase, "let the music speak for itself." . . . Perhaps the greatest service in the cause of aesthetic enlightenment achieved by Toscanini in the years of his conductorship among us has been his conspicuous demonstration of the falsity of this deluding and harmful theory.
>
> If we elected that [the] spokesman [for the composer] shall be some well-disposed and admirably industrious routinier who fancies himself as, let us say, a conductor of Debussy, we shall find that what we are getting when we hear *La Mer* via that conductor is a travesty of the work: that it is Debussy condemned to utter the dull speech and to reflect the commonplace mind and imagination of a mediocrity.

Every aspect of Gilman's tract—including its title, its cover photograph, and its organization—was devised to weld the two notions "great music" and "Toscanini," each being a necessary validation of the other. Where did "great music" end and "Toscanini" begin? None could say—the two entities were fused "inexplicably," "miraculously."

Like his popularizing cohorts, Gilman offered lists and rankings. The great composers were Haydn, Beethoven, Schubert, Brahms, Wagner, Debussy, and Sibelius, each allotted a chapter citing representative masterpieces in tandem with cited excellences of the respective Toscanini performances. Thus, "The Real Haydn" differentiated phony Haydn—"the old and conventional picture of him as essentially a light-hearted classic in a periwig who, oddly enough, was always in good spirits"—from a Romanticized "true picture"—"a master of poignant and affecting musical speech; one who taught Beethoven profounder truths than those of form." Two symphonies—Nos. 88 and 101 (the "Clock")—were briefly applauded. Then to Toscanini: "As Toscanini plays the . . . slow movements of these symphonies, they sound with their proper breadth and gravity and amplitude of speech. Haydn the genial classicist, Haydn the pious bourgeois of the foolish legend, disappears, and we find instead a grave and meditative poet, uttering nobly impassioned speech." In "Schubert in Excelsis," Gilman identified but one masterpiece—the "Great" C major Symphony. However: "If Schubert had written nothing but this symphony . . . his head would be among the stars." And: "If any symphony could challenge the C minor of Brahms for second place after the monarch of them all, Beethoven's Ninth, it would surely be this symphony of Schubert's." And: "Schubert's simplicities have not the profundity of Beethoven's, but they have a sublimity that is their own; and in the last movement they speak with an elemental grandeur that must quicken the breath of any who listen with sensibility." This movement was "Schubert's supreme achievement." The other masterpieces on Gilman's list were, for Beethoven, the Third, Fifth, Sixth, Seventh, and Ninth symphonies plus the *Missa Solemnis;* for Brahms, the four symphonies; for Debussy, *La Mer, La Damoiselle élue,* and the Nocturnes; for Sibelius, the Second Symphony; and for Wagner, excerpts from *Lohengrin, Die Walküre, Götterdämmerung,* and *Parsifal.* As the list was restricted to music figuring prominently in Toscanini's repertoire, it omitted from "great music" all Bach and Mozart, as well as all solo keyboard music, all chamber music, all concertos, and all vocal music save the *Missa Solemnis*—an exaggerated yet essentially truthful distillation of the music appreciation corpus.

Though no other volume bound appreciating music so tightly to appreciating Toscanini, these two enthusiasms proved deeply symbiotic. Whatever Gilman, Downes, Haggin, or Marek wrote, whatever textbook, Baedeker, advertisement, or how-to guide bore an RCA or NBC label, doubly imputed audience expansion and Toscanini worship. Common to both were such ideals as textual fidelity, furnishing the simplest, most accessible of all performance criteria; the canon of acknowledged masterpieces, consolidating supply and demand; and the celebrity performer, mythologizing praxis and thus rationalizing its removal from the home. The performer "must produce what the printed score directs that he produce," Haggin instructed in *Music for the Man Who Enjoys Hamlet* (1944), which elsewhere decried "the vehement plastic distortions of Koussevitzky, the sensationalism of Stokowski" and scorned Bruno Walter's version of the *Eroica* as less "valid" than Toscanini's. For fledgling discophiles, Haggin listed "recorded performances of the works discussed"—in which listing, as in the much longer discography attached to Haggin's *The Listener's Musical Companion* (1956), Toscanini's pre-eminence in Beethoven, Berlioz,

Brahms, Debussy, Mozart, Schubert, Tchaikovsky, Verdi, and Wagner was an article of faith. George Marek, in his inaugural appearance as *Good Housekeeping*'s music columnist, volunteered seven suggestions in reply to a reader wishing to start a record collection with fifty dollars. Marek's "first choice," Toscanini's 1939 recording of Beethoven's Fifth, meshed music appreciation and Toscanini appreciation as follows:

> No other work, I think, has quite such power with such terseness, such ability to engulf all of you, and such final exhilaration. . . . Yet the long-experienced musician still keeps on digging in its structure. . . . *You* needn't dig or look for "meaning." . . . You need only listen. The new Toscanini recording reveals all the blaze of this masterpiece. As has been said so many times, this is not an interpretation, it is the *Symphony* itself.[22]

In Marek's *Good Housekeeping Guide to Musical Enjoyment*—a volume incidentally signifying the homemaker's migration from the spinet to the family phonograph—"Why Is a Conductor?" extolled no conductor but Toscanini, and "Profiles of Composers" extolled no composer later than Wagner or Verdi.

The merger of music appreciation with Toscanini appreciation produced a new music appreciation genre, supplementing descriptions and appraisals of the great symphonies: the great performers described and appraised. These were no biographical vignettes, but reverent popularizations. The leading practitioner was the most prolific of all music appreciation writers: David Ewen, author or editor of some *eighty* music books for the layman. On great performers, Ewen's Opus 1 was *The Man with the Baton* (1936), succeeded by such Ewen volumes as *Men and Women Who Make Music* (1939) and *Dictators of the Baton* (1943). Ewen himself said of *Dictators of the Baton* that it was "a pioneer in describing and interpreting American orchestral music, its orchestras, and their conductors. It undoubtedly helped to bring great music closer to the hearts of the public, to make it more meaningful to listeners everywhere, and to bridge the gap between those who create, those who interpret, those who appreciate." If Gilman taught the canon of acknowledged masterpieces as a proving ground for great interpretation, Ewen taught the evolution of conducting as a teleological progression to Toscanini. In Ewen's revisionist history, Hans von Bülow (1830–1894) was "essentially a theatrical conductor of the twentieth century [sic]"—"profoundly gifted," yet a "pernicious influence" because of his "amazing liberties" with tempo and phrasing. "His method of tampering with the score has created something of a tradition among German conductors which persists until this very day. The frequent use among so many modern German conductors of *Luftpausen* . . . and much of the exaggeration and overstatement that appear in so many performances of classic symphonies can be traced directly to von Bülow." Textual fidelity, as practiced by Toscanini, was the historic antidote which returned conducting to its proper sphere.[23]

Ewen's reconstruction, effectively popularized by himself and others, was cogent as far as it went, but in stopping with Bülow it went no further than it dared. Bülow's "amazing liberties" were themselves traceable to earlier "theatrical conductors," including Wagner, to whom Toscanini-style textual fidelity was anathema. Liszt, like Wagner an influential conductor, also regarded "score tampering" as part of his job. And there are grounds to extend the Bülow-Wagner-Liszt lineage back to the conductor Beethoven.* Since Ewen righteously espoused fidelity to the composer, these interpretive habits of certain composers whom Toscanini interpreted were suppressed. Meanwhile, Bülow's bad example shaped assessments of his successors. In *The Man with the Baton*, Ewen wrote of Mahler, whose conducting he otherwise praised: "Perhaps the severest criticism that has been leveled at Mahler as conductor was the liberties, which he, like . . . von Bülow, took with whatever work he performed." By comparison, Ewen endorsed "scrupulous adherence to the score" as practiced by Karl Muck and Felix Weingartner; the latter's Beethoven, he believed, was unsurpassed "in our time." Ewen found Walter and Klemperer estimable, yet guilty of exaggerations like those of "their predecessor Hans von Bülow." A discussion of Furtwängler, whom Ewen acknowledged "preeminent . . . among modern German conductors," was cut short by information that he "enthusiastically embraced the Nazi artistic policy." Of Toscanini Ewen wrote:

> There are some who believe that in classic symphonies Felix von Weingartner had a vision far greater and a depth more profound than Toscanini; that in the music of the Romantics, Nikisch could be much more poetical. There are some who feel that in the temple of the Wagnerian music-drama, Toscanini must yield the altar to Karl Muck. . . . However, there is no one, intimately familiar with Toscanini's performances, who can deny that in sheer versatility Toscanini is greater than any of his predecessors or contemporaries. . . . There can be no doubt, too, that . . . among the conductors of the world, Toscanini is probably the greatest virtuoso who ever lived. Finally, there will be none to deny that

---

*See page 340.

in certain performances, Toscanini can outstrip the most inspired efforts of any conductor. . . .

Seven years later, in *Dictators of the Baton,* Ewen's views changed. Weingartner was found to have "succumbed to staleness" in old age. Furtwängler was unmentionable. And Toscanini was "The Paragon":

> Toscanini has become a legend in his own lifetime. His career is built around such monumental outlines, his musical achievements have been so fabulous, and his artistic importance assumes such epical stature that it is difficult in speaking or writing of him not to envelop him in legendary glamour. Tales about Toscanini are without number. They highlight his incredible memory, his aural sensitivity, his artistic integrity, and his interpretative genius. The curious thing is that most of these tales are not the inventions of imaginative admirers, but are based on fact. But beyond his musical greatness is the stature of the man himself: his dignity, idealism, and priest-like consecration to the highest ethics, his humility and self-effacement, warmth of heart and understanding—qualities which set him apart from most musicians. Once in a long while is musical genius of a high order married to a personality of such scope and richness. Such a marriage results in a Beethoven; and in a Toscanini.
> . . . He is the greatest musical interpreter of our time.

Between 1936 and 1943—the period during which Toscanini rose in Ewen's estimation from the peer of Weingartner and Muck to the legendary paragon—America was drawn into a war with Germany with momentous consequences for German musicians in the United States; and Toscanini was drawn into an alliance with David Sarnoff and NBC, with momentous consequences for the music appreciation industry, already dispensing Community Concerts and young people's concerts, record guides and guides to the symphony, how-to columns and layman's music courses. When Toscanini was handed the NBC Symphony, *Time,* accounting for "the highest price ever paid a conductor," took pains to explain why a mere baton beater could mean "the difference between a competent and an inspired orchestra." Two years later, *Life* visited Toscanini at home, as it might any celebrity, declaring: "It is a good guess that as many Americans know that Toscanini conducts an orchestra as know that Joe DiMaggio plays center field." *Time* popularized high culture for a readership of 820,000. *Life*'s celebrity cameos, swathed in photographs, used sheer glamour to titillate its audience of 2.5 million.[24]

The NBC Symphony, 1937–45:
The National Context II

*I*n 1915 Van Wyck Brooks, schematizing the "American mind," decried a bifurcation of "highbrow" versus "lowbrow"—the former strain, deriving from Puritanism, seeming "desiccated," "aloof," "fastidiously refined"; the latter, deriving from "catchpenny opportunism," seeming "starkly utilitarian," "two-dimensional," "illiterate." Brooks yearned for a New World renaissance to plug the gap between pious pedantry and the "slang" of contemporary business life: a "middle tradition" on which to base an enduring intellectual identity.[1]

Rather than serving, in Brooks's phrase, "to quicken and exhilarate" the national mind, one "middle tradition" emerging after World War I mainly served to quicken and exhilarate the cultural strivings of the new middle classes. And yet, simultaneously, the intellectual renaissance predicted in Brooks's influential *America's Coming-of-Age* did materialize. These parallel postwar currents, the first urged by popularizers, the second promulgated by artists and scholars, were hostile yet inextricable. Both were energized by the second industrial revolution and urbanization: the new, post–Gilded Age intelligentsia included immigrants' offspring and other hardened city types. World War I was as much a catalyst for the one group as for the other: the new intellectuals were disillusioned by the Great War; men had died, wrote Ezra Pound, "for a botched civilization." The more cultural populists trumpeted optimism and egalitarianism, the more cultural elitists withdrew from Hollywood and radio, from "waves of contagious excitement" stimulated by advertising and public relations. The popularizers gazed aloft at museum landmarks. Critics, poets, and novelists propounded the avant-garde. Each group goaded the other toward greater vehemence.

The first stirrings of the intellectual renaissance prophesized by Brooks were already felt by the turn of the century. Twenty years later, it became possible to speak of American intellectuals as a class, formulating its identity in opposition to previous bifurcation. At war with the "fastidious refinements" of Thomas Bailey Aldrich, William Dean Howells, Charles Eliot Norton, and other genteel culture custodians of the late 1800s, Brooks and his allies championed Dickinson, Hawthorne, Melville, Poe, Whitman. At war with "catchpenny opportunism," they railed against capitalism and what Waldo Frank called the "cold lethal simplicities of American business culture."

Postwar intellectuals despised postwar massification. Consumers, Rotarians, and salesmen were dismissed as so many Babbitts. Chain stores, assembly lines, and installment plans were said to breed robots. Intellectual antipathy for the great bourgeois majority was epitomized by the terrible H. L. Mencken, who dubbed the public "homo boobiens," "gaping primates," "anthropoid rabble." Other, more civil intellectuals were nearly as mistrustful of vox populi. In *Public Opinion* (1922) and *The Phantom Public* (1925), Walter Lippmann found public affairs too complex for public understanding. The rise of fascism provoked even deeper fears. "Representative democracy seems to have ended in a cul-de-sac," wrote Harold Laski in the *American Political Science Review* in 1932. Public opinion, once the province of educated Anglo-Saxons, had come to seem irrational.

A watershed stage was now reached in the history of New World ambivalence toward Old World culture. Within America's disenchanted intellectual community, intense admiration for things European caused many to migrate, chiefly to Paris, after the war. And yet the community's postwar orientation remained Janus faced. Diehard expatriates—Henry James, T. S. Eliot, Pound, Gertrude Stein (of whom James and Stein never turned their backs on America in any event)—were by far the exception, not the rule. And no one could mistake a Hemingway for a European. Back at home, Brooks pined for Europe yet prayed for "a new [American] age." Lewis Mumford was another indispensable twenties gadfly in whom maximum dissatisfaction revealed maximum optimism. Beyond short-range submission to Old World cultural glamour, the long-range New World tendency, in both Paris and New York, was to throw off the Old World yoke, once and for all.

As if in corroboration of this homeward thrust, the thirties saw America's itinerant intellectuals return. In their wake came droves of European artists and intellectuals chased west by Hitler, an emigration including such luminaries as Bertolt Brecht, Albert Einstein, Walter Gropius, George Grosz, Thomas Mann, Erwin Piscator, László Moholy-Nagy, Paul Tillich. The result was an American intellectual community of unprecedented size and force, making the United States, in Virgil Thomson's words, "for the first time an international center for intellectuals," even, as Richard Hofstadter was to put it, "the intellectual capital of the Western world, in so far as such a capital could be said to exist."[2] Brooks and many others now softened earlier impressions of indigenous philistinism, consolidating a positive vision of American arts and letters. Those American intellectuals who remained frustrated at home nonetheless came to care vitally about their homeland. The tensions of provincialism and colonialism, still felt within mass culture constituencies, diminished for scholars and artists. The intellectuals abroad of the twenties came back with none of Mark Twain's 1867 ambivalence. Waning ambivalence meant waning Eurocentrism: in culture's highest precincts, the European-American antithesis lost much of its meaning.

In no creative facet was the influx of talent more impressive than in music. Immigrant performers included Adolf Busch, Otto Klemperer, Wanda Landowska, Artur Schnabel, Joseph Szigeti, and Bruno Walter. Even more remarkable were the arriving composers: in 1933, Arnold Schoenberg; in 1934, Erich Wolfgang Korngold and Kurt Weill; in 1937, Ernst Krenek; in 1939, Igor Stravinsky; in 1940, Béla Bartók, Paul Hindemith, and Darius Milhaud; in 1941, Bohuslav Martinů. Meanwhile, beginning in the mid-twenties, America's own compositional talents—Samuel Barber, Marc Blitzstein, Aaron Copland, Roy Harris, Walter Piston, Roger Sessions, Virgil Thomson—returned home in force. Their prolonged Old World studies, usually in France, signified no defection; rather, as Mumford remarked of Henry James, "absorption in Europe [was] a necessary stage in our common development."[3] Fired with enthusiasm for the "new music" of Schoenberg and Stravinsky, equally eager to sample jazz and other American strains, they would forge a nationalism equidistant from Eurocentrism and chauvinism.

The arrival of this transplanted multinational community in America was welcomed by the League of Composers, founded in 1923. The League's superb quarterly, *Modern Music*, supplemented articles by the leading American composers with reports from Europe, so that an international purview of recent compositions and performances was maintained. The League's crusading concerts, keeping up with foreign sensations, were vigorously debated; as Harold Clurman later recalled: "No matter what was played, how much in earnest the partisans of new music were, or how outraged its detractors, the atmosphere . . . had something giddy about it. They were a sort of aesthetes' prom." But against the larger American backdrop, and notwithstanding enthusiastic support from Koussevitzky and Stokowski, the League was a dissident's enclave. To the arriving Europeans, especially, key New World institutions seemed mired in exclusivity and bravado, unreceptive to composers' counsels taken for granted in France and Germany. The venerable New York Philharmonic, founded in

1842, proved a model of adolescent truculence, hostile to new music in general and new American music in particular. Winthrop Sargeant, among the orchestra's few American-born members, has written: "The Philharmonic hated Gershwin . . . with instinctive loathing. . . . [It] pretended to regard Gershwin's music humorously, made funny noises, and played it, in general, with a complete lack of understanding of the American idiom." With perfect predictability, these same musicians, to whom Sargeant and other American colleagues seemed "alien spies," developed "a sudden and unprecedented upsurge of American patriotism" on tour in Europe, bragging, à la Mark Twain, "that in America we . . . had better sanitation and a far superior standard of living." Of the orchestra's principal conductors, Toscanini had trouble beating complex rhythms and heard no music even in Bartók's *Music for Strings, Percussion, and Celesta;* and Barbirolli was a creature of Arthur Judson, who felt certain nineteenth-century warhorses should be played several times a season and that Philharmonic audiences were unready for Bruckner or Mahler. If the Philharmonic seemed narrow to Schoenberg, Stravinsky, and company, the cultural preachings of David Sarnoff, representing America's largest radio network and its largest manufacturer of phonograph records, exuded a parochialism so profound they unmasked their own millennial pretensions. In the face of rampaging modernism, Sarnoff intoned: "Given a chance, the average man will move slowly, perhaps falteringly, toward a selection of the best." "Every known artist of quality," he maintained, "every orchestra of value, opera, and many other cultural programs of high artistic value are heard over the air time and time again." Speaking specifically of music, he said: "In NBC we are pursuing the policy of giving to our millions of listeners the greatest artists the world has to offer"—from whose ranks America's extraordinary new composers' community was excluded. Coating these ideals was a patina of consumerism. In 1949 Schoenberg wrote to his fellow émigré Rudolf Kolisch: "Fundamentally I agree with your analysis of musical life here. It really is a fact that the public lets its leaders drive it unresistingly into their commercial racket and doesn't do a thing to take the leadership out of their hands and force them to do their job on other principles." Four decades earlier Gustav Mahler, Schoenberg's predecessor as Austria's leading composer, had found American audiences "hungry for novelty," "tremendously unspoilt."[4]

Was Toscanini truly the "First Musician of the world"? Did Walter Damrosch occupy "a position in music that . . . justly places him in the ranks of those who have elevated civilization"? Was the importance of the phonograph to music "parallel to that of the printing press to literature, philosophy, and the whole sum of the world's knowledge"? Was "nearly all the world's great music" really "Victor recorded"? The immigrating and returning musicians did not think so. In its radio column, "Over the Air," *Modern Music* cocked a wary ear toward the surrounding enemy vastness. New York's local WNYC and WQXR, and also Howard Barlow's and Alfred Wallenstein's studio concerts over CBS and the Mutual Broadcasting System, were often singled out for programming adventurous beyond the concert-hall norm. CBS went so far as to commission new American works expressly for radio. Compared with subsequent network practice, these early decades of live concerts and opera, of commentary and instruction by Copland, Abram Chasins, and Deems Taylor, were courageous. But to come-of-age American composers and their expatriate colleagues, the times demanded more than what Copland characterized as "an occasional sop in the form of a prize competition, a few commissions for orchestra works, [and] some specially requested arrangements." "Over the Air" made its chief business designating which of the networks was most musically derelict, with NBC, except during Stokowski's three NBC Symphony years, the usual designee. This was Goddard Lieberson's reaction, in "Over the Air," to Toscanini's NBC performances of Barber's Adagio for Strings and Essay No. 1 for Orchestra in 1938: "It is contemporary [music] only in the sense that the composer is still alive. . . . Maestro Toscanini, in whose hands lies the opportunity to vindicate our native music by his good taste and musicianship, has again shown American music to be what it is most often not—uncreative, colorless, and sub-European." When Frank Black and Samuel Chotzinoff initiated a short-lived "New American Music" series over NBC in 1941, *Modern Music* complained that "most of the numbers are . . . comparatively obvious and simple." Lieberson articulated *Modern Music*'s estrangement from American radio's most high-toned offerings when he wrote of its music commentators:

They are the men who tell me that

is fate knocking at the door. That Bach had innumerable children. What . . . César Franck said to his wife after the first performance of his symphony. Where Saint-Saëns travelled in his busy life. And finally, [they are] the purveyors of the phrases: "The greatest German master," "Sublime in its . . . , etc.," "the great Finnish master," "that rare genius for work," etc. . . . Maybe your experience of radio music has been limited to the amazing fact that Beethoven crossed Napoleon's name from the fly-leaf of the *Eroica*. Or that Brahms wished he could write a waltz like Johann Strauss. But don't tell me you haven't heard how old Mendelssohn was when he wrote the *Midsummer Night's Dream* music![5]

Modern Music's own commentators mainly shut their eyes to the glare of mass culture, seeing no more than they had to. Their antithesis within America's expanding intelligentsia was a handful of German-born social philosophers who maintained mass culture could no more be ignored than Hitler. These were the members of the Frankfurt School, representing the leftist Institute for Social Research (Institut für Sozialforschung). They had migrated relatively early: Erich Fromm in 1932, Max Horkheimer, Herbert Marcuse, Leo Lowenthal, and Friedrich Pollack in 1934; Theodor Adorno in 1938. Distressed by German susceptibility to pernicious authority in general, and to the pernicious authority of mass culture in particular, the Frankfurt analysts discarded the teleological optimism of more orthodox Marxists and rethought Marxism's understanding of culture as an epiphenomenal topping to dialectical-material truth. In the tradition of Hegel and Marx, they insisted on a multidimensional, interdisciplinary perspective—so that Adorno, their music specialist, fastened on the social psychology of music appreciation and Toscanini worship in the context of capitalist radio and recordings, advertising and public relations, business culture and consumerism.[6]

Like all his mass culture texts, Adorno's critiques of symphonic performance and packaging were grounded in the epistemology of Hegel, with its premium on the dialectical interaction of subject and object, ideas and events. "A successful [art]work," Adorno theorized, "is not one which resolves objective contradictions in spurious harmony, but one which expresses the idea of harmony negatively by embodying the contradictions, pure and uncompromised, in its innermost structure." Bona fide novels, paintings, and symphonies possessed "negative truth": internalized tensions promoting an active "critical understanding" of the artwork and its larger milieu (the charged equilibrium binding harmony, counterpoint, and structure in the Classical symphony, in such a view, vindicates symphonic discourse and, in contrast to courtly baroque stasis, reflects a larger dynamic of European upheaval). The opposite of negative truth for the bourgeois epoch was "affirmative" culture, the "official culture" of the masses imposed from above. Ostensibly "ethereal" and "sublime," affirmative culture was homogenized, vapid, estranged. Transformed and disseminated by such practitioners as Toscanini, Walter Damrosch, and Benny Goodman, music became a type of pabulum processed for effortless consumption.

In the holistic world view of Adorno and other Frankfurt theorists, the crux of affirmative culture, accounting for its blandness, was alienation:

cut off from the real world, its "eternal," "universal" values were uncon-
ditionally "affirmed"; its realm of "timeless" beauty was the counter-
image of a material order acknowledged to be tainted, impure. Museum
sanctimony and arbitrary, relentless exposure detached great music from
its source and proper sphere. Under Monopoly Capitalism, breeder of a
"commodity society" in which goods were mass-produced for profit regardless of need, performances of Bach, Beethoven, and Brahms were
mass-produced commodities. Under the guise of promoting universal enlightenment, aspects of the concert hall experience were standardized,
atomized, "fetishized." Among the musical fetishes addressed by Adorno
were the cult-enshrined star conductor, who, alienated from contemporary art, "clings to the heroic-bourgeois past"; the "cult of the master
violins," making celebrated Stradivarius and Amati instruments "into
fetishes . . . torn away from any functions which could give them meaning"; the cult of the singing voice, which, to "legitimate the fame of its
owner . . . need only be especially voluminous or especially high"; the
cult of the "right" concert, whose enjoyment amounted to "being present
at the enjoyment of others, which in its turn has as its only content being
present"; the cult symphony, a category indiscriminately embracing Beethoven, Tchaikovsky, and Sibelius; and, within the aforementioned symphony, isolated themes and moments familiarized by Baedekers and radio
commentators, so that "the climaxes of Beethoven's Seventh Symphony
are placed on the same level as the unspeakable horn melody from the
slow movement of Tchaikovsky's Fifth." This manner of dissecting music
into stranded components Adorno called "regressive listening," arrested
at "the infantile stage."

Not only do the listening subjects lose, along with freedom of choice
and responsibility, the capacity for conscious perception of music, which
was from time immemorial confined to a narrow group, but they stubbornly reject the possibility of such perception. They fluctuate between
comprehensive forgetting and sudden dives into recognition. . . . They
are the new type of listener in terms of the introduction to musical life
of groups previously unacquainted with music. But they are childish;
their primitivism is not that of the undeveloped, but that of the forcibly
retarded. . . .

It is the ideal of Aunt Jemima's ready-mix for pancakes extended to
the field of music. The listener suspends all intellectual activity when
dealing with music and is content with consuming and evaluating its
gustatory qualities—just as if the music which tasted best were also the
best music possible.

Modern Music's columnists complained that radio music ignored Schoenberg and Stravinsky while providing a vulgar context for redundant Beethoven and Brahms. Adorno, inspired by Walter Benjamin's linkages between technology and late capitalism, formulated a more radical critique: that regressive listening was endemic to—indeed, inculcated by—the "radio voice." Compressed dynamics, distorted colors, and flattened textures altered the proper sound of a symphony orchestra. Monaural, living-room reproduction, extinguishable with the flick of a wrist, undermined the enveloping "experience of symphonic space."

> The power of a symphony to "absorb" its parts into the organized whole depends, in part, upon the sound volume. Only if the sound is "larger," as it were, than the individual so as to enable him to "enter" the door of the sound as he would enter through the door of a cathedral, may he really become aware of the possibility of merging with the totality which structurally does not leave any loophole.

Stressing surface over depth, harmony over counterpoint, discrete foreground tunes over the ongoing motivic web, the radio voice could not reproduce the dialectical complexity of Classical symphonic thought, with its intricately manipulated weights and balances. "Structurally, one hears the first bar of a Beethoven symphonic movement only at the very moment when one hears the last bar. . . . The density of thematic interwovenness, of 'antiphonic' work, tends to produce what one might call a suspension of time consciousness." In Romantic compositions, the discourse was more additive, and the interior detail more decorative, less structural. Wagner and Tchaikovsky fared passably over the radio, whereas the Classical symphony was "trivialized" ("The man who in the subway triumphantly whistles loudly the theme of the finale of Brahms' First is already primarily involved with its debris") and "Romanticized" ("They listen . . . as they would to a Tchaikovsky symphony, that is to say . . . to some neat tunes or exciting harmonic stimuli"). Reduced to a sequence of memorizable melodies, symphonic structure was simplified to resemble that of a "narrative" or "ballad." "Radio symphony appears as a medley or potpourri insofar as the musical atoms it offers up acquire the touch of having been picked up somewhere else and put together in a kind of montage." "There exists today a tendency to listen to Beethoven's Fifth as if it were a set of quotations from Beethoven's Fifth." In short, far from wafting symphonic culture to an ever wider audience, the radio voice fetishized the symphony. Deriding apostles of radio enlightenment, Adorno concluded that "the isolation of the main tune, and similar features, [make] a symphony on the air [become] a piece of entertainment. Consequently, it would be absurd to maintain that it could be received by the listeners as anything but entertainment." In a somewhat milder mood, he wrote: "No responsible educational attempt can be built directly upon radio symphony without [giving] the fullest account of the antagonistic tendencies promulgated by serious music in radio."

The Marxist complexion of Adorno's thought ensured his view that "the avalanche of fetishism . . . overtaking music and burying it under a moraine of entertainment" was no gratuitous encumbrance, but a weapon of class warfare. The stronger the contradictions afflicting bourgeois society, the more strenuous existing power and property relations strove to maintain hegemony. Standardization, alienation, fetishization all conspired to preserve the status quo against rightful postcapitalist transformations. In this respect the fetishized symphony was a depoliticizing drug.

> The need for music is present in bourgeois society and this need increases with the problematic social conditions that cause the individual to seek satisfaction beyond immediate social reality, which denies him this satisfaction. This satisfaction is . . . provided by musical life through its acceptance of the bourgeois tendency . . . to flee from social reality and to reinterpret this reality . . . with contents which social reality never possessed or—at best—lost long ago. . . . The ideological essence of musical life is its ability to satisfy the needs of the bourgeois adequately, but to do so by means of a form of satisfaction which accepts and stabilizes the existing consciousness, rather than revealing through its own form social contradictions. . . .

For the exploited classes, the radio symphony was actually soporific. While this was not the conscious intent of the NBC Symphony and New York Philharmonic broadcasts, broadcasters were expert commodity marketers, skilled at persuading the captive listener that Beethoven's Fifth was being played for him and him alone—a privilege compensating for anomie and low wages. Rather than fostering critical understanding, radio music offered "a new function not inherent in music as an art—the function of creating smugness and self-satisfaction." Adorno's favorite analogy for unmasking the listener's pathetic illusion of free choice—a variant of affirmative culture's illusory "rapture of plenitude," an isolationism enabling individuals to "feel good without being so"—was "plugging": the tactic of redundantly programming certain popular tunes until "the most familiar is the most successful and is therefore played again and again and made still more familiar." Consumers of broadcast classical music were likewise made to equate "most familiar" with "best" and "most desirable." The resulting preference for aged warhorses, Adorno believed, infested the concert hall as well as the studio.

> . . . The Philharmonic listener of today listens in radio terms. A clear indication is the relation to serious advanced modern music. In the Wagnerian period, the elite listener was eager to follow the most daring musical exploits. Today the corresponding group is the firmest bulwark against musical progress and feels happy only if it is fed Beethoven's Seventh Symphony again and again.

Elsewhere, Adorno compared the radiophile's demand for Beethoven to the behavior "of the fanatical radio listener entering a bakery and asking for 'that delicious, golden crispy Bond Bread.' " Victimized by "fictitious" supply and demand, the mass culture consumer resembled "the prisoner who loves his cell because he has been left nothing else to love." Again:

> [The listener's] freedom has ceased to exist. This process, however, if it were to work openly and undisguised, would promote a resistance which could easily endanger the whole system. The less the listener has to choose, the more is he made to believe that he has a choice: and the more the whole machine functions only for the sake of profit, the more must he be convinced that it is functioning for him and his sake only or, as it is put, as a public service. In radio we can witness today something very similar to those comic and paradoxical forms of competition between gasolines which do not differ in anything but their names. The consumer is unwilling to recognize that he is totally dependent, and he likes to preserve the illusion of private initiative and free choice. Thus standardization in radio produces its veil of pseudo-individualism.

An outcome of changing methods of production and class relations, the mass musical milieu Adorno denounced as fetishized was, in theory, a necessary component of all capitalist societies. If, with his move from Europe to America in 1938, Adorno's denunciation grew more sarcastic and specific, this might be attributed to the heightened contradictions of Monopoly Capitalism as meted out at the source. Referring only to the United States, he complained that Beethoven's Fourth Symphony was shunted aside as a "rarity," that the "zeal of the belief in property" had produced a singular music commentator (Sigmund Spaeth) whose expertise in tracing "musical larceny" enabled him to "pin his success to the title of tune detective." The most sustained Adorno critique of a specific manifestation of American symphonic culture was his unpublished eighty-nine-page *An-*

alytical Study of "The NBC Music Appreciation Hour." Here, he took radio
to task "as an economic enterprise in an ownership culture . . . forced to
promote, within the listener, a naively enthusiastic attitude toward any
material it offers, and thus, indirectly, toward itself." Fortified by radio's
promotional bias, the language of the "Music Appreciation Hour" was
"barbaric," as in this example, from the 1939–40 students' workbooks, in
which Schubert's lieder catalogue is spoken of "in terms of the output of
a factory": "Schubert was incredibly gifted as a writer of songs; when he
was eighteen he had composed almost 150 of them, and for the rest of his
life, he averaged 40 songs a year." Adorno found the 1939–40 workbooks
riddled with "gross errors and misstatements" arising from their "authoritarian" presentation of simplified knowledge. Of a plot summation of *Tristan und Isolde,* Act II, he complained that its "coy, oldmaidish" evasions
signified a "gerontocratic attitude which does not recognize children and
adolescents as people" ("If one is afraid to speak about adultery, one should
not speak of *Tristan.* One had better not even play it"). Of a "Music
Appreciation Hour" account of the Ride of the Valkyries in terms of
"galloping hoof-beats," "neighing," "the battle song of the maidens," and
their "weird battle cry," Adorno complained that Wagner intended a "musical mythologizing" of the Valkyries' ride, not "primitive naturalistic description," that the passage's naturalistic features appear "only in the sense
in which elements of waking life appear in dreams, not as straightforward
elements of a narration." In turning Wagner into a "musical circus director" ("now come the horses, and now the Valkyries' cry"), the "Music
Appreciation Hour" had confounded the children's expectations and fet-
tered their imaginations. The upshot of such views was a critique of music
appreciation as an aspect of fetishization. Like the "radio voice," music
appreciation treated sonata form as static, standardized, not dynamic, gen-
erative. Like the radio voice, music appreciation fostered quotation listening through spotlighting atomized "themes." Stressing drill and contest,
recognition and identification, the "NBC Music Appreciation Hour"
spawned a generation of commodity listeners who found fun and pleasure
in music as a game of knowing and possessing. The students' workbooks
spoke of making great music "ours," of having it "in our heads." "The
'Music Appreciation Hour' conceives of the 'fun' one gets out of music as
being practically identical with recognition. . . . Actually, what occurs in
the 'Hour' is a shifting of the 'fun' from a life-relationship with music to
a fetishism of ownership of music by rote. The idea is that of the musical
spelling bee."

Adorno regretted the "Music Appreciation Hour" 's personality-cult
marketing of the great composers. He also regretted its marketing of musi-

cal instruments as, in the words of the 1939–40 teacher's guide, "personalities, and not merely disembodied sounds"—a description contradicting Classical usage. He especially regretted the personality cult shrouding the program's famous host, citing such workbook effusions as "Mr. Damrosch . . . turns to the orchestra, waves his baton like a magic wand and instantly beautiful music is heard in hundreds of schoolrooms from Maine to California. No fairy story is more wonderful than this." But the personality cult symbolizing the official musical landscape of American Monopoly Capitalism, equally embodying music appreciation and the radio symphony, was, inevitably, the Toscanini cult. During Adorno's American period, "Toscanini" became his favored code word for "affirmative" musical gloss and consumerism.

> The ruined farmer is consoled by the radio-instilled belief that . . . an order of things that allows him to hear Toscanini compensates for low market prices for farm products; even though he is ploughing cotton under, radio is giving him culture.

> No work of art, no thought, has a chance of survival, unless it bear within it repudiation of false riches and high-class production, of color films and television, millionaire's magazines and Toscanini.

As it was Toscanini who escorted Beethoven into the entertainment arena, his own image blurred the boundaries separating entertainment and art. "Toscanini, like a second-rate orchestra leader, is called Maestro, if half ironically, and a hit song, 'Music, maestro, please,' had its success immediately after Toscanini was promoted to Marshall of the Air with the aid of the radio." With even misguided intellectuals praising jazz for its ostensible newness and vitality, fetishized mass music and fetishized art music became increasingly indistinguishable; in fact, "if one compares the special knowledge of a jazz expert with that of a Toscanini worshipper, the former is far ahead of the latter." In Adorno's lexicon, such Toscanini-cult fetishes as "objectivity" and "textual fidelity" were terms of ridicule. He proclaimed the naiveté of radio-voice broadcasts "executed under the battlecry of the utmost fidelity to the letter." Behind Toscanini's abhorrence of interpolated retards and crescendos Adorno perceived no corrective of corrupt interpretive practice but rather the superficial masking of a deeper corruption wrought by radio, music appreciation, and other mass opiates. "In spite of all talk of new objectivity, the essential function of conformist performances is no longer the performance of the 'pure' work but the presentation of the vulgarized one with a gesture which emphatically but impotently tries to hold the vulgarization at a distance." Adorno approvingly quoted Eduard Steuermann, who dubbed Toscanini's performance ideal "the barbarism of perfection."

> To be sure, passages are not here inflated or climaxes overstressed for the sake of fascination. There is iron discipline. But precisely iron. The new fetish is the flawlessly functioning, metallically brilliant apparatus as such, in which all the cogwheels mesh so perfectly that not the slightest hole remains open for the meaning of the whole. Perfect, immaculate performance in the latest style presents [the work] as already complete from the very first note. The performance sounds like its own phonograph record. The dynamic is so predetermined that there are no longer any tensions at all. . . . What is the point of the symphonic effort when the material on which that effort was to be tested has already been ground up? The protective fixation of the work leads to its destruction, for its unity is realized in precisely that spontaneity which is sacrificed to the fixation.

Underlying Adorno's analysis of the false pretensions of Toscanini's performance style was an analysis of the false pretensions of the celebrity conductor as a twentieth-century musical fetish. Through the end of the eighteenth century, he recalled, composing, interpreting, and improvising were overlapping functions. Only with the victory of the bourgeois class did the composition become a stranded commodity, distinct from the performer. Diminishing opportunities for interpretive freedom were momentarily arrested by such heroic nineteenth-century virtuosos as Liszt and Anton Rubinstein, whose subjectivity corresponded to persistent areas of bourgeois individualism. Under twentieth-century Monopoly Capitalism, however, interpretation was absolutely subordinate to the text. Still, the musical public yearned for the "spiritual," "soulful" individualism of the nineteenth-century Romantics. The result was the celebrity conductor who, expounding his aged repertoire, evoked intoxication and contemplation. "The dream image of vital fullness and uninhibited verve, of animated organic quality and direct . . . inwardness, are provided by him corporally for those for whom capitalist economy denies in reality the fulfillment of all such wishes." Far from liberating the alienated, surrogate wish-fulfillment under the aegis of a podium star could only enslave; as druggist, the conductor became a vehicle of submission for both orchestra and audience. In fact, he resembled the monopoly lord whose canny manner "conceals the rational-mechanical apparatus from the view of individuals in order to control it in his own interest. He dominates irresponsibly and without contradiction. . . ." Combining the concepts of "protective fixation of the work" and total domination of the public, Adorno arrived at his crowning deprecation of the Toscanini-type baton magnate as culturally equivalent to the authoritarian dictator whose ascendancy, like that of mass culture, was guaranteed by capitalist contradictions. This was no superficial equating of tyrannical personalities, but an equating of functions. The conductor, the authoritarian dictator, the monopoly lord represented the all-powerful technocrat/administrator whose submissive subjects are made to feel purposefully occupied while being denied access to negativity and critical intelligence.

[The protective fixation of the work], which seizes on the substance itself, smothers it; the absolute adjustment of the appearance to the work denies the latter and makes it disappear unnoticed behind the apparatus, just as certain swamp-drainings by labor detachments take place not for their own sake but for that of the work [i.e., the labor]. Not for nothing does the rule of the established conductor remind one of that of the totalitarian Führer.*

I have dwelt on Adorno because he is doubly pertinent to understanding Toscanini. For one thing, he and other Frankfurt School members were vital contributors to an emerging mass culture critique within the American intellectual community, and to the post–World War I emergence of that community itself. For another, his analysis, half a century after its inception, retains its pungency: contemporary critics of cultural populism as an aspect of American concert life ignore him at their risk. Partly because Adorno himself was so disputatious, both these achievements—his influence and his enduring merit—have provoked exaggerated claims and counterclaims. He was far from the first to ponder the psychological and cultural costs of modern communications—that had been going on in America since early in the Gilded Age, when the telegraph made the press an eager, undiscriminating news disseminator.[7] Nor was he the first to deplore the combined impact of consumerism and populism on American

---

*More than a decade after the Toscanini-period writings from which I have quoted, Adorno summed up his Toscanini case in "Die Meisterschaft des Maestro" (*Der Merkur*, 1958). Analyzing Toscanini the conductor, he complained that, far from being "true to the composer," protective fixation à la Toscanini steamrolled detail and nuance, compromised counterpoint and inner voices. Analyzing Toscanini the culture-hero, he wrote that "the Maestro . . . replaces the Führer-personality and religion, and also expresses the victory of technique and administration over the music; with him, people feel musically well-tended, safe and sheltered."

music making. Five years before radio, in 1915, Carl Van Vechten, for one, lamented the expansion of symphonic audiences and the redundancy of the standard repertoire:

> In our civilization everybody is supposed to "love" music. Poor though we may be, we send our daughters to the music-masters. . . .
>
> The results are not heartening. The fact is that over fifty per cent of the audiences who attend symphony concerts cannot carry a tune. Naturally they are not averse to hearing Beethoven's Fifth played over and over and over again. . . . There are some overtures and symphonies which every orchestra plays every season to its patrons. Some of this music one also hears in restaurants and in the opera house. It is monstrous![8]

Radio and recordings, godsends to the popularizers, elicited a chorus of hostile outcries from musicians afraid of being put out of work. The American Federation of Musicians authorized spending one million dollars in 1930 to stave off mechanized competition. The American Society of Composers, Authors and Publishers warned its members of automated threats in 1933 with *The Murder of Music*. In 1942 the A. F. of M. imposed a ban on all recordings, forcing an agreement two years later under which royalties from record sales were paid to the union. When the Taft-Hartley Act nullified this pact in 1947, a second recordings ban was declared, to be settled by the creation of the Music Performance Trust Funds. While some musicians fretted over unemployment, others launched broader attacks on the evils of music made "canned" and "mechanized." One notable gadfly, whom we have already encountered denouncing Toscanini's New York Philharmonic concerts ("museums of the past," "fashion-enslaved, prestige-hypnotized minds"), was the composer-educator Daniel Gregory Mason of Columbia University, whose magazine polemics, collected in *The Dilemma of American Music* (1928) and *Tune In, America* (1931), are a bristling condemnation of audience complacency. Challenging the braggadocio of "hurrah-boys," for whom cultural achievement seemed measurable in dollars spent, Mason saw music debased as a "commodity" in American homes, where the "life-giving amateur spirit" had been snuffed out by status-hungry consumers and by American orchestras, whose repetitious concerts required constant advertising to sustain artificial needs. He characterized the core symphonic constituency as "moronic conservatives" transfixed by "rival prima donna conductors." He lampooned radio as a "musical Ford" and "horseless pianoforte," inquiring: "How can any artistic experience have value in which the audience is in a purely passive condition?"* Sounding an alarm widely echoed, he excoriated jazz for exemplifying the "crudity of majority taste" as inculcated by radio and recordings.

Adorno's fulminations were therefore no voice in the wilderness. Lippmann and John Dewey had worried about the democratic "public." Brooks and Mumford had decried philistinism as an aspect of American utilitarianism. Mason had deplored the impact on music of mass media, mass marketing, and mass consumption. What was new in Adorno was his thorough ideological base; to take stock of his permanent contribution to understanding Toscanini is to appreciate the shortcomings and advantages of an inspired ideologue. His shortcomings of tone are unignorable. More often than not, his anger at commodity society seems mainly directed at its victims, whom he holds in contempt. His aversion to the music they like is bloated with hyperbole: "In the field of light music the arrangers are the only trained musicians"; "A sort of musical children's language is prepared [whose harmonies] confine themselves to the three tonic major chords and exclude any meaningful harmonic progression." His notorious rejection of jazz exposes his own Eurocentrism and ill will. He chronically overstates the efficacy of taste manipulation in shaping repertoire preferences;** the

---

*Polemics against radio and other "mechanized" music formats were also issued abroad, notably by the two pivotal contemporary composers: Schoenberg and Stravinsky. A 1930 statement by the former, "The Radio: Reply to a Questionnaire," began: "Quite certainly the radio is a foe!—and so are the gramophone and sound-film." Schoenberg inveighed against "the boundless surfeit of music. Here, perhaps, the frightful expression 'consumption of music' really does apply after all. For perhaps this continuous tinkle, regardless of whether anyone wants to hear it or not, whether anyone can take it in, whether anyone can use it, will lead to a state where all music has been consumed, worn out." Schoenberg was more sanguine three years later in "Modern Music on the Radio," an essay holding out the hope that "many, frequently repeated [radio] performances" of modern works could "educate the public for modern music." Stravinsky, in his 1935 autobiography, had kind words for the phonograph as a means of documenting a composer's own, correct interpretation of his music. But he also worried that

> today anyone, living no matter where, has only to turn a knob or put on a record to hear what he likes. Indeed, it is in just this incredible facility, this lack of necessity for any effort, that the evil of this so-called progress lies. . . . For one can listen without hearing, just as one can look without seeing. The absence of active effort and the liking acquired for this facility make for laziness. . . . Listeners fall into a kind of torpor. . . .[9]

**And thus understates the appeal of the music itself—and not merely as "distorted" by "regressive" virgin ears. As Frankfurt School analysts might themselves have expressed

popularity of Sibelius, in particular, drives him to such paroxysms of pedantry as:

> In the opinion of this writer—and he is prepared to back it by concrete technical analysis—the work of Sibelius is not only incredibly overrated, but it fundamentally lacks any good qualities. . . . It would be very interesting to show: *first,* to what extent Sibelius is played over the radio, and *second,* to what influences his popularity is due. . . . If his great success is really a fact, and not only some sort of manufactured popularity (which is still the writer's opinion), this probably would indicate a total state of musical consciousness which ought to give rise to even graver apprehension than the lack of understanding for great modern music or the preference for cheap light music. . . . If Sibelius' music is good music, then all the categories by which musical standards can be measured . . . must be completely abolished.

But Adorno never undertook a "concrete technical analysis" of Sibelius's language or a study of Sibelius's radio exposure; too often, a suspect paucity of detail and explication accompanies his bullying stridence.* His exposi-

---

it, music appreciation's symphonies and concertos, a product of bourgeois times, inherently addressed bourgeois sensibilities. The works of Beethoven and Brahms, Wagner and Sibelius, speak thrillingly of individual achievement through struggle and competition, of self-denial postponing and finally yielding to climactic resolution. Goal-oriented, imbued with the idea of progress, theirs is the music of the subjective self battling social constraints, of ego versus "other."[10] During World War II, as we have seen, Beethoven's struggle-to-victory scenarios inflamed audiences who recognized in the *Leonore* Overture No. 3 or the Fifth Symphony metaphors for making war against Hitler. More generally, the striving dynamic typifying postbaroque, premodern sonata-form aesthetics—and heightened in Toscanini's tense, militant performances—may particularly have gripped upwardly mobile, new middle-class listeners. That music appreciation inculcated passive culture consumption, placated status needs and inchoate "spiritual" deficiencies, confused high regard with stargazing, art with foreign antiquity —all of this supports Adorno, but does not justify his merciless antipathies. Like Sinclair Lewis's craven culture consumers, his narcotized puppets of Capital are a provocative starting point, not a fair cross-section. Some music appreciation graduates doubtless learned to listen as "critically" as Adorno himself, whose musical purview conspicuously omitted pre-Bach, prebourgeois styles.

*During his 1938–41 affiliation with Paul Lazarsfeld's Office of Radio Research at Princeton and Columbia, Adorno was under constant attack by Lazarsfeld for not grounding his analyses in concrete data. Lazarsfeld, also a prominent emigrant, initiated the first comprehensive studies of radio in America. These were massive data-gathering efforts, using questionnaires and interviews to ascertain the impact of mass media. Given his continued allegiance to Frankfurt "critical theory," Adorno could

tion of the "radio voice" is inexplicably weak; where a well-chosen series of musical examples could pinpoint vital details likely to evade airwave transmission, he offers only the crudest reference points. Like many another historical dialectician, he seems as culture bound as his puppets of history: applied to vindicate Mahler and Schoenberg while rejecting Stra-

---

only reject the behaviorist assumptions of Lazarsfeld's methodology: his papers for the Office of Radio Research disdained quantifiable concepts in pursuit of a critique more fundamental than Lazarsfeld's. At the same time, however, Adorno oversaw music-related Radio Research papers by scholars whose thinking was more statistical, less speculative than his own. Of the empirical studies sponsored by Lazarsfeld's office during Adorno's fitful tenure, the most pertinent to understanding Toscanini was Edward Suchman's "Invitation to Music" in Lazarsfeld's *Radio Research 1941* (a volume also including Adorno's "The Radio Symphony"). Suchman's 1939–40 "Study of the Creation of New Music Listeners by the Radio" sampled the audience for "The Masterwork Hour," a classical music program on New York's WNYC. Responding to a questionnaire, 15.2 percent of Suchman's sample listeners said they "might never have become interested in serious music" if not for radio; 37.6 percent said they became interested "through other sources" but that this interest "would never have grown" without radio; and 47.2 percent said radio was "not the cause" of their interest but had given them "another means of enjoying music." Suchman inferred from additional data that "radio appears to be opening the door to music listening for two significant groups, men and older [i.e., over-thirty] listeners." The men worked during the day and liked to stay home in the evenings; radio made music physically available. The "older listeners," not having developed an interest in music during adolescence, were given a "second chance." Concentrating on the "new listeners" group, Suchman queried further and found: "There can be little doubt as to the importance of the 'prestige' motive . . . a desire to rise in the estimation of one's friends." Scrutinizing musical sophistication, he found (and quantified) a greater fondness for Rimsky-Korsakov, Dvořák, and Rachmaninoff among new listeners than in the other two groups and concluded that radio had fostered "pseudo-interest," "familiarity without understanding," "romantic relaxation or excitement without any concern for the development or the relations of the music." He further found that "among those respondents whose interest developed before the radio, almost every other listener attributes an important part to the concert hall, while more than one out of three listeners played their own instrument. Today, however, among the newly developed music listeners, less than one out of six listeners mention the concert hall or instrument-playing as taking an important place in their development. Similarly . . . the family background as a factor assumes relatively less importance, while the influence of friends grows more important." Some of these observations elaborated Office of Radio Research orthodoxy. In Lazarsfeld's *The Radio and the Printed Page* (1940), for instance, a "gratification study" of the radio program "Professor Quiz" produced respondents who described their culture quest in terms of increased social skills and of "popularity and status in the eyes of one's neighbors or customers." For the most part, however, the mindset informing Suchman's paper is less Lazarsfeld's than Adorno's— his heavy hand shadows tables and statistics in which preformulated conclusions are clumsily rendered "testable." Adorno's own papers, for all their dense circumlocution and abstraction, are more straightforward than Suchman's research, more informative than Lazarsfeld's.

vinsky, his insistence on "negative truth" situates his aesthetic credo within the writhings of German post-Romanticism.

The strength of Adorno's ideological grounding is its heuristic breadth. Working from a general base, he is attuned to issues, even musical issues, that other writers on music overlooked or could not take seriously. It would not have occurred to Daniel Gregory Mason to locate musical consumerism in the "radio voice" itself, or to *Modern Music* to scrutinize "The NBC Music Appreciation Hour." Notwithstanding Adorno's snobbism, his vision of bourgeois anomie illuminates the "spiritual starvation" and psychological dislocations of the twenties and thirties. His persistent denigration of jazz, while obnoxious, confronts the ubiquitous radio presence of new popular music genres. In exaggerating the potency of symphonic marketing, he proved more prescient than Mason and others who, ignoring the lessons of astute commodity salesmanship, feared that with radio the concert supply would outstrip demand. His criterion of "negative truth," despite its historical relativity, furnishes a valuable index, a way of measuring and articulating the defects of the "happy energy" and "chirpy ebullience" of the twenties popularizers, of Billy Phelps's geniality, of Damrosch's stability, of George Marek's reassurances that "you needn't dig or look for 'meaning,' " and of Olin Downes's populism, which vanquished the "elaborate and decaying" music of Schoenberg, Berg, and Stravinsky with the "noble and lonely spirit" of Sibelius. With his yardstick of dialectical abrasion, Adorno could demonstrate that knowledge of Beethoven was not something to be acquired as readily as better muscle tone through five minutes' daily exercise.

Summarizing the "basic dramatic motives" of an artwork whose themes include the nature of art, Downes's *Symphonic Masterpieces* construes *Die Meistersinger* as follows:

> Walther, of course, is Wagner himself. Beckmesser is the prototype of Wagner's antagonists among the critics. Hans Sachs is the virtue and wisdom of the people, prompt to recognize the creative artist and find expression in him. The final moral is that the greatest genius must have its roots deep down in the soil of the race that gave it birth, and that the aristocracy of genius can in turn raise the people to new levels of beauty and understanding.

In thus recycling his own frictionless populism, Downes omits every challenging or disturbing topic Wagner's opera consciously or unconsciously poses: the uses of art in conflict with the status quo; the perils of mass emotional release, whether anarchic or patriotic. Downes's Panglossian "aristocracy of genius" connotes a timeless "great art" whose practitioners are noble, moral, mythic, "affirmative." By rendering Wagner so nutritious, he lends unexpected credibility to Adorno's unforgiving vision of music appreciation as a harmonious anodyne for industrial-age class and economic rifts, a banal evasion of political consciousness.

The direct influence wielded by Adorno and other Frankfurt School emigrants was necessarily restricted. With their convoluted styles, specialized nomenclature, and philosophical grounding, they did not court a large audience. Even within academia, the Frankfurt School was hermetic. In Frankfurt, the Institute for Social Research had already defined itself as an outsider group. In exile on the Columbia University campus, it resisted affiliation with the university's sociology department. Until 1940, its calculated policy was to continue publishing in German. Still, by the mid-forties Dwight Macdonald, Clement Greenberg, and others in America had begun disseminating a jaundiced mass culture perspective palpably influenced by Adorno and Leo Lowenthal. As the American intelligentsia grew in size, confidence, and muscle through the 1930s, its enthusiasm for modernism and Menckenesque disdain for rival "mob man" enthusiasms were bound to filter down from the ivory tower toward mass-circulation newspapers and magazines. The modernists, who advocated Schoenberg and Stravinsky while foreswearing "radio music knowledge" and the Toscanini repertoire, would confront the popularizers, who advocated Toscanini while foreswearing what Olin Downes, denouncing Berg's *Lulu* Suite, called "music which bluffs itself and will bluff us, too." In October 1940, Virgil Thomson, succeeding the deceased Lawrence Gilman, became chief music critic of the New York *Herald Tribune*.

More than a worthy polemicist, Thomson was the perfect embodiment of high-cultural forces ripe for head-on combat with the Toscanini cult and its milieu. As much as any musician could be, he was a member in good standing of America's come-of-age arts-and-letters commonwealth. A Harvard graduate, he had spent many years in Paris, where he not only, like Carter, Copland, Harris, and Piston, studied with Nadia Boulanger, but kept company with Jean Cocteau, James Joyce, Pablo Picasso, and Gertrude Stein. He was a leading composer whose catalogue included an important opera (*Four Saints in Three Acts*, 1934) and an important film score (*The Plow That Broke the Plains*, 1936). He was a practiced writer whose prose was waspish, insouciant, and compulsively readable.

Compared with Gilman and Downes, Thomson was a breed apart. Gilman, self-taught in music, had outside of journalism prepared thematic guides for *Salome* and *Pelléas et Mélisande* and composed an opera he had never sought to publish. Downes's music education was also unsystematic.

As a young man, he had appeared as soloist in one of the MacDowell piano concertos and partly supported himself by playing for physical culture classes; at the *Times,* consistent with *Times* "objectivity" axioms, he made music only in private. Thomson remained a practicing musician, keenly and broadly attuned to the present. He had no use for the "greatest performers" and "greatest symphonies"; as a confirmed Francophile, he harbored reservations about the canonized German masterpieces in any event. Among contemporary composers he found Sibelius and Shostakovich "not adult," saving his shrewd admiration for Bartók, Berg, Copland, Chávez, Ives, Schoenberg, Stravinsky. The conductors he liked included Ernest Ansermet, Beecham, Furtwängler, Charles Munch, and others rarely or never heard in New York. Among instrumentalists, he preferred E. Robert Schmitz to Vladimir Horowitz (the "master of distortion and exaggeration"), Luigi Silva to Gregor Piatigorsky ("fascinating and tedious, impressive and banal all at once"), and almost anyone to Jascha Heifetz ("essentially frivolous"). He thought Artur Schnabel's Beethoven lacked the "voice of authority" and that Arthur Rubinstein's rubatos in Chopin did not resemble "anything Frédéric Chopin ever did or had in mind." He considered France's Orchestre National the "world's best." He called Marian Anderson's demeanor in arias and lieder "that of a very, very, very good student being careful not to do anything wrong." He delighted in not even acknowledging the conventional wisdom that revered what he debunked.[11]

Such heresies could never have found a home at the *Times,* the "newspaper of record," the "world's most influential newspaper," whose publisher, Adolph Ochs, was described by an associate as the personification of "crowd-consciousness," by a 1926 essayist as "the living norm of the median culture of American life." The *Herald Tribune,* by comparison, was a liberal Republican "gentleman's paper" partial to novelty and style. As Thomson later remarked: "With a circulation of only 450,000 [it] aspired to intellectual distinction. . . . On [the *Herald Tribune*] a writer's distinction was judged less by his leadership of public taste—high, low, or middlebrow— than by his skill in handling words, sentences, and paragraphs."* Whereas

---

*In a conversation with me (September 1, 1982), Thomson added: "The *Times* presented a Jewish point of view, rather than, say, a Harvard point of view. And by the twenties and thirties the New York musical public had grown from being a predominantly German public to being a German-*Jewish* public. The intensity of Toscanini worship was like something you would apply to the State of Israel. Because, you see, before and during World War I Jewish people were predominantly German, or Russian, or French. But with the growing anti-Semitism in Germany Jews became aware of being Jewish with an intensity they didn't have before."

The equation linking Toscanini to Beethoven was strengthened by wartime patriotism. This RCA ad ran in *Life* on October 21, 1946.

For Toscanini's famous May 25, 1944 Red Cross benefit at Madison Square Garden, the souvenir booklet contained a photograph making Toscanini into Christ. The most famous Toscanini photographs were by Robert Hupka, who took some fifteen hundred of them for RCA Victor from 1942 to 1949—among the most remarkable pictorial documents of music in performance.

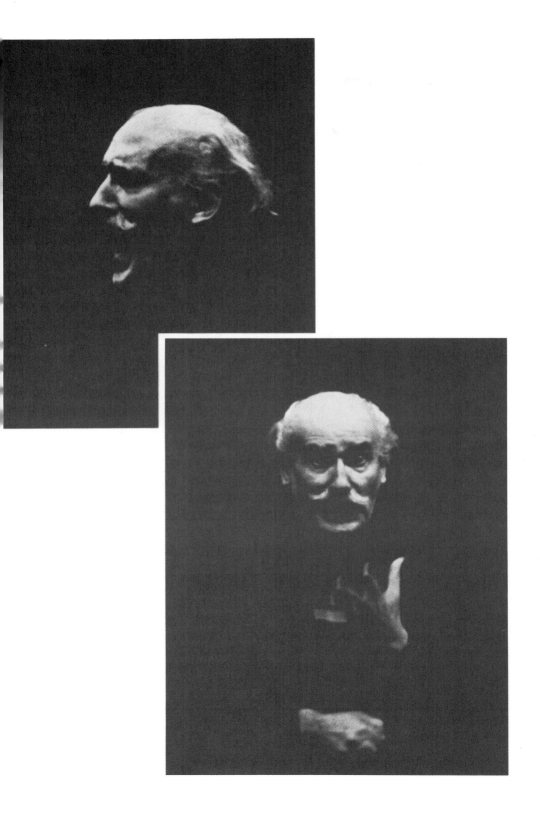

LIFE

TOSCANINI & GRANDDAUGHTER

NOVEMBER 27, 1939 **10** CENTS

Popular imagery of Toscanini shifted during his NBC years (1938–54). Commensurate with the democratized high-culture audience to which NBC/RCA appealed, the "other Toscanini"—kindly, unpretentious, family-oriented—superseded images of imperious, divine authority. *Life*'s November 27, 1939 cover story, in which granddaughter Sonia Horowitz was an ideal prop, repudiated the old Toscanini in favor of one who was "simple," "affectionate," and "unbelievably modest." Photographer Herbert Gehr showed how "the Maestro plays games with Sonia on the lawn" and how "with a switch for a baton, Sonia takes a lesson in orchestra conducting from her famous grandfather."

Time featured the smiling "other Toscanini" on its April 26, 1948 cover. Photographs for the story included "Toscanini Watching a Fight."

NBC televised Toscanini ten times. For the first Toscanini telecast, on March 18, 1948, David Sarnoff appeared on screen to introduce "a great day for radio, for television, for music, and for the public."

Toscanini's 1950 coast-to-coast tour with the NBC Symphony provided countless "other Toscanini" anecdotes. In its May 22 picture story "Toscanini in Texas," *Life* showed him rehearsing in shirtsleeves in a sweltering Austin gymnasium while his tailcoat was being dried by a fan. At Sun Valley, Toscanini rode the ski lift. "On Tour with Toscanini and RCA Victor," a publicity brochure, depicted Toscanini's democratized Saturday-night radio audience.

In conjunction with Toscanini's 1950 tour, RCA's advertisements showed him endorsing its ill-fated 45-rpm classical disks as "fascinating" and "remarkably faithful." Into his eighties, the "other Toscanini" amazed with his tireless rehearsing and gingerly gait. Newspaper photographs frequently showed him in transit at airports.

The Toscanini watch encompassed recipes for his favorite soups (in the July 9, 1950 New York *Herald Tribune*) and a noninterview by gossip columnist Earl Wilson (in the April 5, 1948 New York *Post*).

A typical RCA Victor Toscanini cover from the early 1950s, with twenty Robert Hupka photographs.

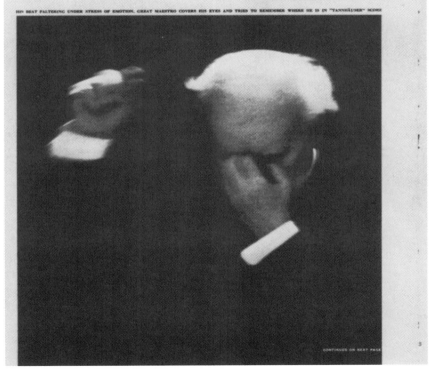

MUSIC

Toscanini Conducts
Farewell Concert

EMOTION MAKES THE GREAT MAESTRO FALTER

Though 87, Arturo Toscanini never faltered musically as he went through his NBC Symphony season this year. But last week he came out at New York's Carnegie Hall for the last time. Few knew it, but the greatest of all orchestra conductors had resigned.

Once or twice Toscanini drove the orchestra into furies of magnificent sound. Once or twice, like a lion rousing himself, he shook his head and roared the melody. But then the firm beat faltered, the infallible memory failed.

Puzzled, he poked at his head (*right*), clutched his forehead (*below*). The musicians floundered. Offstage, his protégé, Conductor Guido Cantelli, shouted, "Cut it off!" The broadcast went off the air for 38 seconds, a record went on for radio listeners. But the maestro caught the beat again, led the musicians to a roaring climax. Even before the last measures ended, Toscanini tottered off, dropping his baton and weeping as he went. The applause went on and on, but he did not return.

TOSCANINI, BEWILDERED, FORGETS HIS PLACE

HIS BEAT FALTERING UNDER STRESS OF EMOTION, GREAT MAESTRO COVERS HIS EYES AND TRIES TO REMEMBER WHERE HE IS IN "TANNHÄUSER" SCORE

CONTINUED ON NEXT PAGE

Life turned Toscanini's final concert into a soap-opera episode on April 19, 1954.

The *Victor Record Review* printed "stories" about new RCA releases, such as this one (November 1940) beginning: "Rarely has it happened in the history of recorded performances that two such artists as Jascha Heifetz and Arturo Toscanini have combined their respective talents (each pre-eminent in his own field) in the interpretation of such a prodigious masterpiece as Beethoven's Concert in D major for Violin and Orchestra, Opus 61." The *Victor Record Review*'s March 1940 Toscanini story quoted Lawrence Gilman on "The Elect Interpreter," and continued: "The truth in

Lawrence Gilman's lines...is brought home most forcibly to anyone who hopes to convey in words something of the grandeur, the sublime eloquence, the electrifying energy, and above all, the utter perfection of Arturo Toscanini's performance of the most dramatic and beloved of symphonies—Beethoven's 'Fifth.'" Four decades later, the Franklin Mint's "Official Family Archive Collection" pledged diehard allegiance to the mostly forgotten Toscanini cult. "Toscanini bookends" were provided without charge to subscribers who acquired all six Franklin Mint Toscanini albums.

RCA's "Toscanini—A Legendary Performer" (1977) included this brown-and-white "picture suitable for framing," with instructions to "cut along dotted line."

Downes wrote third-person appraisals of accredited events at Carnegie Hall and the Metropolitan Opera, Thomson, a spokesman for himself alone, was as likely to cover music at a museum, a nightclub, a movie theater, a church, a university, or a conservatory. His purview frequently led beyond the event to its formulators, promoters, and analysts. He denounced Arthur Judson, whose New York Philharmonic he considered "not a part of New York's intellectual life." He called music appreciation a "racket" and said its practitioners "know only about 20 pieces [and] are merely trying to keep up their own prestige when they pretend that these (and certain contemporary works that sort of sound like them) make up all the music in the world worth bothering about." He considered Theodor Adorno a "brilliant author" and told radio listeners to read him.

Thomson did not dismiss Toscanini; on occasion he called him a "great conductor." But by 1940 Toscanini had ceased to exist for his admirers apart from the cult, and this Thomson loathed. Unimpressed by effulgent patriotism, temperamental genius, or verbatim textual fidelity, he was no finger-in-the-dike Toscanini critic after the fashion of some early postwar opponents of the cult; rather, his writing eschewed any sense of strain:

> Arturo Toscanini's musical personality is a unique one in the modern world. One has to go back to Mendelssohn to find its parallel. A reactionary in spirit, he has none the less revolutionized orchestral conducting by his radical simplification of its procedures. Almost wholly devoted to the playing of familiar classics, he has at the same time transformed these into an auditive image of twentieth-century America with such unconscious completeness that musicians and laymen all over the world have acclaimed his achievement without, I think, very much bothering to analyze it. They were satisfied that it should be, for the most part, musically acceptable and at all times exciting.

Thomson admired Toscanini's "musical efficiency," his "unvarying ability to put over a piece" by virtue of the "detailed clarity, sequential coherence and avoidance of adolescent sentiment" characterizing his readings. At the same time, he asserted: "The maestro . . . needs an appropriate vehicle to make his best effect. For me he is most absorbing in music for the theater, especially the Romantic theater of Wagner and Verdi, and in symphonic literature of not quite first quality. His readings of the great masters often suffer a loss of poetic meaning through the intense objectivity of his approach." Thomson considered the Verdi Requiem—"as sincere a piece of theatrical Italian Catholicism as has ever been written"—to be Toscanini's best vehicle. Toscanini's Beethoven, on the other hand, he found simplified. Of a Toscanini performance of the Seventh Symphony he wrote: "The first movement was the only one that seemed comfortable in its tempo, and that got into some trouble about rhythm along in the middle. . . . The second movement came out as a barcarolle, the third and fourth rather in tarantella vein. In none of them was there any sense of mystery to make the Beethoven fury seem interiorly dramatic rather than merely of the stage."[12]

And these blasphemies enjoyed a regular, respectable forum. They could not be ignored. According to Oscar Levant: "[Toscanini] once passed Virgil in a hall at NBC with no sign of recognition, due to his almost blind eyes. When he was told that Virgil had just passed him, he shouted, 'Where is he? I'll slappa him in the face!' " More typically, the Thomson treatment was considered an optional counterweight to Downes: more brilliant, less "responsible." Notwithstanding an occasional stray broadside, his polemics received scant reinforcement in the mass media; even his own newspaper carried reverent Toscanini notices by others. As Thomson himself recalled many years later, describing a Tocquevillean tyranny of majority opinion: "The same thing happened to Toscanini in his lifetime as happened to George Washington and Abraham Lincoln after their deaths. There was an unspoken conspiracy not to look at the warts. *Privately* musicians talked about Toscanini all the time. Koussevitzky and Beecham were not unhappy about my attacks. But publicly you couldn't say anything against him. I was allowed to because I was able to write with a certain brilliance."[13]

An anomaly among his colleagues, Thomson did not represent a totally new critical type. His worldliness and flair for unexcited heresy evoked the preradio Old Guard. To glance back at the newspaper writings of its leading lights, and at the old *Musical Courier* and *Musical America,* is to appreciate a transformation of critical attitudes in a mere quarter-century. But for Thomson, the armchair aesthetes of the Old Guard, with their amiable curiosities and fine-honed preferences, had been superseded in the daily press by a critical generation given to mounting soapboxes and grabbing sleeves. W. J. Henderson, assessing "The Function of Musical Criticism," wrote: "What we should value most in critical commentary is its point of view, its endeavor to attain an altitude, from which the whole breadth of the subject may be surveyed." James Gibbons Huneker advised would-be critics: "Be charitable, be broad—in a word, be cosmopolitan. He is a hobby of mine, this citizen of the world. A novelist may be provincial, parochial as the town pump, that is his picture; but a critic must not be narrow in his outlook. . . ." Huneker said of his sojourns in Paris, one of many European cities he intimately knew, that they "had lent me aplomb, had rubbed off my salad greenness." Henry Krehbiel researched Wagner's mastersingers in Nuremberg. Philip Hale studied in Berlin, Munich, and

Paris. The Old Guard absorbed as living cultural currency the Germanic traditions Theodore Thomas and Anton Seidl had sponsored in the New World. The Toscanini cultists, with their fondness for churches and soap-boxes, absorbed the Germanic tradition as holy writ while simultaneously absorbing ballyhoo strains once sung by P. T. Barnum and other music salesmen. Like Barnum, the newer critics addressed a vast, massed "other," regaling their audience with excited accounts of celebrity pageantry. The old critics more expressly addressed artists and intellectuals, and wrote of art and of the intellect. As recounted by a fellow critic, Henderson in 1937 recalled

> when he and his colleagues struggled with structural analysis as a part of their reviews, striving to communicate to the reader something intelligible about the first theme, the second theme, the development, and other details of symphonies heard for the first time. This was on the assumption that music criticism was read chiefly by musicians who "knew," or by laymen of studious and ambitious natures, who, thirsting for culture, wanted to know. More than now, newspapers of that time regarded their special departments as for the elect of particular lines; there was much less thought of music as something of a general, perhaps even of a mass appeal. If the reviewer reached the enlightened few, and in a manner that built prestige for the paper among them, he earned his salary. . . .

The "best criticism," Henderson observed in 1915, "will not command a large public. It will perforce address itself to the society of the intellectual." We have already heard Krehbiel complain, in 1919, of the dailies' new taste for "gossip of the foyer and the dressing rooms." Huneker winced before "the glaring badge of 'popularity' " and added, "I have always detested propagandists while admitting their usefulness. I loathe 'movements,' cliques, canacles, anarchs who don't 'anarchise,' but only bellow." Rebuffing the crowd, the Old Guard reveled in individual opinion. Looking back in 1918, Huneker complained that newspapers had "lost their personal flavor." He called "ridiculous" any critic "setting up an effigy of himself and boasting of his 'objectivity.' " But sanitizing "objectivity" was Downes's epistemological beacon, as in his appeal to impersonal "facts" in denouncing "Furtwängler's Conductorship"; it was the *Times*'s imprimatur of respectability, an antidote to the sensationalism of the Pulitzer and Hearst dailies, a status symbol for the successful and aspirant in an age of conspicuous consumption.[14]

Obviously, the Old Guard's high-mindedness was not unproblematic. Its disregard for popular opinion reflected, more than elite standards, elitism pure and simple. Shadowed by John Sullivan Dwight, it exuded a dour, moralistic gentility. Of its front-line members, only Huneker showed an incipient attunement to modernism. He championed Hauptmann, Joyce, Mallarmé, Munch, Strindberg, Wedekind. His account of his first exposure to the music of Schoenberg, a 1912 performance of *Pierrot lunaire* in Berlin, remains one of the best descriptions of *Pierrot lunaire* ever written, beginning: "What did I hear? At first, the sound of delicate china shivering into a thousand luminous fragments." But Huneker disliked Schoenberg's music (which he studied in score) for its "cruelty" and "ugliness."*[15]

Clarifying both the snobbery of the Old Guardsmen and their professional expertise was an exception proving the rule: like Downes, from whom they differed in so many areas, and unlike Virgil Thomson, whom they in these same areas resembled, they produced layman's guides—but of a sort underlining their resistance to messianic populism. Krehbiel, of all people, was the author of a much-read volume titled *How to Listen to Music*, reprinted thirty times between 1896 and 1924. Like music appreciation bibles to come, it surveyed terms and forms, the instruments of the orchestra, the standard repertoire, the mainstream composers. And yet, rather than descending from his accustomed Olympus, Krehbiel merely lowered his sights. Assessing "the majority of the hearers in our concert-rooms"—the readership, that is, of his book—he groaned:

> They are there to adventure a journey into a realm whose beauties do not disclose themselves to the senses alone, but whose perception requires a cooperation of all the finer faculties; yet of this they seem to know nothing, and even of that sense to which the first appeal is made it may be said with profound truth that "hearing they hear not, neither do they understand."

Whereas for Downes the layman would ideally become his "own music critic," Krehbiel portrayed critics and lay listeners locked in "irrepressible conflict." Downes took his cues from the audiences he inhabited; in Krehbiel's view, critical capitulation to public opinion was "ignoble and injurious to good art." Krehbiel in no way anticipated the "cheerful ebullience" and "happy energy" of future popularizers; his reverence for music, he said, rendered him "willing to seem unamiable to the amateur while arguing the need of even so mild a stimulant" as *How to Listen to Music.* Comparable

---

*Two years later, the twenty-eight-year-old Olin Downes, twenty-nine years Huneker's junior, happened upon Schoenberg's Five Pieces for Orchestra as a reviewer for the Boston *Post* and wrote: "For ourselves, we can only say that at present this music is so disagreeable that, whatever its merits, we cannot find the courage to wish to hear it again."[16]

in agenda, but milder in tone, was Henderson's *What Is Good Music?* (1898), intended to enable the "average music-lover" to "make pleasure dependent not on fancy but on judgment." Henderson's prescribed "path of musical salvation" was straight and smooth: "The person who desires to cultivate a discriminating taste in music may acquire the fundamental knowledge in a few short months. After that, one needs only to live much in an atmosphere of good music until the acquired principles become unconsciously the moving factors underlying all attention to the art." This was friendlier advice than Krehbiel's, yet decades removed from George Marek's reassurances that "the listener does not have to be a tutored man," or from B. H. Haggin's ruler. No less than Krehbiel (or Aaron Copland in *What to Listen for in Music*), Henderson volunteered no "how to" regime, no lists of greatest symphonies and performers; versus passive immersion, he prescribed "a few short months" of active study. Notwithstanding his relative geniality, he would have intimidated the thirties radio pupils of Billy Phelps and Walter Damrosch. His discussions of musical structure and aesthetics, sampling the writings of Kant and Eduard Hanslick, reflected his uncompromising respect for intellect. Baedekers produced by Krehbiel and Philip Hale likewise addressed the thinking layman. As in *How to Listen to Music* and *What Is Good Music?*, the concert audience was taken as given. Not until the advent of radio broadcasts and culture consumption, of music appreciation sermons and proliferating orchestras, would the overriding goal of lay music guides come to seem, more than audience education, audience expansion.

Given its genteel odor, the elitism of a Krehbiel, a Henderson, or a Hale was significantly more insular than the breezy elitism of a Virgil Thomson. But the intellectual content of Thomson's music journalism made it a 1940s anachronism.*

---

*The evolution from Old Guard to populist critics parallels an evolution in American cultural ideals described by the cultural historian Warren Susman. According to Susman's *Culture as History* (1985), the "modal psychological type" for the new middle classes of the twenties and thirties, supplanting an earlier idealization of "character," was "personality." "Character" stressed moral qualities; its "key words," culled from self-help manuals, included "citizenship," "duty," "democracy," "work," "honor," "integrity," and "manhood." A radical shift in advice strategies, epitomized by Dale Carnegie's best-selling *How to Win Friends and Influence People* (1936), documented the shift to "personality," with its emphasis on being liked and admired; the new key words were "fascinating," "stunning," "attractive," "magnetic," "glowing," "masterful," "creative," "dominant," "forceful."

The social role demanded of all in the new culture of personality was that of a performer. Every American was to become a performing self. Every work studied

· · ·

In his *Anti-Intellectualism in American Life* (1962), Richard Hofstadter sketched an enduring New World stereotype of the intellectual: effete, impractical, artificial, arrogant, obeisant to European models of learning and manners. A related New World stereotype holds the "genius" to be lazy, undisciplined, neurotic, imprudent, and awkward.[17] Certain long-standing American mores, according to Hofstadter, honor what intellectuals and geniuses supposedly eschew: pragmatism, efficiency, masculinity, spontaneity, unpretentiousness, restless energy, quick decisiveness.

Like Van Wyck Brooks in *America's Coming-of-Age*, Hofstadter traced unsatisfactory features of the American mind to evangelical religion and utilitarian business. Among the evangelists and their adherents he found militantly masculine leaders ingeniously promoting forceful, simple ideas. These ideas included criteria of success and truth. Counting souls was simply counting audiences. Extrapolating doctrine was simply taking scripture at face value. Such textual fidelity reflected a practical bent holding history and analysis irrelevant. Among the businessmen and their adherents Hofstadter found a practical philosophy yielding enthusiasm for machines, and a disdain for contemplation yielding disdain for the past. Henry Ford said: "History is more or less bunk. It's tradition." Andrew Carnegie spoke of "an ignorant past whose chief province is to teach us not what to adopt, but what to avoid." Also "anti-intellectual," in Hofstadter's view, were the twin sources of a new American educational orthodoxy: Edward Lee Thorndike, whose "scientific" understanding of learning reflected widespread enthusiasm for positivism, behaviorism, and other reductionist philosophies; and John Dewey, whose "instrumentalism," based on the

---

stressed the importance of the human voice in describing methods of voice control and proper methods of conversation or public speaking. Everyone was expected to impress and influence with trained and effective speech.

Susman lists as reflecting the culture of personality "comic strips, radio programs, even beauty pageants." He stresses the pertinence of Hollywood, whose movie stars were marketed as personalities, images, and, "to an increasingly sinister extent," as objects. The stunning masterpieces, magnetic performers, and cheerful Baedekers of the music appreciation movement fit the Susman scenario. Toscanini's imagery was the imagery of personality. The Old Guard had exuded "character" virtues handed down by Theodore Thomas and John Sullivan Dwight. Formal, aloof, they meted out earnest, earned knowledge. Students of Krehbiel's *How to Listen to Music* were, like female parlor pianists of the period, infused with notions of duty and honor. Students of "Professor Quiz" and Billy Phelps, of Sigmund Spaeth's tune detections and George Marek's *Good Housekeeping* columns, acquired fascinating and attractive attributes.

notion that no thought is mature until it has passed into action, penalized the contemplative, bookish child in favor of the fledgling pragmatist. Learning was doing and making, not rarefied reading and thinking. "Success," Dewey wrote, "means succeeding, getting forward, moving in advance. It is an active process, not a passive outcome."

While Hofstadter, writing in the wake of McCarthyism, overimpugned the national identity, he did not impugn every contributing influence to anti-intellectualism as "anti-intellectual." A less pejorative catch-all for the attributes he isolates, better describing Benjamin Franklin, P. T. Barnum, Mark Twain, and Henry Ford than "anti-intellectual," is "self-made." Both the positive aspects of American informality, egalitarianism, enthusiasm, and enterprise and their nether side as presented in *Anti-Intellectualism in American Life* crystallize in the self-made American. For the purposes of understanding Toscanini, Hofstadter's discussion furnishes a vital context: his extensive catalogue of self-made traits resonates mightily with the majority of critics and writers espousing the Toscanini cult. Here is Howard Taubman's admiring description of Olin Downes:

> Olin had a solid, sturdy body packed with energy. His head, with its high brow and rough-hewn planes, gave the impression of granitic strength. When, as he did in his later years, he walked with his kind of bearish gait, he looked like a remote and forbidding man. But the appearance was deceptive. When you sat opposite him in his office or across the table over a bit of supper, you discovered at once that he was responsive and outgoing. His enthusiasms were torrential, expressed in vivid and exciting talk. . . .
>
> His education, because of the force of economic circumstances, was far from systematic. He felt that this was a severe handicap. In deepest truth, however, it was an advantage. In his youth he reached out for new ideas, information and impressions with an avidity that made their absorption far more meaningful and lasting than any learning by rote could have been. . . .
>
> Writing came hard to Olin. Part of the trouble, I think, was psychological. He believed that gaps in his formal education had handicapped him. . . .
>
> The recurrent obligation to meet deadlines was like an ordeal by fire. And yet I know that Olin would not have had it otherwise. We discussed often the arguments for waiting a day before writing a review, and he could see that it would relieve some of the pressure. But in the end he felt that there was no better way than to set down one's reactions in the heat and haste of the moment. No time, perhaps, for the ultimate chiselling of a phrase, but the gain was tremendous. There was time only for

honesty and the warm immediacy of the response. There might be occasion in the Sunday article to reflect and expand, but in the review written to a deadline one had to capture the mood and spirit of an event as one still held them fresh in mind.

To which Downes himself, in a 1941 lecture titled "Be Your Own Music Critic," had this to add:

> . . . Many people ask whether it is possible for a critic to write a just estimate of a composition or performance so hurriedly and so soon after hearing it. On the whole I believe that an immediate account of the concert is more inspired, if less finished and dispassionate in its values than commentary written after days of reflection, as is often the case in Europe. What comes out of you when the impression is white-hot is most spontaneous and intuitive. And it happens that vigor, directness, and individual approach are characteristics of the best American musical criticism.

Thus did Taubman and Downes celebrate the self-made man, promoted at the expense of effete intellectuals and neurotic geniuses. Downes's masculinity—his "solid, sturdy" body, "rough-hewn" features, "granitic strength"—complemented his avid, unassuming demeanor. Spontaneity and intuition were catalysts for honesty, vigor, decisiveness, and "warm immediacy"—American virtues, countering the implicit artifice of European "reflection." Formal education was reduced to "learning by rote." George Marek, born in Vienna, wrote in the same vein: "I had received a European education, was crammed full of belles-lettres and pedantry, and had no sense whatever." And again: "I had no training for music (except a few wretched piano lessons) and had no special talent. . . . I enjoyed it with the blessing of ignorance. I plunged into music directly. . . ."[18]

Naturally, the self-made ethos pervaded music appreciation. Its utilitarian bibles pitched their lists and how-to tips expressly to nonintellectuals. Marek was one of many who shielded his novices from "commentaries and explanations which . . . have tended to make music an intellectual exercise." Summarizing his own brass-tacks orientation, he wrote: "There are no critics around, no musical analysts, no wise men who know the symphony by heart. Nobody has heard this symphony before: we are all in here together and it is up to the composer to entertain us." Such pedagogy, savoring tabula rasa, seized on textual fidelity as the basic tenet of interpretation—as with Hofstadter's evangelicals, it held history and analysis irrelevant. And, like Hofstadter's evangelicals, the music appreciators counted converts as an index to success. Popularity measured "greatness." As Marek put it: "Great works of art make an impression immediately on the untutored mind if that mind is not held back by fear or awe." Elitist modernism, perplexing to the untutored, was precious or diseased. For Sibelius, modernism's contemporary antidote, the inevitable accolade was "virile." Like Olin Downes's head, Sibelius's symphonies were a study in "rough-hewn" contours and "granitic strength." Downes, Taubman once recalled, "could not abide what he considered effete."[19]

New World ambivalence toward Old World culture was an inescapable subtext of the self-made syndrome. Downes, who bristled at the natives in Salzburg and Bayreuth, thought "Europe" when he scorned as fatigued the "paler or academic cast of mind," or treated "literati and cognoscenti" as connoting "snobbism," contradicting "rugged individualism." Taubman's bias could be rawer:

It is a pleasant parlor game among the high-brows to flail American audiences for lack of discernment. Some musicians turn up their noses at our tastes and tell us that elsewhere people are more discriminating. Take it from a man like [Vladimir] Horowitz that this high-brow pose is the bunk. He is quite willing to play Tchaikovsky, if that is what the public likes, and he sees no reason to be patronizing about it. "Some musicians keep telling us that in Europe audiences have higher tastes," he says. "Well, I made more money in Germany playing Tchaikovsky than some of the stuffed shirts playing Beethoven and Schubert."

To Toscanini's disciples, America's concert life was not only equal to, but better than Europe's. Marek wrote in 1940: "I believe that the United States is the most musical country in the world today. We started from scratch; but we scratched deeply." David Ewen wrote in 1943 that America was "the musical center of the world—a position, I am sure, it will retain long after a sick and ravaged world is restored to a semblance of normalcy." In particular, the superiority of American orchestras was a contentious article of faith. Ewen dismissed the Concertgebouw Orchestra as "by no means excellent." Taubman wrote that "even the glowing warmth of the Vienna Philharmonic's pre-Hitler glory did not surpass or match" Koussevitzky's Boston Symphony, Stokowski's Philadelphia Orchestra, or Toscanini's New York Philharmonic.[20] Such patriotic proclamations mounted with mounting wartime patriotism.* Downes's

---

*Naturally, World War II stirred visions of decadent or bankrupt European high culture and of compensatory American high-cultural achievement. Even Roger Sessions, a confirmed internationalist among America's come-of-age composers, could write in

anticommunism poisoned his assessments of Shostakovich—but not after Stalin became an Ally in 1941.

The essential pertinence of self-made Americans to understanding Toscanini, finally, is to Toscanini himself. We have already observed Max Smith, in 1914, praising Toscanini as one who, rather than wandering with head in the clouds, "knows exactly where he is going"; who, rather than seeming absentminded, is neat, orderly, and punctilious; who, rather than being "vague," is "eminently sane," a "man of common sense" possessed of a photographic memory any businessman might envy. Other admiring commentaries of the period found him "scientific," self-reliant, and businesslike. Twenty-five years later, as well-known as DiMaggio, "Toscanini" evoked a catalogue of self-made virtues duplicating Hofstadter's list: pragmatism, efficiency, masculinity, spontaneity, unpretentiousness, restless energy, quick decisiveness. Toscanini's world view and methodology fortuitously suited contemporary New World mores. Henry Ford had debunked history as "tradition." To the NBC Symphony, Toscanini said of *tradizione:* "The first *asino,* the first jackass, did it that way, and everyone follow him!" Positivism and behaviorism, speed and precision—these were the sharp tools with which centuries of European tradition were being scraped away. Toscanini, too, disowned the old Idealism. The notes were the notes, nothing more—an empiricism pure enough to please rigorous social scientists, simplistic enough to engage untutored radio listeners. Son of a Parmesan tailor, he was said to deride musicologists who "know everything—except music." Diehard patriot, he interrupted music with politics and—a foible Americans could appreciate—was given to defensive assertions of national superiority, proclaiming Italians the greatest melodists, denouncing German conductors for taking "everything too slow." Not the least of his attractions was his exaggerated masculinity. His ex-

---

1938: "I have not a moment's doubt that the destruction of musical life and tradition in Vienna is final and complete; my experiences and observations in Germany during the first half of 1933 showed me how speedily and how effectively the wreckers do their job. . . . I believe it is quite clear that if music is to have a future, it lies in the United States." While Downes and other music appreciators shared these feelings, they acquired them years before Sessions had cause to: as early as 1924, Downes's first summer as the New York *Times*'s senior music critic, he toured the European festival circuit and surmised: "City after city and festival after festival went by; a wild hope, which in the bottom of the soul was known from the beginning to be hopeless, was formally recognized at last as an illusion. This was the hope of discovering the new and significant talent. The conviction grew all the time that the immediate future in music lay elsewhere and in younger, less exhausted countries." This was a period when Berg, Hindemith, Schoenberg, Stravinsky, and Webern, among many others, were doing "new and significant" work in Berlin, Vienna, and Paris.[21]

tramarital exploits, which might have proved embarrassing before the liberated sexuality of the twenties, were an increasingly open secret. At times, he pursued two or three love affairs at once. At NBC he remained handsome, flirtatious, and sexually active. He still wore tailored suits and polished shoes, and expressed pride that his mouth did not "stink like an old man's." His diversions included watching boxing and wrestling on television; he even met with Primo Carnera, Antonino Rocca, and other Italo-American fighters. Of Beethoven he said: "He was a real man." Of Bruckner he complained that his music showed he "had never had a woman." Jenny Lind—virtuous, mild, evanescent—had embodied Great Music in terms of a prevailing feminization of culture peripheral to Gilded Age realities; Toscanini's masculine imagery registered Great Music's centralization.[22]

Was Toscanini "anti-intellectual"? For the purposes of understanding his New World celebrity, it does not matter. To those who sought a certified token of high-cultural achievement, and needed to mold the token into something familiar, his surface traits suggested an irresistible American likeness.

During Toscanini's Metropolitan Opera years, rival critical camps had traded arguments over whether his Beethoven and Wagner were Italianate. The combat zone was compact, with the battle lines made blurry by shared admiration for the new conductor. Thirty years later, the camps had renounced common ground. Olin Downes preached to the converted; Virgil Thomson preached not at all, and his adherents were mute. Like any sect grown more extreme, the Toscanini cult was growing purer. The loss of the patrician Lawrence Gilman had further simplified its tone. Samuel Chotzinoff and John Royal, among others, orchestrated publicity at NBC, securing a larger, more diverse Toscanini audience. Music appreciation, seizing on Toscanini as the very symbol of the symphony, intensified his mass appeal. His popularized following, equidistant from highbrow intellectualism and lowbrow boorishness, required a customized icon, less rarefied than the New York Philharmonic scourge of years past. With Toscanini himself increasingly sequestered in Riverdale or at Radio City, visible only to a chosen few, his portrait was expediently redrawn. No longer on public view, he was now seen through the eyes of privileged beholders who in reportraying him portrayed something of themselves as well.

The outdated Toscanini portrait had been a study in aloof, imperious authority. Gilman's images of elitist priest and fundamentalist prophet were guiding motifs. The portrait's detail was heroic, never intimate: defiant

temper, prodigious memory, soulful patriotism. It retained useful features
—an "artist" must stand apart—but was too ferocious to hang on the living
room wall. Marek tackled the "musical inferiority complex" of his readers
by knocking the symphony down to size; Toscanini's portrait, too, had to
be made less threatening lest the untutored mind be "held back by fear and
awe."

In the period between 1937, when the NBC Symphony was formed, and
1945, which is as far as our narrative has taken us, the Toscanini literature
undertook a mollifying trend, penetrating Toscanini's forbidding exterior
to glimpse his family and private life "behind the scenes." This is how *Life*
reportrayed Toscanini on November 27, 1939:

> . . . Few people know much about the patrician-faced little Italian musi-
> cian who keeps his private life to himself and, above all, avoids photogra-
> phers. . . .
>
> The world knows Toscanini as a great conductor with a fearful tem-
> per, an unfailing memory and the power to lash orchestras into frenzies
> of fine playing. But only Toscanini's close friends know him as a simple,
> affectionate man, who works hard, is unbelievably modest and never
> understands why people grow tongue-tied when they meet him or why
> musicians grow pale and falter when he comes to hear them perform. . . .
>
> Toscanini gets up at 6 in the morning and goes over scores at the
> piano, usually waking everybody else in the house with his playing and
> singing. He stops for breakfast, works again until lunch. Soup is his
> favorite food. If he has no rehearsal in the afternoon, he goes for a long
> fast auto ride. He has no respect for speed laws. Evenings, he listens for
> hours at the radio to all kinds and qualities of music. Though he reads
> widely in English and Italian and knows the poetry of Keats, Shelley and
> Shakespeare, he likes best to curl up in bed with a good musical score.
> He sleeps only four or five hours a night.
>
> . . . Toscanini's father was an unmusical tailor. His mother was an
> unmusical housewife. None of his known ancestors was a musician.

The occasion for the article was "a great picture scoop"—Toscanini had
invited *Life*'s Herbert Gehr to photograph his daily regime at home. Its
centerpiece was a new, humanizing Toscanini prop: his five-year-old
granddaughter, Sonia Horowitz. In one of Gehr's photographs, Toscanini
and Sonia tenderly hugged. In others she mimicked his podium gestures.
One full-page photo showed Toscanini, attired in his inevitable bow tie,
striped pants, black vest and jacket, circling a large tree Sonia was using as
a hiding place. The text, barely distinguishable from *Life* commentaries on
the domestic affections of certain carnivores, attested:

While the Maestro romped with Sonia, relaxed and at ease as he never had been in front of a camera, Gehr took these enchanting photographs of him. . . . The Maestro was having a wonderful time chasing Sonia around the lawn, arguing with her about conducting, playing hide-and-seek around a big tree. . . . The apple of Toscanini's eye, she grieved him greatly a few days after these pictures were taken by cutting off her hair. Toscanini phoned his friends, moaned to them about the disaster, gathered up Sonia's shorn curls and tied them up in a towel.

A final photograph, of Toscanini and his wife talking with Chotzinoff, was captioned: "At home, Toscanini likes to have friends around him. . . ."

Other newspaper and magazine articles of the early NBC years likewise limned the "other" Toscanini, evoking an unusually warmhearted version of the self-made American, rejecting the "intellectual" and "genius." The other Toscanini identifies and mingles with Italian peasants. He is himself "affable," "fun-loving," and "gentle." He "detests personal publicity" and "never asks for special privileges of any kind." Privately admired as a virile philanderer, he is at the same time a devoted family man who "never tires of praising" his three grandchildren; Sonia Horowitz, in particular, can regularly be found perched on her grandfather's lap. His early-to-rise, late-to-bed routine is efficient, decisive, unostentatious. "He has no valet and dislikes being pawed by barbers. He shaves himself, and Mrs. Toscanini or one of the daughters cuts his hair." He eats simply. He reads late into the night, and "is in the sometimes disconcerting habit of quoting by the yard from the works of Shakespeare, Keats, Shelley and Swinburne." He is "punctual to a fault," and, like many another husband, "frets while waiting for Mrs. Toscanini and complains that she is never ready on time." For diversion, he likes American movies, "especially Mickey Mouse and other Disney products." An avid radio listener, he takes in the news and appreciates "good jazz." He loves to motor at seventy and eighty miles per hour and hopes to be aboard the first commercial trans-Atlantic flight. Not only does he sometimes insist on conducting without a fee; "his private charities and those of his wife . . . have always been, and are now, considerable. Friends in distress and musicians who have fallen on evil days have been comforted by the generosity of the Maestro and his wife, and each summer hundreds of poor Italian children enjoy vacations at the expense of the Toscaninis." His "rough treatment of other musicians has been much exaggerated" and is forgiven by the men who play under him.[23]

Obviously, the other Toscanini was not altogether new. Even the earliest Toscanini anecdotes in the American press had relished his "man of the people" foibles. And the press was not done relishing smashed batons, shredded music, and quaking musicians. But the mildness of the other Toscanini, the close-up vignettes of his home life, the glossy magazine spreads circulating his name added up to more than a retouching. *Life*'s formulaic introduction, rectifying prior misperceptions, said as much. Here is the formula again, employed by David Ewen in the February 1938 issue of *Holiday*:

> The Toscanini legend, as it is repeated from mouth to mouth, places particular emphasis upon his capricious temperament. . . . Here, I think, legends have far outdistanced the truth, and in some instances do not do justice to the man. . . .
>
> [Toscanini] can be the most sweet tempered and docile of men. He demands, of course, the most exacting discipline from his performers, is importunate in his demand for perfection of performance. But he is far from being unreasonable. . . .
>
> Those who know Toscanini well—particularly the musicians who play under him—realize that his temper, when it strikes, is not the expression of a pampered and spoiled prima donna, but the outburst of a profound artist who seeks always to attain perfection in his performances. . . . When performances do not go well, he explodes because he is actually suffering intense physical pain. . . .
>
> . . . Off the platform, he adopts towards his musicians a touching solicitude of affection; when, several years ago, he made his famous tour of Europe with the New York Philharmonic Symphony Society, he personally looked after the comforts of his hundred men as a father might tend a brood of children. . . .

A writer for the New York *Post* portrayed the other Toscanini as follows on November 7, 1938:

> There [is] a side of Mr. Toscanini that the boys have forgotten to tell you about. For years newspaper and magazine writers (in the last couple of seasons the Maestro has even "made" the Broadway columns!) have doled out anecdotes concerning his terrible temper. . . .
>
> [But] those who know Mr. Toscanini intimately find [him to be] the most modest man who ever lived, a man sincerely at a loss to understand the endless fuss that is made about him.
>
> Time and again he has told his friends that he has no fonder desire than to be able to walk about undisturbed, to saunter along the avenue, look into show-windows, do the thousand-and-one common little things that are permitted other human beings. . . .

This was John Royal's behind-the-scenes reportrayal, "The Private Life of Toscanini," published in the May 21, 1938 New York *World-Telegram:*

> To the concertgoer [Toscanini] is a driving force—an impelling personality striving furiously after perfection. He is that, of course, but in addition there is a boy-like side to his nature, and one must be with him as a guest in his home really to understand. . . .
>
> "When I was a boy," he said to me, "I used to spend all my money on Beethoven music. I only had bread and soup to eat. I got so used to eating bread and soup that now I find I don't have to have anything else to eat. I think I could be happy all my life with just bread and soup." . . .
>
> Toscanini has a great affection for children. A year ago, when he was in Palestine, he was given an orange ranch, and when he went out to look it over there were large numbers of children playing under the trees. He stopped and romped with them for a long time. . . .
>
> His castle on San Giovanni Island in Maggiore is one of the most beautiful homes that I ever have seen. . . . Many times while we were there he would go over to the pescatori to ask the men about their day's catch. . . .

Howard Taubman, contributing to the June 1940 *Reader's Digest,* made these distinctions:

> It is the musical autocrat around whom the legends cluster: the conductor who, when he does not get what he wants, throws his baton at his players, smashes his watch, tears up scores, stamps and storms and swears. There is a basis for these tales. Toscanini himself says he is two men, one of whom the other cannot control.
>
> The other Toscanini, the man his friends know, is anything but forbidding. He loves a gay party or an evening of quiet conversation. He does not carry on about music like the highbrows. Indeed, he is fond of a spot of swing. He was surprised one day in his studio, playing "Heigh-ho, heigh-ho, it's off to work we go" on the piano while his five-year-old granddaughter wielded a baton. "Her beat was correct," grandpa boasted.
>
> There is the legend of Toscanini's aloofness. But actually he is gregarious. The National Broadcasting Company provided for him a lavish suite carefully secluded from the turmoil of Radio City. But Toscanini won't use it, except to change clothes. Instead, he wanders around the building, visits other offices, talks with everyone. The more telephone calls, visitors and general bedlam, the better.

Toscanini's love for the pulse of life has much to feed on at home. In his Riverdale house overlooking the Hudson River, vitality spills over. Friends, relatives, even hangers-on, surround him. . . .

Taubman amplified his characterization in a book, *Music on My Beat* (1943), whose chapter "The Glamour Boys at Home" centers on the other Toscanini "letting his hair down" to "have fun with music," devouring practical jokes, excitedly describing kissing Eleanor Powell in Hollywood, and deserting a Radio City "party of bigwigs" to comfort a troubled elevator boy who was "one of his pals."

Toscanini's new American residence lent plausibility to the new, Americanized image. Celebrating his 1939 move from the Hotel Astor to the Villa Pauline, his rented home in Riverdale, NBC's publicists announced: "The Maestro has become an American country squire at last." Some years later, having occupied a second Riverdale residence, Wave Hill, the Toscaninis purchased the Villa Pauline.

Summarizing changes in America's "general attitude toward music" between the end of World War I and the end of World War II, George Marek wrote in 1949:

I have observed it, as everybody else interested in music has observed it. A generation ago an interest in music was in a layman and good citizen almost a suspect quality. It was almost incompatible with "the American way of life." It was certainly not an interest which was thought contributory to success. Music, since it was unable to push you up the ladder toward the goal . . . as previously expressed in the fiction of Horatio Alger, then summarized in the philosophy of "success," . . . was not a useful interest. You may remember with what a belittling smile the "self-made" man of the time would speak of such equivocal pursuits of culture. "Longhair" was the popular term. . . . Music was considered a luxury. The popular attitude, the broad middle-class precept as it was given by parents to their children, was that music did not play an important role in one's normal life. A father speaking to his son would counsel him that an understanding of music could contribute less to his happiness than the ability to drive an automobile well or to play a decent game of golf. . . .

Then, Marek continued, a "new audience" had materialized in the 1930s, after which:

. . . The popularity of music kept increasing. As more homes were equipped with radios, more people listened to symphonic broadcasts. As more people listened, more orchestras took to the air. Attendance at concerts leaped to a new spectacular high during the war, when people had money to spend and needed and wanted entertainment. . . .

The interest in music will grow. For music has turned out to be a useful thing. . . . It has helped "to refresh the mind of man after his studies of his usual pain," as Shakespeare said. . . . To thousands it has proved itself to be entertainment at its most entertaining.[24]

Theodor Adorno and Sinclair Lewis portrayed music's "new audience" in terms of "regressive hearing" and opportunistic self-advancement. Olin Downes perceived "a body of genuinely democratic opinion" destined to create "a new and a better epoch in the life of the world." ("The failure of art overseas" to effect comparable millennial change, Downes explained, "lay primarily in the fact that there was no really democratic diffusion of its essence.")[25] In fact, the new audience did not embody a "scourge of materialism," as Charles Edward Russell, echoing Downes's residual Progressivism, had hoped. Nor did it merely embody recycled materialism as personified by the craven consumers and narcotized puppets of Capital Lewis and Adorno had described. Some new audience members, a minority, purposely used music appreciation to enhance their self-esteem and social rank. Others, also a minority, moved from music appreciation to understanding, fortified by "active listening" and praxis. Suffusing the majority was the excitement of newfound experience, of an unsuspected passion whose rituals included record collecting, radio listening, and starting or supporting a first-class symphony orchestra. To the outside analyst, then as now, this sudden ardor was often naive. In the context of new prosperity, new technology, and upward mobility, of Depression-era fervor, ferment, and idealism, its innocence was at the same time warming, its Progressive faith in "democratic culture" genuine and generous.

But to consider music appreciation's impact on the new audience is not to consider its impact on music. The long view back to the Gilded Age dramatizes the failure to transcend "entertainment at its most entertaining." The ballyhoo tradition's rites of promotion and adulation, the Germanic tradition's "sermons in tones"—these facets of American concert life held on. The New World penchant for virtuosos, noted by Robert Schumann, remained intact. So did the "demand for a brilliant technique" and "method of turning people into celebrities" noted by Ferruccio Busoni. So did the taste for accredited Europeans with an appreciable aura of celebrity. Theodore Thomas's utilitarian arguments for concert attendance (to secure "healthful and elevating recreation") and orchestral proliferation (to "show the culture of a community") echoed and re-echoed. If one blatant difference from pre–World War I conditions was sheer audience size, sheer audience size was judged difference enough.

A singular confirmation of stunted progress was stunted programming. From the time Wagner, Strauss, Dvořák, Debussy, and Sibelius were encompassed by the orchestras of Boston, Chicago, and New York before World War I, the core symphonic repertoire froze for decades. To be sure, Koussevitzky and Stokowski regularly explored nonmainstream fare. But the music appreciation canon—by which Toscanini's repertoire was fortuitously circumscribed—advanced only to the *Parsifal* Prelude, *Ein Heldenleben*, *La Mer*, the Sibelius Second. In effect, the nineteenth-century warhorses were recycled to amass a primer for radio-era listeners. Even if modernism had not been hard to sell, marketing acumen, as practiced by concert managers, radio networks, and phonograph companies, dictated compact, homogenized repertoire bulk. At Community Concerts, the "organized audiences" division of the Columbia management, artists were told what they could and could not play.* The audience increased; the music stayed the same.

If the effects of music's new audience on its own membership were suggested by reverent paeans, by symphonic growth and soaring record sales, the new audience's effects on music were suggested by the experiences of musicians. Artur Schnabel, touring America for the first time in the early 1920s, encountered raw listeners, cordially informal hosts, inadequate instruments, and sketchy arrangements variously attesting to his "longhair luxury" status. Touring ten years later, he found American listeners well behaved and appreciative, the top American orchestras "better" than Europe's, and America itself a complex, invigorating place. But Schnabel's New World success declined as swiftly as it had begun. A radio interview plus soap commercial left him reflecting: "It is depressing to see how these splendid American people are maltreated and exploited, and how they are deliberately isolated from many of the noble things of which they are capable." As the war dragged on, Schnabel came to feel "marooned" in the United States; abandoning professional management and national tours, he turned increasingly to teaching and composing. The fickleness of Schnabel's American following reflected broad but shallow cultivation. Music appreciation was precisely adept at training his listeners to recognize the "Appassionata" Sonata, to respect the solemnity of his recitals, and to

---

*Community Concerts head Ward French at one point forbade recital works longer than seventeen minutes.

honor Schnabel himself as a war refugee and acknowledged "great pianist." But the vast majority remained unattuned to his Schubert sonata and Mozart piano concerto explorations, to his Lieder and chamber music loyalties, and to his own atonal compositions—any of which would have helped foster a more lasting composite imprint.[26]

Schnabel's frustration was redoubled within America's cosmopolitan composers' community, with native-born members excelling native-born conductors and instrumentalists. For the League of Composers, no less than for music's new audience, the twenties and thirties were a period of thrilling symphonic accomplishment—yet American orchestral works barely penetrated the mainstream repertoire.* To Charles Edward Russell in 1927, the symphony orchestra was America's "foremost cultural asset," its "sign of honor among the nations," its one "division of representative art" in which "achievement has gone beyond debate." The cruelty of such claims, extolling re-creators of European art, was not lost on American creative artists. They could not stomach the confused chauvinism of the music appreciators and Toscanini disciples. Olin Downes, in likening post-*Sacre* Stravinsky to "dead or dying European musical pottage," and Mahler and the Second

---

*In *The American Symphony Orchestra—A Social History of Musical Taste* (1951), John H. Mueller found no "established, standard, American repertoire." Surveying his own statistical analyses, Mueller wrote:

> Since 1900, external circumstance and the growing maturity of our own musical resources have contrived to favor a general expansion of American participation in the repertoire. However, when viewed in relation to the total repertoire, the American contribution may still seem somewhat less than impressive. After two world wars, with the attendant inflation of national enthusiasm, the proportion of American music in the symphonic repertoire of all orchestras has attained in 1950 less than seven per cent. In the case of other nationalities, even such a percentage would allow several composers to show a significant position on the popularity pyramid, but American patronage is so diffused among innumerable composers that almost no one achieves a discernible fraction of the repertoire.
>
> In the twenty-five-year period 1925–50 the names of 280 American composers appeared on the regular subscription programs of the ten oldest major symphony orchestras. Of these, 136, or fifty per cent, have been played by only one orchestra each, while only eighteen composers, or six per cent, have been heard in nine or ten orchestras. It is therefore apparent that most of the quota of American composers is consumed in purely token performances of local and regional interest. . . .[27]

Mueller's figures would have been even lower had he not included, as "Americans," European-born composers migrating to the United States at "an early age"—a group including Ernest Bloch. His research is updated and expanded in Kate Hevner Mueller's *Twenty-seven Major American Symphony Orchestras: A History and Analysis of Their Repertoires, Seasons 1842–43 Through 1969–70* (1973).

Viennese School to "elaborate and decaying" Old World culture, took aim
at the colleagues and heroes of come-of-age Americans. Mark Twain had
called the Cathedral of St. Mark "worn out" yet esteemed the Milan Cathedral as a "miracle." Downes, seventy-five years later, eyed his cultural
forebears with incurable ambivalence; enamored of Beethoven, Brahms,
and Wagner, he unexpectedly succumbed to Mahler's *Das Lied von der
Erde,* to Stravinsky's Concerto for Piano and Winds, to *Pierrot lunaire* as
conducted by the composer. Had his aversion to "worn out" music signaled
a sure, timely vision of American maturity, he might have found New
World composers to champion. Though he had kind words for many, he
remained attuned to Old World traditions he cherished and despised. Like
Walter Damrosch and Lawrence Gilman, he chose to champion Sibelius,
whose earnestness reminded him of Beethoven, and whose optimism reminded him of America.[28]

By the forties, the League of Composers' giddy "aesthetes proms" had
paled. Claire Reis, the executive director, later wrote: "In the twenties there
was an atmosphere of adventure in the reception of [new] music; somehow
in 1949 the mood could not be recaptured." Copland, writing in 1941,
celebrated "the increasing sense we [composers] all have that something
vital and important is happening right here in our midst," but added:

> Very often I get the impression that audiences seem to think that the
> endless repetition of a small body of entrenched masterworks is all that
> is required for a ripe musical culture. . . . Needless to say, I have no
> quarrel with masterpieces. I think I revere and enjoy them as well as the
> next fellow. But when they are used, unwittingly perhaps, to stifle
> contemporary effort in our own country, then I am almost tempted to
> take the most extreme view and say that we should be better off without
> them!

The British conductor Eugene Goossens, prominent in America since 1923,
hailed "rapid and significant growth" in the composition and performance
of American music, yet questioned whether American audiences displayed
"a proportionately greater enthusiasm and capacity for intellectual aspiration" as of 1942:

> During the past nineteen years I have guest-conducted every [major]
> orchestra—save one—in the [United States]; not once, but many times.
> On these occasions I have observed audience-reaction very closely, par-
> ticularly at certain times when the resident conductor happened to be
> in charge. I have—regrettably be it noted—watched the vague atmo-
> sphere of suspicion and mistrust creep over sections of the audience

when the performance of an unknown piece of contemporary music has started. . . . In the past 10 years I have watched an audience at Carnegie Hall superciliously condescending to sit through a good American piece whilst deliberately refusing to be carried away by its virtues, and completely intolerant of its intricacies. Equally, I have watched morose audiences in certain other centers of reputedly high culture confronted by the magnificently prepared performance of a work which, while it presented certain problems to the listener, ought, because of the repute of its composer and the high integrity of its interpreter, to have merited at least a sympathetic hearing and an un-biased reception. In all these cases a weak splutter of applause was the reward to the composer for months of labor, and to the conductor and orchestra for long hours of preparation.

. . . There is far too much of the "I-know-what-I-like, and I-like-what-I-know" attitude among our audiences today. It displays itself in a thinly veiled indifference to everything new and unfamiliar—especially American. . . .[29]

The disappointed composers blamed the critics. Copland wrote: "We badly need critical works on the failures and achievements of recent composers, based on intimate knowledge of the composers' works. This kind of knowledge few of our critics possess." He cited, as a lone exception, *An Hour with American Music* (1929) by Paul Rosenfeld, a frequent *Modern Music* contributor of whom Huneker once exclaimed: "You are starting where I left off!" (Copland's own *Our New Music* [1941] was a second such study; Virgil Thomson's *Herald Tribune* writings eventually amassed a third.) Some of Copland's colleagues found his laments a waste of time. Others joined in, lambasting conductors, appreciators, and the Sibelius symphonies. Copland's most trenchant perception, transcending whipping-boy therapeutics, was of the new audience. "The radio and phonograph have given us listeners whose sheer numbers in themselves create a special problem," he wrote in the January–February 1943 *Modern Music*. Somewhat in the spirit of Weill's politicized musical theater, or Hindemith's *Gebrauchsmusik*, or Shostakovich's symphonies, he resolved that "the job of the forties" was to "find a musical style which satisfies both us and them." In *Our New Music,* he similarly argued:

. . . I see no reason why composers any longer should write their music solely with the concert audience in mind. New listeners such as the radio provides may not be cultivated listeners, but at least they have few of the prejudices of the typical concert-goer. Fortunately for us they do not yet know too well what they like. This situation is changing rapidly, of course. The typical radio commentator is doing a pretty thorough job of standardizing and conventionalizing musical taste wherever possible. Nevertheless . . . it is in such unprejudiced hearing of music that our musical salvation lies.

Addressing the networks, Copland recommended the employment of "regular staff composers, very much in the way that Count Esterházy employed Haydn." Addressing his fellow composers, he wrote that the new audience presented "the most exciting challenge of our day":

> The question is: can we composers write a music that will be of interest to these hitherto untouched millions of listeners, and if so, what manner of music shall it be?
> . . . One thing is certain: the new musical audiences will have to have music that they can comprehend. That is axiomatic. It must therefore be simple and direct. But there is no reason why it should not be a music that exploits all those new devices discovered during the first years of the twentieth century. Above all, it must be fresh in feeling. In no sense must it be capable of being interpreted as a writing down to the level of the public. . . . To write a music that is both simple and direct and is at the same time great music is a goal worthy of the efforts of the best minds in music.[30]

Copland's own efforts to be "simple and direct," "fresh in feeling," and consciously "American" included his Music for the Theater (1925) and Piano Concerto (1926)—enthusiastic appropriations of American jazz paralleling Milhaud's *Création du monde* (1923), Gershwin's *Rhapsody in Blue* (1924), Krenek's *Jonny spielt auf* (1927), Weill's *Die Dreigroschenoper* (1928), and the founding of Duke Ellington's "big band" (1923). Later, apparently inspired by the *Lehrstücke* ("teaching plays") Brecht was fashioning abroad in collaboration with Eisler, Hindemith, and Weill, he wrote a young people's opera, *The Second Hurricane* (1937), espousing social responsibility. Around the same time, building on his boyhood fascination with cowboys and Indians (his mother grew up in Texas and the Midwest), he used Mexican and cowboy tunes in the populist *El Salón México* (1933–36), *Billy the Kid* (1938), and *Rodeo* (1942), and wrote for the movies. His Third Symphony (1944–46) was in part a grand patriotic gesture in the Shostakovich mold. And Copland was not alone, among America's leading composers, in aligning himself with the earthiness of the jazz age, with the socially committed art of the Depression, with the patriotism of wartime. Yet all these proved holding actions.

In retrospect, the possibility glimpsed, then lost amid the cultural bustle of what Harold Clurman called the "fervent years" was of a confluence of popularizers and high-culture populists. This opportunity to integrate the spectrum of new American music into the American symphonic curriculum would never recur. Ultimately repulsed by music appreciation's new audience, and influenced by transplanted Europeans uninterested in helping to cultivate the nascent American school, future American composers would increasingly follow Schoenberg's dictum that "all I know is that [the listener] exists, and insofar as he isn't indispensable for acoustic reasons (since music doesn't sound well in an empty hall), he's only a nuisance." Even Copland was using twelve-tone techniques by 1950.*[31]

In England, Handel, Haydn, and Mendelssohn had been honored above all other musicians. Brahms and Bruckner had dominated musical Vienna. Wagner had seemed the most famous musician of his time. Paganini and Liszt, Jenny Lind and Caruso had won fanatic followings. After World

---

*Copland was the most respectable, most influential *Modern Music* contributor to proclaim a new audience whose presence dictated a less elitist compositional posture. Of the more ideological composers to his left, Marc Blitzstein, Hanns Eisler, and Charles Seeger made notable contributions to *Modern Music*. All three belonged to New York's Composers Collective, whose members composed songs for the labor movement. The Collective operated under the auspices of the Pierre Degeyter Club, a branch of the Workers Music League, controlled in turn by the Communist-backed International Music Bureau. Blitzstein, Eisler, and Seeger addressed a new audience weighted more toward the proletariat than Copland's new audience, less toward new bourgeois elements; their music was more overtly political than his. Writing in the March–April 1934 *Modern Music,* Seeger declared that "the proletariat has every reason to look with suspicion upon much bourgeois music, not only of today but yesterday." Beethoven's Third, Fifth, and Seventh symphonies, and the first two movements of his Ninth, stood "as a convenient definition of what is meant by revolutionary content," according to Seeger. "But much of Schumann and Chopin, saving some of the fine tumultuous pieces, should be laid aside for a while. Of Wagner, too, there is much question. Indeed, the morbidity, the servile melancholy, the frenetic sexuality, the day-dreaming flight from reality that permeates much of the music of the nineteenth century cannot be regarded as fit for a class with a revolutionary task before it." As for "recent bourgeois music," it had "ceased to have social value," in Seeger's view; the isolated "liberal" composer necessarily supported the social system "that gives him a tower and allows him to sit in it." In a second *Modern Music* essay, in the May–June 1935 issue, Seeger, a seminal ethnomusicologist, called on America's composers to examine American "grassroots"—songs, hymns, dances—stigmatized by Lowell Mason and other sanctifiers of the Germanic canon. Copland, while not a member of the Composers Collective, contributed to its "workers song books." When he performed his Piano Variations and Piano Concerto (in a two-piano arrangement) at a Degeyter Club meeting on March 16, 1934, Seeger commented that Copland had progressed "from ivory tower to within hailing distance of the proletariat."[32]

War I, however, the most revered, most glamorous of musicians were no longer composers, instrumentalists, or singers. As a writer in the *Atlantic Monthly* commented in March 1938:

> Whether we like it or not, it is the orchestral conductor who has become the important central figure of any musical community. In Europe today the conductor is clearly of greater stature than either composer or impresario. In Germany, for example, Furtwängler has more power than Hindemith; and if Richard Strauss is still a towering figure it is not only owing to his compositions, but also, in some degree, to his extensive career as a conductor. In England a realist would say that Sir Thomas Beecham was more influential than Vaughan Williams, the distinguished composer laureate. In America we bow even more completely to the conductor. . . .
>
> . . . Of all practitioners in this field, none has ever held so unusual a position as Arturo Toscanini. This is the first time that a conductor— and not one who is equally distinguished as a composer—has won the prestige of being the world's most famous musician.[33]

How did the conductor become "the important central figure of any musical community"? Some writers have used political analogies to suggest that in a wartime "age of dictators" Toscanini was music's Roosevelt or Churchill. Adorno's understanding of the celebrity conductor as a twentieth-century musical fetish, functionally comparable to the monopoly lord or authoritarian dictator, is one version of this viewpoint. On a more prosaic level, music itself elevated the conductor's role. Both Wagner's enlarged orchestra and his Romantic ideal of the conductor-interpreter as orchestral nerve and brain center demanded more authoritative, authoritarian leadership. After Wagner, scores written to order for further enlarged concert forces, of which Schoenberg's *Gurre-Lieder* and Mahler's Eighth Symphony furnish extreme examples, spotlit the podium all the more. Concomitant with swelling symphonic scale were tendencies toward larger halls and larger audiences, toward secular religious rites celebrating dead masters and their prophets, toward massification and popularization.

It is here, in the realm of mass spectacle and communication, that the ripest explanatory framework lies, subsuming the "age of dictators" and post-Romantic gigantism. We have seen how music appreciation craved a heroic practitioner to symbolize great music as other personalities had "humanized" great books, and how Toscanini was the obvious choice. Even if Toscanini had not been available—if music appreciation had had to settle for a glossier, more suspect personality, such as Stokowski, or a dimmer, more localized one, such as Koussevitzky—only a conductor could have served. More than charismatic, a proper symbol for "music" had to be broad-based. A celebrity singer or pianist, even a latter-day Caruso or Paderewski, would have seemed parochial, and composers were abandoning Copland's call to reach out to "hitherto untouched millions of listeners." Especially in the United States, where the "symphony orchestra" held sway and opera mattered less, only a conductor could connote the necessary diversity and scale of musical experience, the all-encompassing ritualistic authority.

The first conductor to become the world's most famous musician, Toscanini was more than lionized; he was popularized. During the New York Philharmonic's Toscanini era, Lawrence Gilman, among others, had imagined him a "prophet," a "priest," a "vehicle of revelation" leading New World masses to promised great music. But Moses, who struck the rock and smashed the tablets, proved too aloof and intemperate an image, too close to the arrogant intellectual or imprudent genius. The "other Toscanini" was fashioned to mediate between the people and unadulterated art. Fulfilling a destiny he could neither foresee nor control, Toscanini was made music's golden calf.

The NBC Symphony, 1945–54

By the war's end in 1945 the New World celebrity of Toscanini might have reached its fabulous apogee but for two technological miracles. Like the lightning evolution of radio in the 1920s, and the creation of the NBC Symphony in 1937, these fashioned dramatically new Toscanini showcases. First television and then the long-playing record freshened the aging novelty of regular broadcast concerts by the world's First Musician.

Even more than radio's beginnings, the beginnings of television bore the imprint of David Sarnoff. As early as 1923—only eight years after his "radio music box" prophecy—Sarnoff prophesized that "television, which is the technical name for seeing instead of hearing by radio, will come to pass," that "we will be able actually to see as well as read in New York, within an hour or so, the event taking place in London, Buenos Aires or Tokyo." In 1927, addressing the Chicago Association of Commerce on "Television's Future," he proclaimed "the possibilities of the new art" to be "as boundless as the imagination." Three years later, writing in the New York *Times,* he foresaw "a separate theater for every home," inaugurating "a new era of entertainment and educational services that will far eclipse the achievements of today. . . . There is little in the field of cultural education that cannot be envisaged for the home through the new facilities of electrical communications." One catalyst for Sarnoff's television dream was an iconoscope—an "electric eye" for scanning pictures—exhibited by the inventor Vladimir Zworykin in 1929. Sarnoff seized on the instrument's future and made it his own. To the consternation of both rivals and associates, to whom television signified huge outlays, meager initial returns, and the eventual decline of radio, he poured millions of dollars into his idée fixe, promising television's commercial debut at the 1939 New York World's Fair. As *Fortune* later remarked, television was Sarnoff's "personal mission"; he "bullwhipped his RCA organization into making good on it." Though Sarnoff met his deadline—RCA began telecasting on a limited basis in 1939—it was not until 1945 that peacetime and new FCC rulings set the stage for a television explosion. In 1946, RCA produced five thousand TV sets; in 1950, it produced seven million.[1]

A proud father, Sarnoff oversaw a series of programming landmarks, beginning with the first televised Presidential address: FDR's, at the 1939 fair. Televised sports, a televised national political convention, and a televised Congressional opening followed. Leading radio shows, ranging from "Amos 'n Andy" to "Information, Please," were moved into television berths. The television debut of NBC's most prestigious radio offering was initially delayed by the American Federation of Musicians, which had issued a ban on most "live" TV music. Then, on March 18, 1948, the ban was lifted. Two days later, at 6:30 p.m. Eastern Standard Time, Sarnoff appeared on camera from Studio 8H to introduce "a great day for radio, for television, for music, and for the public."[2]

> Tonight, for the first time in the history of this great science and art of radio, we are televising the great music of Wagner, the great interpretive genius of Toscanini, and the playing of his gifted artists in his orchestra. Never before in the history of the world was this possible. This represents the realization of a dream—a dream we have dreamed for 25 years or more. . . . I wish it were possible for the people in Italy also tonight, particularly during this critical period in the destiny of their nation, to share with us the great privilege and the great joy of seeing and listening to their loyal native son—our own dear Maestro Toscanini.

Ben Grauer now appeared to say "Thank you, General Sarnoff! . . . Our studio has fallen into a hush as we are expecting momentarily the appearance here on our podium of the world-famed Arturo Toscanini." Suddenly, Toscanini was on screen, impatiently threading his way through the first violins, barely nodding to the audience with lowered, inscrutable eyes.* Raising his voice to be heard, Grauer continued: "There is the quickening sound of applause which, as a veteran of many of these broadcasts, I can assure you is even more vigorous and heartfelt [than usual] as the distinguished figure appears. Maestro Toscanini in just a moment will begin our all-Wagner program with the Prelude to Act III of *Lohengrin*." Now the screen erupted with sound and physical energy. A camera (one of two

---

*Upon seeing Toscanini conduct for the first time, Ernest Bloch commented: "I was astonished when I saw this little, sad-looking man come forward; he seemed ill-at-ease before the crowd and had none of that repugnant obsequiousness of virtuosi who seek to flatter the public. . . . I liked that attitude immediately. It revealed a whole side of Toscanini's character which I later found again in his conducting."[3]

stationed in the balcony) panning the NBC strings—first violins, cellos, violas, second violins—showed dozens of men, front desks to rear, straining forward in their chairs, bowing furiously with broad, racing strokes. A third camera showed Toscanini swinging his right arm in arcs of varied force and shape while his left hand gripped his left lapel.

For sixty minutes, the two balcony cameras followed Toscanini from the rear, a compact body with mobile arms and immobile feet, while the third fixed on his hands and face, made visible to millions as only musicians had seen them before. In profile, Toscanini's features were a study in chiseled, aristocratic beauty, his mouth pursed or severely shut, his deep-set eyes lost in shadow. From the front, these same eyes were ceaselessly, hypnotically perturbed. As they passed left and right under Toscanini's flaring brow, no glint of pleasure broke their worried spell. Serving Wagner, they said, was precarious work; at any moment, something might go wrong. During episodes of high excitement, Toscanini's churning right arm whipped his baton in strenuous half-circles, raising it higher and higher on the rebound until it surmounted his left shoulder with each upward thrust. His left hand vibrated convulsively from the wrist, fingers spread. His eyes and mouth strained ajar. The total impression—of the hypnotic, unhappy face, the strong, graceful hands, the relentlessly churning arm—was of insatiable feeling, traumatic intensity, obsessive power.

Sarnoff and Grauer had carefully worded NBC's claims to the March 20 telecast's "historic" precedence. It was, as stated, the first time Wagner, Toscanini, and the NBC Symphony had appeared on television. But it was not America's first televised concert: responding even faster to the lifting of the union ban, William Paley's Columbia Broadcasting System had bested NBC by ninety minutes, presenting Eugene Ormandy and the Philadelphia Orchestra at 5 p.m. Eastern Standard Time the same day. This was the gleeful gist of *Life*'s account of television's first two symphony concerts—that "CBS had beaten NBC to the punch." Culling a second extramusical perspective, *Life*'s article headlined a set of four photographs: "Rival CBS Program FEATURED A MAESTRO WHO ATE COUGH DROPS!" According to the article's text:

> Midway through Rachmaninoff's First Symphony, conductor Eugene Ormandy was seen to make a surreptitious gesture towards his mouth with his left hand. Then, grinning to himself, he began working his jaws furiously. One television fan was heard muttering, "Whatsa matter? His teeth come loose?" . . .
>
> Similar queries poured in, by telephone and by mail, to television stations and to the maestro. . . . The whole matter was set right a few days later by Harl McDonald, the orchestra's manager. "It was," he

grimly announced, "a cough drop. Luden's!" . . . Ormandy had a final word, "I will never, never do it again."*

When NBC next televised Toscanini, on April 3, 1948—a performance of Beethoven's Ninth—the network's research division estimated that 34 percent of all New York City's privately owned television sets were tuned in. Estimates for eight subsequent telecasts, beginning November 13, 1948, and ending March 22, 1952, placed Toscanini's television audience as high as 10 million. For the final telecast, NBC dressed Toscanini in a black, high-collared rehearsal tunic, so that his face and hands emerged from a void à la Rembrandt. Kirk Browning, who directed the concert for television, told the *Christian Science Monitor:*

We try to treat these telecasts primarily from the point of view of the Maestro's conducting. We eliminate a good many of the usual detail shots of the brasses, strings, woodwinds, and so forth. . . . We want the person at the television set to see the whole thing through the Maestro. We are concentrating on his face and hands, eliminating as much as possible all extraneous or distracting elements.[4]

No sooner had CBS beaten NBC's Symphony to the home screen than it beat NBC in a bitter twenty-month rivalry for better-sounding "Micro-groove" phonograph records. In June 1948, CBS's Columbia Records unveiled new, unbreakable "long playing" discs which, with a turntable speed of 33⅓ revolutions per minute, played twenty-three minutes on a side; symphonies that had sold for $7.25 on five 78s could now be had at $4.85

---

*If Ormandy, according to *Life,* mixed cough drops with Rachmaninoff, *Life* itself was a redoubtable potpourri: preceding the "Maestro Who Ate Cough Drops" was "Mary Margaret McBride Zips to New High with Listeners," about a formidable radio personality ("height 5'4", estimated weight 180 lbs.") trapped in her corset ("We had to have a doctor to get it off"). Other articles in the April 5, 1948 issue examined Douglas MacArthur's Presidential possibilities, paraplegic students at UCLA, a seven-month-old baby who could swim ("a sure bet for the 1964 Olympics"), a "church of bones" decorated with skulls, and America's China policy. Considering "homogenized culture" in "Masscult and Midcult" (1960), Dwight Macdonald commented: "*Life* is a typical homogenized magazine, appearing on the mahogany library tables of the rich, the glass cocktail tables of the middle class, and the oilcloth kitchen tables of the poor. Its contents are as thoroughly homogenized as its circulation. . . . Somehow these scramblings together seem to work all one way, degrading the serious rather than elevating the frivolous." For that matter, Toscanini's first NBC telecast directly followed "Howdy Doody."

for a single, twelve-inch LP. NBC's RCA Victor countered with nonbreak-
able, seven-inch 45-rpm records with the same playing time as its standard
twelve-inch 78s. Not until January 1950 did Victor capitulate to the superior
Columbia product and, amid wholesale staff dismissals, begin producing
LPs of its own (a $5 million advertising campaign helped RCA salvage the
45 for the popular market). This implausible "battle of the speeds" was the
capstone to a larger postwar recordings boom. Rebounding from a cessa-
tion of American recording due to wartime restrictions on shellac use, and
to the A.F. of M. recordings ban of 1942–44, RCA and Columbia had
discovered a phenomenal new demand for serious music. An RCA recording of a popular piano concerto that had sold 102 copies in 1929 sold 62,756
in 1946. Even Bach's "Goldberg" Variations, as performed by Wanda
Landowska, sold 30,000 sets within three months of its January 1946 release
date. Record sales for 1947 totaled 275 million discs—more than double the
prewar high. Record sales for 1948 totaled 400 million discs. Stirred by
annual "audio fairs" pitching recordings of thunderstorms and railroad
trains in conjunction with scads of accessories, "high fidelity" enthusiasts
competed for the best amplifiers, turntables, pickups, and speakers. By 1949
American record studios had begun implementing a genuine high fidelity
breakthrough—magnetic tape, guaranteeing longer takes, easier editing,
reduced background noise, and enhanced frequency response. Then came
the proliferating LP. Between August 1949 and August 1954 the number of
American record companies increased from eleven to almost two hundred.
Between 1934 and 1954 American record sales increased from $750,000 to $70
million.[5]

All of this held remarkable implications for Toscanini and RCA, and not
merely owing to the size and speed of the phonographic bandwagon.
Toscanini had always loathed making records. His first experience, in
Camden in 1920, was to see his touring Scala orchestra pared down and
shoe-horned into a cramped wooden studio by the Victor Talking Machine
Company. Notwithstanding numerous retakes, Toscanini found the
finished discs "a pile of rubbish" and swore not to record again. His first
electrical recordings, with the New York Philharmonic, were for Bruns-
wick and RCA Victor in 1926 and 1929; the start-and-stop mechanics of the
four-minute sides again provoked oaths of "never again." In 1931, Victor
used two recording machines to take down a nonstop Toscanini performance of Beethoven's Fifth; Toscanini listened to the masters and rejected
them. RCA's Charles O'Connell considered Toscanini's final New York
Philharmonic recordings, in 1936, "successful" and "pleasant." In 1937, 1938,
and 1939 Toscanini recorded for EMI with the BBC Symphony—and these
sessions, too, proved productive. His relations with RCA, however, deteriorated. O'Connell wanted to record the NBC Symphony in Carnegie Hall;

Sarnoff insisted on using Studio 8H. O'Connell wanted repertoire "in especial need of recording"; Toscanini, in O'Connell's view, insisted on music already in RCA's catalogue or "of secondary importance." Reviewing test pressings for the 1939 NBC Symphony *Eroica*, Toscanini complained that a single oboe note was inaudible. According to O'Connell, the correction of this defect caused Toscanini to insist on numerous corrections ever after, many of them "utterly impossible" to make. Two subsequent projects finalized O'Connell's rift with Toscanini: a 1941 recording of the *Götterdämmerung* Immolation Scene with the NBC Symphony and Helen Traubel, and a series of 1941–42 recordings with Toscanini leading the Philadelphia Orchestra. In the former case, Toscanini withheld approval partly because a rival version with Kirsten Flagstad occupied fewer sides and therefore seemed likely to sell better, partly because certain brass passages seemed obscured. In the latter case, the vagaries of wartime processing resulted in pitted, dim-sounding discs. Aware of O'Connell's high regard for Leopold Stokowski, Toscanini suspected sabotage. The Toscanini family appealed to David Sarnoff, who, at a meeting swiftly convened and concluded, commanded that all unissued Toscanini recordings be placed on the market within three months. Toscanini afterward ceased speaking to O'Connell, who left Victor in 1944.[6]

It was at this juncture that the recordings bandwagon began gathering speed, propelled by the end of the union ban, the high-fidelity craze, magnetic tape, and the LP. For recording Toscanini, tape meant longer takes and easier, more plentiful "corrections." Toscanini's slender RCA catalogue suddenly swelled to accommodate a complete set of Beethoven symphonies, including first Toscanini recordings of the Second and Ninth (1949–52); the complete Brahms symphonies, including first Toscanini recordings of the Second, Third, and Fourth (1951–52); major works by Berlioz, Debussy, Dvořák, Elgar, Gluck, Haydn, Mendelssohn, Mozart, Schubert, Saint-Saëns, Richard Strauss, Tchaikovsky, Wagner; and seven complete operas: *Fidelio* (1944), *La Bohème* (1946), *La traviata* (1946), *Otello* (1947), *Aida* (1949), *Falstaff* (1950), and *Un ballo in maschera* (1954). The promotion of these releases was the most single-minded in Victor's history. In earlier years, the company had democratically bestowed its loyalties on Koussevitzky and Stokowski (both of whose Victor catalogues exceeded Toscanini's), Ormandy and Monteux. With NBC calling the shots following the departure of O'Connell (who had always considered Victor's appropriation by the radio giant a shotgun wedding), Toscanini's recordings came first. Only Toscanini, among Victor's conductors, was called "the Maestro" in advertisements and album notes, or regularly introduced, à la "Heifetz" and "Horowitz," with no first name. The promotional language was that of music appreciation, a longtime Victor specialty, mated, as in

Lawrence Gilman's *Toscanini and Great Music,* with both Toscanini worship and the canon of acknowledged masterpieces. Gilman's metaphors, in
fact, were a frequent motif, as in this 1947 ad for the Toscanini/NBC
Symphony "Jupiter" Symphony:

> Perhaps the most astute observation of the essence of Toscanini was
> made by the late Lawrence Gilman, when he referred to him as "the
> priest of music." Since the historic Rio performance of *Aida* nearly 50
> [sic] years ago, when he hurriedly stepped into the capacity of conductor
> for the first time, Toscanini has been no more than a medium through
> which the great masterworks of music are revealed to the world. . . .
>
> To those who have had the sublime privilege of watching this ener-
> getic person, now in his eightieth year, there comes the revelation that
> this is true greatness—a living example of the fruit of years combined
> with the open naiveté and the freshness of a completely youthful spirit.
>
> It is this fresh quality that dominates his recreation of the aristocratic,
> Rococo lines of Mozart's music. In the "Jupiter" Symphony, the last, and
> to many the greatest of the Mozart symphonies, Toscanini's touch re-
> veals with eager fluency all the dignified charm and grace inherent in
> these magic pages. He takes us through the glowing optimism of the first
> movement and through the haunting dialogue of the Andante cantabile,
> its muted strings singing eloquently—through the poised graciousness
> of the Menuetto and the sparkling virility of the finale. It is the pure voice
> of Mozart that speaks. . . .

Like his rehearsal tantrums, Toscanini's record-making whims were turned
to his advantage, so that each "approved" release documented Victor's
tenacity and acumen:

> Among other good things in the record line, this New Year brings with
> it two beautiful Toscanini recordings, one of which constitutes an event
> of particular importance to music lovers. At long last and after much ado
> the Toscanini version of the great C major Symphony of Franz Schubert
> is available on records.
>
> The magic evoked by the combination of [Toscanini and Schubert]
> has been realized whenever the Maestro has conducted Schubert's music,
> particularly his last symphony. Pleas for recordings of these historic
> occasions have mounted into insistent demands—and we are happy to
> announce that the long-awaited recording is here at last. . . .

Even Toscanini's vetoes aided Victor salesmanship. Who but Toscanini
could have inspired such merchandising as:

The records here consist of the orchestral excerpts from Part II [of Berlioz's *Romeo and Juliet*]. This is the true essence of Berlioz's score and contains the composer's most cherished composition, the impassioned Love Scene. . . .

Unfortunately, the Maestro would not approve the re-takes made of the fanciful "Queen Mab" Scherzo, third section of Part II. Rather than hold back the release of the remainder of this music, we are issuing the album without the scherzo.

There is one point, however, that we should like to make clear. The "Queen Mab" Scherzo will definitely be re-recorded, and will be issued as soon as possible as a single recording![7]

Streamlining Toscanini indoctrination were wartime Atlantic blockades and wartime prunings of the Victor catalogue in favor of proven best-sellers. After the war, some Furtwängler recordings were not widely available to Americans until the early sixties—in effect, reducing Toscanini's phonographic competition. As significant, Toscanini was prevented from competing with his own NBC Symphony. O'Connell, writing in 1947, recalled how Victor's salespeople had found the disembodied "NBC Symphony" to be "sadly lacking in prestige with the public," notwithstanding "Toscanini's prodigiously exploited name." O'Connell had responded by urging Toscanini to record in Philadelphia. Post-O'Connell, RCA imposed a surer, if less exciting, solution, making "Toscanini" and "NBC Symphony" two halves of an equation; Toscanini was not to record with other orchestras. The equation of "Toscanini" with the most canonized, most salable symphonies was nearly as secure. For its post-1949 NBC Symphony recordings of the thirteen symphonies of Beethoven and Brahms, RCA used a standard album cover connoting both equations: twenty photographs of Toscanini's face and hands were aligned in rows of five against a black background; between the rows, the conductor's and composer's names shared the same typeface, with "and the NBC Symphony Orchestra" appended to the former. Toscanini's 1952 Beethoven Ninth—according to an album note, his fifth to be recorded, but first to be authorized for release—was RCA Red Seal's best-selling recording for two years. In 1953, an RCA limited edition of Toscanini's Beethoven was virtually sold out before it could reach the stores. As of Toscanini's retirement in 1954, RCA had sold 20 million of his recordings, for $33 million. When RCA joined forces with the Book-of-the-Month Club to launch the RCA Victor Record Club in 1958, members were offered bargain-priced sets of the Toscanini Beethoven symphonies; in three months, 340,000 customers signed up.[8]

Ironically, while the postwar recordings boom, with its attendant technological improvements, enticed Toscanini to record more, it did not necessarily result in better-sounding Toscanini recordings. In significant respects, his 1936 Carnegie Hall recordings, supervised by O'Connell, were handsomer than all but a few of his NBC Symphony recordings; even as recorded in Carnegie Hall rather than Studio 8H, the NBC Symphony was made to sound dry and coarse. What, one wonders, was Toscanini's response? Samuel Antek has left a memorable description of Toscanini's indifference, exasperation, and withdrawal at NBC Symphony recording sessions. Listening to playbacks, he never commented on the beauty or texture of the sound, according to Antek; his attention focused on tempo, drive, and balance. Others, too, remember Toscanini listening to check the audibility of every instrument, yet indifferent to harsh or dull reproduction. At home, he was a notoriously inept phonograph operator. O'Connell, accounting for the superior sound of Stokowski's recordings, among others, commented: "Toscanini is utterly impatient with, does not understand, and stubbornly refuses to understand, the possibilities or the limitations of recording and reproduction. . . . He will not, by so much as one decibel, modify his dynamics . . . nor will he redress orchestral balance in relation to the conditions under which recorded music is normally reproduced."[9]

Much as NBC's jumble of commercial and artistic aspirations caused network publicists to write about Toscanini with jumbled hoopla and reverence, its recording personnel wound up treating him with jumbled attentiveness and negligence. After O'Connell, no Toscanini producer seems to have offered any but perfunctory advice on repertoire and choice of soloists and singers. EMI's Walter Legge, who, as he was quick to acknowledge, left the richest legacy of any record producer, was asked by Toscanini in 1952 for his opinion of the NBC Symphony's 1946 *Traviata* on RCA. Legge told Toscanini his tempos were too fast. "*Figlio mio,* you are right," Toscanini replied, adding that if he were ten years younger he would have all his records withdrawn and rerecord them under Legge, because Legge was the only man who would not mince words about his performances. Even if this story, told by Legge and Edward Greenfield, is not true, it deserves to be.[10]

"From the very first radio concert of the NBC Symphony Orchestra under Toscanini's direction," Sarnoff announced in 1950, "the National Broadcasting Company and the individual stations which comprise the nation's first network have received thousands of letters from their listeners asking that Maestro Toscanini take the orchestra on a tour of the nation. This year it has become possible to accede to those requests." One reason NBC saw fit to accede to its listeners in 1950 was RCA's capitulation to Columbia's two-year-old LP. The tour's objectives, as RCA's

George Marek later wrote, "were two-fold: to glorify the reputation of NBC, and to stimulate the sale of Toscanini recordings. The record business was just beginning to recover from . . . 'the war of the speeds.' . . . Now, in 1950, [RCA was] beginning to present [its] rich treasure of good music on LPs, and for the Toscanini tour, a special series of Toscanini recordings was put on sale."[11] (Victor issued the new recordings— "among the supreme artistic treasures of all time . . . masterpieces that belong in *every* home library!"—on both LP and 45s; Toscanini was quoted endorsing the latter format as "fascinating . . . remarkably faithful reproduction of recorded music.")

Underwritten by NBC, Toscanini's "first transcontinental concert tour"—his 1920–21 Scala orchestra tour had not reached the West Coast— combined the barnstorming fervor of Theodore Thomas's whistle-stop campaigns with the opulence of Paderewski's rail excursions. Over six weeks, the NBC Symphony gave twenty-one concerts in twenty states—a schedule generously setting aside time for sightseeing and recreation. A special twelve-Pullman train was assembled, including pleasant accommodations for the musicians plus a private Toscanini car equipped with a bathtub, paneled library, and dining room.

Though some at NBC thought the project a corporate self-indulgence, Sarnoff knew what he was doing. All twenty-six works Toscanini took on the road—a heroic number for twenty-one programs—were vintage music appreciation repertoire. Although NBC's press department said that Toscanini and RCA "felt a sense of responsibility toward the music lovers of America to make this tour a great and lasting monument to American culture," no American music was scheduled ("Dixie" and "Stars and Stripes Forever" were added as surprise encores on four occasions). The core traveling repertoire comprised the *Eroica*, the Schubert "Unfinished," Brahms's First and Fourth symphonies and "Haydn" Variations, Tchaikovsky's *Pathétique* and *Romeo and Juliet*, Dvořák's "New World" Symphony, Debussy's *La Mer* and *Ibéria*, and Strauss's *Don Juan*. Just before leaving, Toscanini recorded two tour-program miniatures: Smetana's *Moldau* and Dukas's *Sorcerer's Apprentice*. Within seven months of returning, he recorded *La Mer*, *Ibéria*, *Don Juan*, and a third tour miniature, Saint-Saëns's *Danse macabre*—at which point RCA had recorded Toscanini in twenty-five of the twenty-six tour compositions, the exception being the "New World" Symphony, recorded in 1953.

As Sarnoff must have anticipated, and as NBC's publicists ensured, Toscanini was besieged by reporters, photographers, and fans at every stop. Even in the Deep South, hundreds gathered, climbing on lampposts and atop cars to catch a glimpse and say "Thank you, Maestro." *Life* ran a photo spread on "Toscanini in Texas." Howard Taubman of the *Times* filed firsthand reports of "historic" ovations that were "far from a symptom of provincialism." *The New Yorker* sent a writer aboard the Toscanini train in Virginia and Alabama; he meticulously inventoried the books Toscanini read and the contents of his "concert bag" (four towels, two bamboo fans, Oculav for his eyes, bicarbonate of soda, a family picture, and a silver box containing rock candy). None of this coverage bothered much with music; rather, it embroidered the "other Toscanini." In Washington, Toscanini was greeted backstage by President and Mrs. Truman and became so nervous—"it was said that he had been worrying about this meeting with the President for a week"—he could barely list the program he was about to conduct. In New Orleans, he was observed tapping his foot while listening to jazz. When two hotel maids told him they wanted to attend his concert, he "arranged for folding chairs in the wings and saw they were comfortable throughout the performance." He favored Richmond, Virginia, with a rendition of "Dixie," arousing rebel yells and cheers; Senator Harry Byrd documented the performance in the *Congressional Record.* In Austin, Texas, Toscanini conducted in a university gymnasium so hot that, as *Life* put it, he "broke the rules" and rehearsed without his usual black alpaca jacket. His southern California concerts were, according to Taubman, attended by "scads of Hollywood stars"; in Pasadena, Bob Hope waited ten minutes outside Toscanini's dressing room, and other stars waited "even longer." (It was in Pasadena, too, that Walter Toscanini scuffled with a photographer, getting struck on the head with a camera in return for a blow delivered to the man's neck.) The tour's most publicized stop was Sun Valley, where no concert was given. Toscanini rode the ski lift to the top of ten-thousand-foot Mount Baldy; the musicians cheered when his chair swung into view. Antek remarked, "Maestro, you are a brave man. Some of the boys were afraid to come up"—to which Toscanini replied, "I've never been afraid of anything in my life. I like to try everything."[12]

Sarnoff, quoted in an NBC press release, accurately summarized the tour's first achievement by speaking of "enthralled throngs of Americans who . . . found Toscanini the man to be even greater than Toscanini the immortal legend." Taubman registered the same sentiment in the *New York Times Magazine:* "It is not only the musician who has impressed America. The unaffected simplicity of the man has made new admirers for him wherever he has gone." Taubman also wrote:

> Anyone who has watched [Toscanini] in the course of his transcontinental tour . . . can tell you that there is absolutely no truth to the story that he prefers to isolate himself from ordinary people and the affairs of everyday life. Like so many other myths, this is pure invention.

It is true, of course, that Mr. Toscanini is inexorably exigent as a musician. . . . But in all other respects he is simple, friendly, considerate, and warmly outgoing.[13]

In truth, the tour's musical dividends, if less advertised, were also remarkable. Air travel had yet to homogenize the concert circuit; especially in cities like Atlanta, where people came from as far away as South Carolina and Florida, or Austin, where the applause was described as "shocking,"[14] the NBC visit was momentous. The greatest and least-recognized beneficiaries of the tour's actual music making, however, were the actual musicians, Toscanini included. Liberated from the radio pressure-cooker with its microphones, announcers, and clockwork pacing, from the glass control booth, invited audiences, and rattle-proof programs of Studio 8H, the NBC Symphony became more like a normal orchestra giving normal concerts for normal people. It offered multiple performances of the same programs. It escaped intervals of dismemberment during which the musicians were assigned ditties and fox-trots. In Philadelphia, Baltimore, and San Francisco, it played in proper concert halls with proper acoustics. And, rid of the corporate interface of Radio City, it established a more personal, less formal bond with its conductor. These were among Antek's observations about touring with Toscanini:

As the tour progressed, as the beauty and wonder of our great country unfolded, we realized that the greatest wonder of all was riding on the train with us—our incredible 83-year-old Maestro, Toscanini himself. Throughout the trip, his zest and enthusiasm, his physical and emotional endurance, astounded us all, even those of us who had known and played with him for years. At times the Old Man seemed so tired and gray with fatigue after a concert that we wondered how in the world he would keep going. But the next day he would appear as gay and chipper as ever, looking so fresh we could hardly believe our eyes.

Wherever there was something unusual to see, a famous restaurant to visit, something interesting to experience, Toscanini would be there, enjoying himself immensely. His curiosity seemed insatiable. I had never seen him so happy, so carefree and fun-loving as he was on this trip, so deeply touched and demonstrative in his appreciation of the attention and ovations that greeted him everywhere.

He enjoyed tremendously mingling with the men and talking to everyone about anything, although the conversation invariably turned to music. An enthusiastic, gesticulating figure, he would always be found with a group of us gathered around. Even backstage, before a concert, moving about restlessly before going on, he would engage some of the men in conversation.

As the tour went on, Toscanini seemed to become more and more informal. For the first time he began to appear at rehearsal without the little high-collared black jacket. . . . Rehearsals were brief. Their sole purpose was to get the "feel" and "sound" of the halls we were in.

With Toscanini . . . so relaxed, we all let go *con amore;* everyone played with his whole heart. The performances all along were undoubtedly the finest I ever heard our orchestra give. No wonder Toscanini was delighted and pleased as I had never seen him before.[15]

The summer following his transcontinental tour, Toscanini was informed by Chotzinoff that 8H was being converted into a television studio and would no longer be available for NBC Symphony broadcasts. Toscanini was given a choice between Carnegie Hall and the Manhattan Center. He chose Carnegie, yet was assigned the Center, which he loathed. More rescheduling followed, and Carnegie Hall became the NBC Symphony's new home. The expected acoustical benefits, however, were minimized by engineers who crowded and rebalanced the orchestra with their microphones so that the hall could not be "heard."

Another obstacle to "normalization" of NBC's concerts was that they had acquired sporadic commercial sponsorship as of 1943–44. Even the invited audience was sometimes subjected to commercial "messages" beamed into the hall. Radio listeners and television viewers, meanwhile, were now instructed to equate "Toscanini" and "great music" with "General Motors" or "Socony-Vacuum Oil" or "Reynolds Metals." Billy Phelps had joined Dickens and Thornton Wilder with Swift's "foods distinguished by their excellence"; Ben Grauer, hosting the NBC Symphony, elaborated the art-plus-commerce equation as follows:

The universal appeal of music attains perhaps its most far-reaching expression in these [Toscanini] radio and television simulcasts, heard and seen in millions of homes. Spreading widely, too, is the use of aluminum, the light, strong, rust-proof metal of these modern times. Reynolds Aluminum makes appliances more efficient, makes automobiles safer and more economical. It makes the bright windows of modern homes, and the gutters around the eaves, the lifetime roofs of family farm buildings, the reflective insulation in your walls. Aluminum foil protects the fine foods you buy, just as Reynolds Wrap, the original and genuine, keeps food fresh in your kitchen. . . . Now Arturo Toscanini has just made his entrance on the stage of Carnegie Hall, and now the Reynolds Metals Company invites you to listen as he conducts the NBC Symphony Orchestra in the symphonic interlude from César Franck's *The Redemption.*

And:

Arturo Toscanini and the NBC Symphony Orchestra have performed Rossini's Overture to *William Tell* as the concluding work on our program, presented to you by the Reynolds Metals Company. The Reynolds Metals Company is delighted to have brought you this thrilling performance. Actually, Reynolds Aluminum may well have played a real part in your listening pleasure, for the electric power of your radio, your television, may come to you through Reynolds Aluminum cable now serving millions of homes, and many of the parts of your receiver are aluminum. And now we cordially invite you to tune in again next week at this time for another great concert by Arturo Toscanini and the NBC Symphony Orchestra, again sponsored by the *Reynolds Metals Company, pioneers of progress through aluminum.* Until next week, this is Ben Grauer bidding you good-bye.[16]

In terms of repertoire, the final decade of Toscanini broadcasts propagated the great composers with renewed vigor, the time for patriotic Americana, and for Soviet-American amity, having passed. To the symphonic masterpieces, however, were added seven operatic masterpieces, mostly by Verdi. Performed in concert, two broadcasts per opera, these marked Toscanini's reunion with the genre that had bulked largest through most of his career. One of the broadcast operas, *La Bohème,* was a fiftieth-anniversary celebration of the premiere, conducted by Toscanini himself in 1896; *Time* called it "easily the best performance of *La Bohème* the United States has heard since Toscanini last conducted it at the Metropolitan in 1910."[17] The other Toscanini-NBC operas, broadcast between 1944 and 1954, were as rapturously received—although Virgil Thomson had the temerity to observe that the singers, while assiduously prepared at the piano for weeks on end, were not what they could have been.

During World War II, Toscanini had practically restricted his activities to the United States. Now, with the war ended, he did not return to Germany, Austria, France, or Palestine. In London, he led two concerts in 1952. But he did, inevitably, return to Italy, capping fifteen years of defiance and vigilance. Though rumors of Toscanini's reappearance at La Scala began circulating as soon as peace was assured, he rejected an early invitation rather than return "as a subject of the kings and princes of the House of Savoy." Once a referendum on abolishing the monarchy was announced for June 1946, he relented, arriving in Milan the preceding April: fifty years since he first conducted there, sixteen since his last Milan appearance, with the New York Philharmonic. Scheduled to reopen La Scala with a concert on May 11, he postponed the first rehearsal when, as UPI reported, he found himself as "frightened" as "a little boy going to school for the first time." Rather than reunite with the orchestra onstage, he decided to meet the musicians in a small reception room; there, he and the "old timers" wept openly. The concert, nine days later, was relayed by loudspeakers to tens of thousands gathered on the steps and pavement outside the overcrowded theater, as well as broadcast throughout Italy. Every stage of Toscanini's "return from exile"—the first contradictory announcements, his departure from New York, his delay in Newfoundland owing to inclement weather, his arrival in Geneva, his first tour of Milan's ruins, his first rehearsal—was reported in the American press.[18]

On June 2, Toscanini voted in the referendum that ended the Savoy monarchy. He eventually resumed splitting time between New York and Milan, residing on Via Durini in the latter city from April to October, with holidays at his island villa on Lake Maggiore. He had no intention of again taking charge of La Scala, as some Milanese believed he might. He did conduct there sporadically, however, through 1952. At one 1948 performance, commemorating the thirtieth anniversary of Boito's death, he led staged excerpts from *Mefistofele* and *Nerone*—presiding from an opera pit for the last time. By then, the old fraternal frictions had resurfaced. Toscanini refused to appear at a gala reception in his honor following the historic May 11 concert. Even before, he had offended Milan's mayor by refusing to sanction a short welcoming address at the event, whereupon the mayor declined to attend. Scheduled Scala concerts in Paris and London were canceled by Toscanini when the Allies ceded a tiny piece of Italy to France. Plans for a Toscanini *Otello* went awry. In 1948, Toscanini's two Scala programs were widely criticized as "old-fashioned." The following year, he turned down a lifetime senatorial appointment for having rendered "exceptionally distinguished services" to Italy. Conducting Verdi's Requiem at La Scala in 1950, he received a notably tepid welcome from the stalls and boxes. Four years earlier, a quizzical New York *Times* reporter had noted from Rome that, "as far as can be ascertained here, the interest [in Toscanini's return] is greater in America than in Italy," continuing:

. . . The people in Rome who have been most excited about Signor Toscanini and made the most elaborate preparations to be able to go to Milan for the Toscanini concerts are the Americans.

Most Italians are certainly indifferent, but most persons genuinely interested in music are interested in Signor Toscanini's return. Curiously enough, there is a certain amount of resentment. In the musical world there is a tendency to feel that too much is made of one man. . . .

Afterward, the American press increasingly seized on stories of Toscanini's Italian difficulties as evidence that he was not properly treated there. NBC agreed; not three weeks after Toscanini's arrival in Milan its press department announced: "Toscanini Homesick for U.S.A. Plans to Return Immediately After Final La Scala Concert." George Marek, who covered the Scala reinauguration for *Good Housekeeping,* later summarized:

. . . Much as he loved Italy and firmly though he then hoped for its regeneration, [Toscanini] no longer felt at home in a destroyed city and a morally enfeebled country. . . . He was always "a guest," and he observed with increasing bitterness the cleavage between political parties, the in-fighting, the inability of the Italians to govern themselves, the belief that the substance of liberty consisted of slipping an envelope to the policeman. Perhaps what Walter told me one day in Milan was a reflection of his father's mood: "Now we are strangers here." Their real home lay in Riverdale. His true place lay in front of that orchestra which was unequivocally devoted to him, the NBC Symphony.[19]

A contradictory view was expressed by Toscanini's Italian biographer, Filippo Sacchi, who detailed Toscanini's postwar Italian tribulations yet concluded: "Musically, he was never really happy to be far away from the Scala for too long: and it was in Milan that the true background of his musical life lay. Although he never assumed an official position, he continued to take a fatherly interest in the Scala. . . . His interest in Italian musical life continued to be tireless."

In fact, Toscanini in America and Toscanini in Italy were different Toscaninis. Toscanini in America would never have walked out on an irate audience, as in the old Scala days, or have rebuffed a prominent mayor. Equally implausible is that in America he would have *applauded* an audience, as he did at the Italian premiere of *Pelléas* in 1908; or have formally retracted insults upon being petitioned at home by offended musicians, as happened during his second Scala tenure; or have decided that *Carmen* be sung in the language of the audience, as he angrily advised La Scala in his last years. None of his Milan concerts were reserved for invited guests. None of his New York concerts were relayed to the streets. Toscanini in Italy was a living symbol of national culture, a central actor, a countryman tangled in the daily fray. Toscanini in America symbolized a vital surrogate culture. Off bounds to meddlesome enthusiasts, he commanded NBC's prize sideshow, admired from afar. Toscanini himself (who never chose to become an American citizen) commented in a 1951 letter from New York to Milan: "I'm homesick for my old house on Via Durini. But what can be done? I want to work. I can't in Italy. This alone is my working environment."[20]

The Toscanini cult in its postwar phase inspired reviews as effulgent as any written before or during the war; meanwhile, the escalating celebrity of Toscanini the man inspired a floodtide of national magazine articles in which the other Toscanini was ceaselessly elaborated. "The Perfectionist," *Time*'s Toscanini cover story of April 26, 1948, is one locus classicus of postwar Toscanini iconography. Reiterating long-standing encomiums, *Time* called Toscanini "without question the greatest living conductor"; he had "brought the music of Beethoven, Schubert, Wagner and Verdi to life as no other man has." Reviewing essential pre-NBC Toscanini lore, the article rehearsed Toscanini's humble origins ("Neither his father nor his mother was interested in music"), the details of his debut ("This little scarecrow figi re who closed the score before he started to play looked as if he might furnish some fun"), his rebuke to Geraldine Farrar (" 'Madam, there are only stars in the heavens' "), and his repudiation of Mussolini and Hitler ("Dictators are no match for Toscanini"). Then, fastening on fresher yet equally familiar material, it explained that "there are two Toscaninis" and continued:

> The other Toscanini is the little old man who loves to go to parties, whirl down Manhattan's Hudson River Drive from Villa Pauline, his Riverdale home, to Rockefeller Center in his black Cadillac, and play practical jokes on his family and friends. . . .
> He still has a quick eye for good-looking women, and an obvious attraction to them. . . .

In common with other mass-circulation periodicals, *Time* showed special interest in the other Toscanini's enthusiasm for televised boxing, wrestling, and children's shows—an enthusiasm selected to negate Lawrence Gilman's fading sacerdotal metaphors:

When friends visit. . . . they often find him watching a fight, jumping up & down in his chair like an eight-year-old. When a fighter is knocked down, he leaps up, thrusts his finger at the prostrate figure on the screen, yells at him, "Die! die! die!"

He also likes children's programs on television. A friend recently caught him watching DuMont's program "Small Fry Club," asked him, "What are you watching, Maestro?" Toscanini replied, never taking his eyes from the screen: "Fry Small."

Frequent images of Toscanini identifying with boxers, wrestlers, and children equally served to underline his agelessness. In a *New York Times Magazine* article titled "Ponce de Leon? No! Toscanini!" Howard Taubman revealed that Toscanini took sunbaths, rarely ate meat, ignored drafts, and averaged no more than one cold a year. In a second *Times Magazine* piece, "Toscanini's Secret: Keep Growing," Martin Gumpert, identified as an M.D. "drawn to his study of Mr. Toscanini by a love of music and an expert knowledge of geriatrics," concluded: "Toscanini's secret is unlimited devotion to a limited area of life. Creative passion enlarges the frame of existence almost beyond the point of death."[21] Taubman's Toscanini scrutiny, in particular his coverage of the 1950 NBC Symphony tour, eventually produced a full-length Toscanini biography, *The Maestro* (1951), bulging with "other Toscanini" anecdotes.

Not every portrait of the other Toscanini was scrubbed clean. *Time's* version in "The Perfectionist" showed him encircled by a "little knot of courtiers" who "regard all the Maestro's music with dumb and unquestioning adoration." Of Toscanini himself, *Time* remarked: "He likes to think of himself as shy, humble, unassuming, courteous—and, off the podium, he usually is. . . . Sometimes, he glowers in a corner, refuses to talk, turns away food and drinks and generally casts a pall over everything." Taubman, in *The Maestro,* portrayed Toscanini striving all his life "to live simply and honestly." Certain qualifications were gently posed, however: "He thinks he is above flattery, but there are people in his orbit who apply it so skillfully and with such an air of sincerity that he is fooled occasionally." "He is impatient with vanity. . . . And yet there have been times he has not noticed a touch of frailty in himself." "The autocrat of the concert hall and opera house, for all the mildness of his manner, tends to be tyrannical at home." A more fully sanitized Toscanini characterization appeared in the August 1947 *Reader's Digest:* "At 80 He's Still the World's Leading Musician," condensed from *Liberty* magazine. "Personal publicity is, to the Maestro, extremely distasteful," Ann M. Lingg explained. "This feeling stems from a profound conviction that he himself is unimportant in comparison with the music he conducts." As for the other Toscanini: "The tyrant of the

podium has a soft heart in off hours. He makes a hobby of charities but tries
to keep them anonymous so people will not have to thank him. Recently
he was reported to have sent 30,000 pairs of shoes to Italy."

It was David Ewen who distilled a wholly perfected and simplified
portrait in *The Story of Arturo Toscanini* (1951). Narrating the Toscanini
parables, Ewen was biblical, as in this version of Toscanini's Rio debut:

> "Maybe another conductor will quiet [the audience]," ventured one
> of the singers without actually believing what she was saying.
>
> Another remarked: "Maybe they're so tired of making noise out there
> that they will want to listen to some music, at last?"
>
> A third added: "Unless someone goes out there and tries to conduct
> the opera, we are lost." . . .
>
> It was then that one of the singers came up with a suggestion. It was
> a farfetched one, to be sure, and not likely to be feasible. But an emer-
> gency allowed for even farfetched suggestions. It was simply this: One
> of the cellists in the orchestra, Arturo Toscanini, had time and again
> proved to the company that he seemed to know all the famous operas
> by heart.

As described by Ewen, Toscanini's resignations from La Scala and the
Metropolitan were purged of caprice. His tantrums were the just deserts
of "pampered prime donne and adulated tenors." His controversial first
New York Beethoven's Ninth in 1913 was "decisively" acclaimed. As music
director of the New York Philharmonic, he "devoted himself . . . as completely" to the orchestra as he had to directing La Scala. The men of the
Philharmonic "literally worshiped him." Ewen even misrepresented his
own past, as chronicled in *The Man with the Baton* and other books, when
he wrote that there had "never been a doubt" in his mind that Toscanini
"is the greatest conductor of them all—an artist of such unique grandeur
and of such monumental attainments that no one can be deservedly compared to him." The final chapter of *The Story of Arturo Toscanini*, titled
"The Other Toscanini," is an apogee of sorts.

> . . . The "other Toscanini"—the Toscanini released from the tensions
> of making music—is usually gentle, warm-hearted, sympathetic, and
> sentimental. No one knows this better than the musicians themselves.
> . . . There are some conductors who snobbishly prefer to keep themselves
> at all times at a distance from their men, and have no personal interest
> in them whatsoever. Toscanini is certainly not one of them. He feels very
> close to, and is always concerned with, each one of his musicians. . . .
>
> The "other Toscanini" is known also to his relatives and intimate

friends. In the concert auditorium, his may be an Olympian stature. But in the privacy of his own home, surrounded by those he loves, he is unaffectedly simple and humble. You will never find Toscanini putting on airs of grandeur or temperament. Being of Latin blood, he may at times have an explosive temper or indulge in volatile moods. But that is not the rule. Most often he is gay and easy to get along with, a most charming and considerate companion, and a most devoted grandfather, father, and husband.

Ewen chronicled not only Toscanini the prankster and TV addict but Toscanini the frequent participant in "stimulating conversation on art and politics." "His culture is expansive. His reservoir of information is overflowing, his memory of things read fabulous. Novelists, scientists, statesmen have often been impressed by the flexible range of his intellect." Finally, peeling away every extraneous particle from the other Toscanini, and from Toscanini the self-made genius, Ewen discovered the essential postwar Toscanini—and incidentally produced a new version of the genesis of NBC's transcontinental tour:

> His long stay in America, since 1938, had transformed him into an American. He could no longer live happily, nor function to his fullest capacities, anywhere else. His proud democratic spirit responded sympathetically to the American ideal; his personality and temperament found continual delight in the American way of life. Characteristically, he began more and more to adopt the enthusiasms and interests of Americans: Mickey Mouse films; jam sessions; prize fights. . . .
>
> His increasing identification with the land of his adoption stimulated Toscanini's curiosity in America's geography, people, customs, backgrounds. This curiosity, in turn, awakened a new ambition. He wanted to come more personally into contact with the country in all its variety, to tour it extensively, to visit places he had read or heard about but had never seen. He wanted to conduct living concerts for Americans in their own communities.
>
> The executives of the National Broadcasting Company and RCA Victor Records stood ready to satisfy this ambition. They provided the sponsorship for a nation-wide tour.

Even this was not the culminating reductio of the other Toscanini; the extramusical parameters of Ewen's analysis, while impressive, barely suggested what precincts of stardom the Toscanini cult had invaded. Deferred to by "scads of Hollywood stars," Toscanini enjoyed the same forms of celebrity they did. He turned up on *Time*'s "People" page, beaming while "being congratulated by onetime heavyweight champion Primo ('Old Satchelfoot') Carnera, now a prosperous wrestler." Clementine Paddleford's recipe column in the New York *Herald Tribune* explained how to make "Soup for Toscanini" as prescribed by his own cook, Anna Saccomandi. The gossip columnist Earl Wilson, denied a Toscanini interview, invented one:

> Pretty soon my readers are going to say, "Well, who was it Wilson didn't get an interview with today?"
> Remember my famous non-exclusive non-interview with Garbo?
> So I decided to interview Arturo Toscanini.
> Walking into his dressing room by special permission of a perfect stranger on the street who said it was o.k. with him I wolfed his peppermint, sat on his sofa, peeked brazenly into his refrigerator, and then—
> Aw, who the heck wanted to interview him anyway?
>
> "I don't like publicity," [Toscanini said].
> Offered *Time*'s cover, if he'd see a reporter, he repeated he doesn't see anybody, especially reporters.
> Friends wanted to give him a party when he turned 81.
> "Give me one when I'm 90," he answered.
>
> He fibbed to one reporter, who cornered him, that he doesn't speak English. He has told autograph fans that he's not Toscanini.
> I got an interview last year but some people think this doesn't count, as I asked him only one question, and he didn't answer it.
>
> "Maybe," I said to his son Walter Toscanini, "you'd let me shake hands with him, since I shook hands with him last year and he didn't get poisoned."
> "Oh, no, he's too shy."
> "But you can even shake hands with the President!"
> "I know," said Walter, "but not with my father!"
> Don't miss me tomorrow when I won't have an exclusive interview with General Eisenhower, either.[22]

Toscanini's inaccessibility to reporters and photographers, and his refusal to appear in the movies, had long irked the press. Now, however, every evidence of intractability was made to seem a delightful incongruity. A recipe for rice-and-celery soup was just as good as one for *scalloppine al marsala arricchite*. A noninterview was just as good as an interview. A tussle with a photographer was even better than a photograph. These perverse uses of the celebrity forms seemed actually to enhance their effectiveness. Every apparent obstacle became celebrity fodder.

In one sense, Toscanini's movie-star glamour was elevating. More profoundly, stereotyped probes of his private life satisfied a leveling urge; proportional interest in Toscanini the musician waned. The nineteenth century's ballyhoo tradition had hybridized European talent with American promotional knowhow; the willfully naive metaphors of George Bagby's "Jud Brownin Hears Ruby Play" appointed the New World the measure of all things. Earl Wilson, playing the willfully naive cosmopolite, was 1940s folklore: George Bagby seventy-five years later. Like Jud Brownin's reportrait of Anton Rubinstein, the ballyhooed reportrait of Toscanini as an "American" ensnared Old World culture in a New World milieu—except that Wilson's newspaper audience, and Toscanini's on radio, television, and recordings incalculably exceeded Bagby's or Rubinstein's. And the buttressing merchandising of Toscanini, capitalizing on consumer needs, corporate diversity, and technological change, used methods undreamed of by P. T. Barnum.

If Virgil Thomson's reviews were the sole prominent exception to postwar critical adulation of Toscanini the conductor in the daily press, three notable portrayals of Toscanini the man contradicted the postwar barrage of books and articles testifying to his unsuspected affability and humility. Unlike most "other Toscanini" stories and articles, these were firsthand accounts. Winthrop Sargeant, a New York Philharmonic violinist from 1928 to 1930, wrote a 1944 Toscanini profile for *Life*, later expanded in Sargeant's *Geniuses, Goddesses and People* (1949). Charles O'Connell of RCA included a Toscanini chapter in his book of reminiscences, *The Other Side of the Record* (1947). And Samuel Chotzinoff, Toscanini's NBC factotum, wrote a 1956 Toscanini profile for *Holiday* magazine, barely expanded to book length as *Toscanini: An Intimate Portrait* the same year.

Sargeant's *Life* "Close-Up" was the mildest and least heretical of these dissident vignettes. According to Toscanini orthodoxy, the other Toscanini was "gregarious" and "easy to get along with." Sargeant wrote: "He loves the company of pretty women [but] always looks vaguely out of place in any gathering he cannot lead with a baton." The other Toscanini was so "soft-hearted" he made "a hobby of charities." Sargeant wrote: "He has a reputation for childish helplessness in practical affairs [but] is shrewd enough to bargain closely over his concert and broadcast fees." At home, the other Toscanini "never put on airs of grandeur or temperament."

Sargeant wrote: "In private life he is alternately fussy and playful, head-strong in both his enthusiasms and his hatreds, intolerant of anything in the way of opposition." The other Toscanini was "unbelievably modest." Sargeant wrote: "He is . . . deeply and matter-of-factly convinced that he is the greatest conductor in the world."

O'Connell's Toscanini chapter, subtitled "A Minority Report," black-ened and enlarged every wart drawn by Sargeant. Socially, O'Connell's Toscanini is usually "charming and gracious." But "his conversation con-cerns little but music, and tends to develop into a monologue. . . . He is completely conscious of his importance, and accepts tributes to it with the most disarming simplicity." Rather than "naive" or "shrewd," this Tos-canini is mistrustful.

Toscanini's humors, and humor, are difficult to predict. . . . I do not know whether it is lack of a familiarity with English (even after so many years in America) or sheer lack of humor and imagination that causes him so often to misunderstand and misinterpret. He is quick to suspect those most keenly and most honestly and most disinterestedly devoted to his undertakings; to imagine slights, to look for hidden meanings, to doubt friendship, to accuse of promises unkept when no promise, but only a hope has been given.

More than "headstrong" at home, Toscanini, according to O'Connell's minority report, "loves no one": "I am not speaking of the love for woman or for music; there is evidence enough that he has acquitted him-self, perhaps nobly, doubtless notably, in both directions. I speak of love which is the union of two wills. Toscanini is not interested in a union of wills, but only in the imposition of his own." Regarding Toscanini's self-esteem, O'Connell wrote: "I am sure Mr. Toscanini does not consider himself the greatest conductor in the world. I am sure that he regards himself as the *only good conductor* in the world." A representative O'Con-nell anecdote added:

I was leaving Toscanini's Riverdale home late one night after a long dinner and a longer conference. Usually the family Cadillac was gener-ously assigned to take me back to town, but on this occasion the chauf-feur had gone to bed. I asked permission to phone for a cab, and on being connected required a car to be sent to the home of Mr. Tos-canini. I felt a tap on the shoulder, "MAESTRO, not mister," said Maestro.

O'Connell summarized:

> I believe that Toscanini's obsession with *energy*, with *force*, his pride in possessing them in so full a measure, his idolatrous worship of these qualities, and his relentless application of them in his artistic and personal life, provide a possible key not only to the magical effect he has had upon his audiences and his consequent successes, but to the character of the maestro himself as man and musician. Energy, determination, concentration; these have made Toscanini what he is, and I think somewhat less of each would have made a greater artist and a nobler man. His energy causes him to drive rather than to lead; his determination, to dictate rather than to teach, and the fury of concentration he brings to bear upon the printed score leaves him little time, and apparently less inclination, for gentleness, for tolerance, patience, humility, humanity, or love. I had not known him, in years of acquaintance, countless conversations, and many hours of collaboration, to evidence interest in a book, a growing tree, a burgeoning talent, a picture that lived or a building that leaped to the sky, a work of drama other than that mongrel type, the opera. I do not believe (certain writers notwithstanding) that Toscanini is a student of Shakespeare; he could not be, and remain as simple, as selfish, and as savage as a child.

Samuel Chotzinoff, whose *Intimate Portrait* was written between Toscanini's departure from NBC in 1954 and his death three years later, was an unlikely third source of unconventional wisdom. He was the very leader of the "little knot of courtiers," given to "dumb and unquestioning admiration," to which *Time*'s cover story had referred. Toscanini's retirement, however, impelled Chotzinoff to question his admiration. He now wrote of the Toscanini court:

> The spell that Toscanini cast on everyone around him . . . was powerful and unflagging. . . . They trembled at his frown and basked in his smile. At NBC his every wish was attended to in the spirit of a favor conferred by him. To be allowed to remove his sopping garments was like assisting at a rite. To sit next to him in a motor car or at table, to have him address one as *"caro,"* to attend a concert or a play with him, to entertain him—all these became memorable events. No one stopped to examine and analyze or question his strange and unprecedented power. He ruled over our hearts and minds. His judgments were accepted like articles of faith. We took to our hearts the people he liked and looked askance at those he dropped. We loved the music he loved,

became skeptical about the music he despised, and accepted without question the music that, having summarily cast out, he as summarily restored to favor. When with him we talked about him. We never tired of hearing him talk about himself; when away from him we never ceased recalling his words, looks, gestures, opinions. When he telephoned to one of us, we hastily apprised one another, through a telephone relay, of the happy occurrence. And indeed it was thrilling to lift up the receiver and hear one's name pronounced *sotto voce,* hoarsely, vibrating with the fast tremolo so characteristic of the Maestro's speech.

We spent much of our leisure time in thinking up ways to amuse him. . . .

Toscanini: An Intimate Portrait treated Toscanini's stature as "a great man" and "world's greatest conductor" as assumptions; every scathing rudeness, every exorbitant demand was presumed forgivable. And yet, as if Chotzinoff were forcibly freeing himself from Toscanini's Svengali grip, these rudenesses and demands were mercilessly catalogued. Chotzinoff's Toscanini is rude and bullying. Otherwise "short on humor," he relishes practical jokes played on others. He abuses even his "friends" and is prone to displays of pouting "self-pity" at their expense. "He was naive, crafty, simple, complex, kind, and ferociously spiteful. The moods *inhabited* him without forewarning, and evaporated just as mysteriously." "He was (and is) a law unto himself. I have never heard anyone seriously oppose him to his face on any subject whatsoever." "The plain truth is that all his life he has been forgiven conduct that would have been tolerated in no other artist." The book's most startling anecdotes reduced Toscanini's egomania to juvenile obduracy, as when, dining at the Chotzinoffs for the first time, Toscanini glimpsed two small magnets belonging to twelve-year-old Blair Chotzinoff.

The Maestro, still talking, focused his gaze on the magnets. Presently his words trailed off into an incoherent murmur. He was giving his entire attention to Blair. "That's a magnet, Maestro," I said. "Yes," he said, "a *magneto,* I know." "Would you like them?" He nodded eagerly. "Blair, give the magnets to the Maestro." Blair made no move to obey. "Come on, Blair, hand them over," I commanded. But Blair had put the magnets back into his pocket. "Gee, Dad, I can't," he said. "It don't belong to me. It's my friend Sam's." I spoke more sternly to Blair, who kept doggedly denying his ownership and insisting that he could not possibly do as he was told. The Maestro followed this interchange keenly, his eyes veering from me to my son and back again as if his fate depended on the outcome. The situation grew painful. Blair was plainly determined not to give up the magnets. Concealing as best I could my chagrin at my son's behavior, I finally broke down Blair's resistance with hints of enough money to buy a dozen *magnetos*. The magnets were grudgingly handed over. The Maestro pocketed them with satisfaction and resumed his interrupted anecdote.

At the theater later that evening, Chotzinoff's account continues,

> . . . I saw that the Maestro was not paying attention to the stage. I whispered: "Is anything wrong?" and he whispered back: "The *magnetos*. I have lost them!" I told him not to worry, that he must have dropped them on the floor, and when the curtain came down we would look for them. Until the end of the play he sat, the picture of dejection, his right hand propping up his head, his eyes closed. When the curtain descended, we waited ten minutes for the theater to empty. We then got down on our hands and knees and searched for the *magnetos*. We called over the ushers and they searched the lobbies, but all to no avail. We left the theater and got into the Maestro's car. . . . When the car stopped at our house I suggested that he might have dropped the *magnetos* on our doorstep on the way to the theater. "You think?" the Maestro said, brightening, and he jumped nimbly out of the car and, along with the rest of us, began searching our stoop, illuminated by a street lamp. There the *magnetos* lay in full view. I picked them up and gave them to the Maestro, who hastily put them in his pocket and suddenly decided he was "thirty" (thirsty) and wanted to drink "some*thing*." . . . We went upstairs, where he drank some*thing*, talked for hours, to our delight, played the piano and sang large chunks of operas in his cracked voice. It was six in the morning before he left reluctantly. . . .

More than behaving like a spoiled child, Toscanini, in Chotzinoff's account, was indulged and manipulated like one. "I discovered early that music was the one subject that never failed to dissipate the Maestro's unsocial moods. A disingenuous question on my part like 'Do you consider *Falstaff* a masterpiece, Maestro?' would instantly dispel the blackest depression and set him off on a passionate exposition of the glories of that work." Chotzinoff also discovered that "the mention of something that was certain to rouse [Toscanini's] ire" was an "effective gambit." Some examples: "Maestro, last night I went to the Metropolitan"; "Maestro, why is it that I like *Cavalleria rusticana* so much?"; and "I see the critics are raving about the beautiful tone of the —— orchestra." The same ploys of flattery and deception defined Chotzinoff's professional duties at NBC. If Chotzinoff can be believed, he cajoled Toscanini into returning to America in 1937 by showing

him a magazine article in which canaries were said to have sung in Beethoven's Ninth as led by Toscanini over the radio, then "shrewdly" adding
that "when your music goes over the air . . . everyone who hears will know
the way the composer *meant* the music to be played, [and not] the dreadful
misrepresentations of second-class conductors." When, ten months later,
Toscanini withdrew upon learning that some network musicians would
lose their jobs, it was Chotzinoff who fibbed that not one man would be let
go. When, once ensconced at NBC, Toscanini would terminate a rehearsal
in a rage, Chotzinoff "would surreptitiously countermand his order to the
men and, by applying a psychological treatment that long experience had
perfected, would sometimes mollify him" with "violently diversionary
suggestions."

While Chotzinoff's heretical perception of a juvenile Toscanini partly
reflected the chemistry of their relationship, the press's prevalent "other
Toscanini" was, prima facie, at least as selective an impression. As one who
expected to be the center of attention, he could not possibly have been "the
most modest man who ever lived," or have remained "at a loss to understand the endless fuss that is made about him," or have rejected "special
privileges of any kind." At the same time, Toscanini was obviously no
cold-blooded martinet in the mold of certain Central European conductors.
The uncomplicated affection he inspired in Samuel Antek during the NBC
Symphony's transcontinental tour was felt by many others outside the
inner circle. Robert Shaw, who prepared choruses for Toscanini at NBC,
once took a group of Christmas carolers on a surprise visit to Riverdale.
Toscanini's response was as characteristic as were his tantrums on other
occasions.

> Maestro was in the television room looking at wrestling or something
> as he used to; and he came out, tears rolling down his cheeks. We must
> have sung ten or twelve carols; and when we finished, suddenly he went
> around shaking hands with everybody. Then a door was opened; and
> there was a table full of Italian cheeses and pastries and wines and
> champagne. And he went around and talked to everybody in the group
> —asked where they'd come from and so on—*each one*—which each of
> those forty people has cherished greatly, of course—so that we didn't
> leave until 3:30 or 4 in the morning.
> He was always incredibly sweet and kind and inspiring.

Chotzinoff may have found Toscanini a one-sided genius. Other men, with
other eyes, saw him differently. Alfred Wallenstein, the New York Philharmonic's principal cellist from 1929 to 1936, discovered that Toscanini knew
"the poetry of Shakespeare, Shelley, Keats and Byron; not alone that he

knew them, but that he could turn to the page of the book for the point he was making." In 1936 Ernest Newman, the dean of British music critics, met Toscanini and reported to his wife: "What a brain! What a fascinating man! . . . *There* is someone I can listen to and talk to with pleasure." In Milan in the 1920s, Mieczyslaw Horszowski, a musician of unusually broad culture, discovered that Toscanini "knew everything in Italian literature; he also knew and read English literature." And Ferruccio Busoni in 1911 called Toscanini "the most intelligent musician I have met up til now (with perhaps the exception of Strauss). Tremendously lively, quick, far-sighted, and artistic."[23]

What was Toscanini really like? The conflicting portraits partly reflected changes wrought by age—in 1947, Toscanini became an octogenarian—and reinforced by the shift from turbulent Italy to deferent America. Whisked between Riverdale and Radio City in a chauffeur-driven car, escorted and shielded by an elite coterie, Toscanini rarely strayed from a sanitized social corridor. Erich Leinsdorf, his devoted assistant in Salzburg, was not the only one who found that

> Chotzinoff, like several of the coterie I had met in Salzburg, made my own relations with Toscanini more distant within three years of my [1937] arrival in New York. The atmosphere of a court has never been one in which I breathed easily. As long as I had a firm working schedule with Maestro I was not part of his social life and did not come, but for fleeting instances backstage, face to face with the assortment of jesters, bodyguards, intellectual jugglers, and simple thurifers. . . . I had to lead my own life, which meant my exit from Toscanini's inner circle.

Fritz Busch, who in Europe had counted Toscanini a friend, also watched as "Toscanini, with increasing age, silently withdrew, except for a specially intimate circle, from those who did not force themselves upon him." David Walter, an NBC Symphony bassist from 1940, found Toscanini "more distant" in the later NBC years, during which "the entourage that made itself Toscanini's protector against the intrusion of the outside world included his orchestra among the intruders." Toscanini himself, in a 1943 letter responding to an invitation from Walter Damrosch to attend a reception, wrote: "Please, dear Damrosch, to excuse my growing restiveness to find myself amongst many and many people. More I grow old more I shrink into myself like a snail. . . . Why? I don't know—but I do. . . . Anyhow I am touched by your kindness and I send you my friendly greetings." Two years later, declining an invitation from Sarnoff to attend a party for the conductor Malcolm Sargent, he again wrote that old age had made him "shrink" like a "snail." Toscanini's sporadic correspondence during these years with Clare Conway, a middle-aged (b. 1900) secretary in Chotzinoff's NBC office, evokes a portrait of descending loneliness in old age. She would phone him at Riverdale late at night or early in the morning. His letters, mingling endearments ("A gleam of sun came in my soul when I heard your voice in the morning and received your special delivery just an hour ago with the sweet certainty to bring your thoughts . . .") and confessions ("I am *inheritor from my* mother of this sadness and unhappiness that weighted on me all my life and I doubt that my old age can dissipate that which was my true nature."), are all eagerness and gratitude.[24]

There can be little doubt that the lively Toscanini intellect enjoyed by Busoni, Horszowski, and Newman flourished prior to Toscanini's relocation to New York in 1939 at the age of seventy-two. Generally, Italian reminiscences of Toscanini at La Scala depict a better-spoken, more expansive, more reflective persona than do his American idolators and detractors. A 1924 article in *Il Pianoforte,* for instance, speaks of a "very well-balanced and harmonious intellect. . . . [Toscanini] does not love those who adulate him, nor those who present themselves to him prostrate or fully submissive. . . . He wants colleagues who are intelligent, who know how to argue with him. . . ." Filippo Sacchi, who knew Toscanini, stresses in his biography Toscanini's love of painting and his friendships with many Italian artists. But most of Toscanini's friends, according to Sacchi, were (in contradistinction to Chotzinoff and Sarnoff) not the well-known and successful but "the ordinary run of working musicians with whom he came into contact. . . . When he came back on visits to Italy from America . . . his first thoughts were always for his old companions." Even after World War II, in Sacchi's account, Toscanini in Italy enjoyed a vigorous social life, entertaining at home and attending the opera (which he never did in New York).[25]

As the Toscanini cult peaked in America after World War II, locating the "real Toscanini" behind the cult's sheltered, extravagantly feted icon grew increasingly complex—even, one suspects, for Toscanini himself. It also grew increasingly irrelevant—even to those whose interest in Toscanini was most intense. Far from dulling his presence in the public mind, Toscanini's growing seclusion had facilitated a portrait of the "other Toscanini" as deep and detailed as agglomerated layers of myth would permit. What alterations the portrait underwent were mainly independent of changes Toscanini himself experienced in old age; rather, after the fashion of other celebrity icons of mass renown, the manipulated image obeyed a dynamic of its own. The leveling surge toward Ewen's "American" Toscanini and the colloquialism of Earl Wilson's Toscanini "interview" was the principal current in this dynamic. A fledgling cross-current, conveying contradictory evidence amassed by Sargeant, O'Connell, and Chotzinoff, foreshadowed backlash.

. . .

In 1951 Toscanini suffered a minor stroke while pedaling an exercise bicycle. Though he recovered quickly, the gerontological miracle could not endure forever. By 1953, his eyes, his legs, and his memory were distinctly declining. A contract with NBC for the 1953–54 season was the last he was to sign. According to Chotzinoff in *Toscanini: An Intimate Portrait,* Toscanini "resigned" for reasons of age "almost every year of the 17 he spent at NBC," only to change his mind following "heartfelt emotional pleas" from Chotzinoff and others. The final such crisis, in Chotzinoff's account, began in early 1954, when Toscanini, his face "tearstained," claimed he could no longer remember the words to *Un ballo in maschera,* rehearsals for which were shortly to begin. At Toscanini's insistence, *Ballo* was canceled; his NBC career seemed over. Then, a day later, Toscanini telephoned Chotzinoff to say he could now remember the opera's words. The rehearsals took place, as did the two-part broadcast performance on January 17 and 24. Chotzinoff continues:

> But, notwithstanding this sudden remarkable resurgence of memory, it was clear to the Maestro's family and friends that the time had arrived for him to relinquish his broadcasts. In this the Maestro fully concurred, frowning on any suggestion that he return for another season. His son, Walter, at his father's request, prepared a letter of resignation addressed to Mr. Sarnoff and placed it on the Maestro's desk for his signature.

According to a story told to Alfred Wallenstein by Sarnoff, Chotzinoff and Sarnoff traveled to Riverdale in the fall of 1953 with Toscanini's 1954–55 contract in hand, only to be intercepted by Walter Toscanini, who told them his father could not undertake another season. According to a story originating with the conductor Guido Cantelli, Chotzinoff told Walter Toscanini that the NBC Symphony would be discontinued in the spring of 1954 and that his father might wish to resign for appearance's sake—a suggestion precipitating Toscanini oaths against Chotzinoff and other NBC *"animali."* According to George Marek, Sarnoff's commitment to television had by 1954 predisposed him to abandon Toscanini.

> He was too sensitive to public reaction to act drastically in a situation where he could be made to appear as a money-grubbing Philistine. He might secretly have wished for the end, but he wanted the decision to come from Toscanini, not from him. So Sarnoff pressed him for a decision, instead of waiting patiently as he had done in the past, when Toscanini had sent him those letters of resignation which turned out to

mean nothing. . . . I believe what happened was that Sarnoff kept asking "Where do we stand?," kept asking it fretfully, and that, responding to Sarnoff's obvious impatience, Toscanini finally gave him the not unexpected negative answer. Thereupon Sarnoff had a letter of resignation prepared for Toscanini to sign.

In any event, after a period of apparent prevarication, Toscanini put a shaky signature to a resignation letter dated March 25, 1954—his eighty-seventh birthday. It read:

March 25, 1954

My very dear David:

   At this season of the year seventeen years ago you sent me an invitation to become the Musical Director of an orchestra to be created especially for me for the purpose of broadcasting symphonic music throughout the United States.

   You will remember how reluctant I was to accept your invitation because I felt at that time that I was too old to start a new venture. However, you persuaded me and all of my doubts were dispelled as soon as I began rehearsing for the first broadcast of Christmas night in 1937 with the group of fine musicians whom you had chosen.

   Year after year it had been a joy for me to know that the music played by the NBC Symphony Orchestra has been acclaimed by the vast radio audiences all over the United States and abroad.

   And now the sad time has come when I must reluctantly lay aside my baton and say goodbye to my orchestra, and in leaving I want you to know that I shall carry with me rich memories of these years of music making and heartfelt gratitude to you and the National Broadcasting Company for having made them possible.

   I know that I can rely on you to express to everyone at the National Broadcasting Company who has worked with me all these years my cordial and sincere thanks.

Your friend,
Arturo Toscanini

Sarnoff's letter of reply read:

March 29, 1954

Dear Maestro,

   Your letter, significantly written on your Birthday, touched me deeply. I realize that after more than sixty-five years of absolute dedication to the art of music you have fully earned the right to lay down your baton. Yet I am saddened, along with millions of people in America, indeed all over the civilized world, at the thought that we shall no longer be privileged to look forward to your broadcasts and concerts which for so many years ennobled our lives. That you have made your decision at a time that finds you at the very height of your artistic powers only adds poignancy to our deprivation.

As you know, my own life has been chiefly devoted to the development of instruments of communication. But, however important these may be, they are at best only instrumentalities. Their function is only to transmit. In the final analysis they will be judged by *what* they transmit.

For the last seventeen years radio, television, and the phonograph have done their best to transmit with the utmost fidelity your self-effacing, incomparable re-creations of the great music of the past and present. And those of us who have striven to perfect these instruments feel in the highest degree rewarded for our labors. Happily, these instruments have recorded and preserved for us, and for posterity, the great music you have interpreted so faithfully and magnificently.

During these seventeen years of our intimate and happy association, I have learned from you much that is as vital in industry as it is in music. Your attitude towards your art and especially that human instrument—the orchestra—which realized your musical ideals, became an inspiration to me from the very first time I watched you at work. You proved so convincingly that in striving to attain perfection, the leader who seeks to obtain the maximum from those he leads, must demand the utmost not only from them but also from himself.

I know, dear Maestro, you will carry with you the love and gratitude of your many friends and the great multitude, unknown to you, whose lives you have enriched.

May God bless you and keep you.

> Your friend,
> David Sarnoff[26]

Both letters were distributed to critics attending Toscanini's concert of April 4, 1954, an all-Wagner program thereby identified—but only to the press—as his NBC farewell. As such, it proved as theatrical as his New York Philharmonic "flashbulb farewell" of eighteen seasons past. The final rehearsal, on April 3, was freighted with intimations. For one thing, Toscanini and NBC sanctioned an extraordinary number of guests—the parquet of Carnegie Hall was nearly full. For another, Toscanini began screaming during Dawn and Siegfried's Rhine Journey from *Götterdäm-*

merung, berating his timpanist over a supposed wrong entry. After the passage was repeated, he bitterly exclaimed *"L'ultima prova!"* ("The last rehearsal!") and left the hall. With the audience abuzz, a loudspeaker announcement was made—"This concludes the public portion of the rehearsal"—after which the rehearsal never resumed. The concert the next day was the strangest of Toscanini's career. Conducting the *Lohengrin* Prelude, Forest Murmurs from *Siegfried*, and the *Götterdämmerung* excerpts, he suffered seeming lapses of concentration and was uncharacteristically reliant on the podium railing for support. Then, during the *molto moderato* transition toward the sirens' chorus in the *Tannhäuser* Bacchanale, he ceased conducting. The orchestra momentarily came apart.[27] Guido Cantelli, in the control booth with Chotzinoff, insisted that the broadcast not continue. Technical difficulties were announced, and Wagner's Venusberg languor was shattered by the pounding opening of Brahms's First Symphony in Toscanini's recording. Half a minute later, Toscanini resumed conducting and the *Tannhäuser* broadcast was restored. Frank Miller, the orchestra's first cellist, had to remind Toscanini that the *Meistersinger* Prelude was yet to come. This he led wanly, descending the podium before the final, affirmative chords had ended. He dropped his baton. A musician picked it up and returned it to him. He received it indifferently and walked slowly off stage. He did not return to acknowledge the audience's applause.

The next morning, in addition to Olin Downes's usual review, the New York *Times* ran a front-page story by Howard Taubman announcing what many had suspected: TOSCANINI QUITS SYMPHONY, MAY CLOSE 68-YEAR CAREER. Both Toscanini's resignation and Sarnoff's reply were printed in full. Taubman also revealed that the former letter had sat on Toscanini's desk "almost a fortnight" before he resolved to sign it, that he had changed the April 4 program hours prior to the first rehearsal because he felt unsure of remembering the *Tristan* Prelude and *Liebestod*, that he had been in a "terrible state" the day of the concert, and that NBC had placed Erich Leinsdorf on notice that he might have to conduct in Toscanini's place. As Marek and some NBC musicians have speculated, news of Toscanini's resignation could only have contributed to the mishaps marring his final concert. According to Marek, Toscanini "undoubtedly" knew that some in the hall had been informed he would retire. Having authorized the "My very dear David" letter only nine days before, he conceivably experienced his last broadcast as a humiliating rite of departure. At dinner that night he said, "I conducted as if it had been a dream. It almost seemed to me that I wasn't there." At a postseason party for the orchestra in his own home, he was found upstairs, in tears, exclaiming, "My poor orchestra! My poor orchestra!" According to Marek, he vented his rage on Chotzinoff: "He would no longer see him or speak to him. The interruption of the broadcast had been his fault. Playing the Brahms had been his fault. Giving the news to the journalists was his fault. *Everything* was his fault. . . . It darkened Chotzinoff's life."[28]

In Marek's opinion, Toscanini's retirement "was handled with consummate stupidity" by NBC; the announcement could have been made *after* the final concert. But NBC's timing, if inconsiderate to Toscanini, maximized the drama of the moment. *Life* distilled its essence:

TOSCANINI CONDUCTS FAREWELL CONCERT

—EMOTION MAKES THE GREAT MAESTRO FALTER

Having in 1939 reduced Toscanini's personal life to a "great picture scoop" of "the Maestro having a wonderful time chasing Sonia around the lawn," and in 1948 encapsulated Toscanini's first televised concert as a hairsbreadth competition with "a Maestro who ate cough drops," *Life* now savored a soap opera finale: "Once or twice Toscanini drove the orchestra into furies of magnificent sound. Once or twice, like a lion rousing himself, he shook his head and roared the melody. But then the firm beat faltered, the infallible memory faded. Puzzled, he poked at his head *(right)*, clutched his forehead *(below)*. The musicians floundered. . . ." *Life*'s picture captions included:

"Toscanini, bewildered, forgets his place."

"His beat faltering under stress of emotion, great Maestro covers his eyes and tries to remember where he is in *Tannhäuser* score."

"Suddenly lost in his memories, Maestro stares off into space."

"Leaving the hall, Toscanini avoids the stage door exit to escape a demonstration, his head bowed as he ends already legendary 68-year career."[29]

The departure of Toscanini was not the arbitrary "cashiering" some have made it out to be—his powers were failing, and radio, weakened by television, was well on its way toward abandoning live studio music. It was NBC's tactless efficiency that made Toscanini's exit seem untimely and pathetic.

By 1954, it had been rumored for some years that the NBC Symphony would be retired upon Toscanini's retirement. As of Toscanini's April 4 farewell, NBC was formally offering to keep the orchestra intact, without Toscanini, if a commercial sponsor could be found. But the musicians understood that, in effect, their services were not desired past the forthcoming spring season. In May, an orchestra committee met with Chotzinoff in an effort to change NBC's mind. According to Jerome Toobin, who after-

ward became manager of what was left of the NBC Symphony, the meeting
was a "short, unfriendly" one.

> After they had given their exposition of why they felt the orchestra
> could survive even its great conductor, that it had for 17 years brought
> glory and honor to RCA . . . they concluded . . . on the note that the
> symphony's existence would be the most significant living tribute to
> Toscanini.
>   Chotzinoff listened and, when they were through, said, "Do you
> really want to honor Toscanini? Then die." A pause. "Your orchestra,
> I mean," he concluded, lamely.

After most of the musicians regrouped as the Symphony of the Air, Toobin
himself met with Chotzinoff to propose that NBC carry a concert in memory of Cantelli, widely regarded as Toscanini's heir apparent before perish-
ing in a 1956 airplane crash at the age of thirty-six. Toobin suggested a
memorial broadcast with the Symphony of the Air under several eminent
conductors.

> Chotzinoff sat stolidly before me, a stocky, neckless man who always
> wore a black suit and a black bow tie. I finished.
>   "Well," he said, apparently having heard nothing I had said, "what
> do you want from us?"
>   I repeated the request for a memorial concert, as well as I could in the
> frigid atmosphere.
>   "No," said Chotzinoff. "Next question."
>   I had none.

The Symphony of the Air also unsuccessfully contacted Toscanini, inviting him to lead it whenever he chose. Its first concert, on October 27, 1954,
was played without a conductor, the empty podium signifying "the inspirational memory of [Toscanini's] guiding hands." A checkered nine-year
history followed; the orchestra died penniless in 1963.[30]
    Meanwhile, Toscanini had silently returned to Milan, where his de-
cline continued. Just before leaving New York in early June, he had vigorously conducted two long recording sessions, touching up parts of his
Aida and *Ballo* broadcasts for RCA. But his future conducting plans, including a Milan *Falstaff*, came to nothing. He suffered a mild heart attack
and grew more ashamed of his extreme age. A 1955 return to New York,
where he collaborated on the editing of his recordings, was, in Sacchi's
view, "a sad one. He came back to America as a simple private citizen,

like a man in retirement." His intimates now observed Toscanini con-
tinually scrutinizing his own failing health, testing to see if he could still
hear the ticking of a clock, still distinguish its outline across the room. A
1956 visitor was told: "Do not call me Maestro. I am no longer Maestro."
The pall of Toscanini's withdrawal was broken only by his death, in
Riverdale, on January 16, 1957—an event commemorated, as *Newsweek*
remarked, "as if the head of a state had died." President Eisenhower's
condolence message read: "As man and as musician he gained the admiration of the world. He spoke in the universal language of music, and he
also spoke in the language of free men everywhere. The music he created
and the hatred of tyranny that was his are part of the legacy of our time."
Of the obituaries, *Newsweek*'s was on the mark in calling Toscanini "the
man in all the world most identified with music" and explaining, à la
Adorno:

> . . . More than any other single influence, he made classical music a
> part of popular American culture during his seventeen years with the
> NBC Symphony. His arguments, his legend, his sometimes faultless
> performances did for Verdi, Wagner and Beethoven what Broadway
> song pluggers do for the Hit Parade. All of this effect was incidental to
> his rigidly considered conductor's calling.

More typical was *Time*'s eulogy:

> No contemporary could match his subtlety of nuance—the exquisite
> tenderness, the sweetness, the purity; nor could anyone equal his passion
> and force. Somehow, when the score demanded it, he seemed to coax a
> bigger volume of sound from a given number of instruments; he could
> also reduce the same number to a greater degree of stillness. . . .
> . . . For the majority of musicians, music lovers and critics the world
> over, he came closer to realizing the music of Beethoven, Schubert,
> Wagner and Verdi than any conductor ever did. . . .

During the ghostly thirty-three-month hiatus between Toscanini's retirement and his death, visions of the "other Toscanini" had necessarily faded.
Rather than characterizing Toscanini as affable and gregarious, *Newsweek*
and *Time* drew from Chotzinoff's *Intimate Portrait; Newsweek* retold the
story of Blair Chotzinoff's magnets. The unsigned New York *Times* obituary, by comparison, was unreconstructed. The hand of Howard Taubman
—Olin Downes's successor as the *Times*'s chief music critic upon Downes's
death in 1955—seemed apparent in a paragraph reading:

When Toscanini conducted he was, in a sense, the whole show. This was not because he sought the limelight—all through his long career he did just the opposite—but because of universal respect for his judgment, experience, vast musical knowledge, uncompromising standards and the touch of incandescent brilliance he infused into every performance he conducted.

This hyperbole was matched by accompanying pronouncements accurately, if unwittingly, documenting the potency of the cult: that Toscanini was "the conductor of the [New York] Philharmonic from 1926 to 1936"; that "fear [that Toscanini's NBC appointment] would detract from the popularity and success of the Philharmonic . . . proved groundless"; that Toscanini could correct "any error made by the musicians even in a full orchestral tutti"; that "both as an operatic and symphonic conductor, he achieved a stature no other conductor before him had attained."[31]

Thousands thronged St. Patrick's Cathedral for Toscanini's funeral on January 19; Sarnoff and Taubman were among the pallbearers. His body was flown to his other, truer home for final rites broadcast into the mobbed Piazza della Scala. He was buried in the family tomb in Milan.

Postmortem

*T*oscanini had tolerated no rivals. At the Metropolitan Opera, the New York Philharmonic, and NBC, Gustav Mahler, Willem Mengelberg, Wilhelm Furtwängler, and Leopold Stokowski had challenged his authority and lost. Meanwhile, Toscanini had been tended and attended by Giulio Gatti-Casazza, Arthur Judson, and Samuel Chotzinoff. From these obstacles and supports, David Sarnoff stood apart. Unlike Gatti-Casazza and Judson, he did not administer at Toscanini's mercy. Unlike Otto Kahn and Clarence Mackay, he was no behind-the-scenes Maecenas. To Sarnoff, Toscanini was an honored receptacle for certain of Sarnoff's own communications dreams. The Toscanini token validated his publicized personal mission to see broadcasting become a supreme "cultural service" for "millions of homes." In contrast to Toscanini's previous employers, Sarnoff attended Toscanini from on high, autocrat to autocrat. Then, when certain Sarnoff dreams shifted so that Toscanini was no longer their fit receptacle, Sarnoff disposed of Toscanini. A proper Toscanini postmortem must consider, more than Toscanini's achievement, what Sarnoff achieved with his "Toscanini." To study the Toscanini-Sarnoff relationship is to study the relationship between Toscanini and the New World.

Sarnoff was self-taught, pragmatic, efficient, restlessly energetic, quickly decisive—the embodiment of the self-made man, "the incarnation of the American dream." According to his biographer Carl Dreher, who worked under him at NBC, he "rarely allowed himself an idle, unoccupied moment. For him, no cardplay, no golf, little escape of any kind." Dreher stressed Sarnoff's self-esteem, clarity of mind, power of concentration, relentless drive. A second Sarnoff biographer, his admiring cousin Eugene Lyons, portrayed an "overflowing vitality [manifest] in a genuine involvement in the problem at hand that transmutes a mere job into a challenge. Within [Sarnoff's] personal electromagnetic field, according to those who have felt its vibrations, the seemingly routine and humdrum somehow begins to glow with excitement. 'Part of it,' one of them said to me, 'is his will to win. Even in small things, D.S. starts by ruling out defeat.' " Elmer Engstrom, RCA's president from 1961 to 1965, once remarked that Sarnoff, while "not tolerant of poor performance," was "always interested in the views of others regardless of [their] station in life." Lyons described Sarnoff's aversion to the "pretentiousness" of a formal dinner with Lord Beaverbrook, at which each diner was attended by a butler. Sarnoff's own brand of autocracy was terse and plain, never baronial. According to Erik Barnouw, American broadcasting's central historian:

> Lesser executives . . . hesitated to phone [Sarnoff] about a problem. They addressed him in formal memoranda on which he might pencil brief answers—"Yes!" "No!" or "PSM," meaning "please see me." An appointment was a sort of audience. When angry, Sarnoff could show an icy reserve more frightening than an explosion of anger. The back of his neck would grow red. When he spoke, it was in well-constructed prose, without the slightest hesitation.

Charles O'Connell left this account of Sarnoff's role in the imbroglio over Toscanini's Philadelphia recordings:*

> Mr. Sarnoff is always an interesting person. His rather Oriental countenance can assume the inscrutable aspect of Buddha, the ingratiating smile of Billiken, or the hard-eyed, implacable severity of the great business executive. But he is really at his best when the Napoleonic afflatus is upon him, as it was on this occasion. . . . "D.S." strode furiously up and down the room, discharging vast clouds of cigar smoke along with commands, threats, exhortations, and injunctions upon all present. . . . Ostensibly this meeting was called to enable Mr. Sarnoff to find out why the Toscanini records had not been issued and who was at fault. As it turned out, the boss couldn't wait to hear anybody's explanation, but contented himself with a two-pronged Diktat imposed as of that moment on his quailing guests: first, *all Toscanini records, regardless of any commitment to any other artist or any consideration of the necessities imposed by announcement, advertising, distribution, and the like, must be put on the market within thirty days.* Second, if he could find out that any person in the organization was delaying the execution of this command—well, "that person wouldn't remain in the company for five minutes"; and if

---

*See page 275.

the guilty person turned out to be Arturo Toscanini, well, the maestro
would be fired likewise. . . .

. . . At this point I protested to Mr. Sarnoff that what he demanded
was a physical impossibility. Mr. Sarnoff wanted to know why and then,
with characteristic impatience, didn't wait to discover the reasons but
modified his demand and made it three months instead of thirty days.[1]

Sarnoff could not but identify with Toscanini the self-made man and
tyrannical democrat. From the first, as we have seen, Toscanini was hailed
in the American press for combining inspiration with practicality. "Common sense," "efficiency," and "objectivity" were among the cited Toscanini virtues. His Metropolitan Opera performances were praised for
seeming "scientific." A Chicago newspaper wrote: "He is the man who
knows his business." Toscanini was touted as a new breed of conductor
reflecting a newly rational age; Sarnoff was touted as a new commercial
breed—a practical idealist, a dreamer who yet "knew his business." A
tribute to Sarnoff by MIT's Jerome Wiesner paraphrased the terms in
which Toscanini's greatness was first framed: "The greatness of David
Sarnoff lies in his combination of a visionary and determined builder and
hard-headed industrial leader. He was among the first to recognize the role
that science could play in modern industry and to stake his future entirely
on its promise." In 1927 Sarnoff himself wrote: "The needs of the times will
bring forth perhaps a new type of executive, trained in a manner not always
associated with the requirements of business management. He will have to
reckon with the constant changes in industry that scientific research is
bringing." Max Smith had acclaimed Toscanini for his "neatness, order,
punctiliousness." Among Sarnoff's most publicized attributes was his uncluttered desk, symbolic of orderly thought. Sarnoff doubtless admired in
Toscanini his tenacity and authority, and the down-to-business work habits
that set him apart from the foggy German types Max Smith debunked. Of
Sarnoff's style of leadership Carl Dreher wrote, "We were always conscious
that we fell short of our full capability, as he did not. Thus, when we failed
him, we feared not only his contempt, but our own towards ourselves." Of
Toscanini's leadership style, Sarnoff wrote in his March 29, 1954 reply to
Toscanini's retirement letter: "I have learned from you much that is as vital
in industry as it is in music. . . . You prove so convincingly that in striving
to attain perfection, the leader who seeks to obtain the maximum from those
he leads, must demand the utmost not only from them but also from
himself." When Toscanini died, Sarnoff wrote: "He not only mastered in
every detail the music he was performing, but he also made himself the
master of the human forces he was directing. Orchestras played better for

him than they thought they could; vocalists sang for him as if possessed—
which indeed they were. Each rehearsal was to me a revelation of the
capacity of a dedicated artist to impose his vision and ideals on men and
women." Toscanini's successful tutelage of the NBC Symphony's problematic principal clarinetist was a favorite Sarnoff anecdote, illustrating
how a good executive strengthens the weakest link in a chain.[2] The metho-
dological affinities binding Toscanini and Sarnoff ran as deep as their rude,
subtle personalities. Ever reliant on his own bootstraps, Toscanini had
something like the fervent, New World naiveté bred of Sarnoff's self-
sufficiency. Much as Sarnoff's idealism stoked enough brash confidence to
simplify the job and get it done, the power of Toscanini's textual fidelity
creed lay in its innocence, which bypassed moderation and worldly doubt.
Neither was exactly a creator: Sarnoff took up other men's inventions;
Toscanini, other men's symphonies and operas. Both, in a sense, were
inspired technocrats—managers with a vision, and a genius for making the
team sweat to achieve it.

At the same time, something more than a flattering, inspiring mirror
image magnetized Toscanini in Sarnoff's eyes. As a self-made leader, Toscanini stood for qualities Sarnoff personified; as an entrenched culture
bearer, he stood for something Sarnoff lacked. Sarnoff's remoteness was not
untroubled. The center of attention in any group, genuinely liked by many
of his associates, he nonetheless had, as Dreher put it, "no talent for close
friendship." As an Army officer during World War II, he received the rank
of brigadier general; ever after, it was as "General Sarnoff" that he was
addressed and deferred to. Introverted, nongregarious, unversed in small
talk, he shunned the social milieu of his business acquaintances. With
scientists and engineers he tried, as he once said, "to share their dreams and
disappointments, and to rejoice in their triumphs"—yet he was not one of
them. It was partly as a frustrated aesthete that he felt isolated and incompletely fulfilled. As a boy, he had sung in a synagogue choir and frequented
the uppermost balconies of the Metropolitan Opera. As an adult, his swift
rise cut him off from the respect for learning and high culture he had early
imbibed. In Lyons's view, Sarnoff "felt more at home in a literary-theatrical
haunt like the old Cafe Royal on Second Avenue than in the opulent clubs
of exalted executives. His hunger for intellectual stimulus, for the education
he had missed, drew him to men and women with unusual minds, catholic
tastes, creative impulses." George Marek wrote:

> As with many men, [Sarnoff's] drive for achievement left a hollow in
> him, a blank page on which he did not know what to write but which
> he wanted to fill. . . . Sarnoff knew nothing about music but longed for
> it in a fogged search. . . . He sought the acquaintance of artists and was

on friendly terms with Josef Hofmann, Mischa Elman, Ania Dorfmann, Rosa Ponselle, Jascha Heifetz, John McCormack. To know them gave him greater satisfaction than to know business leaders. When Sarnoff entered a room, you knew that an important personality had entered. He was not in the least humble. . . . In the presence of artists, though, he became, if not self-effacing, unpresuming.[3]

Sarnoff's oft-declared devotion to a "radio art" that would "elevate civilization" while relieving the isolation of small towns and farms was one attempt to fill the "hollow" inside him. On the defensive, he conceded that broadcasting could not "hope to thrill the intellectually overfed." But at times his own dreams must also have seemed shortchanged by the surfeit of crooners, comics, and commercials. His listening tastes, according to Lyons, excluded "comedians, quizzes, westerns, jazz bands."[4] His contribution to radio programming, as he saw it, was to have NBC broadcast learned fare and "the greatest artists the world has to offer." In particular, he took credit for having Toscanini conduct on NBC. As significant, he reached out to Toscanini the man. Sarnoff looked upon Toscanini as a supreme musician, a clear-sighted leader, a self-reliant learner, a champion of democracy, an ally of embattled Jewry—and a friend. Toscanini did not address Sarnoff as "General"; he called him "David." The Sarnoffs and the Toscaninis dined together and exchanged gifts and birthday and New Year's greetings. The frequent assurances of affection and gratitude punctuating Toscanini's letters to Sarnoff transcended convention.

Beyond NBC's image, Toscanini enhanced Sarnoff's self-image. With his appetite for public recognition, Sarnoff neglected no opportunity to identify himself as the man who returned Toscanini to America, and also as a man after Toscanini's heart. His well-publicized reply to Toscanini's retirement letter, refulgent with his own sense of importance, chiefly strove to perpetuate the Sarnoff-Toscanini equation. According to Ben Grauer, with whom Sarnoff frequently conferred about the NBC Symphony broadcasts, Toscanini "was his baby, of course." Late in life, after Toscanini's death, Sarnoff called the Toscanini-NBC affiliation his "main object of pride." As his brash self-sufficiency, his drive for achievement, his material success, his "hollow" were not unique, it was a pride in which all America could share.[5]

Sarnoff's procurement of Toscanini, an inspired personal gesture, at the same time echoed timeworn practices of New World importers and consumers of Old World art. In one sense, Sarnoff resembled the interwar new middle classes writ large, satisfying cultural needs and aspirations more grandiose than any known to Babbitt and his friends. To a degree, he inherited the legacy of nineteenth-century ballyhoo entrepreneurs whose artistic smorgasbords were placarded "the best" and "the greatest." A third class of progenitors comprised Otto Kahn, the Astors, the Belmonts, and other turn-of-the-century millionaire benefactors for whom grand opera, studded with celebrity imports, was "the great vessel of social salvation"— a class also including the New York Philharmonic guarantors whose 1909 procurement of Gustav Mahler was intended to confer unprecedented prestige on New York's symphonic milieu.* Common to all these importers and consumers, as to Sarnoff, was an arm's-length perception of art as essentially externalized, foreign, and embalmed. "It made the creative life synonymous in their minds with finished things, things that repeat their message over and over and 'stay put,' " wrote Van Wyck Brooks in *Letters and Leadership* (1918), thinking chiefly of patrons and collectors of the Gilded Age. "It conventionalized for them the spiritual experience of humanity, pigeon-holing it, as it were, and leaving them fancy-free to live 'for practical purposes.' " It meant, as Lewis Mumford wrote in *The Golden Day* (1926), "over the seas and far away. Whitman was as remote as Dante."[6] The American Dream held out the hope that money could buy happiness and security. Babbitt bought what culture he could afford. Mrs. Jack Gardner and Henry Clay Frick bought Rembrandts. Sarnoff craved music; he bought Toscanini.

Some of NBC's principal stockholders questioned the purchase. Unlike such earlier Toscanini purchasers as Kahn and Mackay, Sarnoff put up corporate money, not his own. In fact, Sarnoff's general priorities were frequently challenged within the financial community. He was criticized for stressing research over sales, for slighting commercial prospects in favor of visionary "firsts"—national broadcasting, television, color television. George Washington Hill, president of the American Tobacco Company, and NBC's largest client, once told Sarnoff what he would do if he owned NBC stock: "I'd fire you for wasting money on symphony music in a mass medium." Lawrence Gilman called Sarnoff "that valiant idealist"—provoking Charles O'Connell to remark that he "might be tempted to enter a dissenting opinion of this point."[7] Was Sarnoff a bona fide cultural philanthropist? A commercialist first and foremost? A king-sized Babbitt? An entrepreneur in the grand tradition? He himself articulated a populist business philosophy: customers could be trusted to opt ultimately for the best. As he put it in his broadcast speech of March 5, 1938, announcing Toscanini's rehiring:

---

*Sarnoff was a member of the Metropolitan Opera's board of directors from 1934 to 1952.

The National Broadcasting Company is an American business organization. It has employees and it has stockholders. It serves their interests best
when it serves the public best. We believe in this principle and we
maintain it as our guiding policy. This is why we organized the NBC
Orchestra and invited the world's greatest conductor to direct it.

Ideally, one could learn something about Sarnoff's role by calculating
whether Toscanini rang up a profit for NBC. As we have seen, *Fortune* was
confident from the outset that Sarnoff's Toscanini investment made business sense—that even without commercial sponsorship, the broadcasts
would adequately reimburse the network in terms of enhanced radio, phonograph, record, and advertising sales. According to Lyons, Sarnoff also
believed that Toscanini "paid off." Marek, however, has argued that Toscanini was not a "commercial success" for NBC—that his radio audience
was relatively small;* that his prestige did not sell radios or phonographs;
that high Toscanini record sales must be understood in the context of high
production costs. But this is a fruitless debate, manipulating variables that
can never be quantified. One thing that can be said, notwithstanding
O'Connell's "dissenting opinion," is that Sarnoff's Toscanini project was
not untouched by "valiant idealism." It was part of his psychological
makeup—part of what motivated his crusading for global electronics as a
communications magnate, and, as a fervently anticommunist advisor to
Presidents, for more propaganda tools and guided missiles.** Halina Rod-

---

*Hooper and Nielsen radio ratings for the NBC Symphony, available only for those
seasons that were sponsored, ranged from 4 to 7, except in 1953–54, when a meager rating
of 2.1 presumably reflected the impact of television (the numbers show the percentage
of homes with radios which had the radios tuned to a given program, and do not
necessarily correspond to broadcasts conducted by Toscanini). A frame of reference is
suggested by the following 1943–44 figures: Bob Hope, 31.6; Abbott and Costello, 24.0;
"Voice of Firestone," 6.0; NBC Symphony, 5.4; Boston Symphony, 2.6.

**Sarnoff's Presidential service included two vital trips to Europe: in 1929, as a member of a
delegation instructed to renegotiate Germany's war debt; and in 1944, as the communications administrator in charge of preparing for press coverage of D-Day and subsequent
Allied advances. In the former capacity, matching wits with Germany's formidable
Hjalmar Schacht, Sarnoff arbitrated between New and Old World political and economic needs. In the latter capacity, he wound up liberating Radio France and preparing a
detailed plan for organizing radio and postal service in postwar Germany. In a shrewd
commentary, Jeremy Tunstall groups Sarnoff with other foreign-born media and movie
"tycoons" with "an interest in demonstrating their success and superiority in Europe.
The easiest way of paying off Europe for its earlier hard blows was for the tycoon to
demonstrate his business pre-eminence to the Europeans in their own turf." Like New
World democracy, New World business and technological acumen were proudly ex-
ported to the Old World, compensating for more tenuous cultural exports.[8]

zinski recalls a dinner conversation about the new NBC Symphony during which "Sarnoff was interested in changing the subject and leaving the table for his study where he could show us the latest electronic marvel: television."[9] In her view, Sarnoff had dollar signs on his mind. In turning from symphony to TV, however, Sarnoff was not turning from art to commerce, but following a single, enthralled train of thought. Once persuaded by Artur Rodzinski that Toscanini would never settle for mere enlargement of the existing studio band, Sarnoff moved boldly to secure the best available talent for the NBC Symphony. He pampered Toscanini. He did not skimp on rehearsals. He saw that the musicians toured in style. He achieved an unlikely accommodation by private industry of a radio orchestra such as governments supported in Europe. All this was the positive side of his ambitiousness. What tarnished and sometimes negated it were countless rudenesses of style and policy: the boastful chatter proclaiming high network purposes, the competitive merchandising and promotional schemes imposed even while lavishing money and loving attention on the Toscanini project.

Put another way, Sarnoff's idealism moved in fits and starts. His influential opposition to public, noncommercial broadcasting shifted the burden of responsibility for premium fare onto swashbuckling "practical idealists" like himself. Manfully self-reliant, he abjured soliciting someone else's integrated cultural purview to shape, refine, and amplify his intuitive vision of "radio art." Rather, he thrilled to the impact of moving in fast and pouncing decisively. His best instincts were noble yet lacked a sound intellectual base. Thinking himself audacious, he betrayed a consumer's susceptibility to brand names: Beethoven and Brahms, Damrosch and Toscanini. In boasting of radio appearances by "every known artist of quality," he revealed an artistic mentality more acquisitive than constructive. With characteristic aplomb, he initially envisioned hiring the seventy-year-old Toscanini not merely to head NBC's new orchestra but to oversee all its "serious music." Given Toscanini's arthritic, Eurocentric repertoire, he was an illogical, even impossible candidate. But Sarnoff's self-reliance, a form of hubris, made him an unreliable entrepreneur. As Virgil Thomson once remarked in the *Herald Tribune*, "The indiscriminate propagation of culture (from whatever noble motives) can operate easily, if not inevitably, toward the destruction of that culture."[10]

A scathing summation of the fate of symphonic music on American commercial radio was delivered in 1951 by the conductor Howard Barlow, whose broadcasting experience was singularly extensive: at CBS, where he first worked for Arthur Judson, he was in charge of the CBS Symphony from 1927 to 1943; afterward, he conducted "The Voice of Firestone" and "Harvest of Stars" for NBC. In Barlow's opinion, the networks were basically indifferent to program content: "Their ideal was to have all their time sold, so that there was no sustaining [i.e., noncommercial] time at all." Only under pressure from the FCC and the public was programming improved, Barlow contended. Studio-based concerts were an attractive sop because "they were the cheapest programs to put on with the talent already hired and the [unsalable] time to fill." The continuing success of soap operas and variety shows nevertheless carried the day: CBS disbanded its studio symphony orchestra; NBC, Barlow predicted, would do the same when Toscanini died or retired. While Barlow's cynicism obscured Sarnoff's sporadic idealism, he captured the spirit of Sarnoff's ad hoc star-corrals in complaining: "The policy of the broadcasting companies, I believe, was catch as catch can, an opportunist policy. I don't believe that they had any definite plan, because their policy changed so often."[11] Transplanted to the air, the concert hall milieu was buffeted, and finally sundered, by changeable corporate brainstorms and trade winds. The case of Toscanini traces the transformation. His sixty-eight-year career was progressively flanked by radio and recordings, music appreciation and organized audiences, press releases and mass-circulation magazines. By the time he joined NBC in 1937, this sheathing shaped more than was shaped by its musical core. Studio 8H, *Life, The Good Housekeeping Guide to Musical Enjoyment,* Earl Wilson, Primo Carnera, David Ewen's *Music for the Millions,* Radio City, "Small Fry," Bob Hope, *Reader's Digest,* Sun Valley, *The RCA Book of the Symphony,* Samuel Chotzinoff, the world's biggest drum, Reynolds Metals— these were the elements articulating the meaning of Toscanini. He had reorganized La Scala to make opera the aesthetic hallmark of contemporary Italy. At the Metropolitan Opera, too, he had superintended every detail of production. At Salzburg, with premium casts and the Vienna Philharmonic in the pit, he had fashioned a defiant yet exquisite cultural leave-taking. Even at the New York Philharmonic, where the music salesman Arthur Judson presided when Toscanini was away, the spreading panoply of commercialism did not yet smother the orchestra, the audience, and the music. To these earlier episodes of the Toscanini career, his NBC employment formed a peculiar coda. Once the nerve center of a nation's performing arts, Toscanini became an appendage to corporate cultural hegemony.

Summing up "Toscanini," adoring Americans saw a different scenario. Olin Downes, in a Sunday New York *Times* column a week following Toscanini's farewell, called "the termination of Toscanini's engagement with the NBC Symphony" the "summit of his career, if not the sum of his achievement." Toscanini obituaries three years later traced the curve of his career as a steady ascent to NBC stardom. Looking back, George Marek called Toscanini's NBC tenure "the most fruitful period of his life." Sarnoff, in a 1963 radio tribute, said: "I have been told by music experts and by music lovers that the Toscanini years at NBC . . . constituted the high water mark of musical performance in America, probably in the whole world." Four years later, in a hundredth anniversary tribute, Sarnoff wrote: "Many people regard the years 1937 through 1954, when the NBC Symphony Orchestra performed under the direction of Arturo Toscanini, as the golden age of the symphony orchestra in America. We had succeeded, finally, in inducing Maestro Toscanini to return to this country for what became the most productive period of his distinguished career." Notwithstanding Sarnoff's vaunted "sense of history," his Toscanini appraisals were typically shortsighted. Lacking, in Barlow's words, "any definite plan" for fostering cultural enlightenment, Sarnoff saw Toscanini as an extension of himself. His sense of history, characteristically American, overlooked the past; it encompassed neither Toscanini's history nor America's own. Though he was correct to sense that Toscanini's NBC tenure represented a historical benchmark, it was chiefly "most productive" in an ironic sense: in marking the genesis of the radio concert hall as a species of megaconcert burying music, it instilled a model that would come to dominate music making in all its venues.[12]

A further frame of reference, joining the latest chapter in our narrative with the first, juxtaposes Sarnoff with the most grandiose musical entrepreneur of a century before: P. T. Barnum. Like Sarnoff in pursuit of Toscanini, Barnum in pursuit of Jenny Lind instructed a European emissary to make an irresistible offer. Like Sarnoff, Barnum reasoned that, since aesthetes sneered at his merchandise, he could afford to lose money "in such an enterprise as bringing to this country . . . the greatest musical wonder in the world." Bypassing Toscanini's musical qualifications, Sarnoff's network endorsed marketing the "other Toscanini." Barnum, who had never heard Jenny Lind sing, set to marketing as the "divine Jenny" a paragon of wholesomeness and philanthropy. When Jenny herself lapsed into irritability and shrewd self-aggrandizement, Barnum conspired to "keep her angel face to the public." As Toscanini's success enhanced Sarnoff's image, so did Jenny's success enhance Barnum's. For Sarnoff, Toscanini endorsed obsolescent 45-rpm discs; for Barnum, Jenny reviewed the ostriches and monkeys of the Great Asiatic Caravan.

And yet the two phenomena were as different as their different American centuries. Barnum's outlandish portrait of "divine Jenny" was drawn nearly tongue-in-cheek; he no more believed that her "every thought and deed is philanthropy" than that Joice Heth, "George Washington's 161-year-old nurse," was "the most astonishing and interesting curiosity of the world." He worked his guile knowingly, whimsically, disseminating with equal gusto favorable notices he had commissioned and hostile gibes increasing his notoriety. He exclaimed: "The bigger the humbug, the more people like it." His autobiography is the very acme of self-promotion without piety.

Beside Barnum's easy panache, paralleling contemporary robber-baron escapades, Sarnoff's ardor seems careworn, decadent. His electronics empire, a precinct of post-Barnum American world mastery, conferred entrepreneurial resources greater than Barnum's, but also a worrying sense of responsibility amplified by needling self-doubt. Barnum's Jenny Lind crusade was blithe. Sarnoff's Toscanini crusade was didactic, sanctimonious, meliorist. Its earnestness combined disturbingly with Sarnoff's arrogance and parochialism. Both Barnum and Sarnoff were self-made, self-reliant managers. Unlike Barnum, Sarnoff allotted himself an educational role his qualifications did not support. While the "other Toscanini" was no less outlandish than the "divine Jenny," it was propagated with insidious religiosity. Barnum's audiences knew they were being humbugged; Sarnoff's did not.

Sarnoff's Toscanini combined the electric charisma of Barnum's Jenny Lind with the dour moral striving of Theodore Thomas. Propositioned by Barnum, Thomas spurned contracting with the devil. Toscanini's pact with Sarnoff foretold times to come when the devilish glamour of television and recordings would ensnare even the most reclusive, high-minded artists.

In the nineteenth century Paganini and Liszt, Jenny Lind and Anton Rubinstein registered galvanizing impressions in person; the resulting portraits were at least superficially apt. In an age of prying mass media, galvanizing impressions could be made to register even when their ostensible source was absent, withdrawn, or irrelevant. Unlike the ballyhoo promoters, whose overt machinations alienated a Theodore Thomas, the new electronics could and would promote anyone. In fact, unlike Thomas, Toscanini lacked the prerogative to ward off promotional advances. Emanating from a broadcast studio, with its synthetic audience and announcer-intermediaries, his stranded image was infinitely manipulable. The nineteenth century could never have produced a popular musical icon at once as respectable and extravagant, as pious and profane as Toscanini.

Four final, failed attempts to bring Wilhelm Furtwängler to America form an essential postscript to the story of Toscanini's American career.[13] After being forced to withdraw as Toscanini's successor with the New York Philharmonic—the 1936 decision *Time* had reduced to "Nazi Stays Home"—and then breaking with Toscanini in Salzburg the following year, Furtwängler found himself increasingly stranded in Hitler's Germany. To some, his insistence on staying put and standing guard for Bach, Beethoven, and Wagner seemed a stoic alternative to emigration; his staunch defender Yehudi Menuhin has likened Furtwängler's chosen wartime fate to "a kind of living suicide."[14] To most people outside Germany, however, his decision to continue conducting there seemed at best naive. The Nazis used Furtwängler but distrusted him; in January 1945, he had to flee to Switzerland to avoid arrest by the Gestapo. Confused American resistance delayed his full "de-Nazification" until April 27, 1947—three weeks following his first postwar concerts, in Italy. His subsequent activities eventually totaled more than six hundred performances in Argentina, Austria, Denmark, Egypt, Finland, France, Germany, Great Britain, Holland, Italy, Sweden, Switzerland, and Venezuela.

An American overture reached Furtwängler on August 10, 1948: the Chicago Symphony wanted him to be its music director. He was interested but could not spare twenty-two weeks per season. Remembering his 1936 New York debacle, he also expressed concern over renewed "calumnies and difficulties of a political nature." The Chicago trustees assured him that times had changed and that Chicago was not New York. In December, Furtwängler agreed to an eight-week commitment to Chicago the following season. A protest campaign materialized, spearheaded by threatened Chicago Symphony boycotts by Vladimir Horowitz, Eugene Ormandy, and Arthur Rubinstein, among others. As in 1936, there were unconfirmed reports of Toscanini's participation or endorsement. Furtwängler was again forced to withdraw from an American appointment.*

In 1951, Rudolf Bing sounded out Furtwängler about opening the Metropolitan Opera's 1952–53 season. He was interested, but Bing soon determined that, based on information he had gathered "from really important persons in public life," it was still too soon for Furtwängler's return to New York. In 1953, plans for an American tour by the Vienna Philharmonic temporarily foundered when the orchestra insisted that Furtwängler lead it. Meanwhile, an American tour by Furtwängler and the Berlin Philharmonic was arranged. With both tours pending, Furtwängler died on No-

---

*In a case with interesting parallels to Furtwängler's troubles in New York and Chicago, the actress Vanessa Redgrave sued the Boston Symphony for $1 million in 1984 after the orchestra canceled her scheduled appearances in Stravinsky's *Oedipus Rex*. The orchestra claimed its decision was forced by protests and threats from Redgrave's political opponents, who objected to her outspoken support of the Palestine Liberation Organization. A jury decided that Redgrave's civil rights had not been violated, but awarded her $100,000 in compensation for career damage. When she appealed the verdict, a federal district judge overruled the jury, deciding that the orchestra owed her only $27,500 for breach of contract.

vember 30, 1954—seven months following Toscanini's farewell concert with the NBC Symphony.

Though American opposition to Furtwängler was understandably exacerbated by the war, his war with Toscanini had long revealed deeper causes. In American eyes, Toscanini personified pragmatism, efficiency, and other self-made virtues. With the full extent of his "American" identity now before us, the full extent of the Furtwänglerian antithesis can be gauged. Gangly, vacillating, self-doubting, visionary, privately educated, Furtwängler more than violated American ideals. Like Mahler before him, he precisely evoked a negative stereotype of the "genius" or "intellectual": neurotic, imprudent, impractical, awkward, arrogant. Examining the "Philosophical Method of the Americans," Tocqueville had remarked: "As it is on their own testimony that they are accustomed to rely, they like to discern the object which engages their attention with extreme clearness; they therefore strip off as much as possible all that covers it . . . in order to view it more closely and in the broad light of day." This strain of the American mind—which gave rise to William James's pragmatism and to the instrumentalism of John Dewey, with its antipathy to contemplative modes—was poles apart from Furtwängler's misty idealism. Among performing musicians, he symbolized what perplexed and intimidated Americans about the Old World. "You can't make out here what people do know," Henry James's Strether says of Europe—a remark that resonates throughout *The Ambassadors*. "[Americans] fall to denying what they cannot comprehend," wrote Tocqueville.[15]

In the United States, Furtwängler was commonly labeled an "intellectual" in contradistinction to earthier or more flamboyant performing types. But he was less an intellectual than a musical mystic. In a revealingly indistinct, mistrustful reference, Chotzinoff's *Toscanini: An Intimate Portrait* has Furtwängler "hover" near Toscanini backstage at Bayreuth, then "vanish like a ghost." Other Toscanini partisans identified Furtwängler's "intellectualism" with pretentious double-talk. Haggin, unable to make Furtwängler out, denying what he could not comprehend, dismissed Furtwängler's "cloudy thinking and imprecise language." In Toscanini lore, the break with Furtwängler at Salzburg in 1937 became a morality lesson in which a little guy's crisp rebukes put a lumbering intellectual in his place. This, for instance, was Taubman's version, in *The Maestro*:

> One day Furtwängler walked into Toscanini's dressing room. As the maestro recalled the meeting years later, he smiled at the way the German, though he towered over him, seemed to be afraid of him.
>
> Toscanini glared at Furtwängler and said, "I don't want to see you."
> "Why?"

"Because you're a Nazi."

"It is not true," Furtwängler protested.

"Yes, you are," Toscanini insisted, "whether you have a party card or not. In London you lunch with Jews to make a good case for yourself so that you won't lose your position in the West. In Germany, you work for Hitler."

Toscanini turned his back on the tall man, who slowly walked away.*

As far as Taubman was concerned, Furtwängler exemplified an unpalatable credo: never mix in politics; live only for art. In *The Maestro*, he grouped Furtwängler with "Karajan, and others who had worked for Hitler and the Nazis"—yet, unlike Furtwängler, Karajan joined the Nazi party, remaining a member at least eleven years. Reporting in the New York *Times* on Furtwängler's withdrawal from Chicago ("Musicians' Ban on Furtwängler Ends His Chicago Contract for '49"—a virtual press release for the boycotters), Taubman misrepresented Furtwängler's de-Nazification as certifying him "not legally guilty" yet "morally culpable." Five years later, in a stern obituary, the *Times* again misrepresented the de-Nazification proceedings. These inaccuracies were standard. David Ewen, among others, wrote that Furtwängler was a "Nazi." Whatever Toscanini's role, his adherents ensured Furtwängler's postwar vilification in the United States.[16]

Hindsight suggests that had Furtwängler lived to lead the trans-Atlantic tours of the Berlin Philharmonic (1955) and Vienna Philharmonic (1956), Americans might have been ready enough to welcome and appreciate him. Though Taubman's reportage created an impression of overwhelming popular antipathy toward Furtwängler's Chicago appointment, letters to the orchestra and comments in the local press were by no means mainly condemnatory; in the opinion of Edward Ryerson, the orchestra's presiding trustee, Furtwängler's "general public relationship" was more improved than injured by the episode.[17] By the mid-1950s, with Hitler ten years dead, much more had changed. Ironically, the very communications revolution that had facilitated the Toscanini cult now facilitated Furtwängler's New World recognition. Airplanes, radio, and recordings were unifying the world concert circuit. Americans' ambivalence toward Old World culture receded, and so did their need for Toscanini. But this puts us ahead of our story.

---

*For "Furtwängler's version" of his last conversation with Toscanini, see Curt Riess's *Wilhelm Furtwängler* (1953).

III · Toscanini on Records

P. T. Barnum said of Jenny Lind: "She was a woman who would have been adored if she had had the voice of a crow." In fact, Jenny's pure, polished soprano more than enhanced her saintly public image. Toscanini's public imagery was as impressive as Jenny's had been: he embodied Art and America both. But to appreciate all his New World celebrity, one must, as with Jenny Lind, finally appreciate the musical accompaniment. Beyond his unquestioned extramusical attributes, Toscanini was an unquestionably great conductor.

If Jenny is remembered as Barnum's prize catch, it is partly because her singing died with her, while the gaudy anecdotage of her celebrity lived after. Toscanini, however, left thousands of hours of recordings. Obviously, these do not re-create the actual sounds of Toscanini in performance. But supplemented by the accounts of those who heard Toscanini "live," they reveal a great deal. The sheer quantity of documentation is daunting. For its archives, NBC recorded all of Toscanini's NBC Symphony broadcasts (as distinct from his many NBC Symphony recording sessions). Toscanini's non-NBC phonographic catalogue includes the fourteen selections he recorded with the touring Scala orchestra in 1920 and 1921, as well as numerous recordings with the New York Philharmonic and BBC Symphony made between 1926 and 1939. In addition to the NBC broadcasts, his vast nonstudio legacy, available on American and foreign labels of varying pedigree, includes three complete Salzburg Festival operas, the 1952 Brahms cycle with London's Philharmonia Orchestra, and much else.

Incongruously, most of Toscanini's studio recordings were made during the last decade of his career. These scorching readings provide a familiar yet lopsided perspective on Toscanini's art. A truer reference point is the pre-NBC decade, when Toscanini's international standing was at its peak and his inevitable physical decline was still far in the future. As none of his Scala and Bayreuth stage performances survive on disc, the Austrian radio's three complete Salzburg recordings are doubly valuable: they document Toscanini's historic collaborations with the Vienna Philharmonic, and they document Toscanini in the opera pit, where his career began and was grounded.

Of Toscanini's Salzburg repertoire, *Falstaff* was, in his assistant Erich Leinsdorf's view, his single favorite work—the opera he performed in a greater number of productions or seasons than any other, beginning one year after the 1893 premiere. In New York in 1909, his first Metropolitan Opera *Falstaff* was deemed "an artistic achievement unparalleled." In Vienna in 1929, the twenty-one-year-old Herbert von Karajan heard Toscanini lead his Scala forces in *Falstaff* and later wrote: "From the first bar it was as if I had been struck a blow. I was completely disconcerted by the perfection which had been achieved." At the first Salzburg *Falstaff* on July 29, 1935, Felix Weingartner, then director of the Vienna State Opera, reportedly leaped into the pit after the first act and exclaimed to the orchestra: "Children, such a performance I have never experienced or dreamed of." Leinsdorf characterized the same performance as one of "unmatchable perfection." George Szell remembered Toscanini's Salzburg *Falstaff* as "perhaps the most unforgettable of all the memorable Toscanini performances I know." This was also the Toscanini *Falstaff* about which Herbert Peyser wrote in the New York *Times:* "astounding . . . from start to finish utterly phenomenal."[1] The Austrian radio recording was made in 1937, when the Salzburg *Falstaff* was two years old and the cast had changed somewhat. Like Toscanini's other complete Salzburg recordings, it was taken down on 8-millimeter acetate tape with a machine called the Selenophone. Compared with contemporary studio norms, the reproduction suffers from distortion, compressed dynamics, and skewed balances. And yet, fifty years later, Toscanini's Salzburg *Falstaff* still sounds "perfect."

This adjective was used by Karajan, Weingartner, Leinsdorf, and countless others for a reason. Of all post-Mozart operas, *Falstaff* seems correct in every detail, without blemish or defect. Its jewellike precision asks for jewellike execution. From the explosive punch and champagne effervescence of the initial orchestral "sneeze," Toscanini's jewellike 1937 performance, with a superb cast anchored by Mariano Stabile, is vividly expressive, breathtakingly secure, instantly "right." The famous transition from Ford's monologue to Falstaff's final Act II, scene 1 entrance, in which a descending horn scale is the bumpy staircase joining Ford's pompous elevation to an Alphonse-and-Gaston exit, shows the range and resourcefulness of Toscanini's perfectionism. The comic contrasts are played for all they are worth—and no more. Weighted, accented melodic strokes following Ford's peroration dissipate to pointed staccatos and feathery trills. Most exquisite of all are the three beats preceding Falstaff's "Eccomi qua," in the course of which the violins' unaccented, sustained attack on the initial piano quarter-note powers the merest flick of a witty portamento from G to D.

As typical as the smart rhythms, razor accents, and pithy ornaments of Toscanini's interpretation is an ineffable, gliding legato reflecting his mastery of the precise contours of sustained tones; the music of Fenton and Nannetta, and of the fairies' sylvan idyll, has never sounded more rapturous. Even in the opera's madcap first scene, Falstaff's sporadic romantic outbursts ("O amor! Sguardo di stella!" etc.) gain unexpected credibility from the ravishing accompaniment. In terms of overall structure, whole scenes are purringly paced and propelled. In terms of overall sonority, the performance's tonal purity and crisp ensemble must have proved diaphanous; critics plausibly reported that "not even a syllable of dialogue is lost." Wilfrid Mellers, commenting on Verdi's "objectification of experience" in *Falstaff*, observes that "although most of the music moves rapidly, the opera seems suspended in time." The serene precision of the Toscanini *Falstaff*, its rarefied coordination and seamless sheathing, are ultimately transfiguring.[2]

If Toscanini was the conductor who most established ideal norms for *Falstaff* in performance, his Salzburg readings of *Die Meistersinger* and *The Magic Flute* reveal attributes not of Wagner or Mozart, but of Toscanini. In the case of *Die Meistersinger*, his interpretation reflected long experience with the score. Of Wagner's operas, it was the one he conducted most often and which seemed to satisfy him most.[3] In 1898, a year before hearing Hans Richter conduct it in Bayreuth, Toscanini opened his first Scala season with *Die Meistersinger*. At the Metropolitan Opera, where an Italian Wagnerian at first seemed exotic, his 1910 *Meistersinger* was acclaimed for its traditional and nontraditional virtues. As preserved on the Selenophone, Toscanini's Salzburg *Meistersinger* matches his Salzburg *Falstaff* in lucidity, precision, animation, and conviction. The fresh, transparent orchestral textures again combine surface detail with surface polish. Toscanini's coursing, lyric legato makes the Mastersingers' Act I entrance mellifluous as well as properly stately. As at the Metropolitan in 1910, the Act II *Johannisnacht* music "exhales exquisite poetry." But the chief "Toscanini shock" comes in the music of Beckmesser and of the apprentices: no other conductor so tellingly projects the darting scherzando staccatos, trills, and grace notes animating David's Act I narrative, or the chattering, giggling woodwinds propelling Beckmesser's frantic Act III, scene 1 pantomime. This application of Italian buffo percolation (Toscanini told the Vienna Philharmonic to think of *Meistersinger* "*come una commedia, non una tragedia* ")[4] illuminates aspects of Wagnerian mischief rarely savored by German Wagnerians.

More centrist *Meistersinger* interpretations, on the other hand, offer aspects of Wagner that Toscanini omits. If, notwithstanding its Italianate lightness and wit, Toscanini's *Meistersinger* is slow enough, it is never at leisure, as Hans Knappertsbusch's is. To a significant degree, the high gloss and forward pressure of the Toscanini *Meistersinger* discourage varied portraiture and earthy warmth (at the Metropolitan, it was said to need "more of the stolidly and ponderously muscular"). More crucial, there is no sensation of "inner space"—of the particular *Innigkeit* James Huneker missed in Toscanini's *Tristan* when he compared it to the "elemental groundswell which Anton Seidl summoned from the vasty deep."* Wagner himself spoke of *Tristan* emanating from "the inner depths of soul events" and "the inmost center of the world."[5] For Wagner the conductor, "deep" subjectivity translated into "deep" structure: the underlying ebb and flow of long-term harmonic rhythms; the combination of single measures into long-breathed phrases. These sustained phrase structures and vertical tensions are what generate the pronounced inflections—the tempo changes and rubatos—Wagner prescribed in *On Conducting* and other writings. In slow-moving music reliance on harmonic stress as a long-range organizing tool dictates extra time; Wagner's model adagio, elucidated in *On Conducting*, "cannot be too slow." In his 1937 *Meistersinger*, Toscanini does not rush the slower episodes, and Wagner's ritardandos and rallentandos are given full value. Toscanini's inflections, however, chiefly articulate the music's surface. The accents are dynamic, rarely agogic (that is, rhythmic). The tempo changes test the pull or slackness of the melodic line, not the deeper writhings of harmonic undertow. Virgil Thomson, in a November 1, 1943 *Herald Tribune* review, complained of Toscanini that "he marks the meter so clearly that every downbeat takes on a slight stress . . . a tiny, tiny dry accent, like the click of a well running machine." I do not hear clicking downbeats in Toscanini's *Falstaff*, but stretches of his *Meistersinger* sound uncomfortably metronomic. Also pertinent is Leinsdorf's comment that in *Falstaff*, Toscanini "felt as if he had an authentic mandate, as if the great composer had charged him with supervising his most minute nuances and all his intentions. Toscanini had known Verdi, and there was an extra

---

*For the cited New York reviews, see pages 58–59.

dimension of personal involvement that was not as obvious in his labors for other composers."[6]

While *Die Meistersinger*'s sunniness minimizes Wagner's "inner space" requirements, Sachs's "Flieder" and "Wahn" monologues fail in Toscanini's performance, and the Prelude to Act III, with its foretaste of the dark "Wahn" refrain, is less stirring than it can be. In the latter, Toscanini accelerates toward the climax of the "Wach' auf" chorale theme's reprise —a surprising reading reflecting his vocal/melodic orientation; he insists on compassing each long phrase within a human breath span. In Knappertsbusch's two recordings of the prelude (Berlin Philharmonic, 1928; Vienna Philharmonic, 1950) he gradually distends the chorale's reprise and so brings to bear a long-term agogic stress on the piece's proper crest: the ensuing fortissimo, *sehr breit* (very broad) return of the "Wahn" theme. In the two monologues, Toscanini skirts the "action": Sachs's puzzlement (in the first case over Walther's song, in the second over the *Johannisnacht* riot), interior quest (Can a cobbler know poetry? Can men surmount "foolish anger"?), and resolution (that Walther's song is true and good, that madness can abet "nobler work"). Part of the reason is Hans Hermann Nissen, a major vocalist but a simplified Sachs. Of more than passing interest, however, is that Nissen was Toscanini's choice for the part after he rejected the scheduled Friedrich Schorr. Schorr was past his vocal prime in 1936, when Toscanini sent him packing. But Schorr's classic recordings of the *Meistersinger* monologues (1929–30) suggest other grounds for Toscanini trouble: a more individual, less malleable singer than Nissen, he punctuates Sachs's cogitation in a manner Toscanini might have prohibited. At the very outset of the second monologue, for instance, Schorr pauses between the first phrase ("Wahn! Wahn! Überall Wahn!") and the second ("Wohin ich forschend blick' . . .")—the instantly intelligible effect of which is to establish two layers of pensive discourse, the first exclamatory, the second narrative.

Toscanini, typically, permits no rhythmic leeway here. Wagner's *"streng in Zeitmass"* ("strongly in tempo") plausibly refers to the passage beginning on the second beat; in any event, Schorr's emotionally fluid reading sounds no less rhythmically stable than Nissen's. Equally telling are the differences between Toscanini's version of the Act II Sachs-Eva duet, with Nissen and Maria Reining, and the classic Schorr–Göta Ljungberg recording. In the latter version, Lawrance Collingwood's subtle tempo modifications accommodate the singers; in the former, the singers must accommodate Toscanini. The exchange in question, in contrast to the succinct, forthright dialogue Toscanini pilots in *Falstaff* (and also to the decisive discourse of Toscanini the man), is layered with innuendo, double meanings, and confused intentions. Conducting Schorr and Ljungberg, Collingwood creates fluid inner space in which Sachs and Eva can seemingly plot and feel as well as speak. Under Toscanini, the instrumental mold attains greater beauty and precision, but, as in Sachs's monologues, the mold's preordained firmness is limiting.

The Magic Flute, the third of Toscanini's 1937 Salzburg operas recorded on the Selenophone, was a work he had not often conducted, written by a composer with whom he was never entirely comfortable. No less than the Toscanini *Falstaff* and *Meistersinger,* the Toscanini *Magic Flute* percolates with buffo diction: clipped phrase endings, spikey accents, prickly staccatos. German conductors, he believed, made this opera too serious, heavy, and slow. At a November 5, 1947 rehearsal of the overture, he cajoled the NBC Symphony: "*Allegri!* With smile! SMILE! . . ." But the scurrying NBC performance sounds driven, charmless. At Salzburg, Toscanini's distance from mainstream Germanic norms proved revelatory in parts of *Die Meistersinger;* his *Magic Flute,* however, sounds merely perverse: Mozart rendered as Rossini. Even the adoring Salzburg audience received it with mixed feelings.

Alexander Kipnis, Toscanini's superb Sarastro, recalled in later years that he and other cast members, fearing a fiasco, appealed to Herbert Graf, the production's stage director, to speak to Toscanini. Graf replied: "It is more possible to move the mountain behind the Festspielhaus than to change Toscanini's mind. If you want to sing this performance, and if you want us to *have* a performance, sing the way he conducts. If you want to change him, the best thing would be to quit."[7] On the 1937 Selenophone recording, the singers' discomfort is audible in nearly every number. Kipnis himself is forced to breathe awkwardly in "O Isis und Osiris" (e.g., "Nehmt sie ' in euren Wohnsitz ' auf"); here, and in the "Isis und Osiris" chorus, Toscanini's rendering of Mozart's "adagio" is astonishingly slow. Most of the other Toscanini tempos, from larghetto to presto, are unusually fast and rigid. In the allegro moderato fioritura of "Zum Leiden bin ich auserkoren," Julie Osváth, Toscanini's Queen of the Night, is momentarily abandoned; only when the orchestra begins collapsing does he consent to slow down and let her catch up. Elsewhere, the relentless accompaniments furnish an obtrusive grid; in Pamina's "Ach, ich fühl's," the orchestra's patterned chords are like iron bars. Tamino suffers most from the prevailing genre confusion, for his story of personal maturing needs inner space in which to grow. "Dies Bildnis" is no moonstruck canzonetta; like Sachs's monologues, this exercise in dawning self-knowledge propounds an internal, puzzlement-to-resolution scenario. Singers attuned to its varied discourse convey the literally quickening pulse of "O wenn ich sie nur finden könnte!" and the measured resolve of "und ewig wäre sie dann mein." No wonder Helge Roswaenge's rendition, under Toscanini's inexorable baton, creates little interest.

The 1937 Selenophone recording of Toscanini's remaining Salzburg opera, *Fidelio,* is unrecoverable. There is, however, a shortwave broadcast of Act I through Leonore's aria. Though the sound is execrable, it is obvious that this was a performance of thrilling urgency. As in *Die Meistersinger* and *The Magic Flute,* Toscanini sounds determined to jettison excess weight: his interpretation is fleet, lithe, direct. As in *Falstaff* and *Die Meistersinger,* the playing and singing are unusually precise and committed. Every number tells. The arias of Rocco (Anton Pavmann) and Pizarro (Alfred Jerger) are singularly clean and mobile. In Lotte Lehmann's ardent "Abscheulicher!", which erupts without a moment's pause after the Pizarro-Rocco duet, "Komm, Hoffnung" is prayerfully poised, "Ich folg' dem innern Triebe" feverishly exciting. The pure lines and tensile strength of Toscanini's *Fidelio* remind us that in this work, revised and compressed following its premiere, Beethoven aspired to a concision akin to Verdi's in *Falstaff.* Lehmann's Leonore, like Stabile's Falstaff, proves that Toscanini's iron authority could tolerate strong, distinctive stage personalities—although it remains relevant that Falstaff and Leonore, unlike Florestan and Sachs, are not disposed to tragic introspection.

Given the many tributes to Toscanini's "textual fidelity," a few additional thoughts regarding the "authenticity" of his Salzburg performances are in order. Habitually, Toscanini at Salzburg avoids conspicuous pulse modifications not indicated by the composer. His freest Salzburg interpretation in this respect, however, is also the one in which he least draws attention to himself: *Falstaff.* Though he sticks closely to Verdi's metronome markings, his tempos are notably plastic. The passage examined earlier following Ford's monologue, for instance, is marked by Verdi "molto più lento, $\rfloor = 8o$," beginning with the last eight measures Ford sings ("Laudata sempre sia . . . "). Toscanini's molto più lento is initially slower than Verdi's, and he makes it slower still as Ford moves toward his grand E flat major cadence on "la gelosia." The ensuing orchestral peroration is eighty to the quarter on the button, as is the horn bridge until Toscanini retards again, this time for the pianissimo E flat major cadence accompanying Falstaff's entrance. The farcical Falstaff-Ford exit music, with its gossamer trills and portamentos, is faster than Verdi's eighty to the quarter.* In *Die Meistersinger,* by comparison, Toscanini is less prone to slow down at harmonic and structural junctures where no ritardando is explicitly sanctioned. The opera's "traditional" allargandos, as at the close of the overture, are also minimized or eliminated. (Toscanini's interpolated accelerando in the "Wach' auf" chorale is atypical.) The tempos, while often somewhat faster or slower than the norm, plausibly interpret Wagner's German instructions (there are no metronome marks) except for the Dance of the Apprentices, which is too fast for a "mässiges Walzer-Zeitmass" ("moderate waltz tempo"). In *The Magic Flute,* Toscanini's understanding of "adagio," "andante," and other speed signals could not be correct unless Mozart's singers were markedly more long-breathed and agile than those of today. In *Fidelio,* as in *Die Meistersinger,* certain conventions are overthrown in the interest of simplicity or fidelity. Thus, the first-act finale (not included on the broadcast) was, according to Kipnis, taken allegretto vivace and alla breve, as marked, rather than at the usual slower tempo. In Leonore's aria, on the other hand, Toscanini allows Lehmann a big retard before "Ich folg' dem innern Triebe." And, notoriously, he has transposed "Komm, Hoffnung" from E major to E flat to help her high notes. As the recitative still begins as written, a new modulation becomes necessary. Leinsdorf later commented: "There were plenty of raised eyebrows over such interference with Beethoven. . . . While the whole enterprise was open to legitimate criticism, I found it a document for Toscanini's approach to a complex masterwork. . . . He was a pragmatist and not a stickler for the printed dot on the i. And it showed that he went to great lengths to accommodate an artist whom he admired and appreciated."[9]

Toscanini himself endorsed the axiom "Blessed are the arts which do not require interpreters" and applied it angrily to the work of such subjectivists as Stokowski. In a 1929 interview he remarked: "Conductors today generally compete to distinguish themselves from each other, so that one can refer to X's 'Pastoral' and Y's *Eroica,* forgetting that Beethoven is the only creator."[10] While these sentiments truly describe Toscanini's interpretive predilections, they must be understood in the context of his time. Scholarly inquiry into historic performance practice was virtually nonexistent. Like other conductors of his generation, Toscanini not only ignored repeats and added dynamics; he also rescored. In Beethoven, especially, he was prone

---

*According to the conductor Gianandrea Gavazzeni, Toscanini himself remarked that "if Verdi approved of the first performances [of *Falstaff*], he could not have accepted his [Toscanini's], if he had been familiar with them. This was on account of the differences which Toscanini noted between his own and those he had heard with the composer present."[8] On the other hand, Arrigo Boito, *Falstaff*'s librettist and an estimable composer in his own right, always praised Toscanini's *Falstaff* performances.

to revise wind and timpani parts. Early in his career, he reportedly went so far as to eliminate the bass drum and cymbals from the alla marcia section of the Ninth Symphony's finale.[11] The majority of his instrumental changes, while perfectly audible, were less conspicuous, their clear intent being not to "improve" the music, but to "make the score sound."*

Between 1926 and 1939—a period encompassing his four years at Salzburg —Toscanini recorded in the studio with the BBC Symphony and the New York Philharmonic. The BBC recordings, mainly of Beethoven, superbly illuminate a bucolic, almost Mediterranean dimension of the First, Fourth, and Sixth symphonies and *Leonore* Overture No. 1. In the *Leonore,* the terse phrasings and turns of the introduction, and the coda's breathlessly accelerating energy, actually suggest Rossini. A striking feature of the "Pastoral" is Toscanini's resistance to rhetorical dalliance: in the coda to the first movement, and during the bird calls closing the "Scene at the Brook," traditional retards and allargandos are serenely rejected, and the solo flute's bridge to the finale is taken strictly in tempo. A particular tour de force is the trio section of the First Symphony's Menuetto, in which the BBC's speeding first violins combine tensile strength with feathery lightness.

With the New York Philharmonic, Toscanini recorded Beethoven's Seventh, the Brahms "Haydn" Variations, Dukas's *The Sorcerer's Apprentice,* the Dance of the Blessed Spirits from Gluck's *Orfeo,* Haydn's "Clock" Symphony, the Scherzo from Mendelssohn's *A Midsummer Night's Dream,* Mozart's "Haffner" Symphony, Rossini's overtures to *Semiramide, L'italiana in Algeri,* and *The Barber of Seville,* Verdi's two *Traviata* preludes, and, by Wagner, the preludes to *Lohengrin* Acts I and III, the *Siegfried Idyll,* and Dawn and Siegfried's Rhine Journey from *Götterdämmerung.* Whereas EMI's BBC/Beethoven recordings have been readily available on LP since 1967, the Philharmonic recordings, a Victor product, were long ago withdrawn in favor of "newer and better" NBC Symphony versions; in recent years, RCA has occasionally reissued the Beethoven Seventh. And yet these are among Toscanini's finest commercial discs— better played, more beautifully recorded, and more persuasively interpreted than the NBC remakes.

Toscanini's Philharmonic was the orchestra in which Bruno Jaenicke, the first horn, and Alfred Wallenstein, the leader of the cellos, regularly rehearsed their sections separately; in which "a continuous psychology of

---

*A short list of such changes, in works by Beethoven, Schumann, Smetana, Ravel, and Tchaikovsky, may be found in Howard Shanet's *Philharmonic* (1975), pp. 261–263.

crisis" motivated the musicians to sweat bullets in rehearsal and study their parts at home. Winthrop Sargeant called it a "hypnotized creature" reflecting Toscanini's "single will." Of its sensational 1930 tour, George Szell, who heard it in Prague, later wrote:

> The clarity of texture; the precision of ensemble; the rightness of balances; the virtuosity of every section, every solo-player of the orchestra —then at its peak—in the service of an interpretative concept of evident, self-effacing integrity, enforced with irresistible will power and unflagging ardor, set new, undreamed-of standards literally overnight.[12]

All this is documented in the state-of-the-art recordings Charles O'Connell produced for RCA. The bloom of the Philharmonic's violins, the realistically recessed winds, the plushly reverberant cello and bass pizzicatos evoke no antiseptic or artificial studio ambience but rather the warm, natural acoustics of Carnegie Hall. What is intermittently inferrable on the Salzburg and BBC recordings is here made gloriously evident: that, beyond maintaining peak standards of discipline, Toscanini secured a luminous tonal sheen yet neither pampered nor manicured the tone; that he obtained precise, transparent textures yet cultivated the richness and warmth of individual strands; that his wispy pianissimos retained color and his roof-rattling fortissimos never shouted; and that—to cite a final paradox, given his aversion to personalized expression—the whole was pervaded by a distinctive, galvanizing electricity.

As in the Salzburg Selenophones, it is in Verdi that Toscanini reveals an "extra dimension of personal involvement" reflecting complete absorption in the idiom. His rapt, minutely detailed New York Philharmonic performances of the two *Traviata* preludes renounce the occasional click track of his Wagner. Toscanini's "vocalizing" of "Wach' auf" proves limiting in *Die Meistersinger;* in *La traviata,* the vocally conceived inflections and phrase groupings are spellbinding. Smoothly diminishing from forte to piano, the intervening short notes as rounded and polished as the strong-beat quarters and halves, Toscanini's cellos *exhale* the Act I Prelude's big tune ("Amami, Alfredo"); their singing is so articulate one can almost hear each pregnant, preparatory intake of breath. Verdi asks that the hushed beginning of the Act III Prelude be played "estremamente piano." Toscanini's rendition, poised "on the breath," trembles with tenderness. His distension of the prelude's crest heaps maximum weight upon the straining line. Even in extremis, the honesty of his reading is self-evident; this is the most incisive, least sentimental Verdi imaginable.

As exquisite is Toscanini's coursing, becalmed *Siegfried Idyll.* This interpretation is not altogether idiomatic—there is no evidence of an "authentic mandate" to interpolate "minute nuances," as in Verdi. It is true that Wagner's melodies do not call for inflamed descriptive detail, as Verdi's do. But, no less than the *Traviata* preludes describe Violetta, the *Siegfried Idyll* describes the Wagner household at Triebschen. We know from Wagner's *Brown Book*, for instance, that the *sehr einfach* oboe tune at measure 91 is a nursery ditty to the words "Schlaf, Kindchen, schlafe," with the accompanying strings impersonating sheep.[13]

In Leo Blech's 1922 recording with the Berlin Philharmonic, the *Siegfried Idyll* evokes Wagner's other Siegfried—his only son, born six months before the music was first presented to Cosima as a Christmas-morning birthday surprise. Blech's playful treatment of the nursery tune, and his drooping string portamentos, variously connoting coy fun and dreamy lassitude, contribute to a portrait of innocence in which are narrated the mother's lullaby, and the infant's drowsiness and slumber. Toscanini, typically, "cleans up" the idiomatic portamentos, and the *Kinder* elements are subdued and abstracted. Compared with the lovable Blech performance, his is more streamlined, less human. But its lyric sheathing is hypnotic. Wagner's nursery images are not erased but made serene and evanescent. The entire family portrait, in fact, is elevated intact to a binding lyric jet stream. Like his Salzburg *Meistersinger*, Toscanini's rarefied *Siegfried Idyll* is not Wagner as the composer would have conducted it; unlike his *Meistersinger*, it constitutes a thorough alternative.

The most ambitious of Toscanini's New York Philharmonic recordings is his Beethoven Seventh, originally on ten 78 sides. Like the Salzburg *Falstaff*, it is a central document of Toscanini in his prime. Of Verdi's operas, *Falstaff*, with its orchestral and ensemble finesse, is especially tailored to Toscanini's operatic skills; of Beethoven's symphonies, the Seventh furnishes an equally irresistible Toscanini vehicle: more than extroverted, its dance energy is physical. Beethoven's tight, tireless motor rhythms showcase orchestral stamina. Toscanini's Philharmonic spews out the dotted figures in flawless streams, modulating from pianissimo to fortissimo with amazing consistency. In such Dionysian stretches as the first movement coda, the sheer agility of the big machine, combining the cruel power of a tank with the fleetness of a race car, is uncanny. In the finale, the knife-edge fortissimos and whipping sforzandos are every time the same. Though, like any conductor, Toscanini modifies his tempos throughout, the changes are so subtle that an illusion of relentless regularity is maintained. As in the BBC "Pastoral," he minimizes or eliminates customary acceleration and deceleration points. The tempos themselves are in two cases unusually brisk. This is because, more than any other prominent conductor of his generation, Toscanini took at face value Beethoven's metronome markings (set down when Beethoven was very hard of hearing, they have long been viewed with skepticism). He really makes the second movement an allegretto with the quarter-note equal to seventy-six beats. And the trio to the scherzo, following Beethoven's eighty-four beats to the dotted half, moves fully one-third faster than the "normal" speed.

To hop aboard Toscanini's Beethoven express discourages criticism; just hanging on is hard work. And yet the performance is undeniably plain. The separate identities of the movements, and of sections within each movement, blur together. The energy is so effortless, so controlled, that Beethoven's abandon seems itself abandoned. Reviews of Toscanini's early New York performances sometimes complained that his Beethoven and Wagner were insufficiently "weighty" or "rugged." The problem was not one of impetus or sheer volume. Rather, his readings sounded streamlined—and with results less satisfying than in the *Siegfried Idyll*. Crucially, as in *Die Meistersinger*, Toscanini's suspect simplicity is internal. As Virgil Thomson put it: Toscanini's Beethoven Seventh is deficient in "any sense of mystery to make the Beethoven fury seem interiorly dramatic rather than merely of the stage."[14] The chords with which the symphony begins are a case in point: Furtwängler, with his notoriously "indecisive" downbeats, makes them well up from a depth, not descend from a height like guillotine chops. Later in the movement, by eschewing an overt allargando just before the recapitulation, Toscanini ensures forward continuity, but forfeits articulating the cumulative strain of the development's harmonic migrations.

To appreciate fully the once forbidding celebrity of this particular Toscanini document, it must be re-experienced in the context of its period.

The familiar image of the podium mastermind is of surprisingly recent vintage. Its origins are bound up in the history of symphonic music itself: as performing forces grew larger, and their individual parts more complex, a new type of leadership was born. The composers responsible for making orchestras harder to coordinate were of necessity themselves the new leaders. Bach, Haydn, Mozart, Beethoven all more or less presided over performances of their own music, but they were not omnipotent "conductors" in the modern sense. Until the mid–nineteenth century and later, orchestras were riddled with indifferent, insolent, or incompetent players; merely synchronizing the notes was the leader's main function. But exceptions emerged: Mendelssohn in Leipzig, Weber in Dresden, Ludwig Spohr in Cassel, François Antoine Habeneck in Paris—all but Habeneck prominent composers—maintained high ensemble standards. A little later, Berlioz brought new charisma to the podium. A turning point, to which I have already alluded, was the example of Wagner, who as polemicist and conductor embodied not just charismatic authority but a new degree of subjective involvement. His *On Conducting* (1869) impugned the "elegant" Mendelssohn and other "time beaters" for mistakenly idealizing their own discreet aesthetic as "Beethovenian Classicism." In Wagner's opinion, Beethoven's symphonies demanded conductors of greater "energy, self-confidence, and personal power," committed to introducing expressive tempo modifications in conjunction with modifications of tone, articulation, and phrasing—that is to say, to a style of interpretation appropriate to his own music dramas. Wagner's podium heirs included Hans von Bülow, Hans Richter, Hermann Levi, Anton Seidl, and, at a further remove, Arthur Nikisch—all but Bülow noncomposers. Beginning in 1895, when the hypnotic Nikisch took charge of the Leipzig Gewandhaus and Berlin Philharmonic orchestras, he was the most glamorous, most lionized podium personality of his day. At the same time, just as Wagner had inevitably been taken to task in some quarters for inserting "distorting" and "exaggerated" nuances, conservative critics such as Boston's Philip Hale found Nikisch's virtuosic approach "overstressed" and insufficiently simple.*

Around the turn of the century, a backlash consolidated around a second tract titled, after Wagner's, *On Conducting.* Its author, Felix Weingartner, defended Wagner for combating "philistinisms that suffocated every modification of tempo" but attacked Wagner's "tempo rubato" progeny. Bülow, in particular, had in Weingartner's view carried Wagner's interventionist principles to a point of caricature, more conducive to serving his "mania for notoriety" than to realizing the composer's text. Weingartner's own, self-effacing ideals combined prudence and practicality; his *On the Performance of Beethoven's Symphonies* (1907), for instance, suggests numerous rescorings to make Beethoven's orchestra "sound," but these are less drastic than Wagner's in "The Rendering of Beethoven's Ninth Symphony" (1873). Compared with such latter-day "Wagnerians" as Furtwängler, Weingartner altered tempos and dynamics with the greatest tact. Upon revising *On Conducting* in 1913—eighteen years after its first appearance—Weingartner gloomily pronounced: "Today the door is open to fantastic caprices . . . to arbitrariness coupled with complete lack of imagination." After World War I, however, consensus opinion, parodied by David Ewen

---

*See page 42.

in *Dictators of the Baton,* * increasingly buttressed Weingartner's revision-ism. George Szell, born in 1897, was one of many young Central European conductors who took the position that "the style of performance usually described by the cliché 'Romantic' had degenerated to mannerism and excess. Historically, this style was . . . handed down to my generation through Hans von Bülow, Richard Strauss, Mahler, Nikisch and Furtwäng-ler. Different as these great personalities were, they had one common characteristic: they interpreted the composer *subjectively* to the point of arbitrariness (and/or distortion)."[15] Among pianists, Artur Schnabel was a pioneering objectivist, preaching strict adherence to the text. An austere, intellectual embodiment of the flight from Romanticism was an interwar aesthetic preferring sober practicality and self-discipline to passionate per-sonal entanglement: Weimar Germany's *Neue Sachlichkeit* (usually trans-lated as "new objectivity"). In music, one representative *Neue Sachlichkeit* composer was Paul Hindemith. The representative conductor was Otto Klemperer, whose performances of Hindemith, Weill, and Stravinsky helped mold his angular, no-nonsense approach to Beethoven.

In Italy, meanwhile, conducting had an even later start. Through the 1860s, it remained common in Italian houses for operas to be led by the first violinist, whose score included vocal parts and orchestral cues. Orchestral standards were famously lax. Mendelssohn, writing home from Rome in 1831, reported:

> The orchestras are worse than anyone can believe. . . . The few violinists play according to their individual tastes, and make their entrances as and when they please; the wind instruments are tuned either too high or too low, and they execute flourishes like those we are accustomed to hear in farm-yards . . . everyone seems so indifferent about it that there is not the slightest prospect [of improvement].

Berlioz wrote from Rome around the same time:

> . . . The orchestras are formidable and imposing in the manner of the Monégasque army, possessing every single quality which is normally considered a defect. At the Valle Theatre the cellos number precisely one, a goldsmith by trade. . . . In Rome the word "symphony" is used, like the word "overture," to designate a certain kind of noise which theatre orchestras produce before the rise of the curtain, and to which no one pays any attention. The names of Weber and Beethoven are

---

*See page 221.

virtually unknown. A learned priest of the Sistine Chapel told Mendelssohn that he had heard mention of "a young man of great promise called Mozart." . . . Instrumental music is a closed book to the Romans. What we call a symphony means nothing to them.

Some forty years later, a written evaluation of the Scala orchestra by Maestro Eugenio Terziana included such comments as "poco disciplinato," "indisciplinato," and "senza attenzione."[16] And instrumental music remained a relatively closed book in Italy. What began opening this book, and making orchestras pay attention, was—as in Germany and Austria—the new music; the impact of Beethoven's symphonies on performance practice in Leipzig and Berlin anticipated the impact of Verdi's operas, with ever meatier orchestral parts, in Rome and Milan. The conductors Franco Faccio, Angelo Mariani, and Alberto Mazzucato, all associated with Verdi, imposed instrumental discipline. In *Otello* and *Falstaff*, Verdi prodded his conductors a step further, raising his orchestra to nearly Wagnerian prominence and virtually eliminating his singers' ornamental prerogatives. This period of late Verdi was the period of early Toscanini: he played second cello in the Scala orchestra when Verdi helped prepare the 1887 premiere of *Otello* and first led that opera six years later; we have already seen how his performances of *Falstaff*, beginning in 1894, earned Boito's approval. Further elevating Toscanini's conception of conductorial authority was his early advocacy of Wagner and of the German symphonic repertoire: he led the first productions by Italian companies of *Götterdämmerung* in 1895 and *Siegfried* in 1899; he made his symphonic debut in 1896.

While by no means "early" (he was already fifty-three and had been conducting for thirty-four years), Toscanini's first recordings, the 1920–21 Victor acoustics with the Scala orchestra, document his impact on Italian music making and clarify his own later evolution. Notwithstanding the cramped quarters in which they were made and Toscanini's dissatisfaction with what he heard on the playbacks, these dim-sounding disks are informative. The hand-picked orchestra, containing Italy's finest instrumentalists, specializes in swift, light-fingered passage work; if a legacy of "Monégasque" bedlam and "senza attenzione" sloth is apparent, it is in passages of mechanical finesse suggesting excess drill. The curt articulation and virtuosic precision of the playing surely contributed to the tonal "translucence" admired in American reviews of the 1920–21 Toscanini tour.* If Toscanini's brisk tempos and forward pressure are at times discomfiting, the studio ordeal of replaying the same short pieces many

*See pages 86–88.

times over could not have been relaxing. Interpretively, Toscanini betrays certain "traditional" predilections: the strings slide more than on his subsequent recordings, and there are rubatos in Berlioz's Rakóczy March and in the Aragonaise from *Carmen* that he would reject fifteen years later. On the whole, however, the Victor acoustics underscore a new Italian regime drastically and permanently overthrowing bel canto norms of individual prerogative and flexible pulse. Three symphonic excerpts—the minuet and finale of Mozart's Symphony No. 39, the first movement of Beethoven's First, and the finale of Beethoven's Fifth—are even more streamlined than Toscanini's Mozart and Beethoven recordings to come. Though the "precious" refinements and "novel effects of tempo" American critics complained about in 1920–21 are not in evidence, Richard Aldrich's derogatory adjectives for the Toscanini-Scala Brahms Second— "small" and "shortbreathed"—fairly describe the two Mozart movements. In the minuet, Toscanini's abbreviated phrase endings at the double bars actually sound callow, and the finale's metronomic click track reduces its sonata-form architecture to the patter of a buffo stretto. In the finale to Beethoven's Fifth, the cutting forte-pianos and supercharged vigor are impressive Toscanini trademarks. But the click-track reprise of the transition from the scherzo lacks mystery. In the coda, the tutti chords are so clipped and hurried that their mass is reduced; in fact, the culminating C minor downbeat, rather than bearing the usual agogic stress, is rushed. On records, Toscanini's 1920–21 Beethoven Fifth does not sound precious or hyperrefined, as some American critics reported, but it does substantiate their complaints of insufficient "weight," "ruggedness," "stolidity," and "muscle" in Toscanini's German readings. Arthur Nikisch's famous 1913 recording of Beethoven's Fifth clarifies the significance of Toscanini's heterodoxy. Conducting the Berlin Philharmonic, Nikisch relishes all of the finale's "traditional" rubatos and tempo changes, and others besides. Where Toscanini's phrasings are terse, Nikisch's are elongated. Where Toscanini's massed chords are staccato, Nikisch's are "rolled." His violins slide more than Toscanini's do. Looking back to Wagner's practice, and forward to Furtwängler's, Nikisch slows down the development to savor its vicissitudes and then accelerates in a manner calculated to retain the added developmental weight. The Berlin players are more vividly spontaneous, the Italians more exactly coordinated. Heard today, Nikisch's performance sounds old-fashioned, Toscanini's oversimplified. But in the context of Weimar culture—of extirpated subjectivity, waning conductor-composers, and proliferating conducting specialists—the Toscanini Beethoven Fifth made a different impression: it sounded "modern." The Russian-American composer Lazare Saminsky, in a revealing 1932 commentary, contrasted Toscanini with "the Romantic and coloristic school" of Nikisch, Furtwängler, and Willem Mengelberg, claiming:

> In purely tonal taste [Toscanini] is entirely a musician of our day, just as much so as a Hindemith, Milhaud or a Poulenc. His very aversion to adorning music, for inflating it with meaning, with extra-musical content, for emotionalizing what is but pure line and form, is the aversion of today's musician. He is bewitched by the very flesh of music, by its sonority and rhythmic flux; their plan and balance entrance him. In this he is a true neo-classic musician, both Hellenic and modern.[17]

Curiously, the conjunction of Italian and German revisionism in Toscanini's Beethoven was partly fortuitous. The locally influential objectivity of Weingartner and Klemperer rebuffed specifically German abuses and was aesthetically based. Klemperer, in particular, espoused aesthetic reform; as the head of Berlin's Kroll Opera from 1927 to 1931, he began his regime by staging *Fidelio* against a stark geometrical set. But Toscanini, who once threatened to desert Salzburg unless Falstaff was shown drying himself in the sun outside the Garter Inn, as Verdi prescribed, rather than in bed under a pile of blankets, was less concerned with espousing new aesthetics than with disciplining errant Italian musicians.* If he presided over radical change, the reasons were not philosophical but temperamental and circumstantial: unlike Weingartner, with his less demonstrative musical temperament, or Klemperer, whose *Neue Sachlichkeit* was at war with his Mahlerian intensity, Toscanini the Beethoven conductor embodied Wagnerian "energy, self-confidence and personal power," yet was an outsider. He did not so much discard tradition as disdain ever acquiring it. The Toscanini/New York Philharmonic recording of Beethoven's Seventh Symphony reflected a self-sufficient literalism unknown north of Italy. In Germany and Austria, where his visits of 1929 and 1930 were revelatory, his interpretation was not admired in every detail—neither Klemperer, who in other repertoire found Toscanini "the ideal representative of objectivity,"[19] nor Weingartner accepted Toscanini's quick tempo for the third-movement trio. His quick second-movement tempo, however, was eventually widely endorsed. And the directness of Toscanini's nonrubato reading, like its shocking ensemble clarity and precision, had a purifying impact; the symphony seemed a dusty facade scorched clean. If Toscanini's Beethoven

---

*Writing to Kurt Weill, Hans Curjel, Klemperer's *Dramaturg* at the Kroll, described Toscanini's Scala productions on tour in 1929 as "musically [wonderful] beyond description, scenically ridiculous."[18]

was not assimilated to the degree his *Falstaff* was, it proved as influential as backlash and corrective.

Toscanini's accidental obeisance to *Neue Sachlichkeit* is not the only ironic take on his Beethoven purification. By spurning tradition and returning to "the source," he may have made most contemporary "tempo rubato" performances sound sloppy, sluggish, and sentimental; but he did not necessarily return to Beethoven's notion of how his symphonies should sound. No composer's instructions fully disclose his intentions. Webern's scores seemingly attempt to notate every performance nuance. Verdi's are less explicit, yet abound in tempo and dynamic changes, articulation marks, and verbal cues to style and temperament. If the scores of Beethoven are less detailed, it is partly because, in a period when composers and performers were still one and the same, many performance conventions were taken for granted. Notwithstanding Toscanini's occasional rescorings, and his singular "Abscheulicher" transposition, his practice, especially in non-Italian music, was to scrutinize the text and use what was there. To what degree was Beethoven's sound ideal notated? The evidence, while murky, does not support Toscanini. "Classical" playing was discovered by discreet Romantics like Mendelssohn; "textual fidelity" came even later. Judging from firsthand accounts of Beethoven at the keyboard, his own playing style was rough, unsteady, and vulgarly expressive by Mendelssohn's or Toscanini's standards. While the testimony regarding interpolated tempo changes is contradictory, several of Anton Schindler's commentaries (in particular, his account of Beethoven's performance of his Opus 14, No. 1 Piano Sonata) suggest that Beethoven was more partial to momentary pulse inflections than Toscanini was. Ferdinand Ries's recollection that Beethoven typically "held back the tempo in his crescendo with a ritardando" points toward the type of allargando intensification Toscanini eschewed. And internal evidence suggests that Beethoven's "espressivo" implies a temporarily slower tempo.[20] To a significant degree, even Toscanini's Verdi deviated from what we can reconstruct of the composer's intentions: though in terms of performance style, the crisp, commanding objectivity of his mobile, external Beethoven bore the stamp of *Falstaff*, it does not follow that the Toscanini style is equally germane to Verdi's earlier operas. (I will return to this point in discussing Toscanini's NBC Symphony opera recordings.)

Toscanini's tabula rasa disposition made him an uncommonly versatile conductor in an era when German and Italian schools of composition and interpretation were nearly as disparate as Wagner and bel canto; though he obviously came to Beethoven via Verdi, his objectivity and good taste usually forestalled blatant Italianisms. Heeding Toscanini's example, some conductors have since achieved a chameleonlike command of diverse idioms unknown to musicians of Toscanini's generation, Toscanini included. In certain respects, not others, Toscanini was more "faithful to the composer" than such forebears as Wagner and Bülow. What better defined his musical achievement was its modernity. He dramatically inspired or reinforced contemporary tendencies in the emergence of the conductor as a performance specialist: toward more dominant personal authority, toward higher standards of precise execution, toward enhanced stylistic flexibility.

As Toscanini's NBC years formed a peculiar pendant to his career, his NBC Symphony recordings form a peculiar pendant to his discography. Coarse and thin, they are among the strangest sounding ever made. Only after 1950, at Carnegie Hall, did Toscanini's broadcast concerts acquire decent acoustics, and only for the benefit of invited guests.

The costs of this anomaly bear pondering. Texture and hue are not ancillary orchestral attributes, secondary to "the notes"; as his own New York Philharmonic recordings make clear, a distinctively lucid, luminous sound-ideal was a Toscanini trademark, at least in those years. In two respects, NBC/RCA's desiccated "high fidelity" stresses Toscanini dimensions his earlier recordings had slighted: the close, multiple miking better defines his orchestra's dazzling articulation, and it clarifies—in fact, over-clarifies—the intense vibrato characterizing the "singing" tone of Toscanini's strings. At the same time, the miking ruins balances, compresses dynamics, and blanches color. Forward winds and amplified pianissimos against a backdrop of dead space transform Toscanini's winged scherzando passagework into thickets of tonal pine needles. The most rudimentary "textual fidelity" is discouraged. In the Scherzo of Beethoven's Second Symphony, the charm of the trio is based on sudden dynamic contrasts; in Toscanini's NBC recordings, the wind lines, variously marked "piano," "sforzando," and "fortissimo," are always loud. In the finale of Beethoven's Eighth, the beginning of the coda—a master-stroke—superimposes gossamer triplets on a mellifluous melody in half-notes. All parts are marked "pianissimo." On Toscanini's recording, the impact of the triplets is grotesquely harsh, as if buzzing insects had infested Elysium. After 1950, RCA began blatantly doctoring its Toscanini recordings with phony resonance, boosted treble, and the like. Without rescuing the skewed balances and dynamics, these "enhanced" versions added fresh falsifications of timbre and perspective. Outside the RCA/NBC time warp, Mercury was already producing orchestral recordings worthy of comparison with any made since; RCA itself made outstanding recordings with Fritz Reiner and the Chicago Symphony beginning in 1954.*

Apart from their dire sonics, the NBC performances defy generalization. Toscanini's NBC Symphony affiliation, his longest anywhere, began in 1937 —in which year he was still active in Salzburg, Vienna, and London—and ended in 1954—by which time he was failing physically and had reduced his commitments to a minimum. Kinescopes of the NBC telecasts suggest the impact of his 1951 stroke and/or other physical inroads: in 1948, he is a "young man" of eighty; in 1952, his features are fleshier, his movements much plainer and less fluid. Though Toscanini's early NBC years are underrepresented in his standard commercial discography, pirated airchecks of his 1939 Beethoven cycle have long circulated. These impressive broadcast performances are comparable to his 1936 Beethoven Seventh— albeit transferred to drier, less integrated acoustics than Carnegie Hall's, and to an orchestra whose winds cannot match the New York Philharmonic's. RCA, however, released only a memorable *Eroica* from the 1939 cycle. Like so many Toscanini LPs, the Beethoven cycle RCA zealously disseminated was made when Toscanini was in his eighties and bears a

---

*Toscanini's own acoustical preferences for broadcasts and recordings remain vague. He is said to have mainly insisted on hearing every instrument. According to Walter Toscanini, his father "liked the unresounding acoustics of Studio 8H in which the purity of the orchestral tone was not marred by hall reverberations and echoes." Further information may be gleaned from Charles O'Connell's difficulties recording Toscanini in the *Götterdämmerung* Immolation Scene. Toscanini had O'Connell rerecord and superimpose the trumpet parts in several places, suggesting a preference for forward, unblended winds normally considered more appropriate to Verdi than Wagner. (As released on Victor, one such trumpet passage, accompanying Brünnhilde's "die den edlen leib der hehresten Helden verzehrt" [m. 1244–1246], is artificially reinforced to the point of obscuring the rest of the orchestra.) Beginning in 1941–42—the season a shell was installed in Studio 8H, under Stokowski's influence—the NBC Symphony broadcasts acquired just such an orchestral mix, favoring the instruments in the rear ranks. Toscanini's Carnegie Hall recordings were engineered, with multiple microphones, to sound much the same. John Pfeiffer, one of Toscanini's Carnegie Hall producers for RCA, later recalled: "We took what we could get and felt any departure from the way it had been done would be disorienting to Maestro"; Toscanini was not directly consulted because "we were scared to death of him." In the opinion of B. H. Haggin, among others, Walter Toscanini—a constant control-room presence and the chief intermediary between Toscanini and RCA's producers and engineers—was responsible for endorsing artificial "enhancement" of the Toscanini recordings on Toscanini's behalf. Privately, Walter was widely considered an unreliable judge of music. When, following the NBC Symphony's demise, RCA's Richard B. Gardner conferred with Toscanini about the orchestra's unreleased recordings, he discovered that Toscanini disliked the "enhanced" versions. Toscanini's preference for forward winds, however, seems indisputable. Even as heard in Carnegie Hall, Toscanini's winds are said to have sounded unusually prominent.[21]

changed interpretive imprint. His 1951 Beethoven Seventh brings the change into focus: it is faster, tighter, stiffer than his Sevenths of 1936 and 1939. Where the texture thins, he is more prone to rush; elsewhere, his beat is more rigid than before. His two "fast" tempos—for the second movement and the third-movement trio—are now faster still, and the consequences are aberrant. The second movement accelerates as it progresses, especially in the A major sections. Toscanini's instability contradicts Beethoven's processional rhetoric; stateliness combines with haste, as in a film run at the wrong speed. The fortissimo perorations of the third-movement trio sound equally self-contradictory: the winds' deep intakes and forceful exhalations over a sustained drumroll connote "breadth," but Toscanini's tempo makes their breathing seem anxious and shallow. The extraordinary payoff comes with the finale's coda, in which Toscanini's prevalent edginess and haste translate into tingling desperation. Accelerating from a headlong basic tempo already exceeding Beethoven's seventy-two beats to the half, he throws the throttle wide open. The playing of the NBC Symphony turns heedlessly coarse, terrifically intense. Although still unconcerned with "inner space" and harmonic undertow, Toscanini's 1951 Beethoven no longer seems lacking in "abandon," "weight," "ruggedness," "muscle," or "stolidity." Sheer, fatalistic ferocity is its dominant motif. In old age, the Great Purifier had become a vengeful Savonarola.

Taken as a whole, Toscanini's octogenarian recordings—concurrent with his transcontinental tour, his meetings with President Truman and Bob Hope, his increasing seclusion, his fulfilled "Americanization"—document final rites of simplification. The equalized surface tension of his earlier style stiffens. Earlier rubatos, as in the first movements of Mozart's "Haffner" and Fortieth symphonies, vanish. Nuances of feeling, tone, and articulation, as in the gentleness and humor, gliding legatos and spikey marcatos of the Salzburg *Meistersinger,* narrow in range and diminish in number. As early as 1937, John Barbirolli, attending a BBC Symphony concert, noticed an increased preoccupation with energy and drive in Toscanini's performances, less attention to polish, and "an almost complete lack of serenity" suggesting "an intense desire to prove to himself, and of course to others, that he is not getting old." At NBC, Samuel Antek found Toscanini sometimes demanding "rough, scratchy, raucous playing, unbridled in spontaneity."[22] So insistent is this "late Toscanini" style that it can be summarized in an all-purpose formula combining American urgency and efficiency with the theatrical *melos* of the Mediterranean: that the strings mold every line, cantabile, as human voices do; that every note convey direction; that every instrument on the page be heard, and at precisely the proper moment; that every player participate with absolute conviction and as much virtuosity as he can muster. Bypassing issues of notation and tradition, indifferent to historic and poetic allusions, the all-purpose formula ensured music making of unsurpassed songfulness and febrile excitation, even where songfulness or excitation was inappropriate. Rather than evoking *Neue Sachlichkeit* sobriety, Toscanini's ultimate imprint had "Toscanini" written all over it.

To Toscanini's adherents, the relative catholicity of his recorded NBC repertoire reflected the versatility of self-effacing "fidelity to the composer." In retrospect, the NBC recordings reflect the versatility of the all-purpose formula.

The formula does not suit all music equally. In the symphonies of Mozart and Haydn, Toscanini's taut tempos and pulsating timbres prove hectic; the minuet from Haydn's "Surprise" Symphony (recorded in 1953) is revealingly violent—Toscanini bristles at its decorum. To the degree that the formula's militance combats humor, Toscanini's interpretations of Beethoven's Fourth and Eighth symphonies (1951, 1952) are idiosyncratically stern (as his bubbly BBC Beethoven is not). To the degree it rejects interiority, Toscanini's "singing" treatment of the Ninth Symphony's slow movement (1952) is idiosyncratically extroverted. Toscanini's Dvořák, Debussy, and Elgar—to cite three composers once frequently cited in proofs of his versatility—are, again, incompletely idiomatic. In the "New World" Symphony (1953), Toscanini savors the fierce "Indian" rhythms, but not the lilting, dancelike themes. RCA's engineers, whose microphones negate Debussy's "ppp," "en dehors," and "très lontain," help make Toscanini's *La Mer* (1950) the least "wet" on records; the distant glockenspiel and harp tones at the close of "Jeux de vagues," intended to blend—as do spray, mist, and wind—into oceanic silence, are like cactus in the desert. The incongruous corporeality of Toscanini's *Nuages* (1952) is partly the result of stressed downbeats contradicting Debussy's diffuse sound imagery. In Elgar, the all-purpose formula's scouring denudes the "Enigma" Variations (1951) of its familiar drizzle and fog, and also of its civilized whimsy. Where Elgar cocks a droll eyebrow, as in describing Richard Baxter Townshend's caricature of an aging amateur thespian (variation 3), Toscanini's all-purpose power cocks a trigger. In "W.N." (variation 8), where Elgar portrays an eighteenth-century house, the Toscanini formula turns a comforting still life into a motion picture—and so provides too animated a prelude for the stately "Nimrod." Elgar's own recording (1926) superbly combines Edwardian whimsy, leisure, and lump-in-the-throat pomp.

When in 1930 and 1935 Toscanini gave the "Enigma" Variations in London with the New York Philharmonic and the BBC Symphony, disparities between his reading and the composer's did not pass unnoticed. In the press, there was talk of individual variations being "clearly misunderstood" and of differing views of the tempo implications of the finale's *grandioso* climax. But England's most eminent critics did not predicate their verdicts on "fidelity to the composer." Neville Cardus likened Toscanini to "a cultivated foreigner speaking the English language," and observed that his "Enigma" "held us throughout even if it departed from English views of the work." Ernest Newman wrote that despite its "slight non-English 'accent,' " the Toscanini "Enigma" Variations "soared to a height and plumbed a depth I have never known it to approach." In fact, gifted performers sometimes uncover facets of a work unnoticed by the composer. If anything, the neutrality of Toscanini's all-purpose formula prohibits fully idiomatic interpretation. But its indiscriminate detergent action makes worn goods emerge glistening clean, and its ballistics ensure excitement and direction. Notwithstanding oddities of sentiment and style, the vast majority of Toscanini's NBC recordings—including his Dvořák, Debussy, and Elgar, if not his Haydn or Mozart—more than put across the music. Even confronted with *An American in Paris* (1945)—an exemplary test of formulaic versatility because its jazz base eluded Toscanini—the all-purpose formula grips and holds. I have heard Russian performances of Gershwin whose inauthenticity takes the form of comic distortion. Toscanini's inauthenticity, while apparent, is subtler and more benign. Rather than fussing over "interpretation," as the Russians do, he fusses over execution. His *American in Paris* is clean, tight, committed. Its active textures and sustained brio make it actually memorable. (Rehearsing the Concerto in F with Toscanini in 1943, Gershwin's friend Oscar Levant pointed out passages where Gershwin's intentions contradicted Toscanini's—to which Toscanini, according to Levant, replied: "Thata poor boy . . . he was a-sick." Yet Levant found the performance "truly remarkable.")[23]

In one respect, the simplicity of the all-purpose formula is misleading: a Toscanini is required to implement it. Maximum precision, commitment, and urgency can be commanded or inspired only by a conductor who is feared or revered—and Toscanini was both. Maximum clarity and cantabile, moreover, must to some degree be plotted and taught. Hearing every note calls for attention to articulation and balance. Singing every phrase calls for attention to bowing and vibrating. When Toscanini exhorted *"Cantando! Sempre cantando!"* he did not have in mind uniformities of sweet tone and smooth phrasing that pass muster in many orchestras today. The vividness of a Toscanini allegro depended on more than clean diction; it depended on the physicality and immediacy of every syllable of song. All this is borne out by Samuel Antek's valuable account, in *This Was Toscanini*, of an NBC rehearsal of Weber's *Oberon* Overture.[24] Adjusting the wind choir one measure after letter A, Toscanini asks for more bassoon and

secures a firmer, less murky sound. At letter B, he changes the winds'
fortissimo to fortissimo-piano ("You kill the strings!"). He insists that
intervening short or soft notes in a phrase carry as much color and impetus
as their neighbors ("Don't eat the notes!" "Sing the small notes!" "Sostenuto—L-o-o-ng short notes!"). Long notes must be held and vibrated for
their full duration. Addressing the overture's adagio sostenuto introduction, Toscanini's somber face and slow, formless baton strokes create a
"forbidding atmosphere," "an intangible tension," "a fourth-dimensional
pianissimo and quietude." As he beats two half-notes to the bar rather than
the customary four quarters, the players are made nervously alert; they fish
for the sixteenth notes in a void. Toscanini supplies no upbeat for the
sudden fortissimo chord prefacing the main allegro con fuoco; his
"whipped, pile-driving, unprepared downbeat" activates a convulsive response. The allegro's first theme consists of a string of sixteenth notes in
the first violins, rising from piano to fortissimo.

Toscanini worries that the first upbeat pair of sixteenths will sound indistinct; he has them played mezzoforte, with accents. He now experiments
with an unorthodox bowing, calling for two speeding staccatos on each
upbow, in order to make the articulation more splintery and mercurial
("*Vita, vita!* Dancing! *Gioia!*"). For the crescendo to fortissimo he demands
broader, driving bow strokes and swirling, writhing arms and torsos. With
Toscanini, Antek comments, "playing loud was not enough; it meant acting, looking loud! . . . You had to get out and shovel! You had to sweat!"
Toscanini next upbraids the second violins, violas, cellos, and basses, whose
accompaniment consists of eighth-note chords ("Play staccato! Use the
bow! You sleep?"). The theme's fortissimo climax, atop a frothing wave of
sound, is now attacked by dozens of hysterically bouncing, ricocheting
bows; "It sounds," Antek remarks, "as though the size of the orchestra had

been doubled." In Toscanini's *Oberon* Overture recording (1952), the buoyant physicality and rocketing articulation are absolutely flattening.

Rehearsing the *Oberon* Overture, Toscanini did not allude to the opera *Oberon*. He used no metaphors to convey the "meaning" of the adagio sostenuto or of the various tunes. To a significant degree, his concerns were purely local: not the contour of a phrase, but the shape, volume, and energy-level of a given particle of sound. This is one reason the range of nuance he demanded does not coincide with a comparable range of feeling. I can imagine an *Oberon* Overture from Toscanini's New York Philharmonic years sounding less stiff jointed, compressed, and violent. I can imagine a more idiomatic *Oberon* Overture, in which the introduction, rather than evoking "a tangible tension," evokes the sylvan fairy kingdom of Weber's opera; in which its juxtaposition with the allegro is not a distracting coup de théâtre; and in which the allegro's lyric subsidiary themes, phrased in proper four-bar units, sound less singsong. But these are second thoughts, picked up after picking oneself off the floor. To paraphrase Ernest Newman: despite his "non-German" accent, Toscanini attains a scathing brilliance previously unsuspected in Weber's Overture to *Oberon*.

If Toscanini's Weber overture recordings are among his most thrilling, it is partly because this repertoire derives from a different milieu than the many symphonies and tone poems he recorded: the stage. As we have seen, it was Weber's Overture to *Euryanthe* that in 1902 provoked one of Toscanini's notable Milan tantrums—his walkout to screams of "*Bis!*" Listening to his NBC Symphony recording (1951), one can understand what the screaming was about, and also something about Toscanini's métier. As in the *Oberon* Overture, he employs "traditional" pulse fluctuations—in particular, for the lyric second subject—more drastic than any he would dare impose on a symphony. The "extra dimension of personal involvement" Leinsdorf observed in Toscanini's *Falstaff* is not imperceptible here: temperamentally, he is no more fiery than in Beethoven; interpretively, he is less inhibited. And when he conducted the NBC Symphony in *Italian* music for the stage, this extra dimension was the more pronounced, and the all-purpose formula less self-sufficient.

Like Theodore Thomas, Olin Downes, and other tastemakers, NBC measured musical culture as symphonic culture. Still, instrumental excerpts from operas by Weber, Rossini, Verdi, and Wagner were integral to the NBC repertoire from the start. On rare occasions, singers, too, participated in excerpts from *Die Walküre*, *Götterdämmerung*, *Mefistofele*, *Orfeo ed Euri-*

dice, and *Rigoletto.* Above all, seven complete operas were given.* In certain respects, this reunion of Toscanini and the theater did not reawaken Toscanini's glory days at La Scala, the Metropolitan, Bayreuth, and Salzburg. NBC's isolationism worked against the greasepaint and adrenaline of the theater, and not merely because the operas were unstaged and split into weekly halves. Cheering and applause between numbers were forbidden. The casts were less distinguished than those Toscanini had previously worked with. To compare the Salzburg *Falstaff* and *Fidelio* with the NBC remakes is to compare opera at the source with opera under glass. (George Szell, among others, testified that Toscanini's Bayreuth performances were also "vastly superior to all of his concert-opera performances of the NBC years.")[25] Stabile, the Salzburg Falstaff, had learned the role for Toscanini in 1921 and was its leading interpreter; Giuseppe Valdengo, the NBC Falstaff, was first coached by Toscanini in *Falstaff* for the broadcast. Stabile sounds ripe and inspired, Valdengo well-drilled and obedient—yet must play a rogue. Stabile and Piero Biasini, the 1937 Ford, are rhythmically incisive but alter the written pitch where a note or word asks for special nuance. Toscanini makes Valdengo read the notes literally—and draws less creative input in return. In the bewitching transition from Ford's monologue, the flicked portamento and subtle tempo adjustments in Toscanini's 1937 performance are simplified or omitted in 1950. In his 1944 *Fidelio,* Toscanini demands commitment from the singers, but not the type of verbal and musical detail he taught his 1950 *Falstaff* principals, and which his 1937 *Falstaff* principals had long assimilated. Only Herbert Janssen's Pizarro comes to life. The absence of applause between the well-defined numbers is disconcerting. The absence of dialogue in an opera whose dialogue furnishes some of its most vibrant moments is crippling—both audience and performers are alienated from the drama. Compared with the Salzburg performance, this *Fidelio* is not only provincial but embalmed; it confuses art with "finished things."

As it happens, *Fidelio* was the least successful of the NBC-Toscanini operas. The most successful, *Otello,* is also Toscanini's most important NBC Symphony recording—the one that comes closest to recapturing Toscanini's revolutionary impact in the pit. Unlike the NBC *Falstaff,* it is not shadowed by a Salzburg Selenophone. More than the other Verdi operas he performed over NBC, *Falstaff* excepted, it calls for a dominating conductor, and its temper suits the Savonarola fury of Toscanini's late years. Notwithstanding Herva Nelli's wind-up Desdemona, it is the best cast of the seven NBC operas. Singing strings, smart precision, and forward

---

*See page 283.

impetus, potential sources of histrionic distraction in Toscanini's German
repertoire NBC recordings, here sound right. In fact, the all-purpose formula is revealed to have its basis in late Verdi: as a source not of neutrality
and versatility, but of authenticity.

Like his Salzburg *Falstaff*, Toscanini's NBC *Otello* is an unsurpassed
centrist reading, an object lesson in interpretation. Trusting Verdi's markings, he finds more meaning in the string motif beginning Act II

than any other conductor: the sudden dynamic surge and ebb, the sinuous,
rounded phrasing, connote cunning and hidden power—and so anticipate
Iago's coming exchange with Cassio. When Cassio departs, Iago sheds his
mask, and the insinuating triplets shed theirs. This is the beginning of Iago's
credo:

A little later, Verdi asks that the accompaniment to Iago's "Temete, signor,
la gelosia!" be played triple-piano, then pianissimo and legato. He shows
phrasings that are long and smooth. The ability of Toscanini's NBC strings
to sing at a soft dynamic without sacrificing tension and phrase-shape
proves ideal. During Iago's "Era la notte" (in which he narrates "proof"
of Cassio's disloyalty), Toscanini's "extra dimension of personal involvement"—his complete identification with Iago, his native familiarity with
the sense and flow of Boito's text—produces a reading of infinite rhythmic
refinement; this time, other conductors, by comparison, sound ensnared in
a click track. Because Toscanini takes nothing for granted; because his
orchestra is at least as articulate as are his soloists; because he thoroughly
commands his chorus, his grip is relentless. He tightens the screws implac-
ably, plotting a continuous descent toward a calamity greater than its
victims.

If an earlier Toscanini *Otello* existed on disc, individual performances
on the order of Stabile's Falstaff and Lehmann's Leonore might have put
NBC's *Otello* in the shade. The reason he can nevertheless dominate his

singers without upstaging *Otello* is that this opera of 1887, more than such middle-period Verdi as *Rigoletto* (1851) and *La traviata* (1853), transcends the sum of its parts. I have already remarked on Verdi's increasingly prominent, increasingly binding orchestra. Verdi himself was the first to recognize that the more he unified his operas, the more he depended on conductors to keep the unities intact. In 1869, the time of the revised *La forza del destino,* he wrote to the publisher Giulio Ricordi: "Keep in mind, my dear Giulio, that the success of our operas rests most of the time in the hands of the conductor. This person is as necessary as a tenor or a prima donna." In 1871, the year of *Aida,* he wrote to Ricordi:

> There was a time when a prima donna and a tenor together with a cavatina, a rondo and a duet, etc., etc., could sustain an opera (if you call it such); today this is not the case. Modern operas, whether good or bad, have quite different aims. You, who run a music magazine, should concern yourself with this subject, which is of the utmost importance. Preach the absolute need we have for talented operatic conductors; demonstrate that success can never be won without an intelligent interpretation; and castigate those asses who are massacring our operas, asses, moreover, who are impertinent to boot. Do you know that a conductor at Naples dared to write on a Mayerbeer [sic] score (*L'Africaine,* I think) something to this effect: "*Omit this aria—it is awful and appallingly written. How could such a Maestro have composed such a monstrosity?*"— Have you understood me?

And, in another letter:

> The way [our conductors] *over-interpret* at every performance . . . leads straight to what is false and contrived. It is the path that led music to the false and contrived at the end of the last century and the beginning of this, when singers took the liberty of creating (as the French say) their own parts, thus producing every kind of chaos and absurdity. No: I want one creator only and I am satisfied when what is written is performed simply and accurately; the trouble is, one never performs what is written! . . . I cannot allow singers or conductors the right to create, for that is a principle which leads, as I said earlier, to catastrophe. . . .

In 1893, the year of *Falstaff,* and six years after *Otello,* Verdi wrote to his friend Italo Pizzi that "everything" in *Falstaff* "springs from the ensemble. . . . Great singers are not required . . . but artists with good intentions. That is why I'm pleased with the performances at Brescia because the singers work as a team—they are not prima donnas but ordinary mortals; they are *de bons enfants.*"[26]

Though Ricordi, for one, disliked Toscanini's 1899 Scala *Falstaff* (he told Verdi it sounded "metallic," "rigid," and "tyrannical"), Toscanini answered the "absolute need for talented operatic conductors" who would command authority without "overinterpreting." When Verdi conducted his Requiem (1874) in Cologne in 1877, it was reported that he favored "sharper, more strident nuances than is customary in Germany"; that "pauses are kept as short as possible, never destroying the sense of rhythm"; that the strings played with "the greatest possible power"; that the quick tempos of the fugues "hardly seemed fast enough for the composer"; that "singers and players are treated as one large orchestra" so that "the solo voice is given its own theme no more or no less than any other instrument of the orchestra."[27] All this was Toscanini's way. (Of his NBC Symphony Verdi Requiem performances, the 1940 version with Zinka Milanov, Bruna Castagna, Jussi Björling, and Nicola Moscona, not the 1951 version issued by Victor, is the one to hear.) To what degree Toscanini's way suited *Rigoletto* or *La traviata* is another question. No recordings exist of his Verdi performances at La Scala and the Metropolitan. Most likely, he was less ruthless in treating "singers and players as one large orchestra" than at NBC. But there can be no doubt that in forging a powerfully unified ensemble, he curbed interpolated cadenzas and high notes and scraped away unwritten ornaments; that he drew the line taut; that he sped up tempos and reduced rubatos. Like Mahler in Vienna, Toscanini admired Wagner's ideal, expressed in *On Conducting* and other writings, of integrated musical theater enforced by enhanced podium authority. As in scorching Beethoven clean, his reforms were timely, yet exceeded the need. The earliest recordings of middle Verdi, beginning in 1898, reveal a style in transition from bel canto, abounding in interpolated notes and elaborate individual nuances. The rhythmic freedom of these recordings, of which many of the best-known are by Fernando de Lucia and Mattia Battistini, facilitate vocal display and personal expression at the expense of steadiness and forward impetus. Do such liberties constitute "abuses" or an elegant exercise of interpretive prerogatives Verdi took for granted? Much recent scholarship leans in the second direction. In *The Record of Singing*, Volume 2, Michael Scott writes:

What we may feel extravagant would to [Verdi] have seemed chaste in the extreme. And Verdi's music cannot be divorced from the manners of his own age, though Toscanini made a great attempt to do so. . . . The singing we hear on records made by artists who worked with him—

Rethberg, Martinelli, de Luca and Pinza for example—so often held up by critics as authentically Verdian, for all its fine qualities, in matters of style and interpretation only tells us about performance practice in the first half of the twentieth century, and little or nothing of the real Verdi tradition.

And Will Crutchfield argues at length that personal liberties with notes, rhythms, and dynamics—"a sudden pianissimo, a lingering rubato, a flash of roulade, even that much-despised stock in trade, the corona on an exciting (possibly unwritten) top note"—are a necessary part of middle-Verdi style; that, taken in context, Verdi's notion of performing "what is written" sanctions these and other "parts of the singer's expressive vocabulary that twentieth century practice has increasingly limited."[28]

Even if such arguments are impugned, aspects of Toscanini's otherwise stirring NBC performances of middle Verdi impugn themselves. Unwritten ornaments—tending, naturally, to relax the pulse—are not part of the vocal style of *Otello*, *Falstaff*, or the Requiem; concomitantly, aria and recitative are fused to obtain an uninterrupted forward flow. But in *Rigoletto*, *La traviata*, and *Un ballo in maschera* (1859), even in *Aida* (1871), the NBC/Toscanini treatment—the taut, simplified lines; the supercharged, goal-oriented accompaniments; the sometimes weak, inexperienced singers (chaste in comparison to those earlier Toscanini-influenced singers Michael Scott finds chaste); the absence of applause to punctuate structure—strips individual set pieces of details necessary for their individual effect; misapplied, uninterrupted forward flow swamps expressive opportunities that can be seized only through lingering. In *La traviata*, especially, Toscanini's forward flow is pre-emptive. Treating singers, chorus, and players as "one large orchestra," he "sings" every role—the soloists stand in, as it were, for his croaky baritone. Scott actually likens Licia Albanese's Violetta (and also that of Gilda dalla Rizza, Toscanini's favorite Scala Violetta) to a "frog march."[29] In Violetta's first-act scena, Toscanini's NBC version exceeds the metronome markings for andantino ("Ah, fors' è lui") and allegro brillante ("Sempre libera").* Verdi's "allargando," "dolce," "a piacere," "pianis-

---

*For all Verdi's operas from *Stiffelio* (1850) on, the autographs contain metronome markings—with the exceptions of *Rigoletto* and *La traviata*. The Verdi scholar Martin Chusid comments: "Since both works were scheduled for performance soon after yet another new opera, Verdi may simply have been too pressed for time to establish metronome readings before his autographs were sent to the publisher. Even for these operas, however, metronomic indications eventually did appear on scores published by Ricordi and on manuscript rental copies of the orchestral scores emanating from its *copisteria*."[30] The scholarly consensus is that the "traditional" metronome markings

simo," and "forte"—not to mention the inflections and ornaments his favorite Violetta, Adelina Patti, doubtless introduced—are also ignored; Albanese struggles merely to spew out the notes fast enough. Verdi portrays Violetta's bewilderment, her dawning susceptibility to Alfredo, her resolve to forget him. Toscanini's portrait is of a soprano in torment— Albanese's manic scalar descent preceding Alfredo's love call actually resembles a scream. Toscanini's American admirers proclaimed his andantes truer than those of German laggards. In Alfredo's "De' miei bollenti spiriti," however, Toscanini's andante is *one-third* faster than the score's sixty beats to the quarter. Jan Peerce is allowed two big rallentandos, but this is not the same as establishing a flexible pulse throughout. Verdi's dynamics range from triple-piano to fortissimo; Peerce produces a steady forte. The aria is made so short, so uneventful, that NBC's applause ban becomes musically apt. In its stentorian simplicity, this performance is neither absorbingly elaborate, as in de Lucia's florid 1906 recording, or *come scritto*, as in Julius Patzak's 1929 recording (as "Ach, ihres Auges Zauberblick"), eloquently attentive to the metronome and dynamic markings. That it comes stamped from a mold is confirmed by the rehearsals of November 28–30 (recordings of which have long circulated underground). Many have testified that Toscanini was more relaxed and expressive in rehearsal,* and a comparison of these *Traviata* rehearsals with the recorded performance of December 1 and 8 bears this out. More to the present point, intermittently singing all the parts himself, Toscanini fashions an incomparably more vivid Act II than with Peerce, Albanese, and Robert Merrill "standing in." With Toscanini as Alfredo, "De' miei bollenti spiriti" sounds not rushed, but ardent. With Toscanini as Violetta, "Dite alla giovine," streamlined in Albanese's performance, sounds starkly expressive. Accompanying Toscanini in Germont's "Piangi, piangi," the NBC violins heave their two-note phrases with short, rapid intakes. This fixed blue-

---

for *La traviata* reflect Verdi's preference as conveyed, directly or indirectly, to Ricordi.

*According to Samuel Antek: "At concerts, Toscanini was invariably tense and controlled, becoming an aristocrat rather than the peasant he had been at rehearsals. This transformation always affected the orchestra's performance. Sensing his tension, the men themselves became tense and nervous and often could not give their utmost. . . . At rehearsal, Toscanini was much more relaxed and, as a result, his gestures were much less inhibited. They were more florid, more free, more expressive and dramatic. The very fact that he could shout, bellow, and sing apparently freed him physically. At concerts he seems to freeze; his movements were smaller, less emotional, more restrained."[31] Antek and many others in the NBC Symphony felt that only during the orchestra's 1950 tour were its concerts "as good as the rehearsals." (See page 281.)

print suits Toscanini's thin baritone; Merrill's needs more breathing space.

If Toscanini's *Traviata* strays further from the metronome markings than do his *Otello* and *Falstaff*, it is partly because the fabric is more sectionalized, less symphonic: as in Toscanini's Beethoven, thinner textures produce a tendency to rush. In *Ballo* and *Aida*, composed six and eighteen years after *Traviata*, Toscanini is correspondingly more at ease. Yet, like *Traviata*, these operas retain individual set pieces; again, Toscanini tends to swallow them. Herva Nelli's Aida evokes the hapless Susan Alexander of Orson Welles's *Citizen Kane*: in place of prima donna glamour, an eerie cipher. Toscanini's penchant for pliant singers increased with age; in casting Nelli in *Aida*, *Otello*, *Falstaff*, and the 1951 Verdi Requiem, he embarrassed himself as well. Zinka Milanov, the Metropolitan's reigning Verdi soprano for most of the forties and an RCA artist, in fact participated in Toscanini's 1940 performance of the Verdi Requiem and his 1944 performance of *Rigoletto* Act III. Her queenly vocal personality loosens Toscanini's autocracy. For this reason, and also because of the terse musical-dramatic unity of the opera itself at this point, the *Rigoletto* extract, issued by Victor, is Toscanini's best middle-Verdi recording.

If I have dwelt on the debits of Toscanini's approach to middle Verdi, it is because in music so rich in unnotated conventions, the equation of literalism with authenticity needs emphatic correcting; and also because a precise correlation of *late* Verdi with Toscanini reveals much about the Toscanini style. Actually, even with every debit tallied, the Toscanini/NBC versions of *Traviata*, *Ballo*, *Aida*, and *Rigoletto* Act III remain among the most gripping on record. The preludes and big ensembles are uniformly memorable. To hear Toscanini's violins recall Riccardo's "La rivedrà nell' estasi" midway through Act III of *Ballo*, or the surge and sweep of their reminiscence of Amelia's "Consentimi, o Signore" during the prelude to Act II, is to forget how disappointingly these tunes were sung; they linger in the ear more poignantly than in any other *Ballo* of my experience. No other conductor so convincingly renders the final measures of *Rigoletto*, in which Verdi's formulaic cadence presents a problem familiar to pianists in Liszt: Toscanini's combination of honest intensity and painstaking, strenuous execution (each grace note carries as much weight as the ensuing quarter) rescues Verdi's rhetoric from cliché.*

Lucia di Lammermoor, a Toscanini specialty he never recorded, seemed similarly "rescued" when he took it on tour with La Scala in 1929. Herbert von Karajan's reaction, in Vienna, was typical:

> I was still a student, and all of us knew that he was coming and prepared ourselves for the event by getting the score, playing it on the piano, discussing it and so on.

Even where Toscanini's style strays too far from bel canto on the continuum toward *Falstaff,* even where he overcompensates for the exhibitionism and sloppiness of egoists and routiniers, the essential drama registers with rare integrity: he identifies with Verdi's stories of jealous husbands, domineering fathers, and betrayed fatherlands. Even where he fails wholly to embrace Verdi's idiom, he identifies, finally, with Verdi himself, who was tough yet shy; who preferred peasants to aristocrats; who wept when moved and raged when crossed; and who in old age seemed miraculously young.

Toscanini's NBC broadcasts of five Verdi operas were a skewed homecoming away from home. Missing were the inspiring stages and singers of Milan, New York, Bayreuth, and Salzburg. RCA's recordings of these broadcasts do not constitute fully realized performances. But no other portion of the NBC Symphony's recorded legacy stirs so much admiration for Toscanini, and for what he had earlier been; no other portion of the NBC repertoire instills such renewed respect for a composer and his work.

With Verdi, opera completed its transformation into a form of popular art. The vitality and rhythmic energy of his music, the red-blooded emotionalism of his stories, were meant to raise the roof, and did. In Italy, waiters, chambermaids, porters, carpenters pushed forward when he ap-

---

And after looking at the score, we all decided that we couldn't understand why he should bother with a work as banal as this. But it took just two minutes of the overture as conducted by Toscanini, to convince us that we were wrong. It was indeed the same score we had studied, but it was played by him with the same devotion and meticulousness that he might lavish on *Parsifal.* And this completely changed my attitude: *no* music is vulgar, unless it is played in a way that makes it so.[32]

peared in public. Organ grinders played his tunes. Enthusiasm in the opera house was barely more restrained. At the premiere of *Rigoletto*, the Duke had hardly finished the first verse of "La donna è mobile" when, according to a witness, "there arose a great cry from every part of the theater, and the tenor failed to find his cue to begin the second verse." When Parma first heard *Aida*, Amonasro's "Rivedrai le foreste imbalsamate" provoked, according to Italo Pizzi, "an almost wild cry, entreating the Maestro to take a bow on stage and asking for the phrase to be repeated." Pizzi's account continues:

> In Germany this would have been an unforgettable scandal. But how can one control—and here Verdi agreed with me—the enthusiasm, I would almost say the delirium, that at certain powerful phrases, at certain melodies that touch and shake every fibre of the soul, takes possession of an entire audience? The Maestro, with undisguised pleasure . . . told me that he remembered that evening very well, and smiled with great contentment.[33]

To understand Toscanini's affinity for Verdi, his strongest for any composer, is to understand essential aspects of his mass appeal—not merely as an embodiment of self-reliance, egalitarianism, masculinity, unpretentiousness, and restless energy (for Verdi, too, embodied all these qualities), but as a *musician*. Rather than introspection, abstraction, or esoteric complexity, Toscanini's art was based in the overt visceral energies of Verdian popular theater. No conductor more instinctively or thoroughly grasped the suspense of a coiled spring, or the thrill of its sudden, tripped release. This is the dynamic of the storm and Gilda's murder in *Rigoletto*, and of Otello's final assault on Desdemona. To hear Toscanini prepare and drive home these fatal thrusts is to hear Verdi's intentions completely fulfilled. To hear Toscanini treat the adagio sostenuto introduction of the *Oberon* Overture as a tingling "fourth-dimensional" foil for a hell-bent allegro con fuoco is to hear Weber interpreted with something like Verdi's intentions. To hear Toscanini treat the adagio introduction to Beethoven's Fourth Symphony as a tingling, fourth-dimensional foil for a hell-bent allegro vivace is to hear Verdian Beethoven; even if Toscanini had not chosen a tempo substantially slower than Beethoven's sixty-six beats to the quarter, it would be obvious that Beethoven had in mind a less portentous, misterioso preamble to a less ferocious first movement. And yet—and this is more pertinent—one's initial, riveting impression is not that Toscanini's interpretation is wrong, but that it works.

No artist of Toscanini's caliber could have cynically calculated such excitement; his immersion in the Verdian idiom was too deep, too sincere for that. Like Verdi, he did not pander to the crowd, yet he pleased it. So, too, with the all-purpose formula—its effect, but not its intent, was to maximize mass appeal. It dispensed with extramusical allusions to art, literature, and language in favor of standardized urgency, efficiency, and virtuosity. As a function of driving rhythms and intense "singing" timbres, of sustained accuracy, precision, and linear pull, Toscanini's NBC performances proved irresistibly exciting. For the purposes of mass consumption, the music—any music—vibrated with a live-wire tension so palpable every receptive novice could plug in.

An earlier section of this book traced the emergence, after World War I, of a mass culture reflecting new prosperity and technology. Shorter workdays and workweeks, and increased separation of the home from the job, resulted in more leisure time. The twenties were a boom decade for new or expanded recreation modes: Hollywood, the automobile, the radio, spectator sports. Critics of the new recreation order, including scholars and clergymen, were quick to deplore a related decline in such pastimes as handicrafts and music making in the home. The monotony of the factory, and of the factorylike office, was held responsible for less reflective, more vicarious styles of pleasure seeking. As early as 1909, Elizabeth Butler, in a classic study of working-class women in Pittsburgh, blamed high nickelodeon attendance on the blue-collar grind: "Dulled senses demand powerful stimuli; exhaustion of the vital forces leads to a desire for the crude, for violent excitation." In the twenties, feature films and palatial cinemas made movies equally irresistible to a wealthier, more respectable clientele. Radio stations and record companies, too, courted the affluent and upwardly aspirant. To Theodor Adorno, "radio music" inculcated "regressive listening" and "spectatoritis," habits of consumption scarcely more reflective than Hollywood addiction; even Beethoven symphonies, he argued, were reduced to "neat tunes and exciting harmonic stimuli" facilitating a soporific flight from reality. To C. Wright Mills, theorizing in the wake of Adorno, "mass leisure" was a characteristically "frenzied" activity whose cause was alienation on the job and whose purpose was to "astonish, excite and distract": "Leisure," he wrote, "diverts . . . from the restless grind of work by the absorbing grind of passive enjoyment of glamour and thrills." To a more recent, representative media critic on the left, Jeremy Tunstall, the "Hollywood grammar" of "pace, brevity and terseness" is intended to capture the attention of a "jaded" public overexposed to glossy entertainments and media hype. Common to all these perspectives on leisure is the notion of feverish yet passive recreation as a narcotic.[34]

To equate Toscanini broadcasts and recordings with narcotic leisure, as Adorno did, is extreme. Still, Toscanini's cult bears mentioning in this context, with qualifications. The all-purpose formula's maximum mass appeal was, as we have seen, a function of Toscanini's NBC years, when his interpretations grew more simplified and taut. Although the formula was based in Verdi, Toscanini's Verdi depended on it less exclusively than his symphonic performances, where the all-purpose approach yielded less culturally specific forms of excitement. To many a lay listener, who turned the radio dial to the NBC Symphony via "Your Hit Parade," "Death Valley Days," or "Saturday Night Serenade," and whose NBC Symphony recordings were shelved beside albums of Frank Sinatra and Benny Goodman, Toscanini's redundant Beethoven and Weber, Dvořák and Elgar were as instantly and effortlessly preoccupying as a drawn six-shooter at the movies or a three-and-two count, bases loaded, at the ballpark. Like the nickelodeon in Elizabeth Butler's study, they offered "powerful stimuli," "violent excitation." Like the "mass leisure" of C. Wright Mills's analysis, their "glamour and thrills" astonished, excited, and distracted. Like Jeremy Tunstall's "Hollywood grammar," they favored "pace, brevity and terseness." Reviewing a 1943 Toscanini concert of Mozart, Haydn, and Beethoven, Virgil Thomson wrote: "one gets hypnotized . . . and forgets to listen to the music as a human communication." Pondering "The Toscanini Case," he wrote:

> Toscanini's conducting style . . . is very little dependent on literary culture and historical knowledge. It is disembodied music and disembodied theater. It opens few vistas to the understanding of men and epochs; it produces a temporary, but intense, condition of purely auditory excitement. The Maestro is a man of music, nothing else. Being also a man of (in his formative years) predominantly theatrical experience, he reads all music in terms of its possible audience effect. The absence of poetical allusions and of historical references in his interpretations is significant, I think, of a certain disdain for the general culture of his individual listeners. . . . His procedure [is] that of directing a melodrama on the stage, character and dialogue being kept at all times subsidiary to the effects of pure theater, to the building up in the audience of a state of intense anxiety that is relieved only at the end of the last act.[35]

To summarize: the mass appeal of Toscanini's NBC Symphony concerts was a function of all-purpose performance excitement correlative with Verdian visceral mechanics. To this equation must be added the inherent excitement of a stirring, striving overture, tone poem, or symphony, plus —not to be forgotten—the excitement of the Toscanini personality. No less than Toscanini's music making, Toscanini the man "hypnotized" through "violent excitation," "glamour and thrills." Proof of the total equation is the Toscanini telecast of December 29, 1951—in its combination of mesmerizing sound and screen imagery, the fullest single rendering of Toscanini's maximum mass appeal in terms of all-purpose excitement, Verdian popular theater, narcotic relief, and extramusical portraiture. This, preserved on kinescope, is what Americans heard and saw:

"Good evening, ladies and gentlemen, and welcome to Carnegie Hall in New York City," Ben Grauer begins. "Today, the Reynolds Metals Company presents Arturo Toscanini and the NBC Symphony Orchestra in a concert which is being broadcast simultaneously over the National Broadcasting Company's radio and television networks. . . . This simulcast, as it is called, is brought to you as a public service by the makers of Reynolds Aluminum, one of America's great producers of aluminum, the Reynolds Metals Company. A public service, in a literal sense, is appropriately used in connection with aluminum, for, inherently, this light, strong, rust-proof metal has immense potential of service to all the public. . . . And now, in a moment, our concert will begin. This evening, Maestro Toscanini conducts the NBC Symphony in a program of the music of Richard Wagner, including the Prelude to Act I of *Lohengrin*, the Forest Murmurs from *Siegfried*, the Prelude to Act I and *Liebestod* from *Tristan und Isolde*, Siegfried's Death and Funeral March from *Götterdämmerung*, and the Ride of the Valkyries from *Die Walküre*. Arturo Toscanini has just come onto the stage, and in a moment he will conduct the NBC Symphony Orchestra in the Prelude to Act I of Wagner's *Lohengrin*." Toscanini has appeared, striding purposefully toward the podium, his eyes fixed on the floor. He acknowledges the audience, turns to the orchestra, and raises both arms high. Grauer has barely finished introducing the *Lohengrin* prelude when Toscanini brings down his stick, beating a slow four with broad, fluid strokes. His unhappy eyes shift left to watch the entering pianissimo violins, forward to watch the entering pianissimo flutes and oboes, then left again to worry over the stratospheric harmonics of four solo violins. As the prelude gathers force, he beats in ever wider arcs, pumping strenuously from the shoulder. The pure intonation of the high strings, the seamless ensemble of the wind choir contribute to a smooth column of sound lengthening and expanding from a precise starting point. With the entrance of the trumpets, whose shiny brilliance drives the dynamic to forte and fortissimo, Toscanini's eyes gape wide and the worry lines of his forehead flare plaintively upward. The prelude's climactic surge, capped by two cymbal crashes, pries his mouth open as he whips his baton toward the floor, then yanks it effortfully aloft as if dragging a weight—a gesture less free than the churning half-circles and convulsive wrist vibrato of his 1948 Wagner telecast,* but nonetheless hypnotic in its controlled violence. Toscanini's jaw slackens during the prelude's denouement. His baton resumes its fluid pendulum swing. His left hand, palm down, admonishes "piano" and "pianissimo." His eyes shift anxiously left and right. The quartet of solo violins recapitulates its perilous ascent. The remaining violins strain to coordinate their exposed thirty-second notes. For the final cutoff, Toscanini holds up his left palm, then flips it forward. The audience bursts into applause, the musicians hastily page forward through their music, and Ben Grauer announces the Forest Murmurs. Meanwhile, Toscanini drops his baton to his side, then grips it horizontally in both hands, then opens one hand so the stick springs upright, then restlessly subdues it, then releases it, then begins conducting. Like the *Lohengrin* Prelude, *Waldweben* unfold in "fourth-dimensional quietude." Staring forward, Toscanini strokes from the elbow in small, left-to-right arcs while his left hand pats the air, palm down. The strings' oscillating eighth-notes accelerate to poised tremolos, surging and receding with gathering force. Siegfried's soliloquy and the song of the Forest Bird are subsumed by a process of steady, threatening intensification mirrored in Toscanini's face. He frets over a stretch of pointillistic scherzando passagework—a hair trigger for the final E major gunshot. He turns to the excited audience, blinking and squinting under the television lights. He shuffles his feet while the orchestra readies itself for the *Tristan* Prelude and *Liebestod.* This begins, yet again, in forbidding stillness. Toscanini's sculpted profile shows drops of perspiration running down his nose, hanging from the tip, and falling. Navigating the three mounting opening phrases, he beats with increasing animation, leaning into the crescendos. The intervening silences, during which he freezes instead of counting the rests, tingle rather than float. Now the prelude mounts its single, writhing arc. Toscanini's pacing, while not fast, is from the start so high-strung that each sharp, intermittent eruption risks pre-empting the next. As the music gathers volume and speed, Toscanini begins rocking both arms forward and back, up and down. His hands, then his forearms shudder at the base of every jagged, convulsive downstroke. The muscles of his face and neck tighten. His burning eyes and straining mouth, ajar as if he were bellowing the notes, make a gargoyle of his features. At the climax, he whips his baton overhead to slash the air with his longest, most violent guillotine stroke. The musical arc recedes, but Toscanini still holds the line taut. He rushes the rests at the close: the English horn, then the bass clarinet enter early. Now for the *Liebestod,* instantly mobile, sonorously sung, an intoxicating rush of euphony. The orchestra's electric tremolos make Toscanini's hands

---

*See page 271.

vibrate. He launches the three heaving preliminary climaxes ("Heller schallend, mich umwallend") full force, relying on instantaneous withdrawals to save more for later. A close-up shows his face and neck glistening with sweat as he propels Isolde's orgasm to its peak. During the subsiding pleasure-waves, a hint of fatigue—his eyelids sag—reveals the beauty of his features in repose. The *Liebestod*'s final pages, however, find his face hungry, his clamp relentless: the closing rallentando and fermata are barely allowed. He turns to the audience while backing off the podium and is gone. Ben Grauer announces: "In this intermission the makers of Reynolds Aluminum are glad to contribute their full time to a subject of fundamental importance to the nation. The subject is the Citizen of Tomorrow, and the speaker is Mr. David W. Armstrong, national director of the Boys Clubs of America." For two minutes and fifteen seconds, David Armstrong advocates "active sports, clean competition, and healthy teamwork" as "a stout defense against the corner gang, a stout defense against the corner preacher of subversive-isms, and—yes—against the corner peddler of evil addictions." Then Toscanini is back to conduct Siegfried's Death and Funeral March. He has dried his face, but his hair, even his bristling eyebrows, has wilted, and he is breathing more heavily than before. Wagner's pointed march rhythms, difficult to coordinate with the stately pulse, are in Toscanini's performance whispered or pounded out with sinister exactitude. Siegfried's funeral music is the fifth consecutive Wagner extract that builds to a terrific climax—this time more sustained, more eventful, more intense than any of the preceding four. A cannonade of massed winds and brass (thirty-one instruments, including five tubas) is piled atop an earthquake of percussion (triangle, cymbals, tenor drum, and two batteries of timpani). Inflamed to fortissimo, the pitiless march tread alternates with a triumphal variant of Siegfried's horn call. Toscanini presides in majesty. His hard, black, vacant eyes now look *through* the possessed orchestra. The worry lines of his brow reverse into lines of power. For thirty seconds, the cataclysm holds him in its grip. Then his mouth sags, his eyebrows quiver, his lids droop, his brow unknits. The retreating march rhythms remain menacingly tight, but Toscanini is tired. He turns to the audience with short, shuffling steps, holding the podium railing, even leaning on it, while Grauer announces the closing Ride of the Valkyries. Grimly, Toscanini sets to work. He marks time with both arms, whipping downward with every upward swoop of the strings. His eyes are closed except to oversee an occasional entrance, after which they clamp shut with sudden force. The orchestra shudders and pounds, stamping out the Valkyrie motif with inhuman stamina. Following the first reprise, a close-up of Toscanini's face explains his closed eyes: they are flooded with stinging sweat; he is conducting blind, wincing in pain. The whipsaw regularity of his plunging arms, of the musicians' streaking bows, of the trilling winds and braying brass, builds unbearably; Toscanini is driving the machine to the breaking point. For the final reprise, he opens the throttle one more notch—not through agogic delays, like other conductors, but by demanding more volume, more intensity, more weight on every crashing downbeat. Even the rigors of the preceding Funeral March were nothing like these five minutes of steady fortissimo pounding, a clangorous, convulsive vortex of sound superimposed on the screaming imagery of Toscanini's disheveled hair, bellowing mouth, clenched brow, and burning, sightless eyes. A careening glissando drives the music to a last, pulverizing downbeat. While the audience leaps to its feet, cheering and clapping, another drama unfolds on screen. Toscanini puts a handkerchief to his face, swabbing slowly. Then he turns to his first violins—and confides a gentle, dimpled *smile*. Rotating further, he smiles at Edwin Bachmann, leader of the second violins. He strides vigorously offstage, mopping his eyes. This rare public glimpse of the eighty-four-year-old conductor in repose, renewed after sixty minutes of calamitous exertion, is more than reassuring; Toscanini's two fleeting smiles acknowledge the ordeal of his sightlessness and evoke a touching camaraderie with his men. In showing his human face, he even humanizes the NBC Symphony. Beyond a doubt, the telecast's softest, most poignant, most memorable impression is not of the dying Siegfried but of the smiling Toscanini.

In fact, to a startling degree, Wagner's imagery makes no impression at all. In Toscanini's performance, the story of the Forest Murmurs sequence —of Siegfried, enchanted by the "deep silence," struggling to picture his unknown mother; of the Forest Bird describing the sleeping Brünnhilde; of Siegfried rushing off to find her—is sacrificed to coiled-spring excitement. The NBC Symphony's active tremolos contradict "tiefe Stille." The anonymous woodwind solos mechanize Wagner's chatty birdcalls. Drawn taut, the music of Siegfried's mother-love, with its aching reference to the dead Sieglinde, conveys neither rumination nor loss. Siegfried's climactic exclamation sounds fiery, not ebullient. Wagner's own prose description of the *Tristan* Prelude identifies an internal narrative in which "gentle tremors of attraction" mount to unslaked thirst for "endless love's delight"; Toscanini's version registers continuous external convulsions. For Wagner, the *Liebestod* attains "the bliss of quitting life, of being no more"; Toscanini's version rejects Wagnerian bliss. In the opera house, an inspired performance of Siegfried's Death, during which Siegfried hallucinates Brünnhilde's awakening, is wrenching. Toscanini's performance is unsurpassed in lyricism but lacks pathos. His satanic declamation of the Funeral March, which evokes no funeral, is actually incoherent; detached from *Götterdämmerung*'s four-hour buildup, so much sound and fury signify, in Virgil

Thomson's words, "an intense condition of purely auditory excitement"; more than "disembodied theater," it is "disembodied music."

In 1951, Toscanini had not conducted *Götterdämmerung, Lohengrin, Siegfried, Tristan,* or *Die Walküre* for more than two decades. This distancing, plus the exigencies of the NBC-period all-purpose formula, could only have exacerbated the inauthenticities of his 1937 Salzburg *Meistersinger*—his only integral Wagner on disc. The mobile, singing lines of his 1951 televised Wagner; the tingling, fourth-dimensional suspense; the "violent excitation" of the pile-driving climaxes—these are elements of Verdian extroversion oblivious to Wagnerian "inner space." Applied to the Forest Murmurs, the *Liebestod,* or Siegfried's Funeral March, they seize as subject matter not the music itself but its potential to excite. With Toscanini conducting, this potential is so considerable as to furnish subject matter enough. His Wagner concert is first and best comprehended as a Toscanini concert to which Verdi and Wagner contribute. Observing his distraught countenance, we fear yet relish his fury (of his tantrums, Samuel Antek wrote: "We were actually relieved. . . . 'He's himself again.' "). Seeing his smile, we appreciate the humility of the "other Toscanini." His convulsively pumping arms and closed, sweat-drenched eyes make him seem fragile; his helpless submission to the music's emotional rigors amazes us. His joylessness inspires reverence for his idealism, pity for his suffering (Antek wrote: "He seemed an unhappy man . . . we always sensed his frustration in reaching for something —a beauty, an understanding—just beyond his grasp. We sensed his despair.").[36] His implausible resilience in old age makes Toscanini the artist seem the more untouchable, Toscanini the man the more touchingly human. One instinctively comprehends why audiences and orchestral musicians loved and honored him, why Chotzinoff and Sarnoff yearned to please him and win his approval.*

During the years of their rivalries in New York, Bayreuth, and Salzburg, Toscanini and Furtwängler were perceived as polar beacons of the symphonic order. Between them, they may not have illuminated the entire Classical-Romantic canon; neither one, for instance, played *gemütlich* music with *Gemütlichkeit.* But in their complementarity, they shed light on each other's achievements. In the case of Toscanini's 1951 Wagner telecast, it is Furtwängler, more than any other conductor, who illuminates what Toscanini obscures.

---

*The psychology of Toscanini's appeal has been pondered by a psychoanalyst, Martin H. Blum. See Appendix B.

No less than their personalities, credos, and podium presences,* their interpretations of the *Lohengrin* Prelude present a study in contrasts. From the start, Toscanini has his orchestra vocalize the melodic lines. Furtwängler, in his 1954 recording with the Vienna Philharmonic, prefers a shimmery, incorporeal sound, with less string vibrato. Toscanini's tempo, while not hasty, is always distinctly mobile. Furtwängler is much slower (his performance takes 9'50" to Toscanini's 7'35") and initially much more relaxed: he makes little of swells Toscanini italicizes, preferring to let the music build cumulatively. Toscanini's pacing is steadier, with many downbeats perceptibly marked. Furtwängler's fluid pacing erases Wagner's bar lines. The downbeats he marks are long-range stresspoints; unlike Toscanini, for instance, he articulates a series of eight-bar phrases beginning with measures 20, 28, and 36. Toscanini accelerates into the prelude's climax, the whole of which (measures 51 to 57) moves at a new, faster tempo. His shiny trumpets, which enter only at this point, dominate the sound. Furtwängler retards into the climax, the whole of which moves at a new, *slower* tempo. His trumpets are darker, making the prelude's crest less sonically distinct. Postclimax, Toscanini resumes his earlier, slower tempo; Furtwängler, his earlier, faster one. Toscanini retards for the full cadence eight measures from the end. So does Furtwängler, but more drastically—rather than a local event, this unprecedented punctuation point registers the harmonic resolution of the prelude's entire, arcing span.** Both conductors retard again at the very close. Furtwängler makes the bigger gesture, stopping all forward motion and diminishing to silence.

No difference between the two performances is more crucial than the contradictory tempo changes at the climax. Toscanini, sensing one-bar units and relying on surface tension to keep the music whole, holds the line with a relatively tight rein. At moments of peak arousal, he grips harder and speeds up. Furtwängler's reliance on four-bar units (or multiples thereof) and sustained harmonic tension allows for more play in the line. At moments of peak arousal, he slows down to give the harmonic tensions space in which to expand and resolve. He can also let the line go slack without stopping long-term musical flow; unlike Toscanini's, Furtwängler's climaxes pre-empt repose and lead to exhaustion. Their slow, weighted pulse might be likened to that of a pendulum swinging with greater force as it spans ever longer arcs. Their visceral impact bears some relation to the

---

*See pages 101–2.

**Furtwängler frequently conferred with the celebrated theoretician Heinrich Schenker. In Schenkerian analysis, whole movements of sonatas and symphonies are shown to elaborate core linear and harmonic progressions.

Hollywood convention of shooting moments of crisis or ecstasy in slow motion. Inner turmoil produces a sensation of temporal dislocation. Time "slows down," even "stands still." In the Prelude to *Lohengrin*, Furtwängler's slow-motion climax seems to exist outside time.

Furtwängler's predication of frequent pulse modification on phrase groupings and harmonic rhythms "beneath" the music's surface follows Wagner's practice. I do not know specific passages in Wagner's writings advocating the slow-motion climax, but his music more than implies it; in *Lohengrin*, the climactic trumpet lines are marked "sehr gehalten"(i.e., held, sustained). The prelude as a whole, according to Wagner, represents a vision in which angels carry the Holy Grail. Furtwängler's performance is ethereal, Toscanini's less so—unless its vibrant timbres are taken to represent Italianate singing angels, as in the Prologue to *Mefistofele* (of which Toscanini was an unsurpassed exponent). The Italian music most precisely evoked by Toscanini's performance of the *Lohengrin* prelude, however, is the similarly conceived prelude to *Aida* (Verdi admired *Lohengrin*, and it is not farfetched to infer Wagnerian influence here). The differences between Verdi's prelude and Wagner's are the differences between Toscanini's Wagner and Furtwängler's: Verdi's is more segmented, more short breathed, more highly strung. The tunes are more vocal. The harmonies are more prone to short-term resolution. The climax is swifter and more pointed.

These Toscanini-Furtwängler differences, and others as well, can be drawn and redrawn for all the Wagner excerpts on Toscanini's 1951 telecast. The excitement of Toscanini's performance is an incidental offshoot of all-purpose intensity and conviction; Siegfried's Funeral Music, in this mode, sounds defiant. The dominant motif of Furtwängler's 1954 performance, by comparison, is a concept: the death of a hero. A binding interior state—call it mournful solemnity—governs considerations of structure and timbre. The Vienna Philharmonic—no radio orchestra, but an opera orchestra versed in the whole of *Götterdämmerung*—is a collaborative presence; the woodwind and horn solos do not lock into step, but spontaneously articulate the evolving threnody. Only with the appearance of the sword motif, which Wagner introduces once the funeral procession has disappeared behind mist, does Furtwängler shift toward heroic declamation. The climax, in Toscanini's performance Everest atop a homogeneous Himalayan landscape, is ephemeral—with the appearance of the Gibichung Hall, Siegfried's march grows veiled and ominous.

It is, finally, in the two *Tristan* excerpts that Furtwängler's immersion in subjectivity and deep structure consummates his immersion in Wagnerian inner space. The prelude begins and ends in enervation, yet pulsates with tireless engines of desire. In the *Liebestod*, completely different, the blended timbres of the 1938 Berlin Philharmonic (versus Toscanini's NBC Symphony, with its discrete choirs and superimposed timpani) complement an orgasmic groundplan culminating in bliss. Yehudi Menuhin might have been thinking of Furtwängler's *Tristan* when he wrote: "In listening to [Furtwängler's music making], it is the impression of vast, pulsating space which is most overwhelming." So might have Josef Krips when he wrote that "one had the impression that the music came from eternity and went back there." In terms of sustained "purely auditory excitement," Toscanini's tingling tremolos and seething linear tension have more to offer; one submits with clenched teeth and white knuckles. To Furtwängler's Wagner one submits more actively, entering into varied, imaginatively re-created worlds of feeling; and the climaxes drive one backward, not toward the edge of the seat.

The interventionist trademarks of Furtwängler's Wagner are generic Furtwängler trademarks. A composer himself, he manifests a composer's distrust of textual fidelity; as he put it in his book *Concerning Music* (1949), he believed Haydn, Mozart, Beethoven, and Schubert were typically treated with such wrongheaded detachment that the music sounded "reported on" rather than re-created. Concomitantly, he believed that "the essence of the creative process is to be found in improvisation, which formed the basis of that which is written down," and that "improvisation is in truth the basis of all genuine music-making." Menuhin has observed:

> [Furtwängler] did not want to impose too stern or too rigid a frame upon his musicians. He preferred to start a piece and let something happen. . . . The total reaction of an intelligent body of musicians [is] more valid and more right than that of any single one of them. Especially is this true when the work is a Classical work in which they are deeply steeped, or [of] which they know the tradition very well. I have always found that a whole orchestra is never wrong. . . . The importance of the conductor is to guide them as a very wonderful rider might guide a horse, which is an intelligent being. It is an entirely different matter from driving a car, which is not an intelligent being.[37]

Furtwängler's reliance on collaborative "improvisation"; his penchant for far-seeing metric and harmonic organization, dictating local and long-term rubatos and slow-motion climaxes; his capacity for absorption in a binding emotional concept achieved striking results in a varied repertoire. In the first movement of Tchaikovsky's *Pathétique* Symphony, it was his inspiration to imbue the famous second subject with *Weltschmerz* and magnify, rather than balance, the prevailing sadness. In Brahms's First, his ongoing re-creative design included slowing the third-movement coda to a standstill and beginning the finale in a void. In the andante of Schubert's "Great" C major Symphony, which he took as an adagio, his long, lofty phrasings facilitated rarefied, slow-motion treatment of the passage in which a solo horn, in Schumann's well-known description, "calls from a distance" like a "heavenly visitant." In Beethoven's Fifth, his rhetorical pulse manipulations* did not preclude unusually truthful renderings of rhythm and metrical structure: more than Toscanini, he articulated the rest with which the first-movement motto begins; unlike Toscanini, he perceived that the scherzo's strong measures are even numbered, not odd (as proved by the accentuation of the returning motto rhythms, beginning at measure 19). Heard today, these memorable readings sound less than idiomatic; for better or worse, they impose precepts of Wagnerian interpretation on non-Wagnerian repertoire. Like Toscanini, Furtwängler merges most completely with the music closest to his time: to Wagner, Bruckner, and Richard Strauss, and to his own late-Romantic symphonies. By the same token, the Furtwängler performances that have aged most are of Bach and Handel. His Beethoven and Schubert possess a revealing or distracting massiveness, breadth, and rhythmic pliancy. Moreover, no less than Toscanini with his Verdian Beethoven and Wagner, Furtwängler betrays a pronounced national bias. His one Verdi recording, of the 1951 Salzburg *Otello*, is effectively Wagnerian, as in the rapturous (and, for the singers, unwieldy) long lines of the first-act love duet, yet cannot bear comparison with Toscanini's coiled, Italianate *Otello*.

Both Verdi and Wagner flourished in an epoch of nationalistic culture, and they knew it. Wagner was a chauvinistic Germanophile. Verdi was not above branding Germans "men with heads but not hearts; a strong but uncivilized race." More realistically, he contended that "an Italian must write as an Italian, a German as a German. Their natures are too different for them to blend"; that "our music, unlike German music . . . is rooted principally in the theater." Toscanini, no less than Verdi, was an Italian

---

*A short history of Beethoven Fifth recordings, beginning with Nikisch's of 1913 (see page 338), would encapsulate a transformation in perceived rhythmic stability. Much as Wagner must have, Nikisch takes different themes or episodes at different speeds: his pulse is flexible throughout. To some degree, Nikisch-like plasticity was once the norm —Beethoven was made to sound elastic; whole pages could be stretched or compressed without violating canons of stylistic decorum. Toscanini signified a turning point toward a new norm: uniform pulse (or its illusion) throughout. Furtwängler's postwar Beethoven Fifths were already a throwback; other conductors of like predilection had mainly died off or (like Bruno Walter, whose American-period recordings are strikingly steadier than his European recordings of the twenties and thirties) switched horses. While Furtwängler eventually exerted a strong posthumous influence, there was no possibility of fully resurrecting his tempo modifications in Beethoven.

patriot. And it was not for nothing that Furtwängler was called by Paul Hindemith "the representative figure of German music," by Leo Blech "the guiding figure of German conducting," by Wilhelm Kempff "the musical conscience of Germany," by Menuhin the "highest expression" of humane German art.[38] Polar opposites in terms of upbringing, appearance, temperament, and interpretive philosophy, Toscanini and Furtwängler both partook of existing nationalistic norms. Only subsequently did more style-conscious interpreters of more multinational bent strive to extrapolate essentially distinct Italian, German, and French performance modes. To the degree Toscanini's orientation was stylistically neutral, he, more than Furtwängler, was a transitional figure. To the degree it was Verdian, Toscanini and Furtwängler were late embodiments of nineteenth-century cultural nationalism, and also of an epoch of specialized-repertoire conductors that had originated with composer-conductors like Berlioz and Wagner.

According to the New York *Times* obituary: "Both as an operatic and a symphonic conductor, [Toscanini] achieved a stature no other conductor before him had attained." The *Time* obituary read: "No contemporary conductor could match his subtlety of nuance. . . . [Toscanini] came closer to realizing the music of Beethoven, Schubert, Wagner, and Verdi than any conductor ever did." Lawrence Gilman called Toscanini "the First Musician of the world," "the greatest musical interpreter who ever lived." To David Sarnoff, Toscanini was "the world's greatest conductor"; to David Ewen, "the greatest musical interpreter of our time"; to Samuel Chotzinoff, "the greatest musical interpreter of our time—perhaps of all time"—in whose performances "masterpieces of music of all ages" achieved "their loftiest, their most perfect expression." With the evidence of Toscanini's recordings and telecasts before us, the justice of these claims may be gauged. In choosing to deify Toscanini, the New York *Times*, *Time*, Gilman, Sarnoff, Ewen, and Chotzinoff deified one of the twentieth century's towering interpretive musicians, in whom commanding integrity and electrifying charisma were combined. His performances of the Classical and Romantic repertoire were unrivaled for urgency and unsurpassed for conviction. They surged with song and throbbed with dramatic intensity. But Toscanini was no Toscanini.

His admirers framed his greatness in terms of self-effacing "objectivity," of "fidelity to the score." It was said of his performances that they were "perfect" renderings of the compositional blueprints, that the music was "resurrected" and "re-created" whole. The *Times* obituary put it this way: "He strove earnestly to realize as exactly as possible the composer's intentions as printed in the musical score." *Time*'s obituary said: "As a conductor, he made fidelity to the composer his watchword." Lawrence Gilman praised his "ideal of lofty and self-effacing service" to the composer. Olin Downes summarized: "He only tries, each season, to come nearer to the wishes of the composer, to be more faithful, if that is possible, to the spirit that is behind the notes on the music paper." Chotzinoff, in an essay entitled "Beethoven and Toscanini," praised Toscanini's "reliance on the printed score or manuscript" as "basic to interpretation," and continued:

> Nothing a composer writes down is insignificant for Toscanini—a sign like < > between two pianissimi is given its just increase, neither more, like ⟨ ⟩ nor less, like < ⟩ . There is for him the nicest distinction between all *shades* of sound. A forte will be fairly loud and each additional *f* a finely proportioned extension of the original sonority. He carefully adheres to the true meaning, as far as he can trace it, of allegro, vivace, lento, adagio, andante, etc. For Toscanini, but alas for very few others, andante means "going," "advancing." . . .
>
> Toscanini gives the most careful consideration and adherence to the entire arsenal of musical symbols—legato, staccato, fermata, rests, the long and short linear tents that encase musical phrases. After all, composers *did* and *do* take pains to write these things down![39]

Tenacious literalism, in Chotzinoff's opinion, was the groundwork for Toscanini's "conscious crusade to rid music of the excrescences left by tradition and the misconceptions of vainglorious interpreters," a crusade culminating in "restorations" of the nine Beethoven symphonies in which "Toscanini sees Beethoven 'plain.' " In fact, Toscanini's objective rendering of prescribed local detail—a rendering pious in spirit, if, given his rescorings and other adjustments, less piously submissive than Chotzinoff indicated—was no absolute interpretive precondition but a possible aspect of truthful interpretation not necessarily eclipsing less localized aspects: the articulation of multiple-bar phrasings and long-range harmonic structure; the empathetic grasp of emotional states, both sustained and incidental; the application of a probing, pertinent cultural base. To ponder "Beethoven and Toscanini" is to ponder Toscanini's outsider status as evinced by Verdian and tabula rasa readings.

No less than textual fidelity, Toscanini's catholicity of repertoire was an article of faith among his adherents. As Chotzinoff wrote: "For Italians, Toscanini is the supreme interpreter of Rossini, Verdi and Puccini. For Germans, he is the supreme interpreter of Beethoven and Wagner; for Austrians, of Haydn, Mozart and Schubert. For the French, he is the very mouthpiece of Debussy and for the English the finest exponent of Elgar." As Toscanini's versatility was taken to demonstrate and validate self-effacing service to the composer, challenges in this arena excited touchy rebuttals. George Marek, in his Toscanini biography, writes: "When he played Smetana's *Moldau* you thought he must have been born in Prague. When he played the 'Enigma' Variations you wondered how often he had strolled down Pall Mall"—and adds in a footnote: "I chose these two examples because some critics felt that he did *not* conduct these compositions in the correct style."[40] In fact, the all-purpose formula facilitated a kind of versatility insofar as it guaranteed febrile excitement yet impeded idiomatic interpretation insofar as guaranteed febrile excitement became a Toscanini signature. To appreciate the potency of Toscanini's reputation for stylistic versatility in the face of his increasing predilection for a compressed, vehement all-purpose style, one must recall its source in the pre-NBC years, when his febrile trademark was yet unregistered and national performance schools were yet ascendant. In 1930 and 1935, Neville Cardus and Ernest Newman might well have marveled at the excellence of an Italian conductor's Elgar (around the same time, Otto Klemperer was raising eyebrows in Berlin for championing the "French" Stravinsky). By 1975, when Marek wrote his Toscanini biography, such skilled, self-effacing generalists as Bernard Haitink had for some time displayed a flexible command of Smetana and Elgar (and Stravinsky and Tchaikovsky) beside which Toscanini's high-strung NBC renditions screamed "Toscanini!" By the same token, the "definitive" label affixed to so many NBC Symphony performances was held over from his years of peak international stature. In Chotzinoff's words, Toscanini 'saw Beethoven plain.' But to the degree Toscanini's Verdian Beethoven approached a plausible idiomatic norm, it predated the ferocious all-purpose mode. Compared with his relatively "plain" BBC Symphony recording, the angry Beethoven Fourth he recorded with the NBC Symphony is compellingly theatrical yet wrong; like his Beethoven Eighth, *Oberon* Overture, *Götterdämmerung* Funeral March, and other excitingly, aberrantly militant NBC performances, it established an insidious model for future generations of American musicians and listeners.

To Olin Downes, Toscanini's NBC years marked "the summit of his career"; to Marek, "the most fruitful period of his life"; to Sarnoff, "the golden age of the symphony orchestra in America." In fact, not only did Toscanini's "objectivity" and "catholicity" diminish at NBC; during this period of peak celebrity, of maximum mass appeal, his artistic stature diminished as well. With the impingement of extreme age, and of extreme isolation, his performance style grew simpler and less flexible. Dislocated from the opera houses and concert halls where he had held sway, he shared an NBC showcase with a part-time orchestra. His dislocated repertoire fixed on accredited symphonic masterpieces from two previous centuries. His belated reunion with the theater also proved dislocated. When in 1962, Otto Klemperer, age seventy-six, undertook recording *Fidelio*, Walter Legge assembled a cast including Christa Ludwig, Jon Vickers, Gottlob Frick, and Walter Berry. Judging from the 1935 Salzburg *Fidelio*, Toscanini in 1944 might have conducted a *Fidelio* recording as enduring as Klemperer's. But his NBC Leonore lacked presence, his Florestan was a lyric tenor specializing in Italian repertoire, his Rocco swallowed and distorted words in a role where Toscanini aimed for revitalizing velocity and crispness, and his Marzelline's creamy soprano incongruously dominated the first-act quartet. The year before Klemperer made his recording, he was coaxed back to the opera house—he led *Fidelio,* and later *The Magic Flute* and *Lohengrin,* at Covent Garden—for the first time in eleven years. The basis of Toscanini's recording was a single broadcast performance without dialogue, given in an acoustically defective studio before a synthetic audience. Klemperer's strong personality was challenged and stimulated by artists such as those Toscanini had worked with at Salzburg and by the opportunities and exigencies of a major staged production. Toscanini presided in vacuo over *Fidelio,* his stranding a microcosm of his lonely eminence at NBC, provided with "a musical miracle . . . an orchestra of unsurpassed attainments" and "the world's largest broadcasting studio," marketed as "NBC's great conductor" and "the priest of music." The historic orchestras and halls of Europe and America, with their audiences and nourishing traditions, ceased to exist for him. He said: "I shrink into myself like a snail."

Of the leading Old World musicians driven to the New World by fascism—an exodus including Bartók, Beecham, Adolf and Fritz Busch, Hindemith, Kleiber, Klemperer, Schnabel, Schoenberg, Stravinsky, and Walter—Toscanini most clearly achieved enhanced celebrity in his new home. No less than the others, however, he did his most fulfilling work at home in Europe. In exile at NBC, he achieved results outstanding by standards other than his own. But his purely musical accomplishments did not account for his continued reputation as an inspired practitioner of "objectivity" and as the "world's greatest conductor"; judged by his best-known NBC recordings, neither encomium fits. The reasons that Toscanini's success was greatest at NBC, and that he flourished where other musical emigrants faded or floundered, are to be found in the disembodied thrills of his NBC performances and in his thrilling personal attributes. Of the several ironies afflicting Toscanini's New World cult—that it peaked as he declined, that its democratic trappings festooned closed-door concerts for an invited elite—this was the crown: that the ostensibly most self-effacing of musicians ultimately gripped his followers as an emanation of self. Spontaneous and unpretentious, the Toscanini personality embodied America; tyrannical and uncompromising, it embodied Art. His Beethoven defied Hitler and Mussolini. His Gershwin confided affection for his "second home" in America. Conducting Wagner on TV, drenched in perspiration at the age of eighty-four, he showed superhuman resilience, then heartwarmingly affirmed his mortality with unexpected smiles. And all this was copiously, extravagantly merchandised and promoted. David Sarnoff was right to ignore Toscanini the musician in observing that "enthralled throngs of Americans" had "found Toscanini the man to be even greater than Toscanini the legend." To metaphrase the New York *Times,* Toscanini did not attain "a stature no other conductor before him had attained"; his personality is what attained unprecedented stature among conductors. And to speak of his legacy is, again, to speak primarily in extramusical terms: Toscanini the conductor influenced mere generations of heirs and epigones; the Toscanini cult, with its unprecedented machinery and machinations, exerted the more lasting impact.

IV · After Toscanini

Collapse of the Cult

Toscanini's heir apparent was Guido Cantelli, whose short fuse and selfless dedication made him seem as honest, obstreperous, and unostentatious as Toscanini himself. The son of a bandmaster, he studied at the Milan Conservatory and later conducted in his native Novara. When World War II intervened, he refused to fight for Nazi principles and wound up in a German labor camp, then an Italian hospital, from which he escaped to live under an assumed name until the liberation. His personality combined impenetrable reserve with boyish exuberance; in New York, he liked attending wrestling matches with Italian-born colleagues. The turning point in his career came in 1948, when Toscanini embraced him backstage following his first Scala concert. He conducted the NBC Symphony four times the following season, after which Toscanini wrote to Cantelli's wife, Iris: "This is the first time in my long life that I have met a young man so gifted. He will go far, very far. Love him well, because Guido is good, simple and modest."[1] In years following, the Cantellis were taken into the Toscanini family. When Cantelli died in an airplane crash on November 23, 1956, aged thirty-six, the news was kept from Toscanini.

Cantelli rehearsed and conducted from memory. A nerve-wracking taskmaster, he once had the Philharmonia Orchestra record Ravel's *Pavane for a Dead Princess* some twenty times in a row. He could not balance the harp to his satisfaction. "He was always shouting '*arrrp! arrrp!*, just like a dog," the orchestra's principal harpist later recalled. "Always shouting before the harp even started to play."[2] The intense concentration and perfectionism of Cantelli's rehearsals were apparent in his performances. While his recordings do not project a fully developed musical personality, he was no Toscanini clone; in particular, he rejected the hypertense simplicity of Toscanini's all-purpose phase. Toscanini said of Cantelli: "I love this young conductor; I think he is like me when I was young." Aspects of Cantelli's recorded performances—their smooth skin, their tonal refinement, their fastidious detail—specifically evoke Toscanini as he must have sounded in youth and middle age. At the same time, Cantelli sounds more cosmopolitan, less Italian, than Toscanini does in his first recordings. In this regard, Cantelli was of his time. To a degree impossible for an Italian conductor of Toscanini's generation, he was not schooled in the opera house, not brought up on Verdi. His repertoire included Hindemith and Bartók.

Beginning in 1951, Cantelli was prominently associated with the New York Philharmonic, but he died too soon to exert an influence. Other Italian conductors associated with Toscanini, including Antonino Votto, who taught Cantelli in Milan, were even less significant outside Europe. As far as Americans were concerned, the Toscanini torch was passed to non-Italians, less like Toscanini in temperament and background than Cantelli, more prone to assimilate Toscanini's imprint as an impersonal ideal. Conductors prominent in the United States on whom Toscanini exerted a formative influence included Erich Leinsdorf and Artur Rodzinski, both of whom we have already encountered. Leinsdorf, after having served as Toscanini's assistant in Salzburg, was music director in Cleveland (1943–44), Rochester (1947–55), and Boston (1962–69), and has been on and off the Metropolitan Opera's conducting roster since 1939. Rodzinski, whom Toscanini helped procure engagements with the New York Philharmonic and NBC Symphony and at Salzburg, was principal conductor of the Los Angeles Philharmonic (1929–33), the Cleveland Orchestra (1933–43), the New York Philharmonic (1943–47), and the Chicago Symphony (1947–48). William Steinberg, whom Toscanini heard conduct the new Palestine Orchestra after the Nazis had forced Steinberg to leave the Frankfurt Opera, came to the United States at Toscanini's invitation to be associate conductor of the NBC Symphony in 1938. He subsequently was music director in Buffalo (1945–52), Pittsburgh (1952–72), and Boston (1968–72) as well as senior guest conductor of the New York Philharmonic (1966–68). Alfred Wallenstein, whom we have encountered as Toscanini's first cellist with the New York Philharmonic, turned to conducting on Toscanini's advice, becoming a leading radio conductor, then principal conductor of the Los Angeles Philharmonic (1943–56). Milton Katims, a violist and assistant conductor under Toscanini at NBC, became music director of the Seattle Symphony (1954–74). Frank Brieff, another Toscanini violist, led the New Haven Symphony (1952–74). For three other conductors whose careers flourished in America, Toscanini, while not a direct connection, was a leading inspiration. To Charles Munch of the Boston Symphony (1949–62) he seemed "of all the great . . . the greatest." To Pierre Monteux of the Boston Symphony (1919–24) and San Francisco Symphony (1936–52), he was "the greatest of all." To Eugene Ormandy of the Minneapolis Symphony (1931–36) and Philadelphia Orchestra (1938–80), he was "the greatest conductor of all times," the "one and only musical influence" of Ormandy's life.[3]

As a group, these ten Toscanini beneficiaries and admirers were diverse in ability and orientation.* But in conjunction with lesser lights, and with George Szell of Cleveland and Fritz Reiner of Cincinnati, Pittsburgh, and Chicago,** they mainly contributed to a symphonic climate seizing and amplifying aspects of the all-purpose formula: objectivity, precision, linear tension. According to the crewcut American musical aesthetics of the fifties, pronounced rubatos and poetic metaphor as an aspect of interpretation were as old-fashioned as side whiskers and beards; high praise was reserved for expression achieved without pulse change or personal signature. Like Toscanini, his United States progeny were for the most part intent on extracting lucid orchestral blueprints and shedding Romantic dross. Unlike Toscanini, most of them betrayed no pronounced national base: Verdian theatrics and vocal inflection were no part of their performance style. At worst, the new norm sounded mechanized in its cruel drive and exaggerated self-effacement.

A glance at Europe's important conductors of the 1950s, and at several important Europeans undervalued in America during this period, reinforces the New World locus of Toscanini's musical legacy. Those without extensive American careers included Ernest Ansermet, Thomas Beecham, Eduard van Beinum, Adrian Boult, Wilhelm Furtwängler, Eugen Jochum, Herbert von Karajan, Rudolf Kempe, Erich Kleiber, Hans Knappertsbusch, Clemens Krauss, Igor Markevitch, and Victor de Sabata. Those whose American careers were impeded included Otto Klemperer, exiled to Los Angeles (1933–39) after being a leading conductor in Berlin;† Josef

---

*All, not so incidentally, conducted the NBC Symphony: Cantelli, 44 times; Leinsdorf, 23; Rodzinski, 12; Steinberg, 14; Wallenstein, 17; Katims, 52; Brieff, 2; Munch, 1; Monteux, 8; Ormandy, 6. No conductor was engaged by the NBC Symphony without Toscanini's approval.

**See pages 379–82.

†As we have seen (page 183), Klemperer sought Toscanini's and Stokowski's New York and Philadelphia posts, but was opposed by Arthur Judson. Klemperer's biographer Peter Heyworth has commented:

> Musical conditions in Southern California were still primitive, and financial restraints limited Klemperer's field of action. He worked conscientiously and with some success to improve his orchestra and to expand its repertory. But his bad relationship with Judson . . . was enough to ensure that other engagements were not forthcoming. It is a significant fact that during the fifteen years that he lived in the United States, Klemperer did not make a single recording.

Krips, exiled to Buffalo (1953–63) after being a leading conductor in Vienna and London (he later conducted the San Francisco Symphony, 1963–70); Bruno Walter, who found the Metropolitan Opera's star system not to his liking; and Dimitri Mitropoulos, whose tenure with the New York Philharmonic (1950–58), which was heretically focused on repertoire rather than pristine execution, was opposed by Howard Taubman of the New York *Times*. As a group, these seventeen conductors were not immune to Felix Weingartner's backlash against undisciplined subjectivity, yet they remained steeped in traditional ways. Some were fervent Furtwängler admirers—to Ansermet, Furtwängler was "the greatest interpreter of the Classics in our century"; to Jochum, an early and persistent role model; to Kempe, "the most remarkable phenomenon" among conductors "of our time"; to Mitropoulos, "the artist I admired most in my life." Others in the group exuded an expansive or relaxed manner equally foreign to American mores; the *Gemütlichkeit* of a Walter or Krips coexisted uneasily with such frowning musical countenances as Leinsdorf's, Reiner's, Szell's—or Toscanini's. Klemperer, while a frowning autocrat, was not an autocratic precisionist. This was a time, too, of proliferating minor American conductors in the Toscanini mold. Winthrop Sargeant said of them: "It suddenly became a crime in symphonic music to deviate from strict mechanical regularity. Conductors . . . began conducting with a rigid, mechanized relentlessness that suggested the goosestep. Some even copied [Toscanini's] most irrelevant mannerisms." To which Virgil Thomson added:

> . . . Young conductors don't bother much any more to feel music or to make their musicians feel it. They analyze it, concentrate in rehearsal on the essentials of its rhetoric, and let the expressive details fall where they may, counting on each man's skill and everybody's instinctive musicianship to take care of these eventually. Poetry and nobility of

---

The nadir of Klemperer's United States career came in 1951, when he arrived from Hungary. His three years at the head of the Budapest Opera had made him politically suspect: his passport was confiscated, effectively limiting his activities to North America. He remained practically unemployed until his passport was returned in 1953, after which a remarkable "second career" based in London made him a revered old master. Klemperer's friend Jascha Horenstein (1899–1973) suffered a similar fate. A Furtwängler protégé in Berlin in the early twenties, he was music director in Düsseldorf until he was forced out by the Nazis in 1933. Beginning in 1940, he lived in the United States for more than a decade, during which Judson found almost no work for him. Horenstein finally enjoyed a European Indian summer, being especially revered in London. It must be added that neither Klemperer nor Horenstein was easy to get along with; Klemperer's difficulties in America derived in part from his notorious emotional instability.[4]

expression are left for the last, to put in as with an eyedropper or laid on like icing, if there is time. All this is good because it makes music less esoteric. It is crude because it makes understanding an incidental matter; but it is a useful procedure and one wholly characteristic of our land and century. . . .

. . . It is noticeable already that lesser conductors analyze music better than they used to and that this simple extraction of a work's formal essence tends to facilitate rather than to obfuscate differentiations of style and expression in the conducting of men whose musical experience is more limited but whose general culture is more ample than Toscanini's. . . .

Toscanini's influence lies, so far, chiefly in America. . . . [Europe's] tradition is too complex for us. We admire the work of the great European conductors but we do not quite understand how it is done. A century of importing them has not revealed their secrets to our local boys. We watched Toscanini work for ten years at the Philharmonic; and now there are 30,000 symphony orchestras in the United States, practically all of them led by the local boys. He is the founding father of American conducting. . . .*

. . . Any influence Toscanini might possibly have on European musical life would be anti-cultural. His ruthless clearing away here, however, of Romantic weeds and unsuccessful implantations has made a space where conductors are already being grown locally. . . .⁵

During the post-Toscanini decade, two American orchestras became virtuoso showcases for Toscanini-like cleanliness and precision: supplanting the orchestras of Boston, New York, and Philadelphia, the Cleveland Orchestra under Szell and the Chicago Symphony under Reiner became known as the most efficient, most prestigious American orchestras, better disciplined than any others in the world. Even in comparison to Toscanini at NBC, Szell and Reiner achieved surpassing feats of instrumental coordination: their winds were better tuned, their rhythms more exact. At the same time, whereas Toscanini was an earthy Mediterranean martinet, Reiner and Szell were aloof Hungarian martinets. Neither endorsed the

---

*Thomson's "30,000" is hyperbole; a more reasonable count of American orchestras for 1942 would be 400. Among the prominent or soon-to-be-prominent "local boys" with orchestras of their own in that year were Victor Alessandro of the Oklahoma City Symphony, Howard Barlow of the Baltimore and CBS symphonies, Saul Caston of the Reading (Pennsylvania) Symphony, Thor Johnson of the Grand Rapids Symphony, Karl Krueger of the Kansas City Philharmonic, Izler Solomon of the Illinois Symphony, and Alfred Wallenstein of the Wallenstein Sinfonietta, a radio orchestra.

humanizing vocal *melos* Toscanini extracted when he exhorted his men to sing.

Szell, born in Budapest in 1897, began as an opera conductor in Berlin, Strasbourg, Prague, and Vienna. World War II drove him to America, where he conducted at the Metropolitan Opera before becoming music director in Cleveland, a post he held from 1946 to 1970. Judging from recordings, Rodzinski had already fine-tuned the Cleveland Orchestra; under the subtler, more sophisticated Szell, it attained its peak reputation, as did Szell himself. As we have seen, Toscanini's integrity, objectivity, and precision made a decisive impression on Szell in 1930; later, in America, he praised Toscanini with such carefully chosen words as:

> [Richard Strauss was] the nearest to a commanding influence in my formative years. . . . There are many others whom I could mention, of course. No one could leave a man like Toscanini unmentioned. Whatever you may think about his interpretation of a specific work, that he changed the whole concept of conducting and that he rectified many, many arbitrary procedures of a generation of conductors before him is now already authentic history. That at the same time he has served as a not too useful model for a generation of conductors who were so fascinated that they were unable to follow him with some sense of discrimination is equally true, I believe.

Toscanini respected Szell sufficiently to invite him to conduct the NBC Symphony six times, only to be offended by Szell's finicky, start-and-stop rehearsal of Beethoven's Second. In Cleveland, Szell's stated objective was "to combine the American purity and beauty of sound and their virtuosity of execution with the European sense of tradition, warmth of expression and sense of style." Szell also said:

> I personally like complete homogeneity of sound, phrasing, and articulation within each section, and then—when the ensemble is perfect— the proper balance between sections plus complete flexibility—so that in a moment one or more principal voices can be accompanied by the others. To put it simply: the most sensitive ensemble playing. Perhaps I can best characterize my idea when I say it should be a chamber music approach. . . .[6]

The vaunted transparency of Szell's orchestra—"I start out with the assumption that everything a good composer writes down is supposed to be heard except in obvious cases where a coloristic impression is intended"—

recalled Toscanini, as did his preference for distinct string and wind choirs. But Szell's "complete homogeneity"—the starting point of his quest for complete versatility and flexibility, mandating matched, anonymous winds and restrained vibratos—risked a sanitizing chastity removed from the urgency of Toscanini's sound. Interpretively, his attention to detail seemed linked to suppressed rhythmic and tonal license. In Mahler's Fourth Symphony, one of Szell's finest Cleveland recordings (1965), his minute observance of Mahler's copious instructions is a tour de force of technique, and his "chamber music approach" capitalizes on Mahler's ingenious scoring. Also, Szell is more relaxed, more expansive than usual. Only a lingering worldliness betrays emotional reticence.

Reiner, born in Budapest in 1888, was already chief conductor of the Dresden State Opera during World War I. Like Szell, he knew and learned from Richard Strauss; he also credited Nikisch with influencing his famously disciplined stick technique. He left Europe in his thirties, conducting the Cincinnati Symphony from 1922 to 1931. He subsequently taught at the Curtis Institute, conducted the Pittsburgh Symphony from 1938 to 1948, and conducted at the Metropolitan. Toscanini had him lead the NBC Symphony fourteen times. Reiner's Chicago Symphony tenure, from 1953 to 1962, had an instructive beginning. Following the Furtwängler debacle of 1948–49, the orchestra was led by Désiré Defauw (1943–47), Rodzinski (1947–48), and Rafael Kubelik (1950–53). Defauw lacked stature. Rodzinski was dismissed following a row with management. Kubelik, in appearance the model of an absentminded professor (his gangly frame and imprecise gestures somewhat evoked Furtwängler), also made important enemies. In particular, Claudia Cassidy, the acid-tongued chief critic of the Chicago *Tribune,* agitated for his removal. Her reviews, like Olin Downes's of Furtwängler twenty-five years before in New York, were themselves a cause célèbre. She found Kubelik's adventurous programming "altogether curious," his performances lacking in "clarity and form." In a farewell to the Kubelik regime, she complained of anonymous hate mail from Kubelik supporters and called the orchestra's deterioration "unspeakably shocking." Kubelik returned to Europe, where his reputation soared. Cassidy hailed his successor as "feast after famine. . . . With Fritz Reiner on the job I don't see how we can have anything but a fine orchestra."[7] Like Cleveland's orchestra under Szell, the Chicago Symphony under Reiner achieved unprecedented celebrity; Igor Stravinsky was not alone in calling it "the most precise and flexible orchestra in the world." Like Szell, Reiner was a harsh taskmaster and poker-faced interpreter; he reveled in power. In his recording of *Ein Heldenleben* (1954), among his most admired, expression arises, as in Toscanini's Siegfried's Funeral March, as a seemingly incidental outcome of arresting, preternatural muscle and exactitude. (Earlier Strauss

specialists, including Mengelberg, Furtwängler, and Strauss himself, vividly characterized the scenarios of the tone poems; Strauss is said even to
have conducted Beethoven symphonies with a "story" in mind.) Toscanini's recorded performances sometimes evoke machine metaphors, but
with a modicum of flesh and blood appended—as if to account for the
strong, nervous grasp of the hand holding the throttle. Reiner's machine
—its parts heroically vast, wonderfully flexible yet firm—sounds self-sufficient.

Around the time Szell and Reiner were perfecting their orchestras in
Cleveland and Chicago, American orchestras acquired a reputation in
Europe for anonymity. This was a reputation never acquired by the New
York Philharmonic under Toscanini, or the Philadelphia Orchestra under
Stokowski, or the Boston Symphony under Koussevitzky.

The Toscanini climate also influenced American rankings of solo instrumentalists. During the forties and early fifties, Jascha Heifetz was regularly
proclaimed king of the violinists, and Vladimir Horowitz king of the pianists. Like Szell and Reiner, Heifetz and Horowitz were imperfect Toscanini
equivalents: not German, but Russian variants of his Italian musical personality. Heifetz's playing was rapid, powerful, tensile, and awesomely precise,
and so could be Horowitz's. If neither emanated Toscanini's integrity—
only Toscanini combined all-purpose electricity with absolute probity—
Heifetz was a notably objective, unsentimental Romantic violinist. If Horowitz was no objectivist, he came closest to Toscanini in his ability to
overwhelm audiences with a species of high-pitched anxiety: his playing
was infused with the theatrics of controlled speed and intensity, and of
astounding power reserves as he pressed speed and intensity toward the
breaking point.

Significantly, both Heifetz and Horowitz were RCA artists, marketed
without qualification as the "world's greatest." And both had additional ties
to Toscanini: Heifetz was Samuel Chotzinoff's brother-in-law; Horowitz
was Toscanini's son-in-law. With Heifetz, Toscanini performed the Beethoven, Brahms, and Mendelssohn concertos, and in 1940 they recorded the
Beethoven for RCA. The recording became an American benchmark for
the work; in the fifties, it appeared on LP as an RCA "Immortal Performance," reissued "in response to widespread popular demand." Heard
today, the Heifetz-Toscanini Beethoven Violin Concerto is a curiosity,
superimposing Heifetz's coy portamentos, teased phrase endings, and flut-
tering spiccatos onto Toscanini's taut, muscular accompaniment. In his
memoirs, Charles O'Connell recalls: "It was rather entertaining to observe
these two men, so alike [as perfectionists], yet so disparate in age, disposi-

tion, and musical outlook, working together during this recording. Outwardly they observed the most rigid punctilio; actually they were as wary as two strange cats, each fiercely resolved upon perfection in every mood and tempo."[8]

With his daunting ego, dour face, and clandestine personality, Heifetz was a less vivid, less malleable celebrity than Toscanini. Horowitz, on the other hand, was intriguingly high-strung and insecure, manipulable both for musical and publicity purposes. As a member of the Toscanini family —he married Wanda Toscanini in 1933, eight months after playing under her father for the first time—he took to displaying Toscanini's photograph on his piano and endorsing Toscanini-like interpretive precepts at odds with his own subjectivist predilections. A much-heralded Horowitz-Toscanini performance of the Brahms B flat Concerto on May 6, 1940, led, three days later, to their first recording, for RCA. Horowitz later said: "Toscanini had his own conception, and I followed it, even if it was sometimes against my own wishes." Edwin Bachmann of the NBC Symphony recalled: "The undercurrent was one of fear—Horowitz's fear of Toscanini." On the recording, Horowitz is heard stuck in basic training; he marches briskly, stiffly through the solo part. The recording's inevitable success—it displaced versions by Artur Schnabel and Arthur Rubinstein— led to a second RCA collaboration between the king of conductors and king of pianists, in the Tchaikovsky First Concerto. This project originated with members of the RCA sales department who were impressed by the popularity of a Rubinstein-Barbirolli recording of the same work. According to Charles O'Connell:

> The salesmen saw that Rubinstein's Tchaikovsky was doing really well; I had also proved by recording a Brahms concerto that the Horowitz-Toscanini combination would appeal to the public with tremendous force. Therefore, it was reasoned that the ideal combination would be Tchaikovsky and Horowitz and Toscanini. . . . Walter Toscanini, who had been employed in the record division at the command of David Sarnoff as a kind of statistician and general handyman, and who on his part seemed to conceive his job as one of observation and special investigation for his father, naturally supported the sales department.

One person not in support was Rubinstein, who turned on RCA when the popularity of the Horowitz-Toscanini Tchaikovsky effaced his own RCA recording with Barbirolli. In his autobiography, Rubinstein describes how he successfully threatened David Sarnoff with deserting RCA for Columbia Records, and even claims responsibility for O'Connell's subsequent "dismissal." He also derogates the Horowitz-Tchaikovsky recording as one in which "conductor and soloist [are] not in accord."* This is true, yet it reflects a healthy assertiveness on Horowitz's part—resulting in an uneasy, supercharged collaboration, in vast commercial success, and in a 1943 rematch: the Tchaikovsky War Bond Concert of Easter Sunday, April 25, 1943, for which ticket sales topped ten million dollars in bonds. This second Tchaikovsky performance, broadcast by NBC, was released on disc by RCA in 1959.[9]

Both Horowitz-Toscanini Tchaikovsky recordings document, as their Brahms recording does not, the complex, layered surfaces of Horowitz's playing, as well as elaborately synthesized "deeper" emotional currents arising from elaborately synthesized voicings and rubatos. Juxtaposed against the omnipresent Toscanini standard, Horowitz's pyrotechnics raised persistent questions of emotional and artistic integrity. His propagandists, including Arthur Judson's publicity staff at Columbia, countered with stories of a "new Horowitz": husband and father (of Toscanini's favorite grandchild), connoisseur of literature (Racine, Molière, Tolstoy), collector of fine art (Picasso, Rouault, Pissarro). The master revisionist was Howard Taubman of the *Times,* whose special access to the reclusive Horowitz resembled his special access to the reclusive Toscanini, and whose masterstroke was to make Horowitz as much like "Toscanini" as possible. Profiling Horowitz for the *New York Times Magazine* on October 17, 1948, Taubman wrote: "The wild volatile virtuoso of 20 years ago has become one of the most mature, responsible musicians." Paralleling Horowitz's artistic stature were his fees ("he is the highest paid pianist in the business") and his "objectivity about his own performances." Contradicting "the old-

---

*Next to Horowitz, Rubinstein was the most celebrated pianist in the United States. He appeared once with Toscanini and the NBC Symphony, in Beethoven's Third Piano Concerto. RCA issued a recording of the broadcast performance; the jacket copy began: "When Rubinstein and Toscanini achieved their great radio broadcast performance of the Beethoven Third Piano Concerto, RCA Victor immediately decided to make recordings of this amazing performance available to the public. . . . Certainly in all of the fabulous history of radio broadcasting the performance of this concerto on October 29, 1944 will stand forth as one of the most brilliant events." Rubinstein also appeared with Heifetz as part of a trio whose third member was Emanuel Feuermann, then Gregor Piatigorsky. With Piatigorsky, this was known as the "million-dollar trio" because, as *Life* explained, "together, as money makers, [its three members] gross more than one million dollars a year." Taking note of the trio's concerts, *Life* commented: "The listeners were enthralled by . . . performances of Beethoven, Schubert and Ravel but would have been completely overcome if they could have attended rehearsals of the million-dollar trio and watched their arguments." The "arguments" were depicted in six photographs, one bearing the caption: "Heifetz won almost all the arguments." RCA recorded the million-dollar trio in the Tchaikovsky, Ravel, and Mendelssohn D minor trios.

fashioned picture of the long-haired virtuoso," Horowitz was "more like a man of affairs than the conventional figure of the musician." He had "a reputation for aloofness" but was "really shy." "Like his father-in-law, he has a charming simplicity in his relations with ordinary people." He had rejected fabulous offers from Hollywood. His "wide interests" included fine art, plus "politics, economics, psychology, what you will." He was full of admiration for the United States, preferring "eager, open-minded" Americans to "patronizing and snobbish" Europeans. Six days after Taubman's article appeared, Horowitz and Toscanini again collaborated in the Brahms B flat Concerto. *Time* wrote:

> Rarely had the men of the NBC Symphony seen their little Maestro in such high humor and fine fettle. . . . For the soloist was a man who calls Toscanini "Maestro" to his face, but "Papa" when he's not around. . . .
>
> Last week, the mob of music fans who stormed into Radio City's modernistic Studio 8-H for the opening concert of Toscanini's eleventh NBC season, heard a concert to be remembered. As usual, shy, nervous Pianist Horowitz almost had to be propelled onstage. But, once there, the power and diamond-hard brilliance of his playing had the studio audience bravoing between movements, despite NBC's standing request to the audience not to applaud until the work is finished. When it was finally over, little, white-topped Papa and slender, dark-haired Volodya stood together, bowing solemnly, as the audience cheered and clapped.
>
> Most listeners had lately found a new maturity and depth—if not yet real warmth—in the playing of Vladimir Horowitz, the sallow, thin-faced Russian who first astounded the U.S. 20 years ago with his mastery of piano technique.

Taubman profiled Horowitz again for the *Times Magazine* on January 11, 1953, announcing "The Transformation of Vladimir Horowitz":

> As a musician, Horowitz believes he has been changing steadily in the last twenty-five years. He remains one of the greatest technicians of piano history, but his technique is no longer an end in itself. He has transformed himself from a fire-eating virtuoso into a self-critical, searching artist. And the most remarkable thing about this transition is that his enormous popularity has not been injured in the least. On the contrary, his audiences have grown in size and devotion. No musician anywhere today surpasses him in drawing power. He can name his own terms, and his fees are the highest in the land.
>
> "We have matured together, the public and I," he says.

Before the year was out, Horowitz had retired from the stage, a victim of nervous collapse. Yet his mystique endured, and so, remarkably, did the "new Horowitz." As Samuel Chotzinoff wrote in 1964:

> . . . Horowitz has read and studied extraordinarily much during his "sabbatical." There is hardly a book on music, ancient and modern, he hasn't purchased and read thoroughly. In effect, he has paused in his career to review his musical knowledge and his approach to music, has thought much, and arrived at interpretive conclusions that represent a new phase in his relation to his art, and not alone in music for the piano. He has arrived at a point which very few virtuoso performers ever achieve, or want to achieve. He has, through study and contemplation, come to believe in the absolute supremacy of the composer, the same belief that was the foundation of the art of his great father-in-law. . . .
>
> Horowitz's feeling for the music of the greatest masters is now broad and deep. In preparation for recording two Beethoven sonatas he made exhaustive researches in the history and the interpretive fates of both works. . . .[10]

The "new Horowitz" never attained the potency of the "other Toscanini"; glimpses of the real Horowitz behaving neurotically, awkwardly, and indecisively skirted an artist-type that Americans mistrusted.

Like the Toscanini cult, the Heifetz-Horowitz hegemony penalized musicians of importance. The instrumental shortcomings of Adolf Busch and Joseph Szigeti were magnified in comparison with America's Heifetz standard, yet both might have furnished saner models of Beethoven interpretation. Among pianists, Artur Schnabel, whose fickle New World following we have already glimpsed, played too many wrong notes; still, his refugee status and textual fidelity helped keep his name before the American public. Alfred Cortot, however, could never have transplanted his career to America, and the same could be said of Edwin Fischer and Wilhelm Kempff. Quite aside from the political ramifications of their continued residence in Europe during World War II, these three pianists, among the foremost of their time, were no more sure-fingered than Schnabel; and all three were cultivated, clear-headed violators of textual fidelity canons, possessing musical imaginations packed with far-flung metaphor. When a generation of gifted American pianists emerged in the late forties and early fifties, they specialized in note-perfect, high-tension performances.

.   .   .

To appreciate the sectarianism of America's musical temple of the gods as of 1950—of Toscanini flanked by Heifetz and Horowitz, a frieze supported by Leinsdorf, Ormandy, Reiner, Rodzinski, and other long-standing pillars—it is only necessary to envision the impact that Furtwängler's Chicago Symphony appointment might have made, had it gone through. The temple crumbled anyway, with Furtwängler playing a posthumous role. Toscanini's retirement in 1954, and his death three years later, dulled the luster of his continued iconography. Meanwhile, postwar European recordings and trans-Atlantic tours interjected the significant conductors, orchestras, and instrumentalists the Toscanini cult had obscured.

During World War II, with imported European recordings cut to a minimum, Columbia and RCA had scrambled to sign up available domestic properties. By 1941, the Rochester Philharmonic and the Cincinnati, Indianapolis, and Minneapolis symphonies were making records. But with the postwar recordings boom—with the LP, magnetic tape, and, as of 1956, stereophonic sound—European orchestras and artists returned in force, more than before on European-based labels with European loyalties. EMI of Great Britain, whose products had previously been distributed in the United States by RCA and Columbia, now established its own American subsidiary: Angel Records, founded in 1953, marketed EMI's ranking conductors, pianists, and violinists without deference to Toscanini, Heifetz, or Horowitz. Beginning in 1947, Decca, another British firm, began shipping its state-of-the-art "ffrr" recordings to the United States, where they were called London Records ("Decca" also being the name of an unrelated American label). Westminster, formed in 1949, was an American firm but heavily reliant on recordings made in Europe by European artists, including *gemütlich* Viennese. Deutsche Grammophon and Philips, with the leading German and Dutch classical catalogues, had their LPs re-pressed and repackaged for America in ever greater quantities; by 1970, both companies had switched to direct exports.

A freshened perspective on the mainstream repertoire was an inevitable result of this incursion. For one thing, the LP format made complete operas and integral sets of orchestral and instrumental works available for home listening as never before. From La Scala, *Tosca* under de Sabata with Maria Callas; from Bayreuth, *Parsifal* under Knappertsbusch; from Vienna, *Die Fledermaus, Die Meistersinger,* and *Der Rosenkavalier* under Krauss, Knappertsbusch, and Kleiber—by 1955, these sets, among others, had altered American standards. Of the many new symphony and sonata sets, Kempff's traversal of the thirty-two Beethoven sonatas, available as of 1952, and Klemperer's Philharmonia versions of the Beethoven and Brahms symphonies, available beginning in 1956, were notable post-Schnabel, post-Toscanini benchmarks. Other early LPs brought unprecedented access to

the major Russian artists: David Oistrakh, Emil Gilels, and Sviatoslav Richter became known to American record collectors before their triumphant
American debuts of 1955, 1955, and 1960.

The most important new phonographic access, however, was to Furtwängler. The first Schwann Artist Issue, for 1953, showed fifteen Furtwängler LPs on the American market;* the eleventh, for 1985, showed thirty-
seven. This growth curve is the more remarkable considering that, as
Furtwängler died in 1954, every Furtwängler recording is prestereo and at
least thirty years old. Also, as Furtwängler's output of studio recordings
was relatively small, any aggregation of three dozen or more Furtwängler
LPs necessarily includes bottom-of-the-barrel material—pirated air checks
in poor or unacceptable sound processed to service or exploit consumer
demand. For Toscanini, who stopped making recordings around the same
time Furtwängler did, and who amassed a core catalogue of studio recording more than twice the size of Furtwängler's, the Schwann shows forty-
three LPs in 1953, seventy-four in 1966, thirty-two in 1985.**

That Toscanini's post-1960s curve inverts Furtwängler's rise is no coincidence: given their rivalry in life as real or imagined antipodes, their posthumous fates could only be linked. Paralleling the Schwann curves, American
music journalism registered a Furtwängler revival tied to a backlash against
Toscanini and his cult. As early as 1954, on the second Sunday following
Furtwängler's death, the New York *Times* printed a eulogy by Henry
Pleasants, an American critic based abroad and versed in European musical
affairs. "In Beethoven, Brahms and Bruckner there was no one quite like
him, in the opinion of some of us," Pleasants wrote. Then, glancing in
Toscanini's direction: "It was not that he played this music more brilliantly,
or even more correctly, in the literal sense. It was simply that he read it
more eloquently, more movingly, more compellingly." Peter Pirie's "Toscanini and Furtwängler: An Empire Divided," in the April 1960 issue of
High Fidelity magazine, acknowledged, then challenged, the continued
Toscanini "Zeitgeist." Two years later, in the *Musical Courier,* Philip
Hart's "Furtwängler in Retrospect" pondered an incipient "basic change
in [American] taste," discovering in Furtwängler "the most prominent

---

*My count is per LP, not per album, and excludes duplicate listings of the same perfor-
mances.

**Schwann excludes many obscure and European labels, and a Schwann listing does not
necessarily mean an album is in the stores. Generally, Furtwängler imports became
more available in the United States in the early sixties. One reason there are fewer
pirated Toscanini than pirated Furtwängler recordings is the Toscanini family's opposition to (and Frau Furtwängler's cooperation with) such piracy.

victim of Toscanini-idolatry." A February 1968 *High Fidelity* piece by David Hamilton, "Furtwängler vs. Toscanini: The Beethoven Symphonies," concluded: "Furtwängler's performances offer a broader, more varied view of Beethoven than the single-mindedness of Toscanini." *Furtwängler Recalled* (1965), a book of reminiscences compiled by Daniel Gillis, and Gillis's *Furtwängler in America* (1970), chronicling his difficulties in New York and Chicago, had printings of only two thousand copies each yet perceptibly reinforced the Furtwängler revival.

Books and articles about Toscanini, meanwhile, mapped a gradual relaxation of the intense sectarianism of the thirties, forties, and fifties. In addition to Samuel Chotzinoff's *Toscanini: An Intimate Portrait* (1956), with its reverent yet resentful anecdotes, the years just following Toscanini's retirement saw the publication of two panegyrics: *Toscanini and the Art of Orchestral Performance* (1956) by Robert Charles Marsh, newly of the Chicago *Sun-Times;* and B. H. Haggin's *Conversations with Toscanini* (1959). These were exercises in dour effusion, tempered by grumblings about certain Toscanini interpretations and, especially in Haggin's case, by a carping disposition toward the NBC/RCA colossus. The best and most adult of all Toscanini tributes (from which I have already excerpted liberally), Samuel Antek's *This Was Toscanini,* followed in 1963. Writing from the vantage point of an NBC Symphony violinist, Antek described what it was like to rehearse and play under Toscanini, to tour with him, to visit him in Riverdale. In terms of musical detail and sophistication, his description of Toscanini's working methods surpassed the efforts of Haggin, Marsh, and all their predecessors. And Antek's portrait of Toscanini the man, if incomplete, was heartwarming and real. With the Toscanini centenary of 1967 came a spate of fresh Toscanini writings, running the gamut from knee-jerk adoration to backlash insurgency. To a notable degree, the tone of these celebrations was intensely admiring rather than worshipful, and the range of substantive commentary was broad. Haggin contributed his best book, *The Toscanini Musicians Knew,* in which seventeen orchestral players, solo instrumentalists, singers, and conductors described making music under Toscanini. The *Saturday Review* of March 25, 1967, presented, as "The First Hundred Years of Arturo Toscanini," a survey of positive opinion, including stentorian praise from its music editor, Irving Kolodin (to whom Toscanini remained "the greatest conductor of his time and possibly the most influential, in action and reaction, who ever lived") and a valuable, more modulated appreciation by George Szell, "Toscanini in the History of Orchestral Performance." A maverick viewpoint was well articulated by Eric Salzman, who in the July 1967 *HiFi/Stereo Review* reassessed Toscanini in conjunction with "a revaluation of the continuing and extraordinary phenomenon of Toscanini-olatry," concluding that Toscanini was limited "[as] both a matter of temper-

ament and a result of a lack of contact with the creative side of musical art."
Harold C. Schonberg, who replaced Howard Taubman as the New York
Times senior music critic in 1960, feted Toscanini on television for the "Bell
Telephone Hour" (March 12, 1967), in a *Times Magazine* tribute (January 8,
1967), and in his 1967 book *The Great Conductors.* Schonberg's praise of Toscanini was more careful than Taubman's or Olin Downes's had been. He
called Toscanini "the greatest single influence on today's conductors" and
"the pivotal conductor of his period." He prefaced his "greatest conductor"
accolades with "Many believed him to be . . ." or "To most, he was. . . ." More
remarkable was that *The Great Conductors,* while centered on America, devoted nearly as many pages to Furtwängler as to Toscanini, noting: "Many
considered Furtwängler the greatest conductor of his time, the only real rival
to Toscanini. It is hard to think of a twentieth-century conductor . . . who
made Furtwängler's kind of mystical impact on an audience."

"The legend of Arturo Toscanini will grow with the years," wrote
Taubman in his 1951 Toscanini biography. After 1970, however, the Toscanini legend rapidly shrank. The critic Michael Steinberg, taking stock in
1975, surmised:

> Now, almost 21 years after Toscanini's retirement and 18 years after his
> death, there are relatively few people around who heard him in concert
> (those NBC concerts with their invitation audiences were anything
> other than accessible), and to most of the musical public he is a transcend-
> ently beautiful face, a bunch of recordings whose sound does not often
> confirm what we read about his mastery of texture . . . and some wise-
> cracking jokes about fast tempos and how he didn't understand singers.[11]

Harvey Sachs's *Toscanini,* superseding all previous Toscanini biographies,
came three years later. Born in 1946, Sachs was, as he noted in his foreword,
the first Toscanini biographer "too young to have met Toscanini or to have
attended one of his concerts." It is clear he considers Toscanini the greatest
conductor of his time, but his book never actually said so. The exaggerations and effusions of previous Toscanini admirers offended him; in a rare
outburst, he criticized "Toscanini criticism" for its "presumptuous stupidity." He distanced himself from NBC and from Chotzinoff, whom he
characterized as belonging to a "clique of sycophants," and whose *Intimate
Portrait* he judged "meretricious" and "malicious." He termed "fallacious"
the "whole notion of 'literal' and 'objective' performance." Though American born, Sachs took no proprietary interest in Toscanini; he lives in Milan
and understands Toscanini's roots. Far from adding to the Toscanini legend, he scraped it away, scrutinizing the evidence in pursuit of hard fact.
Though his reluctance to discuss purely musical questions and disregard of

the Toscanini cult slighted facets of the Toscanini story, his scrupulous research and judicious tone ensured lasting results. Beyond documenting a life, *Toscanini* documented the Toscanini literature come of age.

When in 1982 New York City's Museum of Broadcasting scheduled screenings of the ten Toscanini/NBC telecasts, the museum's kinescopes might have been recovered from a time capsule, so distant seemed the Toscanini rites they preserved. At a Toscanini seminar sponsored by the museum, venerable cult members rejoiced in Toscanini's rediscovery—the screenings had to be extended by three weeks—but lamented the amnesia that had made rediscovery necessary. Around the same time, the critic Harris Goldsmith, an unusually knowledgeable Toscanini diehard, deplored the disappearance of Toscanini's RCA recordings and pondered: "In a few years, Arturo Toscanini may be little more than an obscure name in some music history books. For shame!"[12]

Within two decades of Toscanini's death, the circus days of Toscanini adulation were not even memories. Scattered recordings, stray testimony and opinion preserved remnants of the cult. Some survivors retaliated against imagined enemies. Others were too far gone to notice that Toscanini was no longer a god.

Bitterest of the cult's dregs were the late writings of B. H. Haggin, fulminating against Furtwängler, Chotzinoff, Sarnoff, and Virgil Thomson, among others. "Whereas in Toscanini's lifetime the way to impress one's readers was to admire him," wrote Haggin in an expanded second edition of *Conversations with Toscanini* (1979), "in recent years it has been to attack him—in writing that, whether in admiration or attack, most often represented not perception but invention." Haggin's peak contempt was reserved for Robert Charles Marsh, with whom he had feuded over certain Toscanini matters, and Walter Toscanini, whom he now blamed (and not implausibly) for exiling him from Toscanini's rehearsals after November 23, 1953, and for sanctioning, on his father's behalf, the sonic "enhancements" RCA had inflicted on Toscanini's recordings. Haggin cited a 1963 letter to *High Fidelity* magazine, from one Thomas E. Patronite of Cleveland, characterizing *Conversations with Toscanini* as "the most monumental example of nit-picking of all time," and proceeded to speculate: "While it is possible that Patronite got this description of my book from Walter himself, I think it more probable that he got it through Marsh when he was in Cleveland gathering material for his book about the Cleveland Orchestra."[13]

George Marek, Haggin's temperamental opposite among latter-day hagiographers, produced the friendliest, chattiest of Toscanini biographies, in 1975. Though privy to inside knowledge of RCA's operations, Marek's

Toscanini was an incautious melange of fact and myth. As Harvey Sachs noted: "There are literally dozens of major and minor inaccuracies, mistranslations, chronological and metaphorical mix-ups, and page after page of digressions." Marek produced what Sachs did not: a memoir of the cult, circumscribed by claims to an American Toscanini, buoyed by its warmth and sincerity of embrace. One revealing Marek testimonial stated:

> One or two conductors may well have equaled [Toscanini's] interpretations of certain works, one or two conductors may have performed this or that composition in a juster concept (obviously he had limitations), yet no one rivaled him in the role of inspirator, as a trusted guide, as a teacher to whom we raised our faces. More than a teacher, to us who loved music, he was a father figure. . . .[14]

RCA/NBC, meanwhile, proved the most erratic of longtime Toscanini devotees, vacillating between abandoning the Toscanini business and pursuing it with unreconstructed zeal. For the 1967 Toscanini centenary, RCA reissued (and re-"enhanced") numerous Toscanini recordings on its budget Victrola label, only to begin withdrawing them again. In 1977 came "Arturo Toscanini: A Legendary Performer"—a single, full-priced, luxuriously packaged RCA LP accompanied by an eight-page booklet with photographs and an appropriate Irving Kolodin essay (". . . top rank among legendary performers. Artistically, he ruled the two worlds of symphony and opera on both sides of the Atlantic. . . . His return to New York to direct the orchestra created for him by the National Broadcasting Company in 1937 was the crown of crowns . . . a kingly climax to an imperial career."). The album's crown of crowns was a "picture suitable for framing": a painted portrait ordinary enough for a cereal box, with instructions to "cut along dotted line"—printed on the wrong side of the line. NBC television topped this cult classic with "Live from Studio 8H," a January 9, 1980 Toscanini tribute inexplicably featuring Zubin Mehta, Leontyne Price, Itzhak Perlman, and the New York Philharmonic, and returning symphonic music to what had become the home of "Saturday Night Live" and "Hot Hero Sandwich." Ballyhoo for the telecast included a "high recommendation" from the National Education Association, and a "Viewer's Guide" with "questions and exercises" including:

— How does one listen to a concert? Before your group watches "Live from Studio 8H," compile a list of qualities which characterize a good listener.
— The musical selections tentatively scheduled for this program are:
  • Verdi's Overture *La forza del destino*

- Verdi's "Ritorna vincitor" from *Aida*
- Verdi's "Pace, pace" from *La forza del destino*
- Wagner's The Ride of the Valkyries
- Beethoven's Violin Concerto in D Major, Third Movement
- Mozart's "L'amerò sarò costante" from *Il re pastore*
- Ravel's *Daphnis and Chloé*

Divide your group into research teams to (a) find out the historical background of the pieces, (b) compile biographical information about the composers, (c) investigate the stylistic practices of the period that the composition represents.

— Do these musical selections drawn from Toscanini's repertoire seem to have anything in common? What?

Of all the cult survivors, finally, those placing the highest price on remembering Toscanini as God were members of the Toscanini family. Walter Toscanini had amassed for posterity vast Toscanini archives including scores, correspondence, printed matter, and broadcast and rehearsal tapes. Since 1970—a year before Walter's death—the entire collection had been stored at the New York Public Library's Performing Arts Research Center. The library wanted to acquire the archives, but could not come to terms with the family. *The New York Times*, checking on the negotiations as of April 13, 1982, cited an unidentified musicologist who remarked of the Toscanini heirs: "They've got such an exaggerated idea that we're living in the 1950s, when Toscanini was hot stuff." The family subsequently reduced its asking price, and a settlement was reached late in 1986.* The family also authorized a limited edition of thirty Toscanini recordings, some taken from family archival tapes, issued in 1985 and 1986 by The Franklin Mint and promoted as "the greatest recordings of Arturo Toscanini—Official Family Archive Collection." Subscribers receive Certificates of Authenticity signed by Wanda Toscanini Horowitz, and custom-designed "Toscanini Bookends" inset with gold Toscanini medallions—"an original work of art, designed by the artists of The Franklin Mint exclusively for this collection." According to Franklin Mint advertisements, "Arturo Toscanini was the greatest conductor of the twentieth century. . . . No conductor before or since has ever matched the brilliance of his interpretations or the passion of his art."

---

*A second valuable archival source, opened to the public in 1982, is the Toscanini Collection at Wave Hill, Toscanini's Riverdale residence throughout World War II. The collection's tape copies of sixteen-inch NBC transcription disks are sonically superior to commercial versions of Toscanini's NBC Symphony broadcasts.

. . .

The toppling of the Toscanini deity foretold doom for the twin instrumental deities, Heifetz and Horowitz. By the time Heifetz stopped appearing in public as a soloist, around 1970, most younger violinists preferred a
looser, friendlier playing style. Heifetz's University of Southern California
master class, begun in 1962, dwindled in prestige and appeal; by 1980, he was
advertising for students in the New York *Times*. Horowitz's performing
career far outlasted Toscanini's or Heifetz's. His post-1953 "sabbatical"
ended in a dramatic 1965 Carnegie Hall return, followed by years of sporadic recitals and recordings. At first, his best playing retained its fabled
electricity and élan. Afterward, his rubatos and voicings, always idiosyncratic, grew more mannered to accommodate or mask failing fingerwork.
An entry by Michael Steinberg in the *New Grove Dictionary of Music and
Musicians* (1981), the pre-eminent English-language music encyclopedia
summarized: "Horowitz illustrates that an astounding instrumental gift
carries no guarantees about musical understanding." Glenn Plaskin's 1983
biography, *Horowitz,* offered an even less flattering portrait of Horowitz
the man. Scarcely remarked on was Plaskin's equally unsavory version of
Horowitz's father-in-law:

> Toscanini would pace the floor, foaming with fury when told that rival
> conductors were attempting to imitate him. "We screamed," recalled
> Wanda years later, "but, in the end, we were always right." Indeed, at
> home as everywhere else, the Maestro was determined to have his own
> way in everything.
>   Much of the time, Horowitz was treated like a guest who had no right
> to an opinion. Piatigorsky sympathized with him, terming Toscanini
> "the damndest lump of macaroni to swallow," and Arthur Judson had
> nicknamed Toscanini, more simply, "son-of-a-bitch." *En famille,* Horo-
> witz was astonished both by the steely wilfulness of his wife and the
> tyrannical insensitivity of her father. "It is very sad to have a person like
> that," he reflected years later about him. "It is not an easy person. He
> was a difficult character. Much more difficult than me." Indeed, a friend
> who watched Horowitz's general unhappiness at the time [circa 1935]
> later commented that "the autocratic brutality of Toscanini could have
> killed anyone, and Horowitz simply did not have the resources to com-
> bat such pressure."[15]

Horowitz's American musical progeny suffered a decline as overt as
Horowitz's own. Stressful mechanics employed to emulate Horowitzian
speed and precision, power and turbulence, tended to shorten the life span

of the machine. Both Gary Graffman and Byron Janis, the best known of
Horowitz's students, suffered technical failings in mid-career. Other "Outstanding Young American Pianists" (OYAPs)—Graffman's term for his
gifted generation of home-grown keyboard talent, whose "big brother" was
William Kapell (1922–53)—suffered curtailed or unconsummated careers
suggestive of tense listening and performing habits. The most publicized
victim was Leon Fleisher, a remarkable Schnabel protégé whose poststu-
dent immersion in the high-powered OYAP milieu instilled a craving for
sheer technical proficiency. A year after Schnabel's death in 1951, Fleisher,
aged twenty-four, became the first American to win Belgium's Queen
Elisabeth competition. Swamped with bookings, he began driving himself
pitilessly, practicing up to twice as much as he had for Schnabel. Around
1962, he noticed signs of weakness in his right index finger. By 1965, his right
hand was useless for the piano.[16]

When a post-OYAP generation emerged around 1970, its members—
including Emanuel Ax, Misha Dichter, Richard Goode, Murray Perahia,
Garrick Ohlsson, and Peter Serkin (all born between 1943 and 1949)—
seemed oblivious of the Horowitz-Heifetz-Toscanini pressure cooker.
Goode, Perahia, and Serkin had summered at the Marlboro Festival in
Vermont, where Pablo Casals, Felix Galimir, Marcel Moÿse, Rudolf Serkin,
and Alexander Schneider were dominant influences. Ohlsson, a Juilliard
product, had a closer encounter with the Horowitz mystique:

> I suppose I went through my Vladimir Horowitz phase when I was
> about 15. I was terribly enamored of his recordings, and I sort of thought
> I was a mini-demon myself. Well, as I strove to express intensity and
> emotion I was tightening and tightening and tightening, with my elbows
> locked in at my sides, my arms tense, my stomach muscles in knots, and
> my fingers pounding away like ten little sledge hammers, probably
> making one hell of a racket.
>
> I went on like that until one day I was playing some Scriabin in a
> master class at Juilliard, thumping the basses à la Horowitz, and my left
> arm got into an incredible knot of tension. When it still hadn't gone
> away half an hour after I stopped, I was taken to an emergency room in
> a hospital, where they gave me a shot of something and bandaged me up.
> At that point it became very clear that I was doing something wrong. . . .
>
> With Horowitz you had someone who played with sensational preci-
> sion and focus and fire and temperament, one of the most incredible
> pianists in history. And I suppose that whenever you have somebody
> who does something that is genuinely wonderful, then a host of imitators
> comes along. I would say it was a phenomenon that specifically revolved
> around three Victor recording artists—Horowitz, Toscanini, and Hei-

fetz—all of whom were extraordinarily magnetic and exciting, and who had a fanatical sense of precision and exactness, especially Toscanini and Heifetz. These were musicians who made their careers largely in America, and were not actually taken that seriously in Europe as influences.

At eighteen, Ohlsson adopted new heroes and revamped his technique, dissociating himself from "a whole mechanistic generation [of American pianists], influenced by Horowitz, which forced the piano terribly."[17]

Ohlsson's escape was made simpler—was made, in fact, inescapable—by sped-up cultural dispersion. More than any previous musical generation, his takes for granted the phonograph, trans-Atlantic travel, and trans-Atlantic television. He shares with same-age European colleagues an awareness of Horowitz, Rubinstein, Serkin, Schnabel, and other pianists who came to America to teach or play, and also of those pianists, little known to the OYAPs, who stayed put in Europe and Russia: Cortot, Fischer, Kempff, Walter Gieseking, Vladimir Sofronitzky. More than in name, the intense, competitive OYAPs, infrequently heard abroad during their formative years, seemed "American" in temperament. But Ohlsson and his American contemporaries suggest no American school.

Around the period of Furtwängler's American "rediscovery," he sometimes seemed a unifying figurehead among coming-of-age conductors and instrumentalists. As Winthrop Sargeant observed in the December 16, 1967 issue of *The New Yorker:* "It is a curious thing that younger artists today should be reviving the Furtwängler style in opposition to the Toscanini style, but there is no doubt but this is what is happening." In particular, the pianist and conductor Daniel Barenboim, born in 1942, was observed attempting to reinstate warm Furtwängler sonorities and ample yet purposeful Furtwängler rubatos. More representative was the American conductor Henry Lewis, born in 1932, for whom Furtwängler's ascent signified not a specific new model but a revised general norm. "Here was a conductor who has for me been an object of admiration because of his originality, individuality and honesty," wrote Lewis in the February 1970 *High Fidelity.* "He rightfully freed himself from slavish adherence to the printed note. . . . Thankfully we are emerging from the musicological stage of the fifties, when a critic's highest praise was 'a no-nonsense performance.' This brief but damaging encounter with literalism has ended."

If, Barenboim notwithstanding, Furtwängler produced no "progeny" à la Toscanini and Horowitz, it was partly because his was a harder example to simplify and copy. If, notwithstanding his posthumous celebrity, he produced no posthumous popular cult, it was partly because neither his personality nor performance style rivaled in mass appeal the self-made imagery and all-purpose excitement of Toscanini. More to the point, the sixties and seventies were not the thirties and forties. Jet-age cultural dissemination had desegregated the Schwann catalogue, had refined the Toscanini literature, had broadened the post-OYAP purview, had dispersed the old chauvinism. Post-Toscanini American culture-consumers were too worldly to proclaim Furtwängler (or Bernstein, or Solti, or Karajan) the "greatest conductor of all time," or even "of the twentieth century." The psychological security America's intellectuals had attained after World War I now fortified a broader public. The Old World no longer threatened; the New World no longer boasted and apologized, attacked and defended —no longer needed a Toscanini.

The American reputations of Toscanini and Furtwängler are not done seesawing. Now that backlash against the Toscanini cult has subsided, Toscanini seems due for a moderate comeback, reflecting increased awareness that the Toscanini of the National Broadcasting Company, the New York *Times*, and the all-purpose formula was not the only Toscanini.* Essentially, however, Toscanini and Furtwängler have achieved an enduring parity. This was the clear intent of the "Toscanini" and "Furtwängler" entries in the *New Grove*—entries equal in length (about 2,250 words) and by the same author (David Cairns)—even if lingering backlash tilted the scales in Furtwängler's favor. Cairns set the record straight when he wrote that La Scala "was the artistic focal point of [Toscanini's] existence," and that "in the opinion of many musicians" he reached "the zenith of his greatness" in the thirties. "Energy, single-mindedness, [and] impetuosity combined with an inflexible will, fanatical perfectionism and an almost morbid self-criticism" were listed as "among Toscanini's most remarkable characteristics," with this caveat appended:

> The state of hypertension in which he constantly worked could be adversely reflected in his performances, in a certain relentlessness of tempo and an almost brutal vehemence of attack. This was most evident during the final period of his career. . . . Toscanini's working environment at the NBC . . . was generally less congenial than it had been at the New York Philharmonic in the 1930s. . . . In any case, the positive and far more significant side of his impatience was the electric intensity of his finest interpretations, which, for all their meticulous care for textural detail, gave the impression of being conceived and carried out

---

*Demand for Toscanini/NBC Symphony reissues on RCA began picking up in the early eighties.

as single organic wholes: they seemed in some mysterious way to relive the fiery moment of the music's actual creation.

And Cairns had this to say about Toscanini becoming "one of the great cult figures of his time":

> For many people he was a god who could do no wrong. . . . Toscanini's attitude to interpretation (which was, in fact, more pragmatic than his admirers imagined) had been formed in a natural reaction to the shoddy Italian performing traditions in which he grew up, and this undoubtedly helped to foster the modern spirit of respect for the composer's intentions. But it led in turn to the myth of the objective and therefore faithful interpretation, as opposed to the subjective and wilful one epitomized by Toscanini's rival Furtwängler. Recently there has been a fresh reaction, towards a more flexible conception of interpretation of the printed score, and it is probable that Furtwängler's influence among younger musicians is now greater than Toscanini's.

Long-Term Legacies

Statistics put out by the National Music Club in 1953 showed 30 million annual paid admissions for "concert music" throughout the United States, representing gross revenues of some $45 million; major league baseball, by comparison, played to 15 million and collected $40 million at the gate. These figures, analogizing symphonic concerts to spectator sports, were among the favorite proofs of America's post–World War II "cultural explosion." Survey upon refulgent survey, trailing graphs and charts, documented the continued suffusion of democratized high culture, capping and eclipsing the music appreciation epoch. When ground was broken for New York City's Lincoln Center for the Performing Arts in 1961, its four theaters were predicted to outdraw the New York Yankees two to one.

Since 1965 (the starting point for figures kept by the American Symphony Orchestra League), the number of orchestral concerts has more than tripled, attendance has doubled, and gross income and gross expenses have both increased more than sevenfold. At the same time, Theodore Thomas's venerable dictum equating symphonic and civic culture was outgrown: New World opera acquired a less elitist image. Between 1970 and 1985, the number of American opera companies with budgets exceeding $100,000 increased from 40 to 168, and the number of performances from 5,246 to 10,642. A simultaneous "chamber music boom" saw the number of professional chamber ensembles belonging to Chamber Music America jump from 35 to 450 between 1977 and 1985. As recently as 1950, cities the size of Los Angeles and Atlanta lacked adequate concert and opera facilities. After 1960, Lincoln Center established the mold for dozens of new multipurpose performing arts halls or complexes—not only in Los Angeles and Atlanta, but in Charlotte, North Carolina, and Eugene, Oregon. Longer seasons and proliferating summer festivals ensured year-round access to concerts and opera in many parts of the country. When the cultural explosion was found to have spawned an "economic dilemma"—rising expenditures far outstripped rising revenues—expanded arts funding by corporations and foundations reversed the antipathies of earlier generations of American business leaders (an $80 million program of Ford Foundation orchestral grants was a crucial catalyst in the trend toward longer seasons and bigger budgets). A landmark federal initiative of 1965 established the National Endowment for the Arts, empowered to subsidize orchestras and opera companies, among other performing organizations. Figures released in 1984 by the NEA showed 21.4 million adults, representing 13 percent of America's adult population, attending classical musical performances at least once a year as of 1982, and 5 million, or 3.1 percent, attending opera.*

Aaron Copland and Eugene Goossens, writing in the early forties of music's "new audience," had lamented the lack of commensurate growth in "intellectual aspiration"—Americans seemingly believed that "endless repetition of a small body of entrenched masterworks is all that is required for a ripe musical culture." Today's cultural explosion keeps these issues current. On the positive side, there is less parochialism, less boasting and apologizing. The American antipathy to American music Goossens observed in 1942, a species of inverse snobbery, has abated, and with it has abated unconscious envy of a distinct "parent" culture in Europe. Rather, Americans and Europeans hear the same music, the same orchestras, conductors, and soloists, as never before. And yet the evolution of a less insular musical culture has not notably stimulated adventure and reform. Although the entrenched masterworks are less extravagantly worshiped than in music

---

*In their influential *Performing Arts: The Economic Dilemma* (1966), William J. Baumol and William C. Bowen, applying the tools of skeptical economists, estimated that performing arts events attracted little more than five million Americans, or about 4 percent of the population over eighteen years old. Another skeptic, Philip Hart, upped that figure to a meager 5 percent in his *Orpheus in the New World* (1973). Factoring in population growth, Baumol and Bowen decided that arts attendance was actually diminishing in the United States. And Hart wrote: "In the crucial area of paid symphony attendance during the past generation, it would appear that the so-called 'cultural explosion' has been illusory so far as the orchestras are concerned."[1] While this cautionary perspective has merit, the "explosion" of the seventies, partly powered by federal seed money after 1965, and peaking only after the periods surveyed by Baumol, Bowen, and Hart, is unambiguous. Relative to Baumol, Bowen, and Hart, the NEA's 1982 attendance data, to be found in Harold Horowitz's "Study of an Arts Audience/Study of an Arts Public" (in the *Journal of Arts Management and the Law,* Spring 1985), imply increasing arts patronage paralleling documented increases in the number of concert and operatic performances. (A 1984 Louis Harris poll showing 34 percent of the adult population attending classical music events—as against 25 percent in 1975—was weighted toward an upscale public. A critique of the Harris methodology, plus much additional audience data, may be found in the *1982 Survey of Public Participation in the Arts,* prepared for the NEA by the University of Maryland's Survey Research Center. In general, audience statistics are notoriously unreliable.)

appreciation times, audiences still hew to a canonized repertoire. Compared with contemporary norms for theater, cinema, visual arts, and ballet, orchestras and opera companies still confuse art with "finished things."

In interpreting music-consumption statistics attesting to new audiences, music appreciation, and cultural explosion, certain piano consumption statistics are relevant. According to Arthur Loesser, the compelling central authority in social-historical keyboard matters, the piano's "high plateau" in the United States came during "the few years before 1914." After that, its production and domestic utility fell off—first slowly, then precipitously. American piano factories made 364,545 instruments in 1909, 341,652 in 1919, 306,584 in 1925—during which sixteen-year period the population grew by 22 percent. During the Depression, the piano business nearly died. By 1950, it had picked up: 173,000 pianos were sold in the United States that year. The figures for the seventies fluctuated between 193,814 and 282,172. In 1985, piano sales totaled 151,000. Is it any coincidence that the piano's decline coincided with the rise of mechanical music? A 1924 magazine article entitled "American Pianos" remarked:

> In this age of Victrolas and radios, the piano is fast becoming a rare article in the ordinary home. . . . Few persons now strum the abused instrument. . . . The once ubiquitous instrument is now silenced, for only students of real talent are encouraged. The piano, therefore, is in danger of becoming as rare now as a brougham, a phaeton or a dogcart for the banished horse.

The radio, the phonograph, the movie theater, the automobile doomed longtime parlor music conventions: of "nice girls" playing for "company," of familial singing and chamber music, of four-hand renditions of symphonies and overtures not otherwise audible at home. In the early nineteenth century, orchestras and string quartets were as likely as not to contain amateurs intermingled with professionals; and Beethoven, Schubert, and Weber, like Haydn and Mozart before them, composed *Hausmusik* inviting the attention of talented dilettantes. A century later, the interpenetration of amateur and professional music making was over or ending. Today's orchestras, with their grueling full-time seasons, proclaim an exclusive professional caste. Composers, too, spurn the *Hausmusik* ideal. The amateur is correspondingly condemned to spectatoritis. Granted, an estimated 50 million Americans play musical instruments, a figure increasingly weighted toward electric keyboards and guitars.[2] But for the touted "performing arts" constituency, the dominant trend remains as it appeared to the Lynds in Middletown: "the girl in the crowd who could play while the others sang and danced" is a twice-jaded photograph; "music for adults" has more than ever "ceased to be a matter of spontaneous, active participation."

Equally pertinent today is Aaron Copland's 1943 observation of "listeners whose sheer numbers in themselves create a special problem." To some analysts of the cultural scene sheer numbers of patrons attending Beethoven's Ninth, *Aida, Swan Lake,* or *Hamlet* inspire optimism or delight. But the massive weight of such patronage, however gratifying politically, can be artistically stultifying. To a disturbing degree, the terrain of the cultural explosion is booby-trapped Toscanini territory. Though the Toscanini fetish disappeared after 1970, the smothering fetishism of the Toscanini cult, fixating on personal celebrity and perfect execution, endures. Without Toscanini, there would still have been a new listening audience and a cultural explosion, music appreciation and spectatoritis. With Toscanini, these tendencies acquired an urgent prod and central symbol. It is in this sense, not treating Toscanini as a necessary cause, that I have called certain worrisome aspects of today's music scene "long-term legacies" of the Toscanini cult.

For decades after Beethoven's death, a performance of one of his symphonies was an event, and a good performance was a novelty. Wagner, to his intense frustration, had to wait until 1839 to hear an adequate rendition of the Ninth—by Habeneck in Paris. Wagner's own performance of the same work in Dresden seven years later was the first in that city to establish it as a necessary masterpiece rather than an aberration of genius.

Today, Beethoven's symphonies are as familiar as breakfast cereals. Record buyers comparison-shop among twenty-five brands and more. Bulk-rate boxed sets of the nine symphonies barely narrow the field—there are still eighteen versions to choose from. How to tell them apart? The different orchestras and different sonics matter, but the different celebrity conductors are decisive. Several have even recorded the Beethoven symphonies more than once. At the top of the glamour scale, Herbert von Karajan has put four Beethoven cycles on disc, Leonard Bernstein two. The cover design for Karajan's third cycle, a 1977 Deutsche Grammophon release, is telling: at its center is a photograph of Karajan; higher up, capital letters shout "BEETHOVEN" and "KARAJAN" with equal emphasis. Bernstein's second cycle, a 1980 release also on Deutsche Grammophon, bears a Bernstein photograph and lettering establishing parity between "BEETHOVEN" and "BERNSTEIN." The covers of the booklets inside the two boxes are more candid still. The one shows Bernstein in action, smiling, his arms spread wide; members of the Vienna Philharmonic, and audience members in the Musikverein, are also visible. Karajan, by comparison, is photographed alone. He is not conducting, but immersed in thought, eyes closed. He grips his baton at either end with his fists. His tousled silver hair and stern brow are brilliantly lit from the side; his black jacket and tails blend into a void. If the implied message of the Bernstein portrait is Beethoven-Schiller's *"Seid umschlungen, Millionen,"* Karajan's Rembrandt-like portrayal of the Romantic genius connotes Karajan focused on himself. The contents of the brochures corroborate their covers: in Beethoven-Bernstein, a picture apiece for composer and conductor; in Beethoven-Karajan, three Beethoven pictures versus thirteen huge, imperious Karajan photographs, eleven in color—Karajan studying at home; Karajan brooding in rehearsal; Karajan conducting, clawing the air with curled, Svengali hands. There are also two essays: "Karajan: Artist and Man" and "Karajan Talks About Music." The latter contains one musical observation: that "a sort of recitative" in Mozart's K. 287 Divertimento reminds Karajan of the recitative from the Ninth. The remaining talk—about microphone placement, recording acoustics, seating plans, interpretation, performance psychology— is essentially talk about Karajan.

Wagner, an authoritative conductor, had no inkling of such disembodied conductorial authority. In his day, composers and conductors were allies, if not one and the same. As we have seen, before Toscanini, no conductor of comparable prominence had so concentrated on what was already old and familiar. After Toscanini, his example became the norm. Not the music, but the performer and the performance were new. No previous conductor's record jackets bore such charismatic photographs as Robert Hupka's of Toscanini, his tousled silver hair and stern brow brilliantly lit from the side, his black rehearsal jacket voided à la Rembrandt; one characteristic pose showed him gripping his baton at either end. No previous conductor had recorded so celebrated or lucrative a Beethoven cycle. Essays enclosed in RCA's boxed sets expounded on Toscanini as "artist and man" and on "Beethoven and Toscanini." The leather-bound 1953 limited edition of the Toscanini Beethoven cycle included a bronze facsimile of a medal once presented to Toscanini; on the back was a facsimile of Toscanini's signature. (A limited edition of Karajan's 1977 Beethoven cycle was specially packaged in a hard-plastic slipcase bearing a facsimile of his signature.)

When in 1934 the New York Philharmonic initiated a fund in Toscanini's name in order to raise $500,000, W. J. Henderson, aged seventy-eight, complained that "prima donna conductors" were diverting attention from the music itself: "Critical comment . . . is almost entirely directed to the 'readings' of mighty magicians of the conductor's wand. . . . Can [the public] ever again be trained to love music for its own sake and not because of the marvels wrought upon it by supermen?"[3]

. . .

Henry Krehbiel, writing in 1919, looked back at New York operatic affairs between 1908 and 1918 and observed unprecedented reportage of "the gossip of the foyer and the dressing rooms." Leo Slezak, writing in the 1920s of the Metropolitan Opera between 1909 and 1913, noticed a preoccupation with publicity and press agentry—with "constantly keeping one's name before the public and of not being too particular about the methods used"—then unknown in Europe. Joseph Szigeti, recalling in 1947 his American debut of 1925, remarked on the subsequent prevalence of such "shortcuts to fame" as national news magazines, and radio interviews and performances, resulting in "an appreciable difference in impact and in quick returns."[4]

Slezak's and Szigeti's comments, encapsulating a sudden escalation in the machinery and marketing of celebrity, came in distinguished volumes of reminiscence: Slezak's *Meine sämtlichen Werke* and *Der Wortbruch* (translated as *Songs of Motley: Being the Reminiscences of a Hungry Tenor*, 1938), and Szigeti's *With Strings Attached* (1947). Other musicians of the past who produced books included Thomas Beecham, Fritz Busch, Oscar Levant, Gregor Piatigorsky, and Bruno Walter—all skilled writers with something to say. Walter's *Theme and Variations* (1947) and Busch's *Aus den Leben eines Musikers* (*Pages from a Musician's Life*, 1953) are autobiographies poignantly shadowed by political strife and exodus from Europe. Beecham's *A Mingled Chime* (1943), Piatigorsky's *Cellist* (1965), and Levant's *A Smattering of Ignorance* (1939), *The Memoirs of an Amnesiac* (1965), and *The Unimportance of Being Oscar* (1968) document the after-dinner gifts of world-class raconteurs. Slezak's reconstruction of an *Otello* synopsis allegedly appearing in a Houston program booklet, and Piatigorsky's of his abortive first American tour, as engineered by the impresarios "Discher and Discher," are unforgettable; there is no point in summarizing them here, for the telling—the leisurely pace and fine detail—is all.* Levant, by comparison, was a wicked American humorist with a flair for one-liners: Koussevitzky "is unparalleled in the performance of Russian music, whether it is by Mussorgsky, Rimsky-Korsakov, Strauss, Wagner or Aaron Copland"; Stokowski "be-

---

*But I cannot resist quoting the beginning of the Slezak extract:

The populace are kneeling in prayer for Othello whose ship is in great danger in a violent tempest at sea. The peril is overcome, Othello enters and greets the people with the words:

> Do all your cooking with "Krusto"
> the famous cooking-fat!

came the dandy of orchestral conductors, a veritable musical Lucius Beebe, wearing his scores like so many changes of attire."⁵ The vast majority of famous musicians from pretelevision times, however, produced no written memoirs—presumably, such likely candidates as Adolf Busch, Cortot, Klemperer, Landowska, and Stokowski, among countless others, lacked the gift, the impulse, or the opportunity.

Today, a few such books continue to appear, but none is as touching and urbane as Walter's or Busch's, or as cleverly hilarious as Beecham's, Levant's, Piatigorsky's, or Slezak's (Yehudi Menuhin's old-fashioned *Unfinished Journey* [1977] rates an honorable mention in the former category). Instead, we are inundated by hardbound ephemera: not books for reading per se, but fan and cult books, shortcuts to fame and prerogatives of celebrity whose main purpose is "keeping one's name before the public."

These come in three genres, all new. The first, for coffee-table display, brandishes large photographs, a certain percentage of which capture the artist offstage or in rehearsal. *Life* led the way, as in its 1939 "great picture scoop" of Toscanini with Sonia Horowitz. Though the one *Life*-sized Toscanini book—Samuel Antek's *This Was Toscanini*, with photographs by Hupka—to some degree represented a historic early exercise in coffee-table arts portraiture, its substantive discussion of actual music making placed it on the bookshelf. By comparison, Birgit Nilsson's *My Memoirs in Pictures* (1981) frankly and pleasingly fulfills an essential purpose of the picture-book format as stated by Nilsson herself: to awaken "pleasant memories in some of the people who have given me their applause and their admiration over the years." Whereas Nilsson's home life is depicted in terms of cooking, hedge grooming, and horse nuzzling, John Gruen's *The Private Life of Leonard Bernstein* (1968), with photographs by Ken Heyman, all but unclothes its subject while stalking him at the seashore and in the bathroom; only through acknowledging its own extravagance does Bernstein's private life remain fit coffee-table fare. Bigger, glossier, and more expensive than the Nilsson and Bernstein books, and a shrewder measure of coffee-table etiquette, is *Opera People* by Robert Jacobson (1982), with photographs by Christian Steiner: its ostentation (the glamorous pictures are bloated by the pretentious text) is calculated to gratify culture consumers put off by Nilsson's simplicity or Bernstein's irony.

The second new genre of performing-arts book falls in between P. T. Barnum's souvenir-biographies of Tom Thumb and Jenny Lind, and those dutiful, detached chronicles of artists' lives still produced in Germany. While not "authorized," these pseudobiographies are undertaken in cooperation with their subjects. They do not strive for literary distinction—like musical detail, it would narrow their appeal. Their tone is adulatory yet accommodates caveats enough to feign discretion. Their narratives are larded with innocuous anecdotes and teasing confidences. As much as possible, the subject is made to appear modest, sincere, and likable. Howard Taubman's pseudobiography of Toscanini, *Maestro*, was an early model. Current practice condones greater familiarity: in many cases, the artists are referred to by their first names. Zubin Mehta's pseudobiography, by Martin Bookspan and Ross Yockey, is even called *Zubin* (1978). Kiri Te Kanawa's pseudobiography, *Kiri*, by David Fingleton (1982), serenely abandons even the pretext of substantive personal detail or critical nuance.

Most prevalent and representative of the new genres, finally, is pseudoautobiography. Pseudoautobiographies are readily distinguishable from the first-person writings of such raconteurs and memoirists as Beecham, Busch, Levant, Piatigorsky, Slezak, Szigeti, and Walter, and not merely because they require assisting writers. One giveaway is timing: the older books were typically twilight endeavors; the newer ones are eagerly undertaken in mid-career. While their brisk language and unabashed market orientation ensure a degree of homogeneity, some pseudoautobiographies are more skillfully oriented than others. Marilyn Horne's *My Life*, with Jane Scovell (1983), transcends the genre with its tough veracity, and so lacks glamour. Renata Scotto's *More than a Diva*, with Octavio Roca (1984), lacks tact: she excites herself and turns shrewish. Plácido Domingo's *My First Forty Years*, with Harvey Sachs (1983), is tactful to a fault. The correct approach is epitomized by a single example also epitomizing, in purpose and execution, the entire canon of performing-arts pseudobooks: Luciano Pavarotti's *Pavarotti: My Own Story*, with William Wright (1981). With its deftly apportioned behind-the-scenes detail and opera talk, *My Own Story* steers clear of vapidity and learning. Pavarotti is equally ordinary and extraordinary. William Wright summarizes: "He [has] excelled in an exceedingly demanding and specialized field while retaining a broad range of non-musical enthusiasms: painting, tennis, driving, cooking, to name a few. And he presides over a large and close-knit family that he is determined to keep large and close-knit." A strategy binds and amplifies the book's melange of chitchat and opinion. According to the jacket copy: "Not since the legendary Caruso has an opera personality captured the world's imagination as has tenor Luciano Pavarotti." The Caruso analogy is a constant refrain: Pavarotti is warmhearted, straightforward, democratic, instinctive. As a child, he slept in the kitchen on an iron bed. As a celebrity, he likes simple pleasures, like eating pasta and kissing women. Wright, playing Pavarotti off against singers who are "soulless but flawless," "enigmatic," and "unapproachable," cites Caruso's example, uniting "a beautiful voice and a beautiful nature," and asks: "Could it be that the general public is better at perceiving an essential to great artistry than the people who know and follow voice?" Herbert Breslin invokes the Caruso analogy from a manager/publicist's perspective: "Pavarotti projects a niceness and a lack of guile that people sense right away. . . . His responses are always natural, unaffected, and personal. . . . Right now there is what you might call a Pavarotti explosion going on. . . . When he sings one of his nationally televised performances, just one, he reaches a larger audience than Caruso reached in his entire career." Yet Pavarotti's own version of the Caruso analogy, a rare miscalculation, risks sounding disingenuous for volunteering: "With all due respect, I do not agree with Maestro von Karajan's remarkable comment that my voice is greater [than Caruso's]."

The Caruso-like warmth and charm of "Pavarotti," his high C's, exuberant smile, and photogenic hobbies, constitute an entertainment property tailored to a gamut of celebrity showcases. Some of these are the formative showcases of Toscanini times, now become traditional. In both *Time* (begun in 1923) and *Newsweek* (begun ten years later), he has been the subject of cover stories[6] documenting his girth (he weighed "nearly 300 pounds" as of 1976), fees ($20,000 per recital as of 1979), and Mediterranean élan ("He makes it a point of honor to kiss every female in the same room with him"). *Time* has also marketed Pavarotti on records, in the *Time-Life* mail-order sets "Great Ages of Music," "Metropolitan Centennial Collection of Great Opera," and "Great Performers"; solicitations for the last carried a Pavarotti endorsement ("I was struck by the careful choice of the selections, and by the albums' elegance") and dangled, as a bonus "membership privilege," a 23-by-29-inch Pavarotti poster. Pavarotti's regular commercial recordings, including "King of the High C's," "O Holy Night," "Hits from Lincoln Center," and "Pavarotti's Greatest Hits," have dominated *Billboard*'s classical charts. Hollywood, meanwhile, besieged Pavarotti with offers. He has so far accepted one: MGM's ill-conceived *Yes, Giorgio,* about a famous, charismatic tenor who falls in love with his beautiful female physician. Setting the seal on Pavarotti's superstardom, finally, has been a type of television exposure Toscanini's exhibitors never knew, supplementing televised concerts and operas with more varied and indigenous home-screen formats. Ranked in terms of escalating mass appeal, these include televised master classes ("Pavarotti at Juilliard"), the television documentary ("King of the High C's"), the public affairs show ("60 Minutes"), the network special ("The Luciano Pavarotti Special"), and, crucially, the talk show ("Today," "The Tonight Show"). Toscanini was revered at NBC as a high-culture symbol, yet as the "other Toscanini" was leveled to more common ground. Johnny Carson reserves for Pavarotti a palpable deference he does not normally accord comedians, actors, and starlets; at the same time, the show's invitations to name dropping, flirting, and spaghetti cooking defuse every threatening high-culture stereotype—visibly, demonstrably, Pavarotti is a gregarious fellow of healthy, heterosexual appetites.

The jabbing impact of talk-show pacing, tone, and content has popular print formats scrambling to catch on, if not up. In Toscanini's time, the general-interest picture magazines were *Life* (begun in 1927) and *Look* (begun ten years later). Their successor, as of 1974, is the supermarket weekly *People*. Pavarotti's frequent *People* cameos are Carson replays, percolating with gossip and sexual innuendo. As "opera's Incredible Hulk," "the tenor of his times," and "opera's newest sex symbol," Pavarotti is depicted serving Zubin Mehta his favorite spaghetti sauce, or hobnobbing with Cary Grant, Angie Dickinson, and Rona Barrett. As of December 25, 1978, he is said to be a "shameless flirt," but not a promiscuous one: "I am faithful to my wife, Adua, my angel," he tells *People*. As of November 17, 1980, he confides that Adua "always complains" of his absence: "We are very, very close—for the moment." As of March 14, 1983, he is the subject of "spicy rumors of a romantic liaison" with his protégée, Madelyn Renee. "Why do women find you so attractive?" *People* wants to know. "I think it is my extravagant body. Actually a woman recently wrote me a letter saying just that." "How did you respond?" "I wrote back, 'Send me a picture; I hope you don't have a body like me.' My attitude is: Let them touch." Just as *Life* gave way to *People,* the popular "classical music" monthlies—record-addict magazines stemming from music-appreciation times—have made way for *Ovation,* a fan magazine well distinguished from music appreciation sobrieties by its own publicity:

> Perhaps you have not yet discovered OVATION—the world's most beautiful, most informed magazine for classical music lovers. If not, you're in for a treat!
>
> Here at last is a sumptuous, luxurious magazine which reflects all the color and glamour of the world of classical music and its magnificent artists. . . .
>
> Now you can be a part of the fast-paced, exhilarating world of classical music. . . .

Regular *Ovation* features, in addition to "exclusive interviews with the music giants of our time," have included "Music People," surveying in words and pictures "on and off stage activities of musical personalities," and "Keep Your Eye On . . . ," in which music's rising stars and starlets are identified. Newspapers, too, assimilate talk-show norms. In Henry Krehbiel's day, Sunday music pages commonly scrutinized new operas and symphonies. Today's New York *Times* Arts and Leisure section too often shifts attention onto Pavarotti and other already famous performers—not to scrutinize, but to applaud.

Pavarotti puts in his newspaper appearances, but these are merely obligatory. For him, the icing on the cake has been an advertising campaign beside which endorsements of records and record players by Toscanini and other past celebrities appear parochial. Even Pavarotti enthusiasts have questioned whether a classical-music entertainment property should mainly appear on television on behalf of American Express credit cards. Pavarotti has a ready response. Queried by *People* about his "appearances on commercial TV," he explained: "There are things that will bring this little world of opera to a larger audience, and I don't care how we do it. We have to go to the people, and if someone doesn't understand, it is too bad." And to *Ovation,* asked about Pavarotti the "media personality," he said: "If it would fill a 10,000-seat theater every night for opera, I would sell margarine on TV—and be proud of it." More honest is Herbert Breslin's remark in *Pavarotti: My Own Story:* "I suppose it's an unhappy commentary on our culture, but those television commercials he did for the American Express cards familiarized more people with Luciano than eighteen years of superb singing in the world's opera houses. So these stints are useful for his recognizability."

To focus on celebrity performers is to focus on personality and interpretation. Music per se takes second place, and not least because the celebrity repertoire is so old and familiar, it can only be taken for granted. Many celebrities seem not to mind. Here is Pavarotti, in *My Own Story:*

> The most important way for opera to remain vital among the arts of the twentieth century is through new versions of the great operatic masterpieces, productions that have new insights and a fresh approach that brings the work closer to the modern audience. It is natural that I want, if only occasionally, to be part of this noble effort.

What Pavarotti means is that he prefers traditional repertoire and, with occasional exceptions, traditional mountings of it. A compatible view informs the jacket copy of *Opera People:*

> The history of opera is really the history of the singers for whose voices and expressive gifts the great scores were written. And this has never been more true than now, when—thanks to stunning performances and their dissemination by modern technology—opera is more alive and popular than ever, despite a full half century during which scarcely one new opera of enduring quality has been composed.

This is wishful thinking; a short list of composers who have produced operas "of enduring quality" in the half-century before *Opera People* would include Berg, Britten, Gershwin, Henze, Poulenc, Prokofiev, Schoenberg, Shostakovich, Richard Strauss, Stravinsky, and Tippett. But *Opera People* has a point: in terms of prominent exposure, what celebrity singers do not sing, and what our celebrated opera houses do not produce, does not really count. The track record is at least better than it was: since the retirement of Rudolf Bing, the Metropolitan has welcomed Gershwin and Poulenc, and more enthusiastically accommodated Berg, Britten, and Debussy. Some regional companies even manage to accommodate new works with aplomb. But Opera People remain formidable obstacles to progressive programming.

And the same holds true for violin, piano, and podium People. Itzhak Perlman's TV fame makes orchestras hungry to engage him—and his warhorses. In recital, violinists are the most parochial programmers of all; count the *Kreutzer*s, Brahms D minors, and *Tzigane*s. My own four-season survey of New York piano recitals (1975–76 to 1978–79) showed that each of two warhorse sonatas—Beethoven's "Appassionata" and Liszt's B minor —was being played an average of once every twelve concerts, and that the core repertoire for such events spanned fifty-six years (1804 to 1860) and four composers (Beethoven, Chopin, Schumann, and Liszt). As for our orchestras, with no more than 25 percent of the active symphonic repertoire consisting of music composed since 1900, programming has basically stayed put.[7] When in 1979 Bell Telephone began underwriting domestic tours by American orchestras, it passed unnoticed that for the first year, encompassing tours by six orchestras, a single American work (Jacob Druckman's *Aureole*, performed by Leonard Bernstein and the New York Philharmonic) was programmed alongside truck-loads of Beethoven and Tchaikovsky. When in 1980 the composer William Schuman told a meeting of the American Symphony Orchestra League that "the purpose of a symphony orchestra is to reveal the literature composers have created for it," and that "the most important function of the symphony orchestra is the selection of repertoire," he was enunciating heresies of long standing. The catalyst for Schuman's address was his computation that six out of every hundred composers performed by American orchestras were American. Echoing Aaron Copland's *Modern Music* critiques of forty years before, Schuman articulated his "absolute belief that a country can have the most dazzling array of superior performers, but that its culture, in music as in any other art, will fundamentally reflect the quality of its creative men and women." He proposed a formula: that for every eighty minutes of symphonic programming, fifty minutes be allotted to "the systematic and continuing exploration of the great literature of the past on a rotating basis," with the remaining half-hour reserved for "the introduction of new works, both by established composers and newer ones," plus a "systematic and purposeful effort to develop a repertoire of contemporary works which have already found favor."[8] Two American conductors of chamber orchestras—Dennis Russell Davies, music director of the St. Paul Chamber Orchestra from 1972 to 1980, and Gerard Schwarz, music director of New York's Y Chamber Symphony since 1977 and of the Los Angeles Chamber Orchestra from 1978 to 1986—have regularly assembled programs as adventurous as Schuman's formula. The prevalent antithesis, however, is a diehard curatorial bent that would have stupefied the warhorse composers themselves. Toscanini's backward gaze, fixed on Theodore Thomas's repertoire of fifty years before, beheld the future. The canon of accredited masterpieces is today as contemporary as ever. In fact, never has the cannonade been so intense: anyone with access to a modest record collection and one or two "classical music" FM stations can enjoy round-the-clock exposure without leaving the living room. Orchestras and recitalists parade the warhorses against a backdrop of warhorse wallpaper.

A glance back at Toscanini times shows writing on the wallpaper, but also fewer warhorses. *Modern Music*'s "Over the Air," surveying radio concert fare, had much to complain about, and also something to praise: Alfred Wallenstein, Howard Barlow, the CBS composers' commissions, Stokowski's NBC Symphony premieres. Studio orchestras such as those Wallenstein, Barlow, and Stokowski conducted could, like their European counterparts today, afford to experiment—as "sustaining" (i.e., unsponsored) programming, they sold no tickets or ad time. In the course of the thirties, however, "live" radio music was already in decline. A 1940 Supreme Court ruling, approving the playing of phonograph records over the air without compensation to the performers, eventually undermined both studio orchestras and the distinctive "big bands"—appreciated by Copland and other composers if not by the music appreciators—radio had helped create. A radio-recordings marketing strategy, employing radio "disc jockeys" who called the tune, fostered new musical genres and formats: "country and western," "top forty." Increased reliance on audience ratings, an index to advertising revenues nearing half a billion dollars by 1948, spelled doom for sustaining programs whose listeners were being diverted by television and by the new popular musics.[9] The termination of the NBC Symphony in 1954, and of the "Bell Telephone Hour," last of the "light classical" showcases, in 1968, were landmarks in the diversion of concert music to nonnetwork FM stations. The FM ghetto failed to resurrect "live" radio music; rather, the disc jockey/hit parade format, sensitized to audience ratings and advertising needs, was appropriated from AM. "Classical music" listeners could now casually imbibe familiar symphonies and concertos, bothering to switch the dial only when something "modern" disrupted their reading or eating. Even broadcasts of live concerts came to be taped and delayed, facilitating spliced "corrections" and sonic "enhancements" while sacrificing the consolidated sense of occasion that had once magnified concert broadcasts of significant premieres. National public radio, new in 1970, has addressed some of these problems, but so far seems a remedy too little and too late.

Paralleling the transformation of radio music by hit-parade disc jockeys were proliferating disc warhorses. In the twenties and thirties, when complete symphonies and concertos were new to records, it was commonplace to ask first of a fresh release: Is it already in the catalogue?—and to mean the composition, not the composition-as-performed-by-x. Later, when the LP was new, repertoire replenishment was a central priority: suitable importance was attached to beefing up the Schwann with music previously available only on 78s. The endpoint of the replenishment cycle, however, was a locked groove: infinite re-replenishment. Victor's Charles O'Connell balked at recording Toscanini in repertoire not "in especial need of recording." O'Connell's departure changed that; eventually, Toscanini was recording warhorses even he had already recorded. Today, redundancy prerogatives are taken for granted, with the proviso that the latest sonic gimmickry be cosmetically applied to make the warhorses look a little less tired. Thus criteria of need—Is the "New World" Symphony already in the catalogue? Is it yet on LP?—have given way to bogus or exaggerated marketing yardsticks: Has it been done in stereo? On cassette? In quad? In digital? On CD? Concurrently, the competing marketability of Chubby Checker, Elvis Presley, and the Beatles steadily reduced classical music's share of total record sales: from 25 percent during the post–World War II "recordings boom" to something like 5 percent today. This makes classical labels less inclined than ever to venture outside the masterpiece canon, focusing instead on further nuances of warhorse revamping. Some stratagems, while ephemeral, are at least ingenious: Walter Carlos's "Switched-On Bach" (1968), with its electronic versions of the Third Brandenburg, Air on the G string, and other Bach staples, was the best-selling classical album ever. More often, the stratagems reduce to salesmanship: the best-selling classical lines of recent times, purchasable in supermarkets, drugstores, and discount chain stores, are CBS's Great Performances and other budget-label repackagings of dated warhorse refurbishings. Especially in the United States, where recording costs are higher than abroad, obscure corners of the repertoire have proved of diminishing interest: it seems an eternity since Columbia (now CBS) Records undertook its historic surveys of Schoenberg, Webern, and Stravinsky.

Foremost of all LP survey topics have been the Beethoven symphonies.

Toscanini's RCA cycle of 1949–52 was an early example. By that time, comparing different Toscanini performances of the same Beethoven symphony was already a cult ritual; Toscanini had been steadily programming Beethoven in New York for two decades and had recorded all but the Second and Ninth symphonies on 78s. Then RCA released a third Toscanini *Eroica*—the December 6, 1953, broadcast performance. Haggin, for one, found the first Toscanini *Eroica* (1939) "one of Toscanini's greatest" performances, showing "great elasticity of tempo," while the second (1949) was "an impressive example of the power [Toscanini] would achieve in his later simpler style," and the third seemed "a little more elastic in tempo and plastic in shape" than the second and therefore "finer and more effective."[10] When in 1985 Deutsche Grammophon began issuing Karajan's fourth Beethoven symphony cycle, a "milestone in recording history," the digital technology was new, but the sales pitch, as in the following extract from the press kit, was not:

> . . . These latest versions of the Fifth, "Pastoral" and Ninth Symphonies [bring] new revelations of interpretation. . . . We, comparing the different nuances of expression between one version and another, have a unique opportunity to study in depth . . . the never-ending development of Karajan's views on Beethoven. . . .
>
> . . . It must be emphasized that consistency of interpretation between all four [versions] is very striking, but within the strong and characterful yet direct Karajan approach, there lie fascinating variations. . . . Listeners will find it most revealing to make their own comparisons where they can, mapping the maestro's development, but [in this analysis] all four of Karajan's recorded Beethoven cycles have been brought side by side.
>
> In the first movement [of the Fifth Symphony] the extra spontaneity of expression in Karajan's latest recording is suggested by the very slight variations of tempo compared with the previous versions. The horn entry of the second subject brings a hint of expansion, for example. The approach is a degree more lyrical than it was earlier but just as weighty with even cleaner articulation. The free oboe solo leading back into the main part of the recapitulation is even gentler than before with the rallentando a degree more pronounced. . . .

Here is a daunting task: tracing Karajan's "variations" through his more than three dozen Beethoven symphony recordings—supplemented, at the listener's discretion, by cross-reference to "competitive" Beethoven performances.

Only the language of Adorno-style fetishism—the "cult symphony," the "cult-enshrined conductor"—does justice to an addiction this trivial.

In Adorno's day, relentless "plugging" of mass-produced Beethoven created "a tendency to listen to Beethoven's Fifth as if it were a set of quotations from Beethoven's Fifth." In DG's analysis, and countless others like it, not Beethoven's Fifth but favorite quotations—the opening motto, the unaccompanied horns at measure 59, the oboe's mini-cadenza —are the subject matter of a consumer report. Even if one disregards such evidence of atomized, "regressive" hearing, the sheer surfeit of Beethoven and other music in today's private and public spaces—not excluding beaches, restaurants, elevators, and supermarkets—numbs and disorients. Adorno's perception of alienated, narcotized listening— echoed, as we have seen, by Schoenberg, Stravinsky, and others worried about the impact of radio, recordings, and other audience enlargers—was no ideologue's illusion. Equally atomized and mentally supine is listening focused on visceral subjugation to a favorite knockout climax. The debate over whether "mechanized music" discourages "active listening," vigorously pursued during the thirties, is seldom heard any longer yet remains pertinent.

In 1978 at Carnegie Hall, Georg Solti and the Chicago Symphony, then at the peak of their joint celebrity, gave an unusually loud performance of Brahms's First Symphony. The strings, in particular, thrust forward great sheets of sound in order to hold their own with the winds and percussion. The effect was uncanny, as if someone had turned a knob to obtain a uniform increase in volume. Nearly as odd was the sound's texture, with each orchestral choir cold, forward, and discrete. Rather than mingling or diffusing, the instrumental components of Brahms's First clamped into place like precision-tooled parts. Solti's interpretation was neutral with regard to tempo and articulation, except where the accents seemed exaggerated or the "lyric" phrasings peculiarly musclebound. Mainly the highpowered exterior was distinctive—that and the machinelike vigor and accuracy with which it was pounded out. Afterward, during a boisterous ovation (the man in front of me stood waving his right index finger, naming the Chicago Symphony "number one"), it occurred to me that an electronically dissected orchestra fed through giant speakers could have stirred up the same kind of excitement. The Chicago Symphony under Solti had sounded like a phonograph record.

For decades, recordings were more or less intended to simulate concert performances. Later, a double standard came into effect: "recorded" versus "live." Recorded performances were engineered and edited to ensure clarity, precision, and brilliance; in Carnegie Hall, somewhat less clarity, precision, and brilliance was the rule—until concerts began "catching up." Solti is not the only present-day conductor who realistically simulates recordings in performance.

Toscanini's role was pivotal. For one thing, clarity, precision, and brilliance were Toscanini trademarks. For another, more than any previous conductor, he was recorded so as to advertise his stock-in-trade. By crowding the NBC Symphony with microphones, RCA practically eliminated ambient reverberation in favor of heightened, atomized detail. At Studio 8H, even at Carnegie Hall, Toscanini's very concerts were transplanted to the closed-door, controlled environment of a recording venue. Canceling the hall's "sound," RCA sterilized the sound of the orchestra, then, when sterile sound was found defective, smeared it with additives. This was clumsily done, but something was learned in the process. During the sixties, when stereo redefined "high fidelity," unprecedented "mixing" and "dubbing" opportunities facilitated acoustics combining sharp, segregated instrumental profiles, highlighting "presence" and precision, with surrounding pockets of resonance, suggesting "depth" and "warmth." One cannot say that the musical results strayed ever further from actual concert norms—even, given the preponderance of new halls favoring hard sonic slabs, acoustical norms—because concert and acoustical norms were changing nearly as fast.

With the ascendancy of studio-made music came studio-made careers. Solti's great opportunity was no concert but a recording: his 1959 *Das Rheingold,* produced by John Culshaw as a stereo showcase for sonic wizardry. No staged *Rheingold* had so capitalized on screaming Nibelungs, Nibelheim's industrial racket, or Donner's hammer blow. If Solti's was not a poetic conception, its constant energy seemed volatile and spontaneous. But his later recordings with the Chicago Symphony, like Karajan's later Berlin Philharmonic recordings, are straitjacketed by uniformities of tempo, precision, linear pull, and tingling intensity—easy-to-appreciate Toscanini traits, as indiscriminately applied. Compared with Solti's, Karajan's recordings are notable for their range of color and dynamics, yet the underlying gamut of feeling is narrow, almost nonexistent. In Mozart's and Beethoven's time, unrehearsed performances were accepted as a matter of course; today, rehearsed performances rehearse recordings. In concert and on disc, art is confused with finished things. To Giulio Ricordi, Toscanini's *Falstaff* was "metallic," shearing the score into "identical, immaculate smooth slices." To Adorno, Toscanini's performance ideal suggested the score's "protective fixation"; to Eduard Steuermann, the "barbarism of perfection." But compared with Toscanini, Solti and Karajan are more protective, more barbarically perfect.

"To do it is stupid and a strain," wrote Busoni of recording in 1919. "Not letting oneself go for fear of inaccuracies and being conscious the whole

time that every note was going to be there for eternity; how can there be
any question of inspiration, freedom, swing or poetry? Enough that yesterday for nine pieces of four minutes each (half an hour in all) I worked for
three and a half hours!"[11] And yet Busoni left vital, distinctive recordings
—as did countless others, not excluding Toscanini, who found recording
"stupid and a strain." The chic modern studio, with its mirrors and makeup
tables, is by comparison found seductive. Many of the same artists who rush
to occupy it as often as possible, however, prefer listening to monaural-era
recordings and to pirated concert transcriptions. Music consumers, meanwhile, are urged to survey two dozen post-1960 Brahms Firsts adhering to
a sonic/interpretive norm encouraged and spread by the phonograph itself.
What Adorno wrote of radio listeners in 1945 applies equally to record
listeners forty years later: "The less the listener has to choose, the more is
he made to believe that he has a choice."

When in 1930 Toscanini became the first non-German to conduct at
Bayreuth, many in Germany felt a national shrine had been violated. In
recent Bayreuth seasons, however, German conductors have been in
the minority. More than a gesture of tolerance, such cosmopolitanism reflects weakened local performance traditions in Germany and elsewhere.
Toscanini's example was crucial. Insofar as his musical aesthetic was
recognizably grounded in late Verdi, he was a late embodiment of
nineteenth-century cultural nationalism; insofar as it overthrew "tradition"
in favor of literalism, he was an internationalist. Today Claudio Abbado and
Riccardo Muti are less "Italian" than Toscanini, and also more literal: they
reject rescorings and interpolated notes he permitted. Like their European
and American colleagues, they are fastidious executants, tasteful and, to a
degree, adaptable interpreters. But their up-to-date catholicity exacts a cost.

The interpretive habits Toscanini helped overthrow condoned, as a
seeming complement to sloppiness and self-indulgence, local stylistic bias.
Germany, France, Italy, Russia cultivated distinctive genealogies of performance whose roots were made especially plain when foreign operas
were given in the vernacular. Though Fernando de Lucia performing
"Nun sei bedankt, mein lieber Schwan" as "Mercè, mercè, cigno gentil"
or Richard Tauber performing "La donna è mobile" as "O, wie so trüger-
isch" could be enthralling, this was not the result of any apparent adaptive
effort. Rather, what sounds apparent to modern ears is that de Lucia and
Tauber sang everything the same way. In the "wrong" language and style,
they were endearing vocal personalities. In the language and style they
were born and bred in, they were more than endearing: their idiosyncrasies
melted into impregnated linguistic and aesthetic norms. Today's tenors

sing Wagner in German and Verdi in Italian, and apply stylistic niceties de Lucia and Tauber ignored. But their style consciousness is surface deep, and they themselves blur together.

Evolving within a national musical lineage, de Lucia or Tauber acquired style without trying. But once vital early links faded or vanished following the cultural upheavals of World War II, trying to acquire style became fruitful only to a point. Present-day aspirants to "Romantic" performance practice, reacting against the objectivity of Toscanini, Klemperer, and their followers, painstakingly cultivate rubatos that were instinctive to the Romantics. Aspirants to Classical or baroque performance practice cultivate Classical or baroque instruments, but they and their audiences remain irremediably contemporary. Bach and Beethoven, Wagner and Verdi grow older and more distant every year. At least the gambists and fortepianists promote an enlivening diversity of perspectives. For the most part, however, the mainstream canon sounds reported on from the same neutral outpost. Pungent French woodwinds, burnished German brass, or sunny Italian trumpets, contributory to the orchestral palettes Debussy, Brahms, and Verdi wrote for, today converge toward a single homogeneous mean, and so do French, German, and Italian conductors. In retrospect, even the arch-objective Toscanini seems an arch-individualist whose severe variant of the striving nineteenth-century hero contrasted with a gamut of alternative hero types: the visionary Furtwängler, the magisterial Klemperer, the reckless Mengelberg, the magnanimous Walter. It is not just that the music world gravitates toward more standardized, impersonal norms; this same gravitational force topples swashbuckling individualism in all its manifestations. No current orchestra would tolerate Toscanini's tirades and flung batons; corporate etiquette no longer condones the blatant autocracy of a David Sarnoff.

This suggests one crux of the repertoire problem: what disturbs about the warhorses is not merely the maddening familiarity of their serene, crowding presence, but the diminished potency and relevance of individual audacity as once practiced by Beethoven, Liszt, or Wagner. The desirability of cultivating new repertoire transcends the inherent desirability of change. To work on interpreting the Fifth Symphony or "Appassionata" Sonata is to grapple with standardized performance norms. To work on a new symphony or sonata is to grapple with the music itself—unbroadcast, unrecorded, unformulated except in the ear. Ultimately, such unmediated interaction with the music of one's own time can replenish stale interpretive juices and facilitate unmediated interaction with other music, however old or familiar.

If there already exists a new mode of interacting with the warhorses, a mode operating "against interpretation" somewhat in the sense of Susan

Sontag's influential 1964 essay, its prominent exponents include Pierre Boulez and Maurizio Pollini—performers whose cancellation of the music's own Classical or Romantic instincts is more drastic than Toscanini's aversion to "tradition." As one recent writer observes in finding Boulez "the strongest voice" for "a new, independent style" rooted in contemporary music and contemporary sensibilities:

> His tensile, linear shapeliness of phrase and ethereal, spacy textures represent a philosophical antipathy to thickness and heaviness, bombast and sentimentality. Each instrument keeps the expressive identity of its colors without turning the performance into a light show. If the surface is noticeably controlled, it's because there are powerful impulses underneath to control.[12]

I find my own sympathies more attuned to those contemporary performers who, usually through circumstances of birth and musical upbringing, manage to perpetuate national linkages for an "extra" generation or two. Their obvious breeding grounds are Russia and Eastern Europe, whose musical capitals retained a concentrated cultural life, a nurturing insularity, while Western cultural life was being blurred and dispersed. In the Soviet Union, in Czechoslovakia, in East Germany, orchestras may still flourish that honor tradition over executant hubris, and whose conductors have no distracting commitments elsewhere. And there may still be conservatories, outside the West, whose master teacher-performers are a nation's leading musicians, bent on transferring received tradition, and whose best graduates are to some degree shielded from premature circulation and acclaim. The East German conductor Klaus Tennstedt is an authentic, unwilled tradition bearer. The most gifted of the younger Russians, the violinist Gidon Kremer, seemingly manifests the best tendencies of two worlds: insulated Soviet training and subsequent liberation in the West. Kremer's history also suggests the pitfalls of insularity: he left Russia because he felt trapped. Tennstedt constitutes a holding action, a last chapter in the mainstream German genealogy; another such generation could well prove mannered, decadent.

There is, finally, a third category of warhorse performers who maneuver outside the rut of homogenized discretion and catholicity. Like Boulez, they manifest an "independent" style sidestepping fading German, French, Italian, and Russian pedigrees. But they have nothing to do with the "ethereal, spacy textures" of Boulez's anti-Romantic objectivity. Rather, they are "New World Romantics" whose maverick individualism, ignoring or disparaging Old World decorum, recalls the New England transcendentalists, or Ives, even Gottschalk or Barnum. As interpreters of European music they have nothing in common except a heterodoxy more cocky and complete than any European's could be. The late Canadian pianist Glenn Gould was such an artist, whose engrossing yet self-referential Bach, Beethoven, and Brahms made a virtue of remoteness. The Canadian tenor Jon Vickers, while less remote, is an equally compelling iconoclast, none of whose great roles—Florestan, Siegmund, Otello, Peter Grimes—sounds idiomatically sung as he sings it. And the most important American exponent of the mainstream symphonic and operatic canon is Leonard Bernstein, whose Romanticism is not rooted in Old World national traditions. His Brahms, Tchaikovsky, and Sibelius do not sound particularly German, Slavic, or Scandinavian. Even his Mahler, in which Jewishness strikes a common chord, omits drier aspects of the composer's aesthetic intuitively seized by conductors—Klemperer, Tennstedt—closer to it in time and/or place.

One symptom of Bernstein's success is that, unlike Lorin Maazel, James Levine, and countless lesser-known American conductors, he sounds uninfluenced by Toscanini. Rather, his artistic base is American: American jazz, American musical theater, the come-of-age generation of American composers and their champion, Koussevitzky. If Bernstein does not fully identify with the European canon, complete identification with Europe is off limits to any American. Rather, his New World roots fortify a concentrated musical persona whose formidable depth and range are vitalized by American personal audacity and rhythmic élan, and by Jewish-American emotional chutzpah.*

The NBC telecasts summarized the hypnotic maximum mass appeal of Toscanini the man and musician. Their long-term legacy, public television's "Great Performances," itself summarizes nearly every long-term legacy of the Toscanini cult. Produced in many instances by Kirk

---

*Any account of the Bernstein career must ask: Why has Bernstein, the American champion of Ives, Copland, and other important Americans, failed to establish a role model for American conductors? (For American pianists, the rejected role model was William Masselos.) To what degree does Bernstein's defection to Europe signify the confused rejection by America of this most American of conductors? It is pertinent, I think, that Americans resist being told what to do. A Russian émigré friend of mine once exclaimed: "If Bernstein were Russian, he would be a Russian *institution* by now!" What Shostakovich was and Richter is for the Soviet Union, what Sartre was for France, what Toscanini was for Italy after World War I—there are no American equivalents for these honored arbiters of intellect and high culture. Toscanini was an acceptable American culture-god partly because, unlike Koussevitzky, Stokowski, or Bernstein, he himself propounded no agenda.

Browning of the Toscanini telecasts, today's Public Broadcasting System
concerts fixate on celebrity performers and accredited masterpieces in
search of maximum audience appeal. Correlating size with stature, they
gravitate toward orchestra and opera as signatures of musical high culture, and penalize more intimate formats appropriate to the twentieth
century. Though, as in Toscanini times, they propagate "art" as something old, hallowed, and European, the equation is clinched by promotional glitter, not all-purpose excitement. Equidistant from national
interpretive traditions and revisionist insights, most "Great Performances" are as stale as the repertoire they serve. The same home-screen
showcase in which Toscanini loomed larger than life makes the Great
Performers seem strangely small.

Even television's brief history reveals the possibility of something better. As in radio's early years, sporadic idealism fired early commercial
TV. Both CBS and NBC commissioned new musical works. In addition
to Toscanini's concerts, David Sarnoff, an opera lover, created the NBC
Opera; under Peter Herman Adler, it stressed contemporary and American repertoire, mounting (and in some instances commissioning or pre-
miering) operas by Bernstein, Britten, Dello Joio, Stanley Hollingsworth,
Foss, Giannini, Martinů, Menotti, Poulenc, Prokofiev, and Weill. On
CBS, Bernstein's Young People's Concerts with the New York Philharmonic and his "Omnibus" specials, covering jazz, musical theater, and
"modern music" as well as Bach and Beethoven, proved that music appreciation could avoid every pitfall of the Damrosch patriarchy. Later, symphonic music was ghettoized on public television as on FM radio, its
usual format as of 1968 being an annual Boston Symphony series called
"Evening at Symphony." These Boston Evenings were not Great Performances but ordinary subscription concerts whose serious content and
low-key packaging reflected contemporaneous "educational television"
mores. The soloists for "Evening at Symphony" included many young,
noncelebrated Americans. The repertoire included a fair sampling of
new, American, and otherwise unfamiliar works, by George Crumb,
Charles Ives, Walter Piston, Schoenberg, Stravinsky, and Toru Take-
mitsu, among others. The blandness of Seiji Ozawa, the orchestra's regular conductor, was offset by performances transcending the emerging
"Great Performances" norm: Tennstedt's Bruckner and Mahler, Colin
Davis's Tippett and Sibelius. For two seasons, Michael Steinberg's exemplary Boston Symphony program notes were mailed to interested viewers. The entire undertaking seemed as appropriate to public television as
to Boston's Symphony Hall until the intervention of a new PBS priority:
glamour. As of 1973, Public Broadcasting began airing, as "Great Performances," European tapings of symphonic and operatic staples whose fea-

tured performers were invariably very famous.* In 1976, "Great Performances" inaugurated its own "Live from Lincoln Center" presentations, leading off with Van Cliburn, André Previn, and the New York Philharmonic in Grieg's Piano Concerto and Strauss's *Ein Heldenleben*. This formulaic stress on fame and familiarity doomed "Evening at Symphony," which had been financed by individual PBS affiliates in conjunction with corporate underwriting; after 1978–79—the tenth season of "Evening at Symphony" telecasts—the individual affiliates withdrew support in search of less rarefied, more popular programming, and no corporate underwriter could be found to foot the increased bill.

If public television's music ghetto now offers no concert series as stirring as Toscanini's, and no "educational" features as engrossing as Bernstein's "Omnibus" lectures, many "Great Performances"—Itzhak Perlman plays Tchaikovsky, Pavarotti sings Puccini, Danny Kaye conducts the New York Philharmonic—are "specials" of a sort the commercial networks produced as a matter of course before PBS relieved the burden. In the context of this NBC-PBS continuum, "Evening at Symphony" was an interim aberration, blundering into new territory before "Great Performances" hauled public television back to safety.**

In 1944, an RCA executive proclaimed: "Television has the power to create consumer demand . . . beyond anything we have heretofore known." "Great Performances" manages to shape consumer taste in Art and Culture. The conditioning process is twofold: selecting the pabulum, then larding it with attestations of supreme tastiness. Whereas PBS's television concerts

---

*I am not talking about dance and theater programs on "Great Performances"; like American dance and theater generally, they have been more enterprising.

**In the early years of American public television, the system's proudest achievement may have been its espousal of the maverick documentary filmmaker Frederick Wiseman. *Law and Order* (1969), *Hospital* (1970), and a dozen other Wiseman documentaries—classics of the genre—were premiered and partly financed by public television. With the advent of "Great Performances," however, patient cinéma-verité exposés of American institutions came to seem unacceptably dissident on both political and aesthetic grounds. By 1983, the year of *The Store* (a two-hour perusal of Dallas's huge Nieman-Marcus outlet), Wiseman could no longer depend on support from the Corporation for Public Broadcasting. His denunciation of public television as a "bloated and engorged bureaucracy" in which the enterprising independent filmmaker simply "doesn't fit"[13] spoke the truth; Public Broadcasting's growing fixation on audience ratings, on praising and appreciating, made *The Store* a television anomaly. Patrice Chereau's Bayreuth production of Wagner's *Ring*, also presented on public television in 1983, was so gaudily promoted, tediously explained, and earnestly apologized for by "Great Performances" as to make Wagner's famous cycle, in its most famous contemporary staging, seem the height of poisonous esoterica.

once approximated unbiased samplings of nontelevised symphonic programming, the "Great Performances" music repertoire is preselected to
increase homogeneity. Aesthetic and political heterodoxy are shunned;
even the series's own advisory panel has judged the "Great Performances"
agenda "too geared to the upper middle class."[14] A patina of "smugness"
and "self-satisfaction" was one defining characteristic of Theodor Adorno's
vision of mind-numbing "affirmative" culture. On "Great Performances,"
the thick garnish of propagandistic self-approbation embraces not just the
Great Performers but Public Broadcasting, its audience, and the corporate
sponsor. In *Dialectic of Enlightenment*, Adorno and Max Horkheimer observed: "When Toscanini conducted over the radio . . . he was heard
without charge, and every sound of the symphony was accompanied, as it
were, by the sublime puff that the symphony was not interrupted by any
advertising: 'This concert is brought to you as a public service.' "[15] Later,
when Reynolds Metals sponsored Toscanini "as a public service," aluminum was linked with Toscanini's telecasts—both were "spreading widely,"
with the latter depending on cable made out of the former. The Exxon
Corporation, "underwriting" PBS's "Great Performances" as a "public
service," links gasoline and Lincoln Center with the slogan: "Quality You
Can Count on in the Performing Arts." Summarizing Lincoln Center's
"Twenty-Five Years of Achievement" with clips from "Great Performances" and "Live from the Met" on October 26, 1984, PBS summarized
the praise-plus-pabulum formula. Host Patrick Watson called Lincoln Center "a reflection of the maturing of this country from its period of practical
pioneering to its present international role in the performing arts. . . .
America needed a place for its own performing arts to come of age. . . .
[Lincoln Center is] where night after night America lays claim to its world
pre-eminence in the performing arts." The unconscious irony of these
patriotic boasts was underlined by PBS's preselection from previously
preselected Lincoln Center fare. In the course of nearly two gala hours
("some of the most extraordinary performances originally broadcast live"),
the indigenous music totaled ninety seconds: a minute-long excerpt from
Rhapsody in Blue, and thirty seconds worth of Samuel Barber's *Antony and
Cleopatra* (from a film never shown on public television).

In recent seasons, "Great Performances" has carried the preselection
process to its logical conclusion, staging public concerts specifically for
television. Called "event television," this innovation is not intended to
capitalize on inherent technological possibilities, as were Stravinsky's *The
Flood* (commissioned and premiered by CBS, 1962) and Menotti's *The Laby-
rinth* (commissioned and premiered by NBC, 1963). Rather, the intent is to
maximize glamour and homogeneity, pabulum and praise, by manufactur-
ing superconcerts crammed with superstars. PBS's annual "Gala of Stars,"

taped before a live audience, is one "event television" format, interspersing underrehearsed warhorse extracts with smiling encomiums and urgent appeals for money (as one New York huckster accurately declared during the 1983 gala: "You know very well you wouldn't see a gala like this anyplace else!"). Another "event television" concert, the 1982 "An Evening with Itzhak Perlman," presented the violinist with the New York Philharmonic in three warhorse concertos—the Mendelssohn, the Brahms, and "Winter" from Vivaldi's *The Seasons*. "Because of television, the format of a concert can change," the show's producer, John Goberman, explained in an interview. "The point of this program is to present an evening with Itzhak Perlman; the audience will see him talking, working, and performing the feat of playing three concertos in one evening. In effect, he will be his own host, speaking to the cameras during the intermission segments."[16] In fact, having already appeared on many televised concerts and talk shows, Perlman himself devised the format for "An Evening with Itzhak Perlman," even helping Goberman plan camera placements. Among the telecast's memorable moments was Perlman's backstage assessment following the Vivaldi work (which he also conducted): "Well, that went pretty well, I guess." For that matter, Perlman's personality emerged less in his bland musical performances than in such extramusical banter and in an "intermission visit" showing Perlman fielding questions from his thirteen-year-old son's classmates at New York's Collegiate School.

Q: How do you feel about the commercialism in the arts these days, and do you feel that it leads to any kind of sacrifice in artistic quality?

A: OK. Commercialism in the arts. Can you be more specific?

Q: Things like fur coats and American Express cards. [*Laughter.*]

A: I don't own a fur coat.

Q: I mean, advertising for those, and going outside the arts to find publicity. And then going beyond that, too. There is a lot of publicity on how certain artists give their most when they're going to be on television, because that attracts the widest audience.

A: Ummmmmmmm. Yes. [*Laughter.*] Well, I don't . . . give my most for television only. [*Mugs for camera, drawing laughter.*] I'll tell you: I feel that television has been *phenomenal* for the arts. Absolutely phenomenal. It has brought the arts to so many millions of people who otherwise would not know the experience. I think that the last five years and the next five years will be probably called a golden age in the arts in the United States, and I think that's basically because of television. . . . Whenever I'm in an airport . . . a porter or a bus driver comes and says [*pointing excitedly*] "AIIIII!!!" I mean, there's nothing wrong with that, and if the same fellow sees me on PBS and I'm playing a concerto

... maybe he'll come to the concert. In San Francisco there were a couple of people who came to my concert and said, "This is the first time I've ever been to a concert. I really enjoyed it." Well, I feel that [television plays] an important part in building audiences. . . .

Perlman's arguments in favor of PBS-style high culture are exuberantly endorsed by other superstars, by public television officials, and by arts administrators: that a single Great Performance reaches more people than attend Lincoln Center events all year; that the cumulative "Live from Lincoln Center" audience tops 200 million households; that the impact is "phenomenal," "historic," "incalculable." When Perlman appears on "The Tonight Show," his nightly audience is perhaps 16 million—more than three times the audience for his "Great Performances." Here, his extramusical virtues shine the more brightly. When Johnny Carson plugs Perlman's latest LP and recites his upcoming concert dates, Perlman appears reasonably modest, never self-conscious or indifferent. When Carson feeds him a straight line, he tells his joke spontaneously, craftily. His hearty baritone enhances his outgoing yet relaxed affability. As during Pavarotti's visits, Carson himself seems to have an unusually good time. Perlman gives a honey-toned rendition of a Wieniawski caprice. The studio audience whistles and claps. Carson shakes his head and says: "Wow. Itzhak Perlman. Be back in a minute."

Do Perlman's television fans buy his records and attend his concerts? Are some of them classical music novices? Does this signify a "golden age in the arts in the United States"? Yes, yes, and no. As during the music appreciation decades, some converts are stimulated by new knowledge to transcend music's midculture of warhorses and personalities. For a great many others, however, the warhorses and personalities define Great Performances, denigrating the rest. When Toscanini conducted the New York Philharmonic, Arthur Judson discovered that no other conductors could fill Carnegie Hall. Today, Perlman and other Great Performers penalize their colleagues. As of 1986, Perlman was reportedly making up to $35,000 a concert, Pavarotti up to $100,000—symptoms of a fee structure gone into orbit. (Jascha Heifetz caused a concert-world sensation around 1950 by raising his fee from $3,000 to $3,500, an unheard-of altitude.) Many presenters want Perlman at any cost. Smaller concert managements complain that the market for lesser-known talent is drying up. In one recent season, the major American orchestras engaged piano soloists on 188 occasions, of which more than half were filled by the same eleven pianists. Violinists are even more stratified—and not according to artistic rank. One discriminating manager complains: "There are many people in America who won't go to a concert unless they have seen the performer on TV."

For all the talk of democratizing high culture, "Great Performances," like music appreciation fifty years ago, also inculcates a paradoxical elitism. Rather than great music's aura of exclusivity being negated, partaking in the exclusive aura is made a democratic privilege. Rather than being democratically selected, great music is preselected for the demos. Rather than by a democracy, high culture is propagated by a benign conservative dictatorship; its elections, with their controlled slates and supportive propaganda, are a sham.

The supreme Great Performance to date, bigger than event television (although television proved essential to its packaging), was "Luciano Pavarotti at Madison Square Garden"—two 1984 concerts, of which the first was telecast by public television. The twenty-thousand-seat sports arena was nearly twice sold out at prices ranging from fifteen to fifty dollars. The PBS telecast attracted an estimated 20 million viewers. Since Caruso had sung at an earlier incarnation of the thrice-rebuilt Garden, the Pavarotti-Caruso analogy was played to the hilt. Pavarotti's program biography rehearsed his "direct and appealing nature," his "enormous personality" which welcomed "thousands into his heart." The souvenir program called him "modest," "humble," "a combination of absolute simplicity and authority on the opera and concert stages, as well as in his family life." In an interview prefacing the telecast, Pavarotti declared: "I want people to know I love the public very much. I love people. . . . Audiences love me like I like audiences."

Like Perlman, or Ronald Reagan, Pavarotti excels in televised conversation; even his least plausible lines are delivered with apparent candor, disarming charm. In performance at Madison Square Garden, however, Pavarotti was nervous and self-conscious. His trademark salutation, arms stretched wide, seemed a plea for help. His trademark smile seemed wired with anxiety. He paused during the second concert to tell the crowd: "You have been enjoying yourself. Well, same with me, but even more." His voice sounded worried, his delivery stiff.

The program for both concerts consisted of favorite lyric tenor arias from *Rigoletto, Lucia di Lammermoor,* and *La Bohème,* favorite spinto/ dramatic arias from *Il trovatore, Pagliacci,* and *Turandot,* and Italian songs in a popular vein. The last, including "O Sole mio" and "Torna a Surriento," were underprepared: Pavarotti read the lyrics off a music stand. The Garden's sound system so thickened and amplified his voice that he might have been miming to a record. As for the voice itself, both its condition and deployment documented the costs of celebrity. Pavarotti had advanced in mid-career from lyric to stentorian glamour roles: Manrico,

Radames, Calaf. But his tenor, unlike Caruso's, retained its undesired lyric timbre while losing flexibility and ease. Now he sang everything under pressure, tight and loud. In place of nuances he no longer commanded, he interpolated tricks: extra-long high notes, unintegrated head tones, loud cutoffs to every soft ending, craving applause. His omnipresent handkerchief, a Pavarotti signature, flagged the second evening's nadir: upon misplacing a high note in "Vesti la giubba," he used the handy cloth to smother his face, feigning a sudden surfeit of emotion. All this came accompanied, on both occasions, by an orchestra that looked and sounded underrehearsed and bored. Even the cheering and applause sounded dutiful. Both concerts were simply dull.

In the preconcert PBS interview, Pavarotti felt called upon to deny that his Garden recitals vulgarized high culture. He appealed to earlier tenors—Caruso, inevitably, was the chosen example—who had sung "to the people." "The real tenors of the past, they made popular music. . . . I always love that." To this he appended the familiar populist rationale: "You reach a lot of people. Let's say, the people are scared of serious music. . . . Then little by little they begin to go to the opera . . . and then they begin to love classical music. . . . And with this concert I am able to show that classical music is not something you have to be scared [of]." It is true that Caruso, Richard Tauber, and John McCormack, among others, were hugely successful outside high-culture precincts in Italian, Viennese, and Irish songs. And, as Perlman's TV fans have sampled Avery Fisher and Carnegie halls, many Pavarotti addicts have doubtless been motivated to try the Metropolitan Opera for themselves, if mainly when he was singing there. Still, this part of the Pavarotti-Caruso analogy is as suspect as the rest. Caruso sang "La donna è mobile" and "Lolita" "to the people." Nearly a century later, Pavarotti offered the identical selections at Madison Square Garden—as if "popular music" had never discovered the blues, jazz, or rock 'n' roll. What is more, his style of "popular" singing is as anachronistic as his "popular" repertoire. As every student of popular singing knows, the microphone transformed popular song after 1920. Heavy, formal voices that had lent themselves to "Jeanie with the Light Brown Hair" and "Ah, Sweet Mystery of Life" gave way to light-voiced, amplified "crooners" in "Sweet Georgia Brown" and "Tea for Two." When Jenny Lind sang at Castle Garden, her encores included several Stephen Foster songs. When Adelina Patti sang at Madison Square Garden, her program included "Home, Sweet Home" (with a thousand-voice chorus). The recordings of Caruso include stentorian renderings of "Love Is Mine," "Love Me or Not," and George M. Cohan's "Over There." Mass adulation of Patti and Lind, Caruso and McCormack reflected an absence of competing Sinatras, Garlands, Fitzgeralds, Presleys, and Cashes on radio and recordings: there existed no "pop" singers or songs, no popular music industry such as we have today. In some respects, the appropriate contemporary analogies to Caruso at Madison Square Garden are the Madison Square Garden concerts of Presley and the Rolling Stones.

Compared to Pavarotti at the Garden, Toscanini's 1944 Madison Square Garden Red Cross benefit was in some ways similarly anachronistic, in some ways not. Its emergency philanthropic status rationalized the largest possible audience. Its outsized forces—the NBC Symphony, the New York Philharmonic, the All-City High School Chorus and Glee Clubs—made sense of the huge performing space. Its program—*The Hymn of the Nations,* the third act of *Rigoletto,* "Stars and Stripes Forever," and four Wagner excerpts—was purposefully rabble-rousing, and in fact (as the cheering and applause captured on RCA's recording of the *Rigoletto* extract make clear) roused the rabble to a fever pitch as concentrated and intense as Pavarotti's Garden receptions were mechanical and polite. By any previous criterion, Pavarotti at Madison Square Garden was an arbitrary, even decadent entertainment, "Great Performances" praise-plus-pabulum transplanted from Lincoln Center to sanitize and uplift the lucky sports arena. PBS, with revealing snobbery, pronounced it "perhaps [Madison Square Garden's] finest hour" —better than hockey, boxing, and basketball, better than Ringling Brothers, Barnum and Bailey.

The closer one scrutinizes the Pavarotti/Madison Square Garden conjunction, the more curious it becomes; the more curious it becomes, the more sheer profits and publicity logically explain it. Plácido Domingo's rival "world's greatest tenor" claim had by 1984 been formidably buttressed by a 1981 NBC television special ("Caruso Remembered"), a 1982 *Newsweek* cover story ("King of the Opera"), and an anomalous "crossover" LP ("Perhaps Love" with John Denver) selling more than half a million copies by March 1982—"the quickest rise to 'Gold' by any opera singer." Stung, Pavarotti retaliated in *TV Guide:*

> I know some people criticize me for going on Johnny Carson or making commercials for American Express. They say I am not being "serious." But "serious" is a very elastic term these days, especially if you have a sense of humor. "Bad taste" is also an elastic term.
>
> If anything is in bad taste it's capitalizing on the famous names of others. On a recent NBC show, the tenor Plácido Domingo came out to "celebrate" Caruso. Caruso, at this point in history, does not need celebrating. So who is being "not serious"?[17]

The counterattack continued with "The Luciano Pavarotti Special" on ABC (March 29, 1982), an "event television" Great Performance (with Mehta and the New York Philharmonic, April 4, 1983), and a crossover recording of Pavarotti's own ("Mamma," a selection of popular Italian songs arranged and conducted by Henry Mancini). The mighty knock-out, plugging Pavarotti generally and the "Mamma" arrangements specifically, was the Madison Square Garden superrecitals. Victor Herbert, who knew Caruso, commended him for "the warm glow of his democratic modesty and personal charm." More than *Pavarotti: My Own Story,* more than "Mamma," more than his various "Great Performances," Pavarotti's Garden extravaganzas peg him as a Caruso manqué.

In a sense, one ingredient missing from the Garden concerts was Madison Square Garden itself, which, through four incarnations, traces its history to P. T. Barnum's Monster Classical and Geological Hippodrome at Madison Square. Pavarotti's joyless incursion was oriented to negate rather than savor the Garden's potential abrasion; having actually lost what innocence the Caruso analogy sought to perpetuate, he scorned the healthy vulgarity of his populist locale. In a memorable passage from *Dialectic of Enlightenment,* Adorno and Horkheimer muse that an American strain of "Mark Twain absurdity"—of which certain popular productions of Barnum, Chaplin, and the Marx Brothers are representative—might "be a corrective of art," aglimmer with "negative truth" because of the "effort it demands from the intelligence to neutralize its burdens."

> But of course it cannot happen. . . . Ethics and taste cut short unrestrained amusement as "naive"—naiveté is thought to be as bad as intellectualism. . . . The culture industry is corrupt not because it is a sinful Babylon, but because it is a cathedral dedicated to elevated pleasure. On all levels, from Hemingway to Emil Ludwig, from Mrs. Miniver to the Lone Ranger, from Toscanini to Guy Lombardo, there is untruth in the intellectual content. . . .
>
> The fusion of culture and entertainment that is taking place today leads not only to a depravation of culture, but inevitably to an intellectualization of amusement.[18]

Barnum irreverently appreciated the "Mark Twain absurdity" of his Jenny Lind, Tom Thumb, and Joice Heth shenanigans as surely as the Toscanini and Pavarotti cults have rejected irreverent "negative truth." Like David Sarnoff on behalf of Toscanini, the "fun-loving" Pavarotti is essentially earnest when it comes to preaching that "classical music is not something to be scared of." Like Sarnoff's, his populist sermons sometimes sound defensive; he seemingly struggles against a burden of guilt. Like Sarnoff's, his example embodies what Adorno and Horkheimer debunked as a "fusion of culture and entertainment," what Dwight Macdonald debunked as a "hybridization of masscult and high culture."

Neither Sarnoff nor Pavarotti could carelessly exclaim, after Barnum: "The bigger the humbug, the more people like it." Caruso's cult, like Barnum's Jenny Lind, was blithe mass culture. Pavarotti, who makes Madison Square Garden a "cathedral dedicated to elevated pleasure," is pure midcult.

Conclusion

*T*o close on a personal note:

When I undertook understanding Toscanini some five years ago, I imagined myself extrapolating remedies from the perils of Toscanini's cult. In my fixed-up future, mainstream American high culture, symbolized by Lincoln Center, would be rescued by enlightened musicians, administrators, and critics. The New York Philharmonic would hire a music director identified with certain important contemporary composers, or at least with an important neglected repertoire. The Metropolitan Opera would mount Busoni's *Doktor Faust,* Tippett's *Midsummer Marriage,* Schoenberg's *Moses and Aron*—in English—and regularly engage world-class conductors. CBS and RCA Records, freed of Great Performance hangups, would resurrect the legacy of Goddard Lieberson, who instilled musicianly priorities as head of the former label through 1975. PBS would show half the respect for America's own musical heritage as the National Endowment for the Arts, the New York State Council on the Arts, or the late Works Progress Administration. The New York *Times* culture department would stop playing to the praise-plus-pabulum merchandisers and promote a countervailing focus.

What ended these fantasies, midway through my research, was a sort of epiphany. Walking toward the Lincoln Center subway station, I stopped to study the underground show window of Lincoln Center's Performing Arts Gift Shop. Surveying the napkins, mugs, and umbrellas, all of them decorated with pictures and signatures of the great (i.e., dead European) composers, I realized that as far as music was concerned, Lincoln Center could not be salvaged for living art.*

---

*The New York City Ballet, which makes its home at Lincoln Center's New York State Theater, is excluded from my music-only purview.

In fact, I have practically stopped attending musical events at the Metropolitan Opera, Avery Fisher Hall, and the New York State Theater. To some degree, other American cities have orchestras and opera companies that put repertoire first, that intersect with local composers' communities, that avoid the glare of Great Performances. (If an American test case exists for extending the life span of the orchestra as a central cultural resource, it is probably in San Francisco.) In New York, I find that piano, chamber music, and song recitals in properly scaled halls are most likely to satisfy my appetite for re-experiencing Beethoven and Schubert, Schoenberg and Stravinsky. The New York Rangers, at Madison Square Garden, play with more sustained intensity than the New York Philharmonic. The best musical theater I have encountered in recent years was not at the Metropolitan but at the unpredictable Brooklyn Academy of Music: *The Gospel at Colonus,* the ingenious Lee Breuer/Bob Telson gospel adaptation of *Oedipus at Colonus,* given in 1983.*

To regard Lincoln Center as a lost cause for music does not deny an occasional memorable evening there or the frequent gratification of its undemanding patrons. But Lincoln Center stacks the odds against mystery; it seeks out rather than antagonizes routine channels of feeling and perception. To understand Toscanini is to understand that the central factor transcends who administers, conducts, sings, or plays. Rather, the "performing arts" audience is the Center's massive, immovable base. An outgrowth of music appreciation's democratized "new audience," this core constituency preserves the dichotomy, more pronounced in music than in the other arts, between influential popularizers and fans, on the one hand, and excluded creators and intellectuals, on the other. More than the performing artists, it sets the listening ambience and the parameters for acceptable change. With its conditioned affinity for watered-down high culture, it produces a symphonic quagmire, and quicksand in the opera house. Its expansive bulk demands swaths of space: new shopping centers for the arts, the stocking and merchandising of which enervate higher cultural impulses. Unlike Carnegie Hall, whose ghosts are a palpable presence when inspired music is made there, or downtown Manhattan's La Mama or Performing Garage, where flexible, makeshift performance spaces invite an inquisitive response, Lincoln Center exudes the inherent sterility of new homes for old art.

One lesson of the sixties' "cultural explosion" was that in the labor-intensive performing arts, growing audiences produced no economies of scale. A widening gap between income and expenses forced a widening

---

*And telecast by "Great Performances" in 1985—an auspicious departure.

search for subsidies: private gifts, corporate gifts, foundation gifts, scarce government gifts. In conjunction with union contracts guaranteeing more weeks of work, new subsidy sources promoted yet more concerts, more operas, longer seasons. A necessary part of this vicious circle was an intensified audience search. Lincoln Center and its offspring now use computerized direct mailings, "phonothons," and other professional fund-raising strategies to supermarket glamour, escalating the fatal nexus of overproduction, overpromotion, and overconsumption.* The signature event of every New York Philharmonic season is the Radiothon: a weekend-long fundraising gala, broadcast live, and including "hours of beautiful music, scintillating celebrity interviews, thrilling on-air auctions, and the opportunity to purchase hundreds of wonderful gifts." The 1986 Radiothon gift catalogue, from which the preceding endorsement by Zubin Mehta is taken, was mailed to 175,000 homes. Its forty pages of premiums included specially created Philharmonic sweatshirts and tote bags emblazoned with "Phil the Penguin"; gift certificates for hardware, china, and video games; a blimp ride and a San Francisco vacation; a facial massage, sailing lessons, and a session of hypnosis. The Metropolitan Opera, across the plaza, counters every year with a radio "Met Marathon," supplemented by shoppers' cornucopias including the *La Bohème* music box, inspired by Franco Zeffirelli's Metropolitan production; the Met ceiling scarf, based on the Old Met's ceiling design; the Violetta doll, a porcelain facsimile of Verdi's heroine. Playing for higher stakes, the Philharmonic and the Met compete for PBS exposure: in terms of audience building, a million-dollar magnet beside the mousetraps—Baedekers, young people's concerts, music appreciation lectures—once set to ensnare reluctant Babbitts. The 1979 "Live from the Met" telecast of *Otello*, which may have reached as many as 10 million viewers, elicited this commentary from the company's executive director: "We average 25,000 letters from people who haven't been on our lists with each new telecast. . . . The wider we reach, the more access we have to both federal funding and private contributions." To which the Metropolitan's president added: "We hope to get considerable revenue from electronics of all sorts —cable TV, video discs, cassettes and tapes. . . . We've got to play to the widest possible audience. And with satellite television, the world is there."[1]

At Lincoln Center, on PBS, the dense scaffolding of fund raising and audience expansion obscures the house of culture. Layers of midcult para-

---

*The glamorous "arts center" concept is itself a marketing tool. As the 1984 Louis Harris study "Americans and the Arts" put it: ". . . The more performing arts can be concentrated in centers with facilities for presenting multiple disciplines, the more likely will be the growth of audiences from other performing arts."

phernalia—"scintillating celebrity interviews," pseudoautobiographies, souvenir shirts and bags—insulate the Great Performers from the creative act. Though today's New York Philharmonic has, in Jacob Druckman, a composer-in-residence, and though the Metropolitan Opera has commissioned works from Druckman and John Corigliano, neither institution cultivates an enlightened, open-eared audience, as Koussevitzky and Stokowski tried to. Though the Metropolitan has absorbed *Wozzeck, Lulu,* and *The Rise and Fall of the City of Mahagonny* into its repertoire, these twentieth-century operas remain incongruous where Puccini and Pavarotti are house favorites, holding artistic direction hostage; and where the gaudy, gargantuan house itself—a posthumous embodiment of Romantic grandiosity—promotes performance styles hostile to conversational intimacy and gestural subtlety. To imagine spoken drama screamed at thirty-eight hundred tolerant spectators is to glean the difficulty of conveying Berg or Weill at the Metropolitan. More than Verdi or Wagner, *modern* operas make it seem a mausoleum. This obliterates every pipe dream of renewal. In recent New York seasons, the most satisfying operatic production I have encountered was of Copland's *The Second Hurricane,* by the New Federal Theatre at the Henry Street Settlement Playhouse in 1985. In general, smaller opera companies offer greater hope than does the Met.

In endeavoring to understand Toscanini, I found myself drawn to certain American critics of American culture, eyewitnesses both to the coming-of-age of an American intelligentsia and to the emergence of Macdonald-style American midcult after World War I. Van Wyck Brooks decried "catchpenny opportunism" and "stark utilitarianism." H. L. Mencken perceived a public of "mobmen" and "homo boobiens." Sinclair Lewis mocked civic pride and business acumen. Earlier generations of American self-critics, while less vitriolic, likewise reflected a national relish for self-parody. Mark Twain's ambivalence toward Old World culture bespoke amused or bitter ambivalence toward the New World. George Bagby's "Jud Brownin Hears Ruby Play" embodied a frontier humor parodying fine language and inflated feelings associated with American leaders and institutions. As Edward Martin, a recent historian of American humor, has written: "American audiences enjoyed their own deflation; they liked the boldness of attack, the undisguised ridicule." P. T. Barnum's fabulous appeal depended on his appreciation that "the bigger the humbug, the better people like it."

To cite a truism: For all their satire and contempt, these American critics of America felt a chronic affection for things American. Van Wyck Brooks was one of many come-of-age dissonant intellectuals later to recant in favor of patriotic euphony. Of Sinclair Lewis, a knowing contemporary wrote: "At the bottom [he] is solidly bourgeois. He loves real estate and mortgages and bank accounts. Fundamentally he is a Rotarian, and in spite of his cynical writings about business and business people, he has an immense admiration for the superior executive type of businessman, for people who make money and succeed." Even the terrible Mencken was a child of the middle class in whose prejudices a strain of WASP gentility could be discerned. Edward Martin finds "persistent love and nostalgia for aspects of what they ridiculed" in the rantings of Mencken, Lewis, and other "debunkers." Leslie Fiedler has found America's dissident artists and critics subsumed, en masse, by "the [American] popular mind at its deepest level."[2]

Like Brooks, Mencken, and Lewis, I have fixed my attention on the dangers of the self-made ethos—its anti-intellectualism, and parochial elevation of egalitarianism and efficiency, energy and spontaneity. In their ambivalence toward Old World culture, self-made Americans of Toscanini's time saw Europeans as pretentious and decadent. In part, this was defensive posturing—yet it also conveyed truths. Personally, I have only to visit Europe to re-experience my affection for American egalitarianism and efficiency, energy and spontaneity.

Living in France or Germany, or merely gazing abroad, generations of American writers, painters, and composers have seen greener pastures. Equally revelatory, however, is the testimony of Old World artists abroad in the United States. Even in the context of *Understanding Toscanini*, weighted toward American self-criticism, we have observed how Tchaikovsky, helping to inaugurate Carnegie Hall as Walter Damrosch's guest of honor, was moved to exclaim: "Amazing people these Americans! Compared with Paris . . . the frankness, sincerity and generosity in this country . . . and its eagerness to please and win approval, are simply astonishing"; how Anton Rubinstein, notwithstanding his resentment of American publicity mongers and autograph hounds, called the United States "the land for those who love liberty" and declared he would like his children to be American citizens; how Gustav Mahler found American audiences "tremendously unspoilt," "more eager to learn and more grateful than any European can imagine"; how Alma Mahler, who blamed the New York Philharmonic for undermining her husband's health, could nevertheless write of the solicitude she encountered on the street: "Never in my whole life have I met so much genuine warmth of heart and delicacy of feeling as in America"; how Wilhelm Furtwängler and his secretary, Berta Geissmar, were overwhelmed by the hospitality, wealth, and vitality of New York City and by its "galaxy of musical genius and brilliance."

Like the stereotype of the snobbish, complacent European, the imagery of a brave New World is not wholly mythic. On various occasions, America has embodied a living dream of protean diversity and healthy vulgarity. Mark Twain, P. T. Barnum, Jud Brownin were American originals fortified by innocence. Only in America could Leopold Stokowski, whose naiveté and theatricality predisposed him to experimentation and populism, have found a major permanent post. It was America that produced the composer/critic Virgil Thomson, in whom Kansas and Harvard, Paris and New York, hymn and fugue engendered a dazzling interchange of innocence and insouciant sophistication; that produced Aaron Copland, whose New World innocence found expression in terms of prairie serenity and the urban optimism of jackhammers and skyscrapers; that produced Leonard Bernstein, in whom Copland's unpatronizing populism and the jazzy rhythms of his cityscapes have been perpetuated. These same qualities of invigorating innocence and unfettered personal experience were to some degree perceptible in the personae of the Toscanini cult—in Olin Downes, in David Sarnoff, in Toscanini himself. But every refreshing aspect was so mired in the earnest, parochial cult dynamic that the imagery of a brave New World was defeated. And at Lincoln Center, the midcult spectacle of American high culture praising itself is a spectacle of America denying itself, eagerly embracing the very pretentiousness and snobbery which Mark Twain reviled as "Old World," and the absence of which Tchaikovsky, Rubinstein, and Mahler savored. Inbred, Eurocentric, claustrophobic, the Great Performances syndrome conceives high culture as an Old World enterprise in which superior Americans are privileged to partake.

One proposed antidote to rampant midcult, associated with the Reaganized federal arts endowments and their intellectual accessories, would refine Lincoln Center/"Great Performances" offerings in conjunction with refining—and, presumably, shrinking—Lincoln Center/"Great Performances" audiences. Accredited "masterworks" and "treasures of civilization" would be propounded in an attempt to stem the populist tide. Thus Samuel Lipman, the neoconservative publisher of *The New Criterion*, has taken issue with the National Endowment of the Arts's opera–musical theater program for lumping together opera and Broadway, further diluting endangered high culture standards: "One can only wonder about an artistic and intellectual sensibility that calls the choice between *Fidelio* and *Oklahoma!* a result of 'artificial barriers.' "[3] Lipman's critique, as amassed in *The House of Music* (1984), is full of interest; he acutely perceives the midcult menace. But to counteract the menace by resurrecting traditional aesthetic criteria embodied in *Fidelio* and other treasures risks slighting the very "sense of history" *The New Criterion* would endorse. Audience expansion, and the necessary repercussions for art, are historic facts; audience contraction is a hope as improbable as the contemporary creation of further *Fidelios*

—that is, of masterwork vehicles for Toscaninis and Furtwänglers, Metropolitan Operas and New York Philharmonics.

The "solution" to Great Performances, if one exists, would more likely capitalize on audience expansion, not attack it, and capitalize as well on brave New World imagery—of indigenous innocence, diversity, exuberance, and vulgarity—that Great Performances disdains. At least five worlds of American music were omitted from the curricula of music appreciation and of the Toscanini cult—and therefore withheld from the interwar "new audience" and its progeny. The first was of Koussevitzky, Tanglewood, and *Modern Music:* the come-of-age American composers of the twenties and thirties. The second was a maverick sidebar to the first: rangy American originals in the tradition of Whitman and Melville, beginning with Charles Ives and including Edgard Varèse, Harry Partch, and John Cage. The third omitted world was of American musical theater: Gershwin, Cole Porter, Irving Berlin, Richard Rodgers. The fourth—endorsed by *Modern Music,* Ives, and Gershwin, denigrated by highbrow music appreciators—was jazz, its precursors and forms: gospel, blues, ragtime, swing. The fifth omitted world of music mounted the most thorough attack on the "masterwork" idea, with its elaborate distinctions between "serious" and "popular," "art" and "recreation." Propagated in *Modern Music* by the composers Henry Cowell, Paul Bowles, and Colin McPhee, among others, it prophetically embraced the music of Asia, Africa, and South America, accommodating listening modes more meditative or ceremonial than those of the modern West. McPhee, who took up residence in Indonesia, wrote of "The 'Absolute' Music of Bali" in 1935:

> The original nature of music reveals itself with ever greater clarity as a phenomenon of sound rather than of language, as something springing from the urge to rhythmic expression, spontaneous and physical, rather than as a means for unembarrassed self-revelation.
>
> In conception Balinese music is static, whereas ours is dynamic and generally the expression of a crisis, a conflict. . . .[4]

McPhee's own *Tabuh-Tabuhan* (1936)—his best-known composition, forecasting the "minimalism" of Steve Reich and Philip Glass—is an orchestral toccata appropriating Balinese gamelan techniques.

Each of these five omitted worlds of American music represents a constituency omitted from music appreciation's "new audience." In terms of present-day audience expansion, the omitted worlds represent the possibility of an expansion dynamic based less on snob-appeal marketing, more on the lure of the product itself. In terms of the concert experience, the omitted worlds represent the possibility of audiences less narcotized, more collectively charged. They represent the possibility of abolishing the dated preachiness of Theodore Thomas, Lawrence Gilman, and (as if time stood still) "Great Performances" in favor of a pluralistic art-ideal superseding sanctified "classical music." Whatever one makes of the minimalist movement, it aligns audience expansion with bona fide contemporary aesthetics.

Pondering a new audience whose "sheer numbers" created "a special problem," Aaron Copland envisioned "the job of the forties"—"the most exciting challenge of our day"—as finding "a musical style which satisfies both us and them." He urged his colleagues to reach beyond "the concert audience" to new listeners in other venues. He called for music "simple," "direct," "fresh in feeling," but "in no sense capable of being interpreted as a writing down to the level of the public." Copland's call went largely unheeded yet resounds today. Mass culture shatters the insular creative modes Copland decried and makes the quest for a more egalitarian music less self-conscious.

Is this closing whiff of optimism pro forma? I make no predictions.

When Toscanini first arrived from Italy, symphony and opera in the United States were an evolving mixture of achievement and provincialism, chauvinism and sophistication. His second arrival, after World War I, coincided with America's new international stature, with escalating dreams and realities of high-cultural accomplishment, with an escalating new audience for art. In anointing him their leader, music's new listeners acquired an exciting living sanction to revere dead European masters, a parade of "lofty" or "tyrannical," "serene" or "suffering" Great Music types with Toscanini at their head. The outcome was a popularized version of symphony and opera peculiarly susceptible to modern tools of merchandising and public relations.

To understand Toscanini is to understand the impact of his rabid American following and of the cheerleaders and commentators, advertisements and souvenir booths, microphones and television cameras equipping the grandstands they mobbed. After Toscanini, this equipment, ever more elaborate, became a life support system for ever blander, more aged entertainments. Rather than naturally evolving according to their artistic utility, heroically scaled orchestras and opera companies, legacies of the late nineteenth century, evolved according to publicity and marketing strategies, a survival-of-the-fittest competition in which fitness was predicated on the conspicuous visibility and prestige of name-brand dinosaurs.

At Lincoln Center and other museum/sanitoriums, the dinosaurs are rosy cheeked yet decrepit. Ticket sales to both the New York Philharmonic and the Metropolitan Opera average more than 90 and 80 percent of box office capacity, respectively. These figures, suggesting resilience in the face of ill health, are buttressed by what Patrick J. Smith, chronicling a recent Met season, has termed "ruthless professionalization of the fund-raising apparatus." Smith (since 1985 director of the Opera–Musical Theater program of the National Endowment for the Arts) worries that the Metropolitan's ceaseless creativity in developing new opportunities for giving (the operating loss now totals more than $25 million per season) risks overshadowing its artistic mission.

> Indeed, the inventiveness of the Met in capturing every loose dollar rivals its inventiveness and expertise onstage, and it is not too farfetched to state that as a fund raiser the Met is even more professionally adept than the singers and conductors it presents as end products.
>
> . . . The Met family [including twenty-seven hundred wined-and-dined "patrons," each contributing at least $1,200 a year] likes what it is given, and will permit a few novelties; but it will not tolerate for long any adventurousness—either difficult operas or outré productions. The innate tendency toward the repetition of the core repertory in "Met type" productions is therefore a constant pressure. . . .
>
> All of these developments in fund raising, moreover, have been so widely publicized—as they must be—that they appear to dominate all Met activities, leading inevitably to the charge that the financial tail is wagging the artistic dog. . . .[5]

Actually, there is concern that the performing arts explosion has peaked, that the market is sated, that emerging young audiences have no use for museums and sanatoriums. Compared with music appreciation times, "classical music" is less taught in the schools,* less heard on commercial AM radio, less seen on commercial network television. Around 1940, when more than half the population was reported "liking" to listen to classical music on the radio,** José Iturbi was about to become an MGM bit player, "I'm Always Chasing Rainbows" (after Chopin's Fantaisie-Impromptu) was featured in four movie musicals, and rock 'n' roll was a generation away. To what extent has the post–World War II "cultural explosion" in music tapped new potential within a relatively aged constituency? As of 1982, the average age of Americans whose favorite music was classical was

---

*The number of music teachers for 920,000 New York City public school students dropped from 2,200 in 1974 to 793 a decade later.[6]

**See page 154.

forty-eight years, and Americans who favored opera averaged forty-nine years old.[7] A 1982 survey by the New York Philharmonic found 51 percent of its audience over fifty-five years old, with only 13 percent under thirty-five, and 69 percent reporting incomes of $40,000 or more. Nielsen ratings for PBS's "Great Performances" indicate that viewers over fifty comprise up to 70 percent of the concert/opera audience, with a heavy concentration of women sixty-five years old and older. (PBS's "American Playhouse" attracts a significantly less aged audience.) A 1984 survey of sixth and tenth graders by the Association for Classical Music found "classical music" confused with elevator and ballroom music, associated with "the past" and "old people," condemned as "boring" and "dull."

In 1984, the New York Philharmonic undertook a characteristic response to its perceived need for a younger audience base: a marketing study. The study's recommended "strategies," also characteristic, were for improved marketing. Acknowledging audience antipathy to "new music" as documented in the 1982 survey, the study at no point conjectured that fresher repertoire might entice younger listeners; rather, the orchestra's "image" needed freshening. Alluding to widespread disenchantment with the music director in the musical press, the study inferred that "bad publicity" needed rectifying by "increased publicity support, particularly in the form of selected appearances and interviews by Mr. Mehta and—wherever possible —members of the orchestra." The "Philharmonic experience," according to the study, aspired to fulfill leisure needs by furnishing an "enjoyable" and "stress-reducing" activity. How to communicate the Philharmonic experience? "[Get] on the air more frequently in the New York area . . . in TV and cable and radio."* "High visibility [for] New York occasions, like the Big Ship Parade, a dedication of the Statue of Liberty, a Christmas Show, a New Year's Eve Concert, etc." "Solo appearances by members of the Philharmonic with other area orchestras." "Further development of the management of direct mail and telephone marketing by zip code areas."

In fairness to the Philharmonic, improved marketing probably would enhance the propaganda apparatus that keeps its audience content. Does it represent a plausible long-term survival strategy? One hopes not.

The story of Toscanini in America, as I have told it, is absorbed by the story of an expanding audience whose manipulable needs and aspirations

---

*On December 5, 1984, the Philharmonic board elected Stephen Stamas its new president. A vice-president of the Exxon Corporation since 1973, Stamas supervises its public affairs activities. As the Philharmonic's newsletter put it: "Mr. Stamas has been closely identified with the 'Great Performances' series on public television and the initiation of the 'Live from Lincoln Center' series."

increasingly pre-empted the needs and aspirations of art. The story begins in European courts and salons, where music dilettantes and professionals overlapped, and concerts were relatively private, personal affairs. It ends with PBS and Lincoln Center, where professionals perform and throngs of laymen watch, listen, and applaud.

Democratizing high culture is an enterprise buoyed by good thoughts and deeds. Equally apparent is the risk of a diluted, commercialized high culture that elevates no one.

Writing in *Modern Music* fifty years ago, Marc Blitzstein proclaimed the coming of a "mass audience," including "the entire public—everybody." "It may mean the end of the platinum Orchestra Age," he predicted. "It may mean a participation of audiences in music to a degree unheard of since the Greeks."[8]

If anything like Blitzstein's mass audience is to materialize, it will surely happen outside the precincts of Lincoln Center, beyond the long-term legacies of Toscanini's cult.

Appendixes
Notes
Index

APPENDIX A:
ARTHUR JUDSON ADVISES JOHN BARBIROLLI
ON PROGRAMMING (1936)

Arthur Judson, who managed the New York Philharmonic from 1922 to 1956, was the supreme musical power broker of Toscanini times. When Toscanini left the Philharmonic in 1936, Judson was ready to hire a less expensive, less troublesome, less independent principal conductor, one who would end the Philharmonic's dependency on a single box-office "draw." He fixed on the thirty-six-year-old John Barbirolli, who as recently as 1932 had yet to lead a Beethoven symphony. It was arranged that Barbirolli would conduct the first eleven weeks of the Philharmonic's 1936–37 season—in effect, a trial run for the leading candidate to take over from Toscanini. An exchange of letters (March 5 to September 17, 1936) between Judson and Barbirolli, preserved in the New York Philharmonic archives, illustrates Judson's leverage over Toscanini's young successor.

On March 5, Barbirolli submitted seven weeks of tentative programs for Judson's review, adding: "I should be glad to have your comments on these at your earliest convenience to guide me in such revision as might be deemed necessary and to assist me in compiling the programmes for the remaining four weeks."

In a May 20 reply, Judson offered reactions to Barbirolli's first two programs but elected to defer further advice until hearing more from Barbirolli. His letter ended: "Perhaps you will be kind enough to give the matter of programs a considerable amount of thought and to communicate with me at your earliest convenience. I shall then be glad to offer you any advice which you may ask. I am very anxious to have you make a great success and shall do everything in my power to help you."

On June 22, Barbirolli sent Judson a series of extensive program revisions. His letter ended: "Again, I would be very grateful if you would please submit my programmes to the most candid criticism as I fully realise how vital this question is. . . . If you are still not satisfied with the first programme, please tell me and we will try again."

Judson now replied, on July 16, with a four-page, single-spaced letter. Among his comments:

> I wonder whether you wish to end your first concert with Elgar's ["Enigma"] Variations. I have never found our public very enthusiastic about the "variations" form, probably because the continuity of idea is so broken up. To my mind, it would be much better to end with the Brahms [Fourth] Symphony although, strangely enough, the last movement of that is also variations. . . .

I think this program is very good with the exception of the "Pastoral" Symphony. This symphony has not been successful in New York for many years until Toscanini conducted it. It has been one of his outstanding successes. Why he succeeded with it, I do not know because it is not a favorite but he probably plays it so that the public has not time to get tired of it. I would much rather see some one of the other Beethoven symphonies played—except the Third, Fifth or Ninth.

The William Walton Symphony has been played several times in America and has been totally unsuccessful. Whether you want to play a work of this nature on your first visit to New York and so early in your season, is an open question. If you have a conviction that it is a great work and that you *must* do it, I would give myself two or three more weeks before playing it. . . .

I like this program . . . but wonder whether the whole first half, being by Sibelius, is not a little too much in one color. You will know this better than I.

Do you use the small orchestra or the large orchestra for the Strauss *Le Bourgeois Gentilhomme*? Carnegie Hall seats 2,700 and a reduced orchestra always sounds a little empty. Might it not be a better program if you put the "Emperor" Concerto in the second half and made a first half consisting of the Corelli, Strauss, and Brahms, or, better yet, a more important work than the *Academic Festival* Overture of Brahms to end the first half? . . .

The Sunday program is, I think, good although Berlioz's *Fantastic* Symphony is not a favorite. However, with Hofmann doing the "Emperor," the program as a whole will probably go over.

The American public has progressed rather rapidly because it has heard a great deal of music played very frequently. For this reason, such works as the *Faust* Symphony of Liszt have become worn out and passé. . . . Unless the *Faust* Symphony is one which you do superlatively well and which you feel you can convince the orchestra is a great work, I would do something else.

In an August 25 response to Judson, Barbirolli canceled the "Pastoral," the Walton, the Strauss, the Berlioz, and the Liszt. He repositioned the Elgar, ending with Brahms. He abandoned his all-Sibelius half-program, putting a Rossini overture before the Sibelius First. He repositioned the "Emperor" Concerto on the second half of the pertinent program, and chose *La Mer* as his "important work" to end the first half.

Judson now wrote, on September 17:

I have gone over your programs very carefully . . . and am personally pleased. My only inclination is for the recognized masterpieces of classic literature. I believe that by far the greater part of the public agrees with me but, on the other hand, there is a section of our audiences which desires modern music and which is very insistent and loud with protests when it does not get it.

. . . I want you to make a success and I do not want either of us to leave a stone unturned.

Flavoring Judson's suggestions were such double messages as the following, from his May 20 letter:

What I now have to write about, I trust you will take as advice from one who has had long association with the musical public and who is trying to interpret to you in some measure how they feel about certain things. Also, the American public is very different from the English, German or French public. It has certain likes and dislikes but is very cosmopolitan. Please remember that although I may give you advice, you have complete liberty to accept it or not as you choose. You are the conductor and will be held responsible by the critics and the public. My business as manager is to keep you informed as well as I can, to support you in everything possible and to give you an absolutely free hand in arranging the programs which you conduct.

Judson's July 16 letter closed:

I do not want to be tiresome but allow me to reiterate that after all, although I know something about music, I am only a manager and can give you my reactions to your programs only from the managerial standpoint. It is my desire that you have before you, when you make programs, all of the information which I can give you. On the other hand, you are the conductor and if you are a conductor of great ability, as I believe, you will know what you can do with certain works and certain programs and what effect you can produce on the public. The only question of doubt is the difference in taste of the American public. I have tried to give you a picture of the New York situation so that you may weight your programs carefully, after realizing our difference in taste, but, after all, a musical work of reasonable value, superlatively presented, is always successful and it all comes down to the point of your ability to carry your public with you. This I believe and hope you will do and we will give you every assistance possible.

In the context of Judson's week-by-week proposed revisions, such assurances as these appear disingenuous; Barbirolli wanted the New York Philharmonic and appreciated that Judson would exercise decisive authority over who got it. Judson's professed high hopes for Barbirolli, however, were probably sincere; by then, the other leading contender for Toscanini's job was the intractable Artur Rodzinski.

APPENDIX B:
A PSYCHOANALYST EXAMINES TOSCANINI (1983)

As the NBC Symphony telecasts indelibly document, the Toscanini presence inspired love and unqualified respect, fear and unqualified submission (see pages 359–63). Twenty-six years after Toscanini's death, a psychoanalyst, Martin H. Blum, examined "Toscanini's Relation to His Orchestra" (*Hillside Journal of Clinical Psychiatry* 5:1). The result is a speculative psychobiographical sketch, parts of which may be summarized as follows:

Toscanini's father was "a dreamy, romantic, impractical, and unreliable man," his mother a "grim and hardbitten woman, harried, abrupt, and unaffectionate." Toscanini "grew into an isolated, almost mute, child." He never learned to eat or speak normally. "Separation remained a major theme of his life. He repetitively found reasons to walk out, suddenly and dramatically, on situations, orchestras, and rehearsals. In the same vein, his personal relations were often terminated by his abrupt withdrawal and total refusal to recognize the existence of an offending friend. Even at home, he was frequently wrapped in glowering isolation. . . ." His wife became his "factotum." He was "a failure as a father, without the time or patience for his children. . . ." His son, Walter, became his "valet." "His major emotional relations were with his orchestras"; especially in the intimacy of rehearsal, "he was able to emerge from his isolation and withdrawal and become fully vibrant and alive." In relation to music, Toscanini was a "secular mystic," obsessed with ideal sounds, heard in his head, which he struggled to actualize in rehearsal and performance. This actualization process, never wholly satisfactory, caused him to suffer acutely. Faced with a conductor of Toscanini's bullying personality, acute musical needs, and amazing musical abilities (in particular, his ability to memorize at sight), orchestras experienced "an intense fall in self-esteem . . . recouped either through hostile attack on the intruding object (and some musicians hated and resented Toscanini) or else by an acceptance of the superior as a functional replacement for the former ego-ideal." Abused in rehearsal, the players knew they could not answer back. "This prohibition of any adequate response to an overwhelming stimulus necessarily heightened their defense against resentment which, in turn, increased their feelings of anxiety, lowered their self-esteem, and increased their feelings of guilt"; they became ready "to love the attacking object." Blum concludes:

They always felt that in yielding to him they were nurturing him. Without knowing the details, they sensed that he had been crippled by an impoverished and traumatizing childhood, that his incapacity for ordinary relatedness made him turn to his working relations as a desperate mode of escape from his pain and his rage. . . .

As the providers of the gratifications for which he lived, his performers knew that they were more important to him than his wife, his children, his mistresses, or his audiences. . . .

He was clearly more fragile than they and they needed to solace him so he could lead them. In providing the medium of his states of rapture they guaranteed the materials of their own. What had developed on both sides was a curious kind of love.

Elements of Blum's analysis also pertain to Toscanini's relations with his audience, and to private donors indispensable to American arts institutions. Mahler, Furtwängler, and Klemperer, among others, were notoriously inept in their dealings with American orchestral benefactors, in whose eyes they seemed ill-mannered, awkward, and neurotic. But Toscanini, who did not fit tainted "intellectual" or "genius" stereotypes, seemed at once charming and aloof, vulnerable and intimidating; he could never have been contemptuously regimented by the New York Philharmonic board as Mahler was in 1911. Even Walter Price's October 15, 1941 letter to New York Philharmonic-Symphony Society president Marshall Field (see page 175) reflects long-term toleration of behavior Price would not have endured in a business colleague or in another Philharmonic conductor. Referring to Toscanini's social and professional relations alike, Samuel Chotzinoff truthfully remarks in *Toscanini: An Intimate Portrait:* "All his life he had been forgiven conduct that would have been tolerated in no other artist."

NOTES

TOSCANINI AND THE WAYS OF CULTURE (PAGES 1 TO 10)

1. *Life*, Nov. 27, 1939, and Sept. 13, 1943. *Time*, Apr. 26, 1948. New York *Times*, Jan. 17, 1957.
2. For background on audience evolution, see Henry Raynor, *A Social History of Music* and *Music and Society*, reprinted in tandem (New York: Taplinger Publishing Company, 1978); and William Weber, "Mass Culture and the Reshaping of European Musical Taste, 1770–1870, *"International Review of the Aesthetics and Sociology of Music*, June 1977.
3. On the idea of "culture," see Raymond Williams, *Culture and Society 1780–1850* (London: Chatto and Windus, 1958). On book sales, see Leo Lowenthal and Marjorie Fiske, "The Debate over Art and Popular Culture in Eighteenth Century England" in Mirra Komarovsky (editor), *Common Frontiers of the Social Sciences* (Glencoe, Ill.: Free Press, 1951).
4. The most recent reprinting is in Dwight Macdonald, *Against the American Grain* (New York: Da Capo Press, 1983). The original version was in *Partisan Review*, Spring 1960.
5. See especially Olin Downes, "Be Your Own Music Critic," in Robert E. Simon (editor), *Be Your Own Music Critic* (Garden City, N.Y.: Doubleday, Doran and Co., 1941), pp. 3–38.

SETTING THE STAGE (PAGES 11 TO 42)

1. Leslie Fiedler, Afterword to Mark Twain, *The Innocents Abroad* (New York: Signet, 1966).
2. Justin Kaplan, *Mr. Clemens and Mark Twain* (New York: Simon and Schuster/Touchstone, 1966), p. 30.
3. Kaplan, pp. 356–57.
4. Paris and Pittsburgh quotes from John Tasker Howard, *Our American Music*, third edition (New York: Crowell, 1954), pp. 245, 199–200. Mark Twain quote in Kaplan, p. 207.
5. Phineas T. Barnum, *Barnum's Own Story* (New York: Viking Press, 1927). My account of Barnum and Lind also draws primarily on Joan Bulman, *Jenny Lind* (London: J. Barrie, 1956); Neil Harris, *Humbug: The Art of P.T. Barnum* (Boston: Little, Brown, 1973); Arthur Loesser, *Men, Women and Pianos* (New York: Simon and Schuster Fireside Edition, 1954).
6. For background, see Ann Douglas, *The Feminization of American Culture* (New York: Alfred A. Knopf, 1977). Also see Loesser, pp. 509–64.

7. Max Maretzek, *Crotchets and Quavers* (New York: S. French, 1855), pp. 121–22. Barnum quote from Bulman, Preface.
8. Louis Moreau Gottschalk, *Notes of a Pianist* (New York: Da Capo Press, 1979), p. 239.
9. Loesser, pp. 516–18.
10. Lewis Mumford, *The Golden Day*, second edition (Boston: Beacon Press, 1957), p. 20. Gottschalk, p. 160. Alexis de Tocqueville, *Democracy in America*, vol. 2 (New York: Vintage Books), p. 79. Paul Rosenfeld (editor), *Robert Schumann on Music and Musicians* (New York: Pantheon Books, 1946), p. 81. Hanslick quote from John Mueller, *The American Symphony Orchestra* (Bloomington: Indiana University Press, 1951), p. 22. For background, a concise source is H. Wiley Hitchcock, *Music in the United States: A Historical Introduction*, second edition (Englewood Cliffs, N.J.: Prentice-Hall, 1974).
11. On Paderewski in the United States, see Harold C. Schonberg, *The Great Pianists* (New York: Simon and Schuster, 1963), and Adam Zamoyski, *Paderewski* (New York: Atheneum, 1982).
12. Ferruccio Busoni, *Letters to His Wife* (London: Edward Arnold, 1938), pp. 71, 75, 167, 177, 188. On Busoni in the United States, see also Otto Luening, *The Odyssey of an American Composer* (New York: Charles Scribner's Sons, 1980), pp. 174–78.
13. Gottschalk, pp. 227, 211, 253. Rubinstein quote from Catherine Bowen, *Free Artist: The Story of Anton and Nicholas Rubinstein* (Boston: Little, Brown, 1961), p. 246.
14. Gottschalk, pp. 63, 127.
15. Howard Shanet, *Philharmonic: A History of New York's Orchestra* (Garden City, N.Y.: Doubleday, 1975), pp. 35–37, 109–10. Beyond the history of the New York Philharmonic, this is a valuable source on New York's early concert and opera life.
16. Richard Aldrich, "Theodore Thomas," in Aldrich, *Musical Discourse* (New York: Oxford University Press, 1928). My account of Theodore Thomas in the United States also draws primarily on Charles Edward Russell, *The American Orchestra and Theodore Thomas* (Garden City, N.Y.: Doubleday, Page and Co., 1927); Harold C. Schonberg, *The Great Conductors* (New York: Simon and Schuster, 1967); George P. Upton (editor), *Theodore Thomas: A Musical Autobiography* (New York: Da Capo Press, 1964). The long Russell extract is from pp. 2–3. The Iowa review and New York *Post* editorial are from Upton, pp. 140–41, 138.
17. Henry N. Smith and William M. Gibson (editors), *Mark Twain–Howells Letters* (Cambridge, Mass.: Harvard University Press, 1960), p. 227.
18. Boston, Chicago, and Damrosch quotes from Mueller, pp. 23, 104, 31.
19. Addison and Hone quotes from Henry Krehbiel, *Chapters of Opera* (New York: Holt and Co., 1908), pp. 23, 21.
20. James Huneker, *Steeplejack*, vol. 2 (New York: Charles Scribner's Sons, 1923), p. 32.
21. Chauffeur quote from Stanley Jackson, *Caruso* (New York: Stein and Day, 1972), p. 106. *Rheingold* quote from Schonberg, *The Great Conductors*, p. 185.
22. Montrose Moses, *The Life of Heinrich Conried* (New York: Thomas Y. Crowell, 1916), p. 195. New York *Sun*, Mar. 18, 1906. Herbert quote from Jackson, p. 228. Huneker quote from Jackson, p. 140.
23. Carl Van Vechten, *In the Garret* (New York: Alfred A. Knopf, 1920), p. 244.
24. Mueller, p. 314.
25. *Musical Courier*, Apr. 26, 1911. Finck quote from Shanet, p. 178. Huneker, p. 41. Hale quote from *Musical Courier*, Sept. 8, 1897.

THE METROPOLITAN OPERA, 1908–15 (PAGES 45 TO 77)

1. Rolland quote from Kurt Blaukopf (editor), *Mahler: A Documentary Study* (New York: Oxford University Press, 1976), p. 241. Walter quote from Bruno Walter, *Mahler*

(New York: Vienna House, 1973), p. 83. Critic's quote from Egon Gartenberg, *Mahler: The Man and His Music* (New York: Schirmer Books, 1978), p. 62.

2. Feodor Chaliapin and Maxim Gorky, *Chaliapin* (London: Macdonald, 1968), pp. 146–47.

3. Blaukopf, p. 248.

4. Alma Mahler, *Gustav Mahler: Memories and Letters* (London: John Murray, 1946), p. 107.

5. New York *Times*, Dec. 9, 1907. New York *Sun*, June 8, 1907.

6. Alma Mahler, p. 114.

7. Alma Mahler, p. 107.

8. Knud Martner (editor), *Selected Letters of Gustav Mahler* (New York: Farrar, Straus, Giroux, 1979), pp. 309, 314.

9. *Musical America*, Jan. 25, 1908.

10. Martner, p. 316.

11. New York *World*, Feb. 22, 1909. *Musical Courier*, Mar. 31, 1909.

12. Harvey Sachs, *Toscanini* (New York: J. B. Lippincott, 1978), p. 131.

13. *Musical Courier*, Mar. 5, 1908.

14. Giulio Gatti-Casazza, *Memories of the Opera* (New York: Vienna House, 1973), p. 148. Mahler, *Letters*, pp. 310, 317, 319. Blaukopf, p. 257.

15. Alma Mahler, pp. 137, 122–23. Howard Taubman, *The Maestro: The Life of Arturo Toscanini* (New York: Simon and Schuster, 1951), p. 119. B. H. Haggin, *Conversations with Toscanini*, second edition (New York: Horizon Press, 1979), p. 77.

16. New York *Press*, Dec. 11, 1908. New York *Sun*, Dec. 11, 1908. New York *Telegraph*, Nov. 18, 1911. James Huneker, *Steeplejack*, vol. 2, pp. 40–41. *Musical America*, Apr. 2, 1910.

17. Henry Krehbiel, *More Chapters of Opera* (New York: H. Holt, 1919), pp. 5–7. Leo Slezak, *Song of Motley* (New York: Arno Press, 1977), p. 37.

18. "Leo Slezak" in Harold Rosenthal and John Warrack, *The Concise Oxford Dictionary of Opera* (London: Oxford University Press, 1975). Slezak, p. 39. Boston *Transcript*, Jan. 10, 1910. *Musical America*, Mar. 16, 1912, and Jan. 31, 1912. Orchestra strike from unidentified clipping dated Feb. 3, 1912, from "Toscanini" clippings, Music Division, New York Public Library.

19. New York *Sun*, Mar. 31, 1909. *Musical America*, Nov. 18, 1912.

20. *Century Magazine*, Mar. 1913. *Vanity Fair*, Mar. 1914. New York *Press*, Apr. 14, 1913; Mar. 21, 1915. New York *Press* quoted in *Musical America*, Feb. 24, 1912. *Vanity Fair*, Mar. 1914.

21. *Musical Courier*, Mar. 31, 1909. *Century Magazine*, Mar. 1913. New York *Sun*, Feb. 9, 1910. Unidentified Chicago clipping dated Apr. 10, 1910, from "Toscanini" clippings, Music Division, New York Public Library. *Century Magazine*, Mar. 1913.

22. New York *Evening World*, Mar. 13, 1914.

23. Sachs, p. 128.

24. Sachs, pp. 129–31.

25. *Musical Courier*, Oct. 7, 1915. *Musical America*, Oct. 2, 1915. Boston *Transcript*, Sept. 30, 1915.

26. Gartenberg, p. 159.

27. *Musical America*, Oct. 30, 1909.

28. Blaukopf, pp. 262, 261, 263.

29. *Musical Courier*, Nov. 24, 1909.

30. New York *Tribune*, Dec. 13, 1909.

31. Howard Shanet, *Philharmonic: A History of New York's Orchestra*, p. 214.

32. Otto Luening, *The Odyssey of an American Composer* (N.Y.: Scribner, 1980), p. 178. Luening misidentifies what Busoni played.

33. Alma Mahler, p. 158.

34. Thomas quote from *St. Paul Post-Dispatch*, Dec. 2, 1898 (brought to my attention by Ezra Schabas of the University of Toronto).

35. Alma Mahler, p. 160. *Musical America*, May 13, 1911.

36. John Mueller, *The American Symphony Orchestra*, p. 54.

37. Walter, p. 93. New York *Tribune*, Jan. 2, 1908; Apr. 5, 1909. *Century Magazine*, Mar. 1913.

38. *Musical America*, Oct. 30, 1909.

39. New York *Tribune*, May 21, 1911.

INTERLUDE, 1917–25 (PAGES 78 TO 92)

1. *Saturday Evening Post* and *Alumni News* advertisements from James Mock and Cedric Lawson, *Words That Won the War* (Princeton: Princeton University Press, 1939), pp. 169, 64.

2. Irving Lowens, *"L'affaire Muck,"* *Musicology* 1:3. My account of Muck's debacle also draws primarily on Walter Damrosch, *My Musical Life* (New York: Charles Scribner's Sons, 1923); M. A. DeWolfe Howe, *The Boston Symphony Orchestra*, 1881–1931 (Boston: Houghton Mifflin, 1931); Harold C. Schonberg, *The Great Conductors;* Olga Samaroff-Stokowski, *An American Musician's Story* (New York: W. W. Norton, 1939).

3. George Marek, *Toscanini* (New York: Atheneum, 1975), p. 166.

4. Harvey Sachs, *Toscanini*, p. 125.

5. Kansas City *Times*, Sept. 8, 1917. *Brooklyn Daily Eagle*, Sept. 6, 1917. *Musical Courier*, Sept. 6, 1917.

6. Boston *Post*, Jan. 11, 1920.

7. New York *Telegraph*, July 18, 1920. Souvenir program, "Toscanini" clippings, Music Division, New York Public Library. *Musical America*, Jan. 8, 1921.

8. New York *Times*, Jan. 12, 1921.

9. New York *Sun*, Apr. 14, 1913. *Musical America*, Jan. 8, 1921. New York *World*, Dec. 29, 1920.

10. *Musical Courier*, Jan. 6, 1921. New York *Herald*, Apr. 3, 1921.

11. Sachs, p. 143. Filippo Sacchi, *The Magic Baton* (New York: Putnam, 1957), p. 154.

12. Sachs, pp. 152–53, 150.

13. Sachs, p. 173.

14. Sachs, p. 173.

15. My account of the Toscanini-Mussolini relationship draws primarily on Sachs and Sacchi.

THE NEW YORK PHILHARMONIC, 1926–29 (PAGES 93 TO 110)

1. Howard Shanet, *Philharmonic: A History of New York's Orchestra*, p. 223.

2. Winthrop Sargeant, *Geniuses, Goddesses and People* (New York: E. P. Dutton, 1949), pp. 92–99.

3. Berta Geissmar, *The Baton and the Jackboot* (London: Hamish Hamilton, 1944), pp. 32–33.

4. Sargeant, pp. 114–16.

5. Furtwängler's first Philharmonic concert was reviewed by Downes and Gilman on Jan. 5, 1925. For Downes's review of Furtwängler's second concert, see New York *Times*, Jan. 12, 1925.

6. New York *Times*, Feb. 18, 1926; Mar. 19, 1926.

7. New York *Times*, Feb. 12, 1926; Mar. 25, 1927; Jan. 12, 1925; Jan. 23, 1925.

8. Smith quotes from autobiographical sketch, Max Smith archive (box 4), Yale University Music Library. (The Mackay-Smith-Toscanini negotiations can be reconstructed from letters, telegrams, and other documents in the Max Smith archive and the New York Philharmonic archives.)

9. New York *Times*, Jan. 10, 1926.

10. New York *Sun*, Feb. 8, 1926. New York *Times*, Jan. 15, 1926. New York *Herald Tribune*, Jan. 15, 1926.

11. New York *Herald Tribune*, Feb. 7, 1926.

12. New York *Sun*, Jan. 15, 1926. New York *Herald Tribune*, Jan. 15, 1926.

13. Smith quote in *Century Magazine*, Mar. 1933. Mainardi quote from Daniel Gillis (editor), *Furtwängler Recalled* (Tuckahoe, N.Y.: John de Graff, 1962), p. 176. Wagner quote from Harold C. Schonberg, *The Great Conductors*, p. 279. Geissmar, p. 9. Downes quote from my conversation with Suzanne Bloch, New York City, Nov. 1982.

14. Stefan Zweig, Foreword to Paul Stefan, *Arturo Toscanini* (New York: Viking Press, 1936).

15. Furtwängler quotes from Wilhelm Furtwängler, *Concerning Music* (London: Boosey and Hawkes, 1953), pp. 22, 31; and "Wilhelm Furtwängler Talking About Music," an insert in the recording DG 2740260 (100 Jahre: Berliner Philharmoniker: Wilhelm Furtwängler).

16. My account of the Furtwängler–Toscanini–New York Philharmonic relationship draws primarily on newspaper accounts; New York Philharmonic archives; Harvey Sachs, *Toscanini;* and Daniel Gillis, *Furtwängler and America* (New York: Manyland Books, 1970); and 1926 correspondence between Clarence Mackay and Max Smith to be found in Max Smith archive, Yale University Music Library.

17. New York *Herald Tribune*, Feb. 7, 1927. New York *Times*, Mar. 4, 1927.

18. New York *Times*, Mar. 6, 1927.

19. New York *Times*, Mar. 27, 1927.

20. Gillis, *Furtwängler Recalled*, pp. 139–41.

21. Sargeant, pp. 95–96.

22. New York Philharmonic archives.

23. Judson, Van Praag, and Toscanini quotes from New York Philharmonic archives.

THE NEW YORK PHILHARMONIC, 1929–36 (PAGES 111 TO 149)

1. Winthrop Sargeant, *Geniuses, Goddesses and People*, p. 106. Wallenstein and Zimmerman quotes from B. H. Haggin, *The Toscanini Musicians Knew* (New York: Horizon Press, 1967), pp. 177, 47, 178.

2. On salary figures, see Harvey Sachs, *Toscanini*, p. 208, and Howard Shanet, *Philharmonic: A History of New York's Orchestra*, p. 268.

3. Sachs, p. 199. George Szell, "Toscanini in the History of Orchestral Performance," *Saturday Review*, Mar. 25, 1967. New York *Times*, June 4, 1930 (dateline).

4. Quote from New York *Times*, July 31, 1932. There are conflicting accounts of the incident. See especially Harvey Sachs, "Arturo Toscanini: Some New Discoveries," *Ovation*, Jan. 1982, and Friedelind Wagner and Page Cooper, *Heritage of Fire* (New York: Harper and Brothers, 1945), p. 66.

5. New York *Times*, Oct. 11, 1931.

6. Kreisler quote from New York *Times*, Apr. 5, 1933. Winifred Wagner quote and analysis from New York *Times*, Apr. 8, 1933 (dateline).

7. Fritz Busch, *Pages from a Musician's Life* (Westport, Conn.: Greenwood Press, 1953), p. 217.

8. Toscanini quote from Sachs, *Toscanini*, p. 225. Zirato quote from New York Philharmonic archives.

9. *Time*, Apr. 2, 1934.

10. Burghauser quote in Haggin, *The Toscanini Musicians Knew*, p. 155. New York *Times*, July 30, 1935.

11. New York *Times*, Jan. 12, 1934; Apr. 30, 1934.

12. Wagner quote from David C. Large and William Weber (editors), *Wagnerism in European Culture and Politics* (Ithaca, N.Y.: Cornell University Press, 1984), p. 43. New York *Herald Tribune*, Apr. 24, 1933. Radio address, Jan. 26, 1936; script from "Toscanini" clippings, Music Division, New York Public Library.

13. New York *Times*, Apr. 3, 1933. New York *World*, Feb. 24, 1929. *Brooklyn Daily Eagle*, Apr. 2, 1936; Mar. 6, 1936.

14. Shanet, p. 277.

15. New York *Herald Tribune*, Mar. 11, 1934.

16. Peter Heyworth, *Conversations with Klemperer* (London: Gollancz, 1973), p. 78.

17. Abram Chasins, *Leopold Stokowski: A Profile* (New York: Hawthorn Books, 1979), p. 126.

18. For an overview, see Irene Downes (editor), *Olin Downes on Music* (New York: Simon and Schuster, 1957), and Lawrence Gilman, *Orchestral Music: An Armchair Guide* (New York: Oxford University Press, 1951).

19. New York *Times*, Oct. 11, 1929; Jan. 24, 1936.

20. New York *Times*, Feb. 2, 1934. Chotzinoff quote from "Beethoven and Toscanini," an essay insert for RCA LM 6900 ("limited edition" of the nine symphonies). *Brooklyn Daily Eagle*, Apr. 30, 1936.

21. New York *Times*, Nov. 8, 1929.

22. Shanet, p. 270. John Mueller, *The American Symphony Orchestra*, p. 67.

23. New York *Post*, Feb. 24, 1929; Feb. 14, 1936. New York *Times*, Feb. 14, 1936. Igor Stravinsky, *Stravinsky: An Autobiography* (New York: Simon and Schuster, 1936), pp. 203–5. Winthrop Sargeant quote from *Brooklyn Daily Eagle*, May 3 and 10, 1936. Halina Rodzinski, *Our Two Lives* (New York: Charles Scribner's Sons, 1976), p. 168.

24. Large and Weber, p. 38. William Weber, "Mass Culture and the Reshaping of European Musical Taste, 1770–1870."

25. On Fry and Bristow, see Shanet, pp. 112–13. Thomas quotes from Shanet, p. 167, and George F. Upton (editor), *Theodore Thomas: A Musical Autobiography*, p. 145.

26. Aaron Copland, *Our New Music* (New York: McGraw-Hill, 1941), p. 137. Koussevitzky quote and statistics from Aaron Copland and Vivian Perlis, *Copland: 1900 Through 1942* (New York: St. Martin's/Marek, 1984), p. 109.

27. Shanet, pp. 275–76.

28. Audience estimate from *Time*, Apr. 2, 1934. Recordings history from Roland Gelatt, *The Fabulous Phonograph*, second revised edition (New York: Collier Books, 1977).

29. New York *Herald Tribune*, Nov. 19, 1935. New York *Post*, Nov. 23, 1935.

30. "Toscanini" clippings, Music Division, New York Public Library.

31. Shanet, p. 415.

32. New York *Post*, Nov. 23, 1935.

33. Sachs, *Toscanini*, p. 244.

34. New York *Times*, May 28, 1932.

35. *Time*, Mar. 9, 1936.

36. Daniel Gillis, *Furtwängler Recalled*, pp. 93–94.

37. Yehudi Menuhin, "Furtwängler and Toscanini," *Encounter*, Dec. 1977. Yehudi Menuhin, *Unfinished Journey* (New York: Alfred A. Knopf, 1977), p. 221.

THE NBC SYMPHONY, 1937–45 (PAGES 150 TO 188)

1. Eugene Lyons, *David Sarnoff* (New York: Harper and Row, 1966), pp. 1, 355. The alternative to Lyons's admiring portrait is Carl Dreher's cranky, disorganized *Sarnoff, An American Success* (New York: Quadrangle/New York Times Book Co., 1977). Also see David Sarnoff, *Looking Ahead: The Papers of David Sarnoff* (New York: McGraw-Hill, 1968).

2. For background, see Erik Barnouw, *A History of Broadcasting in the United States* in three volumes titled *A Tower in Babel, The Golden Web,* and *The Image Empire* (New York: Oxford University Press, 1966–70). The trilogy is condensed in Barnouw, *Tube of Plenty: The Evolution of American Television* (New York: Oxford University Press, 1975). NBC statistics from "Toscanini on the Air," *Fortune,* Jan. 1938. Social workers cited in Barnouw, *Tube of Plenty,* p. 72. Sarnoff quotes from Eugene Leach, "Snookered 50 Years Ago," part 2, *Current,* Jan. 28, 1983, and Sarnoff, p. 66.

3. Daniel J. Czitrom, *Media and the American Mind: From Morse to McLuhan* (Chapel Hill: University of North Carolina Press, 1982), p. 81.

4. Barnouw, *The Golden Web,* p. 71. "Toscanini on the Air."

5. "Toscanini on the Air." For ascription to the Davenports, see Harvey Sachs, *Toscanini,* p. 256.

6. New York Philharmonic archives. Ormandy and Koussevitzky figures from Howard Taubman, *Music on My Beat* (New York: Simon and Schuster, 1943), pp. 29–30.

7. David Sarnoff Library, David Sarnoff Research Center, Princeton, N.J.

8. Samuel Chotzinoff, *Toscanini: An Intimate Portrait* (New York: Alfred A. Knopf, 1956).

9. Sachs, pp. 242–43.

10. New York *Times,* Aug. 16, 1936.

11. New York Philharmonic archives.

12. Charles O'Connell, *The Other Side of the Record* (New York: Alfred A. Knopf, 1947), p. 113. Erich Leinsdorf, *Cadenza* (Boston: Houghton Mifflin, 1976), p. 48. Halina Rodzinski, *Our Two Lives,* p. 159.

13. Chotzinoff, p. 70. Leinsdorf, p. 48.

14. All NBC press releases from "Toscanini" clippings, Music Division, New York Public Library.

15. New York *Herald Tribune,* Feb. 6, 1937. New York *Times,* Feb. 6, 1937. New York Philharmonic archives.

16. New York *Times,* Feb. 14, 1937.

17. New York *Times,* Sept. 19, 1937.

18. New York *Times,* Oct. 3, 1937.

19. Sarnoff statement from New York *Times,* Feb. 25, 1937. Rodzinski, p. 159.

20. Samuel Antek, *This Was Toscanini* (New York: Vanguard Press, 1963), pp. 15–16.

21. *Time,* Jan. 3, 1938.

22. Scripts for broadcast speeches in "Toscanini" clippings, Music Division, New York Public Library.

23. David Sarnoff Library.

24. New York *World-Telegram,* May 13, 1938. New York *Times,* Apr. 16, 1938 (dateline); May 8, 1938. For rumors of Toscanini's "Jewishness," see, e.g., Howard Taubman, *The Maestro* (New York: Simon and Schuster, 1951), p. 227, and Alan Levy, *The Bluebird*

of Happiness: The Memoirs of Jan Peerce (New York: Harper and Row, 1976), p. 124.
25. New York *Herald Tribune*, July 24, 1940. New York *Post*, July 29, 1940.
26. Oliver Daniel, *Stokowski: A Counterpoint of View* (New York: Dodd, Mead, 1982), p. 396.
27. Toscanini quote and Burghauser story from Sachs, p. 275. Toscanini letter from George Marek, *Toscanini*, p. 232.
28. Leopold Stokowski, *Music for All of Us* (New York: Simon and Schuster, 1943), p. 309. Daniel, p. 352.
29. Daniel, p. 325. Stokowski, pp. 190–91.
30. New York Philharmonic archives.
31. For Toscanini-Stokowski letters, see Daniel, p. 455, and Sachs, p. 279.
32. Greissle in Daniel, p. 467. Oscar Levant, *The Memoirs of an Amnesiac* (New York: G. P. Putnam's Sons, 1965), p. 211. B. H. Haggin, *The Toscanini Musicians Knew*, p. 225. Toscanini letter to Clare Conway (December 2, 1942) in Conway correspondence, Music Division, New York Public Library.
33. Virgil Thomson, *Virgil Thomson* (New York: Alfred A. Knopf, 1967), p. 465, and my conversation with Thomson, New York, Sept. 1, 1982. Daniel, p. 469. O'Connell, p. 305.
34. Marek, pp. 236–37.
35. New York *Times*, Apr. 20, 1943.
36. *Life*, Sept. 13, 1943.
37. New York *World-Telegram*, Aug. 21, 1944.
38. New York *Times*, May 26, 1944.
39. Souvenir program in "Toscanini" clippings, Music Division, New York Public Library.
40. Marek, p. 105. Antek, pp. 88–90. Taubman, *Music on My Beat*, pp. 70, 42.
41. Stokowski on Philadelphia board from Daniel, p. 340. Peter Heyworth, *Conversations with Klemperer*, p. 77. Rodzinski, pp. 288–93. Winthrop Sargeant, *Geniuses, Goddesses and People*, p. 111.
42. New York Philharmonic archives.
43. Heyworth, p. 78. John Russell, *Erich Kleiber: A Memoir* (London: A. Deutsch, 1957), p. 137. Ronald Crichton, "Fritz Busch," *The New Grove Dictionary of Music and Musicians* (London: Macmillan, 1980).
44. O'Connell, p. 116.
45. Radio scripts in "Toscanini" clippings, Music Division, New York Public Library. Michael Kennedy, *Barbirolli* (London: MacGibbon and Kee, 1971), p. 136. New York *Herald Tribune*, Oct. 28, 1946.
46. Sachs, p. 277. Herbert Graf, *Opera for the People* (Minneapolis: University of Minnesota Press, 1951).

THE NBC SYMPHONY, 1937–45: THE NATIONAL CONTEXT I (PAGES 189 TO 223)

1. Alexis de Tocqueville, *Democracy in America*, vol. 2, pp. 40–41. Frederick Lewis Allen, *Only Yesterday* (New York: Harper and Row Perennial Library, 1964), p. 155. Edward Bernays, *Crystallizing Public Opinion* (New York: Horace Liveright, 1923), p. 195. A useful general introduction is William E. Leuchtenburg, *The Perils of Prosperity: 1914–32* (Chicago: University of Chicago Press, 1958).
2. Helen and Robert Lynd, *Middletown* (New York: Harcourt, Brace, 1929), pp. 201–48.
3. Sinclair Lewis, *Babbitt* (New York: Signet, n.d.) pp. 78, 161, 151, 150.
4. Lynd, p. 247. Allen, p. 183. Warren I. Susman, *Culture as History* (New York: Pantheon Books, 1985).

5. John Dos Passos, *1919* (New York: New American Library, 1969), p. 314. (*1919* is part two of Dos Passos's trilogy *U.S.A.*)

6. James Steel Smith, "The Day of the Popularizers: The 1920s," *South Atlantic Quarterly*, Spring 1963.

7. For NACER vs. NACRE, see Eugene Leach, "Snookered 50 Years Ago," *Current*, Jan. through Mar., 1983. Reprinted (Aug. 1983) as "Tuning Out Education: The Cooperation Doctrine in Radio, 1922–38," a pamphlet available from *Current*, Box 53358, Washington, D.C. 20009.

8. For "Billy" Phelps as popularizer, see Joan Shelley Rubin, "'Information Please!': Culture and Expertise in the Interwar Period," *American Quarterly*, Winter 1983. Also: Joan Shelley Rubin, "Swift's Premium Ham: William Lyon Phelps and the Redefinition of Culture," Catherine Covert and John D. Stevens (editors), *Mass Media Between the Wars* (Syracuse: Syracuse University Press, 1984).

9. "Ten million families" figure (by no means definitive) from Dickson Skinner, "Music Goes into Mass Production," *Harper's*, Apr. 1939. On reduction of "live" concerts, see Daniel Czitrom, *Media and the American Mind: From Morse to McLuhan*, p. 84. On the recordings industry, see Roland Gelatt, *The Fabulous Phonograph*.

10. Charles Edward Russell, *The American Orchestra and Theodore Thomas*, Preface. Thomas and Chicago quotes from George P. Upton (editor), *Theodore Thomas: A Musical Autobiography*, pp. 104, 289. Ganz quote from John Mueller, *The American Symphony Orchestra*, p. 295.

11. Skinner.

12. Howard Shanet, *Philharmonic: A History of New York's Orchestra*.

13. James A. Keene, *A History of Music Education in the United States* (Hanover, N.H.: University Press of New England, 1982), pp. 231–61. Souvenir booklet for Damrosch banquet, Music Division, New York Public Library.

14. Notebooks and other "Music Appreciation Hour" materials, Music Division, New York Public Library. Winthrop Sargeant, *Geniuses, Goddesses and People*, pp. 63–66. Tape of "Music Appreciation Hour" broadcast at Museum of Broadcasting, New York City (May 17, 1938).

15. George Martin, *The Damrosch Dynasty* (Boston: Houghton Mifflin, 1983), p. 369.

16. Reminiscences of Howard Barlow, "Radio Pioneers," Oral History Research Office, Columbia University. Deems Taylor, *Of Men and Music* (New York: Simon and Schuster, 1937), p. xviii.

17. Eileen Simpson, *Poets in Their Youth* (New York: Vintage Books, 1983), pp. 17–18.

18. New York *Times*, April 30, 1934.

19. New York *Times*, Mar. 13, 1985.

20. Gregor Piatigorsky, *Cellist* (Garden City, N.Y.: Doubleday, 1965), pp. 232–3.

21. David Sarnoff Library.

22. *Good Housekeeping*, June 1940.

23. David Ewen, *Dictators of the Baton*, second edition (Chicago: Ziff-Davis, 1948), Preface. David Ewen, *The Man with the Baton* (New York: Thomas Y. Crowell, 1936), pp. 114–16.

24. *Time*, Jan. 3, 1938. *Life*, Nov. 27, 1939.

THE NBC SYMPHONY, 1937–45: THE NATIONAL CONTEXT II (PAGES 224 TO 269)

1. Van Wyck Brooks, "America's Coming-of-Age," from *Three Essays on America* (New York: Dutton, 1934).

2. Virgil Thomson, *Virgil Thomson*, p. 337. Richard Hofstadter, *Anti-Intellectualism in American Life* (New York: Vintage Books), p. 415.

3. Lewis Mumford, *The Golden Day*, second edition, p. xxvii.

4. Harold Clurman, *The Fervent Years* (New York: Alfred A. Knopf, 1945), p. 19. Winthrop Sargeant, *Geniuses, Goddesses and People*, p. 109. Sarnoff quotes from David Sarnoff, *Looking Ahead*, pp. 191, 69, and New York *Times*, Feb. 6, 1937. Arnold Schoenberg, *Letters*, edited by Erwin Stein (New York: St. Martin's Press, 1964), p. 270.

5. Aaron Copland, *Our New Music*, p. 238. Lieberson quotes from *Modern Music*, Nov.–Dec. 1938 and March–April 1938. "New American Music" critique from *Modern Music*, May–June 1941. For background, see Minna Lederman, *The Life and Death of a Small Magazine* (New York: Institute for Studies in American Music, Conservatory of Music, Brooklyn College, 1983). Also valuable is Wayne D. Shirley, *Modern Music: An Analytic Index* (New York: AMS Press, 1976).

6. Adorno quotes from "The Social Situation of Music," *Telos*, Spring 1978 (originally published in *Zeitschrift für Sozialforschung*, 1932); "On the Fetish Character in Music and the Regression of Listening," Andrew Arato and Eike Gebhardt (editors), *The Essential Frankfurt School Reader* (New York: Continuum, 1982) (originally published in *Zeitschrift für Sozialforschung*, 1938); "The Radio Symphony," Paul Lazarsfeld and Frank Stanton (editors), *Radio Research 1941* (New York: Columbia University Office of Radio Research); "A Social Critique of Radio Music," *Kenyon Review*, Spring 1945; Part I (1944) of *Minima Moralia* (London: Jephcott, Unwin Brothers, 1951). Further Adorno quotes from unpublished materials in the Paul Lazarsfeld Collection, Butler Library, Columbia University: Lazarsfeld-Adorno correspondence; "Music in Radio," a 161-page "memorandum" (June 26, 1938) for the Princeton Radio Research Project; "Analytical Study of the NBC Music Appreciation Hour," Princeton University Office of Radio Research. On "affirmative culture," also see Herbert Marcuse, "The Affirmative Character of Culture," in *Negations* (Boston: Beacon Press, 1969). For background, see Martin Jay, *The Dialectical Imagination* (Boston: Little, Brown, 1973).

7. Daniel J. Czitrom, *Media and the American Mind: From Morse to McLuhan*, pp. 3–29.

8. Carl Van Vechten, "Music for Museums," *Music After the Great War* (New York: G. Schirmer, 1915).

9. Arnold Schoenberg, *Style and Idea* (London: Faber, 1975). Igor Stravinsky, *Igor Stravinsky: An Autobiography*, pp. 248–49.

10. My description of a "bourgeois" musical aesthetic is indebted to Richard Leppert and Susan McClary, both of the University of Minnesota.

11. Thomson's *Herald Tribune* articles and reviews have been collected in *The Musical Scene* (New York: Alfred A. Knopf, 1945); *The Art of Judging Music* (New York: Alfred A. Knopf, 1948); *Music Reviewed, 1940–54* (New York: Vintage Books, 1976); *Music, Right and Left* (New York: Greenwood Press, 1969); *A Virgil Thomson Reader* (New York: E. P. Dutton, 1984).

12. For Thomson on Adorno, see New York *Herald Tribune*, Feb. 8, 1942. For Thomson on Toscanini, see New York *Herald Tribune*, Nov. 25, 1940; May 2, 1942; May 17, 1942; Apr. 26, 1943; Oct. 28, 1946; Apr. 27, 1948.

13. Oscar Levant, *The Memoirs of an Amnesiac*, pp. 210–11. Thomson quote from a conversation with me, Sept. 1, 1982.

14. Henderson quotes from "The Function of Musical Criticism," *Musical Quarterly*, Jan. 1915, and Oscar Thompson, "An American School of Criticism: The Legacy Left by W. J. Henderson, Richard Aldrich and Their Colleagues of the Old Guard," *Musical Quarterly*, Oct. 1937. Huneker quotes from *Steeplejack*, vol. 2, pp. 123, 6, 148, 159, 112, 123. For New York *Times* as status symbol, see Michael Schudson, *Discovering the News* (New York: Basic Books, 1978), p. 117.

15. James Huneker, *Ivory Apes and Peacocks* (New York: C. Scribner's Sons, 1915), p. 64.

16. Boston *Post,* Dec. 19, 1914.

17. Irvin G. Wyllie, *The Self-Made Man in America* (Rutgers, N.J.: Rutgers University Press, 1954).

18. Howard Taubman, Introduction to Irene Downes (editor), *Olin Downes on Music.* Olin Downes, "Be Your Own Music Critic." George Marek, *The Good Housekeeping Guide to Musical Enjoyment* (New York: Rinehart, 1949), pp. 13, 4.

19. Marek, pp. 15, 12. Taubman quote from Lloyd Weldy, "The Music Criticism of Olin Downes and Howard Taubman," an unpublished dissertation for the University of Southern California (June 1965), Music Division, New York Public Library.

20. Downes quotes from New York *Times,* Oct. 24, 1937, and Henry and Sidney Cowell, *Charles Ives and His Music* (New York: Oxford University Press, 1955), p. 113. Howard Taubman, *Music on My Beat,* pp. 228, 115. George Marek, *Good Housekeeping,* Oct. 1940. David Ewen, *Dictators of the Baton,* Preface to 1943 edition. David Ewen, *The Man with the Baton,* p. 249.

21. Roger Sessions, "Vienna: *Vale, Ave,*" *Modern Music,* May–June 1938. Downes quote from New York *Times,* Sept. 14, 1924.

22. Toscanini quotes from B. H. Haggin, *The Toscanini Musicians Knew,* p. 134, and B. H. Haggin, *Conversations with Toscanini,* pp. 63, 54; Harvey Sachs, *Toscanini,* p. 314; Erich Leinsdorf, *Cadenza,* p. 53.

23. Quotes from New York *Post,* Nov. 7, 1938; Samuel Chotzinoff, "Toscanini," *Cosmopolitan,* Mar. 1938; *Life,* Nov. 27, 1939; *Reader's Digest,* June 1940; Taubman, *Music on My Beat,* p. 88.

24. Marek, *The Good Housekeeping Guide to Musical Enjoyment,* p. 48.

25. Downes, "Be Your Own Music Critic."

26. Cesar Saerchinger, *Artur Schnabel* (London: Cassell, 1957).

27. John Mueller, *The American Symphony Orchestra,* p. 276.

28. Charles Edward Russell, *The American Orchestra and Theodore Thomas,* Preface. Downes quotes from "Be Your Own Music Critic" and Irene Downes (editor), *Olin Downes on Music.*

29. Claire Reis, *Composers, Conductors and Critics* (New York: Oxford University Press, 1955), p. 45. Copland, *Our New Music,* p. 133. Eugene Goossens, "The Public: Has It Changed?," *Modern Music,* Jan.–Feb. 1943.

30. Copland, pp. 143–44, 233–42.

31. Schoenberg letter to Alexander von Zemlinsky (Feb. 13, 1918), quoted in Henry Raynor, *A Social History of Music,* p. 9.

32. For background, see Aaron Copland and Vivian Perlis, *Copland, 1900 Through 1942.*

33. Alexander Williams, "Toscanini," *Atlantic Monthly,* Mar. 1938.

THE NBC SYMPHONY, 1945–54 (PAGES 270 TO 306)

1. David Sarnoff, *Looking Ahead,* pp. 86–93. Eugene Lyons, *David Sarnoff,* p. 269.

2. Kinescopes of all the Toscanini telecasts may be viewed at the Museum of Broadcasting, New York City.

3. Harvey Sachs, *Toscanini,* p. 146.

4. Audience estimates in George Marek, *Toscanini,* p. 253. *Christian Science Monitor,* Apr. 11, 1952.

5. On the advent of LP, see Roland Gelatt, *The Fabulous Phonograph.*

6. Toscanini quotes from Sachs, p. 145; Gelatt, p. 271. Charles O'Connell, *The Other Side of the Record,* pp. 93–139, 190–97.

7. *RCA Victor Record Review,* Jan. 1947, Jan. 1948, Nov. 1947.

8. For record distribution, see Gelatt, p. 280, and Daniel Gillis, *Furtwängler and America,*

p. 137. For RCA salespeople, see O'Connell, pp. 93–139. For sales statistics, see Gelatt and *Christian Science Monitor,* Apr. 16, 1954.

9. Samuel Antek, *This Was Toscanini,* pp. 111–24. O'Connell, p. 124.

10. Elisabeth Schwarzkopf, *On and Off the Record: A Memoir of Walter Legge* (New York: Charles Scribner's Sons, 1982), pp. 97–98, 112.

11. NBC press materials, Music Division, New York Public Library. Marek, p. 254.

12. Tour accounts in *Life,* May 22, 1950; *The New Yorker,* May 20, 1950; New York *Times,* Apr. 26, May 7, May 14, May 26, 1950; Antek, pp. 97–110.

13. *New York Times Magazine,* May 14, 1950. New York *Times,* May 7, 1950.

14. Dorman Winfrey, *Arturo Toscanini in Texas* (Austin: The Encino Press, 1967).

15. Antek, pp. 97–110.

16. Both advertisements from the broadcast of Mar. 15, 1952.

17. *Time,* Feb. 11, 1946.

18. UPI in New York *Herald Tribune,* May 3, 1946. My account of Toscanini in Italy draws primarily on newspaper stories, Sachs, and Filippo Sacchi, *The Magic Baton.*

19. New York *Times,* May 11, 1946. George Marek, *The Good Housekeeping Guide to Musical Enjoyment,* p. 246.

20. Sachs, p. 301.

21. *New York Times Magazine,* Apr. 17, 1949; Mar. 23, 1952.

22. *Time,* Dec. 13, 1948. New York *Herald Tribune,* July 9, 1950. Earl Wilson in New York *Post,* Apr. 5, 1948.

23. Wallenstein quote in B. H. Haggin, *The Toscanini Musicians Knew,* pp. 179–80. Newman quote in Sachs, p. 243. Horszowski quote from a conversation with me, Feb. 1982. Ferruccio Busoni, *Letters to His Wife,* p. 184.

24. Erich Leinsdorf, *Cadenza,* p. 48. Fritz Busch, *Pages from a Musician's Life,* p. 183. David Walter quote in Haggin, p. 14. 1943 Toscanini quote in Harvey Sachs, "Arturo Toscanini," "Some New Discoveries," *Ovation* January 1982." 1945 Toscanini quote from David Sarnoff Library. Conway letters in Music Division, New York Public Library.

25. *Il Pianoforte* quoted in Sachs, *Toscanini,* p. 149. Sacchi, pp. 150–51.

26. Samuel Chotzinoff, *Toscanini: An Intimate Portrait,* p. 144. Wallenstein story in Sachs, *Toscanini,* p. 307. Cantelli story in B. H. Haggin, *Conversations with Toscanini,* p. 120, and Jerome Toobin, *Agitato* (New York: Viking Press, 1975), p. 88. Marek statement and Toscanini and Sarnoff letters in George Marek, *Toscanini,* pp. 276–78.

27. The broadcast has been issued by the Arturo Toscanini Recordings Association; it is currently distributed by Discocorp (P.O. Box 921, Berkeley, Calif. 94701).

28. Marek, p. 283. Toscanini dinner quote in Sachs, *Toscanini,* p. 310.

29. *Life,* Apr. 19, 1954.

30. Toobin, pp. 86–87.

31. Sacchi, p. 215. The 1956 visitor was Milton Katims, interviewed in "The Maestro Revisited," "Bell Telephone Hour," Mar. 12, 1967 (available at the Museum of Broadcasting, New York City). *Newsweek,* Jan. 28, 1957. Eisenhower quote from New York *Times,* Jan. 17, 1957. *Time,* Jan. 28, 1957.

POSTMORTEM (PAGES 307 TO 320)

1. Carl Dreher, *Sarnoff, An American Success,* p. 7. Eugene Lyons, *David Sarnoff,* pp. 356–57, 132. Engstrom quote from Dreher, p. 254. Erik Barnouw, *Tube of Plenty,* p. 188. Charles O'Connell, *The Other Side of the Record,* pp. 129–30.

2. Wiesner and Sarnoff quotes from David Sarnoff, *Looking Ahead,* Introduction. Dreher, p. 166. Sarnoff's Toscanini tribute from David Sarnoff Library. Clarinetist anecdote from George Marek, *Toscanini,* p. 223.

3. Sarnoff quote from Lyons, p. 342. Lyons, p. 85. Marek, pp. 220–1.

4. Lyons, pp. 130, 190.

5. Reminiscences of Ben Grauer, "Radio Pioneers," Oral History Research Office, Columbia University. Lyons, p. 195.

6. Van Wyck Brooks, "Letters and Leadership," from *Three Essays on America* (New York: Dutton, 1934), p. 135. Lewis Mumford, *The Golden Day*, p. 103.

7. Hill quote from Lyons, p. 201. Lawrence Gilman, *Toscanini and Great Music* (New York: Farrar, 1938), Foreword. O'Connell, p. 114.

8. Jeremy Tunstall, *The Media Are American* (New York: Columbia University Press, 1977), pp. 80–81.

9. Lyons, p. 201. Marek, p. 274. Halina Rodzinski, *Our Two Lives*, p. 172.

10. Sarnoff quote from Sarnoff, p. 69. Hiring plan from David Sarnoff Library. New York *Herald Tribune*, Feb. 8, 1942.

11. Reminiscences of Howard Barlow, "Radio Pioneers."

12. New York *Times*, Apr. 11, 1954. Marek, p. 225. Sarnoff quotes from "Toscanini: The Man Behind the Legend," NBC radio, June 5, 1963, and album notes to the recording RCA LM 6711 (with previously unissued NBC Symphony performances, 1967).

13. My account draws primarily from newspaper stories and Daniel Gillis, *Furtwängler and America*.

14. Yehudi Menuhin, *Unfinished Journey*, p. 220.

15. Alexis de Tocqueville, *Democracy in America*, vol. 2, pp. 5, 4. Henry James, *The Ambassadors* (New York: Signet, 1960), p. 69.

16. Samuel Chotzinoff, *Toscanini: An Intimate Portrait*, pp. 50–51. B. H. Haggin, "Vienna's Great Conductors." Howard Taubman, *The Maestro*, pp. 217, 220. New York *Times*, Jan. 19, 1949. David Ewen, *The Story of Toscanini*, p. 95.

17. Gillis, p. 124.

TOSCANINI ON RECORDS (PP. 321 TO 372)

1. Erich Leinsdorf, *Cadenza*, p. 39. Karajan and Weingartner quotes from Harvey Sachs, *Toscanini*, pp. 191, 239. George Szell, "Toscanini in the History of Orchestral Performance." New York *Times*, July 30, 1935.

2. "Critics" quote from Sachs, p. 191. Wilfrid Mellers, *The Sonata Principle* (London: Barrie & Jenkins, 1973), p. 217.

3. Sachs, p. 220.

4. Sachs, p. 246.

5. Richard Wagner, *Prose Works*, vol. 3, translated by William Ashton Ellis (London: K. Paul, Trench, Trübner, 1892–99), pp. 328–31.

6. Leinsdorf, p. 39.

7. B. H. Haggin, *The Toscanini Musicians Knew*, p. 67.

8. David Hamilton, review of *Falstaff* recordings, *Opera Quarterly*, Winter 1983.

9. Leinsdorf, pp. 40–41.

10. Sachs, p. 197.

11. Sachs, p. 83.

12. Szell.

13. Ernest Newman, *The Life of Richard Wagner*, vol. 4 (Cambridge: Cambridge University Press, 1976), pp. 717–19.

14. New York *Herald Tribune*, May 2, 1942.

15. Szell.

16. Mendelssohn and Berlioz quotes from David Cairns (editor), *The Memoirs of Hector*

Berlioz (New York: Alfred A. Knopf, 1969), p. 186. I am indebted to Will Crutchfield for information about violinist/conductors and the Scala evaluation.

17. Lazare Saminsky, *Music of Our Day* (New York: Thomas Y. Crowell, 1932), pp. 299–300.

18. Peter Heyworth, *Otto Klemperer: His Life and Times* (New York: Cambridge University Press, 1983), p. 293.

19. Peter Heyworth, *Conversations with Klemperer*, p. 90.

20. Kenneth Drake, *The Sonatas of Beethoven as He Played and Taught Them* (Bloomington: Indiana University Press, 1981), pp. 54, 68.

21. Walter Toscanini quote from Walter Toscanini, "The Riverdale Project," RCA publicity brochure (1966), Rodgers and Hammerstein archives, Music Division, New York Public Library. John Pfeiffer quotes from conversation with me, Dec. 13, 1984. Richard B. Gardner, "The Riverdale Project," *High Fidelity*, Apr. 1956.

22. Michael Kennedy, *Barbirolli*, pp. 125–26. Samuel Antek, *This Was Toscanini*, p. 172.

23. Cardus and Newman quotes from Denis Matthews, *Arturo Toscanini* (New York: Hippocrene Books, 1982), p. 69. Oscar Levant, *The Memoirs of an Amnesiac*, pp. 209–10.

24. Antek, pp. 143–82.

25. Szell.

26. Verdi quotes from Martin Chusid and William Weaver (editors), *The Verdi Companion* (New York: W. W. Norton, 1979), and Marcello Conati (editor), *Encounters with Verdi* (Ithaca, N.Y.: Cornell University Press, 1984), pp. 290–91, 349–50.

27. Ricordi quote in Conati, pp. 297–98. Cologne report in Conati, pp. 125–28.

28. Michael Scott, *The Record of Singing*, vol. 1 (London: Duckworth, 1977), p. 135. Will Crutchfield, "Verdi Performance: Restoring the Color," *High Fidelity*, June 1983. Will Crutchfield, "Vocal Ornamentation in Verdi: The Phonographic Evidence," *Nineteenth Century Music*, Summer 1983.

29. Scott, *The Record of Singing*, vol. 2 (London: Duckworth, 1979), p. 84.

30. Martin Chusid, Introduction to *Rigoletto* (Chicago: University of Chicago Press, 1983).

31. Antek, p. 56.

32. Helena Matheopoulos, *Maestro* (New York: Harper & Row, 1982), p. 226.

33. *Rigoletto* story from Charles Rosen, *New York Review of Books*, Oct. 27, 1983. Pizzi quote from Conati, p. 346.

34. Butler quote from Daniel J. Czitrom, *Media and the American Mind: From Morse to McLuhan*, p. 48. C. Wright Mills, *White Collar* (New York: Oxford University Press, 1956), pp. 236–8. Jeremy Tunstall, *The Media Are American*, p. 85.

35. New York *Herald Tribune*, May 17, 1942.

36. Antek, pp. 89, 19.

37. Menuhin quotes from Daniel Gillis, *Furtwängler Recalled*, pp. 40, 180–1. Krips quote from Gillis, p. 122. Furtwängler quotes from Wilhelm Furtwängler, *Concerning Music*, and album note for DG LPM 18742.

38. Verdi quotes from Conati, pp. 190, 153. Hindemith, Blech, Kempff, and Menuhin quotes from Gillis, pp. 56, 33, 133, 41.

39. Samuel Chotzinoff, "Beethoven and Toscanini."

40. George Marek, *Toscanini*, p. 80.

COLLAPSE OF THE CULT (PAGES 375 TO 398)

1. Harvey Sachs, *Toscanini*, p. 295.

2. Laurence Lewis, *Guido Cantelli: Portrait of a Maestro* (San Diego: A. S. Barnes, 1981), p. 98.

3. Munch quote from New York *Times*, Jan. 19, 1957. Monteux quote from Sachs, p. 146. Ormandy quotes from George Marek, *Toscanini*, jacket copy and Roland Gelatt, *The Music Makers* (New York: Alfred A. Knopf, 1953), p. 52.

4. Peter Heyworth, "Otto Klemperer's Turbulent Years," *Keynote*, May 1985. My conversation with Peter Horenstein (the conductor's son), 1985.

5. Ansermet and Mitropoulos quotes in Daniel Gillis, *Furtwängler Recalled*, pp. 27, 116. Winthrop Sargeant, *Geniuses, Goddesses and People*, p. 100. Thomson quote in New York *Herald Tribune*, May 17, 1942.

6. Szell quotes from Paul Henry Lang, "A Mixture of Instinct and Intellect: George Szell on Conducting," *High Fidelity*, Jan. 1964, and Harold C. Schonberg, *The Great Conductors*, p. 339.

7. Cassidy quotes in Chicago *Tribune*, Feb. 28, 1951; Apr. 22, 1953; May 7, 1953.

8. Charles O'Connell, *The Other Side of the Record*, p. 207.

9. Horowitz quote in Glenn Plaskin, *Horowitz* (New York: W. Morrow, 1983), p. 214. O'Connell, p. 249. Arthur Rubinstein, *My Many Years* (New York: Alfred A. Knopf, 1980), pp. 468–70.

10. Samuel Chotzinoff, *A Little Nightmusic* (New York: Harper and Row, 1964), pp. 44–45.

11. *New York Times Book Review*, Mar. 30, 1975.

12. Harris Goldsmith, "Recollections of a Toscanini Addict," *Keynote*, Jan. 1982.

13. B. H. Haggin, *Conversations with Toscanini*, pp. 164, 142.

14. George Marek, *Toscanini*, p. 12.

15. Plaskin, p. 176.

16. Naomi Graffman, "Leon Fleisher's Long Journey Back to the Keyboard," *New York Times Magazine*, Sept. 12, 1982.

17. New York *Times*, Apr. 17, 1977.

LONG-TERM LEGACIES (PP. 399 TO 429)

1. Philip Hart, *Orpheus in the New World* (New York: W. W. Norton, 1973), p. 388.

2. Arthur Loesser, *Men, Women and Pianos*, p. 595. Recent piano statistics from American Music Conference. Magazine article cited in Loesser, p. 602. Amateur musician statistics from "Americans and the Arts," Louis Harris and Associates, Oct. 1984.

3. Howard Shanet, *Philharmonic: A History of New York's Orchestra*, p. 277.

4. Henry Krehbiel, *More Chapters of Opera*, pp. 5–7. Leo Slezak, *Song of Motley*, p. 37. Joseph Szigeti, *With Strings Attached* (New York: Alfred A. Knopf, 1947), p. 248.

5. Gregor Piatigorsky, *Cellist*, pp. 147–50. Slezak, pp. 44–6. Oscar Levant, *The Memoirs of an Amnesiac*, pp. 42, 49.

6. *Time*, Sept. 24, 1979. *Newsweek*, Mar. 15, 1976.

7. Joseph Horowitz, "The Trouble With Piano Recitals: A Polemic," *Keynote*, Nov. and Dec., 1979. Hart, p. 418.

8. Schuman address reprinted in *Symphony*, Aug.–Sept. 1980.

9. On radio music programming, see *Gene Lees' Jazzletter*, Nov. 1983 (P.O. Box 240, Ojai, Calif. 93023) and J. Fred Macdonald, *Don't Touch That Dial!* (Chicago: Nelson-Hall, 1979).

10. B. H. Haggin, *Conversations with Toscanini*, p. 135.

11. Ferruccio Busoni, *Letters to His Wife*, p. 287.

12. Lloyd Schwartz, "Do I Hear a Waltz?," *Vanity Fair*, May 1983.

13. New York *Times*, Dec. 11, 1983.

14. Summary of Program Fund Review Panel, Corporation for Public Broadcasting, July 13, 1983.

15. Theodor Adorno and Max Horkheimer, *Dialectic of Enlightenment* (New York: Herder and Herder, 1972), p. 158.
16. *Lincoln Center Stagebill,* March 1982.
17. *TV Guide,* Mar. 27, 1982.
18. Adorno and Horkheimer, p. 142.

CONCLUSION (PAGES 430 TO 440)

1. Samuel Lipman, *The House of Music* (Boston: D. R. Godine, 1984), p. 287.
2. Edward A. Martin, *H. L. Mencken and the Debunkers* (Athens, Ga.: University of Georgia Press, 1984), pp. 9, 3. Leslie Fiedler, *An End to Innocence* (Boston: Beacon Press, 1952), p. 127.
3. *The New Criterion,* March 1984.
4. *Modern Music,* May–June 1935.
5. Patrick J. Smith, *A Year at the Met* (New York: Alfred A. Knopf, 1983), pp. 194–98.
6. New York *Times,* Dec. 4, 1984.
7. "Public Participation in the Arts, 1982," a survey conducted for the National Endowment for the Arts by the University of Maryland Survey Research Center.
8. *Modern Music,* May–June 1936.

Index

PERMISSIONS ACKNOWLEDGMENTS

JOSEPH HOROWITZ, born in New York City in 1948, was a music critic for the *New York Times* from 1976 to 1980. He currently serves as Artistic Advisor to the Brooklyn Philharmonic, the resident orchestra of the Brooklyn Academy of Music. Since 1981, he has been program editor for the Kaufmann Concert Hall of the 92nd Street Y (one of New York City's major concert halls), where he also presides over an annual Schubert festival. In addition to *Understanding Toscanini,* his books include *Conversations with Arrau* (winner of a 1983 ASCAP Deems Taylor Award for excellence in writing about music) and *The Ivory Trade: Piano Competitions and the Business of Music* (1989). Forthcoming, from the University of California Press, are his *Wagner Nights: An American History* (1994) and *The New Schubert* (1997). His articles have appeared in *The New York Review of Books, Musical Quarterly, 19th Century Music,* and *Opera News,* among many other publications. He lectures frequently at universities and music schools throughout the United States, and has taught at Brooklyn College and the Mannes College of Music. He lives in Manhattan with his wife, Agnes Bruneau, and their six-year-old son, Bernie.

Cultural Studies / Music / American History

During his years with the Metropolitan Opera (1908–1915) and the New York Philharmonic (1926–1936) Arturo Toscanini was regularly proclaimed the "world's greatest conductor." And with the NBC Symphony (1937–1954), created for him by RCA's David Sarnoff, he became the beneficiary of a multimedia promotional apparatus that spread Toscanini madness nationwide. In this boldly conceived study, Joseph Horowitz reveals how and why Arturo Toscanini became the object of unparalleled veneration in the United States. Combining cultural history, biography, and music criticism, Horowitz explores the cultural and commercial mechanisms that created America's Toscanini cult and fostered, in turn, a Eurocentric, anachronistic new audience for old music.

"[*Understanding Toscanini* is] a socioeconomic study of the classical music industry and of the growth, through radio, recording, and television, of musical mass culture. . . . No one concerned with the fate of the arts in our jingoistic and dangerously confused society can afford to ignore Joseph Horowitz's courageous, necessary, and for the most part irrefutable cultural case history."   —Robert Craft, *New York Review of Books*

"A major achievement, the kind of detailed case-study of the role of serious music in a popular culture that has never been attempted before. . . . Should be required reading for all arts administrators, critics, musicians, music lovers and people who care about artistic values."   —Richard Dyer, *Boston Globe*

"One thing that makes *Understanding Toscanini* a significant book for historians and social scientists is the light it sheds on the way aspects of high culture were repackaged as a kind of de facto mass culture during the first half of the twentieth century. . . . *Understanding Toscanini* is a landmark contribution to our understanding of American culture."   —Paul DiMaggio, Department of Sociology,
                    Princeton University

"Absolutely brilliant . . . By examining Toscanini's American career, [Horowitz] states the risks of a commercialized musical culture far more strongly than any theory could."
—Yo-Yo Ma

"A *cri de coeur* about the philistinism and commercialism of contemporary society."
—Edward Said, *New York Times Book Review*

Joseph Horowitz, a *New York Times* music critic from 1976–1980, is Artistic Advisor to the Brooklyn Philharmonic Orchestra. His books include *Conversations with Arrau, The Ivory Trade,* and *Wagner Nights: An American History* (University of California Press, 1994).

Cover photo courtesy of *The National Broadcasting Company, Inc.*

UNIVERSITY OF CALIFORNIA PRESS
Berkeley 94720

9 780520 085428   90000

ISBN 0-520-08542-6